The Catholic Church in World Politics

The Catholic Church in World Politics

Eric O. Hanson

PRINCETON UNIVERSITY PRESS, PRINCETON, NEW JERSEY

Library of Congress Cataloging in Publication Data will be found on
the last printed page of this book

ISBN 0-691-07729-0
ISBN 0-691-02327-1 (pbk.)

First Princeton Paperback printing, 1990

This book has been composed in Linotron Palatino type

Clothbound editions of Princeton University Press books are printed
on acid-free paper, and binding materials are chosen for strength and
durability. Paperbacks, although satisfactory for personal collections,
are not usually suitable for library rebinding

Printed in the United States of America by Princeton University
Press, Princeton, New Jersey

"Somoza Unveils the Statue of Somoza in Somoza Stadium," by permission of Unicorn Press, P.O. Box 3307, Greensboro, N.C. 27402

Quotations from Kim Chi Ha, *The Gold-Crowned Jesus and Other Writings* and Eric O. Hanson, *Catholic Politics in China and Korea*, by permission of Orbis Books, Maryknoll, N.Y. 10545.

10 9 8 7 6 5 4 3 2

To Kathleen, Erin, and Kara,
with love

To Cardinals Franz König, Aloísio Lorscheider, Jaime Sin, and Jan Willebrands,
with respect

CONTENTS

ACKNOWLEDGMENTS

THIS BOOK has benefited from the scholarship and personal suggestions of a great many people. Since it attempts a global integration of Catholic politics, the book relies heavily on many excellent studies of the political and social role of the Catholic Church in particular countries. This debt, as far as I am cognizant of it, is acknowledged in the footnotes. With regard to personal assistance, the primary credit should go to Co-Directors John W. Lewis and Sidney D. Drell and the scholars and staff of the Stanford University Center for International Security and Arms Control. While I have no wish to blame the shortcomings of the book on members of the Center, most of the initial manuscript was written there during a four-quarter sabbatical. In seminars and in informal discussions, members of the Center generously helped me to increase my understanding of many of the political and technical issues treated in the text. Special thanks are due Philip J. Farley, who read the entire second draft and offered many valuable suggestions, and Gerry Bowman. My stay at the Center was supported by a NEH Fellowship for College Teachers and a grant from the Colombia Foundation.

The administration and faculty of Santa Clara University have also been very supportive, especially on questions of national Catholic politics. Special appreciation is expressed to sociologist Witold Krassowski (the church in Polish society) and political scientists Timothy J. Lukes (the American political party system and computer assistance) and Dennis R. Gordon (Latin American politics). University research money has been helpful at various times during the project.

Scholars and political practitioners whom I met on three trips outside the United States, 1983-1984, have also contributed greatly to the text. It would be impossible to list even one-tenth of those who have given of their time and expertise, so I merely list here the conferences and series of interviews, with sincere appreciation to those involved. First, a nine-day stay in Salzburg to participate in the International Federation of Catholic Universities (FIUC)-Club of Rome symposium on "The Peace Movements" provided an excellent opportunity to discuss comparative peace movements with European scholars. Special thanks to Father Joseph Joblin, S.J., and the late Dr. Aurelio Peccei. Second, in August 1983 I represented Santa Clara University at the XIVth General Assembly of FIUC, a marvelous chance to learn from those practitioners of national Catholic politics, university presidents and rectors. Sincere appreciation is due Father Edouard Boné, then FIUC general secretary, who arranged for me to co-chair a panel on "The Catholic Church and Peace" with the dean of American Catholic university presidents, Father Theodore Hesburgh of Notre Dame.

Third, seven weeks in the Soviet Union, Poland, and Western Europe during the summer of 1984 gave me the opportunity to discuss many of these ideas with others. Special thanks to Professors Paul Peachey and Paul Mojzes, who arranged the three-week series of discussions in Moscow, Novosibirsk, Tbilisi, and Leningrad. Soviet academics at the Institute for United States and Canadian Studies and the Institute for the World Economy and International Relations were particularly helpful with their comments on Soviet perceptions of Catholic politics in the United States and Latin America. In other countries I owe a debt of special gratitude to Koos and Rita van der Bruggen, Erich and Brigitte Pilz, and Janina Krassowska.

My brother Kirk (Stanford Graduate School of Business) has taught me quite a lot about the role of multinational businesses in the international system. We both benefited from response to our keynote speech at the Notre Dame Conference on Multinational Corporate Involvement with Religious Groups in April 1985. Finally, it would be inexcusable to fail to mention the assistance of Richard Madsen, James Gifford, Arlee Ellis, Sr. Janet Carroll, M.M., and Fathers David Wessels, S.J., and Gerry Phelan, S.J. Principal assistance during the entire process, came from my wife Kathleen, who helped interview, edit and order the first draft, and assisted with typing.

Throughout this project, the staff of the Princeton University Press, especially Social Science Editor Gail Ullman, have been very helpful. Excellent critical comments were offered by readers Bruce Russett and J. Bryan Hehir. Of course, in the end, despite all this help, the shortcomings of this text remain the responsibility of the author alone.

The Catholic Church in World Politics

"All the News
That's Fit to Print"

The New York Times

VOL.CXXXII .. No. 45,713

Copyright © 1983 The New York Times

NEW YORK, SATURDAY, JUNE 18, 1983

60 cents beyond 75 miles from New York City,
except on Long Island.

Late Edition

Weather: Partly cloudy, humid today;
mostly cloudy, chance of showers tonight. Mostly sunny, warm tomorrow.
Temperatures: today 81-85; tonight 67-
73; yesterday 65-83. Details on page 14.

30 CENTS

LEADERS IN ALBANY AGREE ON MEASURE TO SHIELD TENANTS

UNRELATED RENTERS AIDED

Proposal Prompted by Ruling That Landlords May Evict Unmarried Roommates

By SHAWN G. KENNEDY

An agreement on a bill that would permit two tenants who are not related to share rental housing was announced yesterday by members of both houses of the New York State Legislature, the State Attorney General and the New York Civil Liberties Union.

The measure was introduced in the Assembly yesterday and will be pro-posed in the State Senate early next week. It specifies that tenants named on leases may share their dwellings not only with their families but also with one additional person and that person's dependent children.

The bill, the Occupancy Protection Act, also says that at least one of the tenants covered by the original lease must remain in the apartment; other-wise, the added roommate must rene-gotiate the lease.

Court Decision Prompts Bill

The legislation was drafted after a decision May 9 by the New York Court of Appeals that landlords could evict unrelated people who shared housing without the landlord's consent.

Most leases in New York City limit occupancy of apartments to the person who signed the lease and members of the tenant's immediate family.

The court's decision threatened the live-in arrangements of thousands of tenants in the state, according to the bill's supporters, and broadly criticism

Satellite Tests To Highlight Shuttle Flight

By JOHN NOBLE WILFORD
Special to The New York Times

CAPE CANAVERAL, Fla., June 17— The crew of the space shuttle Chal-lenger reviewed plans today for a flight on which they are to deploy two com-mercial satellites and, for the first

Gen. Wojciech Jaruzelski, the Polish leader, reading a speech of welcome to Pope John Paul II at the Belvedere Palace in Warsaw.

United Press International

Angry Chants And 'V' Signs Fill Warsaw

By JOHN KIFNER
Special to The New York Times

WARSAW, June 17 — More than a million Poles gathered at a soccer sta-dium to hear Pope John Paul II cele-brate mass this evening, and when he was done the crowd saluted him with a

POPE ASKS POLAND TO PUT AGREEMENT OF '80 INTO EFFECT

JARUZELSKI DEFENDS RULE

After Pontiff and General Meet, Regime Says Walesa Will Confer With John Paul

By HENRY KAMM
Special to The New York Times

WARSAW, June 17 — Pope John Paul II urged Gen. Wojciech Jaruzelski today to allow Poland the "renewal" worked out in August 1980. The Polish leader responded by defending the im-position of martial law, which ended the country's brief experiment.

After an exchange of formal speeches and 2 hours and 20 minutes of private talks between the Pope and General

Excerpts from remarks, page 5.

Jaruzelski, the Government agreed to let Lech Walesa, the founder of the Soli-darity union, meet with John Paul dur-ing his weeklong visit.

Solidarity, the first independent union in the Soviet bloc, was founded in Au-gust 1980. The movement flourished under the process known here as "re-newal" until the Polish Government imposed martial law on Dec. 13, 1981.

'Path to Social Renewal'

This evening the Pope celebrated mass before tens of thousands of Poles who displayed signs in support of Soli-darity, which is now outlawed, and chanted Mr. Walesa's name.

"I do not lose hope that this difficult moment may become a path to social renewal, the beginning of which is es-tablished by the social agreements stipulated by the representatives of

John Paul Faces Jaruzelski in Prime Time

IN THE high-ceilinged chamber of Warsaw's Belvedere Palace, Pope John Paul II and General Wojciech Jaruzelski faced each other. The general, his olive-drab uniform encrusted with ten rows of ribbons, represented all the political, economic, and military power concentrated in the leader of Poland's party, state, and army. John Paul, dressed in white robes with a gold pectoral cross, personified all the symbolic power and social legitimacy derived from historic Polish Catholic nationalism. At the beginning of his speech Jaruzelski's hands trembled nervously and one thumb tapped the paper from which he read. However, the general made no apology for martial law, which he presented as the only alternative to the "enormity of human suffering, torment and tears which have been successfully avoided." The Soviets had not invaded. The pope replied by challenging the Polish leader to honor the agreements that had legitimated the union Solidarity. Such action, John Paul observed, was "indispensable for maintaining the good name of Poland in the world." Such liberalization would end Poland's international isolation and improve relations "above all with the United States of America." The general had referred to the Soviet Union with universally understood code words, but the pope openly named the other global antagonist, the United States. This dramatic confrontation demonstrated the complex interconnection among internal ecclesiastical affairs, Polish national politics, and Soviet-American relations.[1]

The purpose of this book is twofold. The primary purpose is to explain the role of the Catholic Church in world politics, with an emphasis on Soviet and American security policy. The secondary purpose is to explain the impact of modern political and technological developments on the internal politics of the Catholic Church.

The first section of this book emphasizes traditional Catholic political culture: historical memory, types of political and social organizations, and traditional modes of thought.[2] An explanation of the contemporary national and international politics of such a traditional institution as the Catholic Church would make little sense without a brief summary of the political history of the Catholic

Church in Europe and an analysis of the political impact of Catholic ecclesiastical organization. By "traditional modes of thought" I mean both conscious ideologies and the habitual paradigms used to analyze specific political issues.

The second section of the book presents a comparative political analysis of the role of the Catholic Church in national political consensus and regional alliances, especially NATO and the Warsaw Pact. In particular, I situate the Catholic Church in the national political cultures of Continental Western Europe, the Anglo-American states, and Eastern Europe. The European and North Atlantic emphasis follows from my focus on Soviet-American relations. If this book were to use significance for the future of global Catholicism as a single criterion, however, the Brazilian church would probably be listed first. Peter Nichols notes that by the year 2000 70 percent of Catholics will live in the Third World that will comprise 90 percent of the global population.[3] Since Soviet-American competition often arises in Third World venues, we will explore this dimension of Catholic politics by including an analysis of Third World Catholicism and superpower rivalry.

The third section of the book focuses on international relations, treating in particular the political role of the Catholic Church in arms control. I use the term "arms control" rather than "disarmament" or "peace" because, while the current Soviet and American governments may well entertain proposals for "arms control," they will embrace "disarmament" and "peace" only in the propaganda sphere. In fact, none of the three terms is satisfactory because each remains loaded with ideological and organizational connotations.[4] I conclude by placing the Catholic Church in its broader international context, and adding a few notes on possible future developments in international Catholic politics.

While an understanding of traditional Catholic political culture is necessary to understand the church's contemporary political activity, it is not sufficient. The postwar technological revolutions in communications, weaponry, and international economics have deeply affected all political and ecclesiastical institutions. The Jaruzelski–John Paul confrontation serves as an excellent media image for the three major theoretical approaches that will inform this account. First, during this highly publicized meeting the general and the pope personified instrumental and expressive powers in the context of Soviet-American relations. Second, John Paul advocated Western values, but he also sought to play a mediational role in both Polish domestic politics and international affairs. Third, in both Poland and the world at large, the pope wished to maximize and balance internal ecclesiastical goals with the promotion of Catholic values within the broader societies.

INSTRUMENTAL AND EXPRESSIVE POWERS: THE ROLE OF THE MEDIA

Rarely in modern history, and never with such complete television, radio, and newspaper coverage, has the difference between instrumental and expressive power been so starkly illustrated as when John Paul faced Jaruzelski.[5] Neither leader derived his particular type of power from the other, and neither could destroy the basis of the other's legitimacy. The Polish Workers (Communist) Party, like its Eastern bloc counterparts, has always claimed both instrumental power (political, economic, and military) and expressive power (articulation of collective ideas, promotion of collective norms, and the representation of symbolic ideas). Through corruption and inefficiency the Polish party has squandered what little popular legitimacy it once possessed. From the 1950s the Polish people had looked to the Cardinal Primate Stefan Wyszyński as their expressive leader. When Józef Glemp became cardinal primate in July 1981 after Wyszyński's death in May, expressive leadership had already passed to Cardinal Karol Wojtyła of Kraków, the first Polish pope. Despite the Polish people's tremendous devotion to John Paul II, however, this pope who inspired the rise of Solidarity could not save it. On the other hand, Jaruzelski proved incapable of legitimizing martial law despite all the instrumental power of the party, state, and army. So the Polish tragedy, exacerbated by East-West tensions, has continued.

The striking photo of John Paul listening to Jaruzelski's speech filled four columns at the top of the front page of the *New York Times* (June 18, 1983). The editors had selected a photo that emphasized the distance between the pope and the general. The paper's leading headline (top right column) stated, "Pope Asks Poland To Put Agreement of '80 Into Effect." The front page also carried a second photo (caption: "The Pontiff blessing the crowd yesterday evening at Warsaw Stadium") and a second story (headline: "Angry Chants and 'V' Signs Fill Warsaw"). In addition, the editors devoted the entire fifth page (including three photos) to John Paul's visit. Thus the *New York Times* and newspapers throughout the West guaranteed that the pope's reference to the impact of his visit on Polish-American relations remained no idle boast. In addition to the massive newspaper and magazine documentation (two *Newsweek* and one *Time* cover),[6] television crews followed John Paul throughout his eight-day journey. Each evening millions of Americans joined the papal pilgrimage via the network news.

The frequent use of photos of the pope emphasizes the significance of papal newspaper articles. It also points to the essentially photogenic character of John Paul's media charisma. For example, the *Times of India* (New Dehli) prints few photos, but in that paper the pope has received more column inches for photos than stories. This pictorial strength makes John Paul extremely effective on television, especially on the American network news with its thirty-second clips. The Vatican advance staff recognizes the media impact of symbol and image. When the pope visited El Salvador, the staff planned no official stop at the tomb of Archbishop Oscar Arnulfo Romero because of a prior assassination threat. However, John Paul made an unscheduled visit. Fortuitously, an Associated Press photographer "happened" to be present and shot a beautifully composed photo of the pope leaving the tomb; a large portrait of Archbishop Romero filled the background. On March 7, 1983, that photo ran on the front page of the *New York Times* and in many other papers.

Such reliance on the Western secular media and the Vatican's own transnational communications network places the papacy on the side of the West in the use of media, even though the Vatican's own media "style" often approximates that of *Tass*. The international debate over the MacBride Report[7] has highlighted the stark differences between Western support for the media as independent political and commercial actors versus Eastern and some Third World emphasis on the role of the media in supporting national construction. Recent advances in media technology have sharpened the debate. The Soviet leadership finds contraband videotapes only slightly annoying, but greatly fears development of future technology that would allow Western networks to televise directly into Soviet homes via satellite. An estimated 70 percent of the East German population already receives West German television, jokingly known as "the class enemy who comes in the evening." Besides providing such popular fare as "Dallas," West German channels beam special weekly documentaries that deal with taboo subjects such as love and sexuality in the German Democratic Republic (GDR) and a consumer report on the East German car. Consequently, citizens of the GDR have become the best informed peo-

San Salvador, El Salvador. Pope John Paul II approaches the tomb of Archbishop Arnulfo Romero at the Metropolitan Cathedral in San Salvador, March 1983. AP/Wide World Photos.

ple in the Eastern bloc. They often write the West German channels to express their opinions on current programming.[8]

The Vatican also operates an extensive foreign radio service.[9] This service remains especially important to persecuted Catholics like the Ukrainian Uniates. In January 1969, the Soviet authorities arrested Bishop Vasyl Velychkovsky for alleged contacts with Ukrainian centers abroad, for anti-Soviet sermons, and for listening to Vatican Radio.[10] Tapes of Western religious programs and Radio Austria's weekly broadcasts of Sunday mass have influenced the current Catholic revival in Czechoslovakia.[11] Media access has also constituted a focal issue in the Polish struggles. During the pope's first visit to Poland in 1979, other Eastern European presses either ignored or decried the pope's visit. Soviet television carried a thirty-second clip on the pope's arrival but did not show the hundreds of thousands who gathered to greet him. The TV commentator warned that "some circles in the Polish church are trying to use [the visit] for antistate purposes." Polish television provided extensive coverage but played down the crowd size and response.[12]

The era of the media in Catholic politics did not begin, of course, with the election of John Paul II. Nor has it always supported the Vatican against criticism from Catholics outside Italy. The Dutch Catholic media, for example, has been crucial to ecclesiastical changes in that country. In 1960 the five million Dutch Catholics could rely on a Catholic press service, 2 national Catholic daily newspapers, 20 local Catholic dailies, 22 Catholic weeklies, 183 Catholic magazines and journals of opinion, 65 Catholic magazines related to the family and education, 42 Catholic learned journals, 22 Catholic magazines related to social or ecclesiastical charity, 70 magazines sponsored by official Catholic organizations, etc. The Catholic Radio Broadcasting Company (KRO), serving the entire population and attempting to maintain its subscription level for public funds, became a major source of news and controversial discussion during the 1960s. Print and electronic media covered the Vatican Council debates in detail, with lively commentary from bishops and theologians in the Netherlands. At the Council itself the Dutch bishops established the only national autonomous information center (DOC), which was entrusted to an independent team from KRO. DOC sponsored press conferences, theological conferences, and the publication of theological working papers. The international theological journal *Concilium* grew out of this experience.[13] Journalists of other countries like Henri Fesquet of *Le Monde* wrote analyses of the Council for their readers.

Americans received their news of the Council through Robert Kaiser of *Time* and a series of spicy letters published in the *New Yorker*.[14] Redemptorist Francis X. Murphy, under the *nom de plume* Xavier Rynne, regaled Catholics in the United States with stories of curial intrigue featuring the machinations of Cardinal Alfredo Ottaviani of the Holy Office.

The Vatican's impact on international public opinion does not derive principally from the Catholic media, but from the coverage of the pope in the secular media of the West. John Paul II's twelve-day trip to Canada in September 1984 generated over 100 hours of coverage from the government-owned Canadian Broadcasting System.[15]

The general impact of modern communications on the Catholic Church has been to increase the institutional church's reliance on expressive rather than instrumental power.[16] As a result, issues of conflict between the Catholic Church and national states have become more complex. From the time of Constantine, control of the appointment of bishops has been the most crucial aspect of the struggle between political and religious authorities. The battles over ecclesiastical appointments and the transnational penetration of missionary personnel and foreign ecclesiastical finances still remain important in both authoritarian and totalitarian political systems.[17] However, liberal democratic states restrict religion to the private sphere and do not seek to control church institutions through episcopal appointments. Church-state conflict in liberal democratic countries focuses on the church's attempt to apply Catholic ethics to political and social issues such as arms control, human rights, and abortion.

ADVOCACY OF WESTERN VALUES VERSUS EAST-WEST MEDIATION

Since the rise of the secular nation state, both church and state have also vied for control of education and other social welfare areas. This struggle to determine national political culture remains most obvious in the Catholic states of Southern Europe. Even in the more secularized Anglo-American and Germanic states, however, both the papacy and national hierarchies attempt to employ the media to shape public opinion on social and moral issues. Such efforts influence the very possibility of national consensus in either a positive or a negative manner.

Despite struggles between the Catholic Church and Western governments, the Vatican had traditionally supported the West against its "godless" Communist enemies. The technological developments in weaponry that have followed the first atomic explosion at Alamogordo, New Mexico, however, have gradually made such a Catholic-led ideological crusade unthinkable. During the Cold War Pope Pius XII (1939-1958) articulated a strong anticommunist position that made the papacy the ideological leader of the Western forces. Since that time, however, the Vatican has shifted its policy. While the church in general remains more sympathetic to Western ideals and institutions than to those of the Eastern bloc, with the accession of Pius's successors the papacy began to place more emphasis on maintaining an independent diplomatic position in order to mediate between the two superpowers. This vision of the Catholic Church as global mediator finds its contemporary precedent in the historical experience of the early 1960s, which brought together the three strong figures of Nikita Khrushchev, John Kennedy, and Pope John XXIII in response to the Cuban missile crisis.[18] The papal intervention began on October 24, when American Jewish publisher Norman Cousins and Belgian Dominican Felix Morlion,[19] both attending the Dartmouth Conference with other Soviet and American writers and scientists, phoned the Vatican to ask if the pope would issue a plea for peace. John XXIII agreed to do so, providing that he had the prior consent of both Washington and Moscow. Khrushchev assented quickly, while the White House agreed to a general plea, provided that Kennedy's prior consent remained secret. The papal text, which was later broadcast over Vatican Radio, was delivered to the Soviet and American embassies in Rome for immediate transmission to the Kremlin and the White House. On October 26 *Pravda* printed John XXIII's appeal on its front page under the heading, "We beg all rulers not to be deaf to the cry of humanity."

John XXIII and Nikita Khrushchev instinctively understood and appreciated each other. Both came from peasant stock and both battled entrenched bureaucracies in order to modernize their respective institutions. For sensitive matters, both leaders often employed high-ranking confidants rather than the institutional chain of command. For example, John XXIII's friend, the German Jesuit Cardinal Bea, served as the leading articulator of the papal position for the next contact with Khrushchev through Cousins.

As editor of the *Saturday Review* and a long-time advocate of disarmament, Cousins had the right credentials for an interview with the Soviet leader. When Cousins stopped in Rome, Bea provided no written instructions but indicated the pope's interest in world peace and religious freedom, especially the release of the Ukrainian patriarch Josef Slipyj, who had been exiled to Siberia for eighteen years. Cousins met with Khrushchev for more than three hours on December 13, 1962. When the editor returned to Rome, he presented the pope with a memorandum covering the principal points of his discussion with the Soviet premier. The memorandum read as follows:

1) Russia desires the pope's mediation, and Khrushchev agrees that it should not be limited to mediation in moments of crisis, but should be a continuous action by the pope in the cause of peace; 2) Khrushchev affirms that he wants to open lines of communication with the Vatican through private contacts; 3) Khrushchev acknowledges that the Church respects the principle of the division of church and state in many coun-

tries; 4) Khrushchev acknowledges that the Church serves all human beings for the sacred values of life and is not only concerned with Catholics; 5) Khrushchev acknowledges that the pope has acted with great courage, considering the internal problems that he faces, just as Khrushchev has internal problems in the Soviet Union.[20]

Six weeks later Cousins received word from Soviet Ambassador Dobrynin that Slipyj was free to leave the Soviet Union. The Soviet-Vatican rapprochement of the early 1960s culminated in a papal audience for Khrushchev's daughter and son-in-law on April 27, 1963. This audience took place despite the disapproval of most of the Vatican bureaucracy, the Italian Christian Democratic Party, and the United States. Washington responded to the new Vatican policy by dispatching John McCone, Catholic Knight of Malta and director of the CIA,[21] to the Vatican to express American objections.

The era of Khrushchev, Kennedy, and John XXIII soon passed. The pope and the president died that year, and Khrushchev was overthrown by Brezhnev in October 1964. In all three cases the succeeding leaders relied less on charisma and more on bureaucratic power. Nevertheless, the Texas Protestant Lyndon Johnson proved much easier for the Vatican to deal with than the Irish Catholic Kennedy from Massachusetts. John XXIII never understood the strong secular tone of the Kennedy Administration, which made it very difficult for the pope to find ways to cooperate with the president. Washington rejected Vatican initiatives as out of character with the "separatist" tradition of American politics.[22] Under the Protestants Johnson, Nixon, and Carter, however, American and Vatican policies toward the Eastern bloc took parallel courses. As the 1960s progressed, the presence of the strongly anticommunist Hungarian Cardinal Primate Mindszenty in the American consulate in Budapest became a greater and greater political embarrassment to both Washington and Rome. Pope Paul VI finally removed him as primate in 1974. Kissinger's *détente* and Vatican Secretary of State Casaroli's *Ostpolitik* set a similar diplomatic tone during the 1970s.

In the early 1980s, increased friction between the superpowers caused difficulties for Western European governments both in domestic politics and in foreign policy. Bonn has had to deal with internal peace demonstrations and a narrowing of foreign policy options vis-à-vis the Soviet Union. In Eastern Europe the reactive stationing of Soviet missiles alarms governments and the public, although even the East German peace movement poses no more than an annoyance to governments in the Warsaw Pact. Soviet-American confrontation has also increased the tension between the Catholic Church and the superpowers. The Reagan Administration, while applauding papal initiatives in Poland, has criticized Catholic positions on arms control and Central America. The establishment of formal diplomatic relations between the United States and the Vatican is perceived by American policy makers as an opportunity to blunt such troublesome "clerical meddling."

Moscow has sought to benefit from papal positions on arms control and North-South economic relations but remains bitterly critical of John Paul II's Polish policy and his advocacy of human rights, especially religious freedom. For example, even before the pope's second visit to Poland in June 1983, the official Soviet news agency *Tass* declared that, in comparison with his predecessors, "the present head of the Catholic Church has taken a much more conservative and rigid position vis-à-vis the socialist world." These comments, excerpted from the Central Committee journal, *Political Self Education*, also tied current Vatican policy to "the growth of aggressive designs of imperialism and the stepped-up activity of the opponents of *détente*," code words for the United States.[23] With Ronald Reagan's Strategic Defense Initiative in the offing, Gromyko met with John Paul II for two hours on February 27, 1985. The Soviet foreign minister tried to persuade the pope to denounce the new American defense program, while John Paul wanted to focus on religious freedom in the Eastern bloc.[24]

The Eastern and Western political systems demonstrate significant differences in their political, social, economic, and religious characteristics. The Western system encourages transnational actors. Such a system suits the Catholic Church, not only because it offers much greater freedom but also because the Eastern system reserves expressive leadership to communist parties nationally and to the Communist Party of the Soviet Union (CPSU) internationally. Vatican financial resources, while less significant to the church than other transnational organizations, remain invested in the Western economic system. Thus, even though the mediational role between East and West remains attractive, it causes some friction with the natural Catholic affinity for Western values. On the other hand, Catholic freedom of operation in the West enables the church to play an autonomous role in Western decision making that is unavailable, for instance, to the Russian Orthodox Church in the East. For that reason alone, the battle for Western European and American Catholic support on arms control remains worth some trouble to both Washington and Moscow. All the political, economic, media, religious, and technological asymmetries of East and West influence the outcome of this particular struggle.

INTERNAL AND EXTERNAL CHURCH POLITICS AND GOALS

Up to this point we have focused on the Vatican's response to Soviet-American foreign policy issues and its attempt to influence them. A complete political analysis of even the single year 1962, however, reveals an intricate relationship between ideological and organizational changes within the church itself and external and internal church dynamics. The same Pope John XXIII who mediated between Kennedy and Khrushchev summoned the Second Vatican Council and issued the progressive encyclicals *Mater et magistra* (May 15, 1961) and *Pacem in terris* (April 11, 1963).[25] Not only did internal changes affect external policy, but external events stimulated internal changes. Monsignor Pietro Pavan, the leading drafter of *Pacem in terris*, commented that the pope's intervention in the Cuban missile crisis had led him to conceive of writing the latter encyclical.[26] Indeed, the Soviet leader received an advance copy of the encyclical (translated into Russian) during Cousins's second visit to him in April 1963.

Major conflicts between internal and external values occur when the Vatican and hierarchies face choices between the maintenance and strengthening of the ecclesiastical institution and the promotion of a consensus for Catholic values within society, such as advocacy of human rights in a totalitarian regime or denunciation of abortion.[27] Only in the defense of religious liberty do these values completely coincide, though certain opportunities do appear for ecclesiastical actions that promote Catholic values and strengthen the church's organizational position in the society at the same time. The American episcopate's deliberations over the peace pastoral in 1982 constituted just such a moment.

Postwar developments in the international economic system and the international penetration of the media have paralleled the influence of the Joannine encyclicals and Vatican Council II (1962-1965) in strengthening national Catholic churches.[28] Prior to the Second Vatican Council, a book such as this would not have placed such strong emphasis on Catholicism at the national level. However, the Council encouraged the emergence of national hierarchies as significant ecclesiastical political actors. National bishops conferences influence each other without necessarily using Vatican channels.[29]

The phenomenal increase in ecclesiastical contacts independent of Rome means that national Catholic Churches have become more and more oriented toward each other.[30] The resulting international ecclesiastical system, made up of relations within the church and of relations between the church and other domestic and international societal and political actors, poses a challenge to scholars and ecclesiastical decision makers.

Even with the recent increase in the political significance of national Catholic Churches, Rome maintains ultimate control and enormous political leverage. First, the Vatican appoints all bishops on the recommendation of the resident papal diplomat. Any cleric with career ambitions constantly considers Roman policy and curial contacts. Second, Catholic institutional socialization remains strong. Most of the important church leaders have studied in Roman ecclesiastical institutions like the Gregorian University. For example, 75 of the 116 cardinal electors in the 1978 papal elections had collected 120 degrees in Roman ecclesiastical universities.[31] Third, changes in Vatican political and social policy have made significant differences in the political and social policies of national churches, which in turn have greatly influenced national events. Pope Leo XIII's encyclical *Rerum novarum* (1891) focused Catholic attention on the concerns of the greatly expanding working class. This encouraged Catholics to found Christian Democratic parties in Europe and Latin America. Fourth, Pope John Paul II has sought to increase the international social and political influence of the church. By means of pilgrimages and modern communications he seeks to contact individual Catholics, thus partially bypassing national structures.

One of the major lessons reemphasized by the SALT II negotiations[32] concerned the intricate causality between domestic politics and international relations. The political composition of the United States Senate greatly influenced the discussions, so that the Soviet negotiators tolerated the intervention of individual senators whereas they never would have tolerated the same intervention by members of their own Supreme Soviet. In the end, President Carter was forced to withdraw a treaty that had no hope of being ratified. Current analysis of Catholic politics must seek to integrate the studies of Catholicism in its national contexts with an understanding of the church at the international level. Such integration poses the special challenge of this book.[33]

Finally, what level of analysis is possible in such a book? The descriptive contribution of this book consists in the way it relates conclusions from various national and regional studies to original research on the role of the Catholic Church in Soviet and American politics. On the explanatory level, the book attempts to account for the mutual influence of the Catholic Church and nation states in the international system and in national and regional systems. This explanation is difficult because the contemporary Catholic Church takes on an openly identifiable political role mainly in periods of great international stress such as the Cuban missile crisis. The strong political stands of the Polish church derive from the fact that Poland suffers from a permanent crisis in political legitimacy. The American Catholic episcopate stepped to the political centerstage when the Democratic Party failed to articulate a unified response to what many Americans perceived as a serious danger of nuclear war in the early 1980s. In more peaceful times and in less polarized political systems, Catholic political influence remains more diffuse and much harder to measure. It has to be analyzed from indirect indicators such as government reactions to hierarchical statements, media coverage, Catholic voting patterns, and survey research.

In this Introduction, I have discussed three major effects of contemporary technology on the global politics of the Catholic Church. First, the pervasive contemporary role of the media has influenced an already primarily expressive institution, the Catholic Church, toward an even stronger orientation to expressive power. John Paul II's use of Western secular media retains particular significance in the Catholic Church's struggle to shape public opinion on political, social, and moral issues, an activity directly related to the possibility of national consensus. Second, the Vatican has traditionally supported Western values and Western institutions. However, since the time of the Cuban missile crisis, the papacy has placed major emphasis on combining this Western orientation with the mediation of East-West, principally Soviet-American, conflict. The worsening of Soviet-American relations in the 1980s has greatly strained this dual role. Third, the year 1962 with the Cuban missile crisis and the beginning of Vatican II serves as an apt illustration of the reciprocal influence of external and internal Catholic politics. While internal and external goals sometimes reinforce each other, the Vatican and national hierarchies are often forced to choose between the internal maintenance and strengthening of the religious organization and the promotion of Catholic values within the larger society.

PART I

Catholic Political Culture: History, Organization, Ideology

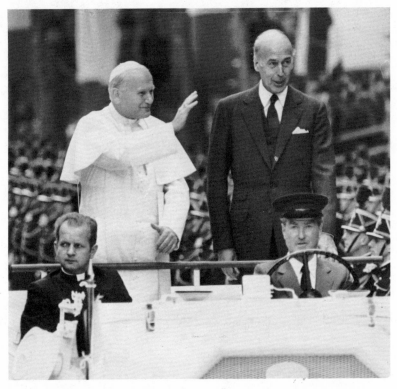

PARIS. John Paul II waves from an open car as he rides down the Champs-Elysées avenue with French President Valéry Giscard d'Estaing at his side after his arrival on a four-day visit, May 1980. AP/Wide World Photos.

CHAPTER 1

A Brief Political History of the Catholic Church in Europe

THE DIVISION OF EAST AND WEST

ON MAY 30, 1980, all the bells of Paris pealed to welcome John Paul II as he descended in a blue and white helicopter into the heart of the city.[1] President Valéry Giscard d'Estaing greeted the pope, who then reviewed the blue, crimson, and silver Garde Républicaine. From the Place de la Concorde Giscard and John Paul rode down the Champs-Elysées, providing Associated Press with an effective photo of the two leaders with the Arc de Triomphe in the background. The pope had come to visit "the church's eldest daughter" for the first time since Napoleon held Pope Pius VII prisoner at Fontainebleau in 1814. Giscard and John Paul proceeded to the 800-year-old cathedral of Notre Dame, where French government leaders, members of the clergy, and a large choir sang a *Te Deum*. The pope then said mass for a crowd of five thousand on the steps of the cathedral.

On his way to Notre Dame John Paul passed along the Boulevard St.-Germain, where crowds thinned out. St.-Germain's "bohemian and leftist"[2] character symbolized the major challenge of this particular papal visit. While 85 percent of the French are baptized, less than 20 percent of the population could be classified as "practicing Catholics." Before leaving Rome for Paris John Paul had spoken of a French national "crisis of belief." Thus the central papal message to France came in the form of a question that served as a keynote the pope's sermon to half a million Catholics at Le Bourget airport, "France, eldest daughter of the Church, are you being faithful to the promises of your Baptism?" This question later became a heading for a section of the French episcopal letter on peace. On the last day of his visit John Paul addressed a strong plea for peace to UNESCO.[3]

Cardinal Marty of Paris invited the various French political parties to send representatives to the ceremony at Notre Dame. The French Communist Party (PCF) sent official representatives, while the Socialist Party (PS) did not. Certain Socialist supporters remain particularly sensitive to the historical legacy of the bitter separation of church and state in 1905. Hence, Socialists could participate in the *Te Deum* and other ceremonies as individuals but not as representatives of the party. Socialist leader François Mitterand attended the government reception the following day at the Elysée Palace, but a Socialist spokesman insisted that members of his party did so in their official government, not party, capacities.

The *New York Times* (June 1, 1980) lead photo (front page, three columns at the top) showed Giscard introducing John Paul and PCF leader Georges Marchais at the Elysée. Communist spokesmen emphasized the importance of papal initiatives to the entire French nation, as well as the presence of Catholics within their own party and the PCF's desire to unite the entire working class, regardless of their philosophical or religious convictions.[4] Desiring to show concern for the French working class, John Paul chose to celebrate mass at the Basilica of Saint-Denis. The mayor of Saint-Denis and other PCF leaders expressed their satisfaction that the pope had chosen one of their strongholds to meet the workers. Also, as another PCF mayor remarked, the pope was a pilgrim of peace in an anxious world, just as Khrushchev had been in his time.

The AP news photo of John Paul and Giscard riding down the Champs-Elysées stirred French memories of an earlier time when the sword of the pope and the sword of the Frankish king cooperated to establish the political-religious basis of Western civilization. The great gothic cathedrals like Notre Dame reflect the historical glories of French Catholicism. France, as no other nation, epitomizes in her history the rise and subsequent disintegration of medieval Christendom. St. Thomas Aquinas and other great medieval philosophers and theologians gathered at Paris. The Protestant Reformation came to France, but in the end Catholicism triumphed because "Paris was worth a mass" to the Huguenot Henry of Navarre. The glorious French monarchy then established that state control over national Catholicism that gave historians the term "Gallicanism." The French Revolution decimated an ecclesiastical institution closely linked to the ancient regime. Subsequent French governments, even the most anticlerical, valued the church principally for its rural clerics who could be sent forth as missionary shock troops for colonial expansion. The 1905 separation of church and state expressed in law the bitter division of French society, with practicing Catholics associated with the political right. French anticlericalism remains particularly strident when compared to the anticlericalism of such Catholic countries as Italy.[5] The French church today inspires little allegiance among the working class or intellectuals. The clergy grows older and older with few replacements. The great cathedrals stand empty. From the Enlightenment to the present time, France best embodies the Catholic Church's failure to respond to the challenges of modern civilization.

Despite the general weakening of French Catholicism, however, individual French Catholic thinkers have pioneered missionary, theological, and organizational experimentation within the church. Nineteenth-century French missionaries set the tone for the political and social development of the Latin American church. Missionary history also demonstrates the importance of the nineteenth-century French church to Asia. In the same century French Catholic liberals such as Fr. Félicité de Lamennais and Count Charles de Montalembert sought to link Catholicism with the values of the Enlightenment. In the twentieth century the French philosophers Jacques Maritain and Emmanuel Mounier have articulated the general Catholic principles that underlie Christian Democracy. And the postwar *Nouvelle Théologie* of Yves Congar, Pierre Teilhard de Chardin, Henri de Lubac, and Jean Danièlou strongly influenced the international church, including papal nuncio to France, Angelo Roncalli (later John XXIII).[6] French postwar Catholicism also stimulated the first postwar intellectual stirrings of the American church.[7]

An understanding of the establishment of Western Christendom through the cooperation of the pope and the Frankish king is essential to the understanding of Catholic politics and East-West relations. The West initially defined itself in reaction against the Eastern empire with its capital at Constantinople (Byzantium). As the historian Walter Ullman has emphasized, "In more than one direction the history of the medieval papacy is co-terminous with the existence of the Byzantine empire. In brief, it was very largely the challenge by Constantinople and the response and reaction by the papacy which in vital and basic respects determined the path of this institution."[8] Some of the major cultural differences which persist between East and West, especially with regard to politics and religion, have roots deep in the period between the fourth and eighth centuries. Hedrick Smith reminds his readers that Russia did not pass through the Renaissance, the Reformation, and Constitutional Liberalism, but "absorbed Eastern Orthodox Christianity from Byzantium, endured Mongol conquest and rule, and then developed through centuries of czarist absolutism with intermittent periods of opening towards the West followed by withdrawal into continental isolation."[9]

Constantine's Edict of Milan (A.D. 313) guaranteed toleration to the Christian religion and allowed its adherents to emerge from the catacombs and to claim ecclesiastical goods confiscated during earlier persecutions. At this time the Roman church "had a somewhat superior but purely moral authority in comparison with other churches, just as Rome itself carried greater weight than, say, Milan or Marseille."[10] The church took on a legal corporate personality under the emperor according to Roman law. In fact, in the following year, the pagan emperor Constantine summoned the Council of Arle. In A.D. 325 Constantine, who took the traditional title of *pontifex maximus* (supreme priest) very seriously, presided over the great Council of Nicaea to put an end to the theological wrangling among Christian factions that was disturbing the empire. The Council condemned Arius and his followers. While over three hundred bishops attended, the Western contingent consisted of not more than four bishops with a fifth, Hosius of Cordova, an imperial appointee. The bishop of Rome was represented by two of his priests.[11]

The vast majority of bishops came to Nicaea from Greek-speaking lands, where theological controversy over such questions as the nature of Christ marked the Christian tradition. The Eastern tradition also focused on the local churches and the liturgical celebration of the Eucharist. The Eastern emperor maintained a strong religious role, and the patriarch of Constantinople who resided in the "New Rome" of this Eastern emperor gained increasing importance. The final religious split between East and West occurred in 1054. The fall of Constantinople (1453) and the subsequent development of the Russian Orthodox Church and the Russian state increased the prestige of the Russian Orthodox Synod, so that at times the rivalry for precedence between the "Second Rome" and the "Third Rome" exacerbated relations with other autonomous national Orthodox churches. These religious questions became part of the essential fabric of Russian and Eastern European history and politics.[12]

In the West, however, the removal of the imperial capital from Rome to Byzantium left Italy in the charge of the exarch at Ravenna with the resulting imperial neglect and political-religious vacuum of power. The barbarian Alaric sacked Rome in A.D. 410, and the city's security remained problematic for several centuries. Pope Leo I (440-461), whom tradition represents as stopping Attila at the gates of Rome, adopted the title of *pontifex maximus*. Leo combined the various preexisting juristic, theological, and biblical arguments to set the foundation for the Roman primacy (*principatus*) during the

Middle Ages. St. Peter, according to Leo's argument, had bestowed the power "to bind and to loose" (expressed in Roman legal terms) to his successor Pope Clement I and to succeeding bishops of Rome, thus separating the power of the office from the sanctity of the individual pope. The traditional binding force of Roman church decretals merely reflected this fact as they imitated the ruling style of imperial rescripts. This papal doctrine received another authoritative statement at the close of the fifth century in a letter from Pope Gelasius I to the emperor at Constantinople.

Having an ideological base, of course, does not automatically create a great bureaucratic organization. The Roman church had been well-organized in the third century, but it was the superb administrator Pope Gregory I (590-604) who built the beginnings of the medieval papal bureaucracy. Gregory imposed order on the far-flung papal economic interests, imported grain to feed the Romans, and sent soldiers against the Lombards. Finally, the eighth-century alliance between the papacy and King Pippin of the Franks established the Papal States and arranged papal support for the political legitimacy of Pippin's family. In 754 Pippin promised to restore to the patrimony of St. Peter the territories, including the old imperial exarchate at Ravenna, which had been seized by the Lombards. In return Pope Stephen III promised to excommunicate any Frankish king not from Pippin's family, and a little later anointed Pippin king at St. Denis. Pippin then crushed the Lombards and donated the conquered lands to the papacy in a solemn document deposited at St. Peter's tomb in Rome in the early summer of 756. The papacy had definitively escaped the political sphere of Constantinople and the insecurity of periodic barbarian invasions through the military prowess of the Franks.[13]

At the end of the century, however, the popes began to fear that they had merely exchanged the interference of Constantinople for the intervention of the Franks. Pippin's son Charlemagne was planning a "Second Rome" at this new capital, Aix-la-Chapelle, where he, like the rival emperor of the East, would have his "chief priest" at his beck and call. In reaction, Pope Leo III hit upon a magnificent and unexpected political and symbolic act to establish the independence and primacy of the papacy at Rome. On Christmas Day in A.D. 800, Leo crowned Charlemagne "Emperor of the Romans," thus transferring that title from the East to the West. In doing so the pope signified that the ultimate legitimacy to bestow and to withdraw that title lay with the papacy in Rome. "Charlemagne's coronation was, so to speak, the final and solemn and public act by which the papacy emancipated itself from the constitutional framework of the Eastern empire."[14]

The Carolingian vision of a "Second Rome" at Aix substituted a Western imperial captivity for an Eastern one. In defending papal prerogatives against both challenges, the popes made skillful use of a forged document called *The Donation of Constantine*, which had been fortuitously "discovered" by the papal chancery for Pope Stephen III in his negotiations with Pippin. According to the *Donation*, when Constantine left Rome for his new capital at Byzantium, he offered to relinquish his crown and imperial authority to Pope Silvester I. He also gave the papacy the right to rule Rome and "all provinces, localities and towns in Italy and the Western hemisphere." Since the Eastern emperors had infringed upon papal rights and thus forfeited the right to be considered Christian emperors, the pope could bestow that trust (*beneficium*) on a more worthy candidate. The *Donation* relied on an earlier *Legend of St. Silvester*, composed between 480 and 490, at a time when Pope Gelasius I (492-496) as assistant to Pope Felix II (483-492) was articulating the basic ideological principles of the papal legitimacy.

THE MEDIEVAL SYNTHESIS: CHRISTENDOM

Leo III's crowning of Charlemagne established the new political-religious relationship of Christendom in the West. This universal vision had its first great thematic presentation in the *City of God*, written by St. Augustine to rebut the pagan charge that the spread of Christianity had led to Alaric's sack of Rome in 410. Augustine related earthly and heavenly spheres by arguing that man always remains a citizen of two cities, the city of his birth and the city of God. While neither city could be precisely identified with existing institutions, Augustine presented the visible church as closely related to the city of God. He thus emphasized the reality of the church as an organized institution with a universal mandate.

The church's universal mandate to include all humanity within its scope imposed rights and duties on the heads of the spiritual and political institutions of Christendom. All matters affected salvation, and thus concerned the church even though different functions belonged to the pope and the emperor. The principal political-religious conflict during the Middle Ages concerned the demarcation of these responsibilities and the sources of legitimacy for these two offices. While nearly everyone accepted the general legitimacy of both pope and emperor, tension arose over their specific rights and duties. This dual organization and control of society in the interest of two great sets of related values became the point of departure for the great medieval struggle between pope and emperor, the investiture controversy of the latter half of the eleventh century. This battle between Pope Gregory VII and Emperor Henry IV occasioned a flood of sophisticated political literature reflecting the rising culture of the time.

The conflict began when Gregory prohibited lay investiture, the participation of secular rulers in the choice of the clergy. In supporting Gregory, the Papalists argued from the concept of the church as a monarchy in the imperial Roman tradition. The pope alone could create and depose bishops, call a General Council, and issue religious and moral decrees. If the pope excommunicated a ruler, that ruler stood outside the Christian body, and, therefore, could not be a ruler in Christendom. This independence of the church had been expressed much earlier by the courageous St. Ambrose of Milan in the fourth century. Ambrose had written the Eastern Emperor Valentinian that in matters of faith "bishops are wont to judge of Christian emperors, not emperors of bishops."[15] Ambrose refused to celebrate the Eucharist in the presence of the Emperor Theodosius because of the latter's guilt in a massacre. He also refused to surrender one of his churches to the Arians upon the order of Emperor Valentinian. The most ambitious statement of papal political power came in the bull *Unam sanctam* (1302) by Boniface VIII, who claimed that the church was the direct source of both spiritual and temporal powers. Papal apologists continued to cite the *Donation of Constantine* until Nicholas of Cusa and Lorenzo Valla exposed it as a forgery in the fifteenth century.

Emperor Henry IV and the Imperialists countered that precedent favored the emperor because, since the time of Constantine, rulers had always had some influence over the selection of prelates. The emperor's power also came directly from God. Imperial apologists also stressed the Christian tradition of passive obedience enunciated by Pope St. Gregory. Faced with the anarchy of the barbarian invasions, this architect of the papal bureaucracy stressed the sanctity of government. In his *Pastoral Rule*, Gregory counsels passive obedience with the words, "For indeed the acts of rulers are not to be smitten with the sword of the mouth, even though they are rightly judged to be blameworthy."[16]

In their fierce political-religious conflict, both Gregory VII and Henry IV denied each other's legitimacy and supported rival claimants. In the end, Henry IV miscalculated politically and failed to appreciate the changed temper of the times. Although his father had deposed and installed a number of popes, Henry IV was forced to undertake a dangerous and difficult winter crossing of the Alps to meet with Gregory at Canossa in January 1077. The pope lifted Henry's excommunication but did not reinstate him in his exercise of government. Canossa and the events leading to it demonstrated that medieval Europe "was in fact ready for the reception of and fertilization with papal governmental ideas."[17] The pope, lacking close military allies, had excommunicated and deposed the most powerful king in Europe for defiance of papal law, thereby forcing the emperor to appear before him as a penitent. The political-religious balance had changed significantly since the time of Charlemagne.

Despite the fierceness of the investiture controversy, Christendom remains more notable for its shared political-religious values than for the constant tension between the pope and the emperor. Both sides subscribed to the basic legitimacy of the other and to a harmonious vision combining earthly and heavenly claims. St. Thomas Aquinas best articulated this sophisticated cooperative relationship. Building on the revival of Aristotle in the West, Thomas separated and balanced the claims of state and church, nature and grace, and reason and faith. The works of St. Thomas and the cathedrals attest to an ordered vision of reality in which each creature and each order of creatures had its specific place, thus creating a universal harmony. According to this vision, society, like nature, consisted of a system of ends and purposes in which the lower served the higher, and the higher directed and guided the lower. Therefore, rulership became a moral trust for the whole community. The ruler laid the foundation of human happiness by maintaining peace and order and providing needed public services. The moral purpose of political rule implied limited authority exercised in accordance with law. Ultimately, this led to heavenly life, but the heavenly realm belonged to the church, not to the ruler.

The weakness of medieval sectarian rebellion illustrates the political power of such a vision shared by church and state. On this question Ernst Troeltsch presents his famous distinction between "church" and "sect." The distinction arises in Troeltsch's discussion of medieval Catholicism in which the universalist church did not allow scope for the radical Christian ideas of sectarianism except as a special monastic class.[18] Asian scholars accustomed to the grand political-religious rebellions of traditional China search in vain for groups like the Yellow Turbans or the White Lotus.[19] Millennial ideology for such rebellions was not lacking. Orthodox

Christian scriptures such as the Book of Daniel and the Apocalypse provided futuristic visions for prophetic interpretation. Sporadic rebellions, generally anticlerical and anti-Semitic, employed such texts to attack the church-state monopoly. These sects rose principally between the late eleventh and the early sixteenth centuries in the valley of the Rhône, Belgium, northern France, and Holland. At that time these areas experienced rapid social and economic change in which the population increased rapidly. But such movements like the Shepherds Crusade and such heterodox preachers like the Drummer of Niklashausen were quashed quickly and easily once the two swords saw them as a threat to the basic legitimacy of Christendom. In the case of the Shepherds Crusade, Pope John XXII excommunicated the *pastoureaux* and called on Seneschal of Beaucaire to destroy those would-be crusaders. Seneschal killed many in battle and hung others in trees in groups of twenty or thirty. The prince-bishop of Wurzburg arrested the Drummer, tried him for heresy and sorcery, burned him at the stake, and threw his ashes in the river. The combined legitimacy of the two swords, either in excommunication plus military force, or in the single person of the prince-bishop, rendered impossible effective medieval sectarian rebellion.[20]

Such an alliance between political and ecclesiastical leaders would seem to be an excellent context for illustrating Vaillancourt's contention that since its inception "the Catholic Church has moved gradually from grass-roots democracy and collegial authority to a vast concentration of power and authority in the hands of the clergy and hierarchy, and especially in the hands of the pope and his curia."[21] Indeed, Vaillancourt follows Antonio Gramsci in seeing vigorous lay protest movements as either destroyed like the Drummer of Niklashausen or coopted into reform by papal integration, as happened with the Franciscans. Part of the difficulty in considering this issue comes from the wide penetration of clerics throughout the medieval elites. Tonsure, ordination, and even episcopal consecration could be received as the prerequisites for political and economic power, without significant loyalty to the papacy or even to the church. As a result, the four variables of church status (clergy or laity), political democratization, ecclesiastical democratization, and degree of corruption all operated independently of each other with a myriad of variations. The most important medieval challenge to papal power came from the Conciliar Movement, which showed its greatest strength at the Councils of Constance (1414-1418) and Basel

(1431-1449). However, the Conciliar Movement did not have popular support, and faded after the healing of the papal schism.[22]

In Leo I's theory on papal legitimacy, individual holiness had been divorced from the legitimate exercise of his juridic power. Later corrupt popes did not shake the ideological basis of the institution. In fact, any layman could become pope, and very few medieval popes were priests or bishops at the time of their election or appointment.[23] Kings and others saw the appointment of bishops and abbots as a normal way of keeping control over their domains. It is easy to see why the ex-monk Gregory VII felt he had to get control of the appointment of bishops if he were to reform the church. Both the Gregorian and Tridentine Reforms contributed to the centralized power of the papacy, not to the mass democratization of ecclesiastical institutions.

THE COUNTER-REFORMATION AND THE CATHOLIC STATES

If peasant sectarian rebellion proved futile, other attacks on the papal and imperial institutions soon surfaced and swept away the universal synthesis of Christendom. The rise of the nation state shook the primacy of the Holy Roman Emperor, while Luther's challenge, following upon the fresh new ideologies unleashed by the Renaissance, resulted in a pluralism of religious institutions in the West. The Catholic Church eventually responded to the Reformation by calling the Council of Trent (1545-1563), but the difficulties experienced in convening the bishops illustrate many of the weaknesses of sixteenth-century Catholicism.

Despite the fact that German Catholic popular sentiment for the Council increased as the seriousness of Luther's challenge became apparent and Emperor Charles I of Spain championed the idea, Charles's rival, King Francis I of France, opposed it. Pope Clement VII (1523-1534) was consistently hostile, but his objections paled when compared with those of his Curia who feared a diminution of their own power.[24] Clement VII's successor, Pope Paul III (1534-1549), found his efforts to convoke the Council entangled with his simultaneous efforts to establish his son Pierluigi among the reigning families of Europe. The pope eventually succeeded in carving out a fiefdom of the duchies of Parma and Piacenza for Pierluigi, and in marrying Pierluigi's son into the emperor's family. Such concerns reflected the decadence of Renaissance worldliness that made the ecclesiastical reforms of Trent all too necessary.

The pope eventually located the Council at Trent, then a prince-bishopric and the first German city outside of Italy on the great thousand-year-old road between Rome and Northern Europe. In summoning the Council, the pope stressed the necessity that the bishops reaffirm Catholic dogma in the face of Protestant challenges, while the emperor focused on the need for internal ecclesiastical reformation. The Council fathers worked on both simultaneously. Paul III appointed three cardinal legates who between them combined administrative experience (Gian Maria del Monte), austere theological learning (Marcello Cervini), and Renaissance humanism (the Englishman Reginald Pole). The great majority of bishops attending (187 of 270 for the three sessions) came from Italian sees. On the question of internal reformation, the common practice of clerics simultaneously holding more than one see, abbey, or parish to extract as much revenue as possible proved the greatest challenge. The response of the "reforming bishops" was to "use the device of the 'automatic' penalty" so that absentee bishops, bishops holding more than one see, concubinary prelates who defied the warnings of a provincial council, etc., were penalized or deposed immediately *ipso facto*.[25] The bishops attacked the generally corrupt and uneducated state of the clergy with provisions for clerical training, especially through special colleges established by each bishop, where selected boys would live and study under religious supervision. These colleges, envisaged as a fruitful seedbed (*seminarium*) of vocations, became the great means of producing a holy and educated clergy loyal to the church.

In terms of dogma, the Council responded to the theological attacks of the Reformation. The main doctrinal treatises, written at a high theological level, defended Catholic positions on Justification and the seven sacraments. Perhaps even more influential was the literary monument of the Council, the so-called *Catechism of the Council of Trent*. Finally, in 1566 a Dominican, Michele Ghislieri, became Pope (later Saint) Pius V (1566-1572). Pius ruled the church according to Trent, vigorously pushing reform. In this, Counter-Reformation popes were aided by a new religious order, the Jesuits, founded by a Spanish nobleman, Ignatius of Loyola (1491-1556) in 1540. Jesuit schools became especially important to the revitalization of Catholicism in Europe. The Jesuits' second general, the theologian Diego Lainez, had been active at the Council of Trent during its last two years. Thus Trent and the Counter-Reformation established the major parameters of internal Catholic life until Vatican Council I (1869-1870).

Theologian Avery Dulles has noted that the major ecclesiastical paradigm from Trent until the encyclical *Mystici corporis* (Mystical Body) (1943) was that of a monarchical institution. The Tridentine reform was directed from Rome, with an emphasis on institutional response, "automatic" penalties, and those concrete signs such as the visible church and its sacraments that were attacked by the Protestants. The Counter-Reformation thus rescued the church from Renaissance corruption and Protestant "heresy," but at the price of separating it from many new trends in European thought. From the time of Trent until Vatican Council I, the Catholic Church was remarkably consistent in rejecting almost every major current of modern life. During that time, Rome came under siege from Conciliarists, Spiritualists, Protestants, Jansenists, Liberals, Rationalists, Darwinists, Gallicans, and other purveyors of novel doctrines.

Secular political and intellectual trends from the sixteenth to the nineteenth century affected different states in different ways, but in general the Catholic Church suffered a severe loss of influence throughout Europe during the eighteenth century. Introducing their series of studies on *Church and Society in Catholic Europe of the Eighteenth Century*, William Callahan and David Higgs point out four general negative characteristics: the "decline in vocations, tension between popular piety and the religion taught by the ecclesiastical elite, the dominance of a wealthy urban church over an impoverished rural one, [and] the difficult relationship between papal and national authority." National Catholic Churches became the captives of powerful monarchs. That the Catholic princes could force "the suppression of the [Jesuit] order by a weak papacy revealed how far the alliance between throne and altar had shifted in the former's favour."[26]

The historian Owen Chadwick stresses the identification of the Jesuits with the Counter-Reformation.

Founded in the age of the Counter-Reformation, intended to be the instrument of its policies, large in historical accounts of its course, engaged with the wars of religion, the Society of Jesus was the symbol of the Counter-Reformation. Anyone who wanted the Church to grow out of the Counter-Reformation suspected Jesuits instinctively, and hardly noticed that Jesuits themselves had been helping the Church to grow out of the Counter-Reformation. They were not only too conservative in higher education. They were a flag, a legend.[27]

The Jesuits' great enemy within the church were the Jansenists, whose order was founded at Port-Royal in France. Outside of France, however, the term "Jansenist" became a general symbol of the desire to reform the church of the Counter-Reformation. Thus, some popular writers divide eighteenth-century Catholics into "Jesuits" and "Jansenists."

Although the Jesuits took a special vow of obedience to the pope and fought to maintain papal prerogatives, incidents like the papal decision against Jesuit missionary tolerance for Confucian ritual in China allowed Catholics to differentiate between papal and Jesuit interests. Chadwick lists that Chinese Rites decision (1704) and the popular backlash against the Jesuit-supported papal bull *Unigenitus* (1713), which roused great controversy by its all-encompassing condemnation of the French Jansenists, as particularly damaging to the reputation of the Jesuit order. Catholics like the great Italian historian and priest Lodovico Muratori (1672-1750) could accept the new principles of the Enlightenment without supporting the Jansenists or losing appreciation for popular piety. However, in general, the Enlightenment in its philosophical principles and regalism in church-state relations hurt both the papacy and the Jesuits.

During the eighteenth century the papacy thus lost control of the various national churches to regalist ministers like Carvalho, Marquis of Pombal of Portugal, who perceived the Jesuits as the major proponents of papal influence within his domain. Pombal also resented the resistance of Jesuit missionaries to his instructions to local bishops during the War of the Seven Reductions in Paraguay. In 1759 Pombal expelled the Jesuits from Portugal. Other Catholic states did the same. Finally, in 1769 Pombal manipulated the election of Pope Clement XIV with the expectation that the new pope would supress the Jesuits. After a series of temporizing moves, Clement finally suppressed the order in 1773. The one monarch who might have saved the Jesuits was the Empress Maria Theresa of Austria. However, the Hapsburgs, deeply conscious of their special Catholic vocation since the defeat of the Turks outside of Vienna nearly a century earlier, had already embarked upon "the most successful of Catholic reforms during the eighteenth century."[28] Such eighteenth-century reforms, even when they served orthodox Catholic goals, increased regal power at the expense of the papacy. While Clement's action against the Jesuits proved very popular in Catholic Europe, the Orthodox Empress Catherine II of Russia, exercising her own regalist prerogatives, refused to promulgate the papal decree of suppression in her dominions, thus providing for a link between the "old Jesuits" and the "new Jesuits" when Pope Pius VII, having just returned from his captivity under Napoleon, restored the order in 1814.

The greatly weakened Catholic Church of the late eighteenth century could not cope with the French Revolution. When Pope Pius VI condemned France's Civil Constitution of the Clergy, French Revolutionary troops marched into Italy. General Alexander Berthier captured the eighty-one-year-old pontiff, and Pius died in captivity. The papacy thus reached the nadir of its political influence.

Papal fortunes rose temporarily with the election in Venice of the cultured fifty-eight-year-old Cardinal Barnaba Chiaramonti as Pope Pius VII in 1800. The pope immediately chose the shrewd Cardinal Ercoli Consalvi as secretary of state, and the two restored relations with France. But when Napoleon demanded full political obedience, Pius refused. The French again invaded the Papal States, captured the pope, and brought him back to France, where he remained a political-religious problem for Napoleon throughout his reign. After the defeat of Napoleon, Consalvi attained the restoration of the Papal States at the Congress of Vienna. Despite the immediate territorial benefits of Consalvi's great diplomatic triumph, however, this arrangement continued the union of papal spiritual and temporal powers, and tied the papacy to the forces of European restoration.

The desire to defend the church's temporal power contributed significantly to the papacy's support for the anti-Liberal position throughout most of the nineteenth century. The French Revolution, allied with secularism, threatened to destroy the church and its moral influence. Many of the revolutionaries were virulently anticlerical. Not only had the church traditionally allied itself with conservative forces, but these forces had restored the Papal States. Metternich, Europe's dominant figure during the first third of the nineteenth century, exerted political pressure to keep the papacy on its anti-Liberal course. In addition, the liberalism and nationalism of the Italian *risorgimento*[29] threatened the pope's temporal power. Following the French captivity of Popes Pius VI and Pius VII, subsequent popes could not conceive of an independent spiritual power without a territorial base.

The political alliance between Catholics and Conservatives produced obvious disadvantages. Support of monarchical and aristocratic privileges ran counter to the social and economic interests of many Catholics. For example, Liberal extension of the franchise could produce expanded Catholic influence in some countries like Great Britain. Nineteenth-century Conservative regimes used all the measures of church control (such as vetoing episcopal appointments) that their predecessors had employed before the French

Revolution. As a result, a Catholic Liberal movement[30] began in the 1820s and lasted through the next two decades. The movement grew strongest in English-speaking countries and in the Netherlands, was weaker in France and Germany, and weakest in Austria and Italy. Even though Pope Gregory XVI condemned its most effective exponent, the French priest Lamennais in 1834, Lamennais's followers Montalembert and Fr. Henri Lacordaire remained in the church to propagate his views.

The Catholic Liberal movement reached its peak in the revolutions of 1848 when Catholics and Liberals cooperated in establishing parliaments in many European countries. Two years before, the cardinals had chosen a well-known Liberal and nationalist, Cardinal Mastai Ferretti, as Pope Pius IX. Liberals everywhere rejoiced at Ferretti's election to replace the conservative Gregory, who had even called on the Catholic Poles to submit to the Orthodox czar during the Polish uprising of 1831. However, in 1848 Pius shocked Italians by refusing to join in the war against Austria. Pius feared the nationalization of the papacy and the loss of his temporal power. When his chief minister, the Liberal Pellegrino Rossi, was assassinated in disorders that also threatened the pope, Pius jettisoned internal reform and fled to Gaeta in the Kingdom of Naples. From Gaeta he called on the Christian powers to restore his position as guaranteed by the Congress of Vienna. This experience of abortive Liberalism set the tone for the rest of his pontificate (1846-1878), the longest since St. Peter. During this time dogmatism grew among both Liberals and Catholics. The growing prestige of science made the Liberals see the church as the preeminent obstacle to human progress. The clash between Catholics and Liberals became especially bitter over control of education. Pius IX enunciated the Catholic condemnation of all things modern in his *Syllabus of Errors* (1864). The *Syllabus* condemned propositions favoring the withdrawal of state-supported schools from church control, the separation of church and state, the abolition of the temporal power of the papacy, and religious toleration. The document summarizes its intent when condemning Error No. 80: "The Roman pontiff can and should reconcile himself with, and adjust to, progress, liberalism, and recent civilization."[31] Pius's attempts to deal with modern nation states resulted in numerous diplomatic failures, from conflicts with Catholic states in Southern Europe and Latin America to the shock of Otto von Bismarck's *Kulturkampf*. When he died, only four countries still had representatives at the Holy See. The international position of the papacy had reached another low point.

After 1849 the pope depended on the Christian powers to preserve the Papal States. The Austrian defeat of 1859 prepared the way for the loss of all papal territory except that around Rome. Finally, the Franco-Prussian War forced Napoleon III to withdraw his troops from Italy in August 1870. Rome surrendered to the Italian troops in September. One month later Pope Pius IX suspended the First Vatican Council, which had been meeting since the preceding December. Pius had summoned the Council "to restate the faith in certain matters where it had been attacked or misunderstood; to review the whole matter of clerical life and its needs; to provide new safeguards for Christian marriage and the Christian education of youth; and to take up in this new age the ancient problems of the relations of Church and State and provide appropriate guidance, so as to promote peace and prosperity in the national life everywhere."[32] Papal infallibility had not been placed on the original agenda, but over 500 bishops petitioned that the matter be considered immediately and separately from its "normal" context within discussions on the nature of the church. On July 13, after prolonged and strenuous debate on the question, the bishops voted: for (451), against (88), for with reservations (62), and not voting (76). The solemn promulgation of papal infallibility took place five days later. Thus, the pope received his strongest religious legitimacy as his temporal empire crumbled.

THE MISSIONARY CRUCIBLE: BRITAIN AND IRELAND

Of the three most impressive "infallibist" orators at the First Vatican Council singled out by the historian Hughes, two represented the British Isles: Cardinals Paul Cullen (Dublin) and Henry Manning (Westminster).[33] From the perspective of the late twentieth century, Cardinal Cullen might be considered one of the two or three most influential ecclesiastics of the entire nineteenth century. Cullen's significance derives from the enormous impact of Irish Catholicism on the formation of the Catholic churches in the United States, Australia, New Zealand, the Union of South Africa, and even Britain itself. It was not just that Irish missionaries staffed these churches, but also that the Irish ecclesiastical model of the last half of the nineteenth century determined the very style of Catholicism in these countries. Rome dispatched Cullen to form the Irish church during the twenty years that preceded the First Vatican Council.[34] It was precisely during the years 1850-1870 that the alliance between European Catholicism and European Conservatism reached its zenith.

Ireland had always had a strong missionary tradition. St. Patrick came to the island in A.D. 432 and quickly converted the inhabitants. Christianity brought Greek and Roman classicism, which, when mixed with a strong native cultural tradition, "made Ireland the leader of Western culture from the close of the sixth century."[35] During the "Dark Ages" Irish monks brought faith and civilization to the European continent. In his book *Ireland and the Foundations of Europe*,[36] Benedict Fitzpatrick includes a map of "Hibernicized Medieval Europe" showing the wide extent of Irish influence. The shaded area of Irish cultural and religious influence reaches east through Central Europe to the gates of Budapest and south to Florence. Charlemagne's empire benefited considerably from the educational, cultural, and religious exploits of Celtic monasticism.

As Ireland had been the starting point for the revival of pre-Carolingian culture in Western Europe, the island was the first to suffer from the new barbarian invasions of the ninth century. Churches and monasteries offered rich and easy conquests to the Viking raiders. Raids led to settlements, and Olaf the White established the Norse Kingdom of Dublin in 851. Following the Norman conquest of Britain, the English began their invasion of Ireland in 1169. King Henry II of England secured papal blessings for this "Christian" endeavor from his good friend, the first and only English pope Adrian VI (Nicolas Breakspeare). The papal bull *Laudibiliter* recognized that Henry had not come to Ireland merely to conquer the "semi-barbarious inhabitants" but also to guide them firmly toward enlightenment and a better life and to achieve "voluntary submission of the Irish Roman Catholic Church and the princes."[37] By 1172 the English held most of Ireland's high ecclesiastical offices and considered the first stage of the conquest a success. However, in the sporadic fighting that continued until the Protestant Reformation, the Irish often triumphed, as when a Scots-Irish force under Edward deBruce overran the original Ulster plantations in 1314. Richard II's grand army of 1399 constituted the last major effort of the Catholic English kings to maintain their sovereignty over Ireland. During the interim, the Irish recovered the greater part of their land, their language, and their culture.

The English Reformation introduced the factor of religious persecution to national struggle. This explosive combination of religion and nationalism resulted in more than three centuries of bitter conflict throughout the island, and inspires violence in Ulster to this day. The Irish risings of 1598, 1641, and 1698 are popularly associated with the Irish Lord Hugh O'Neal, the brutal repression by Oliver Cromwell, and the victory of William of Orange, respectively. Every July 12th since then, Ulster Orangemen have celebrated William's victory with marches, speeches, and often anti-Catholic rioting. In 1695 the British began the passage of a series of laws known as the Penal Code. The Penal Code denied Catholics the right to vote, hold office, learn a profession, own land, etc. Catholic priests were not permitted to travel outside of their parish, and all members of the Catholic hierarchy were exiled. The grave injustices suffered by Irish Catholics roused men like Jonathan Swift, dean of a Protestant cathedral, to come to their aid. Swift did not particularly like Catholics, but he passionately hated injustice. In calling for an end to English rule, Swift formulated the policy of *Sinn Fein* (Ourselves Alone). He attempted to bring Protestants and Catholics together into a movement for Irish nationalism. Such initiatives stimulated the formulation of the Society of United Irishmen, of which the Protestant Theobald Wolfe Tone became the leader in 1791. The Society of United Irishmen called for equality, liberty, and fraternity—the slogan of the French Revolution. In 1793 England declared war on France and attempted to shut down the Society of United Irishmen as well. By 1795 the Orange Society, an anti-Catholic group, began an attack against Wolfe Tone's Society, thus precipitating another civil war. England rushed in foreign mercenaries to keep the peace, and transformed Ireland from a colony into an integral part of Great Britain in 1801.

The Irish Catholic Church supported the Act of Union because the bishops felt that the English Parliament would reciprocate by immediately granting Catholic emancipation. The parliament did not, so the church used its legitimacy and organizational network to aid the Irish politician Daniel O'Connell. O'Connell, who also established his own mass-based party, the Catholic Association, forced the English Parliament to grant Catholics the right to sit as members of that body. However, when O'Connell switched the target of his campaign to a repeal of the Act of Union, the Irish bishops withdrew their support and resources. Thus, this period following the Act of Union set the political parameters for the uneasy alliance of the British state and the Irish Catholic Church during the nineteenth century. This political-religious alliance reserved all political and social questions to the British government, while the Irish bishops controlled the educational, moral, and religious life of their countrymen. Both London and Rome supported the Irish bishops, who fostered a new devotional Catholicism. Cardinal Paul Cullen became the great architect of this new Irish Catholicism, while the British-financed national seminary at Maynooth became the institutional symbol of its religious orientation.

Cardinal Cullen had been the director of the Irish Seminary in Rome, where he made many connections with curial prelates. The Vatican returned Cullen to Ireland as both archbishop of Armagh and as apostolic delegate. Cullen used this concentration of power to isolate the independent-minded bishops among his countrymen. He made sure that only priests who supported his stands became bishops.[38] Cullen's influence thus resulted in a hierarchy and a clergy that reflected his own values of stern discipline, efficient administration, and strong loyalty to Rome.

The cooperation of the Irish hierarchy, British government, and Roman Curia proved so successful because the new Irish Catholicism met the needs of the emerging Irish middle class during the period 1829-1890. At the beginning of this period rural Irish Catholics could be divided into a marginal class (farmers with less than thirty acres of land) and a middle class consisting of farmers with more land and rural merchants.[39] No Irish Catholic urban class of any significance existed. In 1829 the marginal class constituted the most numerous and important Catholic group in Ireland, but it did not have surplus income to devote to national aspirations. By the end of the period, however, the middle class had achieved dominance, and with it the will and means to achieve national independence.

The Great Potato Famine of the late 1840s affected the two classes in different ways. Prior to the Famine the Catholic population had increased rapidly, resulting in a greater and greater proportion of Irish Catholics living at the subsistence level. For example, in 1847, 572,912 of Ireland's 730,009 farmers tilled less than 30 acres of land.[40] The Famine devastated this marginal class. One million starved, and another million emigrated, especially to the East Coast of the United States. Gaelic culture suffered because it had been strongest among the marginal class of the West and South. Thus, the Famine simultaneously deprived Ireland of a quarter of its population and of its primary source of national identity.

The middle-class population remained constant as more and more members of the marginal class emigrated throughout the nineteenth century. As a result, the middle class began to dominate Irish political, social, and economic life. Middle-class social values emphasized frugality and puritanical mores. For example, after the

Famine the Irish married at a much later age. Terence Brown attributes this directly to the Famine:

The Famine, in which the Irish rural population, particularly in the congested districts of the west of Ireland, suffered terribly, confronted the small farmer with the abject insecurity of his position. . . . In the years following the Famine Irish rural life was characterized not by the agreeable carelessness of earlier decades in matters of land and marriage, but by calculated sensitivity to the economic meaning of marriage.[41]

The renewed and redisciplined Catholic Church of Cardinal Cullen grew simultaneously with the Irish Catholic rural middle class. Indeed, this "nation-forming" class provided the enlarged church with most of its new money and manpower. Prior to the Famine the Irish church had been understaffed, with many of its somewhat undisciplined clergy suffering from the vices of greed, lust, and alcoholism.[42]

After the Famine the church's financial position improved dramatically. The Catholic middle-class prospered and contributed as never before. The church tightened its own organization so that bequests given to the church now stayed with the institution and did not get diverted to dead clergymen's families. The British government also became more generous. For example, after the Famine London tripled the annual amount contributed to Maynooth Seminary. Furthermore, the Charitable Bequests Act, passed by the English Parliament at this time, guaranteed the church's right to keep bequests against individual lawsuits. English banks also became much more willing to lend money to the church. With all these resources, Cullen and his clergy embarked on an ambitious ecclesiastical and educational building program, thus greatly strengthening the institutional position of the Catholic Church in Irish society. Despite opportunistic use of British support, Cullen served the church first. He firmly resisted state control of schools. He also refused to cooperate with the British in a nondenominational university system, but built an independent Catholic university at great expense.

With the demise of Gaelic culture, Cullen and his priests borrowed heavily from those Jansenist strains of continental piety which best fit middle-class social values. The great increase in Irish clergy also came from the middle class. While in 1850 5,000 clerics served 5 million Catholics, in 1900 14,000 clerics served 3.3 million Catholics.[43] Thus the middle class, which in most European countries sparked the industrial revolution, devoted its entrepreneurial talent to the Irish church. Success to this class meant the ecclesiastical advancement of a bishopric or at least the well-merited purple of a monsignor's rank. Critics called such collusion "a social order in which church, farmer and grocer and gombeen publican comprise a corrupt and corrupting alliance, intent on social advancement."[44] The episcopal leaders of such a system feared the confusion inherent in rapid industrialization, so many advocated retaining cottage industries. Ireland remained predominantly rural, pious, and sexually conservative. Not only did French Jansenism fit the native social mores of the new clergy, but French Jansenist professors predominated at Maynooth.[45]

The Devotional Revolution of Cardinal Cullen characterized Irish religious life until the 1960s. Weekly mass attendance rose from 33 percent in 1840 to 95 percent in 1890.[46] Cullen borrowed heavily from continental piety and introduced devotions such as the rosary, forty hours, perpetual adoration, novenas, the Way of the Cross, benediction, vespers, devotion to the Sacred Heart, jubilees, triduums, pilgrimages, and shrines. The new Catholic devotionalism provided both the middle class and Irish emigrants with a new sense of national cultural identity following the decimation of Gaelic culture. The noted Dominican friar, Father Tom Burke, remarked in 1872, "Take an Irishman wherever he is found, all over the earth, and any casual observer will at once come to the conclusion, 'Oh, he is an Irishman, he is a Catholic!' The two go together."[47] Thus, the church provided both a new sense of national identity for the Irish and a seemingly endless supply of missionary bishops and clergy for English-speaking Catholics throughout the world.

The Potato Famine drove many Irish to England, Wales, and Scotland in search of employment. Although immigration to Great Britain slowed after 1900, the Irish and their descendents still constitute the largest Catholic group in the British Isles. The Irish joined two indigenous groups, the old Catholic families (Towneleys, Howards, Welds, Stonors) and the converts (John Henry Newman, G. K. Chesterton, Ronald Knox, Evelyn Waugh, Graham Greene). Many of the Catholic intellectuals, e.g. Hilaire Belloc in *Europe and the Faith*,[48] emphasized the part Catholicism had played in the medieval unity of the continent. Numerous theological and literary works offered the romance and legitimacy of an earlier England and inspired English-speaking Catholics throughout the world. The American public television audience of the 1980s was not the first group to be fascinated by Evelyn Waugh's tale of the old British Catholic aristocracy, *Brideshead Revisited*.

John Henry Newman preached his famous sermon on "The Second Spring" shortly after the restoration of the English Catholic hierarchy in 1850. The term "Second Spring" came to designate the renaissance of English Catholicism during the latter half of the nineteenth century. In unifying the Irish immigrants with upper-class English aristocracy and converts, loyalty to Rome played a special role. J. Derek Holmes titles his book on nineteenth-century English Catholicism *More Roman than Rome*.[49] Peter Comen comments that the virulent antipapal prejudice of the preceding centuries "provoked its own antithesis in the special emphasis on loyalty to Rome among English Roman Catholics, although this was usually coupled with strong protestations of patriotism."[50] Comen notes the major role that Roman ecclesiastical education has played in the formation of the English episcopate. For example, in the 1940s twelve of twenty-seven bishops had received at least a part of their higher education while residing at the English College at Rome. Comen then quotes Cardinal John Heenan on his predecessor Cardinal Arthur Hinsley:

The essence of the Roman Spirit is personal loyalty to the Holy Father and a devotion to the Church which is neither national or parochial. . . . But when all this had been said the words remain quite inadequate as a description of "Romanita"—the Roman Spirit. It must, therefore, be stressed that by far the greatest influence in the making of a Roman is the Vatican itself. St. Peter's audiences of the Vicar of Christ and the solemn pontifical ceremonies, exercise an imperceptible but permanent effect upon the young clerics. . . . It is impossible for the Roman-trained priest to return without a pride in the Church of God, an ineffaceable impression of her strength and immensity, together with a consciousness of being, above all things, one of the Pope's men. To be a Roman, in a word, means to possess a width of view which is truly Catholic.[51]

Despite the many diplomatic fiascos of the interminable pontificate of Pius IX (1846-1878), Irish and British Catholicism flourished and demonstrated a strong attachment to the Holy See. By the time of Vatican II, both churches had built strong institutional bases, with a clergy that looked to Rome for guidance.

PAPAL REFORM: LEO XIII TO PAUL VI

The twenty years of Catholic-Conservative alliance, 1850-1870, had in many ways isolated the church from contemporary social and economic problems. With the election of Pope Leo XIII (1878-1903), however, the Vatican began to look for at least a limited rapprochement with many of the changes in European life that had taken place since the fifteenth century. The basic Catholic distrust of democracy remained, but the new pope softened Pius IX's tone of denunciation and called on Catholics to search for practical positive solutions to contemporary social, economic, and political problems. Leo XIII published four encyclicals on the relation of church and state between 1881 and 1890. "In these he confirmed the condemnation of secular liberalism and democracy by his predecessors, but spoke of a Legitimate Liberty while urging Catholics to accept existing political institutions for the common good."[52] Leo's major social contribution lay in his defense of workers' rights in the rapidly evolving industrial societies. In *Rerum novarum* (1891), Leo approved a larger role for the state in the protection of workers, attempted to define a just wage, and emphasized the legitimacy and necessity of trade unions. Such a stand seemed very progressive in the late nineteenth century, especially when contrasted with the popular writings of "Social Darwinists" like Herbert Spencer in Britain and William Graham Sumner in the United States. *Rerum novarum* definitively placed the papacy on the side of the more liberal school of Catholic social thought against the Catholic Conservatives of that period who argued that social problems derived primarily from moral weakness.[53] Catholics now had a social doctrine that differentiated them from their Conservative allies. Leo also wrote to French Catholics in 1885 to discourage the formation of a Catholic party because he feared it would be too monarchist.

Pope Leo's successor, Pius X (1903-1914), presented himself as a religious pastor who distrusted political machinations. Thus he fostered the religious organization of Catholic Action while discouraging Catholic political groupings. Within the church Pius initiated liturgical reform, instituting the practice of frequent communion for adults and first communion at the age of seven. While Leo XIII had cautiously encouraged Catholic thinkers to profit from modern scholarship, certain curialists and Roman theologians under Pius X deplored the "Modernism" of Catholic liberal scholars like Louis Duchesne, Alfred Loisy, and George Tyrell. Monsignor Umberto Benigni, a Vatican functionary of the Vatican secretary of state, Merry del Val, organized a spy system, called the *Sodalitium Pianum* (the Sodality of Pius) in memory of Pius IX. This "Sodality" reported on any slight divergence from papal teaching. The pope issued *Lamentabili* and *Pascendi dominici gregis*, his condemnations of

Modernism, in 1907. The attack on Modernism ranged broadly, even touching the careers of later popes like Benedict XV and John XXIII. After he became pope, John XXIII protested such intolerance by examining the file that had been compiled on his own orthodoxy at the time.[54]

In this milieu Pius condemned the Frenchman Marc Sagnier, who combined Catholicism and Republican politics, while the conservative, anti-Semitic, and monarchist *Action Française* received encouragement from both Pius and the French Cardinal Billot. Eventually, the atheism of *Action*'s leader, Charles Maurras, resulted in the papal condemnation of 1914, but this condemnation was not publicly announced until 1926. Cardinal Billot surrendered his red cardinal's hat rather than withdraw his support for Maurras.[55] Maurras had struck a deep chord in French Catholic Conservatism with his politically motivated appeals to the ancient glory of the church. Pius X broke diplomatic relations with France in 1905 over the French government's separation of church and state. French anticlericalism had become even more heated over the Dreyfus Affair, in which a Jewish military officer was wrongly judged guilty of treason. Although some Catholics had supported Dreyfus, the anti-Semitism of many French Catholics contributed to a hasty verdict.[56]

The election of Benedict XV (1914-1922) signaled the cardinal electors' rejection of the inquisitorial methods of Pius X. Benedict had been a protégé of Cardinal Mariano Rampolla, Leo XIII's secretary of state and the liberal papal candidate in 1903. Benedict halted the antimodernist crusade, and fused the Holy Office and the Inquisition into a single congregation. The new pope spent most of his energy trying to bring World War I to a close, but both antagonists attacked his peace proposals of August 1917. However, President Woodrow Wilson became the first American president to be received by a pope after the two leaders had exchanged considerable correspondence on Wilson's "Fourteen Points." The French and Italian delegations at Versailles opposed the papacy's official participation, although a papal representative did attend the peace talks to negotiate the transfer of Catholic missions in ex-German colonies and to begin discussions on reestablishing diplomatic relations between the Vatican and France. Benedict also sought to establish ties with all the new nations created in the breakup of the Russian and Austrian empires.

Pius XI (1922-1939) had none of Pius X's misgivings about politics. He negotiated with all types of governments to attain as many concessions as possible for the church, which for him constituted a "perfect society, supreme in its own order."[57] The Feast of Christ the King, which he instituted, emphasized the principality of the Redeemer over all mankind. His encyclical *Quadregesimo anno* (1931) was written "forty years after" *Rerum novarum*. As the former encyclical had encouraged state intervention for the rights of workers, *Quadregesimo anno* specified the form this intervention should take. It favored Catholic *Sozialreform* thinkers who called for the corporate organization of society in place of what they perceived as the fatally flawed capitalist and socialist systems. The rival *Sozialpolitik* thinkers had accepted the basic framework of the capitalist system and merely favored a strong social insurance system to reform it. Thus, *Quadregesimo anno* blurred the boundaries between Catholic and Fascist social thinking because of its emphasis on corporatism.[58]

Pius XI and Benito Mussolini solved the Roman Question by negotiating the Lateran Pacts of 1929. From the capture of Rome in 1870 until these treaties, the popes had refused in principle to recognize the Italian state, calling on Catholics to withdraw from Italian political and public life. However, even some Italian bishops showed sympathy for the new government, and the papacy gradually adapted to the new situation without finding a definitive solution. The new Italian republic consisted of a constitutional monarchy whose power lay in the hands of a liberal elite, ruling through a parliament chosen by a small, propertied electorate. Italian Catholic Action provided Catholics with a religious vehicle to oppose this liberal elite state. When the Socialist and anticlerical left grew in strength around the turn of the century, Pius X allowed some Catholic voters to go to the polls in 1904. The Catholic vote favored reliable moderate candidates of the bourgeois parties.

The Lateran Pacts of 1929 resolved the major outstanding issues between the Vatican and the Italian state. They established papal sovereignty over the Vatican State, guaranteed Roman Catholicism as the sole state religion of Italy, gave the church jurisdiction over matrimony, stipulated religious instruction in all state schools, and awarded the church monetary compensation for lost papal territory. On its part, the church recognized the Italian state as the legal and moral embodiment of the Italian people, acknowledged Rome as the state capital, and promised to remain neutral in party politics. The pacts ensured the church's acceptance of Mussolini, which lasted until Il Duce's full partnership with German National Socialism. During this period the church remained the only independent organization within the Italian state. When Mussolini sought to limit ecclesiastical prerogatives, Pius issued *Non abbiamo bisogno* (We have no need) (1931) which denounced Fascist attacks on the church.[59]

In dealing with authoritarian regimes of both the left and right, Pius tried to protect the rights of Catholics by relying on concordats with those regimes. When this strategy proved insufficient, the pope, within a single week of March 1937, condemned Nazi crimes against the church with *Mit brennender sorge* (With burning concern) and atheistic communism with *Divini Redemptoris* (Of the divine Redeemer). Pius groomed his secretary of state, Eugenio Pacelli, to succeed him in dealing with a rapidly polarizing international system.

Pius XII (1939-1958) had spent long years in the papal diplomatic service, which gave him a bias for negotiated solutions to world problems. In describing the pope's activity leading up to and during World War II, Francis X. Murphy comments:

Taking up his predecessor's program for heading off the outbreak of the world conflict, Pius had attempted almost frantically to bring the inimical powers together, and failing in his desire to be the preserver of peace, he stepped up his diplomatic contacts in order to bring strong pressures to bear on both sides of the contest. . . . His man in Turkey was Angelo Roncalli, an old hand in the Vatican service who was on excellent terms with the German ambassador, Franz von Papen, and who used his position to extricate hundreds of Jewish families and persuaded the British to suspend their blockade of Greece to alleviate the starvation of that nation.[60]

In 1936, at the suggestion of his former aide Francis Spellman, Pacelli made a month's trip to the United States, during which he had lunch with President Franklin Roosevelt. With the outbreak of World War II, Myron Taylor became the president's special envoy to the Holy See. Pius's neutrality came under considerable pressure within the church. Cardinal Eugene Tisserant objected to the pope's failure to condemn outright Nazi outrages in the Netherlands. Cardinal Theodore Innitzer of Vienna, on the other hand, was disciplined by Rome for being too supportive of Hitler's *Anschluss*.

Pius XII's diplomatic approach to the Holocaust left him open to strong condemnation by the German playwright Rolf Hochhuth and others. While Hochhuth's *The Deputy*, which was translated into more than twenty languages, lacks some faithfulness to historical sources, charges by scholars like Guenther Lewy raise serious questions about the conduct of the German bishops and the papacy during Hitler's Third Reich. Lewy says:

When thousands of German anti-Nazis were tortured to death in Hitler's concentration camps, when the Polish intelligentsia was slaughtered, when hundreds of thousands of Russians died as a result of being treated as Slavic *untermenschen*, and when 6,000,000 human beings were murdered for being "non-Aryan," Catholic Church officials in Germany bolstered the regime perpetrating these crimes. The Pope in Rome, the spiritual head and supreme moral teacher of the Roman Catholic Church, remained silent. In the face of these greatest of moral depravities which mankind has been forced to witness in recent centuries, the moral teachings of a Church, dedicated to love and charity, could be heard in no other form but vague generalities.[61]

Writing a decade later and with the benefit of the German and British Foreign Office archives, Anthony Rhodes[62] speculates on the probable negative effect of the excommunication of Hitler or of a major papal condemnation of the "Extermination of the Jews" over Vatican Radio. Rhodes also cites the many activities to save Jews undertaken by the Vatican. Controversy over papal conduct during the Holocaust continues to affect relations between the Vatican and Israel.[63]

While Pope Pius XI and Pope Pius XII only gradually came to realize that Hitler's Nazism was not "normal" European authoritarianism, the two popes consistently condemned communism. In the postwar period Pius's strong anticommunism fit perfectly into the Cold War mentality of the West. One of Pius XII's last major documents was *Ad apostolorum principis* (To the Leaders of the Apostles) (1958), which called on Chinese Catholics to resist the control of the Beijing government. The Vatican did not announce the apostolic letter until it had smuggled copies into China.

From the pontificate of Leo XIII Catholic internal ecclesiastical policies manifested contrasting liberal and conservative tendencies. Both tendencies seemed to strengthen under Pius XII so that the pope shortly before his death confided to a European diplomat, "Après moi, le déluge!"[64] Italian curial bureaucracy had grown stronger under the tough leadership of *Il Pentagono* (Cardinals Clemente Micara, Nicolo Canali, Marcello Mimmi, Giuseppe Pizzardo, and Alfredo Ottaviani). On the other hand, Pius XII had issued the encyclical *Mystici corporis*, which challenged the exclusively institutional ecclesiology of the Counter-Reformation. The pope also fostered the biblical and liturgical movements. Reformers at Vatican II would draw upon these resources to challenge the bureaucratic power of the Curia. Under Pius XII German Jesuits became particularly influential on academic questions. The German

Jesuit scripture scholar and later Cardinal Augustin Bea best represents the intellectual underpinnings of Pius's pontificate. Shortly after the election of John XXIII, curial forces led by Cardinal Pizzardo sought to subject all Roman theological institutions to the control of the conservative Lateran University. The Lateran University journal *Divinitas* attacked Jesuit biblical scholarship in its December 1960 issue. When Pope John XXIII read the article, he personally assured the rector of the Biblicum of his full confidence in the Institute's orthodoxy. Pizzardo followed with a letter to Bea pleading no previous knowledge of the article.[65] The transfer of the papacy from Pius XII to John XXIII signaled the beginning of the contemporary era for the church. Bea became one of the leaders of the new reform as the confidante of the new pope, Angelo Roncalli. Roncalli had been papal representative in Bulgaria, Greece, Turkey, and France before becoming patriarch of Venice.

Earlier we spoke of the impact of the Cuban missile crisis on the internal and external politics of the Catholic Church. Just as "Good Pope John" was instrumental in reorienting Catholic policy toward Communist states, his summoning of the Second Vatican Council constitutes the definitive watershed in twentieth-century ecclesiastical reform. The adjectives "pre-Vatican II" and "post-Vatican II" have become common in distinguishing various sets of typologies that attempt to synthesize the tremendous changes that have taken place. John XXIII allowed the Dutch hierarchy to experiment during the most sensitive years for the church in the Netherlands, 1958-1965. When John was dying, he told his private secretary to give to the Dutch Primate Bernard Alfrink a reliquary of the great reformer Pope Gregory VII. The base of the reliquary is inscribed with the words, "May the Church remain free, untainted, and Catholic."[66]

John XXIII died in the midst of the Council. He had written in his diary that he hoped that the cardinals would elect Giovanni Battista Montini of Milan as his successor. The cardinals did choose Montini on the fifth ballot, and the next day the new Pope Paul VI announced on television that the Council would continue. Paul guided it through three more sessions. His most critical intervention came on behalf of the Declaration on Religious Liberty at the fourth session. Paul presided over more ecclesiastical changes than any pope since the Council of Trent, but he lacked the warm charisma of his predecessor. He manifested both liberal and conservative tendencies. He modernized the liturgy, continued the internationalization of the Curia, and launched a series of ecumenical moves with other Christian churches. The pope's conservative pronouncements attacked a married clergy, female ordinations, and the Italian divorce and abortion laws. His name will always be linked with two of his seven encyclicals.[67] *Populorum progressio* (On the Development of Peoples) (March 26, 1967) argues movingly that the rich nations must share with the developing nations or risk "the judgment of God and the wrath of the poor." *Humanae vitae* (On Human Life) (July 25, 1968) ignored the advice of a special papal commission and condemned artificial birth control. The latter encyclical generated a strong negative response, especially in the United States and Western Europe. Third World analysis of *Humanae vitae*, however, was considerably less critical. And Third World spokespersons of nearly all perspectives reacted enthusiastically to *Populorum progressio*. Finally, Paul imitated his namesake by initiating the tradition of papal journeys. He became the first pope in modern times to leave Europe, traveling over 70,000 miles outside Italy and touching every continent but Antarctica.

Montini had served a long diplomatic apprenticeship under the Vatican Secretary of State Pacelli. When Pacelli became Pope Pius XII, Montini continued to serve him until their relationship cooled when Montini failed to follow his mentor's strong anticommunism in the 1950s. Montini's diplomatic flexibility continued with *Ostpolitik*, the diplomatic hallmark of his papacy. Josip Brož Tito, Nicolae Ceaușescu, Podgorny, and Gromyko all visited the pope, and relations between the Vatican and Eastern bloc countries became regularized.

The internal ecclesiastical policy of Paul VI focused on implementing the reforms of Vatican II, including internationalization of the Curia and the cardinalate. He attained greater success in the latter than the former. Although non-Italians took up the direction of certain curial congregations, the bureaucracy remained overwhelmingly Italian. Even where non-Italians directed, their Italian assistants often wielded greater power. The most powerful curial cardinals like Benelli, Sebastiano Baggio, Pericle Felici, and Sergio Pignedoli were all Italians. However, the composition of the cardinalate changed significantly between the papal elections of 1963 and 1978. Paul VI named 110 cardinals, most of them non-Italian. He also limited the age of the electors to eighty. In the August 1978 papal election, Italians constituted only 27 cardinals out of 111 qualified electors. Several non-Italians like Aloísio Lorscheider (Brazil) and Jan Willebrands (Netherlands) were actually mentioned as *papabile* (leading candidates). The nine American cardinals formed the second largest national group, but no one took their chances very seriously. In addition, there were 29 non-Italian Europeans, 12 Africans, 13 Asians, 19 Latin Americans, and 2 Canadians. Increased international representation diluted Italian control. So did the increased travel, media coverage, and international conferences, which ensured that members of the College of Cardinals already knew each other and did not have to depend on curial bureaucrats for introductions.

Despite all these considerations, many compelling reasons favored an Italian candidate. First, the last non-Italian pope, the Dutchman Adrian VI, died unmourned in 1523. Foreign papal candidates had suffered from the "Dutch curse" ever since. Second, an Italian "Bishop of Rome" would understand his diocese better than a "missionary" prelate from another country. Third, the pope must be able to control his mostly Italian bureaucracy, the Curia. Fourth, the prevailing chaos of the Italian political system in 1978 seemed to demand an Italian pope to work out a nuanced arrangement with the Christian Democrats. Fifth, the pope represented the entire church, so he could not be tied to the nationalism of a major power. Italians qualified as neither nationalistic nor citizens of a great power.

The papal elections of August and October 1978 constituted a resounding vote of "no confidence" in the quality of the Vatican bureaucracy.[68] The cardinals sought moderate Italians of pastoral orientation, theological conservatives with a deep social concern for the poor. In August the electors quickly chose Albino Luciani, who died just as quickly thirty-three days later. In the second election the cardinals again sought an Italian candidate. Only when Giuseppe Siri and Benelli failed to attract the necessary votes did the conclave turn to the relatively young (aged fifty-eight) and internationally adept archbishop of Kraków. Karol Wojtyła's fluent Italian, Roman degree, and frequent trips to Italy helped to allay Italian distrust.

A comparison of the two elections is instructive. First, in both elections the cardinals sought a "pastoral" candidate, but the definition had been made more inclusive by the time of the October election. Second, the October electors were willing to take a younger man. In August the cardinals had wanted someone in his mid-sixties to avoid a possible recurrence of the last century's embarrassing thirty-two-year pontificate of Pope Pius IX. Luciani's quick death made the electors realize that the papacy had become a crushing burden and might be better suited to a man in his fifties. Third, the Luciani election resulted from consensus building that partly derived from a bloc against another Italian candidate, Pignedoli. The Wojtyła election, on the other hand, resulted from an impasse between the two Italian front runners which, combined with a paucity of acceptable Italians, forced the electors to look elsewhere. Fourth, due to the rapidity of the August conclave, many electors had spoken of the guiding presence of the Holy Spirit. These same cardinals expressed much greater awareness of human political initiative following the October election. Fifth, increased international tension had strengthened the curial position by October. Vatican bureaucrats argued that "in a collapsing world, the papacy alone should be able to stand up to evil." Sixth, several diplomatic *faux pas* of John Paul I convinced the cardinals that they needed a man more experienced in international relations. Seventh, conservative supporters launched an unprecedented press campaign in October for Cardinal Siri, which produced an equally unprecedented antagonistic campaign by those who recalled Siri's intransigently right-wing stands at Vatican Council II. Siri had termed the Council "the greatest disaster in ecclesiastical history."[69]

Wojtyła seemed to offer something for everyone. He combined pastoral care for the archbishopric of Kraków with extensive international experience. He had visited North America, Australasia, much of Latin America, and most of Europe. He was already fluent in seven languages. The conservatives liked his tough way of dealing with the Polish Communist authorities. At the same time, Wojtyła had been fully committed to Vatican II and understood the difficult church-state problems prevalent in the Third World. He wrote philosophy and poetry, but also skied, acted, and played the guitar. He was the first pope of the industrial age, having worked in a stone quarry and a chemical factory. He had lectured at Harvard on phenomenology and written a book *Person and Act* (1969) on that subject. His charismatic television personality fitted him for the new age of the media. With the exception of the non-Polish Eastern bloc governments, the immediate global public response was enthusiastic. Even the Romans celebrated in St. Peter's Square.

EUROPEAN CHRISTIAN DEMOCRACY

In the last part of the nineteenth century, Leo XIII had successfully extricated the universal church from its conservative political alliance. Leo articulated a distinctive Catholic social theory, but he did not foster Catholic political parties and social organizations. Leo feared such groups might take independent stands, as when the German (Catholic) Center Party faced down the pope by refusing to support Bismarck's military service law in 1887. Leo also discouraged the formation of a French Catholic party. Pius X became even more adamant and broke up the powerful Italian lay movement, *Opera dei congressi* in 1904. Only Benedict XV was generally favorable to Catholic political parties. By the period following World War I politicians across the spectrum were responding to increased mass political mobilization in practically every democracy. As Social Democracy emerged from Liberalism, both Fascism and Christian Democracy emerged from European Conservatism during the period 1870-1920. Before 1870 only Germany had a Catholic political party. By 1920 such a party existed in every continental Western European democracy but France.

Benedict XV allowed the formation of the Popular Party (PPI), the forerunner of Europe's most powerful Christian Democratic Party, in 1919. Father Luigi Sturzo left the directorship of Catholic Action to found the PPI in response to Italian postwar instability brought on by the increasing Socialist and Fascist activity. Sturzo believed strongly in the necessity of a definite separation between the hierarchical sacramental church and a political party inspired by Christian social ideas. Pope Benedict XV agreed to release all Catholic political activity from hierarchical control and withdrew Catholic Action from any direct political involvement. For his part Sturzo emphasized the aconfessional nature of his party, independent of Catholic Action, yet supporting Catholic participation and Christian ideals.[70] The party appealed to the peasant and working masses as well as middle and small bourgeoisie. This wide base enabled the PPI immediately to win 20 percent of the vote and capture 99 seats in the 1919 general election. Unfortunately, this success inhibited the establishment of a stable government because the PPI would join neither the Socialists nor the Liberals to form a government.

When the Fascists rose to power in 1922, the PPI began to polarize along ideological lines. A pro-Fascist group fought with Sturzo's faction and eventually formed a right-wing Catholic splinter party known as Unione Nazionale. Pius XI's desire to reach an accommodation with Mussolini on the Roman Question and to strengthen and centralize Catholic Action led him to discourage the PPI and finally dissolve it on September 9, 1924. Sturzo's successor Alcide De Gasperi had proposed an alliance between Catholics and moderate Socialists, but the pope described such a plan as cooperation with evil. Vaillancourt comments, "Thus Pius XI blocked one of the few moves which might have stopped fascism in Italy."[71] Mussolini declared a dictatorship in January 1925 and dissolved all anti-Fascist organizations in November 1926. He also arrested De Gasperi. The resulting conflicts between Fascist and Catholic organizations resulted in the anti-Fascist encyclical *Non abbiamo bisogno* (1931).

During the war Italian anti-Fascists received some protection from the Vatican, Catholic Action, and the Italian Federation of Catholic University Students (FUCI).[72] Mussolini released De Gasperi just before the Lateran Agreements, whereupon the ex-PPI leader became a librarian in the Vatican until after the war. These leaders of the old PPI and new recruits, especially from FUCI, clandestinely resumed political contacts that led to the foundation of the Italian Christian Democratic Party (DC) under De Gasperi in 1945. With the discrediting of Fascism in Italy and throughout Europe, Christian Democrats solidified power in several countries by a broad-based appeal to both the center and the right of the political spectrum. Both the Vatican and the American government strongly supported the Italian Christian Democrats against both the right and the left in the crucial election of 1948, which gave the DC a majority in both houses.

The party's dominant presence in the govenment enabled it to shape postwar Italy according to its own ideology. The party developed close ties with the state bureaucracy and private industry, a situation facilitated by the growth of *clientela* and *parentela*.[73] Christian Democrats continued to rely on existing ecclesiastical organizations, particularly Catholic Action. The late 1940s marked the entrance of Italy into NATO and active Italian participation in the Cold War rhetoric on the side of the United States against the Soviet Union. These international tensions exacerbated conflicts between the DC and the Italian Communist Party (PCI), Italy's second largest party, over domestic issues of economic and social reform. The DC lost its absolute majority in parliament in the general election of 1953. The party then began a series of dialogues with the Italian Socialist Party (PSI) which eventually resulted in *la apertura sinistra* (the opening to the left) in 1962. This coalition with the PSI received the official approval of Pope John XXIII and the tacit acquiescence of the Kennedy Administration.

John H. Whyte designates the period 1920-1960 as the peak era for "closed Catholicism," characterized by Catholic political parties, Catholic social organizations, and strong clerical guidance. Whyte points out, however, that the rise of Fascism before World War II split continental European political Catholicism into Fascist and Christian Democratic branches. The postwar period allowed Christian Democracy to come into its full force. Whyte lists seven factors that contributed to the strength of "closed Catholicism" during this period: a distinctive Catholic social doctrine, the growth of Catholic Action, the discrediting of the political right, the Cold War, the issue of state aid to denominational education, female suffrage, and the willingness of some hierarchies to give strong political and social guidance. In summary Whyte states, "But for good or ill, organized Catholicism played a more influential role politically on the continent of Europe between 1945 and 1960 than ever before or since."[74] Even French militant Catholics founded a new party based on Catholic social thought, the *Mouvement républicain populaire* (MRP).

The strength of Christian Democracy can be found in the vibrant Christianity of the European religious heartlands. This heartland embraces "Holland, Belgium, French Flanders, Alsace-Lorraine, Westfalia, the Rhineland, most of South Germany and Austria, Switzerland (though here statistics are lacking), and parts of North Italy."[75] While neither Catholic Rome nor Protestant Wittenberg lie within this zone, its political, economic, and military significance for the EEC and NATO are obvious. Postwar Christian Democracy has articulated a vision of Europe united by Christian principles. After 1960 "closed Catholicism" began to decay. Christian Democratic parties became either less powerful or less confessional or both. Many of Whyte's reasons for the decline of European Christian Democracy are the obverse of the reasons for its growth. The Italian Christian Democrats did retain their share of the electorate (approximately 39 percent) until the 1983 election, but this statistic masks a considerable shift in the social base of their support. The contemporary DC has become much less dependent on and less responsive to the Vatican and the Italian hierarchy.

CONCLUSION: THE HISTORICAL PERSPECTIVE

We began this chapter with John Paul II's visit to Paris in order to emphasize the leading role that the French church has played in the development of European Catholicism. The cathedral of Notre Dame filled with political and ecclesiastical dignitaries is an apt symbol for the triumphant glory of medieval Christendom. The empty churches of the working-class quarters of Paris with their Communist mayors signify the European church's failure to respond adequately to the Enlightenment, the French Revolution, and the industrial revolution. We conclude by highlighting European Catholic political history in order to present ten basic points that will be crucial in later analyses. These points concern the European Catholic Church in general, abstracting from the particular national political and ecclesiastical cultures that receive treatment in later chapters.

1. Any analysis of East-West relations must begin with an appreciation of the very different historical and cultural backgrounds of the Eastern and Western European traditions. The initial break between East and West occurred in the eighth century. Later influences such as Protestantism and the Enlightenment in the West and Leninism in the East have added to the basic historical differences between the Catholic and Orthodox cultures, but the split between Moscow and Washington began in Byzantium and Rome.

2. The alliance of pope and Western emperor created Christendom. This medieval synthesis of the two swords produced an idealized vision of the harmonious cooperation of pope and Catholic emperor serving the common good within a Catholic culture. St. Augustine first articulated this relationship of the earthly and heavenly cities, while the vision found its deepest philosophical and theological expression in the works of St. Thomas Aquinas. The idealized vision of Christendom has continued to exercise a powerful hold on Catholic political thought, imagination, and action. Conservative Catholics call for concordats between the Vatican and national states to ensure that Catholic cultures remain Catholic. Ecclesiastical control of education and morality is deemed necessary to protect the sanctity of the traditional family. Conservatives also place strong emphasis on the beauties of Gothic architecture, Gregorian chant, and the Latin Liturgy. Thus, according to this vision, the Catholic faith cannot be completely divorced from its European cultural setting, a proposition that has had a major impact on missionary activity. *Action Française* bolstered French Conservatism by appealing to the glories of medieval civilization, and Pius XI's encyclical *Quadregesimo anno* gave some support to the union of Catholic integralism with corporist social thinking.

Christian Democracy has disputed the claim of Catholic Conservatives to the univocal use of tradition by attacking the static nature of Catholic integralism. Neo-Thomists like Maritain asserted that the nineteenth-century church had saved the shell of Christendom at the expense of its spirit. According to such thinkers, if Aquinas were alive today, he would encourage the church to cooperate with new pluralistic and democratic political forms. Thus Christian Democratic political parties find their inspiration in the Christian moral values espoused by Catholic Conservatives without submitting the church to what they perceive as reactionary ecclesiastical and political policies that provide no defense against Marxism. The historical legacy of medieval Catholicism remains especially relevant in all analyses of Catholic Conservative and Christian Democratic traditions.

3. Christendom's major political-religious struggle concerned investiture, the battle between church and state over control of the appointment of bishops. Control over episcopal selection remains the single most important political issue in authoritarian countries of both the left and right, regardless of whether the state is Catholic like Franco's Spain, or Marxist like Jaruzelski's Poland. State, Vatican, and local church forces all battle to influence important appointments. In addition to the battle over episcopal appointments, authoritarian states seek to prevent Rome and outside national Catholic Churches from transferring personnel and finances to their national church. The Vatican presses everywhere for religious freedom, the issue that joins ethical behavior with its own institutional interests.

In secularized states where the church maintains complete control of the episcopal selection process, struggles tend to focus on religious ideology, with the various candidates' visions of the relation of church and society coming under intense scrutiny. Major actors in these latter decisions tend to be national bishops, the papal nuncio or delegate, the Congregation of Bishops, and in important cases, the pope himself. Of course, the Congregation of Bishops and sometimes the pope himself act on appointments for authoritarian states. A papal representative is not always acceptable in these countries.

4. Neither the ideology nor the organization of medieval Christendom could remain static during the frenetic political, economic, social, and cultural changes of the last six hundred years in the West. As Christendom dissolved, the Catholic Church could only maintain its cultural form by isolating itself from contemporary trends and entering into political-religious alliances with reactionary states. This period from Trent to the First Vatican Council contributed significantly to three contemporary Catholic tendencies relevant for our analysis. First, Catholic political thought continues to harbor a profound mistrust for the modern sovereign nation-state. The nation-state attained its apex during a period of church distress. States professing various ideologies and religions all sought to destroy or limit papal influence. Second, in many cases the national churches sided with their respective states rather than

the Vatican. This historical experience strengthened curial fears of national ecclesiastical organizations in a church whose traditional line of command went directly from the universal church to the diocese. Faced with attacks by the nation-states, the Vatican strengthened its central bureaucratic hold on national churches. Following Trent this central control furthered ecclesiastical reform, thus adding to its legitimacy. Attempts to loosen Roman control were perceived as both politically motivated by the nation states and as antireform. Such perceptions form the basis of contemporary curial ideology.

The third factor concerns the Roman church's reaction to modern culture. At the same time that Catholicism was suffering politically, the new currents of modern thought seriously undermined the church. Faced with the Protestant Reformation, the Council of Trent provided the militant ideology for Catholics to separate themselves from the "corruption" of the later ideas of the Enlightenment and subsequent ideological movements. The Counter-Reformation still offers a rallying point for today's Catholic Conservatives. For example, Archbishop Lefebvre has named his group of conservative priests the Society of St. Pius V, the Dominican pope of the Counter-Reformation.

5. Events in Anglo-American cultures seemed to prove the wisdom of the Counter-Reformation strategy. While prior to the First Vatican Council Catholicism continued to retreat in the traditional Catholic cultures of Southern Europe, Cardinal Cullen fashioned an Irish church that served as the catalyst for Roman Catholic expansion in the increasingly powerful English-speaking nations. Irish missionary clergy established national churches of limited intellectual breadth and strong Jansenist morality. The late nineteenth-century and early twentieth-century combination of Irish organizational and political skills, strong allegiance to Rome, Leo XIII's emphasis on the rights of workers, anticommunist patriotism, and a strong parochial educational system proved highly successful in helping Catholic immigrants find their place in hostile Protestant societies without leaving the church. Catholic questioning of the status quo could wait until European immigrants had attained social and economic equality. Events in Anglo-American and Northern European countries have seemed to indicate the political wisdom of Catholic advocacy of moderate social reform in alliance with progressive members of the rising middle classes.

6. From the accession of Leo XIII, the principal battle for control of the papacy and the Curia took place between those ecclesiastics

who followed the Leo XIII–Cardinal Rampolla line and those associated with Pius X and Cardinal Raphael Merry del Valle. The cardinals elected Benedict XV in protest against the inquisitorial methods of Pius X, but Benedict moved Merry del Valle into the Holy Office. He gave the Secretariat of State to Rampolla's protégé, Cardinal Pietro Gasparri. Gasparri threw his support behind the compromise candidate Achille Ratti (Pius XI) when he realized that neither he nor his conservative opponent Cardinal Pietro Lafontaine had the necessary votes to be elected Benedict's successor. Gasparri remained secretary of state until 1930, when Pius XI replaced him with Eugenio Pacelli, whom Ratti groomed as his successor. Such bureaucratic infighting between two very powerful groups, one of which had a heightened sense of the demands of doctrinal orthodoxy, helps to explain the bitter conflicts of the Second Vatican Council. The Holy Office (now called the Congregation for the Doctrine of the Faith) continues to supervise doctrinal orthodoxy.

7. Starting with the efforts of Benedict XV during World War I, popes have attempted to mediate the major international crises of this century. Both sides resisted papal intervention during the First World War. Archbishop Francis Spellman of New York personified the American Catholic nationalism that President Roosevelt hoped to use for the Allied cause in the Second World War. While American Catholics proved their strong patriotism, Pius XII maintained an official neutrality. The pope's reliance on diplomatic initiatives to help the Jews resulted in postwar charges that the Vatican did not do enough to try to avert the Holocaust. Certainly, both Roman Catholic and Orthodox cultures have experienced a long tradition of popular anti-Semitism, exemplified in the anti-Semitic character of popular sectarianism in the Middle Ages and the Dreyfus affair. Given the distrust of the papacy exhibited by major powers since the eighteenth century, John XXIII's enthusiasm for his mediation between Khrushchev and Kennedy becomes striking, even though the Catholic president remained much more reluctant than the Soviet premier. However, even the Cuban missile crisis did not resolve the enduring papal conflict between taking a neutral stance in international mediation versus upholding religious and cultural values seemingly more fully realized in one political system than the other. The abominations of Hitler provided a starkness to the problem not experienced in most conflicts. In the post-Hiroshima era, moral choices have become much more complicated.

8. Pius XI opted for the concordat strategy in his double battle against Communism and Fascism. To attain certain advantages in

Mussolini's Italy he sacrificed the Popular Party while strengthening Catholic Action. In general, Pius overestimated the force of the concordats and initially underestimated the evil of leaders like Mussolini and Hitler. Cardinal Montini, who personally suffered from Pius XII's strategy, would later encourage the Spanish church to detach itself from Franco. Today authoritarian countries in Eastern Europe and the Third World often demand that the papacy disown certain political and social movements in exchange for limited ecclesiastical freedoms. Such decisions remain extremely difficult, with considerable opportunity for misunderstanding between the Vatican and the national church.

9. Both Communist and Fascist states battered the church between the First and Second World Wars. The European urban workers, especially in Catholic countries, had generally been won over to Socialism or Communism before the First World War. Christian Democracy appealed to progressive European Catholics among both urban and rural middle classes. Christian Democracy provided the stability of traditional Catholic belief, morality, and culture while encouraging Catholics to democratize their political systems and modernize their societies. The old medieval vision of a United Europe, advocated by Christian Democrats, seemed attractive to postwar Europeans who had suffered two global conflicts within three decades. Christian Democratic parties reached their apex between 1945 and 1960. However, since that time, "closed Catholicism" has experienced a number of difficulties. First, the tremendous "economic miracles" of the postwar era encouraged increased materialism, nationalism, and secularism. Today fewer people focus on a Catholic culture as a specific political good, and many doubt the wisdom of further European unification. In some traditional Catholic states like Ireland, the church remains the dominant force in education and morality. In others like Italy, the bishops have suffered major political defeats on moral issues such as divorce and abortion. The whole question of the political viability of a Catholic moral culture remained the unfinished business of the Lateran Treaties.

10. The events and decisions of European Catholic history have deeply influenced the type of Catholicism that has developed in Latin America, Africa, and Asia. The initial missionaries, whatever their nationality, represented Spanish and Portuguese Christendom. Latin American and Asian churches also suffered from the weakening of the papacy during the eighteenth century, with the recall of Jesuit missionaries being particularly significant. Thomas

Bruneau remarks that "The Jesuits were not only the most effective clergy in Brazil, but they were also the largest single order. Not only did the Brazilian Church lose the largest and best contingent of personnel and programs, but they were not replaced by other clergy. In short, a weak Church with little influence became even weaker." Ecclesiastical conditions did not improve with Brazilian independence (1822). Emperor Pedro II (1840-1889), a rationalist devotee of Voltaire, considered the church "nothing more than an ordinary bureau of government."[76] When the Brazilian Catholic Church strengthened itself during the first half of the twentieth century, it did so by employing European models of influence tailored for the rising middle class, a very small percentage of Brazilian society. When Iberian Catholic missionaries left Europe in the fifteenth century to Christianize the new Portuguese and Spanish colonies, they encountered even older civilizations that did not share European cultural values. The resulting conflicts added a deep cross-cultural strain to Catholic politics. The mixture of European and native cultural values raises major questions of religious indigenization and adaptation. In Catholic Latin America political ideologies as diverse as the National Security State and Liberation Theology compete for ecclesiastical influence. All of these questions came to a head at the third meeting of the Latin American bishops at Puebla which serves as the introduction for Chapter Two's analysis of Catholic organization.

CHAPTER 2

Catholic Political Organization: Center, Region, and Nation

JOHN PAUL AT PUEBLA

ON JANUARY 27, 1979, over one million people packed the streets of Mexico City to cheer John Paul II. The papal motorcade proceeded to the Basilica of Our Lady of Guadelupe, the patroness of Mexico. This new basilica stood next to an older church built on the very spot where the Blessed Virgin is said to have appeared to the Indian Juan Diego on December 12, 1583. The pope concelebrated mass with 218 prelates and preached a homily in Spanish. In it he drew a parallel between the preeminence of Our Lady of Guadelupe in Mexico and the place of Our Lady of Częstochowa in Polish nationalism and culture.[1] The pope also mentioned other Latin American national places of pilgrimage and titles of the Blessed Virgin—Altagracia (Dominican Republic), Aparecida (Brazil), Lujan (Argentina)—for he had come to Mexico to attend the third meeting of the Latin American Bishops' Conference (CELAM III) in Puebla. The following day John Paul traveled the 62 miles to the conference by motorcade.

The pope had chosen to make his first foreign trip to CELAM III, just three months after his election, because of the crucial significance of the conference for Catholicism throughout the world. CELAM has become the most powerful regional organization within the Catholic Church. At its second conference (CELAM II) in Medellín, Colombia, in 1968, the assembled prelates and theologians had reoriented the Latin American church to social justice in a final document that employed both "revolutionary" and "developmentalistic" categories.[2] The debate over such issues as Liberation Theology and the ecclesial base communities (CEB) had sharpened since Medellín. Therefore, Puebla constituted a crucial watershed in the development of Catholicism in its most populous continent. John Paul characteristically decided to take personal charge of the event.

The pope opened the meeting with a long and nuanced address to the bishops. He stressed the liberation of humankind, but did not

use the term "Liberation Theology." He insisted that politics properly belonged to the laity, for Christ had not been a revolutionary.
When a Mexican journal commented that such a prohibition could
be used by "governments and paramilitary goons in beating up
clerics demonstrating for their people's rights," the pope reacted by
emphasizing the church's role in working for social justice in his
speech to the Indians at Cuilapan, Oaxaca, the next day. The His-
panic-American theologian Virgilio Elizondo commented:

Listening to John Paul in Mexico was like watching an artist add strokes to
the emerging image of an icon; only when the work is completed is the message clearly discerned. It was fascinating as the entire image gradually appeared, but it was painful as the U.S. press consistently missed or confused
the point. They wanted one-liners, while the pope was slowly constructing
an icon that clearly reveals the divine image in the human and the human
image of the Divine.[3]

Jon Sobrino less diplomatically described some of the press as "incredibly hostile and reactionary,"[4] as both the press and lobbying
groups ran the gamut of Latin American Catholicism.

CELAM III serves as an excellent introduction to this chapter on
church organization because so many levels of ecclesiastical bureaucracy sought to influence the outcome of this conference. The personal role of Pope John Paul II is obvious. The second most significant Vatican actor was Cardinal Sebastiano Baggio. As president of
the Pontifical Commission on Latin America (CAL),[5] he had directed preparation for the meeting. Baggio, a "progressive papal
nuncio during the late 1950s,"[6] derived his principal influence from
being prefect of the Congregation of Bishops. He was one of the curial cardinals who had received votes in the 1978 papal elections.
Baggio supervised Archbishop Alfonso López Trujillo, secretary
general of the CELAM staff. Archbishop López had become prominent in CELAM in the early 1970s as a Roman counterweight to
progressive trends following CELAM II at Medellín. López, who
later became archbishop of Medellín, represented the strong tradition of "un pueblo culto y cristiano" (a civilized and Christian people) developed over long years of church-state cooperation in Colombia.[7] Baggio and López hoped to limit the influence of the great
liberal cardinals of Latin America like Raúl Silva Henríquez of Chile
and Paulo Arns of Brazil. They especially feared the ecclesiastical
clout of the region's most powerful national episcopal conference,
the National Conference of Brazilian Bishops (CNBB). Brazil's
prominence as a nation and as an episcopate had resulted in the

Brazilian Cardinal Aloísio Lorscheider being named president of the conference. However, in December 1977, Baggio and the host Archbishop Ernesto Corripio Ahumada of Mexico City were added as co-presidents, thus strengthening the conservatives.

Baggio and especially López suffered a political embarrassment when the local newspaper, *Uno Mas Uno*, printed a letter of López indiscreetly describing his machinations in blocking the influence of ecclesiastics like Silva and Arns. The letter called the Argentinian prefect of the Congregation of Religious, Cardinal Eduardo Pironio, a "weakling" and the Jesuit Superior General Pedro Arrupe "dangerous."[8] López had developed an animosity against Pironio and Arrupe because he considered the Latin American Confederation of Religious (CLAR), whose headquarters were located close to CELAM's in Bogotá, as his principal regional rival. CLAR came under Pironio's jurisdiction in Rome. Arrupe used his political influence in Rome to defend Jesuits engaged in social action in Latin America. Neither Baggio nor López could control these parallel lines of jurisdiction from Rome to Latin America.

While the papal speech at Cuilapan was meant for a global audience, it was tailored to the local situation faced by the bishop, clergy, and laity in that part of the state of Oaxaca. In addition to international, regional, and national units of ecclesiastical analysis, the individual local dioceses are also important.[9] Individual bishops can articulate positions at variance with their national episcopal conferences. The retired progressive "red bishop" of Cuernavaca, Méndez Arceo, has often taken stands counter to the prevailing policy of most Mexican bishops. His colleagues supported him, however, when he urged John Paul to come to Puebla. Non-Latin American episcopal conferences also sent official observers like Archbishop John Quinn, president of the National Conference of Catholic Bishops (NCCB) of the United States. Thus, the CELAM bishops could directly influence the American church, while Quinn's interviews could help shape American media coverage.[10] Finally, the Catholic lower clergy and laity came to Puebla mainly as the unofficial observers who formed the "Anti Puebla" or "Parallel Conference" at the session. Prominent Latin American theologians like Gustavo Gutiérrez, Jon Sobrino, Leonardo Boff, and Hugo Assmann, although not participants, provided expertise for progressive ecclesiastics like Cardinal Arns of São Paulo.[11] Other less prominent lobbyists focused on attracting the attention of over 3,000 accredited journalists at the event.

THE POPE AND THE VATICAN BUREAUCRACY

Even a quick glance at the Catholic Church's organization chart leaves one with a profound impression of how much authority resides with the papacy. The pope appoints all the bishops.[12] Each bishop exercises complete authority in his own diocese. Every five years the bishops of each country report to the pope in their *ad limina* visits. Traditionally, regional and national episcopal meetings and conferences have held little significance. The pope has handled nearly all church business through his Roman bureaucracy, appointed and dismissed at will. He retains the final power of approval on all policy decisions. "The pope is absolute, and there is no legislature. He is advised, not constitutionally imposed upon, by lawmakers."[13]

Some legislative power does reside with the traditional General Council, the traditional College of Cardinals, and the recently formed Synod of Bishops, but each of these bodies functions under significant limitations. Calling a General Council constitutes the pope's first and foremost method of extraordinary governance, a measure suited to turbulent times like those years immediately following the Protestant Reformation. When John XXIII summoned Vatican II, he did open the church to outside "winds of change." However, both John XXIII and Paul VI maintained control of the Council's agenda and conclusions as curial cardinals fought outside reformers for influence. The College of Cardinals exercises its fullest power in the election of the pope, but the cardinals had to receive their prestigious appointments from a pope. While the pope influences national churches by naming the cardinals, national episcopal conferences elect representatives to the Synod of Bishops held every three years. For example, Cardinal Joseph Bernardin, Archbishops Patrick Flores and John Roach, and Auxiliary Bishop Austin Vaughan represented the American bishops at the 1983 Synod, even though many other cardinals were passed over in American balloting. Since the first Synod in 1967 the popes have kept tight control of the agenda and results,[14] thus preventing the Synod from developing into an ecclesiastical parliament. The 1983 Synod on Reconciliation discussed the sacrament of penance according to the principal position paper by Cardinal Carlo Maria Martini of Milan, while other speakers like Cardinal Lorscheider of Brazil introduced themes of social justice.[15] Other recent topics of discussion have been the family (1980), catechesis (1977), and evangelization (1974).

The Synod first met in 1967 to discuss the international theological commission and several other reforms mandated by Vatican II.

In January 1985 John Paul II announced an extraordinary Synod for November 25–December 8 to review Vatican Council II. The purpose of the Synod, according to L'Osservatore Romano (January 27), was neither a simple commemoration nor an attempt "to shelve the old and bring in the new at all cost." Again, John Paul had activated another channel of personal influence outside of regular bureaucratic channels. The pope used the 26th anniversary of John XXIII's summoning of the Council to give his call some dramatic context. Some liberals feared that the Synod could be used as part of a strategy of ecclesiastical restoration by conservatives like Cardinals Joseph Ratzinger and Silvio Oddi to correct the "abuses" of Vatican II. Ratzinger's approach to the Council, articulated in a series of interviews with journalist Vittorio Messori,[16] seemed especially threatening. However, Cardinal Bernardin diplomatically hailed it as "another moment of renewal," and cardinals like Basil Hume of Great Britain worked very hard to orient the Synod toward the positive aspects of Vatican II. The pope chose Belgian Cardinal Godfried Danneels as the Synod's rapporteur, and Danneels's opening address emphasized the positive results of Vatican II. In the end both conservatives and liberals declared the Synod a success. The conservatives received an endorsement of a universal catechism (suggested by Boston's Cardinal Bernard Law), and liberals rejoiced in the support of national episcopal conferences as "so useful, even necessary." The Synod and its result were quintessentially Catholic in organization, ideology, and style.[17] The Synod was preceded by a meeting of the College of Cardinals, at which the pope defended papal authority and the Curia. The cardinals, who have become the pope's outside financial consultants, also learned that Vatican projected a deficit of $50 million for 1985, compared with $29 million for 1984.

Such meetings also provide an opportunity for international church leaders to meet informally, thus opening more channels of communication independent of the Curia. Cardinal Bernardin mentioned that many of the national representatives at the 1983 Synod had read the American bishops' pastoral on war and peace and discussed it with him. Bernardin has been elected as an American delegate to the last three regular Synods, thus giving him extended contact with Catholic leaders from all over the globe, including Cardinal Wojtyła of Kraków.[18] In 1982 the pope named Bernardin head of the country's largest diocese (Chicago) and named him a cardinal the following January.

One of the major characteristics of John Paul's papacy has been his personal detailed involvement in what he considers to be significant issues. Nevertheless, in the Catholic Church as in all complex bureaucracies, the command of the leader does not guarantee effective policy implementation. Even Pope Pius XII became disenchanted with the Roman Curia during the latter part of his reign. Francis X. Murphy remarks that, at that time, "the pontiff's withdrawal gave the curial bureaucrats control over the conduct of the church's everyday affairs—its dealings with problems of doctrine and discipline; the appointment of bishops and diplomats; its hard line with innovators among the priests involved in worker movements; its monitoring of the church's vast seminary system, and the direction of its worldwide missionary enterprises."[19] Pius XII devoted himself to personal political and intellectual interests aided by his assistants Montini and Tardini. The resulting international episcopal dissatisfaction with the Roman Curia culminated in an attack by Cardinal Joseph Frings of Cologne on the Holy Office at the Council session of November 8, 1963. Many of the Council fathers applauded.[20]

If Vatican II had a villain in the eyes of reformers, it was Cardinal Ottaviani, prefect of the Holy Office. Pope Paul VI, who had served long years in the Secretariat of State and understood the workings of the Roman bureaucracy, began a reform of the Curia even before the Council finished. He removed the presidency of the bureaucracy from the cardinal in charge of the Holy Office (renamed the Congregation of the Doctrine of the Faith) to the Vatican secretary of state. Paul then appointed many non-Italians, including the French Cardinal Jean Villot as secretary of state. However, Villot proved incapable of controlling his own secretariat because of the political clout and craft of his "Substitute,"[21] the Undersecretary Giovanni Benelli of Pistoia (near Florence). Paul VI relied on Benelli to maintain control of the Curia, then appointed him archbishop of Florence in 1977. Benelli's attempts to install northern Italian efficiency in the Curia earned him the nicknames, "Gauleiter" and "The Berlin Wall," and probably cost him the curial votes necessary to win the papacy in October 1978.

Villot's weakness vis-à-vis Benelli points to a principal difficulty with Paul VI's internationalization of the Curia. The Italian staff have demonstrated great staying power, buttressed by familiarity with the Roman style and with Vatican bureaucratic procedure. The traditional curial career begins with "the appropriately unadventurous style of education"[22] at the Roman Seminary, followed by the recommendation of an influential prelate. After he entered the seminary in Pistoia, Benelli was sent to Rome before ordination. Ottaviani came from Rome. He was the son of a bakery worker and went to the Roman Seminary on scholarship. After studying canon law and being recommended to the Curia, he rarely left Rome. Ottaviani eulogized the formative experience of the Curia with these words:

> To those who formed me from the first hours of my priesthood, to their teaching, to their example, I owe the fact that my attachment to the Apostolic See has daily become stronger and more Luminous and, so to say, more instructive and formative. Many people do not know what a great teacher of Christian life and Catholic action this Roman Curia is; it seems a contemporary of the apostles in its glory, so full of life that it seems to have been born yesterday, high and yet humble like a mother, and misunderstood only by those who do not know her.[23]

Such a system fosters strong institutional and personal loyalties. In addition, Italian domination of the Curia has solved the language and cultural problems associated with a widely diversified international bureaucracy like that at the United Nations. Italians offer the extra advantages of a traditionally weak nationalism, the lack of big power status, and a highly developed diplomatic tradition. Ottaviani's contemporary Tardini held that only Romans could properly serve in the Curia, but his colleague Montini (Paul VI) came from the provinces before being recommended by the powerful Cardinal Pizzardo.

One major drawback of the system is the prevalence of the "curial mentality," which Peter Nichols describes as "formalistic, fussy, devotedly jealous." Strangely, according to Nichols, non-Italians have developed some of the strongest cases of "curial mentality." He attributes this to the foreigners' uneasiness in Rome, and designates the worst cases as belonging to Americans, "who lose character and gain fussiness at an alarming rate in Rome's ecclesiastical circles, becoming far more tiresome to deal with than the Italians."[24] For example, the Irish-American Cardinal John Wright of Pittsburgh brought a reputation of social liberalism and theological conservatism to his post as prefect of the Congregation of the Clergy in 1969. Wright had been active in the civil rights movement and was an early opponent of the Vietnam War, but his answer to the many clergy leaving the priesthood consisted of the simple admonition "to go to confession, and right away. They [clergy seeking dispensations] made a promise. They should keep it."[25] The conservative secular institute Opus Dei leaked Wright's letter attacking the "erroneous" theology of the Spanish bishops as part of its campaign to support Spanish ecclesiastical conservatives. The enraged Spanish Cardinal Enrique y Tarancón obtained a statement from the Secretary of State Villot stating that Wright's letter did not represent papal views, and Spanish liberals called publicly for Wright's dismissal.[26] The embittered cardinal died in office in August 1979.

Recruitment poses another obstacle to internationalization of the Curia. While the Vatican bureaucracy holds great appeal for poor rural clerics from Italy's many provincial dioceses, progressive non-Italian prelates object to "losing" bright young priests to the Vatican bureaucracy or being "buried there" themselves. Cardinal Franz König of Vienna would accept the presidency of the Secretariat for Non-Believers only if he could retain his see in Vienna and "commute" to the job. This placed the new secretariat at a great disadvantage in Roman bureaucratic infighting,[27] but did allow König to retain his sanity and serve the church in multiple capacities for many more years. Sometimes "promotion" to Rome also functions as a convenient political mechanism for removing a difficult personality from the national ecclesiastical scene, as with the replacement of Ottaviani by the Croatian Šeper. On the other hand, Bernardin's predecessor, Cardinal John Patrick Cody of Chicago, refused all attempts to "promote" him to the Curia with resulting embarrassment to Cody and scandal to the American church before his death in 1982. Despite these difficulties, Paul VI's internationalization of the Curia has been increased by John Paul II, who has given Eastern Europeans like Władisław Rubin a greater place in the bureaucracy. A Czech priest, Jozef Tomko, replaced Rubin as secretary general of the Synod of Bishops when Rubin became prefect of the Congregation for Eastern Churches. When Agostino Casaroli became secretary of state and prefect of the Council for Public Affairs, another Italian Achille Silvestrini succeeded as secretary for the Council for Public Affairs, but non-Italians, the Spaniard Eduardo Martínez Somalo and the Lithuanian Andrys Bačkis, received the next ranking appointments in the two organizations.[28]

The Curia is composed of various congregations, secretariats, councils, commissions, and offices that have come into being over a long period of time. Some retain their original purposes; others have evolved to oversee new tasks. The ten congregations (Doctrine of the Faith, Bishops, Eastern Churches, Sacraments, Divine Worship,[29] Clergy, Religious, Evangelization of Peoples, Saints' Causes,

Christian Education) all focus in some way on the orthodoxy of Catholic doctrine, though not with the exclusiveness of the Congregation of the Doctrine of the Faith (CDF). For example, López Trujillo complained that Pironio, prefect of the Congregation of Religious, had failed to correct what López perceived as the errors of CLAR.

As in all bureaucracies some curial positions are intrinsically more important than others, regardless of the personalities involved. Among the congregations, the prefects of the Congregation of the Doctrine of the Faith and of the Congregation of the Bishops exercise significant ecclesiastical influence, while the prefect of the Congregation of Saints' Causes exercises little. Cardinal Ratzinger of Munich replaced Cardinal Šeper of the CDF in late 1981. Cardinal Baggio maintained his principal power from heading the Congregation of Bishops until replaced by the African Cardinal Bernardin Gantin in April 1984.[30] In addition, single cardinals like Baggio usually hold multiple offices.

The prefect of the Congregation of Bishops derives his significance from the universal importance of choosing the next generation of ecclesiastical leaders. When an ordinary[31] is to be chosen, the country's papal representative forwards a report with three candidates (*terna*), of whom he has indicated his choice. A staff member of the Congregation of Bishops summarizes the report and presents it to a staff meeting. If the appointment involves the promotion of a man already a bishop, it falls within the competency of the prefect and his staff to make a recommendation to the pope. If the appointment would raise a priest to the episcopate, it must be considered by the full congregation. The undersecretary appoints a cardinal relator who presents the case. The cardinal relator must be fluent in the country's language since the supporting documentation, unlike the papal representative's report, is not in Italian. All 32 members of the Congregation of Bishops receive two weeks' notice of general meetings that consider four or five cases. Noncurial members usually do not fly to Rome for meetings, however, so the 14 curial cardinals have more influence. The prefect presents his and the congregation's recommendations to the pope at a Saturday audience. A few days later the pope informs the congregation of his decision.[32]

THE MAKING OF VATICAN FOREIGN POLICY

Peter Nichols begins his 1968 treatment of the Vatican bureaucracy by remarking how difficult it is to separate the papal court as a political body from the government of the church as a religious organization. "In practice, it is no easier to distinguish between the two than it is to distinguish clearly between the temporal and the spiritual power."[33] The papacy's ability to move flexibly between political and religious issues has always proved a diplomatic advantage. In addition, the Vatican claims that the Catholic Church has no foreign policy in the political sense as all its activities are directed toward the religious good of the faithful. In consequence the pope enters into diplomatic relationships not as the head of the Vatican State, but as the supreme pastor of the Catholic Church. The Catholic Church, according to this theory, which received its classic exposition in Cardinal Ottaviani's *Institutiones juris publici ecclesiae* (Institutes of the Public Law of the Church), remains a *societas perfecta*, "an institution capable of maintaining complete welfare in its own order and, by right, disposing of all the means to achieve that end."[34]

Paul VI's reorganization of the Curia transferred the direction of the Vatican bureaucracy from the primarily religious body of the Holy Office (Doctrine of the Faith) to the primarily political Secretariat of State. The secretary of state constitutes the church's combined foreign minister–prime minister. The secretary can wield enormous influence, as in the cases of the great Rampolla (1887-1903), Merry del Val (1903-1914) and Gasparri (1914-1930). However, the pope can act as his own secretary of state, as Paul VI did while leaving the title with the elderly Cardinal Amleto Cicognani (1961-1969). One reason that present Secretary of State Casaroli works so well with John Paul II is that Casaroli remains willing to follow the papal lead, even in policy areas where he has great experience like *Ostpolitik*. The Secretariat of State has sections dealing with practically all political and religious matters that concern the church, thus constituting its own mini-Curia. These sections, supposedly with anonymity, review the work of the respective congregations, commissions, and other bodies. The secretary of state is also the prefect of the Council for the Public Affairs of the Church, which handles special questions of foreign relations. Casaroli, who had joined the Council (then called the Congregation for Extraordinary Affairs) in 1949, fashioned *Ostpolitik* as its secretary in the 1960s. Casaroli's foreign policy "rival" was not the weak Secretaries of State Cicognani and Villot, but Benelli.

The Vatican, therefore, has five powerful decision makers in foreign policy. They are, in the order of their institutional significance: the pope, the secretary of state, the prefect of the Council for the Public Affairs of the Church, the "Substitute" of the secretary of state, and the secretary of the Council for the Public Affairs of the Church. The present "Substitute" is Martínez Somalo. The Spaniard Martínez will never play the strong role in internal DC politics that Benelli did. Casaroli's replacement as secretary of the Council for the Public Affairs of the Church is the Italian Silvestrini, who represented the Vatican at Helsinki and shares Casaroli's support of *détente*. Silvestrini's undersecretary is Bačkis, whose father was a Lithuanian diplomat.

Holding the institutional title, of course, does not guarantee influence in the Vatican any more than in any other bureaucracy. Each diplomatic decision has its own organizational peculiarities. One could think, for example, of instances when the opinion of the prefect of the Congregation of Bishops (Gantin) or the president of the Commission for Latin America (Baggio) might be the deciding factor. One recently established participant in the formation of political, social, and economic policies has been the Commission for Justice and Peace. Soon after Paul VI established this commission in 1966 it became apparent that its concerns overlapped those of the Secretariat of State. Individual episcopal conferences have also established national offices for Justice and Peace. Both the commission and these national offices have tended to adopt more progressive positions on human rights and social justice than those of career papal diplomats. Paul VI partially muted this competition by his *motu proprio Iustitiam et pacem* (December 10, 1976), which restructured the commission "in modo stabile e definitiva." Cardinal Roger Etchegaray of Marseilles replaced Gantin as president in April 1984. The president of Justice and Peace also oversees Cor Unum (established 1971), the Vatican's umbrella agency for international Catholic relief and development aid, another center of potential political influence.[35]

In some ways the style of Vatican foreign policy resembles Soviet practice. While American foreign policy is plagued with political ambassadorial appointments and other frequent personnel and policy shifts, change in the professionalized papal diplomatic corps comes very slowly. Casaroli has been in charge of *Ostpolitik* since its inception in the early 1960s. Like his Soviet counterpart Casaroli need not fear a legitimate investigative press, but this has contributed to the unreliability of some accounts of the Vatican.[36]

The Vatican's semi-official paper, *L'Osservatore Romano*, enunciates policy; it does not feature late-breaking news. As such, its function approximates *Pravda* or the *People's Daily* more closely than it does the *New York Times* or *Le Monde*. Paul Hofmann remarks that, "To outsiders the large-sized newspaper that comes out in Vatican

City at 3:00 p.m. every weekday seems about as informative and entertaining as the Bulgarian Communist party daily."[37] L'Osservatore functions as a political instrument in the sensitive dealings with authoritarian regimes. For example, at the end of John Paul's second visit to Poland, the pontiff met separately with Jaruzelski and Wałęsa. This second meeting of the pope and the general upstaged John Paul's audience with the Wałęsa family on the morning of his departure. The Vatican itself emphasized the private nature of the audience with Wałęsa and would not release the official L'Osservatore Romano photographs of the occasion nor comment on the reason for not releasing them. On June 24 the Vatican paper featured a front-page editorial by deputy editor Virgilio Levi entitled "Honor to the Sacrifice." Levi praised Lech Wałęsa but concluded that "We can say that he has lost his battle."[38] Two days later the Vatican announced that Levi had resigned his position, and that the article represented only the editor's personal opinion. Newsmen who contacted their Vatican sources for an evaluation of the editorial received assessments varying from a "grain of truth," to the opinion that Levi was sacked for blurting out the truth.[39]

The most successful of recent papal mediations, the Beagle Channel Issue, exemplifies the employment of diplomatic personnel with long experience in a geographical region. In December 1978 Pope Paul VI appointed seventy-three-year-old Italian Cardinal Antonio Samorè as papal mediator. Samorè, archivist and librarian of the Holy Roman Church, had been ambassador to Colombia, secretary for Extraordinary Ecclesiastical Affairs (carrying out Pius XII's Latin American policy), member of the preparatory commission for CELAM I, and both vice-president and president of the Pontifical Commission for Latin America. Samorè's conservative theological background also fitted him perfectly to mediate between the governments of Argentina and Chile in the late 1970s. Principally because of Samorè's mediation, Casaroli was able to preside at the Vatican as the Chilean and Argentinian foreign ministers signed a friendship agreement in January 1984. The foreign ministers came back again in November to sign the treaty which resolved the dispute.[40]

CENTER, REGION, AND NATION: CELAM, CNBB, AND THE POLITICAL DEVELOPMENT OF LATIN AMERICAN CATHOLICISM

The Latin American Bishops' Conference (CELAM) and the National Council of Brazilian Bishops (CNBB) constitute the global church's strongest regional and national ecclesiastical organizations. Their form and political influence reflect various historical trends in Latin American Catholicism. While European Catholicism lost whole nations to the Reformation in Northern Europe, and the combination of the Papal States and foreign intervention made Italian unity impossible, Spain and Portugal extended the medieval ideal of Christendom into the New World. Spain and Portugal had just completed a centuries-long crusade against the Moors to re-establish Catholic dominance on the entire Iberian Peninsula. Lisbon and Madrid then turned their zeal to the newly discovered lands of Asia, Africa, and the Americas. The popes supported Spanish and Portuguese expansion by granting the two kings numerous and extensive ecclesiastical privileges. For example, in 1493 Pope Alexander VI divided the entire new world between the two powers. The pope bestowed the Philippines and the Americas except Brazil on Spain. Portugal received Brazil, Africa, and Asia with the exception of the Philippines. Of course, this papal act of conferring title did not produce actual control, but it did obviate some jurisdictional battles between the two Catholic powers.

The model of Christendom,[41] while theoretically describing the harmonious cooperation of church and state, could result in the predominance of the state or the church, depending on international and local conditions. We have already described the progressive weakening of the European church during the seventeenth and eighteenth centuries. Similar trends fostered state religious prerogatives throughout Latin America. Indeed, so extensive were the ecclesiastical privileges of the Portuguese state in Brazil that "during the whole colonial period (1500-1822) it is probably misleading to talk about a Church." In 1847 the Brazilian Emperor Pedro even turned down the prestige of having Latin America's first cardinal "to avoid subtleties which constantly prevail in the Roman Curia."[42] Up to the fall of Pedro and the establishment of the Republic in 1889, the state limited the church to one archbishopric, six bishoprics, and two prelacies.[43] The First Republic separated church and state in 1891, thus freeing the church to develop at its own pace with strong support from the Vatican.

Following the separation of church and state, however, Rome rapidly multiplied ecclesiastical jurisdictions. By 1920 Brazil was divided into 58 ecclesiastical divisions. By 1930, according to Bruneau, the Brazilian church "resembled a relatively efficient, large bureaucratic organization"[44] based upon the most successful European model of that time, which relied on the bourgeois for societal influence. The Brazilian church built parochial schools, established various ecclesiastical groups and organizations, and emphasized frequent reception of the sacraments. However, the very weakness of the Brazilian church before 1891 meant that Brazil relied to a great extent on foreign, mainly European, ecclesiastical personnel and finances.

The principal political objective of this church institutionalization was to force the state to accept Roman Catholicism in its rightful place as the religion of the country. The great practitioner of this strategy, Dom Sebastião Leme, led the Brazilian church from the time he became bishop (later cardinal) of Rio in 1921 until his death in 1942. He cooperated with his close friend, the agnostic Getúlio Vargas, by initiating ecclesiastical support for Vargas's rule (1930-1945 and 1950-1954) in return for substantial privileges for the church. The Constitutions of 1934 and 1937 reestablished the church and guaranteed it the backing of the Brazilian state. This complete reversal from 1891 constituted a tremendous political achievement for the church, especially when compared with what was happening in other Latin American countries like Mexico. The Brazilian church had not merely recaptured its weak pre-1891 condition as part of the government bureaucracy; it had established a powerful institution, capable of cooperating with the state on an equal basis. Vargas and Leme together constructed the powerful new arrangement of twentieth-century Brazilian neo-Christendom.

The late 1950s and early 1960s brought tremendous political, social, and economic change to Latin America. "In 1961 only one military government remained on the continent (in Paraguay), and the example of Cuba (after 1959) was being felt elsewhere as rural guerrilla movements emerged in several countries."[45] The Brazilian Catholic Church, realizing its weakness in the rural areas of regions like the Northeast, became even more concerned after the Cuban hierarchy's critical attack on Fidel Castro in September 1960. Two years later the Brazilian hierarchy even devised an emergency plan in response to the Cuban situation. John XXIII also asked bishops and religious superiors in Western Europe and North America to send 10 percent of their personnel to Latin America by 1970. The twin motives of social reform and fear of Marxism, especially Castro-style guerrilla movements, mobilized tremendous international and national Catholic resources during this period. For the United States and the Vatican, the great counter-model to Cuba was the victory of Chilean Christian Democrat Eduardo Frei in the election of 1964.[46]

The results in Brazil were mixed. The neo-Christendom model

continued, and "paradoxically, was further strengthened just as the new approach to influence was being refined."[47] The CNBB and Catholic Action led the campaign for a new social Catholicism in Brazil. Monsignor Montini (later Paul VI) of the Vatican Secretariat of State supported Dom Helder Câmara in his formation of the CNBB. In 1952 the Brazilian church consisted of 110 ecclesiastical units. It had had no natural leader since Cardinal Leme's death a decade earlier. The CNBB Secretary Câmara, some progressive bishops from the Northeast, and a small group of clergy and laity constituted the entire organization, but they managed to give the impression that the entire church supported social change. The church also initiated the Superintendency for the Development of the Northeast (SUDENE), the Basic Education Movement (MEB) and rural unions. These efforts constituted part of a new ecclesiastical strategy oriented toward peasants and urban workers. Bruneau terms the strategy "preinfluence" because it sought to humanize Brazilian society so that real religious conversion would be possible. However, social Catholicism during this period remained an elite movement of progressive clerics and laity, without the support of the majority of the bishops or massive participation by peasants and workers. When the CNBB was reorganized to include all the bishops in 1964, Dom Câmara lost his position as secretary general. The military coup of the same year turned the Brazilian government from a supporter of social Catholicism to an opponent.

CELAM II at Medellín (1968) combined elements of reformist Christian Democracy, the more sweeping critiques of Brazilian progressive Catholicism, and the Latin American Catholic radicalism that resulted in the Salvador Allende victory (1970) and the Chilean Christians for Socialism (1972). In the 1960s Bishops Manuel Larraín of Chile and Avelar Brandão Vilela of Brazil played particularly significant roles in activating CELAM as a progressive force in Latin American Catholicism. Eduardo Pironio of Argentina became secretary general of the organization in 1967 and held the same post at Medellín in 1968. When conservatives reacted against the conclusions of the meeting, Rome attempted to "moderate" the organization by naming the young Colombian López Trujillo as secretary general when Pironio assumed the CELAM presidency in 1972. Three years later Pironio, then Bishop of Mar del Plata, was summoned to Rome, probably because he had been designated as a target by right-wing Argentinian terrorists. His Italian descent, Roman education (Angelicum University), and many curial contacts enabled him to influence Paul VI to write a letter to the generally timid

Argentinian bishops encouraging them to protest the violence and repression in that country. Pironio's leadership of the Congregation for Religious helped organizations like CLAR continue the policies of Medellín.

López Trujillo did not disappoint those curial supporters who secured his appointment. He replaced the CELAM staff with conservatives and planned a third meeting of CELAM to repudiate Liberation Theology and other "wrong decisions" taken at Medellín. Moises Sandoval has detailed the political maneuvering that surrounded the meeting itself, from getting John Paul II to name twelve additional delegates with voice and vote (for a total of 187) to planning the physical arrangements of the grand Palafox Seminary in one of Mexico's most historic and conservative cities.[48] López's strongest opposition came from the Brazilian bishops who had prepared for the meeting by issuing a position paper in April 1978 supporting their progressive social Catholicism. The CNBB was particularly sensitive about criticisms of the CEBs, since approximately sixty thousand of them existed in the country.[49]

The pope's presence changed a planned bureaucratic event into one in which charisma played a significant role. John Paul's speeches pleased both conservatives and liberals by stressing the necessity of social justice while condemning Marxism. Liberals rejoiced that the pope condemned neither Liberation Theology nor the CEBs. The bishops' final report encouraged these communities and stressed the political role of the laity to improve the life of the poor. The bishops also sent a shorter "message to the Peoples of Latin America" which stressed Divine Liberation and human rights.[50] The February 18 headline of the *New York Times* read, "Latin Bishops Set Their Course for Political Action." The Brazilian bishops were also pleased by the pope's visit to their country June 30–July 11, 1980. Bruneau summarizes the pope's message by saying that papal words and actions "provided unambiguous support for the progressive sociopolitical orientation of the Brazilian church."[51] The results of Puebla had allowed progressive national hierarchies room to pursue their visions.

CENTER-NATIONAL CONFLICT: THE DUTCH AND
AMERICAN CASES

Earlier we described the historical background of the Catholic Church's habitual suspicion of the sovereign nation-state. The Catholic state did prove troublesome, but the Protestant bourgeois state attacked the church at its religious, political, and economic roots. Catholic ecclesiastical leaders quickly realized the great disparity of values between those held "sacred" by their own institution and by the new Protestant state. "It [the Catholic Church] never quite accepted the bourgeois revolution which it associated—correctly—with Protestant subversion. When, recently, it finally did accept it, it still maintained a critical distance—especially regarding the disintegration of the main institutions of civil society that resulted in the universalization of the commodity form."[52]

Conservative curialists must feel that their distrust of the liberal democratic nation-state has been confirmed by recent experiences with Dutch and American Catholic Churches. During the last two decades Catholics in the Netherlands and the United States have seemed to compete for the unfavorable attention of Rome. Both churches have developed in traditionally Calvinistic cultures that discriminated against but did not fiercely persecute Catholics. While establishing their position in the late eighteenth and early nineteenth centuries Dutch and American Catholics showed a strong devotion to the "rich Roman life." Catholics strengthened their national positions through political, social, and economic organizations to become full partners in highly advanced societies with complex economies and sophisticated media. Both cultures remain very practically oriented, with business efficiency and technical progress held in high esteem. The Netherlands and the United States both suffered considerable political, social, and cultural upheaval during the 1960s. These two NATO countries have developed active Catholic peace movements. The Dutch Pax Christi has become an influential mass movement, while the 1983 statement on peace of the American bishops challenged national hierarchies throughout the world. Conversely, the size and ethnic diversity of the United States mark it as a very different country from the Netherlands (see Chapter Five).

The Second Vatican Council not only legitimized new theoretical understandings of the church but also provided for their embodiment in concrete organizational forms. The most important of these new forms was the national episcopal conference, which was defined as "a council in which the bishops of a given nation or territory jointly exercise their pastoral office to promote the greater good which the church offers mankind, especially through the forms and methods of the apostolate fittingly adapted to the circumstances of the age."[53] In *Ecclesiae sanctae*, the document for implementing the Council, Pope Paul VI further recommended that "bishops of countries or territories which have not yet established an episcopal conference . . . should take steps as quickly as possible to do so and draw up its statutes which are to be approved by the Apostolic See."[54] The exact theological status of these conferences, of course, remains the subject of debate. Curial officials like Cardinal Ratzinger deny that they have a *mandatum docendi* (a mandate to teach).[55] Canons 447-459 of the new Code of Canon Law (1983)[56] describe the purpose (taken directly from the above Vatican II documents) and functioning of the conferences. Since Canon Law generally reflects rather than initiates practice, these thirteen canons indicate the stability of the new organizational form. The canons do not specify the exact theological legitimacy of the conferences, however. These canons merely call on the conferences to foster good relations with other episcopal bodies while insisting that the Apostolic See "must be consulted whenever actions or affairs undertaken by Conferences have an international character" (Canon 459 [2]). Despite the theological controversy, however, the conferences currently do play a leading role in the enunciation of Catholic moral teaching. Most bishops understand national and regional collegiality as an important part of the church's teaching function.

Dutch Catholicism served as the "pilot church" for this new emphasis on the collegiality of a national episcopate. The great change in the Catholic Church in the Netherlands has been described as a movement from the traditional missionary strategy of influence to that of a cultural-pastoral approach. In more colloquial terms, the Dutch primate of the time, Cardinal Alfrink, often contrasted Dutch openness with the bureaucratic spirit of the Roman Curia. Such a stand did not mean that he was anti-Roman, Alfrink said, but that he was "more Catholic than Roman." Thus it was necessary to involve all churches in the implementation of the Council.[57]

Alfrink had originally presided over a very Romanized Catholic Church in the Netherlands. In 1954 the Dutch bishops issued *The Collective Mandatory Letter*, which condemned Catholic membership in Socialist unions and threatened excommunication for significant listening to Socialist radio programs. When Socialists, Protestants, and liberal Catholics reacted negatively to the document, Alfrink traveled the country defending its contents. In the spring of that year, the archbishop proclaimed a "linear, hierarchical, and one way chain of command in the church." Dutch Catholicism had a special tradition of loyalty to Rome, exemplified in the nineteenth century when the Netherlands dispatched more volunteers than any other country to defend the Papal States. Later the Dutch seemed untouched by the modernism that "infected" so many other Catholic Churches in the early twentieth century. Dutch Catholics led Europe in adopting papal reforms on Communion and Gregorian Chant. Indeed, during the period of "Self-Confidence and Triumphalism" (1910-1940), Dutch Catholics lived "the rich Roman life," secure in their church, their Catholic political party, their Catholic social organizations, and their Catholic media.[58]

By 1959, however, Alfrink was championing a much more collegial form of authority. At Vatican II he and the Belgian Cardinal Suenens became the chief spokespersons for reform. The entire Dutch church suddenly became the international symbol of ecclesiastical change. In explaining such a rapid metamorphosis, Coleman isolates four main elements.[59] First, the Dutch Church inherited tremendous mobilizational resources from its period of triumphant *verzuiling* (columnization). All the varied institutions of the Catholic "column," or subculture provided the organizational strength necessary for rapid movement in any direction. Second, the Dutch bishops favored change. Catholicism in other countries had been influenced by new currents in French and native theology, but only the hierarchy of the Netherlands moved in unity to apply these currents to their church. Third, the new collegial model responded to the Dutch political and social crisis of the late 1950s that had been brought about by the negative costs of columnization. Since the Catholic Church constituted the greatest barrier to political and social readjustment in the Netherlands, the entire Dutch society supported and benefited from change in that church. Fourth, among many Catholics an exuberant "collective effervescence" accompanied the initial institutionalization of reform. In addition, Coleman lists seven points drawn from the pre-1853 period which continued to influence the style of Dutch Catholicism.[60] Of these, the method of episcopal selection introduced an incipient collegiality in the various dioceses. The cathedral chapter nominated bishops from priests resident in that diocese. Such a method encouraged input from the lower clergy and discouraged episcopal careerism because no bishop could plot a later move to a more "prestigious" diocese. The compact nature of the Netherlands also encouraged a greater preference for collective pastoral letters and decisions.

The Dutch model, then, did not consist just of the decentralization of ecclesiastical power from the Roman Curia to a national episcopate. The collegial nature of the exercise of power took place at each level. It would have made little sense in this model, for example, for the Dutch bishops to exercise dictatorial control over their priests and laity. The Dutch Pastoral Council, which existed as an experimental body for six sessions between 1966 and 1970, constituted the most coherent organizational expression of this model. Following the six sessions, the bishops commissioned a study group to draw up a definite charter for the Pastoral Council. Rome objected to the charter, which led the episcopate to substitute a National Pastoral Dialogue in place of the Council. The Vatican further insisted that the decisions of the Dialogue be restricted to consultative voice, and that the Dutch bishops attend as individuals, not as a Praesidium. However, the individuals attending and the topics discussed remained the same. Nevertheless, the six sessions of the Dutch Pastoral Council remain the most significant international example of the possibility of combining national collegiality with national hierarchical unity. Thus the organizational arrangements of that period retain considerable significance, even though the Council no longer exists.

The two central Dutch ecclesiastical controversies of the early 1970s concerned Rome's appointment of Bishops Adrien Simonis (Rotterdam) and Jan Gijsen (Roermond) contrary to the traditional prerogatives of the Dutch church. Neither Simonis nor Gijsen was among the three nominees submitted to the papal nuncio by the respective cathedral chapters. Both appointees had conservative reputations but very limited pastoral experience. The bishops had selected Simonis to represent conservative views on the Dutch Pastoral Council, but Gijsen's primary pastoral duties had consisted of a chaplaincy to an order of nuns. The entire Dutch church responded negatively to the appointment and actions of Gijsen. For example, when the new bishop abolished the office of the delegated personnel chief of his diocese and did away with the practice of sending a representative with delegated authority to the National Commission on the Liturgy, the diocese's twelve service bureaucracies, 23 of 24 deans, and the central commission of the diocesan pastoral council published a statement that "cooperation with the bishop at this time has become an impossibility."[61]

The nuncio to the Netherlands at the time of the Simonis and Gijsen affairs, Monsignor A. Felici, had many contacts with prominent members of the conservative *Confrontatie* group. Felici, who spoke no Dutch, walked out of the Dutch Pastoral Dialogue in January 1973 when Gijsen was criticized. His return the next morning "was widely interpreted as a result of a reprimand from his superior officers in Rome for his walkout, and perhaps for his responsibility for getting Rome into the Gijsen mess in the first place."[62] Whatever the reason, Rome appointed the very popular Jan Willebrands to succeed Alfrink as primate in December 1975. Willebrands had been a moderate progressive during his early career in the Netherlands before joining the Secretariat for Christian Unity in 1960. He had an international reputation for pioneering work in ecumenical relations. Both the Dutch bishops and the Vatican seemed pleased by the appointment.

At the beginning of 1980 John Paul took personal charge of the Dutch situation by convening an extraordinary Synod of the Dutch Catholic Church in Rome, January 14-31. At the end of the Synod the pope and the bishops released a 46-point document that John Paul hoped would guide the future development of the Dutch church. When the Dutch bishops made their *ad limina* visit in early 1983 the pope reemphasized the points of the document, focusing on the separation of priestly and lay roles. In May 1985 John Paul himself visited the country. Although small violent demonstrations of leather-jacketed protestors grabbed media attention, the majority of Dutch Catholics stayed home. Even Christian Democratic Prime Minister Ruud Lubbers warned the pope that, "Sometimes Rome seems a very long way from here. Indeed, to be quite frank, simply the word 'Rome' makes some people uneasy if not downright suspicious. . . . We are attached to our democratic tradition and enjoy being so."[63] One thousand demonstrators from Pax Christi met the pope outside the World Court to sing hymns and hold banners supporting disarmament and human rights. The largest crowd came at Amersfoort in the Dutch Catholic heartland where only 25,000–40,000 turned out.

The selection of bishops has continued to be the most crucial and divisive ecclesiastical organizational issue. In July 1983 John Paul appointed Bishop Adrien Simonis to succeed the retiring Willebrands as primate. Simonis remained a possibility for the Vatican because, unlike Gijsen, he had tried to cooperate with his fellow bishops after his initial selection. Coleman remarks, "Even his detractors, who feel that his heart is not in the new church, give him high marks for cooperation with collegiality."[64] Since Simonis had been the choice of neither Willebrands nor the church's clerical and lay boards, the appointment was viewed as a victory for Baggio, who has strong personal ties to the conservative Dutch ex-ambas-

sador to the Vatican, P. A. Kasteel. Kasteel speaks for conservatives, many from large mercantile families.[65] The Dutch conservative group *Confrontatie* gains its strength from "the coalition it seems
to have forged with crucial decision-makers within the international
church in Rome."[66]

The appointment of Bishop Bomers to replace Bishop Zwartkruis
of Haarlem in the following October generated more ill will not only
because local wishes were ignored but because of the insensitivity
demonstrated by Baggio and the nuncio Bruno Wüstenberg toward
the retiring bishop. Zwartkrius had submitted three names suggested by his priests and had been assured the previous month in
Rome by Baggio that no other names were under consideration. In
reality, the post had already been offered to Bomers, a Dutch missionary in Ethiopia. Zwartkruis died of a cerebral hemorrhage
shortly after learning of the appointment. The nuncio then disre-
garded the objections of Zwartkrius's family and insisted on being
photographed by the coffin with Bomers. This embarrassed the
new bishop and further alienated progressive Dutch Catholics.
Wüstenberg died in May 1984.[67]

The papal nuncio or apostolic delegate plays a pivotal role in relations between Rome and the national church. The more intense
the conflict, the more important is his input on the selection of new
bishops. The choice of a Gijsen can incite confrontation, while the
appointment of a Willebrands can restore peace. Many Dutch Catholics resented the activities of Felici and Wüstenberg, who served as
willing conduits to Rome for Dutch conservatives. Nuncios or delegates always represent Rome, but they can also be moderate or
progressive forces in a conservative church. For example, the
change from the conservative apostolic delegates Egidio Vagnozzi
(Washington tour, 1958-1967) and Luigi Raimondi (1967-1973) to the
pastorally oriented Jean Jadot (1973-1980) significantly altered the
character of bishops chosen for the American church.[68] "More than
any individual I can think of," remarked historian John Tracy Ellis,
"he [Jadot] has injected a new openness and warmth in the American Catholic community."[69] Reese reports speculation that "most of
his [Jadot's] recommendations were approved at the beginning of
his term but that toward the end he had more of them rejected."[70]
Jadot's "pastoral bishops" were not proving sufficiently loyal to
Rome for the new pope. Reese's interviewee noted that Jadot was
moved "in a disgraceful haste" when the presidency of the Secretariat for Nonbelievers opened up in 1980. Although Jadot was then

available in Rome, the Congregation of Bishops did not consult him on American appointments, an obvious move if he had remained in favor.

Jadot's replacement, Archbishop Pio Laghi, is an urbane career diplomat.[71] Laghi's first major appointments were Bernard Law in Boston and John J. O'Connor in New York. Both are highly educated, effective speakers, and insistent on firm loyalty to church authority and doctrine.[72] The O'Connor appointment caused controversy, with the unofficial version of events having Laghi objecting to Archbishop Thomas Kelly of Louisville and the American bishops objecting to Bishop Theodore McCarrich of Metuchen, New Jersey. According to the story, the pope called Cardinal John Krol, who recommended O'Connor, a man born and raised in Philadelphia.[73] O'Connor has proved to be very vocal and somewhat combative in defending what he perceives as Catholic positions, even suing New York Mayor Koch over the city's law barring discrimination against homosexuals in city-financed programs, and offending Jews by linking abortion and the Holocaust.[74]

In conflicts between the Vatican and national churches, Rome can employ three methods of influence. First, the Vatican can bring in outside personnel, especially in the appointment of bishops. "Outside" does not have to mean a missionary from Ethiopia (Bomers), but may designate someone without sufficient national support to be chosen (Simonis). The Vatican strongly resists the attempts of any local *groups* to participate openly in the discussion of candidates since traditional Dutch consultations have proved very troublesome. When a Pittsburgh coalition of 15 priests, 24 nuns, and 30 lay people wrote to the apostolic delegate, Laghi replied that "nothing resembling group consultations, canvasses or referendums may take place."[75]

Second, the Vatican may attack the orthodoxy of certain segments of the national church. Rome sought to isolate the Dutch episcopacy ideologically when it ordered no other national hierarchy to give its *imprimatur* to *The New Dutch Catechism* until Roman corrections were included in the appendix. This action, however, did not prevent the catechism from selling over one million copies in six languages between 1966 and 1971. Rome can also declare certain theologians "unorthodox" or "suspect," thus undercutting their legitimacy with certain Catholics, both within the country and internationally. The Vatican's Congregation for the Doctrine of the Faith has continued to scrutinize the writings of the Belgian Dominican Edward

Schillebeeckx, formerly the personal theologian of Cardinal Al-frink.[76]

In the case of the United States, John Paul has emphasized the church's traditional teaching on abortion, divorce, birth control, the ordination of women, premarital sex, and homosexuality.[77] In June 1983 John Paul named three American bishops to investigate the reasons for the drop in religious vocations in the United States. Nuns especially feared Rome would require a return to traditional garb since some American women superiors had been criticized for their lack of "distinctive dress" in a May 9 meeting at the Congregation for Religious in Rome.[78] At the same time the Vatican ordered investigations of Archbishop Hunthausen of Seattle and Bishop Walter Sullivan of Richmond, Virginia. The first announcement was accompanied by guidelines from the Congregation for Religious[79] while all documents related to the two bishops were kept confidential. On November 27, 1985, Hunthausen released a letter from the papal pronuncio Laghi that announced that the investigation "has been concluded and is considered closed." The letter praised many aspects of Hunthausen's ministry, but also included a five-paragraph list of "concerns" that surfaced during the investigation. On December 3, Laghi announced that Donald Wuerl, former secretary to the late Cardinal John Wright and co-editor of the comprehensive adult catechism *The Teaching of Christ*, had been appointed auxiliary bishop to Hunthausen.[80] On September 4, Hunthausen announced that the Vatican had directed him to turn over to Wuerl "complete and final decision-making power" in the above five areas of the marriage tribunal, liturgy and worship, moral issues, clergy formation, and instructions for those leaving or who have left the priesthood.

On February 28, 1984, Cardinal Ratzinger ordered Archbishop Peter Gerety of Newark to withdraw his *imprimatur* from a fourteen-year-old adult catechism, *Christ Among Us*, which had been attacked by the conservative lay group Catholics United for the Faith (CUF).[81] Paulist Press canceled *Christ Among Us*, but continued to publish Philip S. Keane's *Sexual Morality* without its *imprimatur* after Archbishop Hunthausen had been ordered to rescind it. In May 1983 the CDF sent critical "Observations" to Catholic University of America theologian Father Charles Curran. Curran replied in August 1984, received Ratzinger's reply in September 1985, and went to Rome for an interview with Ratzinger in March 1986.[82] On August 18, 1986, Hickey informed

Curran that the Vatican had withdrawn Curran's authorization to teach Catholic theology.[83] The incident is an almost perfect example of the type of Roman intervention most feared by the United States Association of Catholic Colleges and Universities (ACCU) under universal guidelines for orthodox teaching and religious identity at Catholic universities currently proposed by the Vatican Congregation on Education under Cardinal William Baum.

In the case of Brazil, when Ratzinger summoned Franciscan Leonardo Boff to Rome to examine his orthodoxy, Cardinals Arns and Lorscheider accompanied Boff, ostensibly as his personal theologians. The Brazilian hierarchy viewed this action as the most serious Roman attack upon their episcopal conference since the Baggio–López Trujillo position at Puebla. On March 20, 1985, the CDF condemned some of Boff's "options" on the structure of the church in an eleven-page document.[84] When the CDF ordered Boff to withdraw from public life, the theologian went to a Franciscan monastery, but ten Brazilian bishops signed a statement that protested the "grave punishment" from Rome. The CNBB sought to minimize the political damage by acknowledging the existence of "a climate of tensions and doubts over the present situation of our brother Friar Leonardo Boff, but urged the clergy and laity to accept the punishment and avoid the 'spirit of division.' "[85] The Brazilian bishops themselves requested a special meeting with the pope and the Curia at the Vatican. It was held for the 21 senior bishops at the end of the ad limina visits of the 300 Brazilian bishops on March 13-15. The meeting was organized by the prefect of the Congregation of Bishops, African Cardinal Gantin. The prior curial agenda (as published in the conservative Brazilian O Globo) looked formidable, and the Brazilian bishops ended the meeting expressing their "full adherence" to the teachings of John Paul II. However, the pope was conciliatory on Liberation Theology, and the bishops were given a summary of the long-promised second "positive" CDF instruction on the topic that was released in early April. Later that month the CDF also lifted its order of "penitential silence" on Boff. These actions removed the threat of recriminations and deep divisions in the annual meeting of the CNBB in April. In his final sermon to the Brazilian bishops John Paul II advocated "a small step in the direction of unity within the Conference rather than many steps that might break unity."[86]

A third method used by the Vatican to influence national

churches is to encourage criticism of members of the national hierarchy. The role of Dutch conservatives was described earlier. In the Vatican-ordered investigation of Bishop Sullivan by Archbishop Hickey of Washington, Hickey characterized the letters of complaint that sparked the investigation as "the kind of criticism that grows out of efforts at renewal, and I think you could characterize the people [writing the letters] as people who felt uncomfortable with efforts at renewal."[87] While Sullivan received a sympathetic investigator in Hickey, the very employment of such an extraordinary procedure undermines Sullivan's legitimacy. In December 1983 the Congregation for the Clergy appointed Monsignor George A. Kelly as a consultant. The sixty-seven-year-old St. John's University sociologist has been a leading critic of the orthodoxy of American theologians like Charles Curran and Richard McBrien, and scripture scholar Raymond Brown.[88]

National churches have various ways to protect themselves against what they perceive as unwarranted interference from Rome. In the case of the Dutch, the hierarchy relied heavily on national and international theological expertise to defend its pastoral experiments. Schillebeeckx remained particularly effective, both at Vatican II and in organizing the international journal *Concilium* afterwards. In addition, national hierarchies have sponsored experiments which they hoped would gain acceptance over time. The principal example of this was the Dutch Pastoral Council. National churches also defend themselves by changing the venue of the conflict. The Vatican holds an enormous advantage in any closed bureaucratic struggle. The Dutch episcopate's adroit use of the media and public opinion constituted its most effective tactic. Pro-Dutch articles appeared in many influential international journals and newspapers. The Dutch hierarchy became the only national hierarchy to provide an autonomous (run by the Catholic KRO broadcasting company) information center at Vatican II. DOC, as the center was called, "sponsored fourteen press conferences, eight theological conferences, and the publication of forty theological working papers dealing with the key issues of the Council."[89]

The American bishops have a very ineffectual Catholic media when compared with that of the Dutch hierarchy, but *Time, Newsweek*, the *New York Times*, and other outlets do spread religious news to the mass public. While Dutch progressives might put more emphasis on the theological point at issue, the most effective American tactic seems to be to portray Rome as "dictatorial" and "conspiratorial." Leaked memos, such as the summary of the May 9,

1983, meeting between women religious and the secretary general of the Congregation for Religious, can offset Rome's bureaucratic advantage. These tactics of "openness" are all the more effective in Dutch and American societies because they receive reinforcement from basic national cultural values. Such political dynamics should be very familiar to even casual students of incidents like the *Pentagon Papers*.

PARALLEL ORGANIZATIONS: THE JESUITS AND OPUS DEI

Since the Middle Ages religious orders have played critical roles in the internal struggles of the Catholic Church. The mendicant orders—the Dominicans and the Franciscans—have fought to maintain Catholic orthodoxy and religious devotion to poverty. As Italy entered the Renaissance, friars from both orders "were in the forefront of those excoriating the spread of what they called epicureanism or worldliness."[90] Their interventions, of course, were not always appreciated by secular and ecclesiastical princes devoted to the culture of ancient Greece and Rome. The Dominicans have maintained an institutional base in the Inquisition and its successor congregations (presently CDF), while the Franciscans have continued to represent papal interests in the Holy Land.

Since their founding in 1540, the Jesuits have constituted Catholicism's most controversial religious order. Religious orders like the Dominicans, Franciscans, and Jesuits do not fit neatly into the regular ecclesiastical structure. They form parallel hierarchical structures from their generals in Rome to their provincial superiors who head various geographical jurisdictions. Religious orders thus remain exempt from certain types of control by the local bishop. They also project a special esprit de corps from following the spirituality of their founders, such as the Franciscan emphasis on poverty learned from St. Francis. Religious orders and diocesan clergy also have a long tradition of friction.[91]

During the last decade a secular institute called Opus Dei has rivaled the Jesuits for global Catholic notoriety. Many ecclesiastics make the same type of charges against Opus Dei that were made against the Jesuits in the sixteenth and seventeenth centuries: secrecy, greed, elitism, and manipulation of the very young. A comparison of the Jesuits and Opus Dei is useful because of the controversy over their respective political roles, their mutual competition, and their similar origins in the fervent "crusade" piety of the Iberian peninsula. St. Ignatius of Loyola, wounded while fighting for Spain at Pamplona, founded the Society of Jesus during the sixteenth century. The Spanish priest Jose María Escrivá founded Opus Dei in 1928, and it flourished in the Francoist crusading spirit of the Spanish Civil War. In fact, the founding of Opus Dei has been linked to the Jesuit-based Asociación Católica Nacional de Propagandistas (ANCP), founded by Ángel Ayala, S.J., in 1909.[92]

Just as the early Jesuits sought to combine religious orthodoxy with the learning of the Renaissance, Opus Dei has combined traditional religious practice with recent advances in business and technology. The religious ideology of Opus Dei, therefore, matched the integralism of the Franco regime, but provided the emerging business class with the blessings of economic liberalism and integration into the world market. In 1953 the leading Opus theoretician Rafael Calvo Serer minted the phrase "tercero fuerza" to describe the political future of the movement. As the Falangists faded and Catholic Action moved to the left, members of Opus Dei became prominent in the Franco government. The Spanish government of February 1957 contained eight ministers who were either members of or sympathizers with Opus Dei. Opus representation expanded in the governments of 1962 and 1965, and reached a peak in October 1969. However, the Matesa financial scandal shook the Opusdeistas' reputation for honesty, and they declined in 1973.[93] The Opus Dei tie to Spain remains strong, nevertheless, with approximately 40 percent of the members coming from that country. A pro-Opus Dei ecclesiastic who knew Escrivá well explains the organization's secretiveness in terms of Escrivá's experience of the strength of anticlericals and Freemasons in Spanish cultural and political organizations during the late 1920s and early 1930s.[94]

While the Jesuits remain a religious order organized along vertical lines (superior general, assistants, provincials, rectors), Opus Dei took the organizational form of a secular institute made up of priests and laity, celibates and married persons, Catholics and even non-Catholics (among the cooperatores). Among the Jesuits, the professed, who take the special fourth vow of obedience to the pope, serve as an elite core. The Opusdeista elite are the numerarii, who possess university degrees, take vows of poverty, chastity, and obedience, and live in Opus residences. Supernumerari, on the other hand, live in their private homes and can be married. In addition, cooperatores support Opus Dei, but do not play an active role in the internal organization. The cooperatores, the most politically significant part of the organization, generally have Opus priests as confessors, but use "discretion" in making their membership public.[95]

The local church first legitimized Opus Dei in 1941 when Bishop Leopoldo Eijó y Garay of Madrid-Alcalá recognized it as a pious union within his diocese. In 1946 Escrivá and Alvaro del Portillo moved to Rome when they made friends with influential curialists like Tardini. In 1947 Pope Pius XII issued the bull *Provida mater Ecclesia*, which created the secular institute as an ecclesiastical organizational form. This form was conferred on Opus Dei in 1950, and it then became subject to the Congregation for Religious and Secular Institutes. As long as the Opus supporters like Cardinal Ildebrando Antoniutti[96] headed this congregation, the arrangement seemed satisfactory. When Pironio replaced Antoniutti, however, Opus Dei began to lobby for an organizational change. In 1979 some curial enemy leaked confidential documents, which were later published in Spain. These documents included Opus reports and letters employed in its campaign for greater autonomy. In one del Portillo, who became president general in 1975 when Escrivá died, wrote Baggio that John Paul himself wanted the organization made a personal prelature under Baggio's Congregation of Bishops to facilitate Opus Dei's mission as a "mobile corps of priests and laymen" for urgent missions.[97] Opus could count on support from curial cardinal prefects like Silvio Oddi (Congregation for the Clergy) and Pietro Palazzini (Congregation for Saints' Causes). In 1981 69 cardinals and 1,300 bishops signed petitions requesting the canonization of Escrivá, and Palazzini began the process.

Many influential cardinals and bishops, like Pironio and Benelli, however, opposed the creation of the personal prelature. On August 23, 1982, Vatican press spokesman Father Romeo Panciroli announced that "The Pope has decided on the erection of Opus Dei as a personal prelature. However, the publication of the relevant document has been postponed for technical reasons."[98] Three months later Rome did release the document which established Opus Dei as the Catholic Church's first personal prelature, subject to the Congregation of Bishops. Responding to prior episcopal criticism of the independence of the organization, the document specified that Opusdeistas are "subject to the jurisdiction of the diocesan Bishops in everything that the law establishes for all the ordinary faithful."[99] Del Portillo was consecrated as head of the prelature in March 1983.

This analysis has focused on the national background and bureaucratic competition of the Jesuits and Opus Dei, but the global political significance of the rise or fall of these two institutions lies in their considerably different approaches to modernization. In commenting on the future of Latin America, José Casanova remarks, "I think that if the Opus Dei model were to triumph, Catholicism could still serve to modernize Latin American societies in a technocratic-capitalist direction, whereas the traditional anti-capitalist Catholic resistance in Latin America, combined with the impulses unleashed by the Vatican Council could work towards a radically different model of Latin American modernization. In this sense, a lot may be at stake in this seemingly internal conflict between the Opus Dei and the Jesuits." Casanova describes the Opus model of modernization as the combination of a "modern, secular, economic ethos" with the "traditional dogma, the traditional morals and the traditional hierarchic structures of the church."[100] Norman Cooper phrased the same idea by saying that "Escrivá combines the clerical authoritarianism of Pius IX with the profit motive of Henry Ford."[101] For an outsider, an understanding of this vision comes easiest at the Spanish University of Navarre (at Pamplona), the principal intellectual center of the movement. The Opus appreciation for modern business and communications is exemplified in the dean of the Graduate School of Business, Juan Antonio Pérez López, a leading numerary who holds a doctorate from the Harvard Business School. Indeed, Navarre has established the most important schools for business and journalism in Spain. Unlike Harvard, López said that his Graduate School of Business would teach no course whose content was Marxism or "pure materialist liberalism."[102]

Such an approach was bound to appeal to John Paul II, whose support Otto Maduro links to the Polish Catholic respect for "well organized, obedient, structured, modern, and anti-Communist groups within the church."[103] Such a stand also brought Opus Dei and its supporters into direct conflict with certain developments within the Jesuit Order, such as the Christian-Marxist dialogue and public criticism by certain Jesuits of traditional Catholic morality.[104] While Navarre cannot match Jesuit intellectual holdings in Rome,[105] conservative attacks did weaken the Order's standing with the papacy and the Curia. Pedro Arrupe, a Spanish Basque who spent twenty-seven years in Japan, had become superior general in 1965. Arrupe presided over the great outpouring of Jesuit ecclesiastical experimentation following Vatican II. Arrupe himself urged Jesuits to become more involved in social justice. Without publicly approving the actions of American activist Daniel Berrigan, he visited the priest in jail. On the situation in Latin America, he told Italian journalists that while Jesuits were not Marxists, "the possibility of a certain dialogue and also of a critical collaboration with Marxist-inspired groups and movements cannot a priori be ruled out."[106]

The Curia reacted less to calls for social justice than to open challenges to its own authority. In 1972 the Spanish Jesuit José Maria Diez-Alegria, a faculty member at the Gregorian University, published *Creencia y Esperanza*, in which he sympathized with left-wing politics, criticized the Vatican's wealth, and admitted to masturbation in order to remain celibate. In 1973 the British Jesuit Peter Hebblethwaite, in an article for *The Observer*, attacked Cardinal Benelli as a power-obsessed bureaucrat. Arrupe personally apologized to Benelli, and both Diez-Alegria and Hebblethwaite left the Jesuits. In 1974 Pope Paul VI wrote to the Order that he had observed "certain tendencies of an intellectual and disciplinary nature that, if encouraged, would introduce very serious and perhaps incurable changes in your essential structures."[107] In 1979 Arrupe wrote to the Order as a whole that John Paul II had expressed concern about "secularizing tendencies, austerity and discipline in religious and community life, fidelity to the magisterium in doctrine, and the priestly character of our apostolic work."[108] Still, until his stroke in August 1981, Arrupe managed to keep the Jesuit Order united on a moderately progressive course without major curial intervention. When earlier that year Arrupe announced that he wished to resign, John Paul publicly asked him to remain as superior general. As soon as he was incapacitated by a stroke, and one of his general assistants, the American Vincent O'Keefe, was in charge, the pope took action.

Early in October 1981, Cardinal Casaroli visited Arrupe to inform him that the pope was suspending the Jesuit Constitutions and appointing the eighty-year-old Italian Jesuit scholar Paolo Dezza as his personal delegate who would "superintend the government of the Society until an election of a new Superior General." The papal letter carried by Casaroli also named fifty-one-year-old Sardinian Joseph Pittau, a Harvard Ph.D. in Government and ex-Provincial of Japan, as Dezza's assistant. The letter specified that Pittau, whom John Paul had met at Sophia University in Tokyo, would succeed Dezza should he die or be incapacitated. This unprecedented action stirred immediate protests, including a letter from theologian Karl Rahner and seventeen other Jesuits in West Germany which stated that the signers were unable "to recognize the finger of God in this administrative measure."[109] Pittau himself conceded that the papal decision "caused some pain" among the world's over 25,000 Jesuits, but he also described the decision as a "moment of grace."[110] During the interim Pittau traveled to political flashpoints like Central America and Eastern Europe, while Dezza became very active in Vatican politics. In February 1982 Dezza followed the pope's instruction in convening a special meeting of the Order's provincials and assistancy leaders from around the world. John Paul promised that before the end of the year a new General Congregation would be called to elect the next superior general. In December 1982 the pope called the congregation for September 1983.

Unlike the Dominicans, who were simultaneously electing a master general for a nine-year term, the Jesuit leader is elected for life. In addition, the Jesuit superior general appoints assistants and provincials, while the Dominicans elect their provincials and local priors. Thus, the Jesuit election of a superior general can determine the Order's policy for several decades. The 211 delegates elected the Dutch Middle East scholar Peter-Hans Kolvenbach on the first ballot. The fifty-four-year-old Kolvenbach had been provincial in Lebanon before returning to Rome to head the Pontifical Oriental Institute in 1981. This Institute, directed by the Jesuits, depends directly on the Vatican, so someone out of favor with the pope could not have been director.[111] The delegates knew that the American O'-Keefe would not be acceptable, and naming Pittau would seem to indicate that the pope had made the choice.[112]

Kolvenbach responded to the impending CDF investigation of Jesuit Liberation Theologian Sobrino by submitting Sobrino's writings to the conservative theologian Juan Alfaro. Alfaro wrote up his findings that Sobrino's works contained nothing heterodox, and this paper was passed on to Ratzinger, who did not then publicly open up the case.[113] In another case, however, Kolvenbach was forced to dismiss Nicaragua's Fernando Cardenal in December 1984 when Cardenal refused to resign his position as Sandinista minister of education. The general then wrote a letter to all Jesuit superiors in which he recognized Cardenal's "conflict of conscience" and expressed hopes that Jesuits would not conclude that helping the poor meant leaving the society. The Jesuit-run Vatican Radio said the dismissal had taken place "in an atmosphere of mutual esteem and respect on the part of all those involved, but obviously for Fernando, and for many other Jesuits, it was a painful affair."[114] Cardenal blamed the pope and the Nicaraguan bishops.

CONCLUSION: THE ORGANIZATIONAL FACTOR IN CATHOLIC POLITICS

Many aspects of this general overview of the organizational factor in Catholic politics should seem familiar to Soviet and Japanese specialists. For example, the same church leaders appear in different bureaucratic posts over a long period of time. Although the reforms of Paul VI provided for episcopal resignations at age seventy-five and the loss of vote by cardinal electors at eighty, senior citizens play a vigorous role in curial government, usually until they die or are named to one of the Curia's honorary sinecures. For example, in the April 1984 Curia shuffle, Cardinal Opilio Rossi left the presidency of the Pontifical Council of the Laity for the presidency of the Cardinal's Commission for the Pontifical Sanctuaries of Pompeii, Loreto, and Bari. Like the Soviet system, important Vatican leaders serve on multiple congregations and commissions in addition to holding their principal posts. Such interpenetration makes it difficult for even long-time Vatican watchers to pinpoint the curial decision maker on a particular issue. The Vatican bureaucracy itself is usually of little assistance, since, like its Soviet counterpart, it shuns investigative reporters. One of the major complaints against Arrupe's temporary successor O'Keefe was that he talked too much to the American media.

The Vatican's major organizational tension pits one of the world's greatest bureaucratic traditions against a pope elected for life. The active personal intervention of John Paul II is the major distinguishing characteristic of his governing style. This could be seen at Puebla,[115] the Dutch Synod in Rome, the suspension of the Jesuit Constitutions, the Extraordinary Synod of 1985, and the Brazilian Synod of 1986. Such papal interventionism adds a note of unpredictability into the "normal" bureaucratic life of the church. Nevertheless, curial connections and respect remain a *sine qua non* for effective ecclesiastical politics. The Jesuit Order escaped major damage during the suspension of its Constitutions partially through the diplomatic *savoir faire* of the eighty-year-old Italian Jesuit Dezza. John Paul's prior respect for Dezza and Pittau meant that the pope had two Jesuits to appoint after curial officials convinced him that the political costs of selecting a non-Jesuit, the Carmelite Cardinal Anastasio Ballestrero,[116] as acting head of the Order were too great.

Casaroli and Ratzinger are the second and third most powerful political actors and represent two major tendencies in Vatican policy. Secretary of State Casaroli, the architect of *Ostpolitik*, represents continuity with the Italian diplomatic style of Paul VI. Ratzinger, who has been called "John Paul's most important single appointment,"[117] articulates the concerns of those curial officials who would challenge the power of the national episcopal conferences and condemn the "heresies" of progressive theologians. Paul Johnson calls this tendency *The Catholic Restoration*. Indeed, Casaroli took the unusual step of publicly disassociating himself with the CDF's attack on Marxism, which he perceived as counterproductive in Eastern Europe.

Since the same names (Casaroli, Benelli, Baggio, Pironio, Arrupe, Gantin, König, Lorscheider, López Trujillo, Bernardin, etc.) appear often and in different contexts throughout this book, personal characteristics and backgrounds constitute an important consideration in Catholic politics. Not only do these personages move from congregation to congregation within the Curia, but they also move from national and regional posts to curial ones and vice-versa. Cardinal König remained archbishop of Vienna after he became president of the Secretariat for Non-Believers. Cardinal Willebrands retained his curial post when he became Dutch primate. Just as Soviet specialists commented on the political advantages and disadvantages of Khrushchev's prewar return to the Ukraine, Vatican watchers interpreted the significance of Montini's move to Milan (1954) and Benelli's to Florence (1977). Many interpreted Benelli's transfer as Paul VI's attempt to give him pastoral experience, a more necessary quality for prospective popes since Vatican II, so that he could succeed him.

Nationality also remains a factor. Italians still enjoy an advantage in church politics. This Italian advantage even extends in a somewhat diluted form to clerics of other nationalities with Italian descent (Pironio, Bernardin, Mario Revollo Bravo of Bogotá). With regard to non-Italians, the ideal curial candidate would have experience in Italy, a Western industrialized country, and in either an Eastern European or non-European culture. Big-power nationality constitutes a severe handicap, so small European nations like Belgium, Italy, Lithuania, and the Netherlands make excellent backgrounds. In the crucial election of September 1983, the Jesuits selected a Dutchman with Middle Eastern and Roman experience. He succeeded Arrupe, a Basque who had spent long years in Japan. John Paul II had chosen an Italian and a Sardinian missionary to Japan who also had a Harvard doctorate to supervise an Order whose largest numbers are in the United States and India. Dezza replaced the American Vincent O'Keefe, who had been president of Fordham University in New York. John Paul views the United States as the source of much recent criticism of traditional Catholic morality.[118]

In addition to personal and national considerations, church bu-

reaucrats tend to defend the prerogatives of their own organizations, as when Pironio sought to keep Opus Dei under his own congregation. This natural bureaucratic inclination is somewhat
weakened in the Curia by the multiple offices held by high-ranking
prelates. When it comes to ideology, it is difficult to place the major
actors on a single left-right (progressive-conservative) spectrum, especially if the purpose of that categorization is to separate the sheep
from the goats. For example, even Roman progressives missed Benelli's contribution to curial management when the cardinal left for
Florence. Progressives had applauded his opposition to Opus Dei
and his solution to the crisis between Paul VI and Pedro Arrupe of
the Jesuits.[119]

Regional and national episcopal conferences represent relatively
new forces in ecclesiastical politics. CELAM derives its significance
from the importance of Latin America to the Catholic Church, the
importance of the Catholic Church to Latin American national politics, the internal unity of the organization fostered by similar national histories and cultures, and the superb leadership of the Brazilian bishops. In assessing Catholic political influence at the
national level, an analyst must pay close attention to the appointment of bishops. In the Dutch case, Paul VI sought to restrain a national church from taking positions he considered too radical, while
in Spain he sought to break the ecclesiastical influence of a reactionary government. In 1969 Spanish liberals became cardinals, but not
the prestigious Francoist Archbishop Cantero of Zaragoza. When
pro-Franco clergy met in Zaragoza, the Spanish Bishops' Conference declared the conference "unofficial." No cardinal or curial official attended. No usual papal blessing was sent.[120]

Since control of episcopal appointments is so crucial to the control
of national churches, it has also been a central feature of Vatican
concordats with Catholic and Communist states. The 1953 concordat with Spain confirmed Franco's final decision in the appointment
of bishops and the designation of the diocesan boundaries (especially important in Cataluna and the Basque country). Appointment
of auxiliary bishops and apostolic administrators remained completely with Rome. In the battle betweeen Paul VI and Franco following Vatican II, Rome refused to consecrate Franco's candidates
and appointed "temporary" apostolic administrators to some
dioceses, e.g., the liberal Cirarda to Bilbao. Nine sees were vacant
by 1968 when compromises were reached. For example, a liberal
theologian who had refrained from attacking the government,

Archbishop Enrique y Tarancón, became primate and archbishop of Toledo in February 1969.

As national constituencies become politicized, and as Catholic lay organizations become more involved in contemporary political issues, relationships between the hierarchy and lay organizations become increasingly strained. Levine has described this process as it occurred in Venezuela and Colombia:

Venezuelan youth groups and innovative catechisms in Colombia (like other vital Catholic associations such as ACPO [Acción Cultural Popular] or the unions of UTC [Union of Colombian Workers]) were all founded to respond to threats from the outside world. But now the groups find themselves moving into crisis in their relations with the hierarchy, above all as they reach for greater autonomy and move more directly into independent social and political action. As they succeed, they become threatening. This process, which is visible in Catholic groups all over Latin America, points directly to the dilemma of the bishops: they want strong and vital Catholic groups and programs of religious education that really reach and motivate a clientele, but they demand that these be safe and reliable as well. These goals are increasingly difficult to reconcile.[121]

CHAPTER 3

Political Ideology: Catholicism, Socialism, and Capitalism

IDEOLOGY AS POLITICAL CULTURE: JOHN PAUL VISITS NICARAGUA

DANIEL ORTEGA SAAVEDRA, coordinator of the Nicaraguan Directorate, and members of the Nicaraguan Cabinet met John Paul II when he arrived in Managua on Friday morning, March 4, 1983. In his welcoming speech, Ortega told the pope that, "Our experience shows that one can be both a believer and a revolutionary and that no unsalvageable contradiction exists between the two." Ortega also denounced American aggression against his country, specifically mentioning that United States-backed guerrillas had recently killed seventeen Nicaraguan youths. The young men had been buried only the day before the pope's arrival. In his reply to Ortega, John Paul emphasized that he wanted to contribute "to ending the suffering of innocent people in this part of the world, to ending the bloody conflicts, hate and sterile accusations, leaving room for genuine dialogue." He also sent a special message "to the thousands and thousands of Nicaraguans who have not been able, as they wished, to go to the meeting places."[1] This latter remark seemed to refer indirectly to charges by the Nicaraguan episcopate that the junta had hindered some people from attending the ceremonies. Following the opening speeches, the pope was introduced to the Nicaraguan cabinet. John Paul seemed surprised to encounter Father Ernesto Cardenal, the minister of culture, who had repeatedly ignored the request of Managua's Bishop Obando y Bravo that he resign his government post. The Vatican had originally threatened to exclude Nicaragua from the pope's itinerary until Cardenal and four other priests did resign, but a face-saving agreement had been reached whereby the five priests would not be present for the papal visit.[2] Cardenal, dressed in a shirt, slacks, and a beret, knelt to kiss the pope's ring, but John Paul withdrew his hand and shook his finger at him saying, "You must straighten out your position with the Church."[3]

That evening the pope spoke to over 500,000 people at an open

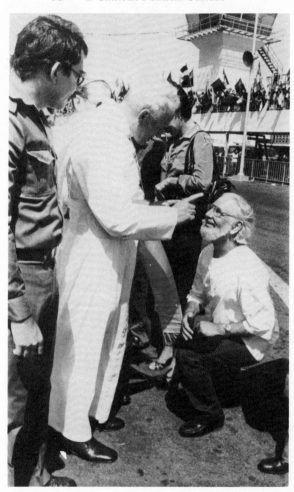

MANAGUA, NICARAGUA.
Pope John Paul II shakes
his finger at the Culture
Minister Ernesto Cardenal
during ceremonies at Ma-
nagua. According to Vati-
can Sources, the Pope told
him "You must straighten
out your position with the
church." March 1983. AP/
World Wide Photos.

air mass. Some of the hearers wore the red and black of the Sandinistas and others wore the papal yellow and white. Both groups carried banners with slogans. In his sermon the pope attacked "unacceptable ideological commitments" and the dangers of
totalitarianism, especially attempts by the Sandinistas to control the
school curriculum. He then cited his pastoral letter of the preceding
June to the Nicaraguan bishops in which he said that it was "absurd
and dangerous to imagine that outside—if not to say against—the
church built around the bishop there should be another church . . .
alternative and as it has been called recently, a people's church."[4]

A variety of responses from the crowd interrupted the pope's sermon. Supporters of the government chanted, "Between Christianity and the revolution, there is no contradiction!" Opponents of the government chanted, "John Paul II, the world loves you." On several occasions during the homily, John Paul called out "Silence!" and was cheered by some for doing so. The event symbolizes the two major sets of issues that dominated the pope's visit to Nicaragua. The first concerned the relationship of the Catholic Church to the Sandinista government. The second dealt with the degree of legitimate diversity within Nicaraguan Catholicism, especially the status of the "people's church" and the case of the priests who had ignored episcopal requests that they resign their government positions. These same two major sets of Catholic political issues are discussed by Brian Smith in his analysis of Chilean Catholicism under Allende.[5] Smith concludes that the solution to the first set of issues is much easier than the solution to the second. The Chilean Catholic hierarchy maintained much better relations with the Allende government than it did with the priests who belonged to Christians for Socialism. John Paul angrily shook his finger at Father Ernesto Cardenal, while he took Ortega's remarks in stride.

In this chapter we will briefly introduce some of the Catholic political ideologies. Earlier, in defining political culture, we included both conscious ideology and habitual paradigms in the category "modes of thought." Here, we focus on the relation between conscious ideology and the other two factors in the definition, historical memory and types of social and political organization. As such, we do not propose to evaluate the truth or falsity of such beliefs, but merely to explain the cultural context of their origins and their present functions in domestic and international politics. In this limited sense of comparative political analysis, ideologies, like other political resources, can be employed for the general legitimacy of institutions or for specific policy objectives. World political leaders have recently become much more interested in the political uses of Catholic thought for both reasons.

When faced with Pilate's interrogation, Christ affirmed that his kingdom was "not of this world." The New Testament offers little systematic political theory and it does not take stands on the foreign policy issues of the day. However, in his Epistle to the Romans, St. Paul did say that "since all government comes from God," Christians "must all obey the governing authorities." This was excellent practical advice for a small Jewish sect that regarded the state as a finite organization due only "that which is Caesar's." Caesar, of course, claimed more. So the early Christians clung to survival in the moderately intolerant atmosphere of the Roman Empire under a *pontifex maximus* who combined both political and religious legitimacy. Only gradually did the church develop systematic theories about itself and its relationship to the outside world. Chapter One treats some of the major historical stages in the Catholic Church's relationships to Western political systems. The church has influenced the basic patterns of those systems and has adopted many characteristics from secular institutions in a complex interaction over nearly two thousand years. During this process prelates and theologians have articulated various understandings of the nature of the church and of its correct relation to society. Throughout the book these ideological positions are presented in their historical and geographic settings.

This chapter draws together some major contemporary arguments concerning the nature of the church and its relation to political systems in an effort to document transnational influences in the current debates over Catholic ideology. In many instances, Catholic ideology from a particular region has influenced thinkers in other cultures. For example, the Korean Catholic poet Kim Chi Ha owes a debt to Latin American Liberation Theology. Such causality should be expected in a transnational organization that takes its doctrinal formations seriously, with or without Vatican mediation.

As James Turner Johnson has pointed out, the word "ideology" is usually used with either a neutral or a negative connotation. Here, the former is intended. Johnson also comments that "A *neutral* sense of this word [ideology], following the usage of Max Weber, merely denotes belief structures wherever and however they appear, without raising the question of the validity of their bases."[6] Each of the thinkers discussed below offers a vision that gives religious legitimacy to political action. When the focus moves from the individual to the church itself, the process becomes more regularized. Unlike classes and individuals, organizations result from conscious creation and therefore demand a more systematic ideology. Like the leaders of the Chinese Communist Party, Catholic leaders devote considerable effort to articulating the ideology of their organization, even though both bishops and theologians believe that the church and its doctrine remains ultimately the work of God.

Catholic ideology is articulated at various levels, from papal encyclicals to the individual positions of bishops, theologians, and the laity. At the universal level the popes usually articulate general principles, such as the dual condemnations of classical liberalism and classical Communism, without applying these principles to specific countries or economic systems. The national episcopal conferences of individual countries may offer more specific encouragements and admonitions. Individual bishops, theologians, and lay experts offer reasoned explanations or "prophetic witness" on particular issues. Since Vatican II more emphasis has been placed on the individual formation of conscience based on a respectful hearing of all of these sources, but different ecclesiastics hold different interpretations of the binding power of specific decrees, so that this latter question also becomes a part of ideological argumentation. The controversy is not open-ended, however, since almost all Catholics agree that there is a minimum "deposit of faith" which constitutes a bond of church unity.

Since this book focuses on the Catholic Church as a political actor, theoretical formulations about the nature of the church (ecclesiology) serve as the central ideological emphasis. Catholics differ considerably in their visions of the church. The monarchical model, with each level completely responsive to the absolute power of the level above it, fit the prevalent theory of the church during the four hundred years from the mid-sixteenth century to the mid-twentieth century. The sharp criticism of this ecclesiastical model during this century has been a major moving force in recent church developments. In *Models of the Church*[7] Avery Dulles offers five different images which all attempt to integrate successfully what Catholics believe about the church and to provide heuristic clues for further understanding. These five models consist of the church as monarchical institution, mystical communion, sacrament, herald, and servant.[8]

In explaining the first model, Dulles cites the definition of Jesuit Robert Bellarmine (1542-1621) that, "The one and true Church is the community of men brought together by the profession of the same Christian faith and conjoined in the communion of the same sacraments, under the government of the legitimate pastors and especially the one vicar of Christ on earth, the Roman pontiff."[9] Bellarmine's definition, which consists solely of visible elements, fits very well with the attempt to defend papal prerogatives from the attacks of the "spiritualist" Reformation. This institutional paradigm, which predominated at the Councils of Trent and Vatican I, guaranteed the prerogatives of the pope within the universal church and the prerogatives of the bishop, a "little pope," within his diocese. In fact, Vatican I went so far as to define papal infallibility as an article of faith.

This institutional paradigm lost its monopoly on the official position in 1943 when Pope Pius XII adopted the ecclesiastical model of the mystical communion in his encyclical *Mystici corporis* (June 29, 1943).[10] The pope declared that the church, identical with the visible Roman Catholic Church, consisted in the Mystical Body of Jesus Christ. The documents of Vatican II employ the images of the Body of Christ and the Sacrament, but the People of God became the Council's dominant model. This latter understanding had deep biblical roots and also harmonized with the Western trend toward political democratization that had been prevalent since the eighteenth century. The models of herald and servant have long Protestant traditions associated with the Reformation's emphasis on the Word of God and Christian service. The latter model appeals most strongly to those Catholics who feel the church must be engaged in social action.

Church leaders currently use many different images to describe the church. The nuances of the various models influence both internal and external Catholic politics. Emphasis on the institution and its visible elements will strengthen internal centralization with a view to enabling this "perfect society" and transnational actor to compete effectively with national states. Use of the People of God encourages decentralization both within the international church and within national churches. The popularity of this model, however, has usually occurred within a Western context which already encourages the activity of transnationals. The emphasis on servant generally influences local Christians to see their religious duty in either revolutionary activity against rightist regimes or in the national construction of leftist societies. Either alternative tends to limit the influence of the Vatican and all other transnationals.

Changes in the Catholic perception of Marxism are especially relevant to Soviet-American competition. *Pacem in terris* promulgated the Joannine distinction between "false philosophical teachings regarding the nature, origin, and destiny of the universe, and movements which owe their inspiration to these false tenets,"[11] which has served as the basis for Catholic participation in the subsequent Catholic-Marxist dialogue. In terms of practical politics, the distinction benefited not only the Soviet Union, but also the Italian Communist Party just three weeks before national general elections. Following *Pacem in terris* certain important Marxist and Catholic theoreticians did turn *From Anathema to Dialogue*.[12] The most famous meetings, initiated by the Paulus Society (Paulus-Gesellschaft), took place at Salzburg (1965), Chiemsee (1966), and Marienbad

(1967).[13] Another external political event, the Soviet invasion of Czechoslovakia brought an end to this phase of the discussions. The French Communist Party (PCF) expelled Roger Garaudy, a leading participant in the dialogue, in 1970. From that time discussions between Christians and Marxists have focused on the political, social, and economic liberation of developing countries, especially in Latin America.

The period 1955 to 1975 thus saw immense changes in the political use of Catholic ideologies. While in the 1950s many Western politicians employed ecclesiastical pronouncements to buttress their Cold War positions, by the 1970s more progressives argued that "real Catholics" must support leftist politics. Kenneth L. Woodward's designation of John Paul II as a "Socialist" (*Newsweek*, June 20, 1983) angered many American Catholic conservatives. *Catholicism in Crisis* retaliated by devoting its entire August 1983 issue to "The Twilight of Socialism." This author agrees with Christopher Wolfe in his article, "The Vatican as Nobody's Ally," in which he asserts the church's tolerance for the broad middle spectrum of Democratic Capitalism and Democratic Socialism while maintaining its prerogative to criticize specific aspects of both, for example, capitalism's greed and socialism's class struggle.[14]

In keeping with our general emphasis on individual ecclesiastics and national cultures, we explore general ideological trends under seven individuals representing seven different nationalities. The choice of the individuals remains somewhat arbitrary, though their utility for explanation should become obvious as the chapter progresses. The identification of specific ideologies with national or regional figures concretizes the connection between theoretical formulation and political experience, thus maintaining our emphasis on comparative politics and international relations, not political theory and theology. Some of these thinkers began their analysis with internal ecclesiastical questions and others originally emphasized the role that the church plays in politics and society. French conservative Archbishop Marcel Lefebvre, Belgian progressive theologian Edward Schillebeeckx, and Swiss ecumenical theologian Hans Küng have begun by examining the internal life of the church. Brazilian professor Corrêa de Oliveira, poets Ernesto Cardenal and Kim Chi Ha, and philosopher Michael Novak start with the place of the church in Brazilian, Nicaraguan, Korean, and American societies, respectively. However, each of these thinkers and the groups they represent remain very aware of the complementary aspects of these issues regardless of their starting point.

TRADITIONAL CATHOLICISM: MARCEL LEFEBVRE (FRANCE) AND PLINIO CORRÊA DE OLIVEIRA (BRAZIL)

In *Challenge to the Church: The Case of Archbishop Lefebvre*, the French theologian Yves Congar emphasizes the continuity of Marcel Lefebvre's views with the whole tradition of French integralism. "What we know of the formation of Msgr. Lefebvre, what we have learnt about his conduct in Dakar, what we have heard about him and know of him at the Council, his declarations since then . . . all these things proclaim him to be a man of the Right, in agreement with the attitudes of the old Action Française." Lefebvre himself sees the pernicious influence of the French Revolution present in many declarations of Vatican II. The revolutionary principles of liberty, fraternity, and equality became manifest in the *Declaration on Religious Liberty*, the *Decree on Ecumenism* and the *Declaration on Non-Christian Religions*, and collegiality, respectively.[15] The deliberations of Vatican II remain highly suspect to Lefebvre and his followers, who revere the Council of Trent (1566), the Latin liturgy standardized by St. Pius V (1570), the *Syllabus of Errors* of Pope Pius IX (1864), and the catechism of the great antimodernist St. Pius X (1912). In 1969 Lefebvre founded the Society of Priests of St. Pius X, which has its headquarters in the seminary of Ecône, Switzerland. From Ecône traditional priests go forth to maintain the faith of Catholics in the above traditions of "Eternal Rome." The contrast between "Eternal Rome" and the current "degenerate" state of the church permeates Archbishop Lefebvre's "Profession of Faith" given in Rome on November 21, 1974.

We adhere whole-heartedly, and with our whole soul, to Catholic Rome, Guardian of the Catholic Faith and of the traditions necessary to maintain that Faith, to Eternal Rome, Mistress of Wisdom and Truth.

On the other hand, we refuse and have always refused to follow the Rome of neo-modernist and neo-Protestant tendencies which clearly manifested themselves in the Second Vatican Council and after the Council in all the reforms which issued from it. All these reforms, indeed, have contributed and are still contributing to the demolition of the Church, to the ruin of the priesthood, to the annihilation of the sacrifice and sacraments, to the disappearance of religious life, to a naturalistic and Teilhardian type of teaching in which is the fruit of liberalism and Protestantism and many times condemned by the solemn Magisterium of the Church. No authority, not even the most elevated in the Hierarchy, can compel us to abandon or diminish our Catholic Faith, clearly expressed and professed by the Magisterium of the Church for nineteen centuries. "If it should happen," said St. Paul, "that anyone should teach you something different from what I have taught you, whether it be ourselves or an Angel from Heaven, let him be anathema" (Gal 1:8).[16]

Such a proclamation of independence alienated even some curial conservatives, to say nothing of Pope Paul VI. Paul had written to the archbishop the previous June 29 demanding his submission. The pope wrote again on September 8, 1975, and August 15, 1976. On June 29, 1976, Lefebvre ordained new priests at Ecône. He did this without the requisite permission of the local Bishop Adam of Sion, who responded by having an announcement read at all masses in the diocese emphasizing that to "remain a Catholic, it is absolutely necessary to recognize the authority of the Present Pope, Paul VI, and of the Second Vatican Council."[17] The Vatican suspended Lefebvre's right to ordain priests and celebrate mass, but the archbishop has continued to perform these acts, now "valid, but illicit" in Rome's judgment. Paul VI did not excommunicate Lefebvre as he did the elderly traditionalist Pierre Martin Ngo Dinh Thuc, former archbishop of Hué and the brother of the ex-president of South Vietnam. When queried on the reasons for different treatment, "a Vatican official cited Thuc's ordination of bishops, his declaration that "the See of the Catholic Church at Rome is vacant" and his refusal to cooperate with an investigation by the Congregation of the Doctrine of the Faith. Lefebvre, on the other hand, met with Paul VI (1976) and John Paul II (1982) and wrote many letters to Rome.[18] While it helps that Lefebvre has constantly lobbied curial conservatives, ordination of bishops would probably constitute the crucial breaking point.[19] In September 1982 the Society of St. Pius X elected the thirty-year-old Father Franz Schmidberger as vicar general with the right of succession. Schmidberger studied at Ecône for three years before being ordained by Lefebvre in 1975. In recent letters to the Vatican, Lefebvre has threatened to ordain a successor bishop.

Although Lefebvre and his followers focus on preserving internal ecclesiastical traditions, the archbishop has at times become linked to right-wing politics. This is not strange given the traditional political orientation of French integralism and the traditional cooperation between missionaries and the state in French colonial Africa. Lefebvre, who had served as apostolic delegate for French-speaking Africa, had written an article in *La France catholique* (December 18, 1959) entitled "Are Christian States Going To Hand Black Africa Over to the Red Star?" The article opposed the movement toward independence and accused Islam, the religion of 80 percent of Senegal's inhabitants, of being a precursor of Communism.[20] On August 29, 1976, Lefebvre gave a heavily political speech to an enthusiastic rally in the sports stadium at Lille. The archbishop called the then-militarist Argentina a model political system. *Le Monde* (August 31, 1976) carried two front-page reports of the event, as well as another front-page story on the papal condemnation of the archbishop. When Lefebvre toured traditionalist seminaries in Latin America in 1980, the archbishop praised the continent's right-wing governments. He stated, "In Central America, the Bishops have yielded to Communism. In South America only countries like Argentina, Bolivia, Chile and Uruguay can join forces for the Catholic fight against communism."[21]

Lefebvre's religious traditionalism adopts its political reaction almost by osmosis in the milieu of its gestation and following, but the Catholic societies for the Defense of Tradition, Family, and Property (TFP) began with a strong political orientation. The TFP societies reflect Latin American neo-Christendom as strongly as Lefebvre reflects French integralism. The ideology of the organization follows Brazilian Professor Plinio Corrêa de Oliveira's *Revolution and Counter-Revolution* (1959), which "shows how certain forces and ideological currents began to unite in the fifteenth century to exterminate Christian Civilization and destroy the Catholic Church, and thus do away with the fruits of the Redemption of Our Lord Jesus Christ."[22] The four stages of this process of religious and civic degeneration are the Renaissance, the French Revolution, nineteenth-century Socialism and Communism, and "the proclamation of the freedom of all instincts." The rebellion at the Sorbonne in 1968 presaged this latter phase.

Corrêa's father was a lawyer, and young Plinio attended the Jesuit Colegio São Luis in São Paulo. He became a militant in Catholic youth groups, and at 24 was elected to the Federal Constituent Assembly by the Catholic Electoral League. Corrêa founded the Brazilian TFP in 1960, four years before the overthrow of Goulart. In the early 1970s the Brazilian bishops separated themselves from this ultra-right organization as they had separated themselves from the ultra-left a decade earlier. Following criticism of the TFP from the conservative Bishop Eugenio Sales in 1970, CNBB President Ivo Lorscheiter sharply attacked the TFP. The February 1972 CNBB statement, "Unity and Plurality in the Church," condemned the TFP and other right-wing groups. Another factor in the demise of the Brazilian Catholic right is the retirement of supporting bishops. Bishop Antonio Castro Mayer, founder of the conservative monthly

Catholicismo on whose editorial staff Corrêa served, finally retired in 1981.

Although each national TFP remains autonomous, they coordinate international campaigns such as the global 1981-1982 TFP attack on Mitterand's policies following Corrêa de Oliveira's denunciation of the French Socialist. The TFP placed advertisments attacking Mitterand's policies in 47 newspapers in 18 countries. When the French dailies refused the ad, the organization mailed 300,000 copies into the country. Despite such European-oriented campaigns, including stands against *détente* and *Ostpolitik*, the major focus of the TFP has been the militant defense of Latin American traditionalism. The Brazilian society, for example, has campaigned for "private property against the two-pronged assault of the leftist Basic Christian Communities and a socialistic and confiscatory agrarian reform." Corrêa attacked the Chilean Christian Democrats in *Frei, the Chilean Kerensky* (1967). After Allende's election, many Chilean members went into exile, where they published the anti-government magazine *Fiducia*, which charged collaboration between Cardinal Silva and the Allende regime. Brian Smith comments that the lack of a "prolonged and sustained attack on the bishops" plus lay leadership diminished the TFP threat to episcopal authority.[23] However, the exiles returned home in 1973 to serve the Pinochet regime. Many Americans learned of the existence of the American chapter of the TFP from a half-page advertisement in the *New York Times* (August 2, 1983) decrying the appointment of Henry Kissinger, symbol of "all the defeatist spirit that led to the handing over of Vietnam," to head President Reagan's National Bipartisan Commission on Central America. The American chapter plus the eleven other chapters in the Western hemisphere sent telegrams of protest to the White House.

TFP reflects its Iberian origins not only in the issues on which it focuses but also in its organizational style. During demonstrations members wear red capes and carry TFP standards which show a golden lion on a red background. Corrêa comments that the cape projects the volunteer into "an ideal and historical perspective" and attracts public attention. TFP piety emphasizes traditional pilgrimages to shrines like Fatima. Thus, Lefebvre and Corrêa exemplify the rich traditions of European and Latin American Catholic integralism, offering the security of long-held established political and religious values in the face of the rapid political, social, and economic modernization since the French Revolution.

PROGRESSIVE EUROPEAN CATHOLICISM: EDWARD SCHILLEBEECKX (BELGIUM) AND HANS KÜNG (SWITZERLAND)

Just as traditionalists like Lefebvre see Vatican II and its aftermath as a betrayal of the Catholic tradition, progressive European theologians like the Dominican Edward Schillebeeckx and the Swiss diocesan priest Hans Küng contributed significantly to the deliberations of the Council and have moved beyond its positions in subsequent writings.[24] In doing so they have incurred investigations by the CDF. Schillebeeckx has been cleared, but on December 18, 1979, the Congregation ruled that Küng could "no longer be considered a Catholic theologian." Adding to the doctrinal controversy was Küng's refusal to meet with the Congregation under its rules (which, he said, violated the rights of the accused), and a critique of the pope's first year in office which covered two-thirds of the op-ed page of the *New York Times* (October 19, 1979). Since the Swiss-born Küng held the chair of Catholic Theology at the German state University of Tübingen, an immediate controversy ensued. Finally, Küng became professor of ecumenical theology under a compromise subscribed to by Küng, the university, the German Bishops Conference, and the Vatican. Küng also lectures frequently in the United States and has been a frequent visiting professor at the University of Michigan in Tübingen's sister-city Ann Arbor. He remains a priest in good standing. In October 1985 Küng broke six years of silence on John Paul's papacy by issuing a 7,000-word statement attacking the Vatican for harassing theologians, thwarting ecumenical efforts, and ending serious dialogue with the modern world. Of Cardinal Ratzinger, Küng says "he fears nothing more than freedom."[25]

Küng is only one of Europe's many theologians who have become prominent in countries other than their native ones. As Küng went to Tübingen, so the Belgian Schillebeeckx served the bishops of the Netherlands. Schillebeeckx became Cardinal Alfrink's personal theologian at the Second Vatican Council. Schillebeeckx's controversial positions irritated curial conservatives, especially those associated with the Holy Office. The Dutch bishops issued a communiqué on October 8, 1968, defending Schillibeeckx, and the Congregation eventually dropped its investigation. Of course, the theologian's collaboration on the *New Dutch Catechism* did not help his relations with Rome. In 1979 the Dominican appeared before the Congregation for the Doctrine of the Faith to answer questions about his book *Jesus: An Experiment in Christology*. The Congregation subsequently declared itself satisfied with the theologian's orthodoxy, provided Schillebeeckx publish the clarifications he gave them. The latest curial inquiries of 1983 have concerned the theologian's views of the priesthood in *Ministry: A Case for Change*.[26]

Schillebeeckx remains head of the Dogmatics Section of the seven-language journal *Concilium*, which has its headquarters at the Dutch Catholic University of Nijmegen. The leading progressive theologians of Vatican II founded the journal immediately after the Council. In October 1983 *Concilium* joined with Küng and Father David Tracy of the Institute for the Advanced Study of Religion at the University of Chicago to sponsor in Tübingen an international symposium on the future of theology. Küng has sought to specify a "new paradigm" which would integrate such diverse currents as the principles of Vatican II and the Protestant Reformation with secular themes like democracy and free scientific inquiry.[27] While both Küng and Schillebeeckx have endorsed feminist theology, one of the three women invited to the conference of seventy theologians commented, "It is ironical that these white, male and overwhelmingly First World theologians look upon themselves as still being the leaders of the theological community. In reality, theological reflection has gone beyond them to the liberation theologians and to others of the Third World and to women."[28] Schillebeeckx himself says that the third volume of his Jesus trilogy will attempt to show "bourgeois" theologians like himself what to do with Liberation Theology.[29]

CATHOLIC POETS OF LIBERATION: ERNESTO CARDENAL (NICARAGUA) AND KIM CHI HA (KOREA)

Progressive European theology has had a great impact on the Anglo-American and continental Western European Catholic Churches; its influence on Third World churches has been less in theological statement than in providing legitimacy for alternative approaches to ecclesiastical thought and organization, thus accelerating the process of ecclesiastical cultural differentiation. As Philip Berryman has observed, "It became clear that Latin American Christians were moving away from European postconciliar concerns."[30] For example, the Uruguayan layman Alberto Ferre criticized the progressive Belgian Cardinal Suenens's modernizing recommendations as strengthening the North Atlantic rich churches at the expense of the poor churches of the periphery. He also denounced Hans Küng's fear that "progressive" European bishops might be outweighed by their counterparts from the Third World because Ferre sincerely believes that Rome protects the poor churches of the periphery against the rich and powerful churches of the (North Atlantic) "center."[31] Although many contemporary European and American theologians have called for the introduction of more social and political analysis, their tradition has remained focused on the life of the church. Even the political theology of a Joannes Metz speaks more to a First World than to a Third World context.

Liberation Theology begins with Latin American political, social, and economic reality. Many of its clerical practitioners studied progressive European theology in either Europe or the United States. When they returned home they found that what they had learned did not fit the traditional popular Catholicism of the people nor the oppressive political conditions imposed by militaristic regimes allied to the United States. Out of the "revolutionary praxis" of activist Christians like the guerrilla-priest Camilo Torres have come theological writings focusing on human liberation. While the guerrilla-priests have been few, many Latin American clergy have worked at "conscientization," inspired by the Brazilian educator Paulo Freire. Philip Berryman says, "It is impossible to overstate the importance of Freire for the Christian left, especially from 1965-1970. Most of the liberation theologians . . . have close personal associations with Freire."[32] Liberation writings also borrow heavily from current socio-economic analysis, especially the theory of *dependencia*,[33] which links Third World poverty to First World exploitation.

Liberation Theology's emphases on class struggle and the conclusions of Medellín differ significantly from the strong theme of reconciliation found in the documents of Vatican II. Since Liberation Theology flows so directly from the experience of revolutionary struggle, these writings do not offer a theological system in the traditional European sense. The seminal basic work for the movement remains Gustavo Gutiérrez's A Theology of Liberation.[34] Gutiérrez points out that any consideration of this topic must start from two facts: class struggle exists, and neutrality in the struggle is impossible. The task of today's Christian is the liberation of humanity. Gutiérrez admits that such a focus on class struggle does pose problems for traditional Christian theology. He traces the different ways in which Christianity and Marxism have been related. Among the "committed," he first focuses on the attempt to find parallels in the two traditions. The danger of this kind of search is that Christianity may be reduced to a revolutionary doctrine or Marxism may revert to utopian socialism. The more frequent solution leaves the dualism of Christianity as "faith" and Marxism as "science." However, such a solution seems to slight the mobilization impact of Marxism. Gutiérrez then distinguishes two levels of political action—science and utopia. Faith and science meet at the level of utopia and thus avoid dualistic juxtaposition. Both Christianity and Marxism are still highly ideologized in the sense of being nonrational and not yet lucid. Both need to become more secular.

Latin American Liberation Theology places considerable emphasis on "praxis," so poets, the "transmitters of direct experience," can articulate this tradition in a special way. Two prominent liberation poets are Ernesto Cardenal of Nicaragua and Kim Chi Ha of Korea. As a priest and a poet, Cardenal acknowledges his debt to his theological and literary studies in North America. He mentions especially the stylistic influence of the American poets Whitman, Pound and Thomas Merton, who was his spiritual director when he spent two years as a Trappist novice in Kentucky, 1957-1959. When Cardenal returned to Nicaragua, he founded the island community of Solentiname to exemplify the spiritual freedom of an alternative vision to the repression of the Somoza-led oligarchy. In 1970 Cardenal went to Cuba to judge a poetry contest for Casa de la Americas, met Fidel Castro, and wrote a generally enthusiastic book about the trip. His poem "Trip to New York" is an interesting contrast to the book on Cuba. In the former poem Ernesto describes a six-day visit to New York in June 1973 to raise funds for the survivors of the Nicaraguan earthquake. In addition to criticizing many aspects of American politics, the poem chronicles Cardenal's encounters with the American Catholic left. The Nicaraguan poet met peace activists Daniel Berrigan and Jim Forest at the Thomas Merton Center, and attended the marriage of Philip Berrigan to Elizabeth McAllister.[35] He also visited the Catholic Worker House in the Bowery where he saw Dorothy Day and wrote,

> she's still beautiful at 75
> I kiss the saint's hand and she kisses my face.

Cardenal's *poesía exteriorista* appeals to people of diverse educational backgrounds who are caught up in social transformation. For example, his short "Somoza Unveils the Statue of Somoza in Somoza Stadium" attacks the self publicity of the dictator:

> It's not that I think the people erected this statue
> because I know better than you that I ordered it myself.
> Nor do I pretend to pass into posterity with it
> because I know the people will topple it over someday.

Not that I wanted to erect to myself in life
the monument you never would erect to me in death:
I erected this statue because I knew you would hate it.[36]

In October 1977 the Somoza government ordered the destruction of Solentiname. Ernesto became a roving ambassador for the FSLN and then minister of culture in the new government.

Despite the strong Latin American cultural context of Ernesto Cardenal's poetry, it shares several major themes with that of the Korean lay Catholic poet, Kim Chi Ha. Both look to the energy and spiritualization of the poor for the true liberation of their country. Kim challenged Park Chung Hee as Cardenal did Somoza. Both ridicule members of the upper class who have sold out their countrymen to ape foreign consumption and pseudo-modernization. In Kim's Ko Kwan, the high Korean official wears "U.S. jockey shorts, a necktie bought in Paris, Chinese green jade cuff links, Scottish tweed pants, and a crocodile belt from the Congo."[37] The same poem features a conflagration in a new Western hotel which has no emergency staircases because the builder had bribed the fire inspector. Korean elites, foreigners, and prostitutes die together as:

Among the dying, some Japanese shouted,
"Is this modernization?
"Is the lack of an emergency staircase modernization?
"Eat shit, you fools! Some modernization," and plunged to hell.[38]

Ko Kwan is the second part of Groundless Rumors, the publishing of which resulted in Kim's second arrest in 1972. Two years earlier the Korean Central Intelligence Agency arrested the poet for Five Bandits, which featured a tycoon, an assemblyman, a government official, a general, and a government minister. The latter and his cronies "command the national defense with golf clubs in their left hands, while fondling the tits of their mistresses with their right." One of the central charges against the Catholic Bishop Tji of Wonju after the KCIA arrested him in July 1974 was that he collaborated with Kim Chi Ha. When the poet came to him, the bishop said, Kim was suffering from tuberculosis and torture. It is no wonder that one of the poet's most celebrated works is entitled Torture Road.

Kim wrote Declaration of Conscience in prison in 1975 to rebut charges that he was a Communist. Among those people and events more influential in his own development, he mentions:

My image of the unity of God and revolution was clarified by Pope John XXIII's encyclical Mater et Magistra: "The mystery of Jesus and the loaves of bread is a temporal miracle which shows the future heaven." I also benefited from the writings of the liberation theologians: Fredrick Herzog, James Cone, Richard Shaull, Paul Lehmann, Jürgen Moltmann, J. B. Metz, Tödt, Hugo Assmann, Reinhold Niebuhr, Dietrich Bonhöffer, and others. Papal statements after Vatican II as well as such encyclicals as *Rerum Novarum* and *Quadragesimo Anno* provided insights. The greatest single influence on my thinking, however, has been my participation since 1971 in the Korean Christian movement for human rights.[39]

In other sections of the *Declaration* he also includes Freire, Fanon, Blanquism, and the Catholic doctrines of original sin and the omnipotence of God. While there are many common themes in Cardenal and Kim Chi Ha, the Korean has produced poetry rich in traditional Korean thought and style. His political orientation owes much to the populist redistributive egalitarianism of Korea's legendary Robin Hood, Im Kok Chong, and to the Tonghak teachings.[40] The concepts and incantations of native shamanism, especially its therapeutic effect, also play a central role. Kim comes from the poor disdained province of Cholla, and he employs many local dialects to singular poetic effect. In short, Kim's liberation poetry results from a highly individualistic synthesis of Eastern and Western motifs.

Although Latin American Liberation Theology has been less influential in Africa, *Pro veritate*, the journal of the Christian Institute began introducing its readers to progressive European and Latin American theologians in the late 1960s. Peter Walshe states:

Although Metz and Moltmann were prominent among the European, and Camara the favourite among the Latin American exponents of "consciencisation" (the awakening consciousness/conscience of an oppressed and exploited people), there were others including de Chardin, Illich and Freire. Freire's educational methods were used by the Institute's Transvaal Community Organiser, Anne Hope, in the years preceding the confiscation of her passport and her one-way exit from the country in 1973. Before leaving she prepared several bibliographies for the Institute which introduced members to these writers as well as to black American and black South African theologies of hope. Freire's methods were also used by the Black Community Programmes that were part of SPROCAS II.[41]

Contact between Latin American, Asian, and African theologians has produced the Ecumenical Association of Third World Theologians (EATWOT), which has held a series of meetings.

It is not coincidental that the works of Cardenal and Kim Chi Ha, Peter Walshe's book on the Christian Institute in South Africa, and the titles of many Third World theologians have all appeared in

English published by Orbis Books. The late Orbis editor Philip Scharper was recruited by the then Maryknoll director of social communications, Miguel D'Escoto. "Our idea," Scharper said, "was to bring Third World theology, reflections on the human condition of hunger, poverty, illiteracy, to the attention of the North American Church."[42] Orbis publishes titles from various perspectives, but the publishing house, *Maryknoll* magazine (1.2 million copies monthly), and the social justice activities of the missionaries have drawn the fire of the political and religious right in the United States. For example, *The Mindszenty Report* charged that Maryknoll "champions radical, self-declared Marxist clergymen preaching guerrilla warfare and violence."[43] Conservative columnists William Buckley and Michael Novak have made similar charges. Orbis Books also published the record of the first Theology in the Americas conference in Detroit in 1975. The conference brought together liberation theologians like José Míguez Bonino, Juan Luis Segundo, Javier Iguíñiz, Enrique Dussel, José Porfirio Miranda, Leonardo Boff, Hugo Assman, Beatriz Melano Couch, and Gustavo Gutiérrez with their North American counterparts.

American Protestant theologian Robert McAfee Brown has become a leading proponent of liberation themes. An early supporter of the work of Gutiérrez, Brown has written *Theology in a New Key: Responding to Liberation Themes*,[44] an overview of Latin American Liberation Theology for North Americans. Following the Puebla Conference, Brown wrote an article on "The Significance of Puebla for Protestant Churches in North America."[45] He chose four topics that related to North American Protestants in special ways: The CEBs, the National Security State, the preferential option for the poor, and the demystification of popes and bishops. Although there was a second Theology in the Americas conference in Detroit in 1980, it would be difficult to specify exactly what constitutes North American Liberation Theology. Rather, according to Sister Marie Augusta Neal, there has been a North American "response to liberation theology."[46]

One of the most interesting documents in the 1975 *Theology in the Americas* collection is a short letter from American theologian Rosemary Ruether to Chilean priest Sergio Torres and other planners of the conference. Reuther rejects complete reliance on Latin Americans for the theological orientation. "In effect, the Latin Americans are to provide the 'theology' and the Americans the 'Devil.' " Reuther advocates exploring the positive resources of critical theology and suggests Robert Bellah's *The Broken Covenant*.[47] Gregory

Baum wrote a similar letter asking for an indigenous Canadian view. Regardless of their sources, North American progressive ecclesiastics have become much more critical of the capitalist system for its part in domestic and international economic, social, and political dislocation. In January 1983 the Episcopal Commission for Social Affairs of the Canadian Bishops' Conference issued a letter on the global economic crisis and Christian values. The letter insists on the priority of labor over capital and technology in the formation of a just economic order. According to the letter, the application of a "survival of the fittest" theory of development has resulted in increasing patterns of inequality and domination.[48] Individual Canadian bishops have gone farther. In 1981 Bishop John Sherlock of London, Ontario, told Catholic university students that "Canadian bishops and, surprisingly, the American bishops are moving to a clear-cut condemnation of capitalism."[49] Conservative columnists like George Will criticized the Canadian bishops' letter for "infantile leftism ('community ownership and control of industries') and, what is worse, an unwillingness to face honestly difficult moral choices."[50] Regardless of the merits of the Canadian letter, it symbolized the continued influence of Third World Catholics on their co-believers in the First World. The Canadian bishops were also responding to the deep unemployment problem in many dioceses and Jesuit-educated Prime Minister Pierre Trudeau's "tough it out" economic message the preceding October. Responding to the same challenge, the American bishops released the first draft of their own ecomonic pastoral immediately following the 1984 presidential election. The debate over that episcopal letter forms the core issue of the next section.

CATHOLIC DEMOCRATIC CAPITALISM:
MICHAEL NOVAK (USA)

Michael Novak, Resident Scholar in Religion and Public Policy at the American Enterprise Institute, has become the most prominent critic of the NCCB's current social policy. Novak is a political convert. During the late 1960s and early 1970s he taught at Stanford University and wrote speeches for Edmund Muskie, Sargent Shriver, and George McGovern. Later he returned to the East and became much more interested in his ethnic (Slovak) roots. The socioeconomic experience of Slovak-Americans and the Czech state persecution of Slovakian Catholics both have served as a counterweight to Novak's earlier participation in the anti-Vietnam War

Movement. Another counterweight has been the rural Iowa background of his wife's family. Novak's major academic interest has been his attempt to formulate a deeper philosophical understanding and defense of the current American political, economic, and moral-cultural systems in terms of traditional Catholic teaching. He himself has commented, "If I've made any contribution it's to look at the liberal tradition—at Adam Smith and John Stuart Mill—with the eyes of a Catholic."[51] Novak's background and academic interests have made him an articulate defender of American policy during the Reagan administration. For example, he served as Chief of the United States Delegation to the U.N. Human Rights Commission in Geneva.

Novak seeks to anchor his own work in the philosophical tradition of the French Catholic Thomist Jacques Maritain. Maritain and his wife Raissa became Catholics in 1906 with the intellectual Leon Bloy as their godfather. Although Leo XIII had declared Thomism to be the official philosophy of the Catholic Church in 1878, Maritain and Etienne Gilson succeeded in again making Thomism a living philosophical force. Maritain defended political and religious pluralism, attacking Franco's "crusade" during the Spanish Civil War. Although many of Maritain's ideas were embodied in the documents of the Second Vatican Council, the French philosopher became disillusioned by the many Catholic philosophers who rejected Thomism, and seemingly, even philosophy and theology altogether. This disappointment is reflected in his last book, *Le Paysan de la Garonne*.[52] Indeed, the battle over the heritage of Jacques Maritain remains an important issue in Catholic ideology.

Toward a Theology of the Corporation and *The Spirit of Democratic Capitalism*[53] lay out Novak's basic position on the morality of democratic capitalism, especially on its most maligned part, the large multinational corporation. Democratic capitalism, he says, consists of three independent, yet interrelated political, economic, and moral-cultural systems. The corporation partakes of all three systems in that it changes political and moral-cultural values, and can exist only in a free political system. Novak calls the business corporation "perhaps the best secular analogue to the church" and later applies Isaiah's passage of the "Suffering Servant" to it.[54]

In discussing Novak's *The Spirit of Democratic Capitalism*, Philip Lawler recognizes Novak's effort "clearly involves a desire to do for twentieth-century America what Thomas Aquinas did for thirteenth-century Europe which was to devise a philosophical and theological system within which the entire society can be judged."

Agreeing with many of Novak's points, Lawler criticizes Novak's explicit statement that the "shrine" (core values) of the moral-cultural system is empty. "Does our society not possess at least some minimal body of common faith? If America's moral fabric is defined by the Judeo-Christian tradition—and it is—is it fair to theorize about a situation in which each individual chooses his own moral postulates?" Novak's position, argues Lawler, "never fully engages the arguments of Solzhenitsyn, and of others who wonder whether freedom and faith are fully compatible."[55]

It is undeniable that Novak's work does celebrate the achievements of American democratic capitalism. This has been the tenor of his testimony to the bishops' committee on the economic pastoral. It infuses the alternative economic pastoral of the lay commission, largely written by Novak. While the latter document acknowledges that the free market may produce some evil effects, it designates the capitalist system and the individual entrepreneur as the main benefactors of the poor and jobless. In response to the charge that North American capitalism bears responsibility for global poverty, especially in Latin America, Novak argues that Latin America has had greater economic resources than North America. The answer to its poverty "appears to lie in the nature of the Latin American political system, economic system, and moral-cultural system. The last is probably decisive."[56] Novak blames the church-state alliance of Latin Catholic economics for stifling capitalist development. In a lecture at the Pontifical University of Santiago in May 1983, for example, Novak attacked both the traditional Catholic teaching advocated by right-wing Latin authoritarianism and the new Liberation Theology because both ideologies ignore "the middle class, the persons of commerce and industry who produce new wealth and are the chief creators of democracy, and who include labor among them."[57]

The preceding section has documented the gradual impact of liberation themes on the North Atlantic Catholic Church. Many United States ecclesiastics felt that the response of the Canadian bishops verged on "economic isolationism," so they set out to formulate their own pastoral letter on *Catholic Social Teaching and the U.S. Economy*, the first draft of which was released shortly following the November 1984 presidential election. The lead story in the *New York Times* (November 12, 1984), which announced the release of the first draft, appeared under the headline "Catholic Bishops Ask Vast Changes in Economy of U.S."[58]

The 120-page episcopal letter proclaimed that, "[t]he dignity of the human person, realized in community with others, is the criterion against which all aspects of human life must be measured." Therefore, according to the draft, all persons have economic rights, and society must take the necessary steps to ensure that no one is hungry, homeless, or unemployed. The document applies this general orientation by means of three priority principles: "fulfillment of the poor's basic needs is of highest priority; increased participation in society by people living on its margins takes priority over the preservation of privileged concentrations of power, wealth and income; and meeting human needs and increasing participation should be priority targets in the investment of wealth, talent and human energy."[59]

The policy applications in Part Two of the draft raised the most controversial political questions. The bishops found the then current levels of poverty, unemployment, and economic inequality disgraceful and morally unacceptable. As a result:

The nation should "make a major new policy commitment" to reduce the unemployment rate to 3 or 4 percent with programs including increased support by the Government to create jobs.

The welfare system is "woefully inadequate" and should be overhauled. The social and economic problems facing the country are made worse by the arms race, which channels "resources away from the task of creating a more just and productive economy."

Government, business and labor should work together to plan and implement economic reforms aimed at the chronically unemployed and others at the margin of poverty.

Labor laws should be changed to help workers organize unions, "to prevent intimidation of workers and to provide remedies in a more timely manner for unfair labor practices."

The direction of United States foreign policy, which under President Reagan has been shifting toward military programs, should re-emphasize basic human needs.[60]

The process of drafting the letter has built on the bishops' experience in the formulation of the pastoral on peace, 1981-1983 (Chapter 8, below). After the bishops released a fairly theoretical and little-read study of Marxism in 1980, Hartford Auxiliary Bishop Peter A. Rosazza, then forty-nine, suggested a sequel on the American economy. Rosazza "says he was stimulated in part by the questions of European priests critical of American economic imperatives."[61] At their November 1980 meeting, the bishops decided to appoint an ad hoc committee to work on a statement, but the peace pastoral received priority. The episcopal committee on the economic letter be-

gan hearings on November 15, 1981, and heard over 120 experts between then and July 27, 1984. The chairman, Archbishop
Weakland, had been primate of the worldwide Benedictine Order.
The other three appointments also represent specific aspects of the
American church. The Latin American experience is represented on
the committee by Bishop William K. Weigand, forty-seven, of Salt
Lake City, who served as a missionary pastor in Colombia 1968-
1977. Bishop George H. Speltz of St. Cloud, Minnesota, seventy-
two, was president of a Catholic conference that dealt with the
problems of rural and farm families. Archbishop Thomas A. Don-
nellan, seventy, of Atlanta, served under Cardinal Francis Spellman in New York, and was bishop of Ogdensburg, New York, for
four years until appointed to Atlanta in 1968.

Catholic Social Teaching and the U.S. Economy follows strongly in
the tradition of American Catholic Nationalism described in Chapter Five, below. Most of the bishops are old enough to have been
educated in the pro-Union, pro-family farm majority American
Catholic tradition. AFL-CIO President Lane Kirkland commented
that he was pleased with the general direction of the document.[62]
The considerable public impact of the peace pastoral had convinced
Catholic lay conservatives of the necessity to organize during the
entire drafting process of the economic letter. On November 6,
1984, the Lay Commission on Catholic Social Teaching and the U.S.
Economy released its own letter "Toward the Future: Catholic Social Thought and the U.S. Economy."[63] The Lay Commission was
formed in January 1984 with former Secretary of the Treasury William E. Simon as chairman and Michael Novak as vice-chairman
and principal author of the response. The other 25 members came
principally from the business community, with noted Catholic conservatives Alexander Haig, Clare Boothe Luce, and J. Peter Grace
the most prominent members.[64]

Political leaders praised the bishops' document in general without committing themselves on specifics. Presidential spokesman
Larry Speakes emphasized the Reagan Administration's agreement
with the pastoral's goals, while failing to comment on specific policy recommendations. Governor Mario Cuomo of New York commented that both the pastoral and Novak's alternative endorsed labor unions and rejected an unfettered free market. Rather than
whether or not there should be state intervention, "[t]he questions
are subtler and more important. They involve emphasis and degree. How much welfare? In what form? How many job programs?
How large should they be?" said the governor.[65] If the Novak letter

had taken a more conservative position, it might have alienated the large body of corporate executives who have come to subscribe to some form of public responsibility for business, "corporate social responsibility." Some of the Lay Commission members also sought to assure the bishops that they wished to play a consultative, not a competitive role. In July 1984 Simon, Grace, and former Secretary of the Interior Walter Hickel had flown to Milwaukee to seek to assure Weakland that, as Novak commented, the letter would be "in the form of an advisory rather than of a comment" on the episcopal letter.[66] Nevertheless, national media coverage almost always juxtaposed Weakland and Novak and their respective letters.

In addition to Novak at the American Enterprise Institute, and various authors at the Heritage Foundation, Ernest Lefever's Ethics and Public Policy Center publishes a steady stream of books and essays by conservative Catholics.[67] Part of the effectiveness of both Catholic and non-Catholic publications of the Washington conservative "think tanks" lies in their short length and readable format. Philip Lawler left the Heritage Foundation to found and become the first president of the American Catholic Conference (ACC), which is modeled on the largely Protestant Institute on Religion and Democracy (IRD). The ACC board includes Claire Boothe Luce, Novak, and James Hitchcock. The Lay Commission on Catholic Social Teaching and the U.S. Economy came out of the New York-based American Catholic Committee (also ACC), whose current president, James J. McFadden, founded the group. However, membership of the two groups is not the same. While the interlocking nature of the memberships of conservative Catholic groups strikes even the casual observer, the ability of the layman Novak to fashion the alternative position to the episcopate is a new phenomenon in American Catholicism. Novak's media connections, especially to national business magazines like *Fortune* (see its comments on the drafting of the economic pastoral in the December 26, 1983, issue) are significant in this regard.

The biggest difficulty faced by the bishops is not the drafting and passing of the letter, but the selling of it to an American Catholic population that has made great socioeconomic advances and that has participated in the landslide reelection of Ronald Reagan, principally on economic policies at variance with the basic orientation of the letter. Sensing the difficulties involved in digesting all of the suggested revisions and preparing the laity for the final draft, the bishops delayed final consideration of the letter until November 1986. The second draft of October 6, 1985, maintained its basic thrust that the fact that "so many people are poor in a nation as rich as ours is a social and moral scandal that must not be ignored." Nevertheless, the second draft became less open to an adversarial interpretation by treating the economic difficulties of the middle-class and by explicitly acknowledging that the government cannot solve many problems. That draft was more explicit, however, in tying present levels of military spending to domestic and foreign poverty. The bishops enthusiastically supported the second draft at their November 1985 meeting.[68] The third draft (June 3, 1986), according to Weakland, "has no main structural alterations from draft two, because that structure was strongly supported by the responses." The most noteworthy five additions, the archbishop wrote, concern the family, education, conversion and personal life-style, Third World debt, and a more extended historical tie-in between the biblical and ethical sections.[69]

CATHOLIC POLITICAL CULTURE: HIERARCHICAL DISCIPLINE AND PUBLIC UNITY IN A POLITICALLY ACTIVE ECCLESIASTICAL INSTITUTION

Historical memory, traditional organizational forms, and conscious ideology all reinforce the values of hierarchical discipline and public unity. In comparison with other world religions, Catholicism has exhibited a striking historical continuity of political involvement. Not only were the popes active in defining the political legitimacy of Christendom, but high-ranking Catholic ecclesiastics have almost always sought to play significant national political roles. In many ways it is easier to understand prelates like Cardinals Wolsey and Richelieu as political figures than as religious ones. Although Christ said that his kingdom was "not of this world," high-ranking ecclesiastics and the papacy as an institution have participated intensely in international and national political struggles since the time of Constantine.

From the reign of Gregory the Great (590-604), the pope has commanded a relatively efficient and highly organized bureaucracy.[70] With the Council of Trent Catholicism became a bastion defending itself against the pernicious currents of the modern world, and this "fortress mentality" intensified when the papacy lost its Italian territories in 1870. The traditional hierarchical style reinforced by the perception of a hostile outside environment caused the popes to prefer "*concordat* Christianity," characterized by legal treaties in which national states guaranteed Catholic privileges, usually in re-

turn for ecclesiastical political support. The papacy fought stren-
uously to maintain its territorial base in central Italy. Defense of papal territory against the *resorgimento* even tended to overwhelm
liberal-conservative ideological arguments during the middle of the
nineteenth century.

With the loss of the Papal States in 1870 and the later accession of
Leo XIII, the church began its adjustment to the modern world.
Gradually, church leaders gave their blessing to a new reformist
agenda or *aggiornamento* which received worldwide ecclesiastical
approbation in the Second Vatican Council. In place of "*concordat*
Christianity," the papacy emphasized human rights, including
freedom of religion. The popes came to prefer Christian Democracy
because this movement maintained episcopal political influence
and a strong Catholic culture while avoiding the disadvantages inherent in clerical-directed Catholic parties. Christian Democracy
proved an extremely effective competitor in Western European politics following World War II. Although its zenith has passed, especially in Italy, the papacy strongly supported the movement until
the death of the quintessential "Christian Democratic pope," Paul
VI. Catholicism's most successful social and political alliances of the
last two centuries have been with the rising middle classes in Catholic societies and with immigrant workers seeking to join the middle classes in traditionally Protestant societies.

Troeltsch's distinction between "church" and "sect,"[71] serves as
an excellent starting point for a brief discussion of the Catholic
Church's political style, its union of organization and ideology.
Catholic leaders have always sought to preach the gospel "to all living creatures" and to include all people in church membership. This
orientation has resulted in a truly "Catholic" religious organization
which has tolerated large variations in the content and style of belief
as long as its members publicly professed ecclesiastical unity and
loyalty to the institution.[72] Such a "church" approach runs directly
counter to sectarian emphasis on purity of belief with concomitant
strict requirements for membership. The natural political impact of
such universality has been a tendency to stress reconciliation
among all people, not prophetic confrontation. Such style contrasts
with traditional Protestantism and classical Marxism, though not
necessarily with some forms of Maoist populism.[73] The internal effects of this tension are obvious in contemporary Latin American
Catholic theory, where many envision true Christianity as an enlightened "vanguard" rather than as an all-inclusive body. Catholic
bishops perceive their loyalty to institutional unity as an integral

part of their religious faith. Just as they take their faith seriously, they take their institution seriously. When circumstances force the pope or bishops to choose between what they consider the survival of essential features of their religious organization and external political or societal goals, a strong presupposition exists that they will choose the former. This is especially true in the twentieth century when celibacy and strong institutional socialization have distanced ecclesiastical elites from close family and state ties.

While John Paul II remains less culturally tied to Christian Democracy than his predecessors, the new pope retains a fierce attachment to the internal hierarchical unity of the church organization. The Polish church could not compete with the Polish state without maintaining its unity.[74] The church's stress on external unity does not derive only from Italian and Polish political and cultural experience. Devotion to public unity also comes from an ideological emphasis on the continuing leadership of the Holy Spirit, "reconciliation" rather than "class struggle," and genuine feelings of episcopal collegiality. Such an orientation can be observed even in highly controversial documents like the national pastorals on peace. The American bishops approved their letter 238-9. The French bishops voted 93-2.

Although we have thus far emphasized internal church developments, none of these developments has taken place in a political vacuum. Even when church leaders sought to isolate their institution from the political, social, and cultural changes in its environment, the form of their reaction was influenced by their perception of the nature of the outside threat. The second and third parts, thus, will focus on the political role of the Catholic Church in national, regional, and international affairs. Specifically, we will describe the interaction between Catholicism and Soviet and American security policy at all three levels: national consensus, regional alliances, and on international issues like arms control. Part Two (Chapters Four–Seven) will analyze Catholic politics in four regional cultures: continental Western Europe, Anglo-American nations, Eastern Europe, and the Third World.

The content of each chapter has necessitated a different ordering of the materials. Nevertheless, certain general questions pertain to the political analysis of the role of the Catholic Church in national politics in all four chapters. What has been the traditional relationship between the Catholic Church and the state, especially with regard to nationalism? What role has the Catholic Church played in political, economic, and social modernization? What is the relationship of the Catholic Church to the political party system? What are the possibilities for Catholic political influence, based on the traditional role in the national culture, the percentage of the population and activity of Catholics, and the quality of ecclesiastical leadership? While these formulations do not exhaust the relevant questions, they do provide a guide for analysis at the national level.

In terms of Catholic influence on regional alliances, the most significant questions concern the impact of Catholic ideology and organization on the stability of the particular alliance. Does Catholic ideology strengthen or weaken the rationale for the alliance? Do Catholic organizations, especially national episcopal conferences, provide alternative communication links that either strengthen or weaken the alliance? Chapter Four begins with a discussion of the papal vision of a united Christian Europe (regional alliance) and a description of papal and episcopal support for Spanish liberalization (national consensus).

PART II

The Catholic Church in National and Regional Politics

CHAPTER 4

The Catholic Church in Continental Western Europe

JOHN PAUL GOES TO THE "ENDS OF THE EARTH"

FIVE HUNDRED thousand Spaniards jammed the shrine town of Santiago de Compostela on the last day of the pope's visit to their country, November 9, 1982. Compostela, revered as the resting place for the remains of Spain's patron St. James, faces the Atlantic. It became known as "the ends of the earth" when Europeans believed that the flat earth ended somewhere out in the ocean. From the early Christian centuries pilgrims from all over Europe have come to this shrine to honor the great apostle and renew their piety. That morning 300,000 Spaniards attended mass at the Labocolla Airport outside the city. Then the pope met with 20,000 fishermen in the cathedral square.

John Paul's final meeting, intended as the highpoint of his ten-day visit to Spain, focused on the Christian unity of Europe. In the Santiago cathedral 5,000 distinguished guests heard the pope encourage European nations to live up to the greatness of their spiritual heritage.

I, Bishop of Rome and pastor of the universal church, from Santiago issue to you, old Europe, a cry full of love: Find yourself. Be yourself. Discover your origins. Give life to your roots. Revive those authentic values that gave glory to your history and enhanced your presence on other continents. You can still be the beacon of civilization and stimulate progress throughout the world. The other continents watch you and expect from you the same response that St. James gave to Christ: "I can do it."[1]

King Juan Carlos of Spain opened the ceremony, described by the Vatican as a "European act." The guests included several Nobel Prize winners, the leaders of the European Common Market and the Council of Europe, and the presidents of the bishops conferences of most European nations. Compostela, the symbol of the fervent Spanish piety of the Iberian Catholic crusade, also signified the common spiritual unity of Europe as John Paul called on all peoples of the continent to build peaceful relations. The pope urged his hearers to reject the "unnatural divisions" and "secularized ideologies" which threatened the traditional Christian moral values. Neither the United States nor the Soviet Union was mentioned directly, though the former might have qualified under the category of "those countries enhanced by European expansion," and the two superpowers certainly were on the pope's mind when he raised the threat of an "atomic holocaust."

King Juan Carlos served as an apt symbol of the difficulties and the possible successes of the nations of "old Europe" seeking national and continental unity amid the complexities of contemporary civilization. The king had played a major role in bringing Spain out of the Franco era into a modern democracy. Indeed, the Spanish Socialist Workers Party under Felipe González had won a sweeping election victory just two weeks before the pope had come to Compostela. Spain had begun the process of reintegration into Western Europe that would lead to the admission of Spain and Portugal to the European Common Market in January 1986. From Compostela such progress in the seven years since Franco's death seemed nothing short of a "political miracle," given Spain's bitter polarization and isolation since the General's victory in the Civil War.

Franco died in November 1975. Carlos Arias Navarro, hated by the left as the "Butcher of Málaga," headed the next government. In July 1976 the king fired Arias and appointed the young Adolfo Suárez Gonzalez, who had been a bureaucrat in the Franco regime, to bring about *reforma sin ruptura* (reform without a break). Together Juan Carlos and Suárez issued a partial amnesty, engineered a national referendum on elections, abolished Franco's National Movement, legalized the Communist Party, and established diplomatic relations with the Soviet Union. The first Spanish elections since the Civil War were held in June 1977, less than one year after Suárez's appointment. Suárez, then forty-four, led his Democratic Center Union (UCD) to victory with 34 percent of the popular vote. The thirty-five-year-old labor lawyer González established the Socialist Workers Party as the viable leftist alternative with 28.5 percent of the popular vote. Both the right-wing Popular Alliance and the Communists led by the recently returned Santiago Carrillo, sixty-two, each got less than 10 percent of the vote. The election thus proved a victory for the political center despite the country's long heritage of bitter political polarization. The king had chosen neither the old men of the Civil War nor the middle-aged technocrats of Opus Dei. Instead, he turned to his own generation for leadership. Both Suárez and González proved themselves handsome and articulate "Kennedy-style" campaigners who knew how to use the media. The Socialist González had attended the Catholic University of Louvain where he learned a considerable amount about political organization from left-wing Northern European Catholicism. As such, he had a strong advantage over his leftist rival, the much older Communist Carrillo whom the electorate associated with the bitter feuds of the past.

Juan Carlos's moderate liberalization had been partially prepared for by the majority position of the Spanish Catholic hierarchy during the previous two decades. As we noted in Chapter Two, the postwar "Catholic Action" concordat gave the church full control of education and morality in exchange for Franco's strong influence in the naming of bishops. Franco and parts of the Spanish church feuded from 1960 to 1975, with Pope Paul VI generally supporting Spanish liberals.[2] By the 1977 election the political position of the Spanish bishops had moved closest to the UCD, although the conservative Cardinal Primate Marcelo González Martín and eight other bishops denounced the Constitution proposed by Suárez in the referendum of December 1978. Cardinal González strongly objected to the "godlessness" of the draft in sections covering education, marriage,[3] human development, and the national role of the Catholic Church. In fact, Prime Minister Suárez devoted his final appeal before the election to rebutting the cardinal. Most bishops, led by the president of the Spanish Bishops' Conference, Cardinal Enrique y Tarancón of Madrid, implied their support for the Constitution by endorsing a statement of the episcopal steering committee which stressed the church's neutrality. The Constitution passed with about 90 percent of the vote, but less than 60 percent of the eligible voters cast a ballot. Both the extreme right and the extreme left urged a boycott of the election.[4] On January 3, 1979, Vatican Secretary of State Villot and Spanish Foreign Minister Marcelino Oreja Aguirre signed a new concordat which brought church-state relations into line with the new Constitution. Juan Carlos gave up the right to appoint bishops, and the church gave up many of its special prerogatives like the right to block civil divorce proceedings. However, the Spanish Bishops' Conference did receive juridical status.[5]

While Basque and Catalán nationalisms, either in themselves or as the excuses for a military coup, pose the most immediate dangers to the newly democratic Spanish state, church-state conflict over public morality challenges the long-term formation of a national political consensus. While John Paul carefully avoided the appearance of political meddling in the 1982 election, Cardinal Primate González represented the minority of the bishops who favored the traditional Southern European alliance between the political right and the religious right in support of a Catholic culture. The program of the Socialist González included key elements opposed by the Spanish bishops, particularly a decrease in state aid to Catholic schools and a liberalization of abortion laws. The Socialists had also supported the legalization of divorce the previous year. In their preelection letter, the Spanish bishops asked Catholics to base their vote on "fundamental points," but named no parties or candidates.

Friction between the Socialist government and the church has centered on education and abortion. The Spanish Ministry of Education banned two catechisms edited by the Catholic Bishops' Conference because these textbooks equated abortion with crime and violence. The Christian Democratic Popular Democratic Party (PDP), currently allied with the right-wing Popular Alliance, vigorously protested the banning of the catechisms. The Bishops Conference urged continued use of the text.[6] On November 18, 1984, hundreds of thousands of mostly middle-class Spaniards marched in Madrid to protest the new Socialist-backed school law that regulated admissions and administration and forbade religious classes and services in private (mostly Catholic) schools that received school aid. The demonstrators, many wearing yellow arm bands and red paper hearts, came in buses from all over Spain. Manuel Fraga, ex-Cabinet minister under Franco and head of the opposition Popular Alliance, marched behind the parent organizers. The Spanish Bishops' Conference did not sponsor the march, but Bishop Elías Yanes, head of the bishops' education commission did remind Catholics of "their right and duty to defend the freedom of education by means compatible with the Constitution and Christian morals."[7] The hierarchy has also objected to a Socialist bill that legalized abortion in cases of rape, danger to the mother's physical or mental health, and serious risk of fetal abnormalities. The latter, like the education bill, has not taken effect pending appeal to the Constitutional Tribunal.

John Paul avoided the Spanish election of October 1982 but challenged González at the Vatican one year later. The pope snubbed the Spanish prime minister by receiving him in a small room off the Synod hall rather than in the papal library. During the visit the pope lectured González about the proposed abortion law and proposed cuts in financial aid to church schools. More alarming to the prime minister was the news that the Vatican was reopening the beatification process of the "Civil War martyrs"—12 bishops and 4,184 priests and religious murdered by the Republicans betweeen 1936 and 1938.[8] Refocusing Spanish attention on the mutual atrocities of the period will not help unify the Spanish polity. Traditional societal conflicts between Socialists and Catholics remain prominent features of the politics of the Southern European governments of France, Portugal, and Spain.

The postwar role of Spanish Christian Democracy illustrates the strengths and weaknesses of this movement in Southern Europe. Christian Democracy has never been strong in Spain, France, or Portugal. After World War II Franco, embarrassed by his Fascist ties, turned to leaders from Catholic Action to build bridges to Christian Democracy in the rest of Europe. His Foreign Minister Alberto Martín Artajo, graduate of the Jesuit Deusto University and close friend of the new primate Cardinal Plá, served brilliantly in preventing Spain's isolation. However, Franco's use of Martín did not mean that the general would encourage the growth of an independent Catholic party. Spanish politics remained frozen in the polarization of the Civil War. Even after Franco's death, Suárez's victory in 1977 resulted from his personal popularity, not the strength of his fifteen-party coalition. The necessity to take positions on questions of education and morality helped to undermine Suárez, and contributed to the splitting up of the UCD.

There are two general contexts in which Catholic politics in continental Western Europe should be considered. In the Southern "Catholic" countries of Spain, Portugal, France, and Italy, major church-state conflicts over education and morality threaten a minimal national political consensus. Political polarization remains a constant danger, with Communists, Socialists, Christian Democrats, and neo-Fascists all operating on the basis of strong ideologies and bitter historical memories. The church has attempted to buttress the Christian Democratic sector of the political spectrum, even in the absence of a strong party, as in Spain.

In the Northern "mixed" countries of Germany, Austria, Switzerland, Belgium, and the Netherlands, national hierarchies have withdrawn from the traditional strategy of close identification with the Christian Democratic party to a more neutral stance on specifically political issues. The bishops tend to view themselves more as an ethical "leaven," primed to articulate specifically religious positions on individual issues. Abortion remains a concern, but the emphasis has shifted to social and economic issues. The more conservative Christian Democratic parties seem to be staging a comeback in these areas. The political system and the Catholic Church's role in it have come to approximate the Anglo-American examples treated in the next chapter.

THE RISE OF SOUTHERN EUROPEAN SOCIALISM: FRANCE, SPAIN, PORTUGAL

The lead photo on page one of the June 25, 1984, *New York Times* shows part of the 850,000 demonstrators who marched in Paris the previous day. This demonstration, called by its organizers "the largest since the liberation," protested the Socialist government's plans to regulate private, largely Catholic,[9] schools. The June protest followed similar rallies in Versailles (March 4, over 500,000 demonstrators) and Nantes (October 22, 1983, 100,000 demonstrators).[10] The school issue placed Mitterand and his Socialist colleagues in a very delicate political situation since opposition to the school bill had overwhelming public support, but Socialist leaders could not soften their public stand without alienating important party activists who had long pushed for the regulation or abolishment of private schools. Thus, the battle over education inherited all the historical bitterness of the basic cultural and political cleavages in French society.

The Catholic-Socialist feud over the control of education dates back to the nineteenth century. Catholic priests monopolized French education until 1882, when leftists succeeded in establishing the *école libre*, free, compulsory, public schools. In 1901 Premier Jules Ferry banned Catholic schools, which were only allowed to re-open during the Third Republic. Finally, in 1959, De Gaulle pleased Catholics and Conservatives by guaranteeing government funding to all private schools that met the minimal requirements of the state curriculum. Private schools remain the target of doctrinaire Socialists and the large teachers' unions. The euphoria surrounding Mitterand's victory in May 1981 led these latter groups to call again for the end to French private schools. The government's actual proposal, called the Savary Project after Minister of Education Alain Savary, envisioned the continuance of both systems, with the state having more control in appointing the directors of all schools. This added control remained unacceptable to the private schools, although Catholic educators did accept the Savary text as the basis for negotiations.

Many Socialist educators felt the proposal was already compromised. Their pressure caused Mitterand's cabinet to approve the bill on April 18 and send it to the parliament where a Socialist majority seemed to assure passage. The previous day Cardinal Jean-Marie Lustiger of Paris had hardened his stand by criticizing the measure for "imperiling the identity of the Catholic school." Passage remained uncertain because even some Socialist legislators were "globally negative" toward the bill.[11] After the Paris demonstration Mitterand and Prime Minister Pierre Mauroy withdrew the legislation. By September the Socialists submitted a new bill which met most of the Catholic objections. The private school victory astounded political and religious observers.[12]

The French bishops, led by Cardinal Lustiger, have taken a generally moderate approach. The church and the state began negotiations in 1982. At the Versailles demonstration, Lustiger called the battle of state versus religious education "a sterile and archaic quarrel." As long as the government recognized the church's "right to teach," compromise was possible. At the beginning of the Paris demonstration, a mild letter from the French bishops urged the participants to act "in calm and dignity, without violence or aggression." The bishops are aware of the weakness of the French church. When Louis Harris (France) interviewed 1,000 French adults in April 1984, for example, 13 percent attended mass each Sunday.[13] Those who do attend regularly tend to support conservative political parties.[14] So the French hierarchy, like their Spanish fellow bishops, knew that the motivation for the educational demonstrations drew on Catholic piety, but also included non-Catholic and purely social elements. The French bishops were also very wary of being perceived as joining political forces with French Conservatives, who saw the schools issue as a marvelous opportunity to bludgeon the Socialists. Jacques Chirac, the neo-Gaulist mayor of Paris, Mme Valéry Giscard d'Estaing, and Jean-Marie Le Pen, leader of the far-right National Front Party, attended the rally at Versailles. Others at Paris were the former President Giscard and the former Prime Minister Raymond Barre. Chirac stated that adoption of the Savary proposal would "lead to the suppression" of a "fundamental liberty in this country."[15]

Rapprochement between the church and European Communist parties had taken a new step forward with the original Eurocommunist declaration of November 18, 1975, which appeared in L'Humanité (Paris) and L'Unità (Rome). The French bishops replied with their own statement on Marxism in June 1977, which admitted the possibility of practical collaboration between Christians and Marxists.[16] The historical bitterness of the relations between French Catholicism and French Socialism prevented the Socialists from adopting the "liberal" position of their old leftist rivals. Southern European Communist openness to cooperation with Catholics has also been fed by the declining fortunes of their parties vis-à-vis the Socialists. The Communists did poorly again in the National Assembly elections of March 1986, which resulted in the "cohabitation" of a Socialist president (Mitterand) and a conservative premier (Chirac) for the first time in the Fifth Republic. The Socialists confounded polls by remaining the plurality party (215 seats), but the two main conservative parties (Chirac's Rally for the Republic and Giscard d'Estaing's Union for French Democracy) joined independents to form a two-seat majority without the help of the far-right National Front. This new institutional arrangement will test whether or not the *Christian Science Monitor* (March 17, 1986) was right in its assertion that the lack of passion during the campaign indicated a new public consensus that France should remain a nuclear power while supporting the Western alliance, and that the French economy should be made more competitive in world markets without dismantling social benefits. The French bishops have certainly positioned themselves to be part of such a consensus.

In Spain the Civil War secured the triumph of a Catholic corporate fascism which had already been established in Portugal in 1926 with Salazar's *Estado Novo*. Franco and Salazar traded church control of education and morality for a politically submissive hierarchy. Rural and small-town Catholic morality and piety, symbolized by pilgrimages to Fatima, Lourdes, and Compostela, constituted the religious-social background of this political alliance. Opposition liberals had exaggerated their anticlericalism, for example, in the liberal Portuguese monarchy of 1820-1910.[17] In both Spain and Portugal the post–World War II Vatican sought to break this alliance between the national church and reactionary politics. Rome favored Christian Democracy as a major force, but the absence of a viable political center made that option impossible. Both national churches have suffered from these reactionary alliances.[18]

The Portuguese Socialists have achieved power with the aid of a coalition with parties to their right. In the election of April 1983 the Socialists led by Mário Soares won with just less than 40 percent of the vote. Following were the Social Democrats (Carlos Mota Pinto), the Communists (Alvaro Cunhal), and the Christian Democrats (Lucas Pires). Soares, vice-president of the Socialist International since 1976, lost the support of the Social Democrats in June 1985. While Social Democrat Anibal Cavaco Silva became prime minister after the October parliamentary elections, the "chubby cheeked"

Soares unexpectedly won the presidency the following February over the youth-oriented campaign of conservative Christian Democrat Diogo Freitas do Amaral.[19] The Portuguese church has taken an official position of political neutrality, although denouncing parties and individuals favoring "atheistic collective Marxism or pure unrestrained capitalism." The Portuguese Bishops' Pastoral before the 1980 election, for example, stressed that between these two forbidden extremes the particular choices of party politics must remain with the laity.[20]

Spain and Portugal will become the eleventh and twelfth members of the EEC in 1986.[21] Even though Spain joined NATO under a center-right government in 1982, significant leftist opposition remains. In October 1984 González announced a national referendum on NATO for March 12, 1986. In July 1985 the prime minister dropped his Foreign Minister Fernando Morán over the latter's coyness about whether or not he would support the campaign for NATO membership.[22] Portugal was a charter member of NATO. Between them these two Catholic Socialist countries house five American and one West German military base. Spanish, Portuguese, and French Socialist defense policies and economic pragmatism, however, has led to the "desencanto"[23] of their respective lefts. For example, Spanish anti-NATO demonstrators in May 1984 wrote González's name on a banner as "an enemy of the working class." The referendum prolonged the political battle, resulting in anti-NATO demonstations like that of the 500,000 who massed in Madrid in February 1986. Anti-NATO demonstrators even massed after the astounding 53 to 40 percent victory of the pro-NATO forces in the March referendum.[24] The vote was a tremendous personal victory for González, who convinced voters that pulling out of NATO would invite national destabilization. King Juan Carlos supported González by publicly voting before television cameras, thus undercutting the boycott of the referendum urged by the conservative Popular Alliance. The campaign against NATO was led by a coalition of radical, Communist, and pacifist forces. González took advantage of the momentum created by the NATO victory to call national elections four months early in June 1986. Although the Socialists lost a few seats, they retained the majority and denied the main opposition party, the conservative Popular Alliance, any additional seats.

Socialist electoral gains in Southern Europe reflect not only the personal charisma of popular leaders and a new economic vision but the significant political liabilities of the other four political traditions contending for power. The church remains an important factor in the political plans of all four opposition groups. Neo-Fascists like France's National Front Party seek to reconstruct the basic political-religious alliance that supported the Franco and Salazar regimes. Conservatives like Giscard and Chirac appeal to traditional Catholic values in morality and education but realize that a post-Vatican II hierarchy will not line up with any government. We have already alluded to the weakness of Christian Democracy, the Vatican's traditional postwar choice. On the far left, Communist parties seek to foster left-wing Catholicism within the party and alliances with Christian Democracy without. However, Communist parties suffer from the traditional Catholic ideological criticism and from voter suspicion about Soviet ties, especially in the case of the more hard-line parties like the French. These two sources of distrust reinforce each other. In analyzing Southern European political systems, therefore, one is struck first by the weakness of all the five general alternatives of Neo-Fascism, Conservatism, Christian Democracy, Socialism, and Communism. The difficult task remains to form practical governing coalitions based on a minimal national consensus.

ITALY: CHRISTIAN DEMOCRATS, COMMUNISTS, SOCIALISTS

In contrast to the rising power of Southern European Socialist parties during the 1980s, Communist parties have been experiencing major electoral reverses. In the late 1970s, however, many political analysts focused on Eurocommunism as the wave of the future on the left. These analysts envisioned Communist parties, independent of Moscow, participating as full partners in the coalition governments of NATO states. The principal example of this possibility was Italy, where the Italian Communist Party (PCI) under Enrico Berlinguer entered into limited cooperation with the Christian Democrats (DC) during the period 1976-1980. The DC always restricted the partnership, however, by refusing to give any cabinet posts to the PCI. The Communists finally withdrew after suffering withering criticism from the extraparliamentary left and a series of electoral defeats. Thus, PCI experience with the DC roughly paralleled that of the PCF with the Mitterand government, although the French Communists had initially been given four minor cabinet posts.

The Italian political system differs from others in Southern Europe in that the Christian Democrats and the Communists are its two strongest parties. The DC and the PCI have approximately the same support among the electorate with the remaining votes split among many other parties. Analysts principally concerned about the country's "governability" have long called for a *compromesso storico* (historic compromise) between these two major parties. According to these analysts, such a coalition would remedy the progressive polarization of the Italian political system with its many parties and extraparliamentary leftist and rightist terrorist groups. Since the DC and the PCI together have always received over 60 percent of the vote, their alliance could bring stability to the entire political system.[25]

Reflecting on the fall of the Chilean Marxist Allende, PCI leader Enrico Berlinguer first proposed the "historic compromise" in 1973. The major obstacle to full PCI participation has been the traditional Italian Catholic distrust of "atheistic Communism." In an effort to allay that distrust, in 1977 Berlinguer wrote "Enrico's encyclical," a 4,300-word reply to Bishop Luigi Bettazzi of Ivrea.[26] Berlinguer affirmed that the PCI not only respected religion, but saw it as a possible stimulus toward building a Socialist society. He also criticized state religious intolerance in Eastern Europe. Cardinal Benelli, long a chief Vatican strategist for Italian politics, defended the traditional church position that "Christian and Catholic principles do not accord and never will accord with Marxist principles." A front-page editorial in *L'Osservatore Romano* offered a more tentative response in remarking that Berlinguer's proposals required "clarification on the doctrinal level and reassurance on the practical level." Berlinguer succeeded in reassuring many because of his strong attacks against the Soviet Union and his personal tolerance for the role of Catholicism in Italian life. He even accompanied his wife Letizia to mass, waiting outside the church as is the custom of many Mediterranean males. Since PCI candidates have won mayoral elections in many large cities, cooperation between them and the hierarchy at the local level has been inevitable. When John Paul II met Rome's first Communist mayor Giulio Argan shortly after his election, the two men embraced. The literary battles between Don Camillo and Mayor Peppone have become political reality in many a Northern Italian village.[27]

The year 1978 was a major turning point in relations between the DC and the PCI. In the beginning of that year Paul VI was pope and his friend Aldo Moro, the leading DC proponent of the "historic compromise," remained a powerful party leader. The friendship

between Montini and Moro represented the best of postwar cooperation between the Vatican and Italian Christian Democracy. Paul
VI was the quintessential "Christian Democratic Pope." His father,
a newspaper editor and early supporter of the Popular Party (forerunner of the Christian Democrats), served three terms in the
Chamber of Deputies. When Montini was a young priest, he served
as part-time chaplain to the Italian Federation of Catholic University
Students, but he lost that position as part of the uneasy bargaining
between the Vatican and Mussolini. While serving in the Secretariat
of State, Montini kept contact with these young Catholic anti-Fascist intellectuals like Moro, Fanfani, and Andreotti who became
leaders in the Christian Democratic Party after World War II.[28] Montini's appreciation for the social and economic distress of postwar
Europe contributed to his policy differences with Pius XII's Cold
War anticommunism. In 1954 Pius appointed him archbishop of
Milan, but without the customary title of cardinal. Montini became
the model of Catholic reform, taking the church to the working
class. He wanted to prove that Italy could combine social reform
with traditional family morality under the banner of Catholic-in-
spired politics.

When the Red Brigades kidnapped and later executed Aldo Moro
in 1978, it was a personal tragedy for Paul. The pope wrote an open
letter to the kidnappers in which he pleaded "on my knees" for Moro's life. Paul personally celebrated the state funeral mass.[29] The
eighty-year-old pontiff died in August 1978. In a three-month period the two Italians most capable of articulating the reforming compassion of Christian Democracy had passed from the political
scene.

The deaths of Paul VI and John Paul I brought an end to the era
of close relations between the papacy and Italian Christian Democrats. John Paul II had neither the experience nor the interest in Italian politics of his predecessors. When the DC suffered its biggest
electoral defeat in thirty years in June 1983, for example, the pope
remained preoccupied with Poland. The Polish editor Jerzy Turowicz rather than an Italian DC politician like Moro benefits from long
friendship with the pope. Furthermore, John Paul's advisers on
Italian politics like the Jesuit Bartoloméo Sorge, editor of *Civiltà Cattolica*, have insisted that today's Catholics have "a legitimate pluralism of political choices." Sorge has also warned the DC that it must
reform itself.[30] Recent appointments to major Italian sees have reflected the pope's desire to distance the church from too close an
identification with the DC. For example, the Communist daily

L'Unità commented that John Paul's appointment of Bishop Marco Cé as patriarch of Venice showed that John Paul II "intends that this line [of reforming the church along the lines of Vatican II] also be reflected in the Italian Bishops' Conference."[31] As general ecclesiastical assistant of Catholic Action, Cé had stressed evangelization and the promotion of human values rather than traditional political ties to the DC. In April 1985, however, the pope seemed to give tacit assistance to the DC when, in a visit to the shrine at Loreto, he urged Italian Catholics to remain united politically so as to serve "the supreme good of the nation."[32]

The new emphasis in Vatican relations with the Italian political system is also reflected in the concordat signed by Casaroli and Socialist Prime Minister Bettino Craxi on February 18, 1984, and ratified on June 3, 1985. The new concordat removed Catholicism as the state religion and took away Rome's designation as a "sacred city." Parents will now have to make a yearly request that their children be given religious instruction in school. The Vatican will no longer have to inform the government of the appointment of bishops, and bishops are no longer required to take an oath of allegiance to the Italian state.[33] Thorny financial arrangements were given to a joint church-state commission, which later recommended phasing out state payments to clergy and parishes (about $180 million annually) by 1990, and giving a $600 deduction to taxpayers for gifts to a newly established Central Institute for the Support of the Italian Clergy, operated by the Italian Bishops' Conference.

The concordat codified the results of the political-religious struggles of the 1970s in which the church lost control over Italian public life. The Italian church faced issues like divorce and abortion earlier than the Spanish church. The Italian Radical Party used a series of referenda to attack the legislation of Catholic positions. The 1974 referendum to legalize divorce won by a large majority. Catholics collected enough signatures to force a counter-referendum in 1978, but the measure lost heavily. During the latter campaign members of the Italian Radical Party brought charges against Cardinal Siri of Genoa for ordering the posting of antidivorce manifestoes in churches. A pending 1976 referendum on abortion led to a national political crisis forcing elections.

The parliament passed an abortion law just prior to the deadline for holding another referendum in 1978. The Radicals opposed the new law as not going far enough, while the uncomfortable Christian Democrats took no party stand. The Communists played a key role when they switched their traditional voting stand of "no" on the basis of protecting the collective welfare (and pleasing the bishops) to voting "yes" to ensure the right of the individual woman. On May 17, 1981, Italian voters faced two referenda on abortion. The Radical Party sought to eliminate many restrictions on abortion contained in the 1978 law. The Movement for Life sought to outlaw abortion unless the mother's life or health was seriously threatened. During the campaign John Paul II journeyed to Bergamo to invoke the memory of native son Pope John XXIII in denouncing abortion.[34] In the end the Italian electorate rejected both 1981 referenda, and left the abortion law as it stood.

With the death of Moro, the most respected leader of the DC, the Christian Democrats faced a series of crises over the notorious corruption of local power bosses. The DC had maintained its plurality by bringing together various types of traditional legitimacy into a bargaining coalition. The political views of its members range from far left to far right, with Catholicism providing the unifying element. However, the lessening of the Vatican's active involvement and the progressive secularization of the Italian political system has threatened the usefulness of religion as a unifying element.[35] Like most successful traditional parties, DC leadership demonstrates a high degree of political shrewdness and a low degree of civic responsibility and moral probity. The DC had survived in power by its political shrewdness in building coalitions with minor parties and in the absence of a viable alternative.

Recently the church has encouraged reform of the Christian Democratic Party and joined in an attack on the Mafia. In October 1982 the Sicilian Bishops' Conference reaffirmed the penalty of excommunication against any Catholic "guilty of kidnapping or unjust and voluntary homicide." The twenty-four bishops deplored "the particular gravity of recurrent episodes of violence which often have as their matrix the Mafia and the ominous mentality that moves and facilitates it."[36] The general political confusion continued until the elections of June 1983, in which the DC suffered a crushing defeat. The Socialists, led by their ambitious leader Bettino Craxi, gained eleven seats (to 73), while the DC lost 37 (to 225) and the PCI lost 3 (to 198). The PSI thus established themselves as the credible third party, while the DC and the PCI continued their decline. After several decades of receiving roughly 40 percent of the vote (38.3 in 1979), the DC dropped to 32.9, only three percentage points ahead of the PCI.[37] The DC's attack on their old allies in organized crime lost them some votes in the south, where many "godfathers" turned to the neo-Fascist Italian Social Movement.

Craxi became the first postwar Socialist prime minister in August 1983, although the DC again held the majority of posts in the five-party coalition.[38] Since becoming head of the PSI in 1976, Craxi had stressed a center-left coalition excluding Communist participation in Italian domestic politics and support for NATO and the EEC in foreign policy. The "historic compromise" lost its most eloquent champion when Berlinguer died at sixty-two in June 1984. The choice of Alessandro Natta, sixty-six, as his successor indicates a desire for continuity in policy, but Natta has neither the charisma nor the international reputation of his predecessor. The PCI faltered in the local elections of May 1985, and their referendum to index wages for inflation was unexpectedly defeated (54-46 percent) in June.

The Socialist governments of the traditional Southern European Catholic states have pursued strong anti-Soviet defense policies. France has retained an independent nuclear deterrent, and resisted the inclusion of that deterrent in the Geneva talks. Spain and Portugal have welcomed Western bases and Italy has begun to deploy its 112 cruise missiles with less popular protest than any other country.[39] The recent decline of Communist parties has also contributed to feeble peace movements in Southern Europe. The generally weak Catholic Churches of the region have devoted their limited resources to internal strengthening and questions of education and public morality. In the 1980s French Catholic leaders speak of promoting Catholic "visibility" on national moral issues. Even when Catholic progressives wish to join the peace movement, they have difficulty articulating their concerns without seeming to join political forces with the Communist parties.

RESURGENCE OF THE CHRISTIAN DEMOCRATS: GERMANY AND AUSTRIA

While the Socialist parties have been gaining in Southern Europe, Christian Democrats staged a comeback in the German and Austrian parliamentary elections of spring 1983. Actually, the thirteen-year rule of the German Social Democrats (SPD) had ended the previous October 1, when the Free Democrats (FDP) deserted Chancellor Helmut Schmidt to support Helmut Kohl of the Christian Democrats. Kohl immediately called elections for March 6, 1983. The Christian Democratic Union–Christian Social Union (CDU-CSU) won a big victory, but fell short of an absolute majority. The CDU-CSU obtained 244 seats with 48.8 percent of the vote. The other parties did as follows: SPD 193 seats (38.2); FDP 34 seats (6.9); Greens 27 seats (5.6). Both the Free Democrats and the Greens surpassed the 5 percent needed to be allotted representation.

The month following the German elections, the Austrian Socialists lost their parliamentary majority. Bruno Kreisky, who had been chancellor since 1970, fulfilled his preelection threat and actually resigned. The Socialists won 90 seats (down from 95), while the Christian Democratic People's Party won 81. The traditionally liberal Freedom Party (FPÖ) won 12 seats to become the key party in forming a coalition, just as the Free Democrats are the key party in West Germany. Unlike the German Federal Republic (FRG), however, two rival Austrian environmentalist parties failed to receive enough votes to be represented in parliament. They did, nevertheless, siphon off some Socialist votes. A United Green Leader Herbert Fux commented, "The Austrians have voted traditionally."[40] The giant shadow of Kreisky continued to influence Austrian politics after his resignation. The Socialists followed his wishes in opting for an alliance with the FPÖ rather than a "grand coalition" with Christian Democrats that would have more closely reflected the Austrian emphasis on social consensus.[41]

The Catholic hierarchies remained neutral in both elections. To avoid the appearance of meddling in the March election, the German bishops delayed the release of their letter on the morality of war until April. The postwar German bishops have traditionally given indirect support to the Christian Democrats, as reflected in a pastoral letter released during the 1980 campaign that provoked strong SPD reaction.[42] A good representative of that conservative political-ecclesiastical tradition is Cardinal Joseph Höffner of Cologne, friend of the Bavarian conservative and leader of the Christian Social Union (CSU), Joseph Strauss. The Vatican appointment of Joseph Ratzinger[43] as cardinal archbishop of Munich in 1977 was widely interpreted as Paul VI's attempt to install a liberal counterweight to Höffner in the German hierarchy after the death of Cardinal Joseph Döpfner in 1976. Catholic support for Christian Democratic policy remains strong, especially among the lay Central Committee of German Catholics, where lower-level Christian Democratic politicians hold many offices. At its November 1981 Plenary Assembly, the Committee reacted to the growing German and American peace movements by adopting a statement "On the Current Peace Discussion." The statement stressed the need to familiarize oneself with the historical and political facts.

However open we Christians need to be for new developments leading towards a greater measure of freedom and self-determination, and however much we pin our hopes on them, for the present the following continues to hold good: the conflict between the communist and the democratic states is essentially due to the fact that the communist side subordinates its policy, both internally and externally, to the command of the totalitarian ideology of Marxism-Leninism. It is an ideology which, in fundamental questions, disregards the ethical norms and misuses the basic concepts that have developed in European philosophical and theological thinking and, over the last two hundred years, have given the liberal, democratic and constitutional state its shape. Marxism-Leninism knows no spiritual and social pluralism and no tolerance. It is symptomatic of this attitude that in the Soviet sphere of power an open discussion of security policy is not tolerated.[44]

The statement praised NATO's two-track decision as "an example of a policy which is aimed at a reduction in armaments and at *détente* and peace by choosing the path of military balance." When the American hierarchy was considering its pastoral letter, Social Democrat and former Minister of Defense George Leber and Christian Democrat Alois Mertes sent a joint letter to the NCCB defending NATO's policy of using nuclear weapons to ward off an overwhelming Soviet attack.[45]

The German bishops are extremely influential in Rome since they receive nearly $2.5 billion annually in tax money to distribute through such organizations as Adveniat. Not more than 65,000–75,000 Germans annually go to the courthouse to remove their names as Catholics, but mass attendance has fallen sharply in the postwar period. Ecclesiastical analysts are particularly concerned about the disaffection of German Catholic youth. Mass attendance dropped from 52 to 16 percent between 1950 and 1980. The Catholic Church thus reflects the strong "generation gap" of the FRG. In an attempt to reach youth, some priests like Tübingen professor Norbert Greinacher have staged *kirch von unten* (church from below) progressive discussions parallel to the *Katolikentag* (Catholic Days) of the Central Committee of German Catholics.[46]

By the spring 1983 elections, German Catholic discussion of the second draft of the American bishops' peace pastoral helped to neutralize the German bishops. In addition, the leaders of both the Christian Democratic and Social Democratic slates were Catholics. In Austria, Kreisky and Cardinal König of Vienna had diffused traditional Catholic-Socialist tension during the 1970s by their adroit handling of issues like education. A third participant in this church-state accommodation was President Rudolph Kerchschläger, an ex-member of the People's Party with excellent relations to König. Kreisky had nominated Kerchschläger rather than a more partisan choice for president.[47]

Moral participation in establishment coalitions—whether they are led by Christian Democrats or Social Democrats—suits well the traditional conservative tenor of Germanic Catholicism, especially now that Catholics constitute a majority (87.9 percent) in Austria and a plurality (46.3 percent) in the German Federal Republic. Since Luther the Germanic Catholic Churches have participated in what Erwin Kleine calls "The War Against the Reformation."[48] The reformers succeeded so immediately and so thoroughly that by the last quarter of the sixteenth century, even four-fifths of the Austrian population had become Protestants. Catholics regrouped, and the Hapsburgs successfully imposed the Counter-Reformation in Austria.[49]

In 1648, the Peace of Augsburg divided Germany into two religious zones, with minority Catholics in the South. At the beginning of the nineteenth century German Catholics tried to overcome their political weakness by forming confessional associations. German Catholics formed the Centre Party in 1870, and the party quickly became embroiled in the quarrel between Chancellor Bismarck and the Catholic Church that has become known as the *Kulturkampf*. Between 1871 and 1875 Bismarck sponsored legislation which brought Catholic schools under stricter state control, banished many religious orders (including the Jesuits), made civil marriage obligatory, and imposed other restrictions on the Catholic Church. In the 1874 elections the Centre Party received 28 percent of the vote, practically every German-speaking practicing Catholic. From 1890 to 1933 the party generally participated in the country's governing coalition, thus defending the rights of the Catholic minority.[50] The result of this history has been a German Catholicism "closer to the country districts and to little towns than it is to the concentrations of big cities which energize and determine modern life. Catholicism, too, is more pervasive in the lower social levels than in the upper strata." Such a narrow Catholicism closed in on the seemingly progressive German bishops when they returned from Vatican II. "Even those bishops who had made a clear decision to move forward were soon worn down by the widespread conservatism of the Cathedral chapter (practically all-powerful in Germany) and by the slow and familiar routines."[51] The recent influx of workers from Italy, Spain, and Portugal has also added to the lower-class composition of the German church, while making Catholicism the largest religion in West

Germany by 1980. Austria maintains a traditional rural, predominantly Catholic culture, especially outside of Vienna.

In both West Germany and Austria, Catholic practice correlates with Christian Democratic voting. In Germany this electoral tendency was set under the postwar leadership of the Catholic ex-mayor of Cologne, Konrad Adenauer, and his successors. The CDU returned political and economic stability to the nation, while avoiding the problems that a reconstitution of the confessional Centre Party would have posed for the bishops. The postwar German and Austrian hierarchies kept the clergy out of politics and encouraged non-confessional parties. For example, in 1946 the president of the Austrian Bishops Conference, Cardinal Innitzer, initiated the slogan, "a free Church in the new State."[52]

The Southern and Northern European political systems differ not only in the relative strengths of party tendencies but also in the importance attached to an establishment consensus among all the parties. In foreign affairs, for example, Germany enjoyed a decade-long consensus under the SPD's Helmut Schmidt. It was Schmidt who proposed the "two-track decision" of December 1979. Schmidt insisted that at least one other non-nuclear-weapon continental NATO member accept a share of the missiles. Italy complied with an offer to take 112 cruise missiles. Other designated countries were Great Britain (160 cruise missiles) and Belgium and the Netherlands (48 cruise missiles each). Only West Germany would deploy both Pershing IIs and cruise missiles. Ironically, the Carter administration initially had strong misgivings about the military and political effects of the two-track decision and had to be persuaded by Schmidt to concur.

This two-track decision not only fragmented the German foreign policy consensus, but it split the SPD. By the spring of 1981 a negotiated settlement seemed unlikely. The rhetoric of the Reagan Administration raised European fears that the Americans were planning to use the new missiles to fight a limited nuclear war on European soil. In West Germany *Der Stern* published a map showing all the nuclear targets in the country. *Der Spiegel*, led by its editor and founder Augstein, gave extensive coverage to the nuclear issue. Finally, many German television viewers were appalled at the nonchalant discussion of nuclear strategy by Schmidt and Minister of Defense Apel at Hamburg's "Churches Day." Massive public protests against the new missiles broke out across Europe, but especially in West Germany, Great Britain, and the Netherlands. As the date of deployment approached, protest activity grew. The four-day Easter weekend of 1983 witnessed major demonstrations in Frankfurt, Dortmund, Cologne, and other major German cities. Two of the keynote speakers were Protestant theologian Helmut Gollwitzer and Oskar Lafontaine, a left-wing Social Democrat.[53]

On October 20, 1983, former Chancellor Willy Brandt attacked the missile decision at a mass rally in Bonn. In November a special party convention voted 400 to 14 to reject the 1984-1988 deployments. Schmidt had been repudiated. When the mass rallies and party votes proved ineffectual, however, the SPD began to edge back toward its former position. The antimissile movement had become much less active, and, as party leader Horst Ehmke contended, the SPD was "trying to prevent the peace movement from going to the direction of radicalization, to prevent a big discussion of the alliance as such."[54]

In Germany, while the Catholic hierarchy identifies with the major parties, especially the CDU, the national policy consensus is under challenge by the left-wing SPD and the Greens. The left-wing Social Democrats and the Greens come from the same sociological background. These activists are mainly middle-class school teachers, university students, and tenured bureaucrats. They are the product of the mass universities, one of the proudest accomplishments of the generally older and more moderate wing of the SPD.[55]

The Greens have proved to be no mere passing phenomenon. As public frenzy over the Euromissile crisis has subsided, the party has returned to its earlier emphasis on protecting the environment and blocking the construction of nuclear power plants. In the June 1984 elections for the European parliament at Strasbourg the Greens polled 8.2 percent of the vote. This surprised many political analysts because of the nearly constant infighting between factions within the party. In the state chapters, which accept little direction from the center, "Realo" and "Fundi" wings feud about the future of the movement. The former favor pacts with the Social Democrats like the present arrangement in the state of Hesse, while the latter hope to see a "grand coalition" of the CDU and the SPD which would leave them an opportunity to expand on the left.[56] The latter scenario presupposes the demise of the Free Democrats, who did fail to get the necessary 5 percent of the vote for the European parliament in the June 1984 elections.

As might be expected, the Greens draw a disproportionate amount of support from the young. In the March 1983 parliamentary elections two-thirds of the Green voters were under thirty-five, and 15 percent of the voters between eighteen and twenty-nine chose the Greens (versus 5.6 percent for all voters).[57] Many members of the German establishment worry about the lack of enthusiasm for regular party practice among the young. Richard von Weizsäcker, president of the FRG, has descried "the failure of my generation to bring younger people into politics." This patrician ex-CDU mayor of Berlin, has set himself the task of articulating the national sense of a single German people, while respecting the postwar political division. "But, apart from the territory, you have the people. And it cannot be seriously disputed that 40 years after the war, as a German, I belong as much to the people of East Berlin as to the people of Aachen."[58] The question of nationalism among the young is complicated. While West German youths are rediscovering German songs and films after the postwar infatuation with American culture, this trend does not seem to have resulted in strong patriotism or pan-German nationalism. There is little support for strong remilitarization, and the numbers of young people registering as conscientious objectors or moving to West Berlin to avoid conscription has risen. The passage of time has lessened any guilt about Germany's Nazi past. This is true even of FRG leaders like Chancellor Kohl, who are in their fifties and were for the most part forced to join Hitler's collapsing war machine.[59]

BELGIUM AND THE NETHERLANDS: COLUMNIZATION AND PEACE MOVEMENTS

Belgian Catholics learned very early that their natural political allies were the liberal bourgeoisie, especially in their joint struggle against a Protestant Dutch monarch. Indeed, this Catholic-Liberal alliance founded the Belgian state in 1830. The resulting Belgian Constitution of 1831 recognized the liberties dear to the church (teaching, association) and to Liberals (opinion, press, and assembly). The Constitution established freedom of worship and separation of church and state. While Vatican officials like the Secretary of State Lambruschini mistrusted such an arrangement, the piety and loyalty of Belgian Catholics kept Rome from major interference.[60] Besides, the arrangement provided for state subsidies for ministers of worship and for religious, educational, and welfare institutions.

The Belgian Catholic-Liberal alliance broke down in 1847, largely because the Liberals feared Catholic control over the Belgian educational system.[61] However, this internal conflict over the control of education did not cause the Belgian episcopacy to lessen its staunch defense of the liberal Belgian state and of the Belgian monarchy.

The Catholic hierarchy opposed the Fascist Rexists between the First and Second World Wars and Nazi demands during the occupation. The Belgian bishops, like their Dutch counterparts, defended the political system because it allowed them to strengthen the Catholic "column" of social, economic, and political organizations. As late as 1969 Jean Delfosse commented:

Belgian society is a strongly segmented society. As Catholicism has occupied a relatively strong position in it from time immemorial, the divisions came into being in terms of the Church or as a reaction to it.

Seen from the outside, the Church appears to be a strongly structured political-religious society in which Christians find an answer to all their needs, not only the spiritual ones but also those on the level of education, health, and the preservation of their social and economic interests. This society is apparently organized in competition with other societies structured around non-Christian political parties. These, doubtless, do not present themselves as counter-churches; yet they organize themselves parallel to the churches and try to meet all the needs of man.[62]

After the Catholic-Liberal split of 1847, the two groups battled for the next thirty years, with the Liberal's opposition seeing itself less as a Conservative and more as a Catholic party as time progressed. Thirty years of Catholic party rule began in 1884.[63] After World War I the Catholic party was reconstructed as the Catholic Social Party. Although formally a nonconfessional body, it constituted the political organ of Belgian Catholicism as the Catholic People's Party did for the Netherlands.

Like the Dutch church, the Belgian Catholic Church has played a major role in international Catholicism during the last one hundred years, especially in providing missionaries and in articulating progressive Catholic solutions to contemporary problems. The interventions of Cardinal Leo Suenens of Brussels-Malines at Vatican II best represent this latter tradition. Suenens was also influential in obtaining the appointment of fellow Belgian and missionary Archbishop Jean Jadot as apostolic delegate to the United States, thus contributing to many of the changes in American Catholicism during the 1970s. However, since the early 1960s the Belgian church has expended considerable energy coping with the internal conflict between Walloon (French-speaking) and Flemish Catholics. Political and religious factors have mixed in this nationality crisis, which began in 1961 at the Catholic University of Louvain (Flemish, Leuven). Louvain, founded in 1425, had become Europe's premier Catholic university by the twentieth century. The university has fostered numerous contacts between theology and the social and natural sciences. Although Louvain was situated in Flemish Brabant, the university had been predominantly French-speaking. More courses in Flemish, however, were introduced from 1911 on.

In 1961 the Belgian government responded to Flemish wishes for more autonomy by proposing new legislation that would have made Flemish the sole language for administration and education in Flemish sections of the country. French-speaking professors at Louvain campaigned to have at least a special arrangement for the university. Partisans of both sides progressively hardened their positions until the Flemish demanded the transfer of the French-speaking section to a Walloon area. On May 13, 1966, the Belgian bishops declared that they would maintain the unity of the university at all costs, but that this unity was no obstacle to greater autonomy for the French and Flemish-speaking sections. This declaration caused "an astonishing explosion of rage among Flemish Catholic youth,"[64] who saw the bishops as siding with the traditionally French-speaking upper classes. Their protest continued until the French-speaking section of Louvain had to move to Walloon territory and establish itself in a new city, Louvain-La-Neuve. In 1972 Pax Christi of Belgium also divided into French and Flemish-speaking branches. While Flemish-speaking Belgian Catholic progressives have demonstrated keen interest in the Euromissile question like their Dutch counterparts, French-speaking groups tend to focus on Third World and North-South concerns like French Catholics.[65] Belgian political parties are also split, with two parties apiece for the Liberal, Christian Democratic, and Socialist traditions. Prime Minister Wilfried Martens, heading a center-right coalition of four parties, comes from the Flemish-speaking (Christian Democratic) Christian People's Party. That party originally voted to delay the March 1985 Euromissile deployment to provide a "chance" for success in Soviet-American negotiations at Geneva. But when Gromyko rebuffed Foreign Minister Tindemans's initiative for more Soviet flexibility, the Belgians finally deployed the first sixteen missiles.[66] In the October 1985 parliamentary election Martens's coalition kept its majority. According to Frank Swaelin, the leader of Martens's party, "The deployment and NATO were not an issue. People voted on economic and social questions."[67] Belgium, like Spain and Switzerland, proves the contemporary political and ecclesiastical relevance of subnational linguistic groups.

Earlier we described the strength of Dutch columnization which resulted in overwhelming confessional support for the Catholic

People's Party (KVP). Between 1918 and 1977 every Dutch cabinet but one (and that lasted only fifteen days in 1939) had Catholic participation. Such a record was not built on an efficient organization with a well-defined program, but on a "loose coalition of individual and group interests" whose major role consisted in "the defense of the subculture's position vis-à-vis Dutch society."[68] Herman Bakvis also notes "definite feelings of inferiority" since Dutch Catholics, unlike their Belgian fellow-believers, remained a minority with a history of persecution and discrimination.

As Dutch Catholics undertook their new confident role in a progressively secularized society, however, the Catholic People's Party went into decline. In 1963 the KVP received 84 percent of the Catholic vote, while nine years later it received only 38 percent. The remnants of the KVP federated with the two major Protestant parties in 1976 to form the Christian Democratic Appeal (CDA). In 1980 the three parties completely merged. The precipitous disintegration of the KVP reflected the low degree of commitment and the lack of a defined program, both factors having been to the party's advantage before 1963. When the hierarchy no longer perceived the KVP as necessary to defend the Catholic subculture, the party fragmented into the many factions it had always embraced. Political scientist Isaac Lipschits identified five separate "streams" within the KVP in the mid-1960s.[69] One of these was left-wing Christians who wanted close cooperation with the Labor Party (PVdA). The PVdA made strong political capital out of a television interview shortly before the 1967 election in which Bishop Bluyssen declared that it was perfectly acceptable for a Catholic to vote for another party besides the KVP. In 1968 other leftist KVP members left the party to form the Party of Political Radicals (PPR).

With the KVP losing such a large percentage of the Dutch electorate, the question of the ultimate disposition of these voters became a very significant issue for Dutch politics.[70] Despite the substantial losses of the KVP, Bakvis refuses to characterize the 1967 Dutch election as a "critical election" in the sense of the American Roosevelt's victory in 1932 because no major realignment occurred. Most of the major parties lost support during the 1960s and 1970s, and none made major gains. Rather, new smaller parties appeared which initially attracted Catholics who had internalized episcopal warnings about the older secular parties, Labor and the right-wing Liberals (VVD). Catholics with opinions on political issues became more likely to leave the KVP than those without opinions. Catholic radicals could join the PPR and Catholic conservatives the Roman

Catholic Party of the Netherlands (RKPN). Some chose not to vote. Over a longer period of time, however, ex-KVP voters seem to be shifting to the PVdA and the VVD, although the newly merged Christian Democratic Appeal has won some of these voters back.

The resulting party system resembles that of Austria, with a left-wing Labor Party (PVdA), a centrist Christian Democratic Party (CDA), and a right-wing Liberal Party (VVD). The parties received 30.4 percent, 29.3 percent, and 23 percent of the votes, respectively, in the September 8, 1982, election. The VVD, capitalizing on the economic issue, greatly increased its vote, while the biggest loser was the left-wing Democrats '66 which dropped to 4.3 percent.[71] However, in the Dutch system such smaller parties as the Democrats '66 do receive representation which is unavailable in the German or Austrian system. The voters' move to the right was reflected in a center-right coalition of the CDA and the VVD with the Christian Democrat Ruud Lubbers as prime minister. The Liberals stressed economic matters and insisted on a pre-coalition agreement that included spending cuts of 12.6 billion by 1986.[72] Both Lubbers and Belgian Christian Democratic Prime Minister Wilfried Martens have pushed through tough economic programs which they believed were dictated by the global recession and national budget deficits. The *New York Times* described the Dutch spending cuts as "far deeper than anything tried by Prime Minister Margaret Thatcher in Britain."[73] When Lubbers ordered a 3.5 percent reduction in public service wages, the workers resisted, but the government won.

Do these political changes signal the end of Dutch columnization? The answer is a mixed one because the KVP always existed for the Catholic subculture, not the subculture for the party. Dutch Catholics retain different degrees of loyalty to different confessional organizations. After examining various social and economic sectors, Herman Bakvis concludes, "the Catholic school system is the institution, other than the church itself, which is least likely to disappear."[74] Education, of course, remains crucial to the formation of the common world view which holds the Dutch Catholic community together. The Catholic Broadcasting Organization (KRO) and the Catholic press, which have long and honorable traditions, have also maintained popular support. The strength of Catholic education and the Catholic media contrasts with most industrialized societies where these same two forces have led the drive for secularization. While the Dutch Catholic media and school system have "modernized" their content, their permanence through the turbulent 1960s and 1970s suggest that deconfessionalization of the Netherlands must be analyzed according to specific issue areas.

During the 1980s the Dutch political system and Dutch society face a serious danger of polarization over whether or not to deploy the forty-eight Euromissiles. On this issue columnization remains relevant because of the long history of a Dutch religious-based peace movement. Hylke Tromp cites three strains of pre–World War II pacifism, and remarks that Christian pacifism, rather than liberal pacifism or Socialist pacifism, "probably had the greatest impact in the Netherlands already in that time."[75]

The contemporary Dutch peace movement received great impetus from the 1962 pastoral letter of the Dutch Reformed Church, which rejected the use of nuclear weapons unconditionally. One year later John XXIII issued *Pacem in terris*, which proved especially important for encouraging Dutch Catholic participation. In 1966 the two major Protestant churches joined the Catholic Pax Christi[76] in forming the Interchurch Peace Council (IKV), and six other Protestant churches affiliated the following year. Thus, the IKV follows the confessional organization of Dutch society by being an "arching" body uniting nine denominations. The fact that it remains the most important peace group in the Netherlands has led one Dutch analyst to speculate on whether or not the Dutch Christian peace movements are "anachronistic relics from the times of denominational segregation." He answers negatively, stating that "the peace movement aims in its cooperation more at non-confessional organizations and political parties than at the 'natural' allies in the Christian organizations and in the CDA."[77] It remains true, however, that Bishop Ernst is president of Pax Christi Netherlands and that since March 1981 Pax Christi representatives to the IKV must be confirmed by the bishops. Both Pax Christi and the IKV had requested the latter procedure as a means of tying the organization closer to the hierarchy.

Pax Christi, however, is both a part of IKV and a member organization of its own. Catholics have more than twice (5.6 million) the adherents than the next largest member, the Netherlands Reformed Church (2.7 million).[78] Pax Christi and the IKV were perceived as "twins" (Hogebrink) during the early 1970s. For the first ten years of its existence the IKV paid attention to a wide range of problems regarding peace and security. It was not until the late seventies that the organization began to concentrate solely on the issue of nuclear arms. Tromp refers to the "Deal of the Age" (1977), the neutron bomb (1978), and the "two-track decision" (1979) as the events which focused the attention of the Dutch public on NATO's nuclear deterrent.[79] The Dutch peace movement became disillusioned with Labor since a Labor government with its Labor Defense Minister Vredeling presided over the "dogfight" concerning which planes should replace the Dutch Air Force's aging starfighters. Surprisingly, although Vredeling's successor came from the right wing of the CDA, he resigned to protest against the introduction of the neutron bomb. In 1977 the IKV adopted a policy advocating the removal of nuclear weapons from the Netherlands and the Dutch Armed Forces. This policy is summarized in the motto, "Free the World from Nuclear Weapons and Begin with the Netherlands." On October 4, 1980, Pax Christi Netherlands presented a report addressed to the Roman Catholic Bishops and the Catholic Community of the country on the IKV policy. Pax Christi hoped that its advisory report could form the basis for an episcopal letter on the subject. The report contains a four-page section on the American episcopacy, which begins with the testimony of Cardinal Krol to the Senate Foreign Relations Committee.[80]

In December 1980 the Catholic bishops initiated a nation-wide consultation on the issues posed in the Pax Christi report. The main question was: "Are you in principle in favor of a unilateral step under the double condition we have formulated in our statement of 1976?" An estimated 40,000 participated in discussions on the topics. This discussion produced more than 2,200 responses, of which 1,037 came from groups and institutions. A majority of these latter responses favored unilateral steps. A summary of the responses formed the appendix to the Dutch bishops letter of June 1983. In the letter, which the bishops wrote after closed discussions, the Dutch episcopate issued a much stronger condemnation of nuclear weapons than before and repeated their opposition to new weapons.

In the 1981 election the IKV focused its political pressure on the PvdA, calling for the party to repeat the resolution of its 1979 congress endorsing the IKV campaign. However, the PvdA leader Joop den Uyl threatened to resign if the party accepted the IKV proposal, so a compromise, which included unconditional rejection of new missiles, was adopted. The CDA "waffled" on the issue, since its leader van Agt had committed himself to the two-track decision, while the CDA left wing opposed new deployment. The election resulted in gains for the left in general, but losses for the PvdA. The resulting coalition of CDA, PvdA, and left liberals from D'66 could not agree on a position concerning the cruise missiles, especially with van Agt remaining as prime minister.

The opposition to deployment, led by IKV, organized a demonstration of 400,000 people on November 21, 1981, in Amsterdam. The center-left coalition did not fall over the question of deployment, however, but over socioeconomic policy. The 1982 election resulted in the gains for the right described at the beginning of this section. The debate over the Euromissiles began to threaten the CDA-VVD coalition as the date for deployment approached. In forming their coalition in 1982, the CDA and the VVD had agreed to deploy the missiles in the absence of progress in Geneva. That decision taken in a period of calm became more difficult to implement as pressure mounted. On October 29, 1983, 550,000 demostrators gathered in The Hague, even eclipsing the numbers at Amsterdam two years previous. The chairman of Pax Christi, Bishop Ernst, gave one of the major speeches.

The CDA-VVD coalition held only the slimmest majority in Parliament, 79 of 150 seats. Not all of the CDA's 45 votes could be counted on. The left wing of the Christian Democrats, including Defense Minister Jacob de Ruiter, opposed deployment. Lubbers and Foreign Minister Hans van den Broek (CDA) favored the deployment. It seemed virtually impossible for the government to assure backing for a decision either to deploy or to reject the missiles. The CDA-VVD coalition would fall, possibly leading to a center-left coalition after elections. On June 1, 1984, the Dutch Cabinet submitted a compromise to Parliament. It proposed to delay deployment until November 1, 1985, and then only if no Soviet-American agreement had been reached, and if the Soviets had deployed more SS-20 missiles than they had as of June 1, 1984. In the meantime, work would continue on control and construction aspects of the deployment program, so that the final date of December 1988 for the siting of the forty-eight cruise missiles could be maintained.[81] On June 14, the Parliament voted 79-71 to adopt the solution. Six left-wing Christian Democrats defected, but the proposal received support from conservative Protestant splinter groups who feared the fall of the coalition. Labor Party leader Joop den Uyl called the compromise "double dealing" and claimed that the offer to the Soviet Union was "not seriously prepared" and could not work.[82]

Lubbers had saved his government and maintained some credibility with NATO. The Reagan Administration officially expressed its disappointment, but a "high-ranking State Department official" also praised the decision as "courageous" and expressed relief that the Lubbers government had not collapsed.[83] The West German government issued sharper criticism, following a Tass report stating that the decision had caused irritation in Washington because of fears it would set off a "chain reaction" among NATO countries.

As the November 1, 1985, date for the Dutch decision approached, the Soviet Union and the peace movement pressed for a rejection of the Euromissiles. Protestors met in the Dam Square in Amsterdam and in front of the parliament building in The Hague. While visiting Paris in early October Soviet Premier Gorbachev claimed that the SS-20 force directed at Europe had been reduced to 243. Nevertheless, the Dutch government accepted the NATO figures which showed that total SS-20 deployment in both Europe and Asia had risen from 378 to 441 since June 1984. The Lubbers government constructed another compromise which accepted the deployment of the 48 cruise missiles while announcing its intention to reduce the number of nuclear weapons it carries on F-16 and Orion aircraft as part of its NATO responsibilities. This reduction would take place in 1988 when the cruise missiles are scheduled to be deployed. In February 1986 the Parliament voted 79 to 69 to approve the U.S.-Dutch treaty allowing the stationing of the missiles. Six members of the CDA voted against the treaty. Lubbers's victory was made possible by the votes of several members of rightist fringe parties. In May 1986 Prime Minister Lubbers led his coalition to victory, despite the prediction by polls of a narrow loss due to the government's austerity measures and public backlash against nuclear power following the Soviet reactor disaster at Chernobyl. The Christian Democrats, campaigning on the slogan "Let Lubbers finish the job," became the plurality party (54 seats, 2 ahead of Labor), while their partners, the Liberals, dropped to 27 seats.

CONCLUSION: CATHOLIC POLITICS IN WESTERN EUROPE AND EAST-WEST RELATIONS

This chapter began with John Paul's appeal to King Juan Carlos of Spain and other European notables to advance European unity on the basis of traditional Christian principles. Exactly eleven months after his pilgrimage to Compostela, John Paul traveled to "Catholic Austria" to join the celebrations of the third centennial of the defense of Vienna from the Turks by the Polish King John Sobieski. As the pope stood in the Heroes' Square of this "window to Eastern Europe," he again stressed the common Christian heritage of the continent "from the Atlantic to the Urals."

The belief that man is made in the image of God, and that he has been redeemed by Jesus Christ, the Son of Man, has founded the respect and dignity of the human being and the respect of his right to a free development in human solidarity, upon the history of salvation. It is thus only logical that the universal rights of man were first formulated and proclaimed in the Western world.[84]

John Paul did not forget to mention, however, those "dark and terrifying traits" of European history which have resulted in so much war and persecution. Cardinal König followed this latter theme by reminding his listeners that Austrian Catholics bear the cross of the banishment of Protestants during the Counter-Reformation and "above all the heavy cross of the persecution of the Jews."[85]

European unity remains problematic. Indeed, the "dark and terrifying traits" of political terrorism and racial and linguistic discrimination still shake the unity of individual European countries. Even the geographical area designated by John Paul is unclear. His phrase "from the Atlantic to the Urals" included a substantial section of the Soviet Union, but it certainly did not indicate a papal preference for any of the specific current political initiatives on the continent. Within the ten nations of the EEC and the European parliament, strong popular support for the interests of the EEC as a whole vis-à-vis national interests exists only in the Netherlands. And 25 percent of all Europeans polled (41 percent in France) preferred that Britain would not be a member.[86]

The political strength of Europe as an independent global actor would have to be based on a strong tie between France and Germany, irrespective of ruling political parties, as in the cooperation between De Gaulle and Adenauer, and Giscard d'Estaing and Schmidt. The current partnership pairs a French Socialist president with a German Christian Democratic chancellor, thus reflecting current political attitudes throughout the ten nations. In the March-April 1984 survey, voters in the EEC in general placed themselves just left of center, with Italians farthest to the left and Irish farthest to the right. The current prevalence of center-right coalitions in Northern Europe could be explained by voter emphasis on unemployment as the major issue. Defense had a generally low priority in all ten nations.[87]

The French-German European axis has been sustained through the postwar changes in domestic politics in both Southern and Northern Europe. Earlier we spoke of Whyte's designation of the period 1945-1960 as the peak of "closed Catholicism" on the European continent. Adenauer in Germany, De Gasperi in Italy, and others fashioned a vibrant Christian Democracy which rebuilt and partially integrated Western Europe with the economic and military support of the United States. From 1960, however, this "closed Catholicism" began to decline. Christian Democratic parties from Italy to the Netherlands could no longer remain secure in power by combining hierarchical support, vague policy positions, and practical distribution of political goods.

The most spectacular manifestations of the decline of traditional politics among the young were the popular protests of 1968 in which hundreds of thousands of European students joined antigovernment rallies, as did hundreds of millions of their contemporaries from Berkeley to Beijing, from Hong Kong to Mexico City. Though these student protests rocked the major European and American universities in 1968, disarmament and peace movements, which began as a protest against American involvement in Vietnam, quickly lost their focus. Student movements fragmented into criticism of the whole gamut of establishment "sins," from nuclear weapons to outdated and unequal school systems to the prohibition of drugs. The "two-track decision" of 1979 finally gave the European peace movement another single major focus which lasted until the first deployments in December 1983.

Many who participated in the Paris protests of 1968 voted for Mitterand in the Socialist victory less than fifteen years later. In French foreign policy, however, the North-South concerns of the demonstrators of 1968 have lost out to Mitterand's desire to assure Washington and the French middle class of his anti-Soviet credentials. Though Mitterand has made such symbolic gestures as verbally supporting the Contadora efforts in Central America and inviting Castro to Paris, the resignation of the French "minister of cooperation" for Third World affairs has "dramatized the fact that Mitterand's Third World policies have become mostly rhetorical."[88] The European Socialist economic program relies more heavily on pragmatic managers than on doctrinaire ideologues. Spain's González, for example, has chosen his fiscal and monetary policy makers from the "lost generation" of the Franco mid-1960s who were forced to study abroad at institutions like Louvain, Oxford, Harvard, and M.I.T.[89] In such a situation, older Communist intellectuals like Carrillo and Marchais, who remind voters of the Civil War and the Cold War, attract fewer and fewer votes. The European Communist parties of Southern Europe are in decline.

What Socialist governments like those of Spain and Italy fear most is the disintegration of their political systems as a result of increased polarization. Spain must avoid military coups and Basque terrorism, while Italy still suffers from considerable terrorism on both the right and the left. Italian universities constitute less a locus for church-state conflict over culture than a fertile breeding ground for extraparliamentary political dissent. Within the Southern European parliamentary systems, compromise remains difficult because the five leading political currents (neo-Fascism, Conservatism, Christian Democracy, Socialism, and Communism) all retain strong ideological roots. The Southern European national hierarchies have supported national consensuses for democratic values. John Paul himself has spoken out against Basque terrorism in Spain and Mafia violence in Italy. Both the Vatican and the Spanish Bishops' Conference played an indispensable role in Spanish liberalization.

Nevertheless, because of the highly ideological nature of Southern European politics, the Catholic Church could contribute to the fragmentation of a national consensus. The main conflicts between the new Socialist governments and the respective Catholic hierarchies concern control of education and public morality on issues like divorce and abortion. These conflicts have weakened Christian Democratic parties, torn between their loyalty to the hierarchy and the national consensus for some movement toward secularization on such issues. Communist parties like the PCI have hesitated to take a strong stand because of a collectivist moral tradition and an unwillingness to alienate the bishops. Neo-Fascists, Socialists, and secularist parties like the Italian Radicals have taken relatively clear and absolute positions on one side or the other. Italy remains a special case in Southern Europe because of the strengths of the Christian Democratic and Communist parties, although the possibility of a "historic compromise" has receded since the kidnapping of Moro by the Red Brigades and the death of Berlinguer. Such a political situation places Southern European Catholic hierarchies in a poor position to influence government policy issues concerning East-West relations, should the majority wish to do so. Italian bishops like Betazzi fight a lonely battle.

What the election of Socialist governments has done for Southern European Catholic hierarchies has been to free them from suspicion of collusion with the state. For example, Lustiger and the French bishops have attained new visibility, despite the continuing internal weakness of the church. The movement to the left of the French government and the movement to the right of French intellectuals have benefited the church's ability to speak out. The French church has less ties to the state than either the Spanish or Italian one. Although the Spanish Constitution of 1978 says "There shall be no state religion," it immediately adds, "The public authorities shall take the religious beliefs of Spanish society into account and shall maintain consequent relations of cooperation with the Catholic Church and other confessions."[90]

In the northern NATO countries of Germany, Belgium, and the Netherlands, however, Christian Democrats presently lead the government coalition. The major political differences in these three systems concern the strength of the respective Liberal parties on the right, and the relative strengths of the established Social Democratic or Labor parties vis-à-vis the more radical groups on the left. While the Vatican and national episcopates such as the German hierarchy have withdrawn from earlier specific support for "the Christian parties," both Rome and the national bishops would prefer Christian Democratic governments because they fear the secularism and anticlericalism of the Socialist tradition even though Northern European Social Democracy shares little common culture with Southern European Socialism. Confessional education remains important, even to "secularized" Dutch and Belgian Catholics.

While Northern European Protestantism had a strong record of antiwar protest in the 1950s, Northern European Catholics have identified with the Christian Democratic governments which rebuilt Europe under the Marshall Plan. German Catholic policy on East-West relations has evolved along with that of the respective governments of the FRG. Kohl has gone to great pains to emphasize the continuity in his foreign policy with that of Schmidt. The head of the Free Democrats, Hans-Dietrich Genscher, remained foreign minister as he had been under Schmidt. Kohl's coalition partner, the flamboyant Franz Josef Strauss of Bavaria's Christian Social Union (CSU) had denounced the *Ostpolitik* of Brandt and Schmidt, but Strauss took center stage in negotiating a West German government guarantee of a new one-billion-mark credit to East Berlin the following summer. Embittered CSU delegates denounced Strauss at the party's July convention.[91] The following month Strauss became the first prominent Western European politician to visit Albania since World War II. Kohl announced the East German credit just prior to visiting Andropov in Moscow to remind the Soviet Union of the value of good relations even after deployment of the missiles.

While German Catholics have remained largely outside the protest movement, Austrian Catholics have been encouraged to join as a means of ensuring a "responsible" peace movement, along with national stability. The spring of 1982 produced considerable trepidation in Austrian political circles as party leaders watched the worsening German confrontation over the Euromissiles. Cardinal König then encouraged Catholic participation in the Vienna rally for peace, and political leaders felt much more at ease. The official Austrian Peace Movement is led by youth representatives of the Communists, Greens, Socialists, and Catholics. The Communists, who are very pro-Soviet and gain less than one percent of the vote in national elections, owe their prominence in the official Peace Movement to party discipline, the support of other leftists, and the better formulation of their proposals.[92] Catholic leaders insisted that Conservative youth also be admitted or they would withdraw from the official movement.

The Austrian peace movement, in both its official and independent forms, plays a much less significant role than its German or Dutch counterparts. This lack of influence reflects not only the less conflictual nature of Austrian society but also the generally progressive foreign policy of neutral Austria under the Socialist Kreisky. Kreisky promoted arms control, dialogue between Israel and the Arabs, and Vienna as the third United Nations city. The major exception to this progressive government policy was the granting of a permit to sell light tanks to Pinochet in Chile. Large demonstrations in the summer of 1980 caused the government to cancel the permit.

Austria serves as the natural conduit to the West for Eastern European countries, especially Hungary. Austria and Hungary, both predominantly Catholic, have a long tradition of mutual influence. In a May 1984 interview Austrian Finance Minister Salcher said current relations are better than during the Hapsburgs' domination because, "We [Austria] export the Western way of living to the East, which has its political consequences."[93] This national political emphasis on East-West relations perfectly fits the Austrian Catholic episcopal emphasis. Cardinal König has been one of the leading proponents and practitioners of Catholic *Ostpolitik*. In the peace "doldrums" following Euromissile deployment, the Catholic peace movement has stressed East-West dialogue by holding conferences with their Eastern bloc counterparts.

As Soviet-American relations have cooled, Central European countries on both sides of the Iron Curtain have begun independent moves to give themselves more diplomatic room despite the intransigence of both Washington and Moscow. When Bonn found itself losing influence on American and Soviet policy, the Kohl government initiated broader contacts with the GDR, resulting in Erich Honecker's scheduling a visit to West Germany in late September

1984. The announcement of this first visit of an East German party and state leader to Bonn generated considerable uneasiness in both the United States and the Soviet Union. Both Washington and Paris feared that the FRG might be willing to accept political neutrality as the Soviet price for reunification. At the present time, however, such a demilitarized reunification would only have the support of the Greens and the left wing of the SPD.

On August 1 a *Pravda* editorial denounced German "revanchism," the favorite Soviet code word for the purported German drive to recover territories lost by Hitler in what is now Poland, Czechoslovakia, and the Soviet Union. The East German Communist paper *Neues Deutschland* replied that Berlin's policy toward Bonn was "determined by the joint desire for peace of the socialist countries." Honecker himself replied that the GDR has always been absolutely loyal to the Soviet alliance, but that relations between the GDR and the FRG have "great significance for European security and the international climate." Instead of demanding withdrawal of the NATO missiles before continuing talks of East-West cooperation as the Soviet Union has specified, Honecker attached "great significance to the dialogue with responsible forces in the FRG." Finally, on September 4 Honecker postponed his trip. The East German statement complained about "unseemly" and "detrimental" declarations by FRG politicians, but Soviet pressure seems to have been the major motivation.[94]

These limited moves between Kohl and Honecker raised some fears of a reunified and armed Germany in both the West and the East. The Polish government remains especially sensitive to traditional German claims to the land beyond the Oder and Neisse Rivers. Polish fears were heightened in the summer of 1984 when President Reagan said (ironically, to an audience of Polish-Americans in Chicago) that the United States "rejects any interpretation of the Yalta agreement that suggests American consent for the division of Europe into spheres of influence." On July 22 General Jaruzelski attacked the claims of some West Germans who had made charges of cultural discrimination against Germans in that part of Poland ceded by the Yalta accords. On August 15, before more than 160,000 pilgrims at Częstochowa, Cardinal Primate Glemp supported Jaruzelski by denying that there were any culturally deprived or genuine Germans in Poland. He chided German Catholics who made such a claim.[95] Glemp's strong remarks were not well received by West Germans, especially the German Catholic bishops who had been among the foremost organizers of aid to Poland after martial law.

Two days later the secretary general of the Council of German Catholic Bishops, Wilhelm Schatzler, began a visit to Poland that the German bishops hoped would calm any conflict.[96]

Such territorial claims come from right-wing Christian Democratic Bundestag members like Helmut Sauer and Herbert Hupka. The main body of the CDU-CSU backs the Kohl initiative for more cooperative relations between the FRG and the GDR, but without any immediate prospect of reunification. In fact, when CDU parliamentary leader Alfred Dregger criticized the recent *Ostpolitik*, his deputy Volker Ruhe quickly reassured an East German Politburo member, and no one supported Dregger, not even CSU leader Strauss.[97] *Ostpolitik* was initiated by the SPD, so the Social Democrats can scarcely criticize Kohl's initiative. What the Social Democrats can say is that the gains of *Ostpolitik* will be limited as long as West Germany continues to deploy the Euromissiles.

Only in the Netherlands, for reasons discussed in the preceding section, do Catholics play a leading role in a strong and politically significant peace movement, the IKV. Philip Everts credits two new developments for "the relative success of the movement so far": 1) its informal coalition stretching from the far left to parts of the political center. The IKV does not seek to function as a "prophetic minority" but to influence the major parties. 2) the IKV's "long march through the institutions," in which peace activists have sought to influence women's, union, and professional organizations, including groups of concerned military officers.[98] Nevertheless, such tactics have not produced a political breakthrough. In fact, when peace organizations tried to influence the 1982 election by issuing a pamphlet advising Dutch "to vote against nuclear weapons," it produced a backlash against both IKV and Pax Christi, even though these organizations had not officially endorsed the pamphlet.

The position on defense of the Dutch ecclesiastical elites, like that of their American counterparts, is considerably to the left of church members. The discrepancy is even greater when the comparison is limited to regular church-goers.[99] Hence, on issues of war and peace, ecclesiastical elites receive their greatest support from nonbelievers. Protestant-lay backlash against IKV-member churches has produced competing organizations like the Interchurch Committee for Bilateral Disarmament (ICTO) of the Gereformeerde Kerken.[100] That there is no comparable Catholic group may be due to conservative Catholic confidence that the bishops, and especially the Vatican, "would simply not allow radical positions." Archconservative Dutch Catholics, including NATO Secretary General Joseph Luns, have influential connections in Rome.[101] Recent episcopal appointments seem to have helped Catholic conservatives. In 1982, Bishop Bär had written an article in the official *NATO Review* criticizing antinuclear tendencies in the church and supporting NATO and ICTO.[102] After the new Primate Simonis met with Christian Democrats in early 1984, he commented that although the Dutch episcopate had pressed for diminishing the role of nuclear weapons, he could respect politicians who felt deployment of the cruise missiles would attain that goal. On the other side, however, the ecclesiastical archconservative Bishop Gijsen has been as uncompromising in his opposition to nuclear weapons as he has in everything else. Gijsen sees nuclear weapons and abortion as twin issues.

In addition to its protests against nuclear weapons, Pax Christi Netherlands has also promoted East-West dialogue. For example, the Dutch have been instrumental in the five rounds of talks conducted by Pax Christi International and the Russian Orthodox Church. These talks took place in Vienna (November 1974), Leningrad (April 1976), London (May 1978), Zagorsk (October 1980), and Antwerp (April 1983). Cardinal Alfrink, then president of Pax Christi International, headed the Pax Christi delegation at the first two sessions. The secretary general of Pax Christi International was also a Dutchman, Mr. Carel ter Maat. For the following meetings the delegation has been led by President Bishop Luigi Betazzi of Ivrea and Mr. Etienne De Jonghe of Belgium, ter Maat's successor.[103]

The traditional European Catholic contribution to peace has consisted not in participation in peace movements, but in fostering East-West dialogue. The FRG's Central Committee of German Catholics is much closer to the West European Catholic majority position than Pax Christi Netherlands. It is no wonder that the first reaction of most European bishops to the second draft of the American letter in November 1982 was one of dismay. In Chapter Eight we will discuss the political interaction between the American and European bishops on arms control. First, however, we will examine the political and cultural background of Anglo-American Catholicism and Eastern European Catholicism.

CHAPTER 5

Anglo-American Catholicism: Immigrant Churches in Western Democracies

THE POPE AND THE NUN

THE FRONT COVER of *Time* magazine (October 15, 1979) blazoned "John Paul, Superstar" above a photo of the pope waving to an immense crowd. John Paul II followed up triumphant tours to Mexico and Poland with a visit to the Anglo-American countries of Ireland and the United States. Certainly, traditional Catholic Ireland would greet the pope with enthusiasm, analysts said, but what about the pluralistic, secular, sexually permissive, and culturally Protestant United States? John Paul's positions on personal morality seemed guaranteed to alienate large segments of the population. America also had a long tradition of anti-Catholic bigotry. Less than nineteen years before, the election of John Kennedy had finally settled the question of whether or not a Catholic could be president. Still, the huge crowds did come, first in Boston, "the most Catholic (and Irish) of all cities," then in New York, Philadelphia, rural Iowa, Chicago, and even Washington, D.C., where a tired and embattled Southern Baptist president tried to grasp some of the pope's magnetism.

The people came, attracted by John Paul's personal charisma. Since Wojtyła had already visited the United States in 1969 and 1976, he felt at home and behaved spontaneously, at one point hoisting a young girl onto the roof of his vehicle at the Youth Concert in Madison Square Garden. His theatrical timing had never been crisper and his staff's advance work had never been more thorough. John Paul's friend, the Polish Catholic editor Jerzy Turowicz, described the objective of the papal visit to the United States as the reunification of a national church whose many groups do not understand each other. "Perhaps what he faces is a problem of language, how to express his vision [of the church] without seeming to take the part of a rigid conservative."[1] On the trip John Paul tailored his emphases to his different audiences. To Americans in general he spoke of peace, brotherhood, and human rights. The highlight of this message was his finely crafted speech to the United Nations which related socioeconomic development and human rights to true peace. "Are the children to receive the arms race from us as a necessary inheritance?" he asked, while the television camera panned the faces of the delegates' children in the hall of the General Assembly. Everywhere on his visit he called on the rich United States to reject a consumerist society and to help less fortunate nations. When he addressed specifically Catholic groups, especially the closed meeting of bishops in Chicago, however, John Paul emphasized papal prohibitions of birth control, divorce, abortion, extramarital sex, and homosexual sex. He reiterated the Latin church's traditional stand against women priests and married priests. John Paul's final message was to encourage Catholics to "stand up every time human life is threatened" by abortion, weakened marital standards, and the limiting of the family size for material comfort.[2]

The most striking confrontation of the papal visit occurred on Sunday, October 7, at the National Shrine of the Immaculate Conception. Before national television cameras, Sister M. Theresa Kane, president of the Leadership Conference of Women Religious (LCWR), challenged John Paul on the role of women in the Catholic Church. The forty-three-year-old Kane, wearing a gray tweed suit instead of the traditional habit preferred by the pope, urged John Paul to be "mindful of the intense suffering and pain which is part of the life of many women in these United States." Sister Kane also linked the church's call for "the dignity and reverence of all persons" to "the possibility of women as persons being included in all ministeries of our church."[3] When she finished, half the audience applauded vigorously, while the other half seemed "to sit on their hands." Fifty-three women religious, dressed in civilian dress, had been standing in silent protest against John Paul's position on women's issues. The pope spoke to Sister Kane after her talk, but he did not depart from the traditional themes of his prepared text to reply directly to her words.

The role of women also caused controversy during John Paul's trip to Canada in September 1984. In Montreal the pope beatified the Canadian mystic Sister Marie-Léonie Paradis, who founded a religious institute dedicated to the service of priests. Although the pope affirmed the importance of women whose form of service "may differ from that chosen by Blessed Sister Marie-Léonie," the symbol of "a woman who washes their [the priests'] floors and does their dirty linen" did nothing to inspire feminists.[4] At the French Acadian cathedral of the Assumption in Moncton, Sister Odette

WASHINGTON, D.C. Sister M. Theresa Kane speaking with the Pope after her remarks at the National Shrine of the Immaculate Conception. October 1979. The New York Times/George Tames.

Léger told the pope that women "count on the confidence and encouragement of the church. Whether we be lay people, unmarried or married women or nuns, we want to share in the apostolic tasks of evangelization, as God calls upon us to do it in our own way as women."[5] Sister Odette's greeting did not challenge as directly as that of Sister Kane's, but the message did come through.

John Paul's difficulty in comprehending the force of Sister Theresa Kane's intervention emphasizes the strong cross-cultural com-
ponent in the interaction between a Polish pope and a newly self-
confident national Catholicism formed in an Anglo-Saxon Protestant culture. Indeed, the American church combines great cultural
differences within itself. For example, Sister Kane's intervention
can be contrasted with the simultaneous comment of the Reverend
Luis Olivares, president of PADRE, an organization of Hispanic
priests: "The Hispano-Catholic relates to the family, not affluence.
Ordaining women is trivia. Birth control or married priests are non-
issues."[6] The Catholic Churches of The United States, the United
Kingdom, Australia, New Zealand, and the Union of South Africa
have only recently become full participants in their respective societies. During the nineteenth and early twentieth centuries, Catholics in these countries suffered political and social discrimination.
The respective cultures have been formed in the tradition of Anglo-
Saxon Protestantism, so the respective civil religions have borrowed heavily from Protestant themes.[7] The political systems have
focused on liberal democratic rights, while the economic systems
have pursued welfare capitalism. At almost every level, different
historical developments have produced major cultural differences
between the continental Western European and Anglo-American
perspectives. Theresa Kane was enunciating the recent American
emphasis on equality of opportunity for both sexes, an emphasis
that does not find comparative support in other national cultures
and national Catholic Churches.[8]

In Chapter 2 we described the historical background of Irish and
British Catholicism. The centuries-long British persecution eventually resulted in waves of Irish emigration which played the principal
role in forming the Catholic Churches of the former British colonies
of Australia, New Zealand, the United States, English-speaking
Canada,[9] and the Union of South Africa. Catholics from other countries also immigrated, but the Irish had the advantage of early and
constant immigration plus English as a native tongue. In addition,
Irish seminaries, especially Maynooth, produced an abundance of
F.B.I. (Foreign Born Irish) missionaries who became episcopal leaders in their adopted countries. South African Catholicism exemplifies an Irish immigrant church in a Protestant society[10] (see Ch. 7,
below).

While the Irish and the English of South Africa cooperated
against the Dutch, the Irish immigrant background of Australasian
Catholics caused conflict with their fellow citizens of British extrac-

tion. In both Australia and New Zealand the Irish national sympathies of most Catholics set them apart during the First World War. The issue of state educational aid for parochial schools also separated Irish and British emigrants, especially during the 1870s.[11] However, Australasian Catholics followed John Whyte's model of Anglo-American "open Catholicism" by never forming a national denominational political party nor strong denominational social organizations. Catholics have tended to belong to the Labor Party in Australia. In both Britain and New Zealand, Catholics supported the Liberals first, and then Labor. The Liberal parties appealed to Catholic immigrants with their early advocacy of Irish independence. Catholics voted for Labor candidates for the same kinds of reasons they voted for the Democrats in the United States. Working-class immigrants supported the party that defended the interests of labor. Whyte places Britain and New Zealand as the two nations closest to his ideal type of "open Catholicism."[12]

As in other Anglo-American countries, the background of the Catholic episcopal leadership in both Australia and New Zealand remains heavily Irish, despite later strong immigration from Southern Europe. Cardinal Reginald John Delargey of Wellington was the only son in a family of six of Irish origin. The late Cardinal James Knox, former archbishop of Melbourne (1967-1974) and prefect of the Congregation for the Sacraments and Divine Cult (1974-1983), was the son of Kilkenny immigrants and a tailor's apprentice when he decided to study for the priesthood. He studied theology and canon law in Rome for five years before being ordained there in 1941.[13]

AMERICAN CATHOLIC NATIONALISM: FROM HUGHES TO SPELLMAN

Dorothy Dohen begins her book *Nationalism and American Catholicism* by repeating a statement Cardinal Francis Spellman made during his five-day Christmas visit to the American troops in Vietnam in 1965. When asked about the role of the United States in Vietnam, he replied, "I fully support everything it does." Then he added, "My country, may it always be right. Right or wrong, my country."[14] The pastoral letter of all the American bishops released the following November showed more hesitation than the cardinal, but nevertheless concluded that on the whole American involvement in Vietnam was justified.[15]

Nationalism is usually treated as an ideological phenomenon,[16]

but in this chapter we will broaden the term to include the conjunction of the majority political and religious values and programs fostered by the ecclesiastical leadership of the American Catholic
Church during the period 1838 to 1967. Here, the term "American
Catholic nationalism" combines both political and religious characteristics. Political attributes include strong nationalistic statements
and patriotic foreign initiatives, virulent anticommunism, and a social policy that fosters unionization. These attributes received their
archetypical expression in the New Deal of Franklin Delano Roosevelt, a personal friend of Cardinal Spellman. Religious characteristics include an autocratic Irish and Irish-American episcopal leadership increasingly trained in Rome, a vigorous attack on national
churches within American Catholicism, a morally based anti-intellectual piety, and a strong emphasis on parochial schools to transmit that piety. In addition, religious and political values reinforced
each other as many eastern and midwestern politicians and prelates
cooperated in serving the interests of the new immigrants.

We have set the period of majority American Catholic nationalism
with the appointment of the Irish-born John Hughes as bishop of
New York in 1838 until the death of Cardinal Spellman in 1967. Another alternative would have been to start the period a decade later
with the Great Potato Famine since that event triggered the first
massive Irish immigration to the United States. As a closing date,
either the election of John Kennedy or the passage of the Declaration on Religious Liberty at the Second Vatican Council would also
be possibilities. Kennedy's election broke down the last major
American barrier to full Catholic political equality. The effective
American episcopal lobbying on behalf of the principle of religious
liberty at Vatican II demonstrated that the hierarchy of the United
States had sufficiently embraced American cultural values to fight
for one of its central tenets against sixteen hundred years of European Catholic tradition. Cardinal Spellman remained the preeminent American ecclesiastic at the Council, making 131 of the 341
American oral and written interventions. It was also Cardinal Spellman who requested the naming of John Courtney Murray, the theologian of religious liberty, as a Council *peritus* (expert).[17] Ecclesiastical historian James Hennesey has remarked, "The principal
national figure among the bishops until his death in 1967 was Archbishop Spellman of New York, close personal associate of Pius XII
. . . and friend of Presidents from Roosevelt to Johnson."[18]

Within New York City, the archbishop's residence had long been
called "the Powerhouse." In the previous century a cooperative as-

sociation had been established with New York political machines. "McCloskey [Hughes's successor and the first American cardinal] and McCloskey's successor, Michael A. Corrigan, were symbols of another lasting pattern—association with Irish political machines."[19] Hughes himself reacted to the nativist burning of Catholic institutions in Philadelphia by stationing in New York churches "an armed force of one or two thousand men 'resolved, after taking as many lives as they could in the defense of their property, to give up, if necessary, their own lives for the same cause.' "[20] Hughes also warned public officials that if a single Catholic church was burned in New York, the city would become a "second Moscow," referring to the devastation that greeted Napoleon in 1812. New York Protestant elites then found ways to control their more zealous brethren.[21] Irish or Irish-Americans (Hughes, John McCloskey, Corrigan, John Farley, Patrick Hayes, and Spellman) presided over the diocese of New York during the entire period 1838-1967.

The other great example of collaboration between Irish ecclesiastics and Irish political machines was Boston, especially under the ecclesiastical rule of the Rome-educated Archbishop and later Cardinal O'Connell (1907-1944). Boston's Mayor James Michael Curley, New York's Boss Thurlow Tweed, and Chicago's Mayor Richard Daley have secured places in history as symbols of Irish-American ward power. The Kennedys came to prominence in this system which also flourished in other Catholic immigrant cities like San Francisco, Jersey City and Kansas City. However, it was indicative of the changing patterns in American politics that Cardinal Spellman did not pass on the same type of local political power to his successor, Terrence Cooke, the son of an Irish immigrant chauffeur and tile layer. Nathan Glazer and Daniel Moynihan, describing the situation, state that, "Spellman was feared, disliked, and heeded. It went on too long by half. His successor, whom he had chosen (having first, some said, laid it down to Rome that either he would be permitted personally to pick the next man or he would refuse to die), seemed almost to sense this and promptly assumed a posture much more in keeping with reality." Indeed, according to Glazer and Moynihan, the Jews ousted the Catholics from New York city government in the 1960s by a "brilliant outflanking maneuver involving the black masses of the city, which combined in inextricable detail elements of pure charity, enlightened self-interest, and plain ethnic combativeness." In this, they were abetted by "the failure of the Italians to make a larger impact on the city scene."[22]

With regard to international and national politics during the period 1838-1967, American Catholic prelates expressed strong nationalism at home and undertook patriotic missions abroad. Despite the paucity of enthusiasm for abolition among Catholic hierarchy or laity at the time of the Civil War, Archbishop Hughes flew the national flag from his cathedral, encouraged Catholics to fight for the North, and joined Tammany Boss Tweed on an unofficial diplomatic mission to Paris to explain the Union cause to Napoleon III. In Rome Hughes met with a chilly reception from the Vatican Secretariat of State which had proclaimed Rome's neutrality. Hughes's frustration with the lack of European support for the Union shows in his report to the American secretary of state to whom he complained, "There is no love for the United States on the other side of the water."[23]

Leading American prelates repeatedly took Washington's side against papal policy in international political events. At the time of the Spanish-American War, Archbishop John Ireland, asked by the Vatican to intercede for Catholic Spain, finally joined all the other bishops except John Lancaster Spalding in supporting American imperialist expansion. American Catholicism with its strong Irish and German traditions had plenty of reasons to stay neutral in World War I, or even to support the Central Powers. However, the assembled American bishops, led by Cardinal James Gibbons of Baltimore, enthusiastically promoted the war. Only four Catholic conscientious objectors surfaced out of a national total of 3,989, and a survey in 1917-1918 could identify no priest or bishop as a pacifist. Over one million Catholics (in a ratio significantly in excess of its proportion in the population) served in the armed forces. Gibbons became honorary chairman of the "League of National Unity," an organization dedicated to prosecuting the war to the finish. Gibbons also moved slowly on presenting papal peace initiatives to Washington because he knew Woodrow Wilson remained unfriendly to Catholic interests.[24]

Franklin Roosevelt became much more friendly to the papacy, a link established by Spellman after he returned to the United States in 1932 from a seven-year tour in the Vatican Secretariat of State. Spellman led American Catholic support of World War II, both as archbishop of New York (from 1939) and as military vicar of the American armed forces. Dorothy Dohen documents Spellman's unthinking "fusion of the themes of Catholicism and Americanism" in speeches and poems like "Magnificat of America."[25] In his capacity as military vicar Spellman began his yearly Christmas visits to the

American troops overseas. Spellman also conducted several diplomatic missions for Roosevelt.

Democrat Roosevelt, unlike Republican predecessors, relied on the Catholic vote for his party's victories in the industrialized state of the East and Midwest. Leo XIII's *Rerum novarum* had provided the American episcopate with the splendid political-religious opportunity to support an anticommunist labor movement that would both benefit their immigrant laity and avoid the Catholic "loss of the working class" that had generally occurred in all of Europe except the Netherlands. Indeed, in 1887, Archbishops Gibbons, Ireland, and Keane had drafted a warning to the Vatican against condemning the American Knights of Labor (founded by a Catholic with a majority Catholic membership) as the Vatican had the Canadian branch the preceding year. This episcopal strategy did not result in a strong direct clerical influence on labor politics, but rather in "the nice harmony between the firm anti-socialist bias of late 19th-century Catholic teaching . . . and the upwardly mobile aspirations of immigrant Catholics, who saw themselves as incipient capitalists, not as members of a proletariat."[26] Besides, the Knights of Labor declined after the Haymarket Square troubles, and were replaced by the American Federation of Labor, whose large Catholic membership was headed by the English-born Jew Samuel Gompers. The labor movement remained nonsectarian, but through it Catholic immigrants were saved for the church, the Democratic party, and the New Deal all at the same time. Of the twelve very controversial social proposals advanced in the 1919 Bishops' Program (written by priest-social theorist John A. Ryan), all but one was adopted by Franklin Delano Roosevelt. At the time of the New Deal, Ryan himself wrote, "Never before in our history have the policies of the federal government embodied so much legislation that is of a highly ethical order."[27]

Spellman's grandparents came from the Irish counties of Tipperary, Limerick, Cork, and Carlow, respectively. His grocer father seemed the very personification of the Irish small businessman described in Chapter 1.[28] Irish episcopal influence can also be seen by comparing the ancestry of the American bishops in 1886: 35 Irish, 15 German, 11 French, 5 English, and one each Dutch, Scotch, and Spanish. Hennesey calls it a "hibernarchy," and also remarks that these Irish had come to America too soon for the Gaelic revival in their own country, leaving the American church with a particularly "narrow, moralistic and bland" variety of Irish Catholicism.[29] German Catholics also benefited from the political advantages of early immigration and pressed to keep their own culture and language. However, the cloud of suspicion surrounding pan-Germanism before, during, and after World War I thwarted these efforts. Quarrels over church property and ecclesiastical jurisdiction among Polish immigrants produced the only sizable and enduring schism in 1907. The Polish National Catholic Church still claims 250,000 believers in the East and Midwest.

As time went by a Roman education became more and more important for clerical advancement. When Cardinal Gibbons was succeeded by the Irish-born and Roman-educated Michael J. Curley in 1921, three of America's four cardinals had been educated and ordained in Rome. One had even served as the rector of the American College in Rome for six years. When faced with the opposition of American-educated Archbishop Dowling of St. Paul, Cardinal O'-Connell of Boston brushed aside the archbishop's opinion with, "To know the Catholic Church and to have those Catholic traditions that enable one to keep the faith intact, one must have been to Rome: have had international experience."[30] The prelates and their clergy transferred their predilection for things Roman to the "fully Roman" and "fully American" Catholic culture of the first half of the twentieth century. Catholic immigrants and their descendants gloried in the "rich Roman life" whose triumphant certitude was unavailable even to the discriminatory Protestant elites educated at Harvard and Yale.

In Rome, the bright and ambitious sons of small businessmen, clerks, salesmen, foremen, and minor executives (5 percent of the fathers of American bishops in 1957 were college graduates) cultivated *romanità* and compiled long lists of church graduate degrees. Roman graduate education offered a literal moralism best exemplified by the promulgation of the Universal Code of Canon Law in 1918. Such a Roman orientation reinforced the anti-intellectual Irish moralism described in Chapter 1. Cardinal Spellman's fervid denunciation of the otherwise eminently forgettable film *Baby Doll* from the pulpit of St. Patrick's Cathedral remains only the most controversial public event in an active moral tradition which produced the Legion of Decency to monitor the movie industry. In 1983 nearly 100 Catholic bishops wrote President Reagan asking that he appoint a federal coordinator to monitor the enforcement of obscenity laws.[31]

In addition to this moralism, Vatican reaction to the putative heresies of Americanism (Leo XIII's encyclical *Testem benevolentiae* in 1899) and European Modernism greatly discouraged independent thinking within American Catholicism. Catholic universities trained the sons of immigrants for professional leadership. They read French philosophers like Jacques Maritain and English novelists like Graham Greene.[32] American Catholic historian John Tracy Ellis attacked this American Catholic anti-intellectualism in a famous article in *Thought* in 1955, which stirred enormous controversy.[33] Gustav Weigel, Thomas O'Dea, and Walter Ong soon joined the crusade, but without noticeable effect on the American hierarchy. Finally, in 1967 twenty-six Catholic educators representing major Catholic universities met at Land O' Lakes (Wisconsin) and issued what has been called the "declaration of independence"[34] of Catholic universities from the American hierarchy.

Moralistic anticommunist piety fostered by autocratic ecclesiastical institutions contributed to the dark side of American Catholic nationalism, the tendency of American Catholics to be "uncomfortably comfortable with authoritarian solutions to the world's problems."[35] From the anti-Semitic radio priest of the 1930s, Charles Coughlin, to the anticommunist ravings of Senator Joseph McCarthy, many Catholics seemed susceptible to rightist demagogues. Mayor Curley termed Boston "the strongest Coughlinite city in America," even though Cardinal O'Connell could not stand the Detroit priest. Senator Joe McCarthy retained his political strength in Massachusetts. On McCarthy the Kennedy family showed more "profile" than "courage."[36] Diocesan newspapers, the *Brooklyn Tablet* and *The Tidings* (Los Angeles), led Catholic support for Senator McCarthy, though other Catholic periodicals and newspapers attacked him. Cardinals Cushing (Boston) and Spellman avoided a specific position, although the latter's appearance with McCarthy at a New York police department breakfast in April 1954 was widely interpreted as tacit approval.

World War II finally proved the patriotism of American Catholics to the nation at large. After the war the G.I. Bill provided many Catholic ex-servicemen with the opportunity to be the first college graduates in their families. Many thousands of these young Catholics left the decaying city neighborhoods they had grown up in, and by the 1950s suburban Catholicism had become a major force in the American church. It was a new kind of Catholicism for any country—young, well-educated, ambitious, uncertain in the new environment, experimental, child-centered, and unprecedentedly affluent. Church attendance increased after World War II. Seminaries thrived. The novitiate classes of the religious communities grew so large that the more popular orders planned new facilities to take care of the influx of recruits. The American euphoria of the Eisenhower and Kennedy years was matched by the euphoria of Catholics of European descent as full partners in the "American way." Not only had Catholics been accepted by their fellow citizens, but they, in turn, voted for the Republican incumbant "Ike" in 1956, as they later voted for Republican incumbants Nixon (1972) and Reagan (1984). In the election of 1960 they gave Harvard-educated Irish Catholic war hero John Fitzgerald Kennedy the more than 80 percent of their votes that he, with the timely assistance of Mayor Daley's Chicago machine, needed to eke out a victory over Ike's heir apparent, the tight WASP Richard Nixon.[37] American Catholics also experienced a greater acceptance from their fellow believers in other countries. The universal church at Vatican II was renewing itself and coming closer to American principles and concerns. In all of this American Catholic euphoria, however, neither the church nor the nation could foresee the confusion and the troubles at the end of the decade.

THE LIBERAL DEMOCRATIC AND RADICAL TRADITIONS IN AMERICAN CATHOLICISM

Despite the predominance of American Catholic nationalism within the American Catholic Church during the period 1838-1967, the United States church maintained minority liberal democratic and radical traditions. John Carroll (1735-1815), the first bishop of Baltimore, was the first major figure in the American Catholic liberal democratic tradition. Liberal democratic values were manifest in the articulate dissent which eminated from the New York priests who opposed parochial schools and contributions to defend the Papal States, and from the brilliant convert intellectual, Orestes A. Brownson. However, such critical Catholic thinkers formed a distinct minority, and they received no support from the universal church. Vatican Council I focused on nineteenth-century European concerns. Not only did Europeans make up the great majority of the bishops attending, but the American ecclesiastics had little to contribute on questions of the Enlightenment, continental liberalism, or the *risorgimento*. The Council's definition of papal infallibility would cause some political problems in Protestant America, but in the end only Americans Peter Kenrick, Augustin Verot, and Michael Domenec joined fifty-two other bishops in leaving Rome before the vote to protest.[38]

In Chapter 1, I alluded to two traditions in nineteenth-century Irish Catholicism. Of these, the middle-class tradition contributed its secure moralistic piety to American Catholic nationalism while the tradition of the revolutionary poor fostered radicalism among American Catholics. Since the beginning of Irish immigration, groups like the Fenians and the I.R.A. have collected substantial sums of money from pubs in Boston, New York, San Francisco, and other Irish-Democratic cities. In 1866 eight hundred Irish-American members of the secret Fenian Brotherhood invaded Canada before being defeated by the Canadian militia and cut off by the American army. Bishop Fenwick of Boston reacted as the Irish bishops did by denying Fenians the sacraments. Rome condemned the movement for its secret oath in 1870.

This Irish revolutionary spirit spilled over into the American radical tradition during the latter half of the nineteenth and early twentieth centuries. According to Benjamin Gitlow, "the American Communist movement owes a great deal to the Irish and Irish-American radicals. . . . From the Irish contingent the Communists got organizers, writers, editors, speakers, trade union leaders."[39] Catholics associated with the American Left were the eloquent priest-socialists Thomas McGrady and Thomas Hagerty, suffragists Mary K. O'Sullivan, Teresa Crowley, Margaret Foley, Evelyn Scanlan, and labor agitator Mary Harris ("Mother") Jones, whose brother was a well-known Canadian priest. Jones had an especially acerbic tongue for the bishops, priests, and nuns "owned body and soul by the Rockefeller interests," but she was buried from a Washington church in a funeral mass she herself had planned. The president of the AFL and the secretary of labor led the official mourners.

During the early years of the Depression all sectors of the church seemed unified in their support for labor, parts of the New Deal, and the bishops' social statements. When convert Dorothy Day, inspired by the itinerant French peasant-philosopher Peter Maurin, founded the Catholic Worker Movement in 1933, most observers saw the movement as part of contemporary Catholic social action. Dorothy Day joined 130 other prominent Catholics in signing the National Catholic Welfare Conference's proclamation *Organized Social Justice* in 1935 as the high point of this "Catholic version of the popular front."[40] Only gradually did it become apparent that Day had founded a genuinely radical Catholic movement. The first issue of the *Catholic Worker*[41] went on sale on May Day 1933. Day had been active in American radical movements before her conversion, but Maurin introduced her to the richness of European Catholic social thought. Other European sources were also significant influences: Emmanuel Mounier's *L'Esprit*, British distributism, and the Russians Fyodor Dostoyevsky and Nikolai Berdyaev. All were examined for their usefulness in the American context as worker houses became the focal point for discussions among Catholic social activists. Despite her many frustrations with the institutional church, Day maintained her communication with the hierarchy, stating that "one must live in a state of permanent dissatisfaction with the Church."[42]

The issue of pacifism during World War II demonstrated how radical the movement would remain. In June 1938 the Chicago Catholic Worker House led by a young unemployed Irishman, John Cogley, began publishing the *Chicago Catholic Worker*, which followed Day's emphasis on religion and poverty but reflected the closer ties to labor and the more liberal atmosphere of the Chicago archdiocese. By early 1940 the question of pacifism was splitting the movement, with the New York and Chicago houses forming the two poles of opposition. In August Day brought the matter to a head by insisting that all houses distribute the New York *Catholic Worker* or leave the movement. John Cogley left. After returning from service in the American forces, Cogley became editor of *Commonweal* and adviser to John Kennedy on religious issues. Cogley prepared Kennedy for his famous appearance before the Greater Houston Ministerial Association on September 12.[43] Other liberals trained in Day's radical movement, like John Cort (Association of Catholic Trade Unionists) and Ed Marciniak (Catholic Labor Association), became closely tied to liberal union activism. The most influential of the Catholic Worker "graduates," however, is ex-*Catholic Worker* editor and Socialist, Michael Harrington, whose *The Other America* (1962) greatly influenced Lyndon Johnson's War on Poverty.[44]

During World War II the Catholic Worker Movement became nearly the sole church support for Catholic conscientious objectors. One writer remarks, "Given the magnitude of the internal crisis and the altered social circumstances during and after the war, it is remarkable that the Catholic Worker survived at all; yet Day and her most ardent followers continued with the movement and the paper without fundamental changes."[45] After the war scholars like Gordon Zahn and Catholic Worker activists like Robert Ludlow developed a more systematic Catholic position on peace. Then came Ammon Hennacy who led Catholic Workers in picketing the compulsory air raid alerts from 1953 until the first massive protests in 1960. Finally, in the 1960s as in the 1930s the Catholic Worker movement became a focal point in American Catholicism. Dorothy Day and her radicals had kept the faith in the meantime.

In the 1960s Day perceived her principal problem to be retaining the Catholic principles of the movement with the large influx of new members. In 1962, in what thereafter became known as the "Dorothy Day stomp," Dorothy cleansed a Catholic Worker apartment of those advocating the "new sexual freedom."

The Catholic peace movement as a whole proved even more difficult to sort out. Day along with Thomas Merton and others had been one of the original sponsors of the American chapter of PAX, founded in 1962 on the model of this English peace group. In September 1965 Day joined other peace lobbyists like Jim Douglass and Gordon Zahn at the last session of the Vatican Council in an attempt to get a strong peace statement which would include support for conscientious objection, the Gospel concept of nonviolence, and a ban on nuclear weapons. She and nineteen other women participated in a fast during the first ten days of October. PAX lobbying helped ensure the passage of a statement proposed by a Swedish bishop, but actually written by Douglass, which condemned "any act of war aimed at the indiscriminate destruction of entire cities and their inhabitants." This compromise statement prevailed over the "hawkish" alternative supported by Spellman, and the "dovish" alternative supported by Cardinal Joseph Ritter of St. Louis. The American chapter of PAX became the American chapter of Pax Christi in 1972.

When Day returned home, she faced an immediate crisis. At 5:20 a.m. on November 8, 1965, Roger La Porte, a former Trappist novice who had worked at the New York Catholic Worker house for only a few months, torched himself on the steps of the United Nations to protest the war. Later, in the ambulance, he declared, "I am a Catholic Worker." Day deplored the event, but even friends like Trappist Thomas Merton, whom Day had influenced with regard to social issues, wrote to protest Catholic Worker association with the burning. Liberal columnist John Leo of the *National Catholic Reporter* commented that the Catholic Worker movement had "never been well-grounded intellectually."[46]

Many young Catholics, however, wanted to move past the lobbying of PAX to direct political action. The Catholic Peace Fellowship (CPF) coalesced in 1965 around the Berrigan brothers and Catholic Workers like Jim Forest, Tom Cornell, Bill Gilliam, Mike Cullen, and David Miller (the first American to go to prison for burning his draft card).[47] Initially, the group focused on providing support for Catholic conscientious objectors, but in time they moved on to symbolic actions at Catonsville, Milwaukee, and other places. Daniel Berrigan became the great hero of this group and the special object of the wrath of J. Edgar Hoover. An F.B.I. posse posing as birdwatchers backed up by a Coast Guard vessel finally captured "the holy outlaw" in August 1970 after two months of hiding interspersed with public appearances. Berrigan's poetry and his play *Trial of the Catonsville Nine* became powerful publicity for the peace movement. In 1965 Berrigan had also joined Rabbi Abraham Heschel, Richard Neuhaus, and John Bennett, president of Union Theological Seminary, to form Clergy and Laymen Concerned about Vietnam (CALC).[48]

Dorothy Day and Daniel Berrigan took different perspectives on the case of Jim Forest. Jim Forest was a Catholic Worker who had become head of the Catholic Peace Fellowship. When Forest decided his first marriage had been a mistake and began another involvement, Day wrote to him urging him to remain faithful to his marriage or to remove her name as a sponsor of the Catholic Peace Fellowship while Forest remained head. Forest sent the letter to both Merton and Berrigan. Berrigan wrote Day, "after witnessing the suffering of so many victims, that in this aspect at least, we have departed from the spirit and compassion of Christ [if we judge Forest]." Merton termed the problem a "terribly difficult" one which reminded him of his own "attempt to resign when Roger [La Porte] burned himself."[49] Despite their differences, Day, Berrigan, Merton, and Forest all remained close friends, and all remained committed to the peace movement. The debate over Vietnam among American Catholics, however, exhibited a special bitterness, even in this contentious period.

AMERICAN CATHOLIC POLITICS

Throughout its development American Catholicism benefited from a strong national tradition which was absent in, for example, the disparate regional development of the South African Church. The American Catholic Church had a significant national tradition before the worldwide founding of national episcopal conferences following the Second Vatican Council. The American clergy had met together in 1788 to elect their first superior (John Carroll), to decide whether he would be a bishop or a vicar apostolic (bishop), and to determine the location of his diocese (Baltimore). The United

States church held plenary sessions of all its bishops in Baltimore in 1852, 1866, and 1884. The last session approved the *Baltimore Catechism*, which, in various revised editions, remained normative for the entire country until 1941 and influential for millions of parochial school students well into the 1960s. From 1890 the bishops had an annual gathering which served for unofficial consultation, but it was not until 1917 that the National Catholic War Council (NCWC) came into being to coordinate the church's patriotic efforts. The Vatican bureaucracy sensed that such a national body might constitute an organizational rival tainted with the dreaded "Americanism," but lobbying in Rome led by Bishop Joseph Schrembs of Cleveland saved the NCWC from curial demolition. In 1922 Pius XI authorized its dissolution but rescinded the decree four months later.[50] Then the NCWC became the National Catholic Welfare Council, or to ecclesiastical wags, "Nothing Counts West of Chicago." The prelates of the major (eastern and midwestern) dioceses continued to dominate the American church since membership in the NCWC remained voluntary and the organization could not legislate for its members.

Following Vatican II the NCWC split into the National Conference of Catholic Bishops (NCCB) and the United States Catholic Conference (USCC). Cardinal Dearden of Detroit, who led the establishment of these new bodies, became the first president of the NCCB (1966-1971). He was succeeded by Cardinal Krol (1971-1974), Archbishop Bernardin (1974-1977), Archbishop Quinn (1977-1980), Archbishop Roach (1980-1983), and Bishop James Malone (1983-).[51] While influence is always sensitive to both personal charisma and the topic at issue, the institutional and public influence of individual bishops derives from both NCCB offices and tenure in major sees. An analyst discussing the most influential American bishops at the time of the 1984 presidential campaign would probably have included at least nine bishops under three categories: 1) Malone as NCCB president; 2) Bernardin (Chicago), Hickey (Washington, D.C.), Krol (Philadelphia), John May (St. Louis), Quinn (San Francisco), and Roach (Minneapolis) for both past NCCB offices and major sees; 3) O'Connor (New York) and Bernard Law (Boston) as having recently been appointed to one of the country's five most important sees. Roger Mahoney (Los Angeles) has since joined the latter group.

USCC political and social policy has combined very liberal positions on international affairs and domestic social policy with conservative concerns about family morality and parochial schools. The

USCC has publicly backed full employment, national health insurance, total unconditional amnesty for Vietnam war resisters, and a federal firearms-control act. It has decried Reagan's budget cuts, military aid to El Salvador, capital punishment, apartheid, and the abuse of human rights in South Korea, Brazil, and Chile. The bishops' foreign policy for the 1970s and 1980s was prefigured in November 1971 when the NCCB, after years of support and hedging, finally condemned continued American military operations in Southeast Asia:

At this point in history it seems clear to us that whatever good we hope to achieve through continued involvement in this war is now outweighed by the destruction of human life and of moral values which it inflicts. It is our firm conviction, therefore, that the speedy ending of this war is a moral imperative of the highest priority. Hence, we feel an obligation to appeal urgently to our nation's leaders and indeed to leaders of all the nations involved in this tragic conflict to bring the war to an end with no further delay.[52]

The statement came so long after other religious bodies and members of the Catholic laity had condemned the war that its tardiness embarrassed the Catholic bishops, but it nevertheless constituted a revolutionary repudiation of American Catholic nationalism, coming four years after the death of Cardinal Spellman. The NCCB's international orientation dates from the 1970s, but contemporary episcopal social policy has strong links to the Bishops' Program of 1919 and the New Deal. Such policy has become more controversial for the laity, however, as they have risen socioeconomically and begun to vote Republican in larger numbers.

The two major conservative issues for the hierarchy continue to be abortion and aid to parochial schools. The hierarchy has maintained a strong position on abortion, and the Supreme Court's decision of 1973 was bitterly received. The great majority of the Catholic laity, however, would permit abortion in the case of danger to the mother's life, rape, or where the fetus is severely defective. They oppose it for reasons of economic distress or personal happiness.[53] In June 1981 a Gallup poll reported an almost even split among American voters (45 percent in favor, 46 percent opposed) on the Supreme Court's ruling that permits a woman to obtain an abortion during the first three months of pregnancy. Protestant evangelicals (30-60) and Catholics (37-56) opposed, while non-evangelicals favored the ruling (51-41).[54]

On the school issue, Irish-American Democratic Senator Patrick

Moynihan of New York charged in a 1978 letter circulated to the American hierarchy that Senate opposition to tuition tax credits for parents with children in nonpublic schools reflected an anti-Catholicism which is the "one form of bigotry which liberalism curiously seems to tolerate."[55] After the great declines in Catholic school enrollment in the 1960s and early 1970s, "the Catholic school system has survived the crisis better than expected, with enrollment increasing in many places, mostly because of an influx of black and Hispanic students who do extremely well in these schools."[56] Cardinal Terence Cooke "made a difference in Harlem" by establishing the archdiocesan tax system which, over a period of five years, redistributed $12 million from all of his parishes to mostly inner-city parishes with schools. Detroit's Edmund Szoka and many others have made the same kind of financial transfers from suburban to inner city parishes with schools.[57]

Cardinal Bernardin has sought to introduce "moral consistency" to Catholic political positions by stressing the "sanctity of life" involved in the issues of nuclear weapons, abortion, and capital punishment. In his Fordham address on the "seamless garment" of all Catholic moral issues, Bernardin even included episcopal opposition to Reagan Administration policy toward Central America. Bernardin succeeded Cooke as president of the Bishops' Pro-Life Committee, and has tried to steer that organization to broader concerns than just abortion.[58] Archbishop Roach made similar pleas to combine all pro-life issues while president of the NCCB.

The issues of abortion and religious in public office combined to present Archbishop Szoka with a dilemma in 1983, when Governor James Blanchard of Michigan appointed Sister Agnes Mansour director of the Department of Social Services. Szoka objected to Mansour's accepting the appointment unless she publicly repudiated the department's financing of abortions for poor women. Mansour, who said she was personally opposed to abortion, would not endorse denying abortions to poor women when it was available by law to all. The Vatican supported Szoka, and Mansour resigned from the Sisters of Mercy.[59] Mansour's case was foreshadowed in 1980 when the Vatican withdrew its ten-year exemption for Jesuit Father Robert Drinan to represent Massachusetts in the United States House of Representatives. Drinan's votes for abortion funding seem to have influenced Rome's position on the case.[60] Drinan has since become president of the Americans for Democratic Action and remains active politically. In May 1984 Arlene Violet, a forty-year-old lawyer for the handicapped, resigned from the Sisters of Mercy to run again for attorney general of Rhode Island.[61]

As we have shown, the political and ecclesiastical views of the American Catholic hierarchy have undergone significant changes since World War II. At the same time the American political system has been evolving at a rapid rate. Scholars have pointed to the pervasive individualism of all sectors of American society, and analysts from all political perspectives have expressed concern about the breakdown of "mediating institutions" like the family, unions, and churches.[62] Some have called for the recovery of the insights of the older biblical and Republican traditions that gave context to the individual. Mainline Protestantism has traditionally functioned as the historical center of American political and moral consciousness, but during the postwar period, especially the 1960s, American mainline Protestantism has suffered in a disproportionate degree from the middle-class malaise and "cultural aphasia."[63]

Political scientists have long pointed to the weakening of political "mediating institutions," especially the American political party system. As early as August 1950, a special committee on political parties of the American Political Science Association (APSA) issued a report calling for the general strengthening of American political parties. The report stressed the role that parties play in meeting the public need "for more effective formulation of general policies and programs and for better integration of all the far-flung activities of modern government."[64] This unprecedented attempt of the APSA to halt history had little effect, and American political parties have lost even more power since 1950.

The weakening of political parties has furthered the atomization of the American public and resulted in at least two modern electoral trends, the influence of the media and single-issue politics. In the absence of a party tradition and organization, each candidate must reach each voter with at least his name and some favorable connotation such as "peace" or "prosperity" so that the voter will recognize and choose the candidate's name on election day. Extensive use of the media, especially television, has become absolutely essential for victory in state and national offices. Media exposure is very expensive, resulting in skyrocketing campaign costs. Dependence on media and enormous budgets is greatest in the most populous states, with California and New York, centers of the American media, considerably in advance of the rest of the nation.

The weakening of political parties has also led to single-issue politics. More and more voters are coming to the polls because they care about a single issue such as abortion or gun control, and voting the entire slate (or failing to vote on particular candidates or issues) on the basis of that question. Single-issue voting is encouraged by professional groups like Physicians for Social Responsibility (PSR) and mass organizations like the National Rifle Association (NRA) that are filling the void left by the demise of the parties at the grass roots level. Abortion remains the best example of the clout of a single issue in American Catholic politics. Thus cultural individualism and a fragmenting party system reenforce each other.

Catholicism, with its traditional emphasis on "church" in both ideology and organization, would seem to be an obvious source of encouragement for a national consensus. An American Catholic contribution to national consensus, however, would demand a prior unity within the church itself, and the major attempt at organizational experimentation in the 1970s had polarized the participants. The NCCB decided to hold a national consultation of clergy and laity in Detroit, October 20-23, 1976, patterned after similar convocations held in 1893 and 1899. Cardinal John Dearden of Detroit was host and chairman, with the USCC under Bishop James Rausch in charge of organizing this "Call to Action." The original aim was to seek representation from all sectors of the church, but, even before the meeting, priest-sociologist Andrew Greeley attacked the final preparatory booklet *Liberty and Justice for All* as "a shabby, shameful, and disgraceful attack on the American people" and "a product of the liberal wing of the American hierarchy."[65] Nevertheless, conservative Cardinal Krol[66] brought a full delegation from Philadelphia and participated actively, "not diminishing for one moment his no-nonsense style." Conservative George Kelly commented that, "Not only were the majority of items proposed relevant to social justice and compatible with 'the teaching of the church, its laws and discipline,' but also they demanded merely the outpouring of fresh determination and organized effort by Catholics."[67] Kelly faults the bishops for not keeping certain controversial issues off the agenda. The 1,350 delegates (nuns and priests constituted 40 percent) ignored episcopal counsels of moderation and adopted resolutions calling for the open election of bishops and priests, married priests, women priests, acceptance of divorce and artificial contraception, equal rights for homosexuals, unilateral nuclear disarmament, a total ban of U.S. arms sales abroad, and divestiture of episcopal "wealth." Such a program split the consultation, but the response of the bishops the following May was mild. They turned over all 182 resolutions to various committees with the exception of

those on celibacy, women priests, birth control, and homosexuality, which they let die. The bishops also set up a committee to monitor compliance with their own five-year (1978-1983) Call to Action
program, "To Do the Work of Justice," but three years later this
committee reported little progress.

Despite a growth in numbers and societal position, an increasingly privatized and secularized Catholicism would still lose political clout in industrialized democracies. In attempting to gauge the
contemporary Catholic impact on the American political system,
Mary Hanna uses Truman's three criteria of strategic position in society, the internal characteristic of the group, and the operating
structure of governmental institutions. First, as Catholic immigrants have progressed socioeconomically, they have also come to
occupy important political posts. In 1986, Catholics constituted the
largest religious group in the House of Representatives and held
important positions, including the Speakership. About three-
fourths of the 122 House Catholics were Democrats. Catholics
formed the second largest religious group (19 Catholics to 21 Epis-
copalians) in the Senate but held few key positions because of generally low seniority. There were 11 Catholic Democratic Senators
led by Edward Kennedy, and 8 Catholic Republican Senators led by
ex-P.O.W. Jeremiah Denton, Reagan confidant Paul Laxalt, and
Budget Chairman Peter Domenici. Ideologically, Senate Catholics
were similar to House Catholics in that Catholic Republicans were
slightly less conservative (based on ACU and ADA profiles) than
fellow non-Catholics, and Catholic Democrats were more liberal
than their fellows.[68] The data are what one would expect of a religious group on its way up in society.

Such numbers, however, do not guarantee unified influence
since Catholic politicians emphasize different aspects of their faith
or deemphasize the specifically Catholic in their campaigns and
tenure in office—"the John Kennedy effect." Hanna shows that
Catholics have often been successful in lobbying for concrete benefits, especially at the local and state level, but have achieved mixed
results on societal values like ethnic heritage, abortion, and social
justice. In addition, she terms Catholic thought on influencing or
changing political institutions as rather "underdeveloped."[69] With
regard to the third criterion of the operating structure of governmental institutions, Hanna emphasizes the force of the American
rules of the game which encourage separation of church and state
and discourage interest group activity, thus limiting Catholic influence.

Previous Catholic orientations do survive in stands on political and social issues, races for the House of Representatives, and, to a lesser extent, in presidential politics. Hanna's analysis stresses the continuity of the views of "White Catholics of European Descent" (WCED) on social and political issues. Though the number of Catholics calling themselves independents has increased, loyalty to the Democratic Party continues, and it is strongest among those who attend church at least monthly.[70] WCED have displayed a continuing economic liberalism greater than that of white Protestants, while challenging American Catholic nationalism by becoming more open to civil liberties and to the questioning of national military policies. This orientation shows itself more clearly in the composite figures for congressional races than in the presidential elections where personality is such a factor. Hanna concluded that American Catholics do operate as a religiously based ethnic political interest group. Despite heterogeneity of background, Catholics do exhibit a common political interest. Even in the case of the split between WCED and the Spanish-speaking, Catholics demonstrate many more similarities in religious, political, and social attitudes than black and white Protestants.[71]

Ethnic politics seems to have a strong future in states like California where high technology and massive immigration combine. The Congressional Research Bureau has predicted that by the year 2000 California will have more than twice as many representatives (50) as all other states except Texas (34) and Florida (28).[72] In geographical terms the Reagan election strategy has been to build on the "megastate" base of these three Sunbelt states while adding more of the 26 states (primarily in the South and West) that have gone Republican at least four out of five times between 1964 and 1984. In terms of target groups Reagan has brought together traditionally Republican upper-income White Protestants with middle-income blue-collar ethnic Catholics.

THE 1984 PRESIDENTIAL CAMPAIGN: CONFUSION IN THE EPISCOPAL RANKS

Catholics had supported Southern Baptist Jimmy Carter with less than their traditional enthusiasm for Democratic candidates in 1976, but Ronald Reagan became the first nonincumbant Republican to win a plurality of the Catholic vote (Reagan 49 percent, Carter 42 percent, Anderson 7 percent). Given the international and domestic political stands of the USCC during the 1970s, the new administration probably did not expect any great assistance from the bishops, despite the large number of conservative Catholics around Reagan. Nevertheless, the public impact of the bishops' peace pastoral shocked both the administration and conservative Catholics. As a result, both have devoted more time in seeking to influence succeeding episcopal statements. In the 1984 election Catholics were slightly less enthusiastic about Reagan than the general public.[73]

Candidate interest in Catholic constituencies surfaced early in the 1984 presidential campaign, as the votes of both WCED and Hispanics were perceived as crucial to victory. The Democrats chose Italian-American Mario Cuomo for the keynote address in San Francisco, and the Republicans chose the Hispanic Kathleen Ortega for their Dallas convention. Ortega's second virtue was that of being a woman, a partial response to archetypical WCED Geraldine Ferraro, if not to Cuomo's oratorical skill. The pious Irish-American, albeit not Catholic, Republican presidential candidate lost no time in embracing all things Catholic. He had last met with the pope at Anchorage in March 1984. In June he sought to capitalize on his Irish background by returning to the town of his ancestors. However, the Irish did not welcome the president as they had the pope five years earlier. When Reagan arrived at Shannon, the local bishop of Limerick did not attend the welcoming ceremony. Both the Irish Primate Tomas Ó'Fiaich and the archbishop of Dublin absented themselves from meeting the president. Bishop Eamonn Casey of Galway[74] openly criticized Reagan's policies, but it was left to Prime Minister Garret FitzGerald to deliver the firm message "that his people had formed strong emotional attachments to Central America through the work there of Irish missionaries and deeply desired that the nations of that region be allowed to develop without outside interference."[75]

Reagan's Catholic political forays at home were much more successful. In early September he attended the Polish-American festival in Doylestown, Pennsylvania, the site of the United States replica of the shrine at Częstochowa. The Polish-American Cardinal Krol, who had given the opening benediction at the Republican convention, praised Reagan for his "sustained effort to reduce and eliminate the ugly blotch of injustice and discrimination" caused by the failure to allow tuition tax credits for private schools.[76] The trip that really stirred Italian-American Democrat Cuomo's blood, however, was Reagan's visit to Hoboken, New Jersey. The *New York Times* photo shows the president helping himself to a plate of spaghetti at St. Ann's Church while Archbishop Peter L. Gerety looks on. Reagan enumerated all the areas in which his policies seemed to coincide with those of the Catholic Church:

We are for life and against abortion. We are for prayer in the schools, we are for tuition tax credits and, in Central America, we are rather more inclined to listen to the testimony of his holiness the Pope than the claims of the Communist Sandinistas.[77]

"It was the spaghetti and Sinatra and the robes that got to me," said Cuomo. "And I'd seen him before, standing in a circle of fundamentalists indicating that he had been born again and spouting morality."[78]

Cuomo decided to attack a statement made by Archbishop O'Connor of New York during a televised news conference the preceding June 24. O'Connor had said: "I don't see how a Catholic in good conscience can vote for a candidate who explicitly supports abortion." Cuomo, like Ferraro, personally opposes abortion but feels he must carry out the 1973 Supreme Court decision. Cuomo said that the archbishop's statement meant that "no Catholic can vote for Ed Koch, no Catholic can vote for Jay Goldin, for Carol Bellamy nor for Pat Moynihan or Mario Cuomo—anybody who disagrees with him on abortion." O'Connor replied that Cuomo had been "foolish" in misrepresenting the implications of his statement, saying that "it is neither my responsibility nor my desire to evaluate the qualifications of any individuals of any political party for any public office, or of any individual holding public office."[79] Cuomo commented that he was "pleased" with the archbishop's clarification. The lead photo of the August 25 *New York Times* shows O'Connor greeting Cuomo at the funeral of Albany Auxiliary Bishop Edward J. Maginn. The two men had met privately two days before.

On August 11, the USCC had issued a statement written by its president Bishop Malone that exhorted Catholics to "convince others of the rightness of our position" but to avoid taking positions "for or against political candidates." The statement also made a strong defense of the church's position on abortion. While it did not mention Cuomo, it did reject the notion that expressing one's private opposition to abortion satisfied morality.[80] Malone was articulating the sense of the NCCB statement of the preceding March that the bishops "did not seek the formulation of a religious voting bloc."

President Reagan highlighted the general debate on religion, morality, and politics during the Republican National Convention. Surrounded by his wife, Vice President Bush, and many evangelical

ministers, the president said that "politics and morality are inseparable, and as morality's foundation is religion, religion and politics
are necessarily related. We need religion as a guide." Reagan's remarks emphasized the major role evangelical ministers played at
the convention, from the content and tone of the platform to the
benediction delivered by the Reverend Jerry Falwell after Reagan's
nomination. In his convention speech Catholic Senator Paul Laxalt
scolded Cuomo: "I can't help but wonder what happened to the
once great Democratic Party when the Democratic Governor of
New York goes out of his way to attack the Catholic Archbishop of
New York. Shame on you Mario Cuomo. What would Al Smith
say?"[81] Indeed, Geraldine Ferraro was not accepted as a replacement for Mondale at the New York Archdiocese's Alfred E. Smith
Memorial Dinner in October. Archbishop O'Connor said he was
"perplexed" by the Democratic presidential candidate's decision to
skip the dinner, which Reagan was attending, but he denied that
Ferraro was being "snubbed." The dinner committee had refused
because its members incorrectly believed that substitutes had
never been allowed. Cuomo said that he was "disappointed that
she [Ferraro] didn't get the treatment that apparently Agnew [who
substituted for Nixon in 1972] did."[82]

On September 12 in Scranton, Geraldine Ferraro met a large contingent of anti-abortion protestors with a statement that her Catholic private opposition to abortion would not influence her actions
on public policy. These remarks were inserted into her speech after
her aides learned that Archbishop O'Connor's successor in Scranton, Bishop James C. Timlin, would give his first public news conference following her appearance. Timlin, who referred to Ferraro
as "Geraldine" throughout the half-hour news conference, called
her position on abortion "absurd," smacking of "secular humanism," and less acceptable to the Catholic Church than that of Republican George Bush.[83] On October 7 Catholics for a Free Choice
(CFCC), an independent Washington-based organization, placed
an advertisement in the *New York Times* which asserted that "there
is a mistaken belief in American society" that total condemnation of
abortion "is the only legitimate Catholic position." Twenty-four
nuns, two priests, and a religious brother were among the ninety-
seven signers.[84]

The hierarchical attack on the Cuomo-Ferraro position was led by
Archbishop O'Connor and Archbishop Law of Boston. On September 5, Law and seventeen other New England bishops issued a stat-
ment that termed "irresponsible" any attempt to keep abortion out

of the campaign "on the pretext that this is a matter of personal opinion and morality." Although the statement also named nuclear arms control an important concern, it added, "While nuclear holocaust is a future possibility, the holocaust of abortion is a present reality." When questioned, Law said he felt "there is a general commitment to arms control" by both parties, and that he did not find anything wrong with Reagan's comments linking religion and politics.[85] At the same news conference Law disclaimed any attempt "to be a political boss," but he felt restrained two weeks later to insist that the New England bishops' focus on abortion as the "main issue" was not a political strategy. In the latter interview he specifically criticized the position of Massachusetts Catholic Edward Kennedy along with his New York colleagues Cuomo and Ferraro.[86]

On September 9, O'Connor had charged that Ferraro had created a "misimpression" that "there are a variety of positions that can be held in consonance with Catholic teachings." The *New York Times* (September 10, 1984) front-page top right-hand headline read, "Archbishop Calls Ferraro Mistaken on Abortion Rule." O'Connor's October 15 news conference, in which he was joined by Mother Teresa (three-column photo), upstaged the NCCB President Malone's attempt to defuse some of the controversy. O'Connor's statement specifically criticized Cuomo's Notre Dame speech of September 14, but it did not designate abortion as the "main issue" of the campaign.[87] Cardinal Krol also issued a diocesan letter on abortion in October that served as the starting point for a question in the nationally televised Ferraro-Bush debate.

Bishop Malone's statement of October 15 reiterated the bishops' political neutrality and urged Catholic voters to consider *all* the life issues. Cardinal Bernardin of Chicago, president of the episcopal Pro-Life Committee, became the chief spokesperson for this "seamless garment" approach to Catholic issues. He did this in a September column for the Chicago archdiocesan newspaper and in a speech at Georgetown University on October 25. The column noted that the bishops "place special emphasis on abortion, on preventing nuclear war and reversing the arms race and on programs which meet the needs of the poor." The speech consciously used parallel language on abortion and the arms race. Instead of demanding that the church's position be immediately translated into legislation, Bernardin said: "I would not want a candidate for public office today to be complacent, passive or satisfied with the level or the dynamic of the arms race or the defense budget," and "I would want candidates who are willing to say, 'The fact of 1.5 million abortions a year is unacceptable, and I will work for a change in the public policy which encourages or permits this practice.' "[88] Pax Christi bishops felt on the defensive throughout the campaign. "It's almost been said that if you vote for the Democratic ticket, you're committing a serious sin," complained Bishop Leroy Matthiesen of Amarillo.[89] However, Bishop Thomas Gumbleton and other Christian and Jewish leaders did condemn "the ideology of a nuclear Armageddon" in a Washington news conference which turned into a debate with leaders of the religious right. President Reagan had used the term "Armageddon" several times during the previous four years in speaking to Christian groups.[90]

Democratic showings at the other levels of the political process, especially the prevention of an "ideological majority" of Republicans and Southern Democrats in the House of Representatives, limited the political effect of the 1984 Reagan landslide.[91] The Catholic bishops were perceived as supporting Reagan-Bush, but this probably hurt the Republican ticket with Catholics. In the Harris poll of September 21-25, 69 percent of the Catholics surveyed reacted negatively to Archbishop O'Connor's "urging Catholics to vote against candidates who are opposed to banning abortions."[92] Following Mondale's victory in the first debate, Harris reported the Catholic vote might go Democratic, partly because of Ferraro's presence on the ticket, and partly as a backlash against O'Connor and Falwell.[93] Reagan sealed his victory with the second debate, but he did not win because Law, O'Connor, and Krol delivered the Catholic vote as their predecessors in Boston, New York, and Philadelphia had at the turn of the century. Despite the Reagan effort, Hispanics remained solidly for Mondale (65-33), although not with the same consistency as blacks (90-9).

During the campaign Catholic liberals felt frustrated by the fact that the first draft of the episcopal letter on the economy, which they correctly surmised would be very critical of Reagan economic policy, was being held until after the election. Given the Catholic response to episcopal initiatives on abortion during the campaign, the strategy was probably helpful, even in the short run. In opening the post-election November 1984 meeting of the NCCB, Bishop Malone contrasted the bishops' united action on the peace pastoral with the episcopal confusion during the 1984 presidential campaign. The NCCB president called for cohesion behind the conference's "broad spectrum" of positions on nuclear arms, abortion, human rights and poverty. "We oppose a 'single issue' strategy," said Malone, "because only by addressing a broad spectrum of issues can we do justice to the moral tradition we possess as a church and thereby demonstrate the moral challenges we face as a nation."[94]

THE NORTH ATLANTIC CONNECTION: IRELAND, CANADA, AND THE UNITED STATES

The political gains of American Catholic nationalism, 1838-1967, become even more impressive when analyzed from the perspective of the differences in the traditional political cultures of the Catholic Church and the United States. American political style features neither "hierarchical discipline" nor "public unity," although American churches have a long tradition of political involvement. Catholic immigrants weathered five major waves of discrimination to become accepted as full patriots by the end of World War II. They participated fully in social and economic modernization as the backbone of the Roosevelt coalition. Despite despised beginnings, American Catholics now constitute a religious plurality whose institutional religious activity compares very favorably with most European Catholic Churches. The current educational background and quality of ecclesiastical leadership has improved markedly, although the precipitous decline in vocations during the last two decades will mean a less educated and/or missionary clergy unless adjustments are made in the recruiting pool.

When Anglo-American Catholicism is compared with churches in countries like France and Italy, the absence of a strong anticlerical tradition is immediately apparent. With the exception of Quebec, where a French-speaking clergy did dominate a predominantly agricultural society, Anglo-American Catholic immigrants have respected their bishops, priests, and nuns. This tradition of respect flows from the Irish experience of British Protestant persecution, which welded Irish nationalism with Irish faith. No amount of Irish ecclesiastical political dealings with the British government during the nineteenth century could shake clerical legitimacy in the hearts of the majority of the Irish people. In fact, the pious middle classes supported papal and episcopal excommunication of the radical Fenians. When Catholic immigrants arrived in the United States, their clergy shared their struggle to become full members of American society, especially in education and unionization.

Since the early 1970s the American Catholic Church, drawing on its previously alternative liberal democratic and radical traditions, has defined itself with a political and ecclesiastical outlook truly independent of the various European Catholic traditions. Demographic trends make the full partnership of Hispanic Catholics the most crucial ethnic issue.[95] In the case of both American Hispanics and Québécois, the minority group was present prior to the coming of the Anglo-Protestant government, speaks a different language, and has remained concentrated geographically. The traditional national support of both ethnic groups for the more liberal of the two major parties has been shaken by the elections of 1984. Both Reagan and Canadian Prime Minister Brian Mulroney have appealed to these groups on the basis of traditionally conservative social values.

Quebec's *Révolution Tranquille* (Quiet Revolution) did not begin with the victory of the provincial Liberals over the *Union nationale* in 1960, although the years 1960-1966 are usually specified as the years of that movement. Many analysts point to the 1950 formation of the magazine *Cité libre* by professors, journalists, and other professionals under the leadership of Gérard Pelletier and Pierre Elliot Trudeau as the origin of the *Révolution Tranquille*. In 1956 *Cité libre* press published *La Grève de l'amiante* (The Asbestos Strike), edited and introduced by Trudeau. In 400 pages a group of young authors from unions, the church, and academia analyzed the famous strike at Asbestos and Thetford Mines in 1949. Trudeau emphasized the gloomy, conservative, and authoritarian nature of Quebec's past, and other authors pointed to the progressive nature of the church's role. Archbishop Joseph Charbonneau of Montreal supported the strike against Quebec Premier Duplessis, and both sides asked Archbishop Maurice Roy of Quebec to mediate. Six months after the settlement Charbonneau left his archbishopric under suspicious circumstances, and many blamed Maurice Duplessis, who held the Quebec premiership, with the exception of the war years, from 1935 to his unexpected death in September 1959. The church seemed a full partner in Duplessis's regime of nationalistic conservatism and unparalleled personal patronage. Other clerical critiques followed *La Grève*. In 1956 an English Toronto paper published an internally circulated ecclesiastical document by Abbés Gérard Dion and Louis O'Neill which criticized the political morality of the Duplessis regime. Four years later the anonymous *Les Insolences du frère Untel* (The Impertinences of Brother Anonymous) denounced severe corruption in education and language. Duplessis had died in 1959, and the provincial Liberals defeated the *Union nationale* the following year. The *Confédération des travailleurs catholiques du Canada* (CTCC) became the *Confédération des syndicats nationaux* (CSN) in 1960. The stage was now set, according to the proponents of the

Quiet Revolution, for Quebec to move toward the secularized society of modern North America.[96]

What did happen was that along with the undeniable economic modernization and secularization of social forms was the incorporation of much of the past into "their so-called revolution. Religion, language, and the family, the traditional institutions of nationalism, became the property of the state. . . . They even appropriated the nation itself and did so quite noisily too. Quebec was not a province like the others and henceforth the state would speak for the nation."[97] However, other groups challenged the *état providence* of the liberals in its claim to speak for French Canadian nationalism. The *Union nationale* came back into power from 1966 to 1970 before disintegrating. The *Front de libération du Québec* (FLQ) espoused terrorist activity to free the "colonized" province from its English-speaking oppressors in Ottawa. Finally, René Lévesque and his *Parti québécois* (PQ) took power in the election of 1976. All this time church attendance and church recruitment declined as young people rejected a church that had been tied to the old corrupt ways of Duplessis. Canadian Catholicism brought particularly heavy historical baggage to the confusion of the Second Vatican Council and its subsequent reforms.

In 1963 Pierre Trudeau succeeded Lester Pierson as prime minister. This French intellectual and Jesuit graduate felt that expansion of French language rights was important, but that Quebec nationalism belonged with other characteristics of the province's reactionary past. As such, Trudeau fit the political needs of the national Liberals who traditionally joined overwhelming national support in Quebec with enough seats outside the province to attain power. Indeed, the Liberals had held power in Ottawa for 62 of the first 84 years of this century. The big sweep by Conservative John Diefenbaker in 1956 had been made easier by the support of Duplessis and his *Union nationale* machine. Trudeau could appeal to the rest of Canada to support French-language legislation as the price for keeping French-speakers like himself in control.

The defection of Quebec to the Conservatives in September 1984 signaled another rout of the Liberals. The Irish-Canadian Catholic Mulroney of Quebec led the Conservatives in winning 211 of 282 seats in parliament, including 58 of his own province's 75 seats. Although Mulroney is a native English speaker, his colloquial French impressed Quebec voters. From poor beginnings he had become a labor lawyer and a business executive. He graduated from St. Francis Xavier University in Antigonish and received his law degree from Laval University in Quebec City. Mulroney says he was influenced by St. Francis Xavier's pioneering work in cooperative movements and Third World development. His pledges to maintain Canada's extensive social service network place him much more to the center of the political spectrum than President Reagan in the United States. Mulroney's wife was born in Yugoslavia, tying him to the massive European postwar immigration to Canada, especially to Ontario. Catholics now make up 45 percent of the province. Over one-fourth of Ontario students are enrolled in Catholic schools. In June 1984 Ontario premier William Davis announced that he would press for funding of these schools equal to that provided to the public system.[98] While the immigrants have been mainly Italian,[99] Portuguese, and Spanish-speaking, older English-speaking Canadian Catholics tend to be Irish.

Quebec Premier René Lévesque and the PQ have continued to press for separatism, despite being defeated in a 1980 referendum on the issue. In the recent recession, however, the PQ has tried to allay the fears of the business community. Many businesses reacted to the 1976 election by transferring their headquarters to English-speaking areas. Quebec unemployment exceeded 13 percent in May 1984, and the provincial Liberals led the PQ 69 to 23 percent in a Sorecom opinion poll.[100] Party membership had dropped from 300,000 to 110,000 in the three years prior to Lévesque's resignation as head of the PQ on June 21, 1985. Another indication of the changed political environment was the reelection of Robert Bourassa as head of Quebec Liberal Party the previous year. Bourassa seems certain to become Quebec's premier in the next general parliamentary elections.

On his visit to Canada in September 1984 John Paul paid special tribute to the long history of the French-speaking Catholic Church in his address at the stadium of the University of Laval, founded by the church in Quebec City in 1852 and named after Canada's first bishop. The pope often evoked the motto of the province, *Je me souviens* (I remember). But Quebec Catholics no longer demonstrate the fervent piety of their ancestors. A recent *Montréal Gazette-Le Devoir* poll indicated that 38 percent attend mass regularly. The percentages disagreeing with official church positions on birth control, women's ordination, and abortion were 70, 60, and 42 percent, respectively.[101] The pope encouraged French-language rights not just in Quebec but also in Manitoba, where the issue remains much more controversial in that predominantly English-speaking province. John Paul, who received over 100 hours of television coverage during his twelve-day visit, urged his listeners to reject the attractions of a "perfect" technological society to care for the unemployed, Indians and Inuits (Eskimos), the handicapped, and the Third World.

The pope had delayed his visit until after Mulroney's election. American newsmen seeking to apply papal remarks to their own November election came up with mixed results. The emphasis on taking care of the poor and unemployed seemed to fit the Mondale campaign, while John Paul's call for state funding of church schools touched on a Reagan theme. The pope gave both speeches the same day, September 12, to fishermen at the Atlantic village of Flat Rock and to Catholic educators at the Basilica of St. John the Baptist in St. John's, Newfoundland. When the papal spokesperson Panciroli was asked about the education speech, he said that pope did not intend his words specifically for the United States, but for "all types of schools in any country in the world."[102]

In terms of the political significance of the Catholic Church to the North Atlantic Alliance, the most obvious fact is that Catholics constitute pluralities in the United States, Canada, West Germany, and the Netherlands. Catholic majorities exist in France, Belgium, Italy, Spain, and Portugal. Strong transnational conduits of influence and information exist between Catholic organizations within and among all these countries, although their direct international influence is not always utilized.

Papal and episcopal denunciations of terrorism benefit members of the North Atlantic Alliance by strengthening national consensus and removing pretexts for regional disruptions. The case of Northern Ireland is especially important to Great Britain and other English-speaking nations. John Paul II preceded his trip to the United States in 1979 by visiting Ireland. The pope stood in a natural amphitheater in the historic town of Drogheda north of Dublin and issued a strong condemnation of violence to 200,000 Irish:

I join my voice today to the voice of Paul VI and my other predecessors, to the voices of your religious leaders, to the voices of all men and women of reason, and I proclaim the conviction of my faith in Christ, and with an awareness of my mission, that violence is evil, that violence is unacceptable as a solution to problems, that violence is unworthy of man, that violence is a lie, for it goes against the truth of our faith, the truth of our humanity.[103]

The pope did not mention the IRA by name, condemn conditions in Belfast's Maze Prison, nor call for Irish reunification. John Paul had planned to go to Ulster to celebrate an ecumenical mass at the an-

cient primate's see of Armagh, but the assassination of Lord Mount-
batten raised fears for papal security. When the Armagh trip was
canceled, the Reverend Martin Smyth, president of the Orange Order, wrote an open letter which said: "We can only conclude that
your refusal to visit Northern Ireland stems from a political unwillingness, so long nurtured by the Roman Catholic Church in Ireland, to recognize North Ireland as part of the United Kingdom."[104]
At Drogheda the pope said, "May not Irish Protestants think that
the Pope is an enemy, a danger or a threat. My desire is instead that
Protestants see me as a friend and brother in Christ."

The Irish Cardinal Primate Ó'Fiaich has also condemned the IRA
in the strongest terms. For example, in November 1981 he stated:

> Most of these murders have been claimed by the IRA. Let me therefore
> state in simple language, with all the authority at my command, that par-
> ticipation in the evil deeds of this or any other paramilitary organization
> which indulges in murder, wounding, kidnapping, destruction of property
> and other forms of violence is a mortal sin which will one day have to be
> accounted for before God in judgment.
>
> To cooperate in any way with such organizations is sinful, and if the co-
> operation is substantial, the sin is mortal.[105]

In Northern Ireland, the two most important dioceses are Derry and
that of Down and Connor (which includes Belfast and has over
300,000 Catholics). Both Bishop Edward Daly of Derry and Bishop
Cahal B. Daly of Down and Connor have also condemned the "violent option."[106] Cahal Daly, a specialist on the "troubles," has written *Violence in Ireland and the Christian Conscience* (1973) and *Peace, the
Work of Justice* (1980). He has said that members of the IRA "cut
themselves away from the community of love which is the Christian
Church."[107] The latest attempt at political compromise is the Anglo-
Irish treaty signed by Prime Ministers Margaret Thatcher and Garret FitzGerald on November 15, 1985. The treaty gives Dublin a
mechanism for pressing its views on Catholic minority rights in Ulster. FitzGerald said he hoped that Catholic support for the IRA
would be "eroded" when the treaty took effect.[108] The treaty has
helped John Hume's moderate Social Democratic and Labour Party
against the IRA's political partner, Sinn Fein. In June 1986 FitzGerald
miscalculated, however, as voters in the Irish Republic overwhelmingly rejected the prime minister's proposed referendum to legalize
divorce. The Republic's bishops, who had opposed the referendum, thus made it more difficult to convince Unionists that Irish Re-

public participation in Ulster's affairs did not also entail the importation of Catholic morality.

Despite all this national, regional, and international activity by Anglo-American Catholics, the central question articulated three decades ago by Jewish ecumenist Will Herberg in *Protestant, Catholic, Jew*[109] remains. Herberg sought to explain the coexistence in American culture of the pervasive secularization of American consciousness with the religious revival of that period. He contrasted the role religion played in the lives of first-, second-, and third-generation immigrants and argued that, by the 1950s, each of the three major religions had become a specific way of being American. When church attendance declined in the 1960s, the academic discussion turned to "American Civil Religion," that overarching civic piety built on Protestant themes which binds the nation together. Robert Bellah has cited the inaugural address of John Kennedy as illustrating concepts belonging more properly to American civil religion than to the Catholic faith per se.[110]

Have the Anglo-American Catholic Churches, then, come of age by becoming merely a sociologically acceptable way to express the political nationalism and the cultural secularism of their respective countries? In some cases, yes. However, in other cases Catholic values have directly challenged prevailing societal norms. Mel Piehl distinguished between the Catholic Worker movement and the liberalism of the World War II period by stressing that the former held to its basic orientation, regardless of the views of the surrounding culture. This made Catholic Workers unpopular in the early 1940s and popular in the late 1960s. The fundamental importance of the movement, according to Piehl, lay in that "it offered within American culture a model of socially and intellectually engaged Catholic spirituality. In doing so, it signaled the beginning of a deeper relationship between Catholicism and American culture, a mark of the maturing of the American Catholic community."[111]

CHAPTER 6

Catholic Poland and *Ostpolitik*

"THE WORLD'S MOST FAMOUS POLE"[1] RETURNS HOME

ON OCTOBER 16, 1978, eight men labored to ring the great Zygmunt Bell, rung only on historic occasions, at Kraków's Wawel Castle, the traditional home of Polish kings. More than one thousand years after the conversion of Poland to Christianity, the universal Catholic Church had elected a Polish pope, Kraków's own Cardinal Karol Wojtyła. The Polish people exulted. In Kraków, the historic political and cultural center of the nation, thousands of people jammed the streets, singing and shouting and hugging one another. All the bells in Warsaw's churches pealed joyously. Poland's three top party leaders cabled the new pope to tell him of their "great satisfaction" and lifted travel restrictions so that six thousand Poles could attend Wojtyła's installation. Catholics throughout Eastern Europe proclaimed their faith with a new boldness. In the Polish village of Ople Stare, the people reacted to the election by building an illegal church dedicated to the Franciscan victim of the Nazis, Blessed Maximilian Kolbe.[2] The villagers then organized guard patrols and installed a bell system loud enough to summon three thousand defenders from six neighboring communities in case the government should try to tear it down as had been threatened.[3] A few weeks after the pope's inauguration, five Lithuanian priests called a press conference in Moscow to proclaim that "the Church of Silence is no more because a pope from Poland is speaking."[4]

Polish television telecast the pope's complete inauguration to the entire nation. President Henryk Jabłoński, who attended the ceremony, commented that the pope was welcome to visit his homeland, but that the government would issue no official invitation. However, Cardinal Primate Wyszyński acted on behalf of the Polish bishops in inviting John Paul II to come to Poland in May 1979 to attend the 900th anniversary celebration of the martyrdom of St. Stanislaus, archbishop of Kraków. Wyszyński chose the May date because this patron saint of Poland, murdered by King Bolesław the Bold in 1079, remains a national symbol of church autonomy and protest against the state. Eastern European party leaders, cognizant that the enraged Polish people then forced King Bolesław to retire to a Hungarian monastery, favored neither the papal visit nor the proposed date. The massive popular reception given John Paul II in Mexico the next January made these leaders even more nervous. But Polish Party Secretary Gierek, whose government would have fallen in 1977 without Wyszyński's timely intervention, could not deny the pope a visa. Further pressure came when the Polish Bishops' Conference composed a special prayer read in all of the nation's churches on February 2 petitioning God that John Paul be allowed to visit his homeland. Finally, the party and the church reached a compromise which brought the pope to Poland in June.

As John Paul arrived in Warsaw on June 2, church bells began to peal throughout the nation. The pope made three dozen public appearances in nine days. He visited Warsaw, his home town of Wadowice, Kraków, Częstochowa, Poland's holiest shrine, and Auschwitz, "the Golgotha of the modern world."[5] Wherever he went, the people had walked and driven for miles, and then had stood for hours, shoulder to shoulder, some even dropping in exhaustion, merely to glimpse the man. John Paul spent three days at Częstochowa, where he led the ceremony of national consecration to Our Lady, "Queen of Poland." Częstochowa's Jasna Góra (Mountain of Light) Monastery holds the painting of the Black Madonna, attributed to St. Luke the Evangelist, which was found at the monastery in 1382. The Black Madonna had defended Poland from the Swedes in 1655 and from all her enemies since.

While the pope never mentioned the Soviet Union nor the Communist Party by name, he constantly challenged the Polish government to give the church the necessary freedom to accomplish its mission in the world. On the first day he greeted Party Secretary Gierek, "It is [the church's] mission to make man more confident, more courageous, conscious of his rights and duties, socially responsible, creative and useful. For this activity the church does not desire privileges, but only and exclusively what is essential for the accomplishment of its mission." John Paul II presented himself as the first "Slav Pope," sent especially, not only to Poles, but to Czechs, Slovaks, Slovenes, Serbs, Croats, Bulgarians, Ukrainians, and Russians. Referring to would-be pilgrims from other Slavic countries who were turned back at the Polish border, John Paul said, "It would be sad to believe that each Pole and Slav in any part of the world is unable to hear the words of the Pope, this Slav."[6] The most significant political effect of the visit did not consist in the pope's carefully nuanced statements, but in the popular euphoria of a total national experience. Before the visit the Poles were doubtful and cynical about the possibility of reforming their political system. Now they felt they could change the course of public events. When Italian journalist Oriana Fallaci interviewed Lech Wałęsa in Warsaw in February 1981, the Solidarity leader not only talked about daily mass, his rosary, and the image of the Black Madonna on his jacket but added: "We also have to consider the election of Pope Wojtyła, his travel to Poland and the continuous obstinate, smart work of the church. Without the church nothing could happen."[7] Four years after the pope's first visit when Wałęsa's wife, Danuta, returned from Stockholm with Lech's Nobel Peace Prize, they and their parish priest, the Reverend Henryk Jankowski, drove to Częstochowa to dedicate the medal to Our Lady. There it joined other patriotic artifacts of Poland's history such as the memorial to the Home Army partisans of World War II. The front page of the *New York Times* (December 14, 1983) shows Wałęsa dedicating the medal.

In August 1980 workers in Gdańsk struck in response to a rise in food prices. From its initial victory in September until martial law was imposed fifteen months later, the independent trade union Solidarity and its leader Wałęsa revolutionized Polish politics. The union's membership grew to ten million (nearly one-fourth of the country), including many Communist Party members. The fact that General Jaruzelski still feels it is necessary to assert that his government honors the state-Solidarity accords of August 1980 indicates the enduring public support for the union's ideals.[8]

While the success of Solidarity was inconceivable without the optimistic popular atmosphere created by John Paul II's first trip, the exact relations between the church, the party, and Solidarity up to the time of martial law remain the subject of debate. European socialist Daniel Singer criticizes "the ideological hegemony of the Catholic Church," and says he would prefer posters featuring Rosa Luxemburg to Pope John Paul II.[9] Although most of Solidarity's leaders were devout Catholics, Wałęsa himself stressed the nondenominational character of the union. "In our union there are believers and unbelievers and for this reason we do not call for the construction of churches. But should there be a lack of churches, we shall also ask for them to be built."[10] Some Polish workers and intellectuals have also offered tactical criticism of the church, especially for its caution in the initial strikes. These critics particularly objected to a sermon of Cardinal Wyszyński's, broadcast on state television, that seemed aimed at getting the workers back on the job.[11] Throughout this period the Vatican and the Polish church under Cardinal Wyszyński and his successor, Józef Glemp, sought to play a dual role. The church fostered the independence of the union and at the same time sought to mediate strife between it and the party in the interests of national stability.[12] John Paul placed his prestige behind Solidarity in a widely publicized audience on January 15, 1981. In front of the international media the pope embraced Wałęsa and conferred his blessings on the formation of the union. John Paul said: "The creation of the free union is an event of great importance. It shows that there does not exist—because there should not exist—a contradiction between such an autonomous social initiative of working men and the structure of the system that hails human labor as the fundamental value of social and state life." Then the pope indirectly warned the Soviet Union that the Polish labor movement "is truly, and will continue to be, a strictly internal issue for all Poles."[13]

At the same time, Cardinal Wyszyński was also looking for a compromise position. Shortly after John Paul's audience with Wałęsa, the Polish Bishops' Conference set three criteria for the attainment of labor peace: unfettered possession and expression of truth and freedom of opinion; individual ownership of land and farms; and freedom of association of citizens in independent worker representations and self-governing bodies in keeping with the teachings of the Second Vatican Council.[14] Wyszyński also entered the government's negotiation with Solidarity at specific points. For example, during the March 1981 crisis Wałęsa left stalled talks with the government to meet with Cardinal Wyszyński for one and one-half hours. They were joined by an informal adviser to Party Secretary Stanisław Kania, Stefan Bratkowski, who played the role of go-between in many government-union crises. Shortly before the meeting, Jerzy Ozdowski, Polish deputy premier and a Roman Catholic, was seen leaving the cardinal's palace.[15] The negotiations did produce some hopeful signs. The Extraordinary Party Congress of July 1981 under Gierek's successor Kania, for example, introduced democratic reforms without challenging the preeminent position of the party or Poland's role in the Soviet defense system. While there were many personnel changes in the Politburo and the Central Committee, the delegates reelected Kania to carry out the moderate program. The church's policy of defending Solidarity while fostering a national consensus seemed to be succeeding. The possibility for this dual role was grounded in the complete identification of Catholicism and Polish nationalism.

CARDINAL WYSZYŃSKI AND POLISH CATHOLIC NATIONALISM

Cardinal Primate Stefan Wyszyński remains one of the great ecclesiastical figures of the twentieth century and the symbol of traditional Polish national Catholicism. The cardinal, who endured the suspicions of three popes and their Curias and witnessed the fall of four Polish governments during his thirty-three years as archbishop of Warsaw, certainly fit the Polish historical mold of the politically powerful primate who managed national affairs in the interregnum between one monarch and another. Wyszyński was born in northeast Poland in 1901. After being ordained for the Warsaw diocese at twenty-three, he went to Paris and Rome for studies. At this time he was influenced by the church's lay movement and became an expert on labor relations. When the Germans attacked Poland he was performing pastoral duties in a parish outside Warsaw. He joined the underground and continued his pastoral duties in secret. Following Soviet occupation of Poland, Wyszyński became chaplain of the Catholic University of Lublin and then archbishop of Warsaw in 1948.

In January 1953 Pius XII named Wyszyński cardinal, but he refused to go to Rome to receive the red hat because he feared he would not be able to reenter Poland. Wyszyński then accelerated his attacks on the Bierut government. When the Primate Wyszyński refused to admonish three of Poland's bishops for publicly criticizing the government, Soviet soldiers arrested him as he returned home from saying his nightly mass. The Bolesław Bierut government detained him for three years in four different monasteries. Bierut's fall in 1956 brought about the cardinal's release and a more liberal policy toward the church by the second Gomułka government.

While Wyszyński was under detention he reread the Polish classic *The Flood*, inspired by Poland's famous victory over the Swedish invaders in 1655. Later, he sought to embody the book's religious and nationalistic spirit in the Program of Religious Revival, a ten-year (1956-1966) celebration of Polish Christianity which climaxed at the Polish millennial celebration in 1966. The history of Poland and the history of Polish Catholicism had begun together. The first historical leader of Poland was Mieszko of the House of Piast. Since the Germans of that time felt it was their "Christian duty" to convert Poland by conquest, Mieszko understood the strategic necessity of adopting Catholicism voluntarily from another source. In 965

Mieszko married Dubravka, a princess from his Slavic neighbor Bohemia, which had been Christian for some time. One year later Mieszko received baptism and decreed the Christianization of his nation. Now, Poland stood as the outpost of Western Catholicism against pagan Tartars, Orthodox Russians, and Muslim Turks. God had called this nation to missionary zeal in defending and spreading Catholicism. At this time Poland tried to unify all central Europe into a sphere of national Catholic influence, but even the papacy opposed creation of so strong a state.

Poland looks back to the period 1370-1572 as its Golden Age. The church served as a source of political cohesion and fostered a high level of culture. The Catholic clergy participated in the Polish Enlightenment, and the Reformation caused little upheaval. Internal disorder occurred in the years 1572-1795, during which Poland turned to a more democratic political system whereby the nobility elected the king. The nobility usually maximized their own power by choosing a weak monarch. In 1683 the Polish king John Sobieski rescued Vienna from the Turks. This expedition served papal interests by saving Catholic Austria, but hurt Polish national interests by rescuing a dangerous neighbor. Finally in 1795 the strong monarchies of Lutheran Prussia, Catholic Austria, and Orthodox Russia partitioned Poland. Poland ceased to exist for 124 years.

The Prussians ruled the northwest corner of Poland. They kept efficient, stern, and thorough control over this part of the country, attempting to Germanize the area by not allowing the people to speak Polish. Austria exercised control over the southern section of Poland. The Hapsburgs then ruled over an unstable multicultural empire and conceded some home rule to most of their subjects. Universities and schools in the Austrian section kept alive the Polish culture. The Russian sector contained the remaining two-thirds of Poland. The Poles constantly revolted against the czars, but were put down in bloody slaughter. Throughout this entire period Polish nationalism coincided with the Catholic faith. To be Polish was to be Catholic. Conversely, czarist Russia identified Catholicism with Polish nationalism.

Although all Poles identified with Catholic nationalism, the people traditionally perceived the church as a hierarchical institution of considerable wealth and power. Peasant resentment of the clergy found expression in such sayings as: "A priest's Kith and Kin will never grow thin," and "This shepherd only cares for the sheep he can shear: We have no wool for him."[16] During the twentieth century, however, the clergy more closely allied themselves with the suffering of the people. In 1926 the Cardinal Primate August Hlond declared that his primary interests would be the social progress and welfare of all Poles and the adaptation of the church to the needs of the people.[17] Hlond thus shifted the church attention more toward the urbanized proletariat. But the church did not fully earn its present high status as "champion of the people" until the Nazi occupation. Many clergy joined the underground and died for their country. Eighteen percent of the Catholic clergy were killed during the war. The Warsaw diocese alone lost over half of its clergy. Cardinal Wyszyński's ten-year celebration of Polish national Catholicism drew upon this rich thousand-year tradition.

Polish Catholics still glory in a traditional church whose strongest embodiment is the conservative peasant. Over the centuries religion has become an integral part of the Polish peasants' practical interests and folk customs. Farmers pray in the morning upon rising and again at midday, kneeling in the fields when they hear the sound of the church bells. They stop at roadside shrines which cover the countryside to cross themselves or kiss the feet of a statue of Jesus. Hail Marys are said to ward off evil spirits, and throughout the day the customary peasant greeting can be heard, "Praised be Jesus Christ," and the reply, "World without end." Sundays bring rest and prayer and an opportunity to socialize with one's neighbor at church. For the peasant, regular attendance at mass, receiving communion, and going to confession are all part of being a "good" Catholic. The church building itself represents God, Christ, and the saint to whom it is dedicated. For this reason construction of churches is a vital point of contention with the government. Pilgrimages also remain a very important part of life for the Catholic peasantry. Each year the entire community travels as a group to the shrine of the Black Madonna at Częstochowa. Poland defers only to Italy in the number of ecclesiastical holidays. Epiphany, Lent, Easter Week, and Mary's Assumption are observed with mass peasant pilgrimages. The pilgrimages and their destinations are not announced outside the village. The peasants board up their farms and follow their parish priest into the countryside for up to a week. Thus the entire life of the Polish peasant centers around his religion.[18]

The political uses of these traditional religious symbols can be appreciated by analyzing John Paul II's second trip to Poland in June 1983. The pope came to celebrate the 600th Anniversary of the Black Madonna of Częstochowa, and his itinerary proceeded from one shrine to the next. In Warsaw John Paul celebrated a memorial mass for Cardinal Wyszyński "who had made the church and the nation strong in the midst of the trials and experiences of history." He visited the Church of the Capuchins, which keeps an urn containing the heart of the Polish hero-king John Sobieski. At the monastery at Niepokalanów the pope celebrated a mass in honor of the newly canonized St. Maximilian Kolbe, martyr of Auschwitz. He again spent three days at Częstochowa, where the "tear-filled and sad" eyes of the Black Madonna caused the pope to reflect on his country's history. In Poznań, John Paul beatified Sister Urszula Ledóchowska, a Polish educator who organized schools before World War I. In Katowice, the pope celebrated mass under the image of Our Lady of Piekary, a madonna much beloved of the region's coal miners. Finally, in Kraków John Paul beatified Rafael Kalinowski and Adam Chmielowski, both participants in the 1863 uprising against the Russians. Kalinowski and Chmielowski, said the pope, learned a spiritual strength "more powerful than any situation, not excluding the arrogant use of power." When the pope returned to Kraków, the great Zygmunt bell tolled again.

The people responded not just with Solidarity banners and other banners in Solidarity's distinctive script, but with religious badges that have become common political symbols as well, for example, the Black Madonna against a red and white national background, the Polish eagle superimposed on a cross. The government has finally torn up Old Town's Victory Square to prevent any more floral crosses being left there in the heart of Warsaw. Correspondent John Kifner has singled out Nowa Huta's Queen of Poland Church as "the most breathtaking example" of Polish national Catholicism: "From the red and white flower beds, the national colors, on the outside to the figure of the Madonna in the basement chapel cast from shrapnel and bullets taken from the casualties among the Free Polish Forces in the battle of Monte Cassino in Italy in World War II, it is a monument to a synthesis of Roman Catholicism and Polish nationalism."[19]

POLISH STATE RELIGIOUS POLICY

Polish governments fell in 1956 (Bierut), 1970 (Gomułka), and 1980 (Gierek). In each case the primary occasion was public demonstrations over government food policy, while state religious pressure played a secondary role. In each case the succeeding political leader sought the good graces of Cardinal Wyszyński to support his new regime, and offered concessions to the church. The party secretaries then hardened ecclesiastical policy as they solidified their power. Finally, the process was repeated. The demonstrations against Gierek in 1976 showed the importance of church support for the Polish government. In December 1976 Gierek raised food prices 40 percent, and Gierek's government appeared to be about to fall. But the party secretary had not completely cut his ties with the church. In fact, when Wyszyński bitterly objected to three clauses in the Constitution of 1976, the party either adopted church amendments or dropped the clauses.[20] When riots threatened in response to Gierek's food policy, the church arranged a compromise which rolled back prices. Gierek then made a visit to Pope Paul VI as a way of propping up his political popularity at home. When Gierek again raised food prices in August 1980, however, he was forced to resign.

Forty years of conflict have forced both the Polish Workers Party and the Polish Catholic Church to accept the permanent existence of the other. However, this practical political recognition lacks the force of law since the state has refused legal status to the church. The state Ministry of Religion reserves to itself the right to veto assignments of bishops to particular dioceses. In one particularly outrageous case, the ministry rejected twenty candidates before accepting the supposedly "safe" Henryk Gulbinowicz. Former Minister of Religion Kazimierz Kąkol once joked, "The church knows the way we function so the simplest thing would be for them to put their favorite candidate last."

Church-state conflicts have focused on episcopal appointments, government denial for permits for church construction, media censorship, and the role of the church in education. The independent Catholic press is led by the respected *Tygodnik Powszechny*, edited by John Paul's lay friend, Jerzy Turowicz. The paper has at times been limited to eight pages an issue and a circulation of 40,000. Turowicz currently prints 80,000 copies, which are read by about one million Poles. The Polish party is ambivalent about its censorship since it doesn't want to drive all readers to the extensive underground press.[21] The introduction of religious education into the public educational system has been a major goal of the church. The state's new mandatory educational system introduced in 1976 produced the opposite result. The ten-year plan emphasizes technical and scientific subjects while avoiding morality and ethics. Religious instruction remains optional, relegated to after school hours. Both parents must give written consent. Local government officials often pressure parents not to enroll their children. Many commentators link Poland's rising rates of alcoholism, drugs, crime, divorce, and abortion with this lack of moral instruction.[22] Others tie these prob-

lems to the contagion of Western liberal values or the cavalier attitude toward law which was encouraged as a patriotic stance during
the Nazi occupation.

These general concerns have shaped Polish church-state relations
during the entire postwar period. However, each party secretary
has projected a slightly different emphasis in his religious policy.
And the policy has tended to be tougher at the end of a government's tenure than at the beginning. The fiercest attacks against the
church came under the Stalinist Bierut government, 1953-1956. In
February 1953 the state issued a decree giving it control over all hierarchical appointments and suspending many Catholic publications. In September Bierut imprisoned Cardinal Wyszyński and
other bishops. The government closed most seminaries and severely restricted Catholic educational institutions.[23] It also attempted to split the church from within by fostering PAX, a group
of clergy and lay people loyal to the regime. PAX Chairman
Bolesław Piasecki and other leaders denounced the hierarchy.[24] Until October 1985 there were three associations of lay Catholics represented in the Sejm (parliament). In addition to PAX, there were
the Christan Social Association (ChSS) and the Polish Catholic Social Union (PZKS). The hierarchy worked with PZKS under Janusz
Zabłocki, but even this group became suspect when Zabłocki was
dismissed as chairman in May 1984.[25] In the October 1985 elections
Glemp refused Jaruzelski's offer of a few seats for orthodox Catholics.

Following the fall of the Bierut government, Gomułka took a
much more conciliatory approach. While the state continued to restrict church actions and foster the largely ineffectual PAX, it released Wyszyński and the other bishops. The primate received sig-
,nificant concessions in return for his support. The government
guaranteed freedom of expression for non-Marxist Catholics, an independent press, independent activity for Catholic social and intellectual groups, and freedom of religious teaching in the schools.
The clergy was so successful in its "get out the vote" campaign in
January 1957 that twelve open adherents of Catholicism were
elected to parliament. Gradually, however, Gomułka responded to
criticism by other East European bloc countries by increasing pressure on the church. He increased church taxes and reduced church
building permits. He also ordered the elimination of religious instruction in the schools, appealing worldwide to Protestants and
liberals, "we want a secular society . . . no more, no less."[26]

If the arrest of Wyszyński was the hallmark of Bierut's hard line, secularization has been the main thrust of more conciliatory approaches. Secularization attempts to privatize religion by sponsoring the scientific study of religion in its social, psychological, and historical dimensions. The goal is to relativize Catholicism as just one rather traditional phenomenon in modern Poland. With Poland's rapid postwar industrialization, Gomułka's strategy seemed propitious, even though the same comparative criticism could be used by Catholics to attack Marxist dogma. In light of the party's decades-long stress on secularization of the workers and the intellectuals, however, the strong religious fervor of the new industrial towns constitutes a major embarrassment.[27] One of Cardinal Wojtyła's most significant victories as archbishop of Kraków was the erection of a modernistic concrete and steel church at Nowa Huta, a steel town designed to provide no church for its 200,000 residents. The permits and building took twenty years. When John Paul II returned to Nowa Huta on June 22, 1983, he consecrated the new town's sixth parish church, with three more under construction.[28]

The "War of the Crosses" in spring 1984 shows just how little progress the government has made in its attempt to secularize Poland. Neither governmental nor ecclesiastical leaders stirred up the controversy, and both sought the diplomatic compromise which ended it. In fact, Cardinal Glemp was traveling in South America when protesting students at the Stanisław Staszic complex of agricultural colleges in Mietnow first appeared in a three-column lead photo on the front page of the *New York Times* (March 9, 1984). The previous December the government had issued an order that crucifixes and "other religious cult objects" must be taken down from the walls of public schools, but the decree generally attracted much grumbling and little compliance. Nevertheless, the local director of the Staszic complex, Ryszard Dobrynski, removed the crucifixes in the school's seven lecture halls. The students objected. The turmoil spread as parents, priests, and the local bishop backed the protesting students, while party and state officials supported the director. Crosses were put up and taken down several times.

The *New York Times* photo shows some of the 3,000 students attending a protest mass at the local parish church three miles away in Garwolin. The night before a line of police had turned back the students from the church. Two hours before the protest mass, riot police arrived at the college dormitories with several buses, apparently hoping to drive the students to church, thus avoiding a protest march with photos for the international media. The students scattered across the fields, but the riot police cornered most of them in the walled cemetery. The students then rang a chapel bell, which brought a delegation of priests who negotiated their passage to the mass. Bishop Jan Mazur of Siedlce told the students that he had ordered a declaration, which called on all adults to petition General Jaruzelski on their behalf, to be read from all the pulpits of the diocese. Many of the students wore crucifixes, and near the altar a large red and white sign proclaimed "There was no room for you, O Christ, in our school." At the end of mass the students sang the traditional hymn "God Who Protects Poland" with their hands raised in the "V" sign of resistance. Two days later about 500 students from the Garwolin region arrived at Częstochowa and were admitted into Jasna Góra Monastery to pay their respects to the Black Madonna. Bishop Franciszek Musiel of Częstochowa reminded the students that the cross was a symbol for which many Poles would choose to die. All of the symbols of nationalism supported the students, while the government argued for a secular society.[29]

National state and ecclesiastical authorities could no longer ignore this regional issue. The secretary of the Polish Bishops' Conference, Warsaw Auxiliary Bishop Bronisław Dąbrowski met with Bishop Mazur on March 11. Glemp returned to Poland on March 12, and two days later the nine-member Main Council of the Polish Bishops issued a statement saying that crucifixes should be returned to the school and "defended." That night Glemp spoke in St. John's Cathedral in Warsaw saying that most Poles wanted the crucifixes displayed in classrooms as a symbol of nationalism. "Whom is this cross disturbing so much? Is the law right that sweepingly and rather deeply hurts the feelings of the majority of believing society?" asked Glemp. The cardinal further argued that even secular institutions "should be based on the principle of the reality of social and national feelings."[30]

Government spokesman Jerzy Urban remained adamant that the crucifixes must go, but six days later the Minister of Religious Affairs, Adam Łopatka, met with Bishop Mazur and told him that the government would no longer insist that parents sign a pledge supporting the secular character of public education before the school was reopened. Łopatka's concession followed correspondence between himself, Glemp, and the church's secretariat. When the school reopened a week later, however, school authorities did demand pledges, and most of the students again left the school. Bishop Mazur began a fast on bread and water until the issue was settled. The Polish episcopate, after a two-day meeting under

Glemp, issued another statement, "The cross should remain where the faithful desire it to be." This statement was followed by a pastoral letter read from every pulpit in the country the next Sunday, which recalled "the devoted and untiring defense of the cross by its believers, the adults and youth."[31]

Finally, the church and the state reached a compromise at a meeting of Bishop Dąbrowski and Internal Affairs Minister Czesław Kiszczak. In the intervening week more than 450 clergymen had joined Bishop Mazur in his fast, and it looked as if the pastoral letter might ignite a national movement, which would present major diplomatic difficulties for both governmental and ecclesiastical leaders. The compromise specified that crucifixes would be allowed in reading rooms and dormitories but not in lecture halls. The government dropped its insistence that the students or parents sign any pledge and promised no reprisals. The hierarchy discouraged priests from speaking publicly about the ban. Neither side would comment on the general meaning of the law nor its enforcement. Bishop Mazur ended his fast and congratulated the students, "You were the ones who came to Christ and calmly stood by the cross. Stand by Him all your lives."[32]

The incident had proved embarrassing for the government, and the church leadership did not want to delay parliamentary approval for Glemp's privately administered agricultural aid program or legal status for the church. The incident proved a political advantage to the cardinal because he could stand up to the government on the crucifix issue while he opposed ecclesiastical militants by insisting on the transfer of Father Mieczysław Nowak, the pro-Solidarity priest who had ministered to workers at the Ursus tractor factory.[33] In comparison with Wyszyński, however, Glemp relies much more on the consensus decisions of the country's leading episcopal figures who belong to the Main Council, the small "Politburo" of the Polish episcopal conference.

THE SOVIET FACTOR

Control of Eastern Europe remains the first line of defense for the Soviet Union. When that control was threatened in Hungary (1956) and in Czechoslovakia (1968), Warsaw Pact tanks rolled into the streets of Budapest and Prague. Recent events in Poland have caused Soviet leaders considerable anxiety and brought the Soviet Union to the brink of intervention several times. The high international costs of such intervention, the well-known "stubborness" of the Polish people, plus concern over the reaction of the Polish army inhibited Moscow. Finally, Jaruzelski's declaration of martial law in 1981 seemed to stabilize the situation.

Polish-Russian relations have been strained since the Middle Ages. While Poland accepted Roman Catholicism, Russia embraced the Eastern Orthodox tradition from Constantinople. Tsarist rule of two-thirds of Poland, 1795-1919, combined terror, oppression, inefficiency, and corruption. In 1920 the Soviets attacked Poland, but were routed in the "miraculous" battle of the Vistula River. Then came Stalin's cynical pact with Hitler which dismantled the country in 1939. Finally, the Soviet troops sat outside Warsaw while the Nazis massacred the Polish underground army in 1944. John Paul II recalled that event during his 1979 visit when he mentioned that the city was "abandoned by the Allied powers." His listeners all knew that only one ally was involved. Poles harbor a special hatred for Russians which is obvious to the Soviets. Moscow's response has been to give the Polish government wider discretion in internal affairs in return for unswerving international and military strategic support.

The election of the staunchly anticommunist Slav Wojtyła to the papacy worried the Kremlin. Soviet Foreign Minister Andrei Gromyko initiated a visit with John Paul in January 1979 because the Soviet government was anxious "to take the measure of the new Polish Pontiff." Gromyko was later quoted in the Italian press as saying that he feared John Paul's visit to Poland would have "the same effect on the masses as the Ayatollah Khomeini had in Iran." The Soviet leadership became more and more alarmed at papal influence in Poland. In November 1979, for the first time in many years, the Soviet embassy in Rome invited no Vatican representatives to its November reception. With the founding of Solidarity the following August, the czarist identification of "Catholic" and "Polish" became the guiding principle of Soviet perception of the Vatican. The following fall John Paul II wrote secretly to Brezhnev assuring the general secretary that "Poland will help itself," and the church would continue to assist as mediator. This letter "was probably the factor that changed Brezhnev's mind and precipitated the withdrawal of the invasion order, but the Soviet troops stayed in their temporary tents around the Polish borders throughout most of the winter months."[34]

It is doubtful that objective evidence will ever settle definitively whether there was Soviet complicity in the attempted assassination of the pope. This is especially true after the Italian court acquitted the three Bulgarians and three Turks "for lack of proof," a judgment of neither guilt nor innocence. After Mehmet Ali Agca, an escaped Turkish convict, wounded John Paul II in Saint Peter's Square on May 13, 1981, Agca claimed he had acted alone. Later he changed his story to implicate the Bulgarian and Soviet intelligence agencies. In a surprise encounter with journalists on July 8, 1983, Agca himself said, "I have been several times in Bulgaria and in Syria—and in the attack against the Pope even the K.G.B. took part."[35] Soviet spokesmen reacted angrily to Agca's charges, made the more sensitive because General Secretary Yuri Andropov was head of the K.G.B. at the time of the assassination attempt. Tass charged that such "slander" came from those who wished to "sow more seeds of distrust between East and West at this already tense moment in the international situation," and thus divert attention from "the true organizers and inspirers of acts of terrorism, who are closely linked with neo-fascist circles and the American CIA."[36] The Bulgarians were more restrained, combining point-by-point rebuttal of the complicity charges against Bulgarian airline official Sergei Ivanov Antonov with relatively low-key counterallegations that the affair was part of Reagan's crusade against communism.[37] In May 1983 the pope received with considerable courtesy a high-ranking Bulgarian delegation which was not received by the Italian government.[38]

Regardless of the facts and the Vatican's disinclination to use the assassination for propaganda, widespread perception of Soviet guilt has increased East-West tensions. The years following the assassination attempt also witnessed repeated Soviet attacks on the political role of the Catholic Church in Eastern Europe. On August 21, 1982, Tass reprinted an article from the Czechoslovakian weekly *Tvorba* which attacked the Vatican for trying to dissolve the government-sponsored PAX, which the Vatican considered too political, while encouraging Solidarity, which the Kremlin considered too political. A much harsher attack came in an October issue of *Literaturnaya Gazeta*. One paragraph charged, "The Catholic Church thus gives to Fascist thugs the right to impunity and is financially maintaining the counter-revolution. So much for the pastoral mission."[39] A more nuanced approach came from the head of the Soviet Communist Party's International Relations Department after an August 1983 visit to Poland. Leonid M. Zamyatin said on Soviet television that elements of the Polish Catholic Church backed counterrevolutionaries, but that "[c]ertain parts of the clergy" were "more soberminded" and maintained a degree of cooperation with the Polish government.

Within the Soviet Union Catholicism constitutes a nationalities problem in the areas contiguous with Poland, especially Lithuania, Byelorussia,[40] and the Ukraine. Catholicism is thus linked to one of the Soviet Union's most significant political problems, the ethnic diversity of its citizens. With "Greater Russians" constituting a little more then half of the Soviet population, ethnicity enters into many Soviet political decisions. While Catholic ethnics do not form a large group, they are associated with the Soviet Union's most intractable ethnic areas. Both Lithuania and the Ukraine, where Catholic nationalism remains a sensitive issue, have been united with Poland at different historical periods. The Soviets are especially concerned about "Polish contagion" spreading across the border into Lithuania. Moscow has pressured the Polish government to resist Catholic radio and TV broadcasts because they might encourage Lithuanian believers. The Soviet government forbade Lithuanian Catholics to go to Poland during the pope's visits. It is no wonder that the Soviet government denied the pope permission to visit Lithuania for the 500th anniversary of the country's patron St. Casimir.

The Baltic states of Lithuania, Latvia, and Estonia were among the most advanced and Westernized nationalities when they were forcibly incorporated into the Soviet Union in 1940. Lithuanians fought an eight-year guerrilla war against Soviet forces, 1944-1952. Lithuanian poet Tomas Venclova, a member of the Helsinki Group in Lithuania, points out that "although Lithuania was the last country in Europe to embrace Christianity [late in the fourteenth century], the Christian faith has deeply penetrated the nation's life style and culture. During the Czarist occupation [1795-1915], the struggle for national self-determination was indistinguishable from the struggle for religious rights. Similarly, today, the Catholic Church in Lithuania has supporters who are not primarily religious believers, but who are aware of the Church's historic role."[41] In January and February 1972 more than 17,000 Catholics signed letters protesting religious restraints to CPSU Secretary Brezhnev and UN Secretary General Waldheim. Mass riots followed in May in Kaunas, the nation's second largest city, sparked by the self-immolation of Romas Kalanta, a young student-worker protesting Soviet domination and religious persecution. Over 500 of Lithuania's 708 priests, including Bishop Julijonas Steponavičius, apostolic administrator of Vilnius, signed protests against the 1976 Decree on Religious Associations.[42] By 1976 apostolic administrators headed all six dioceses because the Soviet government refused to allow the naming of any regular bishops. The government did permit the country's sole seminary to increase its students from 50 to 72 in

1978. The first priest ordained in an underground seminary, Father Virgilijus Jaugelis, remains a hero of Lithuanian Catholic nationalism. The Soviet authorities denied him permission to enter the regular seminary each year from 1966 to 1970 and arrested him in 1972 for duplicating the *Chronicle* and collecting signatures for a "slanderous document" that appealed to UN Secretary General Waldheim. Jaugelis, who was ordained in 1978, died of cancer in 1980. Although the government has continued to denounce Jaugelis since his death, Lithuanian Catholics regularly visit his grave.

Church-state relations became partially regularized in July 1982 when the government permitted the appointment of two new apostolic administrators, Vincentas Sladkevičius (Kaišiadorys) and Antanas Vaičius (Telšial). These two bishops plus Liudas Povilonis, apostolic administrator of Kaunas and president of the Lithuanian Bishops' Conference, and Romualdo Krikščiunas, apostolic administrator of Panevėžys, were allowed to make the first Lithuanian *ad limina* visit to Rome since 1938. The four left Moscow on April 6, 1983. The Tass report did not mention why they had been to Moscow, merely commenting that "the aim of the trip is to pay a traditional visit to the Vatican, which is made once in five years."[43] Bishop Julijonas Steponavičius, who has reportedly been under house arrest since 1961, did not make the trip because he feared he would not be able to reenter Lithuania. This partial regularization of church-state relations was accompanied by a crackdown on dissidents throughout the Baltic states.[44] Since Latvian Catholics constitute only 10 percent of the population, and Lutherans are three times as numerous, the Latvian authorities do not perceive the Catholics as a major threat. When John Paul named Bishop Julijans Vaivods, then eighty-eight, as cardinal in February 1983, Vaivods said he felt that the pope wished to use him as a "bridge between the Vatican and Moscow."[45] Vaivods's five volumes on theology earned him a two-year deportation to Moravia in the 1950s, but he has been allowed to go to Rome occasionally since 1964.

An estimated 5-6 million Ukrainian-Rite Uniates reside in the Soviet Ukraine, although in 1946 the government convened the Sobor of Lvov, which officially abolished the separate church and placed all believers under the Orthodox patriarch. This synod followed the arrest and deportation of Archbishop Slipyj and four other Uniate bishops. Although the Soviet government "pardoned" Slipyj in February 1963, it was left to the papal representative Monsignor Willebrands to convince him to leave the country without full exoneration. In describing the incident Stehle remarks that Slipyj could not have known that "the papal church was in the process of revising its centuries-old concept of 'orthodoxy.' . . . [T]he idea of union in the sense of conversion of the Orthodox, that concept by which the Catholic Church repeatedly (and with tragic consequences) had become entangled in the nationalistic quarrels of Eastern Europe, was gradually being filed among the historic documents."[46] Slipyj excoriated the new policy in a famous speech to the 1971 Synod of Bishops in which he castigated Russians and Poles, Moscow and the Vatican: "No one defends the Catholic Ukrainians," he said. "Now, because of the diplomatic negotiations, they are put aside as embarrassing witnesses of past evils."

Paul VI three times (1971, 1975, 1976) refused petitions from the 1.5 million Ukrainian exiles in the West that he appoint Slipyj patriarch of the Ukraine as a sign of encouragement to a "church condemned to death which has been waiting for thirty years for a word of comfort from Your Holiness." Such an appointment would have infuriated both the Soviet government and the Orthodox patriarch. Slipyj rejoiced in the election of a fellow anticommunist Slav to the papacy and renewed his requests for the title of patriarch and a review of "dialogue with the Russian Orthodox Church, which is based on false premises."[47] John Paul II refused both, but sent the archbishop a courteous letter on March 19, 1979. In September, against Slipyj's wishes, the pope named Miroslav Lubachivsky as Uniate Metropolitan in Philadelphia, which resulted in a cool reception by Ukrainian emigrants during John Paul's visit to the United States.

The Ukrainian Uniates held a synod which opened on November 25, 1980, in Rome. Cardinal Władysław Rubin, a Pole who then headed the Congregation for Eastern-Rite Churches, represented the pope. After the synod the pope named Archbishop Lubachivski of Philadelphia as coadjutor with right to succession to Cardinal Slipyj.[48] Slipyj died on September 7, 1984, at ninety-two years of age. Nine days later, while John Paul was addressing Ukrainian emigrants in Winnipeg's Cathedral of Vladimir and Olga, the pope broke off from his prepared text to describe Slipyj as a "noble hero" who "gave his life for the good of the church and his nation."[49]

OSTPOLITIK: THE VATICAN IN EASTERN EUROPE

Strong historical antipathy existed between Catholic Poland and Orthodox Russia. Religious affiliation with Rome or Constantinople (later Moscow) defined the line between Eastern and Western civilizations in Europe, especially in the Balkans. During the Greek

Revolution of 1821 against the Turks, for example, Greek Roman Catholics did not support their Orthodox fellow nationals but attempted to remain neutral until forced to profess loyalty to Greece rather than to the Sultan. The papacy also decided not to support the rebels because it feared that an Orthodox-ruled Greece would be less tolerant toward Catholics than the Turks.[50] Rome's traditional policy of seeking to "convert" the Orthodox had also produced embattled minority Uniate churches in the Balkan nations of Romania and Bulgaria.[51] When the state of Yugoslavia was formed, however, it combined fiercely Catholic Croatia with Orthodox Serbia and other non-Catholic nationalities. The Croatians have always been Rome's bastion in the Balkans, as the Poles and Lithuanians have been Latin Christianity's line of defense farther north. The Croatians constitute roughly one-third of Yugoslavia and are separated from their Serbian countrymen by religion, alphabet, and nationality. Thus, Yugoslavia has faced significant tension among the nationalities since its founding. Tito's death produced considerable anxiety about the danger of a regional break up, but the political system passed that crisis without major ill effects.

Because of its multireligious character, Yugoslavia has been the Balkan state most receptive to separation of church and state.[52] Of course, any party which must ideologically justify its monopoly of power is going to have disputes with the Catholic Church, but many of these have concerned national rather than religious differences. Casaroli and Milutin Morača, the president of the Federal Committee for Religious Affairs, signed the first Vatican-Yugoslavia "protocol" in Belgrade on June 25, 1966. During the two years of negotiations the Holy See had hardly consulted the Yugoslav bishops, and Cardinal Franjo Šeper of Zagreb traveled to Rome on May 25 to try to persuade Paul VI to remove the protocol's formulation in which the "Holy See" condemned "any act of political terrorism or similar criminal forms of violence, no matter who uses them" (Art. II, 2).[53] Paul replied that the protocol assigned such clerical cases to church jurisdiction, thus preventing false suspicions. Besides, Croatian national terrorist activity had been a legitimate concern of the Yugoslav government.

At the suggestion of Cardinal König of Vienna, the pope brought Šeper to Rome to be prefect of the CDF on January 8, 1968, just three days before the official visit of Yugoslav Prime Minister Mika Špiljak. Yugoslavia became the first Eastern European country to establish postwar diplomatic relations with the Vatican in 1970, which resulted in an official state visit of Tito to the Vatican in 1971. The

Yugoslav situation looked even better when contrasted with Albania's closing of all churches in 1967 with the intent of "total liquidation" of all religion in imitation of China's Cultural Revolution.

Pope John XXIII moved to change the Vatican's policy toward Eastern Europe for several reasons. First, he perceived that Communist power in the region, backed by the Soviet Union, seemed secure for the immediate future and Catholicism would only suffer in continued confrontation with it. Second, after Stalin's death, both internal and external considerations gradually compelled all communist European regimes, except Albania, to seek improved relations with the Vatican. Third, *Ostpolitik* was part of the church's cautious reappraisal of its traditional antipathy to Marxist and socialist ideologies. Paul VI defined the main purpose of *Ostpolitik* as obtaining "sufficient living space" for the church in Communist Europe.[54] Stehle summarizes the new Vatican policy under four theses:

1. Classical concordatory policy is no longer a model for agreements with Communist governments, for it presumes a greater degree of mutual accommodation than is desirable for either side. . . .
2. Partial solutions, even those unwritten or only of a trial nature—because they can effect concrete results—are to be preferred to universal agreements, which are much more difficult to achieve and then usually remain all too unstable. . . .
3. It is not positions of prestige, not political resistance nor collaboration that must be secured, but rather the practical ministry of souls. This includes not only freedom of worship, but also freedom of confession and instruction. . . .
4. Theoretically, the relationship to the Soviet Union takes precedence, although this is the most difficult to regulate. . . .[55]

The man chosen for the conduct of *Ostpolitik* was Archbishop Agostino Casaroli, the current secretary of state. When John XXIII named him undersecretary of the Congregation for Extraordinary Ecclesiastical Affairs (now the Council for the Public Affairs of the Church) in 1961, Casaroli had already spent eighteen years in that body (1940-1958) before teaching diplomacy for three years at his alma mater, the Pontifical Ecclesiastical Academy in Rome. Casaroli's diplomatic suavity and his links to *détente* have gotten him the nickname, "the Vatican's Kissinger." Casaroli has been assisted by other Vatican diplomats like Achille Silvestrini and Luigi Poggi, giving Vatican policy to Eastern Europe the same stability of personnel as Soviet diplomacy under Gromyko. Cardinal König, both as archbishop of Vienna and president of the Secretariat for Non-Believers, has also played a prominent role.

Eastern European prelates like Archbishop Slipyj, who had experienced the Stalinist years, strongly opposed *Ostpolitik*.[56] Cardinal Wyszyński of Poland articulated a more measured opposition. The Polish primate did not object to the Vatican talking to Communist governments, but he did criticize the negotiations as too diplomatically oriented to produce tangible concessions for the local churches. By 1977, however, the policies of Paul VI and Wyszyński had grown much closer together, demonstrated by the cardinal's intervention to save Gierek. Wyszyński even broke his thirty-year-old rule not to attend Polish state receptions when he sat at the same table with Gierek, Casaroli, Italian Christian Democrats Aldo Moro and Giulio Andreotti, and Italian Communist Enrico Berlinguer at the Grand Hotel in Rome a few days before the Polish party secretary's audience with the pope.[57]

Ironically, the strongest criticisms of *Ostpolitik* came from the primate of the country that has proved to be the policy's greatest success. In 1949 the Hungarian government had conducted a show trial of the Cardinal Primate Mindszenty after drugging him to secure his confession to treason. The court sentenced Mindszenty to death, but imprisoned him until he escaped to the American legation in Budapest during the revolt of 1956. The Hungarian regime's desire to increase its domestic and international legitimacy[58] provided impetus for the Vatican-Hungarian agreement of September 15, 1964, which was the first public accord signed between the Holy See and a Socialist state. The negotiations preceding the agreement took almost 18 months, with the status of Cardinal Mindszenty the major issue. Finally, the two sides agreed to remove the question of what to do with the cardinal from the agenda. The negotiations then produced agreement on the consecration of five new bishops, the first such Hungarian consecrations since 1951, and the exact wording of the oath of allegiance to the state that the new and subsequent appointees must take.[59] The accord also secured the return of the Hungarian Papal Institute in Rome, formerly controlled by Hungarian émigré priests, to the Hungarian Bishops' Conference, and included an extensive unpublished protocol on the extremely delicate issues of religious instruction, ecclesiastical administration, clerical freedom and others.

Mindszenty vehemently opposed the improvement of Vatican-Hungarian and Hungarian-American relations. When the United States raised its legation to an embassy in 1967, the cardinal consid-

ered the diplomatic move a personal insult and threatened to em-
barrass all parties by walking out of the embassy. At the last moment the pope sent Cardinal König to Budapest with an urgent
command to desist. Finally, in 1971 after many similar difficulties,
the Hungarian Foreign Minister János Péter tied any further improvements of Hungarian-Vatican relations to a solution of the
"Mindszenty problem." The United States embassy in Budapest
also wished to get rid of its "aristocratic" guest of fifteen years. The
Curia, represented by Monsignor Giovanni Cheli of the Secretariat
of State, convinced the cardinal to go to Rome. At the Vatican, however, conversations with Cardinal Slipyj convinced Mindszenty to
leave papal supervision and return to Vienna. Mindszenty committed several more diplomatic *faux pas* and bluntly refused to resign
before the pope finally removed the cardinal as archbishop of Esz-
tergom and primate of Hungary on February 5, 1974.[60] Mindszenty
died on May 6, 1975, in Vienna. John Paul II made a silent visit to
Mindszenty's grave on the papal visit to Vienna in September 1983,
but "pointedly ignored a microphone that had been placed at the
tomb in case he wanted to make a public comment."[61]

Mindszenty's successor as Hungarian Primate, László Lékai, became apostolic administrator as soon as Paul VI removed the cardinal.[62] After protracted negotiations that involved several trips by
the special papal envoy to Eastern Europe, Archbishop Luigi Poggi,
the Budapest government permitted Lékai to become archbishop
and to accept the cardinal's red hat. That accord also named bishops
to all of Hungary's vacant sees. When Kádár visited Paul VI in June
1977, the pope characterized their meeting as "almost the comple-
tion of a slow but uninterrupted process which, in the last 14 years,
has little by little brought closer the Holy See and Hungary."[63] In
August the Hungarian government granted the church permission
to expand its religious instruction of youth, to begin extension
courses in theology for interested laity and religious, and to establish a retreat center. These steps, while not eliminating the concerns
of the 1964 protocol, represent one of the few instances in which
Ostpolitik has resulted in substantive concessions to the local church
beyond ecclesiastical appointments. The church has reciprocated in
supporting government legitimacy. The Hungarian and United
States Bishops' Conferences sought the return of St. Stephen's
Crown (the symbol of Hungarian political legitimacy) from the
United States to Budapest. The request of the Hungarian bishops
allowed the Carter Administration to blunt the fierce criticism that

came from anticommunist Hungarian-American émigrés, especially those who fled in 1956.

Recent conflict within the Hungarian Catholic Church has been between Lékai and a base community leader, Father György Bulányi, because Bulányi has advocated conscientious objection and avoidance of military service. John Paul has urged members of the base communities to obey the bishops, while prodding the bishops to take a stronger stand toward the government. In a letter to Lékai Casaroli said that base communities "in order to call themselves truly ecclesial, must above all be firmly united to the local Churches . . . and through them to the universal Church, working always in communion with and under the guidance of their respective bishops." The letter specifically mentioned the base community directed by Bulányi and asked the Hungarian bishops to make "a pressing personal invitation to Father Bulányi and his followers to submit to the guidance of the bishops in channelling their activities."[64] In June 1983 Cardinal Lékai and the bishops suspended Bulányi from his right to celebrate mass, and eight other priests allied with him were removed from parishes. The state, in the person of Chairman Imre Miklós of the Office of Religious Affairs, has expressed unconcern about the controversy. "They want to make the world believe that we are worried by this movement. We are not worried, and we are only interested insofar as it is likely to disturb the calm of our society."[65]

Both Kádár and Lékai feared disruptions like the Polish conflict. Commenting on Poland, Lékai described the Hungarians and Poles as "brother peoples," but "the Poles decide their history and we decide ours in full autonomy. . . . It is clear, therefore, that the influence of the two Churches in their respective societies is different and that, therefore, their methods would also be different." In response to a follow-up question about martial law in Poland, Lékai replied, "I've already said too much."[66] James Markham of the *New York Times* (January 23, 1984) reported that neither Lékai nor the party's Miklós sounded enthusiastic about a papal visit to Hungary.

The two principal successes of *Ostpolitik*, Yugoslavia and Hungary, offer different approaches to negotiations. In the case of Hungary, the 1964 agreement emphasized principles of relations, with controversial points confined to an extensive unpublished protocol. The Yugoslav agreement emphasized questions of detail because the Belgrade government "thought that a formal contractual 'special regulation' with a single confession contradicted the constitutional principle of religious equality."[67]

Relations between the Yugoslavian government and the Catholic Church have worsened since the death of Tito in 1980. After their annual meeting at Marija Bistrica in October 1981, the Yugoslavian Catholic bishops issued a declaration criticizing the government for presenting Marxist atheism to school children as the "only scientific conception of the world."[68] The government has been particularly concerned about an alleged series of apparitions of Our Lady to six children in the Croatian village of Medjugorje that began on June 24, 1981. The government arrested the local parish priest, and the party expelled eleven persons for visiting the site and warned forty-eight others. The local bishop, Pavao Žanić of Mostar, defended the priest and the children without certifying either the apparitions or the reported accompanying miracles.[69] By November 1985 three million pilgrims from all over the world had come to the village, presenting quandaries to both church and party. With a foreign debt of $20 billion, any source of foreign exchange seemed welcome. Dušan Dragosavać, a member of the Praesidium of the League of Yugoslav Communists (Politburo equivalent), remarked "Yugoslav and foreign tourists attend such manifestations. . . . We have no illusions. Religion is here and will be here for a long time."[70]

The party has stepped up criticism of the former primate Alojzije Stepinac[71] since Jakov Blažević, president of the Croatian Communist Party Praesidium, published a book charging Stepinac with collaborating with the Nazis and also criticizing the present hierarchy. The Zagreb daily *Vjesnik* attacked Stepinac in its May 28-30, 1986, editions. The articles also tied Stepinac to the current archbishop of Zagreb, Cardinal Franjo Kuharić.

John Paul's emphasis on the importance of national ecclesiastical strength in *Ostpolitik* is most evident in Czechoslovakia. Under Paul VI Casaroli negotiated an offer to the imprisoned Archbishop of Prague Josef Beran to go to Rome to receive the cardinal's hat, but not to return.[72] The government accepted František Tomášek as Beran's replacement because he was not perceived as a strong leader. In fact, on January 23, 1977, the Catholic newspaper *Katolické Noviny* (Catholic News) contained a declaration signed by Tomášek on behalf of all the Czech bishops disassociating themselves with Charter 77, the Czech human rights group. While the statement did not explicitly condemn Charter 77, it was perceived as indirect criticism. The famous Czech theologian Josef Zvěřina, survivor of Dachau and professor at the Catholic seminary of Litoměřice during the Prague spring, wrote a reply calling on Tomášek to "Take into your care those who are helpless to whom you gave a bad example, those half-broken characters who have given in to false promises, threats, pressure, weakness and cowardice!"[73]

After the Warsaw Pact troops had marched into Prague in 1968, the Husák regime had controlled the church through issuing and revoking licenses for priests to perform their pastoral duties. If a priest ignored an official ban, he risked up to two years in prison for "obstructing state supervision of the church" (Article 178 of Penal Code). In addition, the government sponsored the association Pacem in Terris. Member priests, called "Paxterriers" by more traditional Catholics, included Bishop Josef Vrana and eight vicar capitulars.[74] On March 8, 1982, two days before the Czech bishops arrived in Rome and three days before they met with John Paul, the Congregation of the Clergy released a "Declaration on Some Associations and Movements Forbidden to the Clergy," directed against such movements as Pacem in Terris. Vrana refused to comment on the document, but Cardinal Oddi, prefect of the Congregation of the Clergy, said of Bishop Vrana, "For a bishop to take part in this association is even worse than a priest."[75] John Paul stated that the declaration applied to Pacem in Terris. Rome had decided to try to strengthen the leadership of the Czechoslovakian church, even at the risk of worsening relations with the Czechoslovakian government.

Czech church-state relations in the early 1980s were patterned on those of the earlier Stalinist period in other Eastern bloc countries. The result was a weak hierarchy with little popular legitimacy. However, many of the priests and laity ignore the official hierarchy, and there are also secretly consecrated bishops and priests who encourage an underground church. In addition, there are as many as 500 priests who have been denied licenses to perform pastoral duties. Catholicism remains an integral part of traditional Slovak nationalism. Among the Czechs in Bohemia and Moravia the Catholic Church is traditionally associated with the oppression of the Germanizing Hapsburgs who rooted out the Protestant nobility. Although nearly 70 percent of the Czechs are nominally Catholic, the church has not been influential among the secularized elites of Prague.

The early 1980s added two factors to this Stalinist church-state pattern which greatly alarmed the government. First, Prague and other Eastern bloc capitals feared the spread of the "Polish contagion." Second, greater numbers of young people began seeking religion. This revival took place disproportionately in the secularized large cities where the Catholic Church had been weakest. The joint suffering of agnostic intellectuals and Catholic clergy and laity in

Charter 77 had partially closed the gap between these groups. Cardinal Tomášek has emphasized the importance of the religious revival in this new setting.[76]

The cardinal, who turned eighty-seven in June 1986, has spoken out strongly since returning from Rome. When some Pacem in Terris priests complained about the Vatican ban, he condemned their "serious violation of church discipline." Membership in Pacem in Terris has been reduced to 5 percent of the Slovak clergy and 7 percent of the clergy in Bohemia and Moravia. Tomášek first charged Communist authorities with discriminating against religion in his reaction to a television program which attacked the church.[77] When the Communist weekly *Tvorba* (March 28, 1984) attacked John Paul as "one of the century's most reactionary popes," Tomášek accused the editorial board of "unobjective demagogy" in a letter which he also distributed to Western journalists. Tomášek formally invited the pope to visit Czechoslovakia in 1985 to mark the 1,100th anniversary of the death of St. Methodius, the country's first archbishop.

Such church-state conflict has definite disadvantages for both the church and the state. Ten of the thirteen Czech dioceses lack residential bishops. Tomášek will not live forever. The fact that state-approved clerics have little popular legitimacy and the recent religious revival among youth and intellectuals encourage a strong Catholic underground. Karel Hruza, as head of the Czech Secretariat for Church Affairs, accused John Paul of conducting a "Cold War" against Czechoslovakia by issuing the declaration against Pacem in Terris and appointing "secret bishops" to fulfill vacancies in the country's hierarchy.[78] The first break in the conflict came with a letter from Casaroli to Tomášek and the other bishops expressing the Vatican's willingness to resume talks on church-state relations which had been suspended in 1981 by the Czech government. On December 7, 1983, John Paul received Czech Foreign Minister Bohuslav Chňoupek, and Archbishop Poggi visited Prague in March.[79] Conflict continues within Czechoslovakia while Rome and Prague search for the functional diplomatic equivalent of the Hungarian compromise. At Christmas 1985 the state attempted to strengthen its hand with a crackdown on the underground church and a strong attack on Cardinal Tomášek.

THE POLISH TRAGEDY

Since the eighteenth century Poland's "geopolitical reality" (Jaruzelski's code words in his reply to John Paul) has caused the country much suffering. International political pressures have taken various forms. Of the three nations that divided Poland in 1775, Austria lost her status as a major power after the First World War. Of the two powers that occupied Poland in 1939, Germany herself has been divided. Now the Soviet Union remains to set the parameters for Poland's existence as a nation. However, Poland retains strong economic ties to Germany and cultural and religious links to Austria. The mass migration of Polish refugees to the United States has produced strong kinship ties to that superpower. Therefore, in seeking a solution to its contemporary political, economic, and social problems, Warsaw must look, not just to Gdańsk and Kraków, but also to Moscow, Frankfurt, Vienna, and Chicago. Since the rise of Austria following John Sobieski's rescue of Vienna from the Turks, the "Polish problem" has also been an international problem.

The visit of John Paul II in June 1979 changed the nature of Polish politics. The new Party Secretary Stanisław Kania was faced with the unenviable task of finding a new political and social order which would satisfy the union Solidarity on one hand and the Soviets on the other. The church under Wyszyński and Glemp sought to play the dual role of supporting Solidarity and mediating the national crisis. Kania failed, and was replaced by General Wojciech Jaruzelski as party secretary in October 1981. On December 13, Jaruzelski, citing the necessity to reestablish law and order, declared martial law. Solidarity had given the general a pretext when it called for free democratic elections which would test the party's leading role in Polish life. Wałęsa had had trouble controlling the more activist sections of the movement, but he blames the disorder on the authorities who "never supported me. They never gave me any ammunition to use in arguments against the most nervous people in the union."[80]

Jaruzelski's declaration of martial law received the immediate approval of the Soviet Union and the immediate condemnation of the United States. As such, martial law demonstrated that the Polish army, but not the Polish Workers Party, could control Polish society. The general has used the army to attack party corruption, and has created the Patriotic Front for National Rebirth (PRON) in an attempt to draw some mass support for the government.[81]

While the Polish army could guarantee martial law, neither the party nor PRON could gain public support. At the same time, the death of Wyszyński meant that the church and the country had lost its strongest arbiter. Although the fifty-two-year-old Glemp, a one-time laborer who had earned two Roman ecclesiastical degrees, had spent twelve years on the cardinal's staff and had been Wyszyński's choice as successor, no successor could hope to match Wyszyński's prestige.[82] Glemp's negotiating experience made him acceptable to the party. When the Vatican named Glemp in July 1981, Party Secretary Kania immediately joined the Polish president and premier in sending congratulations. The government newspaper declared that the new primate "enjoys the sincere and warm approval of the state." He was less acceptable to some Solidarity activists and their clerical supporters, who had taken to calling him "Comrade Glemp" for what they perceived as his overly conciliatory attitude toward the government. The cardinal met with 300 such priests in December 1982 and received strong criticism from the group.

Glemp denounced the imposition of martial law as a "blow applied to the hopes and expectations of society and the government was terrorizing the nation," but many criticized the primate for not being strong enough. Glemp's words, however, merely echoed John Paul II's call to Poles "to do everything in their power to build a peaceful future and that Polish blood must not spill." Later the pope again expressed support for the workers in Poland (and other countries), declaring "the church is on the side of the workers." In the face of marital law the church had very few options. It wished neither to support Jaruzelski nor to call for a civil war which would invite Soviet intervention. Glemp did solve some minor difficulties, as in January 1982 when he declared that Poles might sign the government's loyalty oath without scruple, since coercion made the oath invalid and meaningless.[83]

The church had continuously urged talks between Solidarity and the government, but it was not until April 1982 that Glemp formally presented a list of proposals to achieve social accord. This ten-page letter, prepared by the archbishop's Social Council, was sent to all the bishops and the government authorities. Priests then read it at all masses on Easter Sunday. The letter emphasized four points: the release of all internees, amnesty for the people arrested for political offenses, a reactivation of Solidarity, and a dialogue between the authorities and labor union leaders. When Solidarity called a nation-wide strike for November 10, 1982, Glemp disapproved the action because he said it would only bring more repression to Poland. However, he added that this was only his own personal opinion, not the position of the bishops. During the strike Glemp did call all the bishops together for a three-day retreat at Częstochowa, thus distancing the church from the protest. The day before the strike Glemp and the government announced an agreement on the second visit of John Paul II for June 1983. The strike failed. Few people turned out, and government forces quickly broke up the demonstrations. On November 13, the government released Lech Wałęsa, who immediately went to consult with Glemp. Thus Glemp chose limited cooperation with Jaruzelski for limited gains, with the second visit of the pope as a key issue.

Jaruzelski agreed to the visit of John Paul because he hoped that a successful papal visit would add to the internal legitimacy of the government, demonstrate to the Soviets the correctness of Jaruzelski's policies, and ease relations with the United States and Western Europe. Religious Minister Adam Łopatka blatantly stated the hope of Polish officials that the visit would influence the Western nations to abandon the economic sanctions imposed in December 1981.[84] Soviet response to the visit had indicated displeasure. The Soviet journal *Novoye Uremya* (New Times) attacked the Polish journal *Polityka*, edited by "moderate" Vice-Premier Mieczysław Rakowski, for its "revisionist" content. The attack was thought to be instigated by the Polish ambassador to Moscow, hardliner Stanisław Kociolek, through his contacts with Soviet hard-liners unhappy about the papal visit and PRON.[85]

Both the government and the church sought assurances that the trip would not be used politically against their respective institutions. The government had forbidden papal visits to the cities of Gdańsk, Szczecin, and Lublin, while the Vatican had refused to provide advance copies of papal speeches, or to rule out a meeting with Wałęsa. The pope began with strong criticism of the government and continued it throughout the eight days. In his opening remarks to Jaruzelski John Paul said that he hoped "the social reforms announced on many occasions, according to the principles so painstakingly worked out in the critical days of August 1980 and contained in the agreements, will gradually be put into effect." After his first meeting with Jaruzelski, it was announced that the pope would meet Wałęsa. At Częstochowa John Paul described the creation of Solidarity as a "testimony which amazed the whole world, when the Polish worker stood up for himself with the gospel in his hand and a prayer on his lips." Later that day the pope first used the forbidden word "solidarity," and the 750,000 young people who had gathered for a special mass cheered loudly and waved red and white kerchiefs. The pope's first direct mention of the banned labor union by name waited for his address to a crowd of 1.2 million at the steel-producing city of Katowice in the Upper Silesian mining region. Huge enthusiastic crowds attended every mass. As many as one-half of the Polish nation may have seen John Paul personally during those eight days. Such a tremendous popular response from a "weary and cynical people" confounded both church and government analysts.

Government leaders, especially moderates who had been optimistic before the visit, became alarmed. Rakowski criticized "educators who treat history in an uncritical manner" and encourage youths to accept "myths, legends and half-truths." Government spokesperson Jerzy Urban warned that the visit might damage church-state relations. "We did not rent him the country for a week," snorted Urban. By the end of the trip even prelates like Glemp became concerned that the pope might have been so forceful that Jaruzelski's credibility with Moscow might have suffered fatal damage. Then it was announced that the church had requested a second meeting at Kraków's Wawel Castle between the pope and the general. The Vatican press secretary, Father Romeo Panciroli, blamed all political interpretations of the "exclusively religious and moral" visit on Western reporters. Glemp repeated the latter charge in Rome.[86] Jaruzelski's second meeting and the denial of the visit's political implications by both church and state salvaged some prestige for the Warsaw government, which immediately announced that the papal visit had been a huge success. For example, Łopatka told parliament that the pope's visit was of "enormous positive value," despite the efforts of some, aided by Western radio stations, "to use the religious congregations for ignoble political ends." *Polityka* praised the pope personally and commented that John Paul "can help Poland overcome the political boycott in which the visit makes another break, and the economic boycott forced through by the United States, inflicting so many losses on us."[87]

The papal visit did demonstrate conclusively where Polish popular support lay, but it did not solve the Polish political stalemate. In addition to the tension between church and state, both Jaruzelski and Glemp continue to face significant opposition within their respective institutions. Furthermore, both the Soviet Union and the United States must concur in any permanent settlement. Moscow could forcibly remove Jaruzelski, and the lifting of American sanctions is necessary for the full reconstruction of the Polish economy. Pressure from the two superpowers has been a major factor in decisions about the release of certain dissidents.

Just as Jaruzelski heads institutions made up of members with a wide spectrum of political views, so does Glemp. Activist priests like Lech Wałęsa's spiritual adviser, Henryk Jankowski and the late

Jerzy Popiełuszko of Warsaw had been particularly galling to the authorities. When Jaruzelski and Glemp met for five hours on January 6, 1984, Glemp agreed to try to moderate the statements of these priests about the government, although Glemp told the general that "priests like Jankowski and Popiełuszko did not surface of their own or the church's accord, but as a result of errors and injustices committed by the authorities, especially in the field of human rights." Jaruzelski undertook to free political prisoners and end political trials. The Warsaw newspaper *Życie Warszawy* said that the meeting between Jaruzelski and Glemp "finally and irrevocably disposed of allegations of growing tension between the church and the state."[88]

At the end of January bishops met with Glemp and issued a statement pledging a continued struggle against domestic oppression, but encouraging the people to cooperate with the authorities when food prices went up the following Monday.[89] Both the general and the cardinal tried to prevent the "War of the Crosses" in March from becoming a national political issue. Jaruzelski did not comment directly on the controversy but said "Neither the state nor the church needs a conflict. It would only suit Poland's enemies, and would bring our country irreparable losses." He also conceded that there had been "misunderstandings and frictions, especially in the context of the principle of separation of church from state, which is constitutionally sanctioned in all the modern states in the world." Contrasted with the moderate tone of these remarks to 1,700 party delegates to a national congress, Jaruzelski sharply criticized "converted" antigovernment activists who used the church's prestige, and priests who "have confused the pulpit with the Radio Free Europe microphone."[90]

The church-state modus vivendi received a severe test, however, following the kidnapping of the thirty-seven-year-old priest Jerzy Popiełuszko by three security officers on October 19, 1984. Interior minister General Czesław Kiszczak announced on television that he had arrested members of his own ministry who had abducted and possibly killed the priest.[91] Both Glemp and Wałęsa issued appeals for calm. Glemp told worshipers at St. John's Cathedral that the "tragic abduction" might have been an attempt to provoke opponents of the government. Wałęsa said: "We won't let anybody pull us into brawls in which we will lose. We simply cannot let anybody manipulate us into any situation. If somebody assumed it would be a revolution, I won't give him a bloody revolution. I am for peaceful evolution."[92] Popiełuszko's body was recovered from a reservoir on the Vistula River on October 30. The following day John Paul II spoke to Polish pilgrims, calling for restrained reaction. "May the great moral eloquence of this death not be disturbed by anything."[93] The event seemed to move the church and Solidarity closer together and blunt a government press campaign against the church. Both Glemp and Wałęsa spoke at the funeral mass.

Although the arrest and sentencing of Popiełuszko's murderers partially mollified the public, church-state relations remain cool because of the Jaruzelski government's continual pressure against political dissidents and activist priests. Glemp and Jaruzelski did not meet between January 1984 and June 1985. The latter meeting was held as an attempt by both sides to keep relations from getting even worse. According to the final communiqué, the two sides "discussed the principles of church-state relations and the significant issues of public life," but no progress was reported on any outstanding issues.[94] When Foreign Minister Stefan Olszowski hinted at Warsaw's readiness for diplomatic relations with the Vatican, John Paul II dismissed the suggestion as not "appropriate." Jaruzelski could not hope that Glemp would tell Catholics to vote in the October 13, 1985, parliamentary elections as Wyszyński had for Gomułka in 1957, but the primate did go to Rome during the voting. However, the changed conditions were reflected in the fact that the cardinal declined an official offer of a few seats for orthodox Catholics, and discouraged some prominent laymen from standing on their own. Thus, for the first time since 1957 the Polish parliament has no official church representation. Despite some calls by remnants of the Solidarity underground for a boycott of the election, the government got a good turnout at the polls. Jaruzelski used this mandate the next month to strengthen his hold on the party. Olszowski, long regarded as the most powerful of the pro-Soviet hardliners, and Mieczysław Rakowski, the most prominent of the party liberals, were both removed from the Politburo.[95]

CONCLUSION: THE CATHOLIC CHURCH AND SOVIET POLICY IN EASTERN EUROPE

The Polish tragedy remains so difficult to solve because it involves very complex and intertwined political, economic, and social issues. At the level of political legitimacy, the Eastern bloc's weakest Communist party is no match for Europe's strongest church, so the Polish army has been forced to intervene to maintain order. None of the external governmental arrangements even approximates the realities of political legitimacy, thus permanently disorienting the entire society. The Polish government has lacked the legitimacy to introduce needed economic reforms, either a complete restructuring of prices or the firing of incredibly greedy, corrupt, and inefficient state managers. Although the country was forced to follow Soviet-style development after World War II, poor planning and heavy borrowing during the 1970s have been the immediate causes of the current economic crisis. Western bankers, with West Germany holding the largest portfolio, fear that the Poles may never reform their economy sufficiently to pay off their huge international debt. Poland has abundant fertile land, but until lately farmers have been given no incentive to produce. Every time the government raised food prices, it courted political disaster. Private peasant farmers cultivate more than 80 percent of the arable land, but the government has always discriminated against the private sector in favor of inefficient state farms. The cynicism of Polish workers finds an outlet in alcoholism, lack of discipline, and the glorification of cheating the system.

Even in a favorable international climate, such national problems can only be resolved through the cooperation of the Polish army and the Polish church. However, Jaruzelski and Glemp, each "good Poles in their hearts," both have significant political difficulties in controlling their own institutions. Much hard bargaining remains over the exact role of Wałęsa and other Solidarity activists. The remaining negotiations will be difficult enough, but peripheral crises can intrude into Polish national politics at any time. They can come from the local level of Polish politics, as in the "War of the Crosses," or the murder of Jerzy Popiełuszko. They can also derive from international politics, as when Moscow criticizes Polish party moderates or when the United States fosters the collapse of the Polish economy.

Although the Soviet Union is the principal foreign influence in Poland, the role of the United States is also significant. The Jaruzelski government, following the words of John Paul II when he first met Gierek, has perceived the treatment of the church and Solidarity as connected with American foreign policy. When the Polish government released nearly all the political prisoners, including the eleven Solidarity and KOR activists in the summer of 1984, it anticipated that the amnesty would open the door to an end of United States economic sanctions. The Reagan Administration had originally set three conditions for the lifting of sanctions: the abolition of martial law, the freeing of political prisoners, and the resumption of a dialogue with the church and Solidarity. The United States gradually stopped speaking of Solidarity. While the church position was not publicly announced,[96] the Chicago-based Polish-American Congress switched its position to advocate the lifting of sanctions. Its president, Aloysius A. Mazewski, made it clear that he was making his recommendation to Reagan only after consultation with the church. "Like all of us, the Polish church is cautious," said Mazewski. "But the church is inclined toward removing one of the substantive sanctions."[97] In its attempts to improve its domestic economy, the Polish government sought commodity and trade credits, readmission to the International Monetary Fund, and reinstitution of most-favored-nation treatment for Polish exports. Reagan, however, merely lifted the bans on Polish airline flights and scientific and cultural exchanges, leaving the substantive penalties in place. The United States argued that the amnesty had not been fully observed, and that the government had to establish a "dialogue with the whole nation."

By the end of September 1984 Polish spokespersons began attacking the United States for not fulfilling its part of the arrangement. American failure to respond more substantively was giving party hardliners an issue to use against Jaruzelski. Many of Poland's creditors in Western Europe wanted to see Poland readmitted to the IMF to encourage economic stability.[98] In October Western European nations moved to end Poland's diplomatic isolation. Austria's Foreign Minister Leopold Gratz led the way, followed by representatives from many NATO powers.[99] Finally, on December 8, the government released Solidarity members Bogdan Lis and Piotr Mierzejewski, who had been under investigation for high treason. Nine days later the United States announced that it would no longer oppose Poland's attempt to rejoin the IMF. In early 1985 British Foreign Secretary Howe visited Warsaw, but he also layed a wreath at the grave of Popiełuszko and visited Solidarity activists. Later visits by Belgian, Irish, Danish, and Spanish foreign ministers were canceled because the form of the visit could not be agreed on. Jaruzelski made a diplomatic breakthrough in December 1985 with his visit to Mitterand in Paris and former German Chancellor Willy Brandt's visit to Warsaw. Brandt did not meet with Wałęsa, his fellow Nobel Peace laureate, but with four Catholic intellectuals, two of whom have links to Solidarity.[100] On April 24, 1986, Jaruzelski and Glemp held five hours of talks, their first meeting in ten months. The general and the cardinal called for the lifting of Western economic sanctions, said that full Vatican-Polish diplomatic relations would "serve the nation," and pledged to continue work on an agreement that would grant the church legal status.[101]

Both Jaruzelski and Glemp have sought a modus vivendi in the interests of the Polish nation. Critics of the current malaise in the Polish political, economic, and social systems often point to Hungary as an example of what national concensus can do for an Eastern European country. In the years following the abortive revolution of 1956, János Kádár has moved the nation toward economic and some political liberalization. At the time of the Polish price increase of 10 percent in January 1984, the Hungarian government raised prices by 20 percent without the fear and trepidation experienced in Warsaw government circles. The key to Hungarian economic liberalization has been agricultural reform. The government still harrasses dissidents, especially those associated with the *samizdat* press, but even the activists themselves admit they have more freedom than elsewhere in the Eastern bloc.[102] Budapest has staged the continental European première of the musical "Cats" and has produced its own rock-opera movie, "Stephen the King," in imitation of "Jesus Christ Superstar," presumably as the original king sought to imitate Christ.[103] The focus on "Stephen the King" emphasizes the importance of Catholic tradition to Hungarian nationalism. Cardinal Lékai and the government worked out a modus vivendi, and neither was anxious for a papal visit that would disturb it.

With the exception of Hungary and Yugoslavia, the tangible political benefits of Paul VI's *Ostpolitik* have remained so few that analyses of these relations often read like the travel diaries of Vatican and Eastern European diplomats. Such a characterization is especially valid after the regularized bureaucracy of Brezhnev's government replaced Khrushchev's improvisation which allowed for semi-private contacts and agreements. Foreign Minister Gromyko arranged to see Paul VI at the United Nations in 1965, and then visited the pope at the Vatican in 1966, 1970, 1974, and 1975. President Podgorny visited Paul VI on January 30, 1967. Casaroli first traveled to Moscow in February 1971 to sign Vatican adherence to the Nuclear Non-Proliferation Treaty. Casaroli's major interest concerned making direct contact with those responsible for the USSR's policy toward the Catholic Church.[104] The Soviet representatives reacted in a manner which "resembled the thinking of the czarist era. Catholics actually existed almost solely in the Baltic republics, which had bishops, and competent comrades as well, they said."[105]

Such contacts have demonstrated conclusively that the Vatican and the Soviet Union retain different agendas in their relations. Rome seeks to attain greater freedom for the national churches, as Moscow directly controls Soviet religious policy and indirectly influences the religious policy of the entire Eastern bloc. Paul VI requested greater religious freedom at each of his four meetings with Gromyko.[106] On the other hand, Gromyko's interest in the pope stemmed from Paul's call for peace at the United Nations, which echoed Soviet concerns.

For the Catholic Church the accession of Gorbachev has both advantages and disadvantages. No longer can Eastern European politicians and ecclesiastics count on the weaknesses of the Soviet "interregnum" (1979-1985) to open opportunities for independent action. Recent Soviet moves short of significant concessions to better relations with China and Japan can be seen an attempt by the new Soviet leadership to secure their Asian front while restoring discipline to Eastern Europe. On the other hand, Gorbachev better appreciates the political value of expressive institutions like the Catholic Church, and he went out of his way to strengthen Jaruzelski during 1986 Soviet and Polish Party Congresses.[107] In his dealings with Glemp the Polish party leader will be able to get a clear "da" or "nyet" from Gorbachev without worrying about the machinations of Polish and Soviet hardliners.

The impact of John Paul's assertiveness in *Ostpolitik* can best be examplified in the case of the Polish and Czechoslovakian churches. The Slavic pope inspired the movement that led to Solidarity and galvinized Tomášek's resistance to government control of the Czech church. The curial attack on clerical involvement with Pacem in Terris was particularly significant. External papal policies like *Ostpolitik*, of course, provide only limited support to national churches. The main determinant of whether or not Catholic Churches can obtain concessions from their respective Eastern European governments remains the internal strength of the churches. The forty-fourth issue of the *Chronicle of the Catholic Church in Lithuania* comments, "The priests and faithful of Lithuania long ago understood the truth expressed so beautifully by Pope John Paul II when he said that the faithful will have as much religious freedom as they win for themselves." The major factors which contribute to that strength include the percentage of the population that is Catholic, the fervor of that faith, the strength of the ecclesiastical organization, the quality of the hierarchical leadership, and the identity of Catholicism with nationalism. The Polish church under Cardinals Wyszyński and Glemp has rated high in all five categories.[108]

Poland, Hungary, and Czechoslovakia all have majority Catholic populations. Unlike Poland, however, the episcopal tradition in Hungary and Czechoslovakia has been that of cooperation with the empire of the Catholic Hapsburgs. Czechoslovavia also unites two different Catholic traditions, the historical Catholic nationalism of the Slovaks and the Germanizing ecclesiastical control of the Hapsburgs over the secularized Czechs. With regard to the Slovakian tradition, many political parallels exist with the Croatian Catholic tradition in Yugoslavia.

Both Eastern European governments and Eastern bloc churches would benefit from a lessening of Soviet-American tensions. Polish Foreign Minister Olszowski and Romanian Foreign Minister Andrei made speeches to this effect to the United Nations in September 1984.[109] The greater the tensions between the superpowers, the more the Soviet leadership perceives Polish Catholic nationalism as threatening to their hegemony in Eastern Europe and as setting a dangerous precedent for the Lithuanians and Ukranians within the Soviet Union itself. Therefore, worsening Soviet-American relations decreases the internal bargaining power of national Catholic Churches in Eastern Europe. In fact, one high-ranking Polish Catholic politician told me that any definitive solution to Polish tensions must await the return of *détente*.[110]

CHAPTER 7

Catholicism and Soviet-American Competition in the Third World

CATHOLIC POLITICS IN THE MIDDLE EAST: JOHN PAUL MEETS YASIR ARAFAT

ON SEPTEMBER 15, 1982, John Paul II met with PLO leader Yasir Arafat in a twenty-minute private audience. This meeting followed the PLO's summer debacle in Lebanon when the Israelis had forced the evacuation of Arafat's main force. Few details of the meeting between the pope and the guerrilla leader were released, but the news photo of the white-robed pontiff and Arafat, wearing a black and white kafiyeh headdress and an olive green uniform, made practically every major newspaper in the West and the Middle East. Later in the day the pope called for Israel and the PLO to "accept the existence and reality of the other." A PLO spokesman called the audience "a turning point" in favor of the movement.[1] When the Israeli government had learned of the proposed meeting several days earlier, Israel cabinet spokesperson Dan Meridor said, "If, in fact, Arafat meets the Pope, Israel would view the meeting grievously."[2] Ranan Naim, one of Israel's seven delegates to the same Interparliamentary Union meeting that Arafat was scheduled to attend, said he would also request a meeting with the pope and threatened to demonstrate outside the Arafat meeting.

Another "senior Israeli official" stated that the Roman Catholic Church had not spoken out against the Holocaust or the killing of Christians in Lebanon but that now the pope wanted to meet the guerrilla leader sworn to destroy Israel and thus complete the work of the Nazis. These remarks infuriated curial officials, who issued an official communiqué that castigated such statements for ignoring all that the church had done to save Jews during World War II. This "outrage," asserted the Vatican communiqué, had been expressed "in language so little respectful of a Pope of whom one cannot ignore what he has said on numerous occasions, and particularly during his visit to Auschwitz, to condemn and abhor the genocide directed by the Nazis against the Jewish people (and not only against them)."[3] When the John Paul–Arafat meeting actually took place,

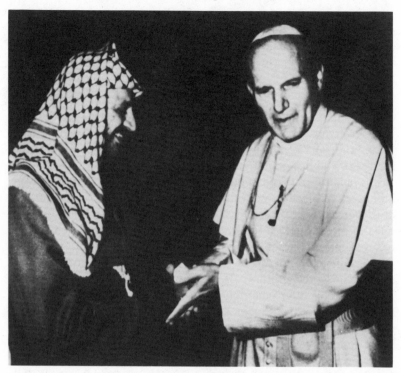

VATICAN CITY. Pope John Paul II shakes hands with Yasser Arafat, during a private audience at the Vatican, September 1982. AP/Wide World Photos.

the Israeli Foreign Ministry termed it "revolting." Major Saad Haddad, commander of the Christian militias in southern Lebanon and a firm ally of Israel, claimed that Arafat was responsible for killing at least 100,000 Christians, and "We wonder how our spiritual father can receive our killer."[4]

The Middle East is one geographic area where the policies of the Vatican and the United States have diverged since the founding of the state of Israel in 1947. While the United States has fostered the Israelis as the West's primary outpost in this volatile region and only very recently has come to consider any role at all for the PLO, the Vatican has always placed primary emphasis on solving the Palestinian problem by providing the Palestinians with a secure homeland. American Monsignor John Nolan, president of the Pontifical Commission for Palestine (Vatican relief agency for the Palestinian refugees), stated:

The core problem in the Middle East is the Palestinians, not only those living in Lebanon—the site of recent Isareli air raids—but also the million refugees in Syria, Jordan, the Gaza Strip and the West Bank. A solution agreeable both to them and the Jews must be reached if there is to be lasting peace.[5]

The Vatican's call for the internationalization of Jerusalem has also challenged American and Israeli policy. On April 19, 1984, John Paul wrote an apostolic letter to the Middle East in which he reaffirmed official Vatican support for a Palestinian homeland, security for Israel, and designation of Jerusalem as an open city protected by "a special, internationally guaranteed statute so that one side or the other cannot place it under discrimination."[6] Some Polish members of the Curia have pressed for the diplomatic recognition of Israel, but the foreign policy apparatus led by Secretary of State Casaroli has resisted such a move. The pope, whose strong repugnance for anti-Semitism might make him sympathetic to the international symbolism of recognition, also reaffirmed the position of the April 1984 apostolic letter when he received the credentials of the Egyptian ambassador in October 1984.[7] The Vatican currently has diplomatic relations with Algeria, Egypt, Kuwait, Lebanon, Morocco, Syria, and Tunisia. This position has brought the Vatican into consultation with moderate Arab states like Egypt and Jordan. For example, on June 18, 1979, Egyptian Foreign Minister Boutros Ghali led a delegation to see John Paul II, Casaroli, and Archbishop Achille Silvestrini, secretary of the Council for the Public Affairs of the Church. Vatican press spokesman Father Romeo Panciroli said the meeting dealt with "the urgent need to bring about the legitimate rights of the Palestinian people" and the status of Jerusalem. The Vatican, of course, opposed the July 30, 1980, Knesset vote which proclaimed the city the indivisible capital of Israel. John Paul met with King Hussein of Jordan on September 1, 1980, to discuss this particular issue.[8]

While Vatican Middle East policy has been closest to the moderate Arabs, the papacy has also emphasized maintaining communication with Israel. John Paul II met with Israeli Prime Minister Shimon Peres for forty minutes on February 19, 1985. After the meeting Peres reiterated his country's resolve, despite Vatican opposition, to keep Jerusalem as its capital. Speaking for the Vatican, Joaquin Navarro Valls commented that the meeting had been "cordial" but that the positions of Israel and the Vatican on the Middle East were "not identical."[9] The significance of Israel for Soviet-American relations is magnified by the fact that the three largest Jewish populations exist in the United States (nearly 6 million), Israel (3.4 million), and the Soviet Union (1.6 million).

Jewish emigration from the USSR remains the major Soviet issue for American Jewish organizations. On May 5, 1985, the same day that President Reagan visited Bergen-Belsen, New York Jews sponsored a "Solidarity Sunday" demonstration to encourage administration officials to press for the rights of Soviet Jews. The quarter-page *New York Times* (May 8, 1985) advertisement quoted Archbishop O'Connor's remarks to the march, "It is my passionate conviction that as long as Jews are not free, the entire world lives in slavery." At a dinner the following November honoring the cardinal for his work in interfaith relations, Edgar M. Bronfman, president of the World Jewish Congress, used his introduction to urge O'Connor to "please convey to Rome the importance to Jews everywhere of normalizing relations between the Vatican and Israel, which is home for so much of Jewish culture and so many of the world's Jews."[10] The Vatican has made a special effort to develop contacts with American Jews. The pope saw a delegation of American Jewish Committee leaders and issued a strong condemnation of anti-Semitism in February 1985. When the pope visited Rome's main synagogue on April 13, 1986, the city's chief rabbi called the decision "courageous and coherent," while the Israeli Foreign Ministry hoped it might be a prelude to recognition.[11]

The Vatican's primary diplomatic emphasis on a solution to the Palestinian problem has resulted in active Catholic support for a continued Palestinian presence on the West Bank occupied by Israel in 1967. This support has brought Catholic institutions directly into conflict with the Israeli military which administers the West Bank and with Jewish fundamentalists who wish to secure the area politically by Jewish settlements. In addition to Catholic relief efforts for the Palestinian refugees, Pope Paul VI founded Bethlehem University in 1973 to help stem the tide of Christian emigration from Palestine. The university, which has a student body of 35 percent Christians and 65 percent Muslims, has had a series of difficulties with the Israeli Ministry of Defense. According to the university's vice-chancellor and chief executive officer, American Christian Brother Thomas Scanlan:

> The major problems are mainly political because we operate in an occupied territory. We only deal with the Israelis through the Minstry of Defense because the military is responsible for the occupied territories. So a

fundamental orientation is lacking in that we do not deal with Israel's Ministry of Education or its Ministry of Religious Affairs.

The history of all the universities (Catholic Bethlehem, Protestant Bir Zeit and Muslim Al Najah) in the occupied West Bank of Palestine and their relationship with the Israeli military, especially under the Likud party, has been a series of conflicts. I think the reason is that the universities bring stability and development directly into this area.

The Israelis who wish to annex the West Bank, however, must enact policies which tend to increase the rate of emigration. And that is why there is a conflict between the West Bank universities and the present government of Israel.[12]

Syrian Melkite-Rite[13] Archbishop Hilarion Capucci has caused even greater friction between the Vatican and Israel by his active support of the PLO. An Israeli court convicted Capucci of gun-running for the Palestinians in 1974. Israel released him from prison in 1977 following Vatican guarantees that he would not return to the Middle East nor publicly discuss political issues of the region. The Vatican Congregation for Eastern Rite Churches then appointed him as visitor to the Melkites in Latin America, and as visitor for Western Europe in 1979. The Israeli embassy in Rome protested the second appointment. Capucci met Arafat in Madrid in September 1979, and first visited post-revolutionary Iran in January of that year.

Vatican spokespersons have denied that Capucci represents Vatican policy at various times, but the Syrian archbishop has undertaken papal missions to radical Islamic leaders.[14] Capucci was also involved in an attempt to mediate the American hostage crisis in Iran in April 1980. The more moderate Iranian officials such as Prime Minister Abolhassan Bani-Sadr and Foreign Minister Sadegh Ghotbzadeh, were looking for a way out of the crisis created when Islamic militants stormed the American embassy and took the hostages. The Iranian officials hoped to use Capucci, Iran's Papal Nuncio Annibale Bugnini, the Swiss Ambassador Erik Lang, and the Argentinian lawyer Hector Villalón as a mediation team. However, the Ayatollah Khomeini rebuffed Bani-Sadr by leaving the hostages in the control of the militants. President Carter then cut off diplomatic relations. Had the mediation proved successful, it would have greatly benefited Carter, Bani-Sadr, and Ghotbzadeh, all of whom subsequently lost heavily because of the continued crisis.[15] Thus, Capucci plays the ambiguous diplomatic role of Vatican contact with the more radical Islamic leaders, while leaving the Vatican free to disown any potentially embarrassing initiatives. Capucci

ROME. Pope John Paul II is escorted by Rome's chief Rabbi Elio Toaff as they enter Synagogue. It was the first recorded visit by a pope to a synagogue, April 1986. AP/Wide World Photo.

himself has deflected questions about his relationship to the Vatican with "the Church of Rome is a great mother, and I am a son of this mother."[16] He termed his Iranian initiatives humanitarian, denying that they had violated the Vatican-Israeli accord because that agreement only banned permanent residence in the Middle East.

The Vatican's primary diplomatic emphasis on a solution to the Palestinian problem is also related to the church's primary organizational interest in defending Middle Eastern Catholics. Most of these Middle Eastern Catholics belong to non-Latin rites and strongly support a Palestinian homeland. The principal Catholic groups in Lebanon belong to the Maronite and Melkite rites. Both the Maronite and Melkite patriarchs have called a solution of the Palestinian problem the key to peace in the Middle East.[17] While Vatican policy differs significantly from United States and Israeli policy with regard to the Palestinian problem, all three countries are vitally interested in the political stability of the Lebanese Maronite community.[18] The Vatican, the United States, and Israel have all been embarrassed by the sectarian brutality of the Maronite Phalangist Party and the Christian militias. The Syrian and Israeli interventions increased the factionalism among Maronite groups. In 1978 the Lebanese Forces, the Phalangist militia that had been built up by Bashir Gemayel attacked the summer home of the rival Maronite chief Suleiman Franjieh. The surprise assault, led by Samir Geagea, gunned down Franjieh's eldest son, Tony, and his wife and baby daughter. In 1980, in what is euphemistically termed the "July 7 corrective movement," the Phalangist militia attacked another Maronite leader Camille Chamoun's personal militia and destroyed it as an effective fighting force. Throughout this period Bashir Gemayel used such tactics until he alone could represent the Maronites.[19] It is no wonder that rumor in Beirut had had papal representative Cardinal Paolo Bertoli muttering, "These people are not Christians,"[20] as he left the city in November 1975 after his first attempt at mediation.

The Vatican was not represented when the leaders of various Lebanese factions met in Geneva in November 1983 in an attempt to reach an agreement that would end the fighting. The bitter intrasect factionalism is exacerbated by the strong role that outside forces play in the Lebanese situation. At Geneva, for example, the Syrian observer, Foreign Minister Abdel Halim Khaddam, exercised considerable clout. A "senior pro-Syrian Christian" said, "All the Lebanese can do here is cosmetics. We have to get the frame set first and that frame can only come through an outside agreement between the Israelis, Syrians, Americans and Soviets. They are the dynamic forces. Without them, this conference will be a mess. It will be nothing more than a masked ball."[21] The Israelis worked out of their consulate. The American delegation, led by special Middle East envoy, Richard Fairbanks, told participants it would permit no tampering with the May 1983 Israel-Lebanon accord. The conference ended with Lebanese President Amin Gemayel traveling to various capitals to search for ways to persuade Israel to withdraw from southern Lebanon despite his government's repudiation of the accord. He met separately with John Paul II and Italian Prime Minister Craxi on November 28 before going on to Washington.[22]

Within the Catholic Church, the political spectrum stretches from militant Maronite monks at one end to the pope and the Curia at the other. The Maronite patriarch generally stands for moderation within Lebanon, but he also plays a major role in the Maronite consensus, so that some of his statements sound less moderate than the pope's. One of the leading ideologues for the Maronite militias is Father Paul Naaman. "We might," the monk concedes, "have a less developed form of Christianity than you people in the West. But at least we fiercely cling to our Christian traditions." He also argues, "What we have had till now may have been a dictatorship exercised by the Christians, but is that any less just that the dictatorship of the majority?"[23] Naaman had a close relationship to Bashir Gemayel and gave a eulogy at his requiem after Bashir's assassination.[24] Church officials, who had been guaranteed the right to visit their churches and monasteries in Israel by the 1949 armistice agreement, were the only Lebanese civilians freely allowed to cross the Israeli-Lebanese border. Naaman did not hide his connections to Israeli officials.[25]

The current Maronite Patriarch Antoine Pierre Khoraiche, who was also made a cardinal in 1983, has consistently called for moderation and compromise. When the Phalangists again attacked Franjieh's forces in July 1980, the patriarch released a statement in *L'Osservatore Romano* vigorously condemning the "atrocities" and "abominations" committed during the fighting which claimed more than 300 lives. He said that there were reports of "mistreatment of prisoners, disrespect for corpses and the murder of innocent citizens and the destruction of homes." The patriarch also praised commentary elsewhere in *L'Osservatore Romano* that reminded warring factions that "there are human and Christian motivations which must have absolute priority over every other consideration of differences or political dissent."[26]

Syrian President Hafez al-Assad's intervention on behalf of the Maronites had left Syria as the dominant influence on the Lebanese government. The rise of Bashir Gemayel, however, and the losses of Syria's client Franjieh increased Israeli influence. Israel first invaded Lebanon in March 1978. Although American President Carter reacted forcefully, Israeli Prime Minister Begin did not withdraw his troops until June, leaving his client Major Haddad and the Christian militias as a buffer zone. The United Nations Peacekeeping Force established another buffer zone to stabilize the military situation. Nevertheless, Arafat and the PLO continued to reside in a fragmented Lebanon in which Israel's enemy Syria played the major role. The Israelis attempted to solve their Palestinian problem once and for all with a full-scale attack on Lebanon in June 1982. The Israeli army swept all before it, and the PLO guerrillas were forced to withdraw from Lebanon and to split up into many different contingents throughout the Arab world. Begin seemed to have solved the Lebanese problem without the participation of the United States, the Soviet Union, or Syria.

The Israelis, of course, had not planned to occupy and administer Lebanon permanently. They hoped that their Maronite allies, under Bashir, could now maintain control. The United States also began to pressure Israel to withdraw, and joined France, Britain, and Italy in sending a Multinational Peacekeeping Force to the area, hoping to stabilize Lebanon under a Maronite-led administration without the participation of Syria or the Soviet Union. The United States sponsored an Israeli-Lebanese Accord as the keystone of this policy. When the newly elected president Bashir Gemayel was assassinated on September 14, 1982, his brother and the new president Amin Gemayel signed the accord.

The situation, however, continued to deteriorate. Many Muslims and their allies the Druze[27] perceived the Multinational Force as employed for the benefit of the Maronites. Terrorist attacks increased, especially against the American and French forces. Many militant Maronites sought to seize the opportunity to control Druze sections, especially in the Shuf Mountains.[28] The Druze refused to permit the Christian-dominated Lebanese army to reenter the area, and the stage was set for a mini-civil war in the Shuf. The Syrian-supported Druze militia decisively defeated the Maronites, thus altering the balance of power around Beirut. Amin Gemayel then realized that no solution was possible without Syrian participation. The Multinational Force of the Western Powers, symbol of the United States–Israeli policy to exclude Syrian influence, began leaving Lebanon in February 1984.[29]

The period February 1975–February 1984 produced many losers in the Lebanese situation: the Lebanese people, the Maronites, Israel, the United States, and the PLO. Israel expelled the PLO from Beirut, and Syria expelled Arafat from Damascus while fostering discord within the guerrilla organization. The Vatican joins the list of losers. Not only is the survival of Maronite Catholicism still threatened, but Arafat, whom the Vatican perceived as part of a moderate solution to the Palestinian question on the West Bank, was greatly weakened. John Paul continues to support Amin Gemayel in his attempts to regain Lebanese independence in both domestic and international affairs. On October 23, 1984, Gemayel visited both the pope and Italian Prime Minister Craxi. It was Gemayel's third audience with John Paul. The pope had just received a letter from Franjieh requesting that he press the United

States to get Israel to withdraw from Lebanon and the West Bank. Gemayel hoped to use Craxi's influence to get fellow Socialist and Druze leader Walid Jumblatt to agree to security arrangements within Lebanon.[30]

The clear winners were the Lebanese left, Syria, and the Soviet Union. Any permanent solution to power sharing will have to reflect the growth of population and the increased fighting effectiveness of the Shiites.[31] Syria has reestablished its dominant position in the country. Recent events have also reversed the decline of Soviet influence in the Middle East that followed the Arab-Israeli War of 1973. The Soviets launched no major initiatives, but merely waited for American policy to fall apart. In early April 1984 a high-level Soviet delegation was sent to Beirut. Two months earlier Amin Gemayel had warned President Reagan that, if United States Marines were withdrawn, "There would not be a new president to replace Amin Gemayel, but a revolutionary council under Soviet control, or chaos."[32] The revolt of the Lebanese Forces against Gemayel in March 1985 added to the chaos. Any lasting solution to the Lebanese question will demand the participation of the Soviet Union, the United States, Syria, and Israel.

The growing isolation of the Maronite community in Lebanon has worried Vatican policy makers and other Catholic leaders concerned with the Middle East. The United States church has maintained contact with the Middle East through the Near East Welfare Association, traditionally headed by the archbishop of New York. In June 1986 Cardinal O'Connor traveled to Lebanon, where he met with Sheik Hassan Khaled, the spritual leader of the Sunni Muslim community. The Vatican said that O'Connor's visit was not part of a Vatican peace mission but was designed to show solidarity with the Maronites. The cardinal did stop in Rome, however, on his way back to New York. Although the cardinal was unable to deliver family messages to American hostages held by the pro-Iranian Shiite Jihad (Holy War), this terrorist organization did release American missionary Father Lawrence Jenco on July 26, 1986. Jenco received phone calls from President Reagan and John Paul II before going to Rome to see the pope.[33]

CENTRAL AMERICA: CATHOLICISM, THE WESTERN MEDIA, AND HUMAN RIGHTS[34]

When John Paul visited Managua on March 4, 1983, his sermon focused on internal church matters, failing to mention such recent national political events as the deaths of seventeen youths killed by the Contras. This distressed all the Sandinista supporters in his audience, but especially about fifty mothers of "heroes" (those who had died for the Revolution) who sat in the front row within reach of the crowd microphones. During and immediately after the sermon, according to the usually reliable newsletter of the Historical Institute of the Nicaraguan Jesuits,[35] a spontaneous demonstration began with the mothers chanting, "We want peace." At the same point, junta members who had remained respectful up to that point, added their own revolutionary slogans from the stands on the side. Government supporters and opponents both used the microphones. According to one eye-witness, the demonstration broke out when one petitioner prayed for mercy for Sandinista political prisoners and Nicaraguans in exile.[36]

The various news reports of the papal visit to Nicaragua reflected the political divisions within the crowds, and thus advocacy of this or that news report became a political event in itself.[37] Costa Rican Archbishop Román Arrieta Villalobos, president of the Central American episcopal secretariat, issued a formal statement excoriating "the behavior of the Sandinista mobs, who, duly organized and skillfully directed, showed disrespect for the Vicar of Christ and turned the Eucharist celebrated by His Holiness . . . into a political meeting." L'Osservatore Romano stressed the responsibility of "Sandinista militants" who manipulated the sound system. Daniel Ortega Saavedra spoke for the junta when he described the mass as "a massive dialogue between the people and the Pope." Father Ernesto Cardenal called the incident 'a counter-revolutionary meeting.'"[38] On the whole, according to Jon Snow of British Independent Television News, Sandinista crowd manipulation did occur, but nothing so sophisticated as suggested by L'Osservatore. The crowd contained both supporters and opponents of the government. The pope, relying on his briefing by Archbishop Miguel Obando y Bravo, misjudged the tenor of the situation, especially the deep feelings about the deaths of the youths.

Although the papal trip to Central America did not demonstrate the political deftness of John Paul's trip to Poland three months later, most Central American Catholics, even those who were discouraged by his theological positions, experienced the trip as a significant religious event. Even the politically disappointing visit to Nicaragua retained a positive accent. The pope visited eight countries in eight days, the most sensitive visits being those to Nicaragua, El Salvador, and Guatemala—countries shaken by political violence whose Catholic hierarchies were in some conflict with their respective governments.

In Guatemala the pope focused on human rights. He reprimanded the Protestant dictator Rios Montt for executing six opponents after the Vatican had made a special plea for their release. In his homily during the mass in Guatemala City he said, "When you trample a man, when you violate his rights, when you commit flagrant injustices against him, when you submit him to torture, break in and kidnap him or violate his right to life, you commit a crime and a great offense against God."[39] He encouraged greater solidarity among the various Guatemalan Indian tribes as a means of strengthening their resistance against exploitation. The pope also strongly challenged the Haitian regime of thirty-two-year-old Jean-Claude (Baby Doc) Duvalier for repression and social injustice. John Paul's words strengthened the Haitian church, which was channeling and organizing opposition to the Duvalier family rule.[40] Three years later Duvalier had fled, and most analysts focused on the church, rather than any political party or labor union, as the principal local catalyst.[41]

The pope used Archbishop Oscar Romero's theme of "reconciliation" as his keynote in El Salvador. John Paul pleaded for a dialogue that was not a "tactical truce," but a "sincere effort to respond to the search for agreement, to respond to the anguish, the pain, weariness and fatigue of the many, many that yearn for peace." Both the rich and the terrorist must change. "No one must be excluded in this effort for peace." The pope did not call for negotiations with the leftist opposition, a position opposed by both the American and Salvadoran governments, but he did emphasize "dialogue and reconciliation." In his welcoming speech, provisional President Alvaro Magnaña pledged that his government would hold elections within the year. Thus, John Paul emphasized a different theme in each country: El Salvador (peace and reconciliation), Guatemala (human rights), and Nicaragua (church unity).[42]

Many American Catholics began to pay attention to Central American politics as a result of secular media coverage of the assassinations of Archbishop Romero in March 1980 and the four American Catholic women missionaries less than nine months later. The kidnapping and murder of Maura Clarke, Jean Donovan, Ita Ford, and Dorothy Hazel generated not only immediate and extensive television and print coverage but also documentary treatment ("Roses in December") on ex-Texas Congresswoman Barbara Jordan's PBS series and a TV movie. The United States government reacted immediately but seemed unable to obtain action from the Salvadoran government. The United States learned of the women's murder on December 4, 1980, two days after the killings, when church officials informed U.S. Ambassador Robert White, who went immediately to the gravesite. The Carter Administration suspended military aid to El Salvador the following day. One week later a special U.S. Presidential Commission concluded that the Salvadoran authorities knew "that four women were brutally murdered and had cause to believe that they were Americans—yet provided no information to the [U.S.] Embassy. There is a high probability that an attempt was made to conceal the deaths." Finally, on May 24, 1984, a Salvadoran jury convicted five former members of the National Guard of aggregate homicide. This constituted the first time any Salvadoran jury had ever convicted any member of the armed forces of a killing that had political overtones.[43]

The assassination of Archbishop Romero remains unsolved, despite the fact that former Ambassador White has charged the Reagan Administration with supressing evidence linking the head of the conservative ARENA party D'Aubuisson with the killing. The linking of D'Aubuisson to the murders certainly contributed to heavy American government financial support for his Christian Democratic rival Napoleón Duarte in the 1984 Salvadorean elections and D'Aubuisson's eventual resignation as head of ARENA.

Both Maura Clarke and Ita Ford were Maryknoll sisters. Maryknoll, the Catholic Foreign Mission Society of America, has played a major role in shaping the perception of the American Catholic community toward foreign events. In the early part of the century American Catholics learned about China and the dangers of Asian Communism from returned missionaries and the *Maryknoll* magazine. While Maryknoll priests, sisters, and brothers have long been active in Latin America and the Orient, their work for social development and human rights in Latin America, the Philippines, and South Korea has become especially pronounced since the mid-1960s. Maryknollers have tended to locate in rural areas where native clergy are not available, so the order has been among the first foreigners to document the impact of twentieth-century Western-style development on the rural areas of the Third World. When the Bolivian government removed two area military commanders and the mayor of Riberalta for brutality and incompetence, for example, Maryknoll Father William Coy agreed to serve as mayor for four months.[44] The Maryknollers have worked in the area since 1942.

In the last two decades Maryknoll has become more outspoken

and influential on Third World issues. For example, in June 1982, the Maryknoll Fathers and Brothers issued a statement asking the United States government "to refrain from covert activities and military conflict in Nicaragua." The statement also defended Maryknoll priest Miguel D'Escoto, Nicaragua's foreign minister:

Father D'Escoto is a priest in good standing with Maryknoll and, contrary to some reports, is not under orders to leave his political office, neither from Maryknoll nor from the bishops of Nicaragua, nor from the Vatican. In his priestly ministry and now in his political office, we have always known him to act honestly and with integrity in seeking peaceful development for his people.[45]

Democratic Speaker of the House Tip O'Neill, a leading critic of Reagan Administration policy toward Central America, had an aunt who was a Maryknoll sister who died in 1981 at the age of ninety-one. According to O'Neill:

I have great trust in that order. When the nuns and priests come through, I ask them questions about their feelings, what they see, who the enemy is, and I'm sure I get the truth. I haven't found any of these missionaries who aren't absolutely opposed to this policy.[46]

The issue of human rights in the Third World also finds strong support among people who left groups like Maryknoll during the "great departure" of priests and religious during the 1960s and early 1970s. Those who left tended to be theologically and politically progressive, and many retain strong friendships with those who remain as missionaries. Many also have used their linguistic and cultural training to emerge as local opinion leaders in their new contexts in the United States. For example, ex-Maryknoll priest and UCLA Latin American history professor Blase Bonpane has organized delegations of prominent Americans to visit Nicaragua at the request of Rosario Murillo, the wife of Nicaraguan junta leader Ortega.[47]

Jean Donovan of the Cleveland diocese was just one of the many laity and clergy who have represented the American local church in Latin America. Cardinal Cushing of Boston, in response to the call of Pope John XXIII for missionaries, founded the St. James Society, which sent diocesan priests to Latin America for five-year tours. Many of these priests now hold important positions in the American church. "Fast track" ecclesiastics tended to request such assignments as their secular counterparts of the same period joined the Peace Corps. In Guatemala these foreign missionaries have been prime targets of intimidation and assassination. With the July 28, 1981, slaying of U.S. missionary Stanley Rother (Oklahoma City diocese) and the February 13, 1982, slaying of Christian Brother James Miller, at least twenty other catechists, lay workers, Protestant and Catholic missionaries had been killed since 1976. Moreover, more than 200 priests and religious left Guatemala during the period 1980-1982.[48] Most had worked with poor Indians in the rural areas.

Many American Jesuits who teach at the order's twenty-eight colleges and universities in the United States have personal friends and acquaintances among missionary and native Jesuits who teach at Latin American Catholic universities or serve in the rural areas. Many Latin American Jesuits have studied in Europe and North America. All of Central America constitutes a single Jesuit province, so the province acts as a focus for interchange on regional problems and strategies. The provincial of that province from 1976-1982 was César Jerez, a Guatemalan of Indian origin. Since he cannot return to his country because of death threats, Jerez has become director of planning and research projects at the Jesuit University for Central America in Managua. When Jerez visited Great Britain in late fall 1983, he said:

You have to live in Managua to feel just how far the Reagan administration is the decisive factor in Nicaraguan politics. People are asking: "If Grenada can be invaded, then why not Nicaragua?"[49]

On April 29, 1983, a group of forty-seven American missionaries in Nicaragua criticized the Reagan Administration's emphasis on military aid rather than negotiations. The statement expressed support for the Managua government, even if it did not "deny problems, nor mistakes—but we must not confuse errors with systematic repression." The Sandinista Revolution resulted from poverty, hunger, and injustice, according to the missionaries, "with or without the Soviet Union."[50] The *New York Times* printed the entire letter the following day.

Missionary connections, of course, do not always benefit critics of American policy. In the case of the Nicaraguan government's treatment of the Miskito Indians, the Reagan Administration has sought to bolster its policies by identification with the Indian's bishop, a Capuchin missionary from Wisconsin. On Christmas Day 1983 President Reagan himself called Bishop Salvator Schlaefer to tell the prelate that his three-week exodus into Honduras with 1,300 Indians showed that the people of Nicaragua, especially the Indians, wanted democracy. "They showed it with their feet," said the president. Earlier the State Department had expressed concern over the whereabouts of Schlaefer and his American Capuchin companion, since both had been reported killed.[51]

The major Catholic input on American policy toward Central America occurs in the United States Congress. Archbishop James Hickey of Washington, D.C., represented the USCC in testifying before the Senate Foreign Relations Committee on March 5, 1981, and March 7, 1983. In the latter testimony Hickey said that he was "profoundly disappointed" that the Reagan Administration was proposing more military advisers and military aid for El Salvador. Hickey advocated peace talks instead, rejecting the suggestions by Secretary of State Shultz and Vice President Bush that some church leaders seem to favor Marxists.[52]

Major political battles have been waged in 1985 and 1986 over the Reagan Administration's plan to provide military aid to the Contras. On April 16, 1985, the president claimed that the pope had been most supportive of "all our activities in Central America." At issue was a papal letter for Reagan given to Republican Senator Robert Dole when he and other senators visited John Paul. The following day the Vatican Embassy in Washington issued a statement which said that the pope wanted to "exclude the possibility of his support or endorsement of any concrete plan dealing in particular with military aspects."[53] Archbishop Hickey, testifying before Congress for an indisposed Archbishop O'Connor, who was to represent the NCCB, also opposed military aid. The sharpest Republican cross-examination quoted the charges of Archbishop Obando that the Sandinistas were "totalitarian enemies of the church."[54] Sandinista attacks on Obando grew virulent in the following January and February when Obando, eight months after being made a cardinal, went to the United States. He met with church officials and United Nations Secretary General Pérez de Cuéllar, to denounce persecution of the Nicaraguan Catholic Church. The Nicaraguan government condemned Obando and tied his trip to the congressional battle over military aid to the Contras.[55] The USCC position has remained the moderate one of deploring human rights violations by the Sandinista government, while opposing military aid to the Contras.

On June 25, 1986, after extremely heavy presidential lobbying, the United States Congress passed a $100 million Contra aid package. Prior to the vote there seemed to be some hope for better relations between the Sandinista government and the Nicaraguan bishops. The Nicaraguan episcopal letter of April 7, 1986, had showed some limited movement toward the government position. Earlier in June Nicaraguan Vice President Sergio Ramírez Mercado returned from Europe saying that his "cordial" visit with John Paul II had "opened the possibility of a space for understanding with the ecclesiastical hierarchy." Immediately following the congressional vote the Nicaraguan government refused to allow Father Bismarck Carballo, one of Cardinal Obando's chief aides, to reenter the country, and, six days later, expelled the vice president of the Nicaraguan Bishops' Conference, Bishop Pablo Antonio Vega. Both the pope, traveling in Colombia, and USCC president, Bishop James Malone, denounced the government actions. A Maryknoll statement said, "It is difficult to see how this act [Vega's expulsion] and the earlier banning of Father Bismarck Carballo can serve the Nicaraguan people's need for peace and reconciliation. . . . Maryknoll joins the U.S. bishops in opposing U.S. military action against Nicaragua."[56]

Critics of Obando have charged that the cardinal is being supported by right-wing money from the United States. In 1983 Obando stayed with Cardinal Cooke when returning from Rome to Managua. That stay resulted in an internal memo of the W. R. Grace company which suggested that Obando's Commission for Social Promotion in the Managuan Archdiocese (COPROSA) provided an independent context for the training of opposition leaders. When the memo was leaked, COPROSA affirmed that it had received money from AID and the German bishops (Miseror and Adveniat), but "The only assistance we received from W. R. Grace was a box of rosaries, and these never made it through customs. We don't know where they are."[57] Funding is always politically sensitive. Salvadoran Catholic officials turned down AID money to clean up five refugee camps in February 1984 because they considered the money "politically tainted."[58] The degree of "taintedness" would run along a spectrum beginning with the CIA and companies having large investments in Latin America like W. R. Grace, through AID, whose humanitarian projects serve United States policy, to foreign ecclesiastical organizations like Misereor and Adveniat which favor basic developmental educational and health programs, but eschew revolutionary politics. In addition to foreign governmental and conservative business support, the Central American right has been aided by the rise of Protestant sectarianism throughout the region, the "prophet motive."[59]

The USCC has been criticized by the lay lobbying group, the American Catholic Conference. For example, on March 16, 1984, the ACC sponsored a special White House briefing chaired by Robert Reilly, President Reagan's liaison to the Catholic community. The speakers were ex-Maryknoll sister Geraldine O'Leary de Macías,[60] ex-*La Prensa* Editor Humberto Belli, Langhorne Motley of the State Department, and ACDA head Kenneth Adelman. The ACC cooperates with the ecumenical Institute for Religion and Democracy (IRD), which pressures American churches to take tougher stands against Communism in the region. Three weeks before the American presidential election, for example, IRD organized a press conference for Archbishop Arrieta, in which the archbishop, following a White House visit, praised "all the things he [Reagan] has done to strengthen justice, peace, freedom and democratic solutions in the area."[61]

Salvadoran Christian Democratic President Napoleón Duarte's primary American Catholic connection has been Theodore Hesburgh, president of the University of Notre Dame. In May 1985 Duarte received an honorary doctorate in engineering as "the only graduate of this university to become a head of state, the first elected civilian President of his country in half a century." Duarte then gave the main commencement address, in which he credited Hesburgh with inspiring him to enter public life.[62] Hesburgh was one of the international poll watchers who certified the March 28, 1982, elections for the Constituent Assembly. These elections, in which the opposition declined to participate, were also supported by the Salvadoran bishops.[63] Throughout the conflict, the Salvadoran episcopate has denounced the violence and human rights violations by both the right-wing death squads and the guerrillas. Archbishop Arturo Rivera y Damas continued the Sunday homilies of Romero. In his homily of February 8, 1981, the bishop called on "our sister nations in Central America" and "our neighbors Cuba and the United States" to halt arms shipments into the country.[64] The bishops have also urged a negotiated settlement without taking the position that the guerrillas have the same political standing as the government. However, Rivera y Damas has defended priests who do pastoral work among the guerrillas.[65]

The archbishop has long been a critic of right-wing terrorism. In the fall of 1983 the archbishop and his auxiliary bishop Gregorio Rosa Chávez stepped up their denunciations of right-wing terrorism. On September 11 the archbishop expressed his outrage at the Secret Anti-Communist Army which the preceding week had planted explosives in a Jesuit residence at the UCA, in a faculty member's house, and in the truck of a labor leader.[66] At Christmas Chávez attributed 4,736 of the country's 6,093 political killings in

1983 to the armed forces and right-wing death squads. "It is almost a rare thing to die a natural death in this country. It is almost a miracle," said Chávez.[67] Both Rivera y Damas and Chávez received public death threats for spreading "disinformation about our country."[68]

Duarte's victory in the May 1984 elections enabled the church to increase its role as mediator between the government and the guerrillas. In commenting on several successful prisoner exchanges, Chávez said, "The arrival of the new Government has facilitated many things."[69] The most dramatic of the church's mediational efforts came in arranging the meeting between Duarte and Salvador's two leading rebel officials, Guillermo Ungo and Rubén Zamora at La Palma on October 15, 1984, in which Bishop Chávez acted as the designated mediator. Duarte took advantage of the period prior to the American elections to make his offer of negotiation. Ungo and Zamora would have had difficulty refusing, and with their acceptance, Secretary of State Shultz hailed the peace bid.[70] The peace talks produced little, but Archbishop Rivera y Damas was able to arrange the release of Duarte's kidnapped daughter, Ines, in October 1985. Duarte's major internal political problem results from his tenuous control over the military, especially the air force. On January 12, 1986, Rivera y Damas condemned the indiscriminate bombing of civilians by the air force and the destruction of homes and crops in army sweeps of rebel-held areas.[71] In an effort to regain the political initiative and halt his loss of moderate support, Duarte offered a third round of peace talks on June 1, 1986.

Thus, the political crises continue in El Salvador and Nicaragua, as in Lebanon. The progressive polarization of the national political systems continues to polarize the national churches. In each of the three cases, however, the Catholic Church remains a major political actor, with strong transnational links to Western public opinion through Catholic organizations, especially episcopal conferences and missionary groups, which affect United States congressional votes directly by lobbying and indirectly through the major American secular media.

BRAZIL: POLITICAL AUTHORITARIANISM, POLITICAL LIBERALIZATION, AND THE CONSOLIDATION OF THE POPULAR CHURCH

In this section we will compare the experiences of the Catholic Church under authoritarian regimes and will discuss the Catholic role in Brazilian *abertura* ("opening" to democracy, or liberalization). Argentina's recent liberalization[72] under Raúl Alfonsín has also been very significant for its neighbors, but the relatively weak Argentine Catholic Church did not play a major role in that liberalization. In analyzing Catholic political activity under authoritarian regimes, Argentina before Alfonsín, Chile under Pinochet, and the Philippines under Marcos would make excellent comparisons for Brazil after the coup of 1964.

The previous section described the missionary connections between the United States and Central America provided by diocesan organizations, Maryknoll, and other religious groups. These links constitute independent sources of information on human rights abuses in all the countries of Latin America. Both governments and churches remain strongly linked to the international system. The governments continue to be major debtors in the international banking system, while the churches remain dependent on foreign personnel and aid within their countries, and on ecclesiastical and media publicity of human rights abuses in the international system.[73]

In his comparison of the impact of the churches on human rights in Chile, Brazil, Paraguay, Bolivia, and Argentina up to 1978, Brian Smith observes that Catholic human rights strategies were basically reactive, "responding to unforeseen crises in secular society."[74] The abuse of human rights forced national hierarchies, who were often the only institution that could speak out, to take stands against their governments. The detention and assassination of clergy produced the strongest episcopal reaction, but government action against ecclesiastical programs for the poor, or a government attack on a political group particularly close to the church like the Chilean Christian Democrats, also moved the bishops to action.

In the cases of Chile, Brazil, and the Philippines, the bishops acknowledged the need for social order and reserved judgment during the initial stages of martial law. Immediately following the September 1973 coup in Chile, the Catholic hierarchy offered some moral legitimacy for the regime. The first official reaction was somewhat critical, but church leaders in general felt that the coup was necessary to prevent the chaos of civil war. The Brazilian episcopate's respose to the coup of 1964 was even more positive. There was general popular support for a return to stability to ensure that Brazil attained its economic potential as a major power.[75] In the beginning the Brazilian military did not emphasize repression. Only a few Brazilian bishops led by Dom Helder Câmara had advocated a strong social commitment for the church. When Ferdinand Marcos declared martial law in the Philippines on September 21, 1972, the Catholic hierarchy's reaction was also "restained: applauding the President's reforms as essential but deploring human rights violations."[76] In all three countries conservative archbishops like Emilio Tagle (Valparaíso), Geraldo de Proença Sigaud (Diamantina), and Julio Rosales (Cebu) became apologists for the official anticommunism, despite the more restrained stands of the national episcopates. Tagle read a television statement thanking the government for saving the country "from falling irrevocably under the power of Marxism."[77] In February 1977 Sigaud accused two fellow bishops, Casaldáliga of São Felix and Balduino of Goiás Velho, of being Communists because of their action in defending the land claims of peasants and Indians. The government used Sigaud's accustion in a campaign which almost succeeded in expelling Casaldáliga (a Spaniard) from the country. Cardinal Rosales remained so conservative that when he represented his country at the World Anti-Communist League meeting in Asunción in April 1979, the Paraguayan bishops, who had issued a strong denuncation of Latin America's oldest continuous dictator Alfredo Stroessner (1954-) in June 1976, refused to welcome him.[78]

In April 1974 the Chilean bishops began a cautious criticism of the undeniable violations of human rights by the Pinochet regime. Cardinal Raúl Henríquez Silva wished to avoid the appearance of episcopal disunity that characterized the initial phase, so document texts were framed in a way that they could be supported by all the bishops. The Episcopal Conference issued "Reconciliation in Chile" (April 1974) and "Gospel and Peace" (September 1975). A second phase of church reaction in Brazil was stimulated by a substantial increase in government repression during 1968. The regime suspended habeas corpus and tolerated widespread torture. Repression began to affect Brazilian ecclesiastical institutions and personnel. The CNBB published its first major public criticism in May 1970.

The Brazilian military's goal of economic development produced the most consistent record of human rights abuses in the Amazon and other underdeveloped regions. In 1973 the Northwest and Centerwest Conferences of Brazilian bishops issued pastoral letters employing a structural criticism of the Brazilian economic model. *I Have Heard the Cry of My People* and *Marginalization of a People: Shout of the Churches*[79] caused such a negative reaction among the elites that the next year a confidential report of the Second Army concluded that "the clergy are the most active of the enemies which threaten our national security."[80] The period 1974-1978 was particularly tense, with three spectacular incidents of state repression of the Brazilian church occurring in the last half of 1976. In July in the Amazon, landowners and their armed band killed Father Rudolfo Lunkenbein and two Indians. In September armed paramilitaries kidnapped Bishop D. Adriano Hypólito of Nova Iguaçu. They stripped him and sprayed him with red paint, after which they tied him up and abandoned him. In October the police shot and killed Father João Bosco Burmier when he and Bishop Casaldáligna protested murders and rapes of the Indians.

Direct government attacks on clergymen also became significant in the Philippines. The Philippine Bishops' Conference (CBCP) remained divided over Marcos' social and economic problems, but even Cardinal Rosales responded strongly to the detention of Filipino priests and the deportation of foreign (mostly American) clergy and religious. The celebrated August 1974 raid on Sacred Heart Novitiate and San Jose Minor Seminary in Novaliches unwittingly netted the Jesuit superior in the Philippines, Father Benigno Mayo. Cardinal Jaime Sin reacted by holding a prayer vigil for peace and justice and releasing a CBCP letter calling for the end of martial law. In late 1976 a series of raids plus a government document designating 155 clergy (including four bishops) and laity for arrest prompted 66 of the 74 Philippine bishops, even those usually supportive of the government, to sign a strongly worded statement against government interference in church evangelization.

The recent increased authoritarianism and polarization in Chile is running against the tide in the rest of South America. Church-state tension in Brazil increased after the coup in 1964 until the end of 1976. It was still severe two years later but has decreased since the liberalization beginning in January 1979. One explanation of the Brazilian government's policy of liberalization in 1979 places first emphasis on the government's loss of popular legitimacy due to the social implications of Brazil's economic model.[81] The Brazilian "economic miracle" had resulted in even greater maldistribution of income. The anticommunist legitimacy of 1964 had faded with the threat of subversion and the increase of diplomatic pragmatism. The military as an institution had found it increasingly difficult to maintain its unity through fourteen years of expansion into all sectors of the society. Economic modernization had produced a large middle class, a very highly qualified industrial working class, and a large entrepreneurial group. Finally, military repression had damaged Brazil's reputation in the United States and Western Europe.

What has been the effect of liberalization on the internal politics of the Brazilian Catholic Church and on church-state relations? First, liberalization with its lessening of tension in the political system has made it easier for the church to maintain its own unity, but ecclesiastical unity had already been consolidated during, in advance of, and independent of liberalization. The period prior to liberalization saw the unified adoption of progressive positions by the Brazilian episcopate. "The CNBB . . . with Dom Aloísio Lorscheider as president and Dom Ivo Lorscheiter as general secretary, enjoyed the confidence of the overwhelming majority of the bishops— irrespective of their sociopolitical views."[82] The bishops' conference reelected both men in 1974. They organized the conference into a series of commissions, institutes, and seminars which institutionalized ecclesiastical conflict and maintained a unified church position on almost all issues. By March 1977 the bishops voted 210 to 2 to approve their pastoral letter "Christian Requirements for the Political Order." The changed relationship could be seen in the fact that Cardinal Eugenio Sales of Rio, long a defender and personal friend of President Ernesto Geisel, would no longer meet with Geisel for "mutual understandings." In February 1980 the bishops passed their politically explosive document "The Church and Problems of Land." The vote was 172 for, 4 against, and 4 abstentions. One of the four voting against, Archbishop Luciano Cabral Duarte, CELAM's first vice-president, charged that the document was "Marxist," but the CNBB's new president, ex-General Secretary Bishop Ivo Lorscheiter, pointed out that it followed previous CNBB statements.

Brazilian unity was demonstrated after the Puebla Conference when the leading spokesperson for Brazilian conservatives, Archbishop D. Vincente Scherer of Pôrto Alegre, stated that Liberation Theology had many positive elements, as long as it did not reduce religion to politics. "We have commitments and obligations towards all, rich and poor alike. But the poor have the right to preferential treatment."[83] This episcopal unity benefited from the progressives' earlier strong commitment to the CNBB, even after their leader Câmara was voted out of office. Progressives never issued a document critical of the CNBB or even of conservative or reactionary bishops. Rather, they formed a group which they opened to all interested bishops.[84] The issues which destroyed ecclesiastical unity in Chile under Allende and in Nicaragua today have not split the Brazilian church.[85] Brazilian progressive thought has always been very conscious of the limits of the church's political activity.

For this reason, Brazilian progressive theologians are equivocal about the term "Liberation Theology," since it usually denotes a degree of religious politicization that is seen as undesirable in Brazil. Scott Mainwaring has commented, "As liberalization permitted the rebirth of political institutions, the popular Church became critical of excessive involvement in politics. Not only was this option no longer necessary, most progressive bishops came to believe it could threaten the Church's identity."[86] Pastoral agents could spend less time on political issues and more time on specifically religious tasks, even as the bishops as a whole adopted more progressive political positions.

Such an episcopal stance, however, does not immediately solve all Brazilian religious-political dilemmas. Most of the Brazilian church has easily reached the conclusion that priests and religious should not run for office, participate in political parties, or tell others how to vote. However, the bishops have strongly encouraged people to vote, especially in the elections of 1982. This encouragement ranged from pamphlets with a more favorable evaluation of progressive parties (São Paulo) to pamphlets with no evaluation (Rio) to no pamphlets (most moderate and conservative dioceses).[87] The separation of the political and the religious has extended to the popular grass-roots organizations, which have remained in close contact with the bishops. "Perhaps more than any other characteristic, this harmony between the base and the hierarchy has made the Brazilian Church unique in Latin America."[88]

Although Brian Smith ranks Argentinian human rights organizations as the least effective of the five he studied,[89] the Ecumenical Movement for Human Rights (MEDH) and the Permanent Assembly for Human Rights (APDH) have documented cases of "the disappeared" and the torture of prisoners and provided aid for their families. As in Brazil, the security forces have murdered and imprisoned priests. Bishop Enrique Angelelli Carletti of La Rioja was killed while collecting evidence on the deaths of two of his priests. The Argentine bishops have issued pastoral letters denouncing human rights violations, but the church remains a weak institution with no past history of social commitment. Both the Argentinian bishops and the Vatican criticized the 1983 government "White Paper" on the Disappeared.[90] Argentinian human rights organizations have been wary of substantial international funding lest they seem to be manipulated by outside forces.

The Catholic Church in Latin America and the Philippines is the archetypical example of what this book terms the "primary ethical broker,"[91] an institution which is traditionally recognized by the majority of a national society to have the responsibility to articulate the primary ethical concerns of that society. The Catholic Church in Latin America has become involved in the denunciation of torture and other human rights abuses because these abuses are the principal unethical byproducts of dictatorial regimes of both the right and the left. Brazil's National Security State of the early 1970s and the present Sandinista government have both challenged the role of the national episcopal conference as primary ethical broker. The strong hierarchical tradition and the necessity to represent the ethical concerns of the majority of society mean that national episcopal conferences will be deliberate—critics would say slow—in taking ethical positions. However, the ethical positions taken will be politically and culturally significant for the entire society. The last section of this chapter offers a detailed analysis of the political impact of the Catholic Church on human rights in the Third World.

CATHOLICISM IN AFRICA: TRIBAL POWER AND APARTHEID

In May 1980 John Paul landed in Kinshasa, Zaire, to begin an eleven-day visit to six countries in Central Africa. Cardinal Joseph Malula and fifty-three Zairian bishops in their white cassocks and purple sashes met him at the airport. Bampende, Ekonda, and Watusi dancers in leopard skins and body paint welcomed him. When the papal motorcade reached Kinshasa's Notre Dame Cathedral, John Paul summarized the promise and the frustrations of this potentially rich country when he said, "This nation has a long way to go to forge its unity, develop its personality and culture, realize its potential and to actively insert itself in the concert of nations. And for this, Africa needs independence and it needs peace."[92]

Le Monde's coverage of the event focused on the political significance of the enthusiastic welcome by President Mobutu Sésé Séko. Mobutu had had his second marriage blessed in church by Cardinal Malula the evening before the pope's arrival. His first wife had died in October 1977, and he already had four children by his new wife Bobi Ladaocia. On television Mobutu explained that in marrying he was following the sage counsels of the various ministers of God. *Le Monde* commented that the picture of the president being married by one of the most prestigious African cardinals could not help but reinforce his political legitimacy.[93]

Relations between Mobutu and the Zairian church have been spotty. Periodically the president has sought to emphasize ancestral traditions and purify the country of foreign influence. Once, in his attempt to reinstate native "authenticity," Mobutu attempted to remove Christmas from the calendar. Mobutu, whose official title is "the all-powerful warrior who, by his endurance and will to win, goes from contest to contest, leaving fire in his wake," has presented himself as the traditional all-powerful chief of his nation. The evening television news in Zaire, for example, has begun with the swelling of angelic music and heavenly clouds parting to slowly reveal the face of the president. Mobutu, symbol of wisdom and mystical strength, then stares benevolently at his viewers.[94]

The central political issue in the Catholic missionary expansion into Africa has concerned the relation of an independent episcopal hierarchy, developed over more than one thousand years in Western Europe, to native political leaders, who have also claimed religious legitimacy over their people. Often, these Catholic bishops have been Europeans themselves. In the case of Zaire, "the eldest child of the church in black Africa," however, Malula and his bishops constitute Africa's largest native hierarchy, known for its independence and local (not Roman) education.[95] Four of the eight new bishops consecrated by the pope during his tour also came from Zaire.

John Paul came to Central Africa to celebrate the hundredth anniversary of the evangelization of black Africa. In 1880 Cardinal Charles Lavigerie, founder of the White Fathers, organized a caravan out of Zanzibar to the great lakes region of Central Africa. Five years later King Leopold II of Belgium received clearance from the European powers to establish the Congo as his personal fiefdom. The Vatican assigned Belgian missionaries to the area. In the next sixteen years the Jesuits, the Trappists, the Sacred Heart Fathers, and the Mill Hill Fathers all came to evangelize the area. The successor state of Zaire is 43 percent Catholic. Despite the fact that church leadership has passed to native bishops, the missionaries have not returned to Belgium. "Behind every Zairian bishop even today is a fleet of rock-ribbed, loyal Flemish clergymen. Known for hard work, endurance and organizational skill, they persist in every corner of Zaire." Many of the missionaries are engaged in educational and welfare work. The Zairian Catholic Church's social and political influence derives from its 5,000 schools, 36 hospitals, and 200 maternity centers. Despite the riches of Zaire's mineral deposits, this developing country, which has suffered severely from civil wars, could not afford to lose such a social infrastructure.

On his African journey the pope visited five other countries: the

Congo (Marxist state, 40 percent Catholic); Kenya (one-party state, 17 percent Catholic); Ghana (democracy, 12 percent Catholic); Upper Volta (westward-leaning military dictatorship, 7 percent Catholic); Ivory Coast (one-party state, 10 percent Catholic). The itinerary avoided the political problems of Zimbabwe or South Africa and omitted Lusophone Africa.[96] The pope denounced racism from Kinshasa, the most southerly capital on the trip. The only African cardinal accompanying the pope was Cardinal Bernardin Gantin, a native of Benin and then president of the Pontifical Commission for Justice and Peace. Gantin's influence seemed to be evident in John Paul's emphasis on "justice, security, and concord" in his speech at the Kinshasa airport.

The African continent's key "justice" issue is apartheid. The South African Catholic Church, generally weak at the national level because of its immigrant status and regional development, suffered further disequilibrium with the founding of the Republic in 1948. Power passed from their political allies the British to the Nationalist Party, which was strongly influenced by the Afrikaner Church.[97] The Dutch Reformed (Nederduitse Gereformeerde or NG) Church has historically provided the biblical justification for government racial policies, referring to the Africaners as God's "chosen people." Although in 1974 the Dutch Reformed Church rejected the notion that blacks must remain in permanent servitude, the NG Church has found a biblical basis for the "separate development" that would maintain the current racial system. In contrast, a small minority within the NG have questioned apartheid. This questioning became focused in the Christian Institute, founded in 1963 by Dr. C. F. Beyers Naudé, then moderator of the Southern Transvaal Synod of the NG. During the fourteen years of its existence the Institute membership grew to 2,000, which included prominent clergy from both Protestant and Catholic groups.[98] Some black and Coloured churches are also historically related to the Afrikaans Reformed "family." Reverend Allan Boesak, president of the World Alliance of Reformed Churches, has been instrumental in securing the condemnation of apartheid by many Reformed churches worldwide. Boesak was also a major figure in the creation of the United Democratic Front to oppose the new South African Constitution adopted in 1984. The government arrested Boesak during the 1985 protests.

Black Protestant clergy like Nobel laureate Archbishop Desmond Tutu and Boesak have provided the main religious leadership in the struggle against apartheid in South Africa. South African Catholic Archbishop Denis Hurley supported the South African Council of

Churches (SACC) and the Christian Institute from the 1960s.[99] Hurley was heavily criticized by fellow Catholics in the early 1960s when, "[w]ith very few exceptions, the largely expatriate hierarchy and clergy lacked a prophetic social vision and were incapable of applying the principles of the Church's pastoral letters." The Catholic bishops had condemned apartheid in 1957, 1960, and 1962, but the church in general "was no exception to this syndrome of an impoverished, nominal Christianity enmeshed in the prevailing culture of racial discrimination."[100] Catholic seminaries remained segregated in 1963. It was a full ten years later that the Catholic Church first opposed the government on segregated schools. That year the South African government asked Catholic schools to educate the children of black diplomats residing in South Africa. Local blacks protested that they could not attend these same schools, and finally the church decided to defy the government and open all white parochial schools to blacks in 1976.

One of the most creative student initiatives was the foundation of the ecumenical University Christian Movement (UCM) in July 1967 in consultation with representatives of Methodist, Anglican, Congregational, Presbyterian, and Catholic Churches. Reverend Basil Moore, a Methodist from Rhodes University, was its first president. The general secretary was Catholic priest Colin Collins, chaplain to the National Catholic Federation of Students, and past general secretary of the SACBC. The UCM evolved quickly "under the influence of its black caucus, the continuing leadership of Moore and Collins, and the charismatic presence of Steve Biko and Barney Pityana."[101] At the UCM's conference in July 1968, a caucus of sixty African, coloured, and Indian students formed the nucleus of what became the South African Students Association (SASO) in December. The focus of the UCM and SASO on Black Consciousness was partially stimulated by trends in Liberation Theology in other countries.

Student demonstrations in the black township Soweto erupted in June 1976, changing South African race relations forever. The demonstrations and the subsequent army and police repression created shock waves within the Catholic Church. Bishop Mandlenkosi Zwane of Swaziland told his fellow white bishops of the South African Catholic Bishops Conference (SACBC) that, "after June 1976 the possibility of building bridges between black and white in the normal way no longer belongs to us."[102] A difficult struggle for justice, said Zwane, would have to precede any reconciliation. This struggle would be painful to any "bourgeois affluent" elements within the church. In February 1977 the SACBC issued a "Declaration of Commitment" which confessed that "the Catholic Church in South Africa is lagging behind in witness to the Gospel in matters of social justice." The Declaration promised to desegrate all church hostels, orphanages, hospitals, dispensaries, and other institutions. It also criticized police brutality during the Soweto riots of the preceding year.[103] In 1981 the SACBC appointed a "banned" black priest, Smangaliso Mkhatshwa, as their general secretary. The government had arrested this graduate of Louvain[104] in August 1976 for allegedly disturbing public order. A five-year banning order was served on him in June 1977. He was detained again without trial from October 1977 to March 1978. In August 1986 Mkhatshwa's testimony in a Pretoria court provided the first detailed evidence of police torture during that summer's detentions.[105] The SACBC now includes 34 bishops from South Africa, Namibia, Botswana, and Swaziland. Fifteen are black or Indian, as are 400 of the 2,500 priests in the four countries.

The February 1977 statement of the SACBC was especially welcomed by those refusing military service in the South African Defense Forces (SADF) on grounds of conscience. The statement read: "In this matter of conscientious objection we defend the right of every individual to follow his own conscience, the right therefore to conscientious objection both on the grounds of universal pacifism and on the grounds that he seriously believes the war to be unjust."[106] In South Africa conscientious objection is intimately bound up with the morality of SADF strikes in Namibia and other areas. The SACBC statement was endorsed by the Anglicans in April, and the Methodists and Congregationalists in October.

Prime Minister P. W. Botha has sought to stabilize South African politics by combining overtures to neighboring black states, forced removal of domestic blacks to native homelands, and introduction of Coloureds and Indians into the parliament. The 1984 constitution angered blacks because it seemed to be the definitive statement of their exclusion from South African society by even "centrist" elements of the Nationalist Party. Right-wing members of the Nationalist Party and the security forces, on the other hand, had opposed giving any power to Coloureds and Indians. In analyzing black opposition to the constitution, Paul Van Slambrouck singled out the United Democratic Front (UDF) and the Azanian People's Organization (AZAPO) as the most important groups. Van Slambrouck also commented that the "most significant development since the government squashed most black political activity in 1977 has been the emergence of a black trade union movement."[107]

In June 1984 Prime Minister Botha made a trip to Europe to seek support for his new "liberal" policy. On June 11, he visited the pope with his wife and Foreign Minister Roelof F. Botha (photo *New York Times*, June 12). Unfortunately for the prime minister, forty-eight hours earlier police in Namibia had arrested thirty-seven leaders and supporters of the Southwest Africa People's Organization (SWAPO) at a quiet barbecue on the grounds of a local Catholic mission. Although all were subsequently released, the arrests by right-wing elements compromised any diplomatic possibilities Botha might have sought with the pope and European leaders like Helmut Kohl. As soon as the two South African leaders left the papal audience, the Vatican took the unusual diplomatic step of issuing a condemnation of apartheid, while insisting on independence for Namibia. After the SWAPO arrests, Kenneth Abraham, a member of the Namibian Independence Party, appealed to the pope to secure the release of the SWAPO leaders. Five black priests wrote an open letter to Archbishop Hurley protesting the pope's "insensitivity" in giving a gift to the prime minister to whom they would not offer "as much as a glass of water."[108]

The two most important national hierarchical supports for the South African bishops come from the United States and Great Britain. The USCC has consistently lobbied for American government pressure on Pretoria.[109] Jesuit ex-congressman Robert Drinan wrote two articles in the Jesuit magazine *America* in 1979 urging readers to protest the banning of Father Mkhatshwa to the South African ambassador. Mkhatshwa was rearrested in the Ciskei homeland in October 1983 and released five months later. In June 1984 friends and admirers held a reception for him at the USCC.[110] The American debate, like the British one, has focused on the effectiveness and advisability of economic sanctions.

While P. W. Botha was being sworn into office as the first president under the new constitution on September 14, 1984, police were using tear gas and rubber bullets against protestors in Soweto and other cities. In the ceremony Botha invoked the Afrikaner religious vision of "God's great design" as he addressed members of the white, Coloured, and Indian chambers. A black-robed NG minister quoted Scripture that those who rebel against authority "rebel against what God has ordained."[111] Botha's policy toward surrounding black nations was represented by the presence of Jonas Savimbi, leader of the Angola guerrillas. At the same time, black protests over rental increases in Sharpeville had forced four South African cabinet members led by Minister of Law and Order Louis Le Grange to abandon a tour of the township.[112] Since the inauguration the Botha government has stepped up arrests, especially of the leaders of the United Democratic Front, which claims to have 1.5 million followers. Battles between various opposition groups have also reduced the possibility of peaceful change and indirectly benefited the government. Bishop Tutu has sought to unify opposition to Botha, as in a May 1985 church service for leaders from the UDF, the rival Azanian People's Organization, and Zulu Chief Gatsha Buthelezi's Inkatha movement. The other major black ecclesiastical group is the more conservative Zion Christian Church, with five million members. Botha was invited to address its Easter 1985 assembly.

In response to increased political polarization, the South African and international business communities have become more active. On August 29, 1985, the predominantly English-speaking companies of the Association of Chambers of Commerce of South Africa, the National African Chamber of Commerce and Industry, the South African Federated Chamber of Industries, and the Urban Foundation responded to the suspension of trading on foreign exchange and stock markets in South Africa by calling for major steps to end political instability, including accommodating blacks in the political system. One month later ninety-one business leaders, representing English-speaking, Afrikaner, and foreign corporations, placed advertisements in English-speaking and Afrikaner newspapers under the heading, "There is a better way." The statement advocated negotiation with "acknowledged black leaders" on sharing power.[113] The United States Corporate Council on South Africa reprinted part of the statement with its own endorsement in the October 21 *New York Times*.

Religious leaders throughout the world have also taken stronger stands. During summer 1985 Reverend Leon Sullivan, speaking for himself as a Protestant minister, not for the Sullivan Principles signatory companies, advocated withdrawal by all American companies from South Africa if significant progress was not made in ending apartheid. The Interfaith Center on Corporate Responsibility (ICCR) has selected twelve American companies, and stated that, "We believe that if there has not been significant progress toward these goals [end "homelands" policy, restore full political rights to blacks, end influx control, etc.] by the end of 1986, these corporations' continued presence in South Africa cannot be justified."[114]

Concluding its December 1985 emergency meeting on South Africa, the World Council of Churches called for increased church pressure and mandatory economic sanctions against the Pretoria government, along with the resignation of Botha. Delegates were impressed by the strong speeches of South African labor leaders, who advocated sanctions even though they would be among the first to suffer. WCC officials and ten South African white student leaders also met with leaders of the outlawed African National Congress.[115] Pope John Paul II called for an end to apartheid at The Hague on May 13, 1985, and in Cameroon on August 11. The polarization of South African politics has led to increased activism by business and church groups both within the country and through transnational links.

THE CATHOLIC CHURCH AND THE PEOPLE'S REPUBLIC OF CHINA

History and culture, not political ideology, still dominate the style and outcome of church-state relations in the PRC. My earlier book (1980) on Catholic politics in China and Korea summarized the effects of Chinese state religious intervention under four propositions:

A. In times of a strong Chinese state, only a religion with deep rural sectarian roots could effectively resist national government pressure.
B. The Chinese elite tolerated foreign religious influence only during periods of social, economic, and political crisis. Buddhism, Catholicism, and Protestantism all found their initial strong acceptance during such periods. The more the old legitimacy failed to provide security and sustenance, the more the people were disposed to accept both universal religions and heterodox sects.
C. The more organizationally cohesive and complex a religion, the better able it was to resist Chinese state penetration, regulation, and control.
D. A strong Chinese state did not tolerate an independent Catholic Church. At such times the church had to choose between the equally unsatisfactory alternatives of state penetration, regulation, and control, or underground sectarianism. Penetration assured that national government loyalists held positions of ecclesiastical leadership. Regulation limited the number of clerical ordinations and new members. Control enabled the state to use

the ecclesiastical organizations for political goals. It is especially in this last aspect of active social control through campaign mobilization that the People's Republic has differed from its predecessor governments.[116]

State penetration, regulation, and control of the church organization became the crucial church-state issue at both national and local levels. The People's Republic won the national battle only when it successfully established the Chinese Catholic Patriotic Association and forced consecration of government-sponsored bishops. Furthermore, the more radical the general orientation of Chinese state policy, the more strongly the national government attacked the Catholic Church. In other words, state policy toward the Catholic Church has followed the alternations in general policy in the PRC. For example, state pressure mounted in both the Great Leap Forward and the Cultural Revolution, when party cadres attacked "orthodox" and "patriotic" Catholics alike.[117]

The political victory of Deng Xiaoping at the Third Plenum of the Eleventh Central Committee in December 1978 introduced an exciting new period in Chinese politics. Many of Deng's supporters interpreted his new political and economic clout as signaling an era of general liberalization following the oppressive years of the "Gang of Four." The general euphoria of the time resulted in Beijing's "Democracy Wall," that shrine to "the Fifth Modernization" (democracy), which would inevitably accompany Deng's other four modernizations in agriculture, industry, defense, science and technology. The high point of the political thaw came in February 1979. On March 16, Deng warned a small group of high-ranking cadres that the Democracy Movement had "gone too far," threatening the "stability, unity, and the Four Modernizations." On March 29 the police arrested the movement's leading figure, Wei Jingsheng, who later received a sentence of fifteen years.[118] The movement could continue, the party said, but only under official direction.

Similar events took place with regard to state religious policy.[119] In January and February 1979 those who had suffered during the Cultural Revolution presented their grievances against the then operative religious policy of the "Gang of Four." In Shanghai especially, both "orthodox" and "patriotic" Catholics had experienced significant persecution. The party first indicated its new religious policy on March 15 in the *People's Daily* in a series of replies to (unpublished) letters. The new policy distinguished between superstition and "proper" religious activities in which believers "must conform to the policies and laws of the government. They may not interfere with politics or education or revive the system of feudal oppression and exploitation that was abolished after Liberation. Much less is it permitted to the class enemy to use religion to carry on counter-revolutionary or illegal activities. The government organs therefore must strengthen the administration of religious organizations."[120]

Such a policy meant a return to the party orientation which preceded the Great Leap Forward. In keeping with the strategy of a "United Front," practice of religion would be permitted, providing it took place under the supervision of party and state organs. The most relevant organs were the United Front Department and the Religious Affairs Bureau,[121] which had disappeared during the period of radical domestic politics. As in numerous other sections of the party and state bureaucracies under Deng, these two organizations were reconstituted by bringing back many cadres who had lost their positions in the Cultural Revolution. Ulanfu, the former boss of Inner Mongolia, headed the United Front Department. At the first meeting Ulanfu announced that its former director, Li Weihan, had been rehabilitated. The Religious Affairs Bureau came under its last director, Xiao Xianfa. These cadres began immediately to extend their bureaucracies and reinstitute "moderate" Chinese religious policy, which allowed for opening churches and theological schools, establishing research institutes, and appointing clergy.

The keystone to this policy was an approved association for each religion. The Chinese Catholic Patriotic Association, founded in 1957, held its third national conference May 22-30, 1980. The fact that its last national conference had been in 1962 under the same Xiao Xianfa as director of the Religious Affairs Bureau emphasized the continuity of Chinese state religious policy with the pre-Cultural Revolution era. The party did, however, make organizational improvements. During the "moderate" period prior to the Cultural Revolution, many Catholics objected to the leading role of the Chinese Catholic Patriotic Association in determining ecclesiastical policy. Catholic tradition did not provide for direction from such a body, many of whose members were lower clergy or lay persons. To meet this objection, two new Catholic organizations came into being at a second meeting, May 31–June 2. The Chinese Catholic Bishops' Conference deals with "doctrine, regulations and exchange." The Chinese Catholic Religious Affairs Committee deals with "religious affairs in the spirit of independence, self-government, and self-administration." The relationship between the Patriotic Association and these two groups is still not clear, but the Patriotic Association and the Bishops' Conference issued a joint letter to all Chinese Catholics at the conclusion of the meeting. Jinan Bishop Zong Huaide heads the Patriotic Association, with Bishop Zhang Jiashu of Shanghai (eighty-eight at his appointment) leading the other two groups.[122]

Beijing's newly appointed bishop Fu Tieshan was passed over because it was common knowledge that he was married, thus raising questions of legitimacy among many Catholics. Fu's appointment to Beijing, which had been without a bishop since 1964, was widely interpreted as an instance where the party placed political reliability over conformity to the traditional Catholic criteria for religious legitimacy.

As China emerged from the Cultural Revolution the Vatican began to look for a way to regularize its relations with the PRC, especially in light of its experience with *Ostpolitik* in Eastern Europe. Rome downplayed its diplomatic ties to Taiwan, replacing the apostolic nuncio (technically a pro-nuncio) with a chargé d'affaires. In March 1980 two high-ranking ecclesiastics, Cardinals König of Vienna and Etchegaray of Marseilles, undertook personal visits to China. The cardinals visited both Ulanfu and Xiao Xianfa.[123] When John Paul visited Asia in February 1981, he turned down an invitation to visit Taiwan, but from Manila addressed an emotional appeal to all Chinese for reconciliation with Rome. The pope praised Chinese culture, expressed his "deep admiration of the testimonies of heroic faith [of both 'orthodox' and 'patriotic' Catholics during the Cultural Revolution]," and omitted any denunciation of the Chinese Catholic Patriotic Association. At the conclusion of the papal visit to Asia, Vatican Secretary of State Casaroli went to Hong Kong to visit with Bishop Dominic Tang (Deng Yiming) of Guangzhou.[124] Bishop Tang, arrested at the height of the Great Leap Forward in 1958, had been released the previous June and restored to his former bishopric. Later the government approved his application to go to Hong Kong for medical treatment and to visit relatives. In a joint press conference with Casaroli, Tang said the Chinese Catholic Church would support the "Three-Self Principle," but that such self-government, self-support, and self-propagation did not constitute independence from Rome. Casaroli stressed the flexibility of the Vatican diplomatic position, including the issue of diplomatic recognition. In reply to a question the secretary of state indicated that the Vatican "would attach no special conditions for the normalization of relations with the Chinese Church, such as the release of certain clergy." This latter statement referred principally to orthodox Bishop Gong of the Shanghai, who had been in prison since 1955.

When Casaroli returned to Rome on March 5, he remained cautious in commenting on the Chinese situation. He seemed willing to accept the Chinese Catholic Patriotic Association as "an association of a civil, and not of an ecclesiastical character," thus needing no Vatican approval. He also said he hoped "that Monsignor Dominic Tang may have the opportunity to come to Rome himself to fulfill not only his own desire but also that of the Pope, who wants to meet him and express to him his affection and gratitude, and at the same time to hear directly from him all that can be said about China."[125] Often the most difficult problem in *Ostpolitik* has been finding bishops acceptable to both the Vatican and the state. Obviously, Casaroli thought he had the episcopal keystone for a new relation with the PRC in Bishop Tang.

On June 6, 1981, John Paul elevated Tang to archbishop of Guangzhou. The Chinese bitterly denounced the appointment. The first statement came from Bishop Michael Yang Gaojian, but his sentiments were soon echoed by the Religious Affairs Bureau, and clergy and laity throughout the country. The Guangzhou Patriotic Catholic Association and the Guangzhou diocese dismissed Tang as bishop on June 22. Bishop Yang's statement said: "The Holy See's move rudely interferes in the sovereign affairs of the Chinese Church. This cannot be tolerated."[126]

A diplomatic move undertaken to advance Sino-Vatican relations had ended in denunciation. What happened? The Vatican probably thought it had more Chinese support than it did. In early May Bishop Tang had paid a courtesy call on the PRC Embassy in Rome and had been cordially received. The Religious Affairs Bureau, however, had become progressively more alarmed since the liberalization of early 1979. The Chinese authorities were astounded at the resilience of traditional piety. For example, the hill of Zose outside Shanghai had long been a place of pilgrimage for people, especially fisherfolk from East China. Many of the pilgrims came from families converted in the seventeenth and eighteenth centuries. In October 1979 some groups of Shanghai Catholics on pilgrimage reported that they had seen a shining light and heard a message that the light would reappear on March 15, 1980. The Shanghai Communist press denounced this "superstition," with the result that Catholics from all over East China thronged to the shrine in early

March. The environment for state acceptance of a Vatican-approved bishop became less and less favorable as time progressed.

In terms of the actual appointment itself, Father John Tong, Director of the Holy Spirit Study Centre in Hong Kong, attributed the fiasco to mistakes by both Rome and Beijing. The Holy See moved too quickly and "failed to take into consideration the historical background and feeling of the Chinese." The Chinese Catholic Patriotic Association replied with a crescendo of strident accusation, without waiting for Bishop Tang's explanation of the event. The bishop, according to Father Tong, was not even accorded the hearing given to the nefarious "Gang of Four."[127]

In November 1981 the Shanghai police arrested four Jesuits, the most famous being Father Zhu Hongshen. Father Zhu, known in the West as Vincent Chu, comes from an old Shanghai Catholic family.[128] He had already spent many years in prison, but had been free in Shanghai during the two preceding years. At the April 1983 trial Zhu received the longest sentence of the four, fifteen years. The formal charges against the Jesuits listed collusion with foreign countries, collecting intelligence, fabricating rumors, and subversion.[129] Father Zhu had received foreign Catholic visitors and had refused to join the Chinese Catholic Patriotic Association. Amnesty International has taken up the case of the four Jesuits, as it had of the jailed "orthodox" Bishop Gong of Shanghai.

The "Catholic problem in the South" will become even more complicated at the end of the century when the PRC takes over administration of Hong Kong with its active Catholic diocese. Bishop Tang is held in high esteem by Hong Kong Catholics, who resent the attacks against him. Bishop Wu of Hong Kong, who has expressed the desire to play the role of "bridge-builder" between the church in China and the universal church, visited Beijing and Shanghai in March 1985 and was assured that the Hong Kong Catholic Church will not be interfered with after 1997, and that it may continue its international contacts. The return visit to Hong Kong and Macao of eight Shanghai Catholics, led by Auxiliary Bishop Jin Luxian, came in July. Bishop Jin, a respected Shanghai Jesuit, said he had prayed for six months before he had decided to cooperate with the Chinese Catholic Patriotic Association and accept his former position as rector of Sheshan. Jin was consecrated bishop in January 1985.[130] On July 3, just before the Hong Kong visit, the government released the orthodox Bishop Gong of Shanghai. It was claimed that Gong had "admitted his crime," but only an oblique remark attributed to him suggested that he was repentant.[131] Northern Catholics, led by Bishop Fu Tieshan of Beijing, visited Belgium in November. Fu is less acceptable to orthodox Catholics than Jin.

My earlier work on Catholic politics contrasted the church in China with the church in Vietnam. Despite a similar Confucian traditional political-religious culture, the numerical strength of Vietnamese Catholics meant that Hanoi had to deal with a national church in union with Rome.[132] Recently, Hanoi has been attempting to impose much stronger state control on the Vietnamese church in moves reminiscent of Chinese Catholic policy in the early 1950s. For instance, in November 1982 the police rearrested Archbishop Francis Xavier Nguyên van-Thuân, coadjutor with right of succession in Ho Chi Minh City. On April 27, 1983, Vatican Radio reported preparations for the trial of four Vietnamese Jesuits, including the regional superior, Father Joseph Nguyên Cong Doan (forty-two). Cardinal Joseph Marie Trinh văn-Căn of Hanoi and Archbishop Philippe Nguyên Kim Diên of Huê were also reported as being under house arrest. The following November the Vietnamese government founded a Patriotic Catholic Committee in Hanoi. The deterioration of Vatican-Vietnamese relations could be seen in John Paul's visit to a Vietnamese refugee camp during his stay in Thailand in May 1984. He had refrained from making a similar visit while in the Philippines in 1981 at the request of Hanoi.[133] It would be difficult to find two governments more estranged at the present time than Hanoi and Beijing, but they certainly agree that the respective Catholic Churches should be subject to national state policy.

CONCLUSION: THE CHURCH AND HUMAN RIGHTS
IN THE THIRD WORLD

In this chapter, we have focused on the Catholic impact on Third World regional alliances with the Soviet Union and the United States, and the influence of the Vatican and various national Catholic Churches on the national political coalitions in their respective countries. Unlike Western Europe, where analysts weigh the chances for different majority coalitions in the formation of governments, in countries like El Salvador, Nicaragua, Chile, Lebanon, South Africa, and South Korea, the question is not which of the several viable coalitions will prevail, but whether or not *any* political solution exists which will provide political stability and economic growth, let alone human rights. In each of the above cases United States foreign policy plays a significant role.

On May 22, 1977, President Jimmy Carter made a major speech

on human rights at the University of Notre Dame commencement exercises. Receiving honorary degrees with the president were Cardinal Stephen Kim of South Korea, Cardinal Paulo Arns of Brazil, and Bishop Donal Lamont of Rhodesia. These three ecclesiastics represented Catholic commitment to human rights on their respective continents. After the ceremony Cardinal Kim said that Carter's comments were "very encouraging," though South Korea's human rights problems would have to be solved by the Koreans themselves. "Our problems can be changed by ourselves, but he can encourage us." Bishop Lamont praised Carter for reintroducing "integrity of conscience" into politics. During a television interview of the three prelates, the bishop said that although it was not the function of churchmen to provide solutions to political problems, the church "must implement social justice with its message."[134] Because of the Notre Dame ceremony, their respective national governments became less likely to arrest Arns and Kim. These ecclesiastics returned home with added American media exposure, the prestige of a major United States university honorary degree, and the acquaintance of the president of the United States. When Carter visited Brazil, Cardinal Arns accompanied him to the airport. When Carter went to Korea, he met with Cardinal Kim and other religious leaders to demonstrate his concern for human rights. When the former president visited Brazil again in October 1984 after the beginning of liberalization, many civic and ecclesiastical leaders like Cardinal Arns welcomed him. Carter experienced a degree of respect from Brazilians that has eluded him in the United States.

During the years immediately preceding the Carter presidency, American allies in Latin America had produced some particularly repressive regimes. In contrast with the "democratization" of the 1960s, national security states held power in most of the nations of the continent. In most of these countries, the Catholic Church had moved from its initial cautious approval of the regimes to becoming the major institutionalized opposition. Thus United States policy and national Catholic policies pursued similar courses on human rights during the Carter administration. The election of John Paul II meant that the church would take a stronger stand on all its policies, including human rights. After the conclave Cardinal Arns remarked, "It is as if a Third World Cardinal had won."[135] Arns felt the new pope understood the difficulties of working with authoritarian governments from his experiences in Poland.

After the election of Ronald Reagan, the first two heads of state to visit the White House came from Argentina and South Korea, two dictatorships with abysmal records on human rights. The president's first nominee for assistant secretary of state for human rights and humanitarian affairs, Ernest Lefevre, had such a controversial record that the Senate refused to confirm him. The juxtaposition of the 1981 visits of John Paul and George Bush to the Philippines demonstrates that period's (Alexander Haig and early George Shultz as secretary of state) divergence of policy between the United States and the Vatican. While John Paul challenged Marcos to improve his treatment of the people, Bush enthusiastically gushed, "We love your adherence to democratic principles and democratic processes."[136] During the same period anti-Americanism grew among students, especially in Latin America, the Philippines and South Korea.

American and Vatican Latin American policies most closely approximate each other in the support of Christian Democratic regimes like those of Eduardo Frei and Napoleón Duarte. Such a similar approach has been tenuous, however, under administrations like those of Nixon and Reagan which have focused on security interests. In general Vatican policy makers have taken a much more European approach which gives priority to North-South relations. The Soviet Union's main "Catholic card" consists of its connection through the Cuban government to Latin American political and ecclesiastical radicalism. These radicals may despise the current Soviet Politburo, but Moscow still profits from the disruption of Washington's sphere of influence.

The same holds for South Africa, where since the Soweto riots of 1976 the Catholic hierarchy has actively joined Archbishop Tutu and others in resisting apartheid. The pope showed willingness in June 1984 to discuss Botha's new policies with the prime minister, but not to be identified with his repressive policies. In both Latin America and South Africa, the policies of the Reagan Administration have been more difficult to harmonize with national and international Catholic interests than those of the preceding administration. In the Middle East, on the other hand, Reagan's attempt to move American policy to a more neutral position brings it more in line with the Vatican's orientation toward the moderate Arabs. Nevertheless, Israel's security remains the focus of United States interests, while the Palestinian problem continues to be the central concern of the Vatican. Both Washington and the Vatican demonstrate considerable anxiety about the future of Lebanon.

The Vatican, like the United States, has a "two China problem." During the Cold War period of the 1950s both Rome and Washington supported Taipei against what seemed to be the implacable opposition of the Beijing government. Following the Cultural Revolution both sought for some rapprochement with the PRC as the Sino-Soviet split and more moderate Chinese domestic politics seemed to offer new possibilities. Nixon visited the PRC in 1972, and Carter recognized Beijing in January 1979, providing encouragement for the new policies of Deng. The Vatican, however, had less to offer in political legitimacy and military and economic assistance. Even if the Holy See broke, rather than downplayed diplomatic relations with Taiwan, the results would be uncertain. In fact, the greatest danger to current "moderate" PRC religious policy comes from the far left, party Maoists who lump "religion" and "superstition" in the same category.

Neither the United States nor the Vatican is ready to join a crusade against their old ally, the Kuomintang (KMT), regardless of their desire to bargain with Beijing for their own strategic interests. Even in international politics, loyalty and old friendships count for something. In addition, an anti-KMT crusade would hurt the United States economically. The Vatican would suffer in terms of government pressure on the local church. As United States–Taiwan cooperation has survived President Reagan's trip to Beijing, so the Catholic Church in Taiwan could survive a papal visit to the PRC. However, the two separate China problems of the Vatican and the United States place definite limits on the closeness of relations with the antagonists on both sides of the Taiwan Straits.

The various national Catholic Churches differ enormously in their political orientation, internal strength, and their position within the national culture. With regard to political orientation, Father Naaman's traditional perspective in Maronite Lebanon and my own studies of Asian Catholic peasant sectarianism show the Catholic Church acting as a minority sect focused on preservation of the group in a hostile environment. Such an orientation militates against a national consensus. In most of the countries discussed, however, religion forms a bond at the national level. This study has dramatized the importance of the presence of an organization which is recognized by a majority of a society to be articulating the primary ethical concerns of that society. The presence of such a primary ethical broker is already the first step toward solution of serious moral crisis within the society. The absence of such an actor is an indication of grave fragmentation of the cultural and/or institutional system. A comparison of South Africa, Chile, and South Korea reveals that a different Christian group functions as the primary ethical broker. Protestant churches grouped as the South African Council of Churches provide moral leadership in South Africa. The Chilean Catholic Church and the ecumenical cooperation of Protestant and Catholic churches in South Korea perform the same function in their respective countries.

Various Catholic Churches differ considerably in terms of their internal organizational strength. The Argentinian General Jorge Videla may be a more devout Catholic than Pinochet, but he also faced a much weaker church. While Catholicism is peripheral to Castro's Cuba, it is central to the Nicaraguan culture, as Cuban advisers posted to Nicaragua have painfully discovered. For that reason, the refusals of the Nicaraguan bishops to attend Somoza's inaugurations in 1972, 1975, and 1978 constituted significant political statements. Nevertheless, Nicaragua has never had the extensive resources or level of intellectual activity of the Brazilian church. Nicaraguan basic Christian communities developed in conjunction with the revolution so that they frequently forge strong links with the Sandinista government. In addition, Nicaragua lacks the multiplicity of viable opposition political movements found in Brazil. Such a situation makes it much more difficult to separate political and religious groups.[137]

In Chile under Pinochet, the Catholic Church has used its transnational contacts, especially papal, Vatican, and national episcopal statements on Chilean human rights, to support its role as the national counterweight to government repression.[138] In both Central America and the Philippines missionary activities have linked the countries to the United States. In Chile the most important international contributions to the church were money and materials. This flow could be hindered, but not completely blocked by authoritarian regimes heavily dependent on Europe and North America for loans and credits. In the case of missionary personnel, however, governments like Brazil, Paraguay, Bolivia, Rhodesia, the Philippines, and South Korea have expelled large numbers of foreign clergy and religious. Such expulsions remain a serious threat to churches which are heavily dependent on missionary staffing. In addition, the governments and right-wing death squads can create such a climate of violence that priests and religious leave the area. For example, Bishop Juan Gerardi of El Quiché, president of the Guatemalan Bishops' Conference, withdrew eighteen priests and twenty-five nuns from his diocese in 1980 lest they be murdered. Gerardi then traveled to Rome to see John Paul. The Garcia government banned the bishop from reentering the country when he returned, although he is a citizen.[139]

Missionary organizations have been particularly active in linking the American Catholic Church with the human rights concerns of churches in client states of the United States. An independent information network has provided groups like the USCC with the documentation necessary to lobby Congress and influence public opinion. One only needs to compare the lack of public reaction to the CIA-orchestrated coup in Guatemala in 1954 with the Sanctuary Movement and public protest against arming the Contras in Nicaragua to realize the major changes that have occurred in American perceptions, especially American Catholic perceptions.

With regard to both leftist and rightist governments, the church has attempted to maintain its institutional independence, so that some of the political dynamics remain similar in both cases, regardless of the state's ideology. For example, both the Nicaraguan and Philippine bishops have issued pastoral letters critical of their respective governments. All the priests of these countries read these letters to their congregations on a particular Sunday. Both leftist and rightist governments have used some similar tactics to stop this independent flow of information. The Nicaraguan government canceled the weekly televised Sunday mass of Bishop Obando, while Salvadoran rightists blew up the KSAX transmitter to halt Romero's sermons. Under Allende, Father Raúl Hasbún used his position as director of the television station at the Catholic University of Santiago to criticize socialism, leading the government to refuse Hasbún permission to expand his network.[140]

The rightist governments have been much more dependent upon violence to silence the church. Right-wing death squads, employing some military and security personnel, have distinguished themselves for their brutality. The most violent South American regimes mentioned have been Argentina (with two bishops and many priests killed), and Brazil before 1978. In Central America, prelates like Rivera y Damas have denounced violence from both the right and the left, but Guatemalan and Salvadoran rightists have been particularly brutal. In the cases of Argentina, Brazil, Guatemala, and El Salvador, the militaries have perceived a massive threat from the left. In Guatemala and Brazil the church has been defending Indians against rural oligarchies, a particularly difficult task. However, the murdering of priests and religious has certain political disadvantages. The killings unite the national church and hurt the government's international image. The assassination of Archbishop

Romero may have succeeded in terms of short-term national politics, but the great succession of anniversary masses and pilgrimages in the United States, not to mention all the books and newspaper articles, has certainly restricted American military aid. Archbishop John Quinn of San Francisco, then president of the NCCB, attended the funeral of Archbishop Romero and issued a statement for the American press. The murder of the four churchwomen constituted an unmitigated political disaster, regardless of morality.

Leftist violence against church personnel in Latin America has been oriented toward discrediting the clergy through the manifestation of the "people's" anger, as in the jostling of Bishop Obando and the damaging of his car. Also, the Nicaraguan and Cuban governments have substantially more control over popular organizations than the Salvadoran executive has over the death squads. The church, then, has battled both leftist and rightist governments over access to the media and institutional independence. The major struggle with authoritarian governments centers on the right's use of violence to protect economic and social privilege. Church conflict with leftist governments, on the other hand, focuses on maintaining control of Catholic educational and youth programs.

PART III

The Catholic Church in the International System

CHAPTER 8

Arms Control as a Catholic Political Issue

JOHN PAUL AT HIROSHIMA

THE WHITE-ROBED pope stood before the memorial in Hiroshima's Peace Park. Twenty-five thousand Japanese had gathered in the bright sunshine that followed a light snow on that February day in 1981. The "eternal flame," lit when the park was completed in 1958, burned behind John Paul, who began his message in Japanese, and then continued on in English, French, Spanish, Portuguese, Polish, German, Russian, and Chinese.

To remember Hiroshima is to abhor nuclear war. To remember Hiroshima is to commit oneself to peace. . . . Let us promise our fellow human beings that we will work untiringly for disarmament and the banishing of all nuclear weapons; let us replace violence and hate with confidence and caring.

The terrible destructiveness of nuclear weapons, the pope said, constituted a new stage in the history of war. "In the past, it was possible to destroy a village, a town, a region, even a country. Now, it is the whole planet that has come under threat. This fact should fully compel everyone to face a basic moral consideration: from now on, it is only through a conscious choice and then deliberate policy that humanity can survive."[1] The crowds stood in quiet respect. The pope's use of ten languages underscored his desire to speak to the entire world. Despite the fact that Japan's 406,000 Catholics make up only approximately one-fourth of one percent of the nation's population, the papal words received a wide hearing. Japan's leading newspaper *Asahi Shimbun* editorialized, "Will it be possible to make the Pope's visit to Japan a turning point, not only for Japan but also for the world?"

The detonation of the first atomic bomb at Alamogordo, New Mexico, on July 16, 1945, began a new era in global politics. While the subsequent explosions at Hiroshima and Nagasaki did make an immediate temporary impact on international public consciousness, political and religious leaders only slowly realized that splitting the atom had changed war qualitatively, not just quantitatively. Pope Pius XII frequently referred to the dangers of ABC (atomic, biological, and chemical) weapons, but his discussions of the morality of their use remained anchored in the just war tradition. Pius reaffirmed the traditional position that a nation must "suffer injustice" rather than violate just war norms, but he merely raised the question as to whether these new weapons would necessarily violate those norms:

What we have just discussed applies especially to ABC warfare—atomic, biological and chemical. As to the question of knowing whether it (ABC warfare) can become clearly necessary in self-defense against ABC warfare, let it suffice for us to have posed it here.[2]

According to Pius, warfare becomes immoral when it "involves such an extension of evil that it entirely escapes from the control of man." The use of weapons which cause "the pure and simple annihilation of all human life . . . is not permitted for any reason whatsoever."[3]

This papal position did not lead to any major Catholic institutional reevaluation of the ethics of war in light of the new weapons. Following the just war tradition, Pius also emphasized the duty of a nation to defend its citizens against the unjust aggression of other states. A nation might even have the duty to defend neighboring states:

A people threatened with an unjust aggression, or already its victim, may not remain passively indifferent, if it would think and act as befits a Christian. . . . Among (the) goods (of humanity) some are of such importance for society that it is perfectly lawful to defend them against unjust aggression. Their defense is even an obligation for the nations as a whole, who have a duty not to abandon a nation that is attacked.[4]

Given the state's duty to defend its citizens from unjust aggression, and the citizen's duty to work for the common good, it is easy to see why Pius rejected absolute pacifism as an option for the Catholic citizen.[5] With regard to the international political impact of the papacy at this time, the above moral positions on nuclear weapons were not as significant as Pius's strong anticommunism which reinforced the motivation necessary for the strategic arming of the West during the 1950s. Protestants, not Catholics, participated prominently in the peace movements of that decade. Pius's moral positions became significant, however, for later church documents like the American pastoral. Pius's two important statements on the morality of nuclear weapons were addressed to the Internation Office of Documentation for Military Medicine (October 1953) and the Eighth Congress of the World Medical Association (September 1954), thus foreshadowing the alliance between ecclesiastical and medical professionals during the early 1980s.

In the Introduction we noted the significance of John XXIII's encyclical *Pacem in terris* in dampening the universal Catholic anticommunist crusade. That encyclical did contain a broad stricture against nuclear war:

In an age such as ours, which prides itself on its atomic energy, it is contrary to reason to hold that war is now a suitable way to restore rights which have been violated.[6]

However, it is obvious from his other writings that John XXIII did not intend to rule out all nuclear weapons. Neither he nor succeeding popes have attempted a detailed analysis of when and under what conditions such use would be justified.[7]

American bishops were among those supporting both the "hawkish" and the "dovish" resolutions on nuclear weapons at Vatican II. The compromise final text of the *Pastoral Constitution on the Church in the Modern World* (*Gaudium et spes*) allowed for legitimate national defense but condemned the indiscriminate destruction of whole cities:

Every act of war directed to the indiscriminate destruction of whole cities or vast areas with their inhabitants is a crime against God and man, which merits firm and unequivocal condemnation.[7]

Paul VI articulated this new sense of urgency in the international church in his address to the United Nations General Assembly in 1965. He raised both arms and cried, "No more war! War never again." Fourteen years later, on October 2, 1979, John Paul II addressed the General Assembly on the same theme. "The continual preparations for war demonstrated by the production of ever more numerous, powerful and sophisticated weapons in various countries show that there is a desire to be ready for war, and being ready means being able to start it. . . . It is therefore necessary to make a continuing and even more energetic effort to do away with the very possibility of provoking war."[8]

The United Nations has since held two special sessions on disarmament (1978, 1982). Although the 1982 session was addressed by four heads of state (including Ronald Reagan), one vice-president, thirteen prime ministers, two deputy prime ministers, and forty-four foreign ministers who all insisted on the urgency of the issue, few analysts have claimed that either session accomplished much. The senior foreign policy spokespersons Gromyko and Casaroli represented the Soviet Union and the Vatican, respectively. Casa-roli read a statement from John Paul II which in its most important section dealt with the morality of deterrence:

In current conditions "deterrence" based on balance, certainly not as an end in itself but as a step on the way toward a progressive disarmament, may still be judged morally acceptable. Nonetheless in order to ensure peace, it is indispensable not to be satisfied with this minimum which is always susceptible to the real danger of explosion.[9]

This formulation was eventually adopted by the American bishops to solve the difficult problem of the morality of deterrence in their own pastoral. The spirit of the American letter, however, took its lead from John Paul's speech at Hiroshima. Thus the popes have employed the symbolic settings of Hiroshima and the United Nations as the context for important statements on strategic weapons.

In the Introduction, we mentioned the separate difficulties associated with choice of the terms "peace," "disarmament," or "arms control" to designate the area of Catholic politics that forms our central focus. The popes and the Vatican Councils have called for "peace," whose positive vision has a long tradition in the scriptures and Catholic theology. *Gaudium et spes*, for example, defined peace as "more than the absence of war." Peace is "the fruit of that right ordering of things with which the divine founder has invested human society and which must be actualized by man thirsting after an ever more perfect reign of justice."[10] Pius XII also insisted that any true peace was a peace based on justice, hence the obligation of states to defend their citizens from unjust aggression. Catholic documents have approached peace from both philosophical and theological traditions. John XXIII's *Pacem in terris*, for example, primarily employed the philosophical argumentation of natural law, considered by the church to be the common heritage of humankind. *Gaudium et spes* stressed the Catholic theological heritage of scripture and tradition.

"Peace," then, is the focus of Catholic ecclesiastical discussion of the topics in this chapter. The term, however, has certain disadvantages. The breadth of its usage in both Eastern and Western political systems combines with the richness of its ecclesiastical tradition to produce many different meanings. The meaning of the terms "arms control" and "disarmament" are difficult enough to specify, but they have a more restricted use in the literature on international politics. "Arms control" has the disadvantage of bringing with it for many members of the peace movement all the connotations of the failed negotiations between the United States and the Soviet Union, especially the unratified SALT II agreement. Supporters of arms control, on the other hand, dislike the connotations of "disarmament" with its suggestion of the peace movements of the 1950s. The Freeze Movement of the early 1980s sought to avoid the political disadvantages of both terms since "freeze" could be, and was, used in either an "arms control" or "disarmament" scenario. For our purposes, it is not so important which of the three terms is used as that the reader is cognizant of the connotations involved. This book uses "arms control" to emphasize the political, not theological or philosophical, nature of this chapter, and because the positions of the Soviet Union and the United States approximate "arms control" much more than "disarmament" or "peace."[11]

THE PEACE MOVEMENT, POLITICAL PARTIES, AND AMERICAN CATHOLICISM

In the late 1970s, world concern over nuclear weapons increased. Carter withdrew the SALT II Treaty from the Senate when the Soviet invasion of Afghanistan made its passage impossible. The failure to ratify SALT II destroyed the public confidence that the superpowers would gradually regulate strategic weapons. Not only had progress on disarmament halted, but the arms race seemed to be heating up. On October 2, 1981, President Reagan called for a major increase ($1.6 trillion over five years) in defense spending to respond to an alleged Soviet military superiority. Even more alarming was the accompanying rhetoric. As L. Bruce van Voorst commented, "Whether National Security Decision Directive (NSDD) 13 of November 1981 actually goes much beyond the old Presidential Directive (PD) 59 of the Carter Administration in projecting a 'winnable' war can be known only to those privy to the documents, but certainly the cavalier attitude of many senior Reagan Administration officials toward nuclear issues has contributed significantly to the widespread fears outside government."[12] Van Voorst also pointed to the growing American perception of the nuclear vulnerability of the United States as contributing to the contemporary timing of this moral debate, whose basic features came into existence with the explosions at Hiroshima and Nagasaki. The lurid descriptions in Jonathan Schell's *The Fate of the Earth*[13] affected one segment of the American reading public because for the first time that public realistically perceived a nuclear holocaust as "America's fate."

Theoretically, the United States political system provides a chan-

nel for such situations of serious public concern by structurally encouraging a single opposition political party which can unify and articulate the dissenting position. However, this theory of effective
two-party politics has become less and less tenable as the parties
themselves have become weaker and weaker and single-issue and
media politics have prevailed. This new American political situation
holds true not just at the national level but also for state elections.
In the November 1982 congressional elections, nine states voted on
the Nuclear Freeze Initiative, but the political commentators focused on California, the nation's most populous state. President
Reagan and many of his cabinet members and aides come from California.[14] California also contains the largest concentration of major
defense contractors, from the Lawrence Livermore Laboratory to
Lockheed Corporation.

California government has led the nation in an anti-party tradition. The Reform Movement of the early twentieth century sought
to ensure that the evils of Eastern machine politics would not rule
the Golden State.[15] The California ballot lists party affiliation for
very few of its offices. Even in the cases where the affiliation is
listed, Californians regularly split their ballots, so that often the
governor and at least one senator come from different parties. In the
last two elections the governor and his second in command, the
lieutenant governor, have come from different parties. The state
constitution encourages citizens to take specific issues "to the people" by collecting enough signatures to qualify a proposition for
state-wide balloting. These initiatives, e.g., Proposition 13 on property taxes (1978), are seen by national politicians as trend-setting
referenda on volatile issues.

Proposition 12, the Nuclear Freeze Initiative, began in 1979 as an
idea by Randall Forsberg, a graduate student in political science at
MIT, who was searching for an idea simple enough to sell the American public on arms control. Early in 1980 Forsberg wrote and circulated a document entitled, "The Call to Halt the Nuclear Arms
Race." Anne Sutherland, director of the Pasadena, California Interfaith Center to Reverse the Arms Race received Forsberg's publication in the mail, and discussed it with Harold Willens, a Los Angeles businessman, who had become increasingly frustrated in trying
to popularize opposition to nuclear weapons. Willens chaired the
group that collected over 800,000 signatures (346,000 properly registered voters were needed to qualify the measure), and then supported Proposition 12 in the general election.

Willens and other Freeze leaders sought to detach the initiative from party politics. They formed their own grass-roots single-issue organization by appealing to other nonpolitical, especially religious and professional, groups. Women were particularly active in the organization. The media campaign, featuring well-known television and sports personalities, appealed to the voter at large. Proposition 12 passed with slightly over 52 percent of the vote. California's traditional North-South split was evident in all the balloting. The North traditionally votes more liberal and Democratic, while the South votes more conservative and Republican. The high-tech Santa Clara County is regarded as one of the state's "swing counties," especially in presidential elections. The greatest political challenge to a Democratic candidate or an initiative like the Nuclear Freeze is to win the "swing counties" and to get enough votes from the more populous Southern California to add to a strong margin in the North. Urban Los Angeles County is the best source of these votes in the South, while largely suburban Orange and San Diego Counties remain extremely difficult for any Democrat. The Freeze won in the Bay Area counties of San Francisco (nearly three to one), Marin, Alameda, Contra Costa, San Mateo, Santa Clara, and Santa Cruz. In Southern California, it won in Los Angeles County (1,096,337 to 907,648) but lost in Orange and San Diego Counties. It also lost in most of the state's rural counties. Despite the fact that Freeze leaders worked diligently to insulate the issue from party politics, they won with a traditional Democratic strategy that showed a natural ideological affinity between the Freeze and traditionally Democratic voters.

The Nuclear Freeze Initiative did not, however, rely on the California state Democratic organization. The Freeze belongs to the new pattern in American politics which deemphasizes political parties. Instead, the campaign relied on a specific group formed to get the signatures necessary to place the initiative on the ballot. In addition, many special interest groups like Educators for Social Responsibility, Lawyers for Social Responsibility, and Computer Professionals for Social Responsibility have been formed to pursue disarmament. The most influential of these single-interest professional associations has been Physicians for Social Responsibility (PSR), at that time led by the charismatic Australian pediatrician, Helen Caldicott. These doctors have made it their mission to convince everyone of the medical horrors of nuclear war. "The Last Epidemic,"[16] a video featuring Caldicott and retired Admiral Gene R. LaRocque of the Defense Information Center at the PSR convention in San Francisco, was extremely effective in enlisting grass-roots support for the Freeze. The new VCR technology had facilitated widespread home use of this graphic presentation. The doctors have also focused on attacking the Reagan Administration's Civil Defense Program as an attempt to fool the public into thinking that there will be survivors after a nuclear attack. The above professional associations remain largely nonpolitical and new to citizen action. However, the Northern California campaign headquarters of the Freeze was located on College Avenue in Berkeley, thus relating it to the antiwar movement of the late 1960s and the environmental movement of the 1970s. Just down the street is the Sierra Club, which provided the first Northern California manager of the Freeze, Pam Nichols. Thus, the California political climate, even more than the United States in general, encouraged professional, single-interest, nonparty organizations.

The Catholic Church, especially in the Northern California dioceses of San Francisco and Stockton, became another nonpolitical interest group backing the Freeze. The leadership of Archbishop Quinn of San Francisco, past president of the NCCB, set the tone for the church throughout the state. Two days after President Reagan's announcement of his new strategic weapons package, Quinn took the occasion of the feast of St. Francis, the city's patron saint, to issue a pastoral letter condemning the arms race. In the letter Quinn supported the Nuclear Freeze, urged Catholic medical personnel to oppose the "Civilian-Military Contingency Hospital System," and encouraged Catholics to develop creative proposals for converting military weapons technology to civilian uses. On the same day, the establishment newspaper of "Silicon Valley," the *San Jose Mercury News*, began a fourteen-day series entitled, "Reagan's $180 billion strategic weapons package: Will it make us safer?" Quinn continued to be a major sponsor of the Freeze, testifying before the United States Senate Foreign Relations Committee in January 1982, and facing the conservative San Francisco Commonwealth Club on July 2.[17]

Bishop Roger Mahony of Stockton wrote a strong pastoral letter on war in the nuclear age on December 30, 1981. Mahony's letter focused on linking the arms race to the plight of the world's poor. In the notes Mahony thanked theologians from Berkeley's Jesuit School of Theology and others for their contributions to the letter. Besides Mahony, the much more conservative Cardinal Timothy Manning of Los Angeles criticized the arms race. The Los Angeles archdiocesan newspaper, *The Tidings*, and the more influential *Los Angeles Times* carried full coverage on the development of the pastoral letter by the national bishops' conference. The Catholic

Church's general position and expression of urgency was clear when Californians went to the polls to vote on the Freeze in November 1982. This Catholic position placed the California bishops along with mainline Protestant leaders against Protestant fundamentalists. Conservative evangelist Jerry Falwell, for example, mailed his California supporters a warning about the "Freezeniks" in their state.

At a time when the public perceived the arms race as a grave crisis, important segments of the Catholic Church in California led by Archbishop Quinn joined other nonpolitical professional groups to pass a single-issue initiative, the Freeze. The initiative passed, despite a strong concentration of arms industries within the state and the overwhelming support of the state's voters for President Reagan in 1980 and 1984. The vote and the subsequent fragmentation of this broad coalition as an effective political force demonstrates some of the political strengths and weaknesses of the contemporary Catholic Church in American state politics presently characterized by strong media and weak political parties.

THE DEBATE OVER THE AMERICAN PASTORAL LETTER

Shortly after the November 1982 vote, the American Catholic bishops met in Washington to consider the second draft of their pastoral letter on peace. This second draft expressed many of the concerns of those who voted for the Freeze. Its adoption would have placed the bishops considerably to the political left of the majority of the American laity and European bishops on this issue. The eventual high degree of unanimity of the American episcopate surprised many observers who were quite aware of the enormous differences of opinion within the episcopate. It is obvious that each bishop had his own nuanced position, but for the purpose of analysis, we will group the bishops into five categories.

Religious Protest. These bishops were the ideological heirs of the American Catholic radical tradition discussed in Chapter 5. By fall of 1982, fifty-seven bishops belonged to Pax Christi. The head of the American chapter, Auxiliary Bishop Thomas Gumbleton of Detroit, has said, "My position is simple to state. I am a total pacifist. I would not accept the use of any form of violence in my own defense." Bishop Gumbleton mentioned Thomas Merton, Dorothy Day, and Gordon Zahn[18] as influential in the formulation of his position. Not all the clergy in this category would have taken so uncompromising a stand. Archbishop Hunthausen of Seattle, for example, has said, "I've always said that I'm a nuclear pacifist; but given our present world, it is unrealistic to talk about conventional war." Whatever the exact ideological nuances of the archbishop's position, Hunthausen deliberately withheld 50 percent of his income taxes as a protest against America's continuing involvement in the race for nuclear arms superiority. This, of course, meant that Hunthausen had broken the law just as the Jesuit Daniel Berrigan did when he damaged warhead cones in Pennsylvania.[19]

Bishop Leroy Matthiesen of Amarillo united Hunthausen's criticism of the local arms establishment with Berrigan's concern over warheads. Just as Hunthausen characterized the Bangor Trident submarine base in his diocese as "the Auschwitz of Puget Sound," Matthiesen called on the 2,400 workers at Pantex, final assembly point for United States nuclear weapons, to quit their jobs. *Life* magazine (July 1982) had a full-page picture of Matthiesen, a "good old Texas boy," galloping along on a white horse. The bishops in this group have been referred to as the "peace bishops" by their supporters and the "war bishops" by their detractors. The presence of such a large group of bishops deeply committed to the peace issue has greatly influenced the rest of the hierarchy, both in pressing them to examine their own positions, and in moving the final compromise to the left so as not to lose their support for the final document. Pax Christi and the USCC did split on the SALT II Treaty. The USCC supported it as a positive step, while Pax Christi reflected American radical sentiment that the treaty only slowed down and disguised, not halted or reversed, the arms race.

Establishment Liberalism. This position was associated with the dynamic new leadership of American Catholicism as evidenced in Archbishops Roach, Quinn, Bernardin, Hickey, May, Weakland, and Malone. All were in their fifties or early sixties at the time of the peace pastoral. Only Bernardin has been named a cardinal, but the leaders of this generation have already been elected by their fellow bishops to important national posts. Castelli singles out Quinn and Hickey, both past chairmen of the NCCB Doctrinal Committee, as being the two leaders of the progressive forces at the final meeting in Chicago.[20] Many share Quinn's concern about Third World areas like Central America, thus uniting the two major concerns of the liberal wing of the Democratic Party.

The "Polish Position." If the ideology of any American prelate corresponds to that of John Paul II, it is the Polish-American Cardinal

John Krol of Philadelphia. Despite his well-earned conservative reputation on church doctrine and discipline, Cardinal Krol, then sixty-nine, represented the American bishops before the Senate Foreign Relations Committee in testifying for the ratification of SALT II in 1979. His intervention at that time was specifically quoted in the final text of the pastoral letter. The text states:

In 1979 John Cardinal Krol, speaking for the USCC in support of SALT II ratification, brought into focus the other element of the deterrence problem: the actual use of nuclear weapons may have been prevented (a moral good), but the risk of failure and the physical harm and moral evil resulting from possible nuclear war remained.

"This explains," Cardinal Krol stated, "the Catholic dissatisfaction with nuclear deterrence and the urgency of the Catholic demand that the nuclear arms race be reversed. It is of the utmost importance that negotiations proceed to meaningful and continuing reductions in nuclear stockpiles and eventually to the phasing out altogether of nuclear deterrence and the threat of mutual-assured destruction."[21]

Krol, whose name means "king" in Polish, is no more retiring than Wojtyła. In fact, Krol suggested that the pope's term "acceptable" (Second Special Session on Disarmament) would have been better expressed as "tolerated." Rather than himself changing his position on arms control over the last decade, Krol claims that the bishops have finally come around to his opinion. The cardinal says that his Spring 1982 address to Philadelphia's Interfaith Witness to Stop the Nuclear Arms Race did not differ basically from his 1969 address to the Veterans of Foreign Wars urging support for disarmament. "We advocate disarmament—not unilateral but reciprocal or collective disarmament, proceeding at an equal pace, according to agreement and backed up by authentic and workable safeguards."[22] Cardinal Krol demonstrates that theological conservatives can support disarmament. When a reporter asked him about President Reagan's charge that members of the peace movement were Soviet dupes, Krol replied, "Don't talk to me about that. I am a Pole." In any case Krol's leadership has given disarmament legitimacy among older, anticommunist, theologically conservative prelates.

Just War Self-Defense. This position predominated in the archdiocese of New York, which for a long time was also the Military Vicariate of the American Armed Forces.[23] The military vicar, Cardinal Cooke of New York, criticized the various drafts of the letter for ignoring the Soviet threat and for deemphasizing the legitimate right of national self-defense.[24] Cooke's major initiative consisted of a personal letter to all the Catholic chaplains of the armed forces emphasizing that the bishops' second draft supported Catholics in the military and upheld the right of the nation to legitimate self-defense. The most controversial sentence in Cooke's letter said: "As long as our nation is sincerely trying to work with other nations to find a better way [to maintain peace], the Church considers the strategy of nuclear deterrence morally tolerable; not satisfactory, but tolerable." More than sixty priests, religious, and laymen of the New York Archdiocese wrote a rebuttal letter, citing Krol's testimony, and terming Cooke's intervention "a positive disservice to our Church." Cooke wrote a second letter to transmit the bishops' final document to the Armed Services. The Army and Air Force Chiefs of Chaplains, both Catholics, mailed Cooke's letter and the bishops' pastoral letter to all their chaplains, regardless of faith.[25] The bishops in this fourth group cannot be characterized as blind and reactionary conservatives. Cooke's support was crucial to the joint letter of the American and Panamanian bishops urging support for the Panama Canal Treaty, thus making him a sort of "ecclesiastical Howard Baker (R-Tenn.)." O'Connor, whose election by the American bishops to head their Social Development and World Peace Committee terrified peace activists, has expressed doubts about the MX, the B-1 bomber, and the Pershing II missile. On June 26, 1984, O'Connor and Bernardin testified before the House Committee on Foreign Affairs. The two archbishops, representing the USCC, questioned both the MX and President Reagan's space-based defense plan on the criteria of their impact on the arms race and their cost. When Catholic Republican Congressman Henry J. Hyde criticized the pastoral letter of the American bishops as pacifistic unilateral disarmament and "bluff deterrence," O'Connor replied that he knew of "no bishop who would advocate unilateral disarmament," but neither did he know a bishop "who is not scared to death about what could happen if that power was unleashed onto the world."[26]

American National Anticommunism. Bishops in these last two categories both had legitimate reasons to claim ideological descent from Cardinal Spellman. Prelates like Cooke and O'Connor served the same conservative and military constituencies, and maintained their predecessor's acute appreciation of the Soviet threat. Nevertheless, they had moderated Spellman's nationalistic positions as both the American bishops and American Catholics in general had moderated theirs. And in the end, both Cooke and O'Connor voted for the pastoral letter. A few bishops, notably from the South, carried Spellman's strident anticommunist nationalism into the 1980s. Archbishop Philip Hannan of New Orleans became the most outspoken episcopal critic of the letter. In Chicago Hannan proposed fifty amendments to the letter, of which the bishops approved thirteen minor ones. Hannan even personally criticized the Chair, Bernardin, a grave exception to the usual (even exaggerated) courtesy that pertains among episcopal collegiality. Castelli relates:

Hannan then attacked the pastoral's statement urging that it be used as a teaching document. Shouting, he cited Cardinal Ratzinger's comments on the limited authority of national conferences and accused Bernardin of disobeying Rome's desires. Finally, exasperated in defending his belief that the pastoral was, in fact, in line with Rome, Bernardin yelled back, "I was at the meeting."[27]

After the adoption of the pastoral, Hannan issued a seven-page rebuttal to the letter, objecting to the tone and a number of the specific conclusions.[28] Van Voorst also singles out Hannan as "particularly vocal on the dangers of a Soviet system as a fate worse than death," but mentions only Archbishop Oscar Lipscomb of Mobile as making a similar argument.[29] Lipscomb, and Auxiliary Bishops Patrick Ahern and Austin Vaughan of New York are mentioned by Castelli. Vaughan was the only bishop to speak against the final document. These bishops retain their political importance not because of possible significant hierarchical support, but because of the fact that Spellman's anticommunist nationalism remains a viable current among the Catholic laity. On arms control, the median position of the episcopate remains to the left of the median position of the laity.

THE PROCESS

The process of the pastoral letter began with the responses of three bishops (P. Francis Murphy of Baltimore, Edward O'Rourke of Peoria, and John Whealon of Hartford) to the annual request for new business to be taken up at the NCCB meeting in November 1980.[30] All three bishops, starting from different perspectives, requested that the NCCB reexamine and systematize its teachings on war and peace. When the bishops met, Ronald Reagan had just been elected president of the United States. The 1980 presidential campaign had given a new sharpness to the national debate over military preparedness. When the topic was introduced, several bishops, most notably Pax Christi President Thomas Gumbleton, urged serious consideration of the topic. In January 1981 the new NCCB President Roach named a committee headed by Archbishop Bernardin (then of Cincinnati). The committee also included Gumbleton and Auxiliary Bishop John O'Connor of the Military Vicariate, along with Bishop Daniel Reilly of Norwich, Connecticut and Auxiliary Bishop George Fulcher of Columbus, Ohio. The last two appointments were perceived as representing the broad middle ground between Gumbleton and O'Connor. The staff also consisted of five persons: a representative each from the American men and women religious; Father J. Bryan Hehir, director of the USCC Department of International Justice and Peace; Edward Doherty, adviser on political-military affairs for the USCC; and Professor Bruce M. Russett of Yale. Russett, a Catholic and editor of the *Journal of Conflict Resolution*, eschewed the title of "author" but accepted the designation of "principal consultant." Hehir recruited Russett and served as the principal object of conservative criticism during the process. Russett remarks that the choice of an episcopal committee "that covered most of the American foreign policy spectrum was no coincidence." Pastoral letters require a two-thirds majority, but the "informal, but very real, decision rule is more like 85-90 percent of all members present and voting."[31]

The committee held hearings at which many experts, from theologians to political scientists, from peace activists to military officers, testified and answered questions. Former and then current government officials interviewed included Casper Weinberger, Lawrence Eagleberger, Eugene Rostow, Edward Rowney, Harold Brown, James Schlesinger, Gerard Smith, Helmut Sonnenfeld, Herbert Scoville, David Linebaugh, and Roger Molander.[32] Bishop Fulcher remarked that the turning point for him was the sessions with the former Secretaries of Defense Schlesinger and Brown, whom he called "gifted, talented, sensitive people." "Here are these men who have had to make these decisions, who were put in the position of having to justify the use of the bomb. What a horrifying thing that is."[33]

Episcopal concern had been growing after Reagan's military buildup speech of October 2 when the NCCB met again in November 1981. Arms control was not the principal topic of the meeting, however, which focused on the bishops' decision to support the Hatch amendment that would have given the states and the federal government concurrent power to regulate abortion, with the strictest law prevailing. Bernardin gave an interim report on his committee's work. He concluded his speech with the strong words that,

"the very created order is threatened by nuclear war. We must learn
how to evaluate war with an entirely new attitude."[34] The bishops
not only gave Bernardin a standing ovation but also elected him as
one of their delegates to the 1983 Synod of Bishops. In the discussion period that followed Bernardin's report, the bishops heard
strong speeches from representatives of all five of the episcopal categories listed above.

Bernardin distributed the first draft of the pastoral in June to
about 250 American bishops attending an eleven-day assembly at
St. John's University in Collegeville. After responses from the bishops and others, the second draft was presented in late October for
the November meeting. The second draft was divided into four sections: 1) Peace in the Modern World: Religious Perspectives and
Principles; 2) War and Peace in the Modern World: Problems and
Principles; 3) The Promotion of Peace: Proposals and Policies; and
4) The Pastoral Challenge and Response. Media coverage focused
on the second section because it posed a direct challenge to American strategic policy. The document ruled out counterpopulation
warfare, initiation of nuclear war, and expressed grave doubts
about the possibility of a limited nuclear war. The moral acceptabil-
ity of deterrence was conditioned by three criteria: a) it must exist
only to prevent the use of nuclear weapons by others, not to encourage war fighting capabilities; b) "sufficiency," not superiority is
the goal; and c) each strategic weapon or doctrine must be judged
in the light of whether or not it facilitates arms control and disarmament. In light of these principles the draft opposed "first strike"
weapons,[35] strategic planning that sought a nuclear war fighting ca-
pability, and proposals which had the effect of lowering the nuclear
threshold and blurring the difference between nuclear and conventional weapons. The document supported a bilateral nuclear freeze,
negotiated bilateral deep cuts, especially of destabilizing weapons,
a Comprehensive Test Ban Treaty, and removal of nuclear weapons
from border areas along with strengthening of command and control procedures to prevent accidents. The many differences between this document and the official position of the United States
government became obvious immediately. The bishops in general
reacted positively to this second draft. In an informal survey by the
NCCB, 195 bishops replied they were "basically in agreement," 71
said they had "major reservations," and 12 were in "basic disagree-
ment."[36] The bishops voted overwhelmingly to meet again in Chicago in May 1983 to consider what became the final draft of the document.

If the bishops were basically positive, a deluge of negative response came from the Reagan Administration, American Catholic conservatives, and some European bishops. National Security Adviser William P. Clark articulated the Administration position in a letter delivered to all 285 bishops at the November meeting. Clark served as Reagan's Catholic spokesperson on this issue because both he and his wife Joan, a Czechoslovakian émigré, remain traditional Catholics who prefer the Latin Mass. Clark had attended Stanford, Santa Clara University (Jesuit), Loyola Law School (Jesuit), and the Augustinian Novitiate to explore a vocation to the priesthood. In the letter Clark, "on behalf of President Reagan, Secretary Shultz, Secretary Weinberger, Director Rostow, and other Administration officials,"[37] argued that the Administration's position was guided by compelling moral considerations. The Clark letter defended the concept of deterrence and praised the arms control initiatives of the Reagan Administration.

The Clark letter did not sway the bishops. In fact, the net effect was probably negative since many bishops objected to the fact that the letter had been released to the press before they had received it. Besides Clark, other important Administration Catholic spokespersons were Edward Rowny, chief negotiator at START, and John P. Lehman, Jr., secretary of the Navy.[38] The second draft outraged American Catholic conservatives. Former Labor Commissioner James J. McFadden offered his New York-based American Catholic Committee as a "lightening rod" for Catholics concerned that the bishops were steering the church away from traditional Catholic political positions. "The net effect of this [the second draft]," said McFadden, "is that the bishops are going to politicize the church." Twenty-four Catholic congressmen, led by Henry Hyde (R-Ill.), wrote an open letter to Archbishop Bernardin in which they strongly criticized the Soviet Union, against whose corrupt ideology Alexander Solzhenitsyn "has come to us as a spiritual witness."[39] The Congressman's letter was reproduced in *Catholicism in Crisis*, a new magazine started by Ralph McInerny (Jacques Maritain Center, University of Notre Dame) and Michael Novak (American Enterprise Institute). Novak was instrumental in drafting a competitive document, "Moral Clarity in the Nuclear Age: A Letter from Catholic Clergy and Laity."[40] The letter went through three drafts and was publicized to obtain supporting signatures.

When the third draft of the bishop's letter was released in April, conservatives rejoiced. Novak praised the new text as an example of the "open church." State Department officials asserted that the new draft "explicitly endorses many of the far-reaching objectives the administration seeks." Daniel Berrigan, receiving the Pacem in Terris award at Georgetown University, said he felt "betrayed" by the draft. Jesuit Peter Henriot, director of the Center for Concern in Washington, D.C., merely said the new draft was "unfortunate" in that the treatment of the just war theory was "clouded by extraneous material supportive of U.S. military policy and by the addition of the concept of comparative justice, which has no basis in the classical discussion of just war theory." Henriot did praise the increased emphasis on international cooperation and interdependence. The *National Catholic Reporter* offered an alternative simple one-page draft and editorialized that it would be better to issue no letter than to release the third draft.[41]

Had the bishops softened their position? This 150-page document (the longest to that time) retained the same general orientation as the second draft, but it became less specific in three areas important to administration policy. First, the adamant prohibition of the first use of nuclear weapons was softened to provide for at least a theoretical possibility of such use as a last resort. Second, the draft remained skeptical about deterrence, but it did not brand it as immoral. Third, the bishop changed the specific wording calling for a nuclear freeze. This latter change had strong political significance because of the imminent vote on the nuclear freeze in Congress. Representative Hyde wrote a letter to his colleagues stating that the bishops, "after careful deliberation, have refused to endorse the nuclear Freeze."[42]

How did these changes come about? Eight meetings on the draft were held between November and the release of the document on April first. Only the committee attended five of these. On December 21, Hehir and Russett met with "staff level" members of the Reagan administration to discuss United States strategic targeting. On January 6-7, the entire committee met with higher level officials at the State Department. On January 18-19 Bernardin, Roach, Hehir, and Monsignor Daniel Hoye met with European bishops and Vatican officials in Rome (see following section). The full committee of five bishops met four more times before sending the document to the general secretary on March 25. Hehir commented that changes were influenced mostly by brother American bishops, then by the Rome meeting, with only two small changes coming from the administration. Bishop O'Connor took the lead in proposing changes within the committee.

Part of the media interpretation came from a Bernardin press conference, in which he said that the committee had tried to be "sensitive" to the Reagan administration and that it had produced a more "flexible" third draft. While Bernardin's comments were technically correct, they encouraged headlines indicating that the bishops were backing down in the face of administration criticism.[43] The administration had also learned from the mistakes it had made in November when every protest merely emphasized the difference between the second draft and American policy. On April 7 the *New York Times* ran a front-page headline that read, "Administration Hails New Draft of Arms Letter—Says Bishops 'Improved' the Nuclear Statement."

Most of the committee and many bishops were distressed about the general press treatment of the letter, which emphasized the agreement between the new draft and the Reagan Administration's positions. Bernardin and Roach called a press conference in which they rejected "any suggestion that there are relatively few and insignificant differences between U.S. policies and the policies advocated in the pastoral."[44] The pastoral had removed some specifics such as a mention of the MX, but the more important political reality at the time concerned the widespread impression that the American bishops had retreated under pressure from the administration and the Vatican. The changing of the word "halt" to "curb" concerning nuclear weapons became the symbol of this public perception, since the freeze occupied congressional and national debate at the time.

This perception of retreat fueled efforts to rework the letter in Chicago. The bishops first voted to change "curb" to "halt," adding a sentence which disclaimed endorsement of any "specific political initiative." As has already been mentioned, Archbishops Quinn and Hickey led the attack on changes that seemed to soften the third draft. Quinn believed that use of nuclear weapons could never be justified and felt the third draft afforded too many loopholes that would allow such use. Quinn won support for some of his amendments and was defeated on others. However, he was surprised at how well his proposals fared, while the conservative Hannan became more and more discouraged. Castelli characterizes the voting of the bishops:

As the afternoon went on, the sophisticated pattern of the bishops' voting became clear—they approved virtually everything that strengthened the document, while consistently stopping short of saying that there was no conceivable situation in which the use of nuclear weapons could be morally justified. They rejected efforts which would have either given the document a more pacifist tone or given any suggestion for using nuclear weapons.[45]

This episcopal approach almost fragmented with initial passage of Quinn's Amendment 68 which specified, "Nevertheless, there must be no misunderstanding of our opposition on moral grounds to any use of nuclear weapons." The amendment was reconsidered, and Bernardin argued very strongly against it. It was then defeated.[46] Finally, after three days of debate, the bishops passed the pastoral letter 238-9. The next day the House Freeze resolution, to which critics attached an amendment setting an indefinite time limit, passed 278-149. Catholic Democrats backed the resolution 82-4, while Catholic Republicans voted against it 23-15.

The American bishops, despite being as politically fragmented as the Democratic Party, came to adopt by near unanimity a very progressive document. How did this happen? Most importantly, of course, the episcopate perceived their process not primarily as political bargaining but as an exercise of collegial religious and moral responsibility. Common liturgy and prayer had nurtured this hierarchical unity. Several bishops mentioned the eleven days of prayer at Collegeville in June 1982 as a profound common experience.[47] In addition, several nonreligious factors were significant. First, the American hierarchy felt it had lost moral authority by waiting so long to take a stand on the Vietnam War. Now they seemed to be retreating from their earlier strong stand in the second draft because of criticism from the Reagan Administration. They would end up looking worse than they had on Vietnam. Second, as Chapter 2 has pointed out, there had been a tremendous number of new bishops, selected on socially progressive criteria, appointed during the tour of the progressive apostolic delegate Jadot. Third, the international church had been emphasizing peace. While some European bishops were uneasy about the second draft, John Paul had named Bernardin a cardinal on January 15, and had restricted himself to general suggestions in the January 18-19 meetings. Bernardin felt sure enough of his own position to finesse curial intervention. Fourth, the bishops in general feared a split with the fifty-seven Pax Christi bishops. As long as the general thrust of the document stayed within what I have termed "establishment liberalism," and that it was made clear that various parts of the draft carried different moral binding force, most conservative bishops would vote for the final draft as an expression of episcopal unity.

What practical impact has the letter had in the United States church and political system? Within the church, the bishops charged a committee under Bishop Fulcher to disseminate the letter. While the letter has raised consciousness generally throughout the American church, different bishops placed different emphases in their own dioceses, as was obvious from comments following the May meeting. This diversity was encouraged by the section of the pastoral letter which specifically states:

We wish to explore and explain the resources of the moral-religious teaching and to apply it to specific questions of our day. In doing this we realize, and we want readers of this letter to recognize, that not all statements in this letter have the same moral authority. At times we state universally binding moral principles found in the teaching of the church; at other times the pastoral letter makes specific applications, observations and recommendations which allow for diversity of opinion on the part of those who assess the factual data of a situation differently. However, we expect Catholics to give our moral judgments serious consideration when they are forming their own views on specific problems.[48]

What was the political impact of the letter? The educational value of the process is probably more important than the specific conclusions of the third draft. The debate on the second draft during late October and November strengthened nuclear freeze proponents in the nine state initiatives. The November debate on the second draft became a major media event, with Archbishop Bernardin on the cover of *Time* (November 19, 1982). One month later the House of Representatives, traditionally a bastion for defense "hawks," handed President Reagan a stinging foreign policy defeat by deleting production funds for the MX missile. The vote was 245-176, despite extremely heavy lobbying by the White House. The future of the MX remains uncertain three years later. It passed the latest funding hurdle in March 1985, despite opposition from the bishops.[49] The Reagan Administration won by launching a massive campaign which tied the weapon to the Geneva arms talks.

The continued dissemination of the Catholic peace policy continues to undermine a hard line on nuclear weapons, despite the administration's attempt to coopt its lofty sentiments. When President Reagan was asked about the inconsistency between the position of the pastoral letter and administration policy in his May 4, 1983, press conference he replied, "They're looking for a way toward peace and promoting world peace. And that's what we're also looking for."[50] This political strategy seems a more effective approach for the administration than drawing attention to the discrepancies, as in the Clark letter. After all, said the president at the same press conference, "As I say, I have not seen it yet and 45,000 words are a lot to digest." The president hoped to bury the document with polite praise for peace. One approach to gauging the impact of the letter would be to analyze the reaction of sympathetic non-Catholic commentators within the political establishment. The editors of the *New York Times* in an editorial also reprinted by the *Christian Science Monitor* praised the bishops' "sense of moral challenge" and some of their strategic judgments, e.g., that nuclear war can never be winnable. However, the editorial questioned the strictures on targeting Soviet cities and retaining a nuclear option to a massive Soviet attack in Europe. The fundamental defect of the letter, according to the *Times*, is its attempt to eliminate rather than control nuclear weapons. Thus they have strayed "far from the prevailing theories of the arms control community."[51]

The next month McGeorge Bundy, a charter member of the establishment arms control community, wrote an article in *The New York Review of Books* in which he contrasted the pastoral letter with the Scowcroft Commission report. Bundy praised the bishops for making a "signal contribution" to the task of living with nuclear weapons without considering deterrence as an adequate long-term basis for peace. He commented that the letter does not address the questions of what to do if deterrence fails, but "it is at least a partial defense of their omission that a bad answer to this question is worse than none at all." Bundy contrasted the long-term thrust of the Scowcroft report toward survivability and arms control with its endorsement of the MX, which he says, has precisely the opposite effect. "Yet," Bundy predicts, "I think that in the end the sensible recommendations of the commission will overtake its illogical endorsement of MX, just as I think the basic conclusions of the bishops will prove more durable than the debate over the degree of their enthusiasm for specific proposals like the freeze or (to take one I myself resist) the idea of a 'peace academy.' "[52]

CATHOLICISM AND ARMS CONTROL IN NATO

Bruce Russett, the principal consultant for the American pastoral, has pointed out that defense of Western Europe provided the central problem faced by the United States bishops in writing their letter.

The central problem for the bishops' analysis is not deterrence of attack on the United States, but of attack on allies or neutrals under American protection. This of course has also been the central function of American nuclear deterrence since its inception. Nuclear deterrence, furthermore has been extended to deterrence of *conventional* attacks on our allies, a policy promoted by the relatively inexpensive nature of nuclear weapons (more "bang for the buck") and the difficulties of raising adequate conventional defense forces against the "Eastern hordes." Thus a key element of some acceptable resolution of the bishops' dilemma is their strong advocacy of a "no first use" posture. It is not quite an unequivocal rejection of first use ("We do not perceive any situation in which the deliberate initiation of nuclear warfare, on however restricted a scale, can be morally justified"), but it comes very close. In doing so, the bishops oppose the idea of using nuclear weapons for extended deterrence, and require that non-nuclear attacks be resisted by other than nuclear means.[53]

It is no accident that the last section ended with McGeorge Bundy's comments on the American pastoral, since Bundy joined Robert McNamara, George Kennan, and Gerard Smith in the very influential *Foreign Affairs* article (Spring 1982) which advocated a no first-use policy in Europe. The American pastoral, therefore, benefited from the general critique of existing NATO strategy among more liberal members of the arms control establishment. It was these members who provided much of the necessary strategic and technical expertise for the letter. Bundy mentions the difference between the American and some European hierarchies over whether or not NATO should use nuclear weapons to respond to a Soviet conventional attack. He then remarks, "but it takes an unnecessary and even unbecoming lack of American self-confidence to suppose that this particular difference makes the American bishops wrong."[54]

The impact of the American pastoral on the plausibility of NATO strategy concerned both the Catholic hierarchies and the national governments of Europe. The German bishops became especially sensitive because of their traditional closeness to Christian Democratic governments, and because officials of their own governments had criticized the second draft of the American bishops' letter. In response to these European concerns of the NATO bishops, Father Jan Schotte, secretary of the Pontifical Justice and Peace Commission, called a meeting of representatives from American and six European churches (West Germany, England and Wales, Italy, France, Belgium, and the Netherlands), along with Vatican officials. The meeting took place January 18-19, 1983, in Rome. Archbishops Roach and Bernardin, Father J. Bryan Hehir, and Monsignor Daniel Hoye represented the American church. Cardinal Basil Hume led the British delegation. Although a cordial atmosphere prevailed, Cardinal Joseph Ratzinger of Munich attacked the competency of a national bishops' conference to write such a document. Other concerns were also expressed, especially about the degree of moral binding force attached to specific recommendations. Schotte's report of the meeting, dated January 25, mentions "fidelity to the tradition of the church and the teaching of John Paul II" as the criterion for sound doctrine. The pope, however, did not intervene in the formal meeting, and the Schotte memo does not detail his position. Secretary of State Casaroli offered a personal commentary on the pope's June 11, 1982, message to the United Nations. "He did so," according to the memo, "not as an authorized interpreter of the Holy Father's statement, but on the basis of his knowledge of the text and context of that message."

The Schotte report, which praises the American bishops for their "courage and humility" for agreeing to go to Rome for this "open exchange," arrived in Washington on March 9, with the indication it would be distributed to all the American bishops. Schotte summarized the January meeting of the American and European bishops, denying that bishops' conferences have a mandate to teach, and reporting that the participants made comments like the following:

1. When bishops propose the doctrine of the church, the faithful are bound in conscience to assent. A serious problem arises on the pastoral level when bishops propose opinions on the evalution of technical or military factors. The faithful can be confused, their legitimate freedom of choice hindered, the teaching authority of bishops lessened and the influence of the church in society thus weakened.
2. When differing choices are equally justifiable, bishops should not take sides. Rather they should offer several options or express themselves hypothetically.[55]

While Bernardin felt certain of his own understanding of his conversations with Ratzinger, Casaroli, and John Paul, this "staff report" could cause difficulties, especially when joined with Bishop O'Connor's increased militancy. Therefore, he and Roach obtained apostolic delegate Archbishop Laghi's permission to distribute the Schotte memo with a cover letter of their own expressing confidence that they had met Vatican concerns. As expected, the memo and letter were leaked immediately, depriving conservatives of a possible Vatican intervention just prior to the Chicago meeting. In this environment O'Connor influenced the committee to change "halt" to "curb," although the other members saved the specifics in the deterrence section.

The roles of John Paul II and Vatican Secretary of State Casaroli remain unclear. According to a report from Great Britain, some European bishops felt Casaroli's remarks exonerated the Americans since he made it clear that national hierarchies remained free to go beyond the pope, as long as they quoted the pope correctly. The Schotte report mentions no intervention by John Paul himself, but Archbishop Bernardin told the American bishops in a closed-door session at Chicago on May 1, 1983, that John Paul had expressly discussed the second draft with the American bishops in January. The pope's points included:

—Various hierarchies of the world should be united, because if they are divided on issues, one would have to disavow the other;
—A distinction must be made between principles, i.e., the teachings of the church, and the principles' practical applications, which do not have magisterial force;
—The draft's conclusions "must be logical";
—The impression should not be given that the church supports pacifism;
—The responsibility of both superpowers to negotiate must be stressed;
—The point must be made that Russia does not accept the church's moral authority.[56]

Whenever the American delegates asked about specifics, the pope stayed with generalities. All this ecclesiastical bureaucracy resulted in detaching the pope from specific responsibility, encouraging the American bishops while setting parameters for their letter, and indicating to the European bishops that they must come to grips with this issue.

The various European hierarchies did issue their own letters. During 1983 the bishops of the NATO countries of West Germany, the Netherlands, and Belgium wrote joint pastoral letters, while Cardinal Hume of Great Britain wrote a letter to *The Times* of London. The French, Irish, Scottish and Austrian bishops also wrote joint letters.[57] The geopolitical importance of France and Germany made the German and French episcopal documents the most significant. The German bishops issued *Gerechtigkeit schafft Frieden (Out of Justice, Peace)* on April 27, 1983, between the German elections and the final debate on the American document. The letter, released by the president of the (West) German Bishops' Conference, Cardinal Joseph Höffner of Cologne, called the arms race and the expansionist aims of Marxist regimes the chief threats to world peace. The letter was divided into four main sections: an exposition of biblical perspectives on peace, an analysis of traditional Catholic teachings on war and peace, a "comprehensive peace stragegy," and a series of recommendations. Compared with the American letter, the German pastoral put more emphasis on the Soviet threat, the necessity of international social justice, and human rights. It avoided discussing specific weapons policies or strategies, such as the deployment of the Pershing and cruise missiles. The letter did not state a direct judgment on NATO's first use of nuclear weapons but implied that a limited Western nuclear response might be justifiable under certain conditions.[58] The West German government welcomed the pastoral letter, commenting that deterrence is a necessary peaceful policy that makes arms negotiations possible.

The French bishops issued *Gagner La Paix* (*Winning the Peace*) at Lourdes on November 8. *Le Monde* (November 10, 1984), which gave the event a three-column head at the top of page one, headlined its front-page editorial, "A chacun son pacifisme" (to each his pacifism). The editorial pointed to the surprising fact that the French bishops were "less to the left" than their American colleagues, but attributed the difference between American "idealism" and French "realism" to the differing church-state and political contexts. Indeed, in an earlier *Le Monde* interview, the priest Gérard Defois, who played a major role in preparing the draft, took a similar approach. Defois avoided criticizing the American pastoral, noting that it was "the point of departure" for discussions of the arms race within the church. Differences in American and French viewpoints could be accounted for in terms of the different political and military situations, especially the old, traditional role of churches in American life and the rhetoric of the early Reagan Administration.[59]

With regard to the specificity of the recommendations, the Dutch, Belgian, and Irish episcopal letters all fall between the general principles of the German treatment and the more concrete applications of the American letter. In interviews, however, the leaders of all national churches have emphasized the broad agreement of the documents, and downplayed any differences. Following the passage of the American pastoral letter in Chicago, for example, Cardinal Ratzinger gave a long interview to the German magazine *Der Spiegel*, in which he defended the United States pastoral letter and attributed differences between the American and European hierarchies to the different national contexts involved.

France's situation is different. Its atomic weaponry, in quality and capacity, can never be used aggressively. Thus it is defensive in the world power struggle. Mitterand can't do the same thing as Reagan for world policy. In this respect the moral position of that country's bishops is also different, naturally. And the historical responsibility of the Germans is likewise of a different nature.[60]

While the British bishops did not write a joint pastoral on peace, Cardinal Hume's letter appeared the London *Times* on November 17, 1983. In it Hume stated that the "acceptance of deterrence on strict conditions and as a temporary expedient leading to progressive disarmament is emerging as the most widely accepted view of the Roman Catholic Church."[61] Hume's letter was published in the midst of the public turmoil over the deployment of the Euromissiles. The cardinal recognized that "in a free society, the peace movements play an important role. They bring before us the terrible questions we might otherwise ignore but which must be answered."[62] Inevitably, however, according to Hume, these movements pressure Western governments more than those of the East. All must obey the law, respect "democratic processes" and the "institutions of a free society," and retain their right to conscientious beliefs.

British Catholic intellectuals had a much stronger tradition of advocacy for disarmament than their American fellow-believers.[63] Catholic Monsignor Bruce Kent, head of the Campaign for Nuclear Disarmament (CND), led the British struggle against the deployment of the Euromissiles. Kent had been vice-president of Pax Christi International and a major figure in the meeting between Pax Christi International and the Russian Orthodox Church in London in 1978. Under Kent's chairmanship, the CND grew from 3,500 in 1980 to 54,000 three years later. Kent's prominence introduced considerable political conflict into the British Catholic Church. For example, Catholic M.P. Michael Brotherton remarked that, "for someone with such a senior title as 'monsignor' to be doing as Bruce Kent does the work of the Kremlin, which is an organization which is patently anti-Christ is to me something that is totally repugnant." In April 1983, at the height of the British election campaign, Cardinal Hume renewed his consent for Kent to remain general secretary of CND, but warned that recent developments had caused him "serious misgivings." If CND became too political, Kent would have to resign.[64]

Archbishop Winning of Glasgow defended CND against charges by the British defense secretary Michael Heseltine that the majority of the organization's national coucil were advancing Socialist or Communist causes: "Is he [Heseltine] saying that Pope John Paul II is a tool of Russian propaganda?"[65] The apostolic pro-nuncio Bruno Heim entered the controversy with a letter to British conservatives criticizing Kent and implying that those who support unilateral disarmament are "useful idiots" of the Soviet Union. On May 20 the Vatican distanced itself from Heim's letter, which it termed the pronuncio's personal initiative. Heim's letter angered Cardinal Hume, who had taken a leading role in the European peace movement by presiding over a four-day meeting of forty Catholic and forty Protestant and Orthodox leaders from Western and Eastern Europe at the Cistercian monastery of Logumkloster, Denmark, in late 1981.[66]

The British ecclesiastical conflict was exacerbated by the fact that the British opposition party and the British peace movement took much more radical stands than their American counterparts. The Labour Party, for example, voted two-to-one in favor of unilateral nuclear disarmament. The CND staged some imaginative demonstrations, as when it joined the Women's Movement for Peace in forming a fourteen-mile human chain which surrounded the Trident base at Greenham Common and two other weapons facilities. British youth, however, do not manifest the huge generation gap of West Germans when their perceptions of the United States are compared with those of their elders. In the end, Labour's stand for abolishing Britain's nuclear deterrent proved too extreme for the electorate. Margaret Thatcher invoked the previous year's victory in the Falklands as the Conservatives won a smashing victory.[67]

The British CND worked closely with the European Nuclear Disarmament Campaign (END), which began on April 28, 1980. END, with its advocacy of a nuclear-free Europe from Poland to Portugal, has constituted one of the four major approaches to arms control and disarmament found among peace movements in the NATO countries. The American Freeze is the second. The Dutch IKV has called for unilateral first steps, focusing on removing nuclear weapons from the Netherlands. Fourth, the Belgian peace movement, with significant European backing, has supported a *Security Zone* in Europe. This Security Zone, made up of all nonnuclear countries in Europe, would freeze present nuclear deployment and then begin withdrawal according to terms to be defined.[68] While each of these movements still maintains its greatest support in its country of origin, each also maintains an international liaison body in support of its objectives. For example, END founded the Internation Liaison Committee in Rome in November 1981. The Dutchman Willem Bartels is president of both the IKV and the International Peace Communication and Coordination Centre (IPCC), established in September 1981 following a conference in Copenhagen. In January 1983 Pax Christi International brought together representatives of all four groups at a meeting in Antwerp.[69] In December the president of Pax Christi International, Etienne De Jonghe sought to use the concept of a Euro-Freeze as the central focus for a pan-European peace movement following the deployment of the Euromissiles.[70]

As we mentioned in Chapter 4, the Austrian government, Catholic hierarchy, and Catholic peace movement have all emphasized their roles in bringing together the principal antagonists from East and West. The 1983 peace pastorals of both the Austrian and Hungarian bishops stressed the necessity of dialogue and discussion in slowing down the arms race and in achieving normal relations between states. Cardinal König joined Father Theodore Hesburgh in sponsoring a meeting of religious leaders at Vienna on January 15, 1983. The religious leaders met to respond to the "Declaration on Prevention of Nuclear War," a statement which had been framed by fifty-five scientists, twenty of whom were presidents of national scientific academies, who had met September 22-24, 1982, under the auspices of the Pontifical Academy of Sciences.[71] Catholics, Protestants, Orthodox, and Muslims attended the Vienna meeting. Such an initiative stands out by reason of its attempt to join scientific expertise to religious leadership, rather than by the content of the statement. The Vienna meeting was also significant in that American Catholics were represented by Archbishop Roach and Father Hehir, who within a week were facing the objections of the European bishops to the Americans' pastoral letter in Rome. When the American bishops decided on the final text of the pastoral in May, the president of the Pontifical Academy of Sciences, Brazilian Carlos Chagas, praised the American hierarchy "because thay resisted many pressures, beginning with those from their government." The United States episcopate, Chagas said, had rightly gone beyond the Academy's first 1981 report because "the U.S. bishops were dealing with a more specific problem, namely President Reagan's military development programme, which was ruining the country's social development programme."[72] In October 1984 thirty-three scientists and four clerics met under the auspices of the Academy to consider "the impact of space exploration on mankind." The group issued its report to the Curia the following January. In its section on armament, the report recommended "banning the placement and testing of all weapons in outer space." By July the Vatican had still not released the report, despite heavy Soviet lobbying for its release. The United States, of course, urged the Vatican to withhold it. When questioned, a Vatican spokesperson issued a one-line statement which declared, "The Pontifical Academy of Sciences has examined this problem, which is still under study."[73]

CATHOLICISM AND ARMS CONTROL IN THE WARSAW PACT

The Catholic Church has no monopoly on calling meetings of religious leaders to support peace. Soviet officials perceive such conferences as opportunities to strengthen the peace movement in the West and thus place domestic political pressure on NATO arms procurement. On May 10-14, 1982, religious leaders from more than one hundred countries gathered in Moscow for a conference grandly entitled "Religious Workers for Saving the Sacred Gift of Life from Nuclear Catastrophe." In his opening greetings Soviet Premier Nikolai Tikhonov accused the West of "whipping up war hysteria." Russian Orthodox Patriarch Sergei M. I. Pimen also charged "certain powerful circles in the West" of "blackening the honest and open peace-loving policy of our fatherland." As Bishop David Preus of the American Lutheran Church took his turn as chairman, he noted that the conference was "becoming a political forum heavily tilted against the country I represent."[74] Evangelist Billy Graham, whose presence guaranteed extensive Western media coverage, called on both Brezhnev and Reagan to set nuclear disarmament as the clear priority for the rest of the century.

The Vatican secretary for Christian Unity was represented by observers Father John Long, S.J., and Jean Larnaud, secretary general of the International Catholic Centre at UNESCO. Following the meeting Long described the conference as "worthwhile" and "pretty well balanced." On the patriarch's opening address, Long did note that the lengthy talk contained "a couple of paragraphs supporting Soviet policy," but that the majority of the patriarch's words marked him "as someone who really does care about the issue of disarmament."[75] Long also praised the role of Billy Graham, who had been sharply criticized by some Western ecclesiastics for not placing more emphasis on human rights in the USSR. Over 10 percent of the nearly 500 participants were Catholic, including several priests and bishops from Eastern European countries. The Czech Catholic bishops did not participate since the Vatican had recently condemned Pacem in Terris.[76]

Throughout the Warsaw Pact nations, Catholic Churches, engaged in bitter struggles over their freedom to operate in Socialist societies, have not devoted scarce political resources to supporting official peace initiatives, nor have they received governmental trust to do so. Protests against nuclear weapons have appeared in Solidarity and Polish church writings, for example, but such protests remain a minor theme. Cardinal Glemp did condemn the spread of nuclear arms in Europe in his sermon of January 6, 1984, after a joint communiqué on the subject followed a Glemp-Jaruzelski meeting of the preceding week.[77] PZKS established a Centre for Peace Research, headed by the priest-professor Joachim Kondziela, which cooperates with the Polish hierarchy. PZKS, ChSS, and PAX jointly sponsored the "Warsaw Christians Forum for Peace in Europe" September 1-2, 1979, with the "circumspect blessing" of Primate Wyszyński.[78] Cooperation with the Polish government on peace initiatives has also traditionally been the activity of PAX, thus tainting such activity with the connotation of collaboration.[79] A similar situation has existed in the Soviet Union in the bitter relations between the Soviet government and Ukranian and Lithuanian minorities. State officials are not anxious to give such Catholics any official pretext for organization. However, weaker national denominations like the Latvian Catholic Church present little danger of a peace movement causing disturbance. For example, the Washington bureau of the Soviet news agency Novisti used an interview with the Latvian Bishop Julijans Vaivods, apostolic administrator of Riga, to support its SALT II campaign.[80] As noted earlier, Vaivods perceives his own cardinalate as a "bridge between the Vatican and Moscow."

The positions of various Eastern European churches on peace are thus strongly influenced by their respective relations with the state. The Dutch Reformed scholar J. A. Hebly has presented a comparison of three models of Eastern European church-state relations for analysis of religious bodies belonging to the World Council of Churches.[81] They are the Russian Orthodox Church in the Soviet Union, the Protestant churches in Hungary, and the Federation of Evangelical Churches in the GDR. This text substitutes the Romanian Orthodox Church for the Russian Orthodox one in order to limit the discussion to Soviet clients. After presenting each church in Hebly's classification, the text presents its Catholic counterpart. Throughout the comparisons, the impact of church-state relations on the respective peace movements receives emphasis.

The Romanian church remains a majority (85 percent of the population) religious body closely allied to an authoritarian state which has the most independent foreign policy in the Warsaw Pact.[82] Such a church plays a strong role in a Romanian nationalism that can oppose some Soviet initiatives, but it would not be expected to foster or shelter independent peace activists. The Ceauşescu government has been particularly outspoken on the arms issue. For example, in November 1983 Romania party leaders issued a statement which deplored the Soviet decision to station new missiles in East Germany and Czechoslovakia as much as it criticized the deployment of the NATO Euromissiles. The statement said, "the U.S. and the U.S.S.R. should resume the Geneva negotiations with the aim of reaching a general agreement conducive to the halting of the placement of new medium-range missiles, and the withdrawal and scrapping of the ones in place."[83] Prior to the NATO deployment, the Bucharest government gave permission for Eastern Europe's largest peace demonstration. Banners denounced both Soviet and American arms buildups.

There is really no Roman Catholic analogue for the Romanian model, unless an analyst wishes to designate the Czechoslovakian Pacem in Terris prior to Vatican condemnation. The possibility of Roman intervention, however, always creates a different climate in church-state relations. And the Prague government has not taken the independent line that the Bucharest one has.

The Hungarian Protestant and Catholic examples are closer. The Reformed bishops have been so supportive of the Kádár government that Hebly comments that "[n]ot only is a critical attitude rejected, but the prophetic task of the church has been reduced to conformism to the new order."[84] Such a church, he says, cannot be expected to shelter independent activists like the Peace Group for Dialogue. Hungarian Catholic bishops have more political leverage against the government than their Reformed counterparts, however, because of their majority position, the threat of Vatican intervention, and the identification of Hungarian nationalism with the Catholic tradition. The joint pastoral letter of the Hungarian Catholic Bishops in 1978 listed abortion, violence, and nuclear arms as the three main threats to human life.

While Budapest has not been as outspoken on foreign policy as Bucharest, the Hungarian government has taken some independent positions as when it praised the proposed visit of East German leader Erich Honecker to West Germany. The government has also allowed Eastern Europe's freest *samizdat* press, but the arrest of Gábor Demzky, the Hungarian publisher of E. P. Thompson's *Beyond the Cold War*, demonstrates that limits remain. The fifty-member independent Peace Group for Dialogue, which had organized an independent peace demonstration on May 9, 1983, disbanded when its members could not agree on whether or not to join the official Peace Council as the latter became more active. András Bárd, head of the official Youth and Student Peace Commission, admitted that official groups had undergone a "process of invigoration." "One should never be ashamed," said Bárd, "of accepting good ideas from others."[85] The dissolution of Dialogue left only Father György Bulányi's pacifist group outside the official organization (p. 219, above). In Hungary church and state march together along the path of moderate liberalization. Bulányi, who spent nine years in prison during the post-Stalinist repression, has said that his group will "not retreat one millimeter" from its stance that "[w]e would rather sit in jail than kill another man."[86] With ecclesiastical censure, the state will probably not have to make the priest a martyr by taking him at his word. In addition, the government has instituted a new policy allowing conscientious objectors to do civil service in place of military training.

The GDR, the most important Warsaw Pact ally of the Soviet Union, presents an even more complicated situation as the intricacies of inter-German relations and significant economic and military power are added to considerations already relevant in the case of Romania. The East German population of nearly 17 million is nominally 47 percent Protestant, 45 percent without religious affiliation, and 7 percent (1.2 million) Catholic. Since 1978 the strict East German government of Erich Honecker has regarded the loyalty of the Lutheran Federation of Evangelical Churches as one of the important keys to the popular credibility of its administration. On March 6 of that year Honecker publicly advocated an open role for the churches in the country's future and equal civic rights and privileges for all believers. The East German state rehabilitated Luther in 1981. Honecker himself chairs the Luther "Committee from the Society," which expended considerable effort in commemorating Luther's 500th anniversary in 1983.[87]

The Lutheran Churches in turn have fostered a sporadic and loosely organized peace movement, a radical undertaking in East German society. Church leaders have called for a social-service alternative to the military draft and for East German disarmament. East Berlin Lutheran minister, Rainer Eppelmann even petitioned for the removal of all nuclear weapons from German soil, and the eventual withdrawal of all occupation troops from both Germanies. This "Berlin Appeal," which received 2,000 signatures, produced an angry reaction from the government, and some church leaders warned against the "misunderstandings" that might arise from taking the Appeal too seriously. The Berlin-Brandenburg church leadership secured Eppelmann's release after his February arrest, but also criticized the analysis and the form of the "Appeal." Timothy Garton Ash comments, "Thus it seems so far that the church hierarchy will not support any initiative which places among its aims the central goal [a nuclear-free Europe] of END."[88] The government also banned a "Swords-into-Plowshares" peace patch even though it was designed directly from a statue the Soviet Union had presented to the United Nations.[89]

A small pacifist movement, which has openly questioned the stationing of Soviet missiles in East Germany, remains. But the Lutheran *Kirche im Sozialismus* (Church in Socialism) adheres to a limited cooperation with the state similar to the arrangement between the Hungarian state and the Hungarian Catholic Church. Too much emphasis on pacifism and conscientious objection may result in state oppression without official ecclesiastical support. Four current issues of contention are paramilitary training in schools, military exemption for conscientious objectors, freedom of assembly for peace activists, and protection of the environment. For example, the government has allowed "peace seminars" to be held in churches, but has not allowed public protests.[90]

The smaller East German Catholic Church has generally limited itself to pastoral activities. The majority of the 1,200 priests in the GDR, and this is true of the 4,000 Protestant ministers as well, serve in parishes and in social service institutions, including hospitals and facilities for the aged, children, and the disabled. The one notable Catholic exception was the episcopal letter on peace issued on January 1, 1983. The letter took a strong stand supporting conscientious objection and criticizing the militarization of education and public life. If this statement was forthcoming only with the "command of the Vatican,"[91] then the GDR would provide another example of Rome stiffening Catholic resistance in the Eastern bloc, as it did in Czechoslovakia. Erich Honecker met with John Paul II in Rome in April 1985 in the first meeting between a pope and a head of the GDR.

The Soviet response to the NATO deployment of Pershing IIs and cruise missiles was to announce the stationing of SS-22s in the GDR and Czechoslovakia. When the Czech press announced the preparation of Soviet "operational tactical missile complexes" on October 24, 1983, many Czechs reacted negatively. *Rudé Právo*, the Communist party daily, received "stacks of letters" from readers concerned about the increased threat to the country.[92] While Pacem in

Terris, which supported the party position, was in disarray, the heads of the seven Catholic dioceses in Slovakia stated, "We declare with one voice that the production, stationing, and deployment of nuclear weapons is a crime against humanity and must be condemned from the ethical and theological point of view."[93] The Czech government discouraged any independent reactions to the Soviet deployment by warning activists from Charter 77 that any attempt to oppose the agreement would be treated as "subversion," entailing a sentence of up to ten years.[94] At present the Warsaw Pact government most concerned about further SS-22 deployments is Bulgaria. Bulgaria, which has no Soviet troops and has recently pursued some economic reform, advocates a nuclear-free zone in the Balkans.

The Federation of Evangelical Churches in the GDR and the Polish Catholic Bishops' Conference both constitute the major independent centers of power in their respective countries. The Lutheran churches have provided a space for independent peace activism, without directly challenging the state. Many German Protestants have remarked that they would be uncomfortable with as strong and as combative a church as the Polish Catholic one.[95] The Polish Catholic bishops could shelter a major independent peace movement, but such an initiative is not a high priority, and it would greatly alarm the Soviets who have been allowing relative freedom on domestic issues in return for support on foreign policy.

ASIAN SECURITY AND THE JAPANESE CATHOLIC CHURCH

John Paul II's appeal for peace at Hiroshima in February 1981 made a strong impression on the Japanese bishops. Since the call came from the Holy Father, the episcopal response had to be unanimous, incorporating "even the bishop of Nagasaki, leader of an old and patient church that had been told that the bomb was a punishment for their sins."[96] The Japanese Catholic bishops launched a signature campaign in support of a complete ban on nuclear weapons and total disarmament. The statement stressed the following four points:

1. To impart the horrors of being nuclear victims and to appeal for a complete ban on nuclear weapons. 2. To abolish nuclear weapons as being a crime against humanity. 3. To bring about world disarmament. 4. To convert the vast sums of money spent for armaments around the world into use for man's total development.[97]

The Japanese bishops' petition was signed by 500,000 Japanese and 25,000 resident non-Japanese from forty other countries.[98] This petition was part of an effort by peace organizations in eight countries to collect signatures to call for action by world leaders at the United Nations Second Special Session on Disarmament in June-July 1982. Pax Christi Italy represented that nation in presenting the petitions to Secretary General Pérez de Cuéllar on May 25.

Archbishop Peter Shirayanagi of Tokyo led the Japanese delegation which consisted of Bishop Aloysius Nubuo Soma of Nagoya, three priests, two nuns, two laymen, and two laywomen. The only non-Japanese member of the delegation was Maryknoll Father John Vinsko, representing the male religious Superiors' Conference of Japan. The bishops held a press conference in Washington and later went to Capitol Hill to meet with Senator Edward Kennedy, one of the two principal sponsors of the Senate's Nuclear Freeze Resolution. At the press conference Archbishop Shirayanagi expressed his conviction that, "There can be no such thing as a 'just war' using these (nuclear and other indiscriminately destructive) weapons."[99] In support of the Japanese initiative the Asian bishops passed the following resolution at their October 1982 meeting:

This body expresses its condemnation of the arms race among the nations of the world and the proliferation of nuclear experimentations and deposits of nuclear waste especially in the Pacific Basin, creating the dangers of ecological imbalance in our Asian countries; and appeals to the nations concerned to come together to a sincere dialogue to eliminate or control these situations.[100]

There had also been earlier statements on peace by individual Japanese. For example, in the fall of 1980 Bishop Nobuo Soma, moderator of the Japanese Council for Justice and Peace, warned about the mounting pressures for rearmament. "Elements in the government," said the bishop, "are waiting for this gradual erosion of public sentiment. This erosion has begun and pressures are mounting for rearmament and a revision of the 'Peace Constitution.' "[101] In fact, three issues have been particularly significant for Japanese Christians in the postwar period: religious liberty, peace, and the Yasukuni Shrine. The last issue combines concerns about religious liberty and peace.[102]

Bishop Soma's statement about rearmament came at the height of the Yasukuni Shrine controversy. On August 15, 1980, Prime Minister Suzuki and nineteen cabinet members visited the Yasukuni Shintoist Shrine dedicated to the Japanese war dead. Although Suzuki insisted that the government officials had merely made a private visit, the government soon began to press for nationalization of the shrine. During World War II Japanese military spirituality held that a soldier's highest honor was to be worshiped by the emperor as part of the heroic dead enshrined at Yasukuni. In fact, Kamikaze suicide pilots used to bid farewell to each other by saying, "Let's meet at Yasukuni." Many Japanese perceived the Suzuki visit and the bill for nationalization as part of the psychological preparation for remilitarization. The Japanese Catholic bishops opposed the bill on the basis of safeguarding the constitutional separation of church and state. In a letter to Suzuki they wrote:

The principles of freedom of belief and of separation of religion and politics affect one of the foundations of the Japanese Constitution. Recently the news is spread that once again a bill concerning the nationalization of the Yasukuni Shrine will be introduced in the Diet. As the aim of this bill runs counter to the basic ideas of the Japanese Constitution, the Catholic Bishops' Conference of Japan declares that it opposes this bill.

We request that within the Government the importance of the principles of freedom of belief and of separation of religion and politics be deeply recognized and that discretion be used so that this importance is not threatened.[103]

The Japanese Catholic hierarchy was criticized from both within and without over its other interaction with nationalistic Shinto during the same period. The scheduling of a World Religionists' Ethics Conference (WOREC) for the anniversary dates of the Emperor Meiji and the prominent Shinto shrine dedicated to him raised protests from political and religious groups. These groups charged that this conference of Christians, Buddhists, Shintoists, and Hindus on nature, ethics, and culture would be used to further the conservative nationalism that produced wartime militarization. Japanese Protestants declined invitations, and the Japanese Catholic Council for Justice and Peace circulated position papers opposing the conference. Finally, the sponsoring Japanese Conference of Religious Representatives changed the dates of the conference from October 1980 to June 1981. The Catholic bishop of Kyoto, Kenichi Tanaka, vice-president of the Japanese Conference of Religious Representatives, gave public assurances that the discussants would avoid political topics. Two weeks before the conference, Japanese Protestants and Catholics met and agreed on the importance of interreligious dialogue and the necessity of preventing it from being used for unworthy political ends.[104] Some Protestant leaders refused to meet the pope in February 1981 because John Paul met with the Emperor Hirohito. "There is no hostility toward the Catholic Church," said a Protestant spokesman. "Rather, this is a specific stand on the emperor system."[105] The Catholic Church had never been as critical of Shintoism and the emperor system as most Protestants. The Vatican's decision of 1939 which reversed the eighteenth-century prohibition of the Chinese Rites also permitted Japanese participation in official "civil" Shinto rituals.

When the Japanese episcopate wrote its pastoral "The Desire for Peace: The Gospel Mission of the Japanese Catholic Church" (July 9, 1983), the bishops produced a document that fit the Japanese culture and historical experience. Of all the Catholic peace pastorals the Japanese one is most insistent on the complete dismantling of all nuclear weapons and linking the East-West confrontation to North-South differences. These two themes are joined in the letter's fifth and sixth paragraphs:

What is more, nuclear weapons are not confined within the East-West camps. There is a tendency to try to spread them to Third-World nations, afflicted as they are with various problems, as if this provided a simple way to settle disputes. In this sense, we can say that the crisis of nuclear war is a hard reality that transcends the ideologies and social systems of the East-West camps. Nor can we very well deny that behind all this there stands interposed between them a military-industrial complex sharing enormous interests.

We have experienced the violence brought to human life and dignity by the use of nuclear weapons, and are thus able to relate the story to the world and hand it down to our descendants. So leaving all political considerations aside, we demand the world's greatest and utmost efforts in establishing a nuclear-free zone in East Asia, that would eventually extend to the world, in order to stop all experiments, production, and deployment of new nuclear weapons, and in order to abolish all existing ones.[106]

The eight-page (in English translation) Japanese letter is addressed to the hearts of the people, and makes no attempt to arrive at specific moral judgments about deterrence like its American counterpart. It calls for an individual breaking away from the materialism of consumer society, even mentioning the enormous number of used chopsticks discarded daily.

Nuclear disarmament is important so talking about a trifling matter like used chopsticks might perhaps provoke indignation. Used chopsticks, however, serve as a good example to show that, with our insatiable desire for material abundance, no matter how rich we become, we continue with an unending thirst to demand an even more abudant material life, and so fail to notice that this is indirectly related to poverty and the destruction of nature.[107]

The Japanese bishops make use of the Vatican II concept of the "signs of the times" to locate the mission of the Japanese Catholic Church with regard to peace. The bishops mention Japanese responsibility for World War II, the bombings at Hiroshima and Nagasaki, the Peace Constitution, and the visits of John Paul II to Hiroshima and Nagasaki. "We clearly recognize that these 'signs of the times' map out our destination. What is more, if we cannot discern the directions we're to follow, we lay ourselves open to the charge that Japan is lazy and insincere. It can be said that we bear that much responsibility for the future of the world."[108] The words "diligence," "sincerity," and "responsibility" represent very strong cultural norms to the Japanese. The document's emphasis on personal conversion echoes a response of Bishop Soma when asked about the American pastoral letter:

True, the nuclear issue is a serious problem in today's world. However, I don't think that this is the most important issue. What we are facing as humankind today is the problem of lack of trust and mutual understanding. If there were trust even nuclear war would not be a threat and isn't this precisely what the Gospel is supposed to do? It might be a difficult task for you, but you should tell people to trust even Russians.[109]

The initiatives of the Japanese bishops on the issues of peace and human rights mark a startling departure from the traditional Japanese Catholic silence on public issues. Japanese Catholicism has a long history of state persecution, which made Japanese Catholics reticent about playing public political and social roles in nineteenth and early twentieth century Japan. As in China, Protestants played a leading part in the modernization of the country while Catholics concentrated on building up local communities. Many of the prewar leaders of the Japanese Socialist Party were Protestants. Tetsu Katayama (1887-) became Japan's first Socialist prime minister in 1947. His resignation nine months later was motivated principally by his fear that General Douglas MacArthur would order him to restore the Japanese armed forces.[110] Other Christian prime ministers have been Liberal Democrats Yoshida (baptized a Catholic after his death), Hatoyama (an inactive member of an independent Protestant church), and Ohira (an inactive Protestant). Ohira's death in 1980 stirred great public sympathy.

Although the direct involvement of Christians in Japanese politics has been minimal,[111] this is a case of the lack of significant religious input on public policy in general. As Edwin Reischauer has remarked, "Before the seventeenth century it [religion] did play much the same role in Japan as in the West, but the trend toward secularism that has recently become marked in the West dates back at least three centuries in Japan."[113] However, the polarization of Japanese society has at times contributed to the polarization of Protestant churches, as in the cases of the 1960 Security Treaty debate and the vigorous societal struggles that began in 1968 over many issues including Vietnam. Both periods polarized the largest Protestant church, the United Church of Christ in Japan (UCCJ) (Kyodan), but most Catholics avoided the period of trauma after 1968 "by 'bending with the storm' when necessary but then by reinstituting what seemed like reasonable controls afterward."[113]

The traditional locally oriented characteristics of Japanese Catholicism would seem to prepare its adherents to support the Liberal Democratic Party (LDP) in national politics. On the issues of peace and North-South redistribution, however, episcopal statements come closer to the views of the opposition parties, although up to now the LDP-led governments have put into practice the consensus view of moderate increases for the Self Defense Force, no nuclear weapons, and significant aid for Third World countries. Critics of militarization have sought to limit defense spending, with the figure of 1 percent of the GNP as a limit assuming an almost mythical significance. Prime Minister Sato signed the Nuclear Nonproliferation Treaty in February 1970. Despite misgivings about American reliability in a crisis, the ruling Liberal Democrats still adhere publicly to their "three nonnuclear principles" of not manufacturing, possessing, or permitting the introduction of nuclear weapons onto Japanese soil. Prime Minister Nakasone, with American encouragement, has attempted to increase Japan's defense role, but so far he has succeeded only in attaining gradual increments. What Prime Ministers Suzuki and Nakasone both promised in Washington has proved very difficult to shepherd through bureaucratic consensus, especially in the Ministry of Finance.

CONCLUSION: ARMS CONTROL AS A CATHOLIC ISSUE

Jonathan Schell begins his second series of two articles for *The New Yorker* by citing the speech of John Paul II at Hiroshima.[114] Schell uses the pope's "deceptively simple statement" to structure his own discussions of: 1) "conscious choice" (January 2, 1984); and 2) "deliberate policy" (January 9, 1984). "Conscious choice" refers to the hundreds of millions of individual decisions made by men and women faced by the realities of the nuclear age. These decisions, which belong to the moral and spiritual realm, produced that surge in human activity known as the "peace movement." The pope's second category, says Schell, refers to the various political policies designed to combat the terrible threat of human extinction.

We cite Schell here to demonstrate the media penetration of John Paul among peace activists at the sophisticated level of the *New Yorker*, and to highlight the categories of "conscious choice" and "deliberate policy" for use in our own analysis. Traditionally religious leaders have preached "peace" to encourage individual "conscious choice" but have been wary of espousing particular policy options like unilateral disarmament or the SALT II Treaty. At Hiroshima the pope appealed for peace as he stood near the epicenter of the world's first nuclear attack. It would be difficult to imagine a more apt or forceful symbol for this particular "expressive" message. Papal speeches to the United Nations have also been particularly effective media presentations. Such expressive activity remains the principal thrust of international Catholic activity on peace, but it always leaves itself open for Stalin's biting query about the strength of the pope's "divisions."

Catholicism also has a fairly strong tradition of advocating specific conceptual frameworks (the just war theory) and specific policies (the medieval "Truce of God"). John Paul's message to the United Nations did set the parameters for national episcopal conferences on the question of deterrence. Following June 1982 no bishops' conference could entertain embracing either unilateral disarmament (if any ever did) or permanent acceptance of the *status quo*. As such, papal "deliberate policy" combines short-term "arms control" with long-term "disarmament."[115] Among the national pastorals, the American episcopal letter makes the most detailed attempt to consider policy questions, thus necessitating its declaration that "not all statements in this letter have the same moral authority." The American bishops have continued their policy activity, as in their letter against funding the MX. Most other national episcopates have shied away from such concrete statements. The German letter of April 1983, for example, does not even mention the imminent deployment of the Pershing II and cruise missiles.

Direct papal mediation on arms control, the institutionalizing of "Good Pope John's" vision after the Cuban missile crisis, seems dead under John Paul II. While the Irish-American Protestant Reagan willingly embraces all things culturally Catholic as his Irish-

American Catholic predecessor Kennedy could not, the pope's aggressive stances on Solidarity and human rights have directly challenged the Soviets in Eastern Europe. The Vatican's impact on arms control policy is more likely to be politically efficacious in indirect ways than merely through the general statement of the papal position. The worse Soviet-American relations become, the more important are regional initiatives by the national Catholic Churches of the NATO and Warsaw Pact countries. These regional initiatives have had some success. The Vatican's foreign policy in Europe most closely approximates Catholic Austria's attempt to bring together European nations of East and West in their common interest. In the Vatican's case, this policy originated in Casaroli's *Ostpolitik* which benefited from the general relaxation of tension accompanying the *Ostpolitik* of Brandt and Schmidt and the *détente* of Nixon and Brezhnev. With the rigidity, malaise, and distrust of the superpowers in the early 1980s, European states, including the Vatican, have sought to promote a mini-*détente* on the continent.

Catholics constitute majorities in the Warsaw Pact countries of Poland, Hungary, and Czechoslovakia. While all Eastern European churches have issued at least individual episcopal statements supporting peace such as Cardinal Glemp's, national hierarchies like the Polish episcopate fear government cooptation in state-controlled peace organizations like Czechoslovakia's Pacem in Terris. The closest political-religious collaboration on the peace issue obtains in Hungary where the Budapest government has pursued a moderately independent foreign policy and moved to coopt independent peace movements within an "invigorated" official movement. The "Catholic model" of European *détente* is most closely realized at the present time in relations between Catholic Austria and Catholic Hungary. Throughout continental Europe only in the Netherlands do Catholic organizations (in that case, Pax Christi) play an aggressive role in the peace movement.

1983 was the year of the national Catholic peace pastoral. Hierarchies in the GDR, Hungary, West Germany, the United States, the Netherlands, Belgium, Ireland, Japan, and France issued letters. The pope certainly encouraged such efforts, notably in the Japanese case. However, it was the American church's second draft that particularly challenged European churches to clarify their own positions on nuclear weapons. The principal national causality on arms control has been the influence of one national Catholic Church on another. The principal actors have been the episcopal conferences themselves, but semi-independent transnational groups like Pax Christi have also been effective.

In summary, the Catholic impact on arms control has been most significant in three areas: John Paul II's expressive activity most vividly shown at Hiroshima; the Catholic links of the NATO and Warsaw Pact nations; and the peace activity of the American bishops. Of these, the reorientation of the entire Catholic Church toward support of the status quo in postwar Europe has been the Catholic Church's greatest contribution to world peace. While the Vatican's *Ostpolitik* has had its political and religious costs, the alternative to the Helsinki Accords would be a NATO crusade to free Eastern Europe. Such a crusade, almost inevitably involving nuclear weapons, could only be nourished by the uncompromising anticommunist ideology of early twentieth-century Catholicism.

CHAPTER 9

The Catholic Church, Soviet-American Relations, and International Politics

INTERNAL CATHOLIC POLITICS: ORGANIZATION AND IDEOLOGY

THIS BOOK analyzes the internal and external politics of the Catholic Church, a transnational ecclesiastical institution strongly rooted in the traditional culture of Western Europe, as it adjusts to the technological revolutions of the latter half of the twentieth century. Of these technological challenges, advances in electronic communications, computers, and weapon yields are particularly significant for the analysis of Catholic political influence in the formation of national consensus, regional alliances, and arms control. In this chapter we will summarize and relate the conclusions of previous chapters and make some tentative predictions about future trends. As Part One focused on internal Catholic political culture, the first section of the chapter discusses Catholic organization and ideology.

The historical emphases on the internal hierarchical discipline and the external public unity of the Catholic Church remain strong factors in the contemporary politics of this very publicly active ecclesiastical institution. These factors are exhibited in the working style of the Curia and the continuity of personnel within the entire organization. The rapid internationalization of Catholic organization and ideology constitutes the principal change within the church during the last twenty years. This internationalization of organization and ideology, however, has not had a great impact in the "Eternal Rome" of Vatican politics. The addition of more non-Italians to the Curia has produced few major changes in governing style at the ecclesiastical center. The intense personal style of John Paul II marks the major organizational hallmark of the current pontificate.

On the periphery national hierarchies have become significant national and international political actors. Often, the most significant contemporary transnational Catholic connections bypass Rome. The modern media has increased the political impact of the national bishops' conferences on ethical-political issues such as arms control, North-South relations, and human rights. Attention to these issues also introduces indirect criteria for bureaucratic efficiency into the national hierarchies and, to a lesser extent, into the Curia. Catholic public opinion, informed by the national mass media, applauds and criticizes episcopal and papal activity on global issues. Organizational and ideological struggles are often intertwined, as with Cardinal Ratzinger's dual attack on the writings of Boff and the prerogatives of the Brazilian bishops (see p. 83, above).

In the mid-1980s the Catholic Church's central organization combines Eastern European and Italian traditions as its dominant political-cultural forces. The Vatican by its historical tradition and present modes of operation remains a European entity. The principal question at present concerns whether the central institution will continue in its delightfully and irritatingly inefficient and demonstrative Italian bureaucratic behavior, or become a stronger and more assertive force on the cultural model of Polish Catholicism. Much depends on the length of John Paul's pontificate and the character of his successor. What if there is a rapprochement between the Polish Catholic and Eastern European Orthodox traditions so that the resulting unity becomes the central cultural context for the Vatican? How would such a relatively conservative Slavic orientation relate to the liberal democratic and positivist West, or to a Soviet state that combines fading nineteenth-century Socialism with Russian nationalism, or to Third World nations pursuing modernization amid tremendous social, economic, and political upheavals? In the next fifty years Third World ecclesiastics should play a stronger role as the numerical dominance of Third World Catholics and Third World clergy grows.[1] A scenario based on the strong internal influence of various Third World ecclesiastics would predict the continuance of a fairly traditional ecclesiastical institution, its leadership socialized in Roman ecclesiastical universities, whose primary ethical concerns would be North-South relations and human rights, espcially political freedom for the Catholic Church as an independent religious institution.

Many commentators have noted the great dichotomy between John Paul's stress on dialogue between the church and society and his more authoritarian approach to internal ecclesiastical organization. The pope follows the logic of his Polish experience in which a unified disciplined church based on traditional cultural and family values stands as the great institutional bulwark against state oppression and foreign (Russian) domination. His Slavic distrust of a soft and greedy West does not dispose him to a sympathetic hearing on questions of divorce, contraception, and priestly laicization. Those in the Western democracies who worry about the new pope's vision are haunted by the similarities between Wojtyła's first days and the beginning of the pontificate of Pius IX. European liberals rejoiced at Pius's election, but the church hemorrhaged during Pio Nono's long reactionary reign. In 1979 Gary Wills argued that "this Wojtyła Pope seems too good to be true, and probably is." Wills predicted that as Pius IX's "Liberal political views fell victim to theological conservatism," so will John Paul's.[2] John Paul's first seven years have maintained this tension, however, as demonstrated in the outcome of *l'affaire* Boff.

We began the main discussion of this book by stressing three aspects of contemporary Catholicism: 1) the difference between instrumental and expressive powers, and the significance of the contemporary media for the Catholic Church as it increases its expressive role; 2) the tension between the Catholic Church's traditional advocacy of Western values and institutions and its current attempt to mediate East-West conflict; and 3) the tension between internal and external church politics and goals.

With regard to internal Catholic politics, the contrast between Catholic traditionalism and the use of contemporary media is not just a matter of political style. It also pertains to the content of the message. Nevertheless, John Paul is forced to rely on independent secular and Catholic media to bypass the curial bureaucracy, national episcopal conferences, and local bishops to influence directly individual Catholics on matters of faith and morals. The Western Catholic media remain weak, except in a "columnized" country like the Netherlands, where the very strength of the Catholic newspapers, radio, and television reinforces their independence from Rome. For the pope, however, the potential influence of the secular media can be worth the gamble. In late March 1985 Pope John Paul II appeared live from Rome on NBC television's "Today." The Vatican spokesperson Joaquin Navarro Valls compared it to performing "without the net beneath, as in the circus."[3] Such a live appearance constitutes the complete antithesis of traditional bureaucratic style, which restricts access to and familiarity with the leader. Papal media politics focuses on persuading Catholics and their fellow citizens to embrace the church's moral positions, while traditional processes of bureaucratic control predominate in internal personnel matters.

We can examine points 2 and 3 by analyzing the tensions between three categories of values for the leaders of the Catholic Church. These categories are: A) the maintenance and growth of the ecclesiastical institution; B) a national, regional, or international consensus for Catholic values; and C) the maintenance and growth of national, regional, or international political systems, as in John XXIII's mediation in the Cuban missile crisis. This entire book has illustrated how difficult it is for Catholic leaders to make judgments which maximize values in all three categories. For example, Cardinal Wyszyński criticized *Ostpolitik* under Paul VI because the Polish cardinal primate asserted that the Vatican's initiative sought illusory gains in categories A and C at the expense of very real concessions in categories A and B. To make matters worse, said Wyszyński, a real national consensus for the values of Polish Catholic nationalism already existed. Only the greedy and corrupt party bureaucrats, sustained by Soviet arms, constituted the opposition.

This type of tension between the values in all three categories often becomes acute because the Catholic Church, like the CPSU, sees the maintenance and progress of its own institution as an integral part of its central ideological orientation. Neither the Curia nor the Politburo can envision the internationalization of its highest values apart from the survival and growth of its own institution. Nevertheless, the significance of the values of the three categories runs along a spectrum from a minority sectarian national church like the Maronite or Vietnamese Catholic Church to a majority primary ethical broker like the Brazilian Catholic Church. The former would stress categories A, B, and C in that order, while the latter would give greater weight to categories C and B. In terms of the time dimension of a single Catholic Church, immigrant American Catholicism during the mid-nineteenth century would fit the former model, while the current NCCB, with its pastorals on peace and the economy, more nearly approximates the latter. With regard to the book's three central issues, Catholic and national political cultures most strongly affect national consensus, and their impact lessens progressively for regional alliances and arms control. As the influence of political cultures lessens, technological constraints become more significant, so that weapons development is an important independent variable in arms control.

THE TECHNOLOGICAL CHALLENGE: MODERNIZATION AND MEDIA

Although the Catholic moral tradition retains its cultural orientation toward the small European peasant village, the increasing speed of technological change is rapidly destroying much of what is left of traditional agrarian society all over the globe. Traditional cultures are breaking under the strains of industrialization, urbanization, and immigration. Instantaneous communications raise communal expectations, posing major challenges for national political and religious institutions, especially in the Third World where many nations have recently emerged from colonialism or traditional autocracy. The popular resistance movements which gain independence for these new states demonstrate their greatest unity at the moment they overthrow the colonial power or indigenous despot. Maintaining national unity during subsequent social and economic development in a hostile international environment has proved excruciatingly difficult.

The basic internal political challenge has been to select the right combination of traditional cultural (often heavily religious) expressive values and contemporary political and social structures necessary for rapid national integration and economic development. The expressive values derive from the traditional village and the instrumental structures from the secular city, capitalist or communist. This problematic thus transcends Soviet-American ideological debate. Both rightist and leftist dictatorships have fallen because they have failed to include enough traditional values in their program and/or excluded traditional sectors from politics and the economy.

The Shah of Iran, for example, brought about his downfall by modernizing too quickly and ignoring traditional Islamic values. He also slighted traditional power groups like the bazaris and the mullahs. The Shah's fall discredited Western secular modernization in Iran and left three competing visions for Iran's future: the traditional conservative orientation of the Islamic Republican Party (best exemplified in the assassinated mullah Behesti); the combination of enlightened Islam and technical progress of the Mujahedin, the Islamic Socialist movement (supporting Bani-Sadr); and the strongly secular and nationalistic vision of technical progress espoused by the Iranian Communist Party. After mediating between the first and second alternatives following the revolution, the Ayatollah Khomeini finally supported the mullahs. Bani-Sadr disappeared and his partisans clashed with those of Behesti. Islamic Socialists responded to political executions by blowing up Behesti and over one hundred other leaders of the Islamic Republican Party, but the government eventually controlled the militant Socialists as it had the Communists. It is doubtful, however, whether such a fundamentalist vision will be able to contribute to the modernization of the

Iran, especially as its dogmatism continues to add fuel to the conflict with Iraq.

Nineteenth-century Japan constitutes the world's most successful model of a non-Western society modernizing to meet the technological challenge of the West. Japan succeeded because it found the right combination of traditional values and modern technology. The ex-samurai who directed the Meiji Restoration proposed political centralization and economic modernization in terms of returning to Japan's traditional political system. These ex-samurai argued that the Meiji Restoration would reestablish the emperor in his rightful position. Even when Japan felt it was necessary to adopt a constitution in imitation of the West, the leaders chose the German Constitution as a model because its values most closely approximated traditional Japanese values. The Japanese economic miracle has continued to be fostered by the right combination of traditional values and modern technology in the spirit of national unity and loyalty. Abstract ideology is the least important consideration in Japanese politics.

Recent Chinese leaders like Deng Xiaoping have praised Japanese successes. Mao is criticized for major policy mistakes beginning with the Great Leap Forward in 1957.[4] However, in the first half of the twentieth century Mao and the Chinese Communist Party produced the world's most successful model of agrarian revolution. Mao borrowed from Marx and Lenin, but adapted these borrowings to an agrarian society and traditional Chinese values. He emphasized the unity of the Chinese people. Mao said that the revolution should unite the vast majority (usually 90 percent) of the people against the feudal power-mongers and "running dogs" of imperialism. Mao thus stressed a "democracy of the whole people," not an apocalyptic class struggle. The national unity of political center and political left fostered reconstruction in the early 1950s. During the Cultural Revolution, however, the Red Guards vigorously attacked the "four olds" (ideology, culture, customs, habits) in their youthful attempt to remake Chinese civilization. Chinese politics fragmented into the two great lines of Mao and Liu Shaoqi. This split had disastrous effects on China's development. It was the earlier version of revolutionary unity and cooperative reconstruction that was so attractive to many Third World countries. Only Albania espoused radical Maoism. In the post-Mao period China has returned, often with the same rehabilitated bureaucratic leaders, to a more moderate economic policy. The current major political struggle pits "eclectic modernizers" against "all-around modernizers" like Deng.[5]

The political leadership of most developing countries like Iran and the People's Republic of China feel it is extremely important to retain control of the national media, so as to maintain political control and to focus public attention on "Socialist Construction," "The Four Modernizations," or similar programs. While internal media control is relatively easy for a Third World single-party system, major powers control international communications as they control international politics and international economics. For example, the news agencies AP, UPI, Reuters, Agence France, and Tass usually constitute the major source of international news to Second and Third World countries. As the latter have called for a New World Economic Order, they have also called for a New World Information Order. UNESCO's MacBride Report, generally supported by Second and Third World countries, has encountered enormous criticism from both government and media organizations in the First World.[6]

The examples of Iran, Japan, and China raise questions about the effect of Catholicism on modernization in Third World countries, especially in Latin America and the Philippines. In most traditionally Catholic countries only a comprehensive religious vision can unite village peasant and urban technocrat in the transformation of a national society. John Paul II has demonstrated a mastery of the modern media in the support of traditional Catholic village morality. Vatican Radio and Roman ecclesiastical universities play significant roles in forming Third World Catholic public opinion and socializing Third World Catholic leadership. Nevertheless, it is uncertain whether papal charisma and Catholic bureaucratic organization can stimulate Catholic nations to maintain traditional Catholic values while encouraging national social and economic construction.

The post-Marcos Philippines, with its enormous political and economic problems, should prove an interesting test case. In contributing to the ouster of Marcos, Filipino church leaders adroitly combined contemporary democratic and traditional religious values. Cardinal Sin's mass of appreciation for the independent vote-counting organization NAMFREL took place on February 18, the fifth anniversary of the beautification in Manila by John Paul II of the seventeenth-century Filipino martyr Lorenzo Ruiz de Manila. Both national and international media organizations played major roles in the demise of the Marcos regime. Cardinal Sin's Radio Veritas constituted the major source of independent information for supporters of Corazon Aquino, and the capture of the government television station by anti-Marcos forces was a crucial event. The wide coverage of the February 7 election by the television networks prepared American public opinion to support the change in United States policy. *Washington Post* columnist Tom Shales, commenting that "Filipino political fates were played out in interview after interview on U.S. newscasts and discussion programs," mentioned television newsmen Tom Brokaw, Peter Jennings (both of whom went to the Philippines), Ted Koppel, David Brinkley, and even Johnny Carson. Marcos, who had been challenged to have elections the previous November by newsmen George Will and Sam Donaldson, thought he could use the American media against his critics. "Instead he became the star of a continuing saga that played like a real-life version of 'Sins,' " said Shales.[7]

In the end, of course, it was neither Cardinal Sin nor David Brinkley who defeated Marcos, but the Filipino people who lay down in front of the tanks and hugged Marcos's soldiers to protect military commanders Fidel Ramos and Juan Ponce Enrile after their defection. Sin did use Radio Veritas to issue the initial call urging the people to mass around the rebel soldiers. The cardinal also strongly supported NAMFREL (see photo of the cardinal autographing a cap at NAMFREL in the *New York Times*, February 12, 1986), which was organized by businessman José Concepción, Jr., president of the nationwide Council of the Laity. Sin shunned Marcos throughout the campaign, but the day before the election he visited Aquino to praise her as an honest and sincere woman who "will also make a good president." Sin continued, "I am tempted to ask: Is this a presidential election or is this a contest between good and the forces of evil, a fight between the children of light and the children of darkness?"[8]

The Philippine episcopal conference (CBCP) was less partisan, but it did play a very significant role following the election. President Reagan's initial reaction to the election at his press conference on February 11 emphasized the strategic importance of the American bases, leading to speculation in both countries that the United States might stick with Marcos regardless of the election fraud. The presidential remarks thus cheered the beleaguered Marcos and alarmed the American State Department. The CBCP issued a statement on February 14 which condemned "fraudulence and irregularities" in the election, resulting in a "forcible seizure" of power which "cannot command the allegiance of the citizenry." The entire text of the episcopal statement appeared in the following day's *New*

York Times.[9] When the Senate voted 85 to 9 to condemn the election fraud on February 19, the nonbinding resolution included a paragraph which began "Whereas the Catholic Bishops Conference of the Philippines judged the elections to be "unparalleled in the fraudulence of their conduct."[10]

The ouster of Marcos was a model nonviolent revolution based on a disparate coalition. Following the assassination of Senator Aquino, Cardinal Sin had striven to bring together non-Communist popular movements, traditional political elites, legitimate business interests, and reformist sections of the military. All these groups are now represented in the post-Marcos cabinet.[11] The church thus provided an alternative source of national legitimacy (versus Marcos's authoritarianism), media distribution (versus the state media), and grass-roots organization (versus Marcos's party [KBL], the army, and local cronies).

The Vatican's major contribution to the situation was to refrain from action despite the urgings of the papal nuncio to the Philippines, Archbishop Bruno Torpigliani. In an interview with *Asian Focus* (February 28, 1986), Cardinal Sin said:

The nuncio calls Rome every day and tells Casaroli what he (the nuncio) thinks should be done here. The nuncio thinks we bishops should shut up and leave Marcos alone. Casaroli agrees with the nuncio for the sake of peace but he doesn't interfere with us here in any way. The nuncio is too much. The First Lady (Imelda Marcos) runs to the nuncio and tells him what she wants, he calls Rome and passes it along as his own suggestion and then he would come here to tell me what to do. He has stopped coming because he knows my mind is made up.[12]

Prior to the CBCP pastoral of February 14, Imelda Marcos visited both Cardinal Sin and Cardinal Vidal in an attempt to stop the letter. Throughout the Philippine crisis the pope was very cautious in his remarks, but Cardinal Sin's major advantage in Roman ecclesiastical politics is the continued personal trust of John Paul.

The major losers in the Philippine events were the local Communist left, which encouraged its followers to boycott the election, and the Soviet Union, whose ambassador was the only ranking diplomat to congratulate Marcos on his election victory. The United States and the Vatican came out well in both the Philippines and Haiti. In both these predominantly Catholic countries the ouster of the dictator came after a papal visit (1981, 1983) which emphasized human rights, church organization of grass roots opposition, the adroit use of church media (Radio Veritas, Radio Soleil), the defection of parts of the military, intensive treatment by American media, and the abandonment of the dictator by the United States State Department. The major spill-over effect in Asia concerned renewed questions about the legitimacy of Chun Doo Hwan in Korea. On March 9 Cardinal Kim Sou Hwan of Seoul devoted his midday sermon in the historic Myongdong cathedral to supporting opposition calls for swift constitutional changes that would permit direct presidential elections. Opposition leaders Kim Dae Jung and Kim Young Sam sat in the front row.[13]

THE CATHOLIC CHURCH AND SOVIET-AMERICAN COMPETITION IN THE THIRD WORLD

The previous section focused on the contemporary challenges to traditional political culture brought on by social and economic modernization. In this section we discuss the resulting political role of the Catholic Church and its influence on Soviet-American competition in the Third World. Third World civil crises invite the disruptive interferences of Washington and Moscow, which usually lead to further polarization within the country involved and also increase the global tension between the United States and the Soviet Union, thus making arms control and other security agreements less likely.

In Chapter 3 we pointed out that national Catholic hierarchies could theoretically embrace political positions all along the broad middle of the ideological spectrum, from Democratic Socialism to Democratic Capitalism. International and domestic political conditions, however, considerably narrow the actual choices. Chapters 6 and 7, treating Poland and superpower competition in the Third World, respectively, make a parallel comparison because in each case the disruption of one superpower's sphere of influence is aided by certain segments of the Catholic Church. American presidents have lauded papal trips to Poland and enjoyed the Soviet discomfort at Catholic influence throughout Eastern Europe. These same presidents have been considerably less enthusiastic about Marxist guerrilla-priests in the American spheres of Latin America and the Philippines.[14] In these latter areas the Catholic hierarchy has shifted from being a bastion of the status quo to a supporter of progressive change, with a minority of its clergy even advocating revolution. The Soviet Union and Cuba, of course, have praised such radical leftist Catholics to the annoyance of the United States. In each case certain specific domestic political events can cause the superpower to move from criticism to intervention. The call for free elections in Poland and the elimination of centrist business elements from the Nicaraguan government initiated reactions by the hegemonic superpower. The hegemonic superpower can respond by economic or military sanctions, or by forcing domestic political changes, as in the case of Polish martial law.

What factors affect national political stability in such a situation? First, different Soviet and American administrations have shown different degrees of toleration for political ambiguity in their client states. The 1980 election of President Reagan was perceived as bad news for the government of Nicaragua and the democratic opposition in the Philippines, South Korea, and Chile. The replacement of Secretary of State Haig with George Shultz has given democratic oppositions a slightly better chance for American support. Riding on the crest of foreign policy successes in the Philippines and Haiti, President Reagan declared to Congress on March 14, 1986, that the United States opposed all dictators of both the right and the left. While National Security Adviser John Poindexter commented that there was "nothing new" in the presidential message, and that its political context was the president's attempt to win funding for the Nicaraguan Contras, the rationale of the declaration had come a long way from the Haig-Kirkpatrick years. In the Soviet sphere of influence, Eastern European political and ecclesiastical leaders watch promotions, demotions, and deaths in the Politburo with keen interest. The rise of Mikhail Gorbachev has strengthened Soviet policy in Eastern Europe after five or six years of comparative drift. Despite all the above similarities in American and Soviet spheres of interest, Vatican-American and Soviet-Vatican relations are not completely symetrical. In both Poland and Latin America, the most significant transnational Catholic links are from the local church to the Vatican and to the United States government through American Catholic groups, especially the USCC. In addition, whatever the government, reduced global Soviet-American tension gives individual nations more opportunity to pursue a "third way" independent of Washington and Moscow.

In general, the dictatorial rule of a small sector of the right or left, even with the active support of the relevant superpower, faces significant difficulties in attaining political stability and economic growth. In these situations the twentieth-century Catholic Church joins the opposition in its insistence on at least the limited restoration of human rights. Within the American sphere, a center-right coalition tends to receive United States support and thus remains more stable. Within the Soviet sphere, a center-left coalition would tend to be more stable, if one defines "left" as the national political grouping that includes hardliners within the Communist Party. Center-left coalitions in the United States sphere and center-right coalitions in the Soviet sphere only have a chance for stability in times of *détente* and a "tolerant" superpower administration. Poland and Nicaragua have been unstable during the early 1980s because the superpowers have been disturbed by the political rise of a coalition between the center and the opposite political tendency from the superpower. Solidarity, while it included many reformist members of the Polish Communist Party, also comprised radical elements dedicated to ending the monopoly of that party. Somoza was overthrown by a coalition of the left and the center. In both cases the Catholic Church served as the opposition ethical broker as it worked to stabilize and unify the opposition coalition. The opposition superpower or its clients sought to destabilize the coalition by sponsoring selective violence from the other side of the political spectrum, for example, the death squads in El Salvador and the murder of Father Popiełuszko in Poland. The political "necessity" for such instrumental force increased as the local client government lost expressive legitimacy.

Cardinals Wyszyński and Wojtyła have served as the center of ecclesiastical and political legitimacy for Poland. This has involved the dual roles of ethical broker for the opposition and mediator between the opposition and the local government. Wyszyński assisted Wałęsa in the formation of Solidarity, but also encouraged the union to moderate its demands on the Polish Communist Party. At several junctions in the negotiations, the church has served as a mediator. The Polish episcopacy unites the ecclesiastical center with the ecclesiastical right. Association with PAX and other government-sponsored religious initiatives has tarred the ecclesiastical left. However, like other revolutionary situations, the national bishops' conference seeks compromise between an entrenched state establishment and the political opposition. The church serves as the symbol of Polish unity and seeks to maintain that unity in the face of the Soviet threat. The cardinal primate enunciates what is possible politically in terms of domestic and international politics. He maintains a national consensus because the people trust the church.

John Paul II and the majority of the Latin American hierarchy retain a reformist, as opposed to a radical, political position. Such a position emphasizes socioeconomic development along with political and civil rights. Unfortunately for the pope and the bishops, reformist political groups remain weak in most Latin American countries. Christian Democracy could not repeat its postwar European successes in Latin America. Unlike Europe, the Latin American far right remained politically viable, while only a few countries have possessed the large prosperous middle class needed to form the basis of the movement. Only in Chile and Venezuela have South American Christian Democratic parties come to power. The hierarchical response in countries like El Salvador has been to seek an alliance between progressive business interests favoring a Christian Democratic solution and peasant and worker groups favoring more radical change. Just such a coalition between the political center and the political left overthrew Somoza, but has been unraveling ever since under the dual polarizing influences of American military and economic interference and the radicalization of Sandinista ideology.

The Nicaraguan coalition of the political center and the political left was possible only because of a corresponding cooperation between the ecclesiastical center and the ecclesiastical left. The ecclesiastical center is constituted by the principal member of the hierarchy or the president of the episcopal conference speaking in the collective name of the national episcopal conference. This cardinal or archbishop must combine the altruistic concerns of social justice with *real politique* and decide what is politically prudent in a particular instance. The ecclesiastical center practices "critical collaboration"[15] by refusing to identify with a particular political form or government. The ecclesiastical left refers to prophetic bishops, clerics, and laity who cry out for social justice. They sometimes do identify very closely with a political party in a revolutionary situation. In Nicaragua, only the reconciliation of Bishop Obando (ecclesiastical center) and clerics like the Cardenal brothers (ecclesiastical left) could help maintain the political unity necessary for national reconstruction. The failure to maintain this unity has produced traditional-modern fragmentation analogous to the Iranian situation, inviting rightist reaction and American support for the Contras.

In Chile the lack of cooperation between the political center (Christian Democrats) and political left (UP) brought about the tragedy of Pinochet's coup. The Cold War climate of the international political and ecclesiastical systems precluded center-left rapprochement. The strongly anticommunist Pius XII dominated the church when the PDC was founded and the strong ideological anti-Marxism present in the early education of the leadership remained a central focus of the party. The statement of the Chilean bishops, *Social and Political Duty in the Present Hour*, buttressed its position by quoting from Pius XII and also from Pius XI's famous encyclical *On Atheistic Communism*. The Marxist tradition of the 1950s was equally critical of Christian Democracy. The left brought down the PDC by pushing hard on all its own programs so that compromise and a reformist political solution became impossible. Nor did the ecclesiastical center and the ecclesiastical left cooperate. Great antagonism existed between the Chilean episcopal conference led by Cardinal Silva and the Christians for Socialism. The rightist coup brought terrible sufferings to Christian Democrat and Marxist alike. After the coup the ecclesiastical center and the ecclesiastical left have cooperated in aiding the victims of repression through the church's Vicariate of Solidarity and its successor organizations.[16] Brazilian political development has proceeded in the opposite direction from that of Chile. Unity of the ecclesiastical center and the ecclesiastical left in the CNBB has encouraged movement toward political liberalization.

In South Africa the national hierarchy has encouraged cooperation between the more progressive (mostly British) government and business leaders and a strong black labor movement. Since the Soweto riots in 1976 the Catholic bishops have taken strong stands while identifying with moderate leaders like Desmond Tutu rather than more violent groups. In May 1986 the SACBC first endorsed "economic pressure" against the Botha government, but offered no specific strategy. In September the NCCB called for divestment by American Catholic Institutions. Daniel F. Hoye, USCC secretary general, wrote a letter to United States senators advocating economic sanctions.

Based on the above cases and others, especially three nations (Chile, South Africa, and South Korea) from three separate continents, this book offers the following hypotheses about a core solution for political stability and economic progress within the United States sphere of influence:

1. A core solution, be it a center-right coalition (1964 Chile election), centrist coalition (Frei strategy, 1964-1970), or center-left coalition (Nicaragua 1979), must include representation by over half of the political spectrum. Political representation from the urban middle class, which must not fragment for ideological (Chile 1967) or personal (Korea 1980) reasons, is necessary for all solutions. All solutions require at least the neutrality of the primary ethical broker,

the military, and the United States. In all cases the primary ethical broker must take a strong unified stand. The continuance in power by an uncompromising authoritarian like Somoza, Marcos, or Pinochet makes any solution less likely because of militarization of the society and the progressive polarization and weakening of the liberal democratic urban middle class. In this sense, the ousting of Marcos was a political "miracle."

2. A center-right coalition is most probable, especially under the present U.S. administration. It must be led by a centrist (Aquino, Frei, Duarte)[18] who can guarantee the basic human rights of the left. This guarantee is the basic condition for the necessary support of the primary ethical broker. The primary ethical broker must represent a strong unified ecclesiastical center-left coalition (Brazil 1970-) that continues to press for a fairer distribution of economic resources and the guarantee of basic political and civil rights.

3. If it is a centrist coalition, the solution will require strong United States support to prevent defections on the right wing and strong united support from the primary ethical broker to prevent defections on the left wing. Frei received neither in the crucial period 1967-1970. In both centrist and center-left solutions American multinational corporations may have to endure some nationalization, and the United States public certainly will have to develop a tolerance for some anti-American rhetoric.

4. If it is a center-left coalition, centrists must be represented in the primary ruling group (first Nicaraguan junta). The economic rights of the urban middle class and the moral freedom of the primary ethical broker must also be guaranteed. And the United States may have to relocate some of the society's far-right elements in London, Miami, or Hawaii in exchange for guarantees of its security interests.[19]

The Middle East, a battleground in neither the American nor Soviet spheres of influence, presents different problems and different policy choices for the Vatican. In terms of the good of its own organization, the Vatican wishes to preserve the freedom of Maronite Catholics and to attain the internationalization of Jerusalem. The Vatican's support for Palestinian "self-autonomy," symbolized by John Paul II's meeting with Arafat, has caused friction with Israel, which still is not recognized by the Vatican. Centering its policy on the moderate Arabs gives the Vatican a basic orientation toward a unifying coalition that solves the Palestinian problem while guaranteeing the security of Israel.

The above national cases presuppose a strong transnational organization that can support the national church against the national state. Rome has always opposed claims of absolute sovereignty by regimes of either the right or the left. This opposition is especially important in the appointment of bishops as evidenced in the Vatican's refusal to transfer complete control to a national government as in China. The local hierarchy, missionary personnel, and outside ecclesiastical finances thus tend to limit the arbitrary power of local authoritarian and totalitarian governments and their superpower patrons, while offering possible mediation toward national consensus.

THE UNITED STATES AND THE VATICAN

On January 10, 1984, the United States and the Vatican established full diplomatic relations after a hiatus of 117 years. Washington withdrew its last minister to the Vatican, Rufus King, in 1867. Widespread American anti-Catholicism and public objection to Pope Pius IX's obstruction of Italian unification led to a congressional ban on diplomatic relations with the Vatican. Franklin Roosevelt began the practice of appointing a personal representative as a way of bypassing the Congress. In 1951 Truman nominated General Mark Clark as ambassador but had to withdraw the nomination because of public outrage. In November 1983 Senator Richard Lugar (R-Indiana) succeeded in attaching a rider to the State Department appropriation bill that repealed the 1867 ban. In a later interview Senator Lugar said that he had not discussed the issue with the president at the time but felt that Reagan would avail himself of the opportunity, though not as quickly as the president actually did. Lugar said that he knew Reagan admired John Paul II, especially for his actions in Poland, and that the president's personal friend and personal representative to the Vatican, William A. Wilson, strongly favored the upgrading of his mission. Wilson proved to be an independent operator who resigned on May 20, 1986, after a major political controversy over his unauthorized dealings with Libya.[20]

Lugar himself seemed to be acting from the perspective of American interests in Europe. The senator stressed the integral diplomatic role of the Vatican in European politics and its value as a source of diplomatic intelligence. He had visited the Vatican on his European trip the preceding summer but had not discussed the establishment of diplomatic relations with curial officials. Lugar commented that he was surprised at the public debate in January 1984, since there had been little controversy the preceding November.[21]

Public opposition to the resumption of diplomatic relations with the Vatican came from religious groups like the World Council of Churches, the Seventh-day Adventists, and the Baptists. Even among Fundamentalists, however, opposition remained a pale reflection of the 1951 attack. Jerry Falwell remarked, "I wonder whether Mecca will want one. I told the White House if they give one to the Pope, I may ask for one."[22] Falwell also suggested that maybe the Vatican should have to recognize Israel as a condition for United States recognition of the Vatican. American Catholic episcopal reaction was restrained. NCCB President Bishop James Malone commented, "It is not a religious issue but a public policy question which happily, has now been settled in this context."[23] Such a lukewarm reaction by the American hierarchy led to speculation that American progressives feared a conservative cabal by Reagan and John Paul II. Political speculation centered on the president's need for the Catholic vote in the November election.[24]

This reestablishment of diplomatic relations merely raised the level of contact already in place under the president's personal representative, Wilson, and the Vatican's apostolic delegate in Washington, Archbishop Pio Laghi.[25] The United States and the Vatican have a long history of informal cooperation. In his article on the Catholic Church as a transnational organization, Ivan Vallier adds a speculative note on East-West relations in which he contrasts the Communist system where the state plays both expressive and instrumental roles with the more differentiated West in which Western governments play the instrumental role and the Judeo-Christian system the expressive one. Then he suggests that the primary matrix of transnational developments in the West is the changing relationship between the Roman Catholic Church and the United States.[26] Of the seven Western economic powers, Catholics constitute a majority in France and Italy, and a plurality in West Germany, the United States, and Canada. Four of the seven countries currently have Catholic heads of state. Many of the other NATO countries also have Catholic majorities or pluralities. It is no wonder that Senator Lugar, then chairman of the European Affairs Subcommittee of the Foreign Relations Committee, sponsored American recognition of the Vatican.

The Introduction traced the evolution of relations among the Vatican, the United States, and the Soviet Union into the present decade. In the early 1980s worsening Soviet-American relations have been paralleled by worsening Soviet-Vatican relations. Trouble between the Kremlin and the Vatican has not automatically forced the

White House and the Vatican closer together. One of the asymmetries of Soviet-American relations is that Washington's ties to the
Vatican are more important than Moscow's ties to the Vatican. One
need not accept Vallier's thesis at full value to recognize the significance of the Vatican to American legitimacy in Europe or the importance of the Catholic Church to national consensus in the United
States. In international affairs, Vatican positions on arms control,
North-South relations, Central America, and Israel differ significantly from current American policies.

The Vatican can prove useful to the Unites States, however, in denying legitimacy to international and national terrorist groups, and
in limiting conflict between American allies. In May-June 1982 John
Paul II visited both Britain and Argentina, and the two episcopates
issued a joint letter in an effort to mediate a settlement in the Falklands dispute. While in this case the Vatican was no more successful
than the United States, papal diplomacy solved the conflict between
Argentina and Chile over the Beagle Channel. The Filipino people's
ouster of Marcos, mediated by Cardinal Sin, saved the United
States an immediate diplomatic debacle, even if long-range development remains a grave concern.

As we saw in Chapter 5, the United States bishops articulated the
compromise opposition position to Reagan's military buildup when
the fragmented Democratic Party proved unable to reach a consensus. Later that same year Democratic Chairperson Charles T. Man-
att, after consulting his party's seven presidential candidates and
congressional leadership, articulated general support for the bishop's letter.[27] American Catholicism could contribute a set of policies
taken from the USCC and a political style borrowed from the NCCB
as a model for the reconstitution of a strong Democratic Party. On
policy, this would mean stressing peace and human rights; cutting
defense spending and maintaining basic social programs for the
poor, the elderly, and minorities; advocating public morality and
urban neighborhood security and rehabilitation for the "old ethnics"; and articulating an internationalist economic posture emphasizing the national development of technology for the business
community. The latter policy, of course, would generate some tension with an old ally, organized labor, but the "whole cloth" resurrection of the FDR coalition is neither possible nor desirable. Organized labor, as indicated in Chapter 3, is generally pleased with the
pastoral on economics. Catholicism has an internationalist tradition, and in this sense, remains more suited to this task than the

Japanese communitarian ethic currently being touted in the business community as an antidote to American individualism.[28]

Catholic political activity in American domestic politics will continue to be significant for three reasons. First, the continued decline of political parties and the rise of media politics increases the significance of independent "expressive" institutions. The United States hierarchy seems willing to exercise that national social role, although the bishops will not be as influential on every issue as they have been on arms control. Second, American Catholics who are knowledgeable, conscious, and proud of their distinctive Catholic tradition have joined the political and economic elites in greater numbers. The differences in "Catholic awareness" between politicians who happened to be Catholic like John Kennedy and Catholic intellectuals like Cuomo and Moynihan is striking. Third, not only do Catholics constitute a plurality in the United States, but White Catholics of European Descent (WCED) and Hispanics constitute a significant block of the "swing vote" in the most crucial electoral states like California, New York, Texas, and Ohio.

The NCCB, of course, is not going to endorse either the Republicans or the Democrats. Nevertheless, the American Catholic political vision could significantly contribute to a new national consensus primarily articulated by one or other of the major parties. Historically, the Democrats would seem to have the edge. It is significant that the Jesuit Father Robert Drinan, who left Congress at the Vatican's request, remains head of the Americans for Democratic Action. The principal "new blood" for Democratic resurgence would come from the "socially responsible" business community, the politicization of members of the new professional groups like the Physicians for Social Responsibility, and increased minority representation through unions like César Chávez's United Farm Workers. The Catholic Church remains especially relevant for the Democrats because Catholics have traditionally voted Democratic, and the church has been successful in bridging the old and new ethnics on certain issues. For example, Robert Kennedy and César Chávez received communion together at the conclusion of Chavez's fast during the UFW Grape Boycott. That California event had special impact for politics in the increasingly powerful Western states because most Hispanic and many Vietnamese immigrants are Catholic.

Should the Democrats fail to reconstitute their center-left coalition under an "old ethnic" like Cuomo, Republican senators like Peter Domenici, Robert Dole, Paul Laxalt, and Richard Lugar might move to the left to form a partnership with the WCED and Jewish voters. Such a coalition would tap the traditions of European Christian Democracy, joining the "Catholic interests" of Senators Laxalt and Lugar, whose progressive roles in the Philippines crisis received general acclaim,[29] to the concerns of Senator Patrick Moynihan (D-N.Y.). Although Reagan did benefit from a majority among Catholics in 1980 and 1984, Catholic percentages trailed those of white Protestants. The security and economic policies of the Reagan Administration seem too far right to underwrite a long-term Catholic coalition. In both the Democratic center-left and Republican center-right coalitions Catholic ethnic politics would play a significant role. These alternative coalitions, partially based on the communitarian values of the Catholic tradition, would constitute a response to the contemporary American overemphasis on the individual, so well documented by Bellah et al. in *Habits of the Heart*.

This vision of Catholic participation in the formation of a new American social and political consensus depends upon the continued unity of the NCCB, and its continued legitimacy among Catholics. This, in turn, depends upon at least the acquiescence of the Vatican. Despite the Hunthausen case, the greatest danger does not lie in irrational episcopal appointments like Gijsen of the Netherlands. Bernardin (Chicago), Law (Boston), O'Connor (New York), and Mahony (Los Angeles) have all brought at least some values to the vision of a new consensus. The greater danger lies in Vatican pressure bringing about the alienation of the United States bishops from their best "middle management" and intellectuals, and from the laity, especially women.

COMPETING SLAVIC VISIONS: THE SOVIET UNION AND THE VATICAN

John Paul II's fourth encyclical, *Slavorum apostoli* celebrated the 1,100th anniversary of the death of St. Methodius, who along with his brother, St. Cyril, brought Christianity to the Slavs and devised the Cyrillic alphabet. In this encyclical (July 2, 1985), the pope stressed his solidarity with the Slavs and called for religious tolerance in Eastern Europe. The latter concern was presented, according to Czech Vatican official Cardinal Jozef Tomko, "not by accusing but by praying."[31] The document also stressed two other Joannine themes: the desirability of closer ties with Eastern Orthodoxy and the common Christian heritage of both Eastern and Western Europe, "one of the most solid points of reference" for those who would unite Europe.

The worsening of Soviet-American relations in the early 1980s did pose serious diplomatic challenges to the Vatican in its relations to Moscow. Just as Cold War tensions make Vatican relations with Washington more difficult, they add significant complications to Soviet-Vatican relations. To these tensions derived from superpower relations in themselves has been added John Paul II's active role in supporting Solidarity. Any lasting rapprochement between the Polish government and the Polish church depends upon a return to Soviet-American *détente*. In that sense the Vatican experiences the negative effects of superpower tension as the tiny Western European state that it is. The Vatican like other European states has fostered increased East-West contacts as a means of lessening tensions. The Evangelical connection through Berlin (FRG-GDR) and the Catholic connection through Vienna (Austria-Hungary)[32] have both served as unofficial diplomatic conduits. Should Soviet-American relations continue to improve, then Polish Catholicism itself might play a significant role in linking East and West.

In Poland the Eastern bloc's weakest Communist Party faces Europe's strongest Catholic Church. Intervention of the Polish army was necessary to maintain the political monopoly of the party. Jaruzelski and Glemp seek to maneuver within the straightened circumstances presented them by current Soviet-American relations. Both the general and the cardinal also face opposition within their own institutions. Hungary constitutes the principal contrast to the Polish confrontation since in Budapest both government and church cooperate more closely. Neither is anxious for a papal visit. In general, five factors determine the political strength of the Catholic Church of a particular Eastern European country: the percentage of the population that is Catholic, the fervor of that faith, the unity of the ecclesiastical organization, the quality of the hierarchical leadership, and the degree of identification of Catholicism with nationalism. Even in the case of a relatively weak church like the Czech one, however, the Vatican attack on PAX decimated that government-sponsored organization.

Whenever possible the Vatican has followed the Eastern policies of the West, especially West Germany's *Ostpolitik* and America's *détente*. The Vatican participated intensely in the Conference on European Security and Cooperation in Helsinki to incorporate strong statements on religious freedom into the final accords.[33] Indeed, the principal European diplomatic value of the Vatican to the Soviets has been the Vatican's participation and strong defense of the Helsinki Accords. While the human rights concerns of Basket Three[34] have proved troublesome to Moscow, the Accords do guarantee the legitimacy of the political boundaries of postwar Europe. Support for Helsinki comes not just from the Vatican, but also from the Polish bishops through the German bishops to the German Christian Democratic Party. On February 27, 1985, German Chancellor Kohl made his strongest statement pledging to "respect" Germany's present border with Poland, despite his usual domestic political bow to his party's right-wing Association of Expellees.[35]

In addition to Vatican and Polish Catholic defense of the Helsinki Accords, Soviet leaders remain interested in discouraging Western armaments and encouraging Western peace movements through their Catholic connections. When *National Catholic Reporter* editor Michael Farrell of the United States visited the Soviet Union in the summer of 1983, Georgi Arbatov expressed Andropov's desire for "normalizing relations . . . and a return to detente." Arbatov continued, "[Andropov] has a high opinion of the efforts which are being made by many representatives of different churches in the United States, including American Catholics, to bring this very urgent message to humanity to do something now. It is really an urgent task to stop this race to oblivion toward which we are heading."[36] Arbatov, director of the Institute for United States and Canadian Studies and a leading Soviet expert on American affairs, was joined in the interview by Deputy Director Vitaly Zhurkin, Department Head Yuri Zamoshkin, and Secretary for International Relations Vladimir Krestianov.

Where John Paul and Soviet leaders find some common vision is in their blistering attacks on the evils of Western society. The cultural context of such papal criticism approximates that of fellow Slav Solzhenitzyn. Both Slavs have attacked the morally enervating "consumerism" of contemporary Democratic Capitalism. While John Paul's Italian predecessors have all attacked the dual ideological evils of Manchesterian Liberalism and atheistic Marxism (both forms of "economism"), the present pope retains a special Eastern European sense for the cultural decline of the West.[37]

The pope's defense of free labor unions and other civil and political rights,[38] however, directly attacks the Soviet system on the vital issue of the role of the proletariat. The encyclical *Laborem exercens* was originally intended for the ninetieth anniversary of *Rerum no-*

varum in May 1983, but the papal assassination attempt delayed its release until September, an extremely tense period between Solidarity and the Warsaw government. This third encyclical focuses on labor as the source of the specific dignity of man's life. John Paul II thus places himself within the general social tradition of the church following *Rerum novarum*, provided allowance is made for the gradual development of a critique of Capitalism to match the earlier strong denunciations of Communism and Socialism. Despite such continuity in social doctrine, however, the change in cultural perception from Montini to Wojtyła is striking. Polish-born political philosopher Alfred Bloch describes John Paul's vision as the "Third Rome" of Christian unity supported by the philosophy of the "new humanism" based on man's redemption by Christ. This Wojtyłan vision, says Bloch, rejects the Panslavism led by the Greek cross (Dostoyevsky) or the Red star (Lenin) for one which returns to the ancient Christian unity.[39] On his first visit to Poland, the pope said he came to preach not just to his countrymen, but to all Slavs. Most Slavs are Orthodox so unity with the Orthodox churches takes on even more importance than ecumenism with the Protestants.[40]

John Paul II did not originate the vision of Orthodox-Catholic unity. There has been a series of contacts between theologians in Leningrad (1967), Bari (1970), Zagorsk (1973), and Trento (1975). Finally in 1978, the Orthodox Metropolitan Nikodim represented the Moscow Patriarch at the funeral services of Paul VI. Unfortunately Nikodim died of a heart attack during pastoral discussion with John Paul I.[41] Wojtyła's fierce Polish nationalism and his Panslavic vision both pose a direct challenge to Soviet ideology, especially since the vision of a great Christian unity on the edge of Islam is a seductive vision for Russian nationalism. John Paul II has not forgotten that it was the Turks from whom the Polish king John Sobieski saved Vienna in the seventeenth century.

Whether or not Politburo alarm at a competing Slavic ideology or John Paul's support for Solidarity resulted in Soviet complicity in the attempted assassination of the pope, it is difficult to imagine this particular pope being perceived as a neutral mediator by the Kremlin. Veteran Italian Vatican diplomats like Cardinal Casaroli, the original architect of *Ostpolitik*, and Archbishop Luigi Poggi receive a warmer welcome. In July 1985 the Czech government received Casaroli, but refused to let the pope come to Prague to celebrate the anniversary of Ss. Cyril and Methodius. John Paul was forced to remain in Rome and content himself with issuing an encyclical. However, a meeting between Gorbachev and the pope is expected to occur in 1986 during the secretary general's visit to Rome.[42] If the meeting takes place, Gorbachev would be the first Soviet leader since President Podgorny to visit the pope, an indication of the secretary general's appreciation of the significance of "expressive politics" conducted through the international media.

THE CATHOLIC CHURCH AND A NEW ARMS CONTROL AGREEMENT

American Secretary of State Shultz and Soviet Foreign Minister Gromyko met in January 1985 to resurrect the process of arms control negotiations. Arms control agreements are notoriously difficult to conclude because the negotiating process includes many disparate factors from ethics to politics to physics. Furthermore, the rapidity of technological change and the media-enhanced volatility of the Western, especially American, political systems results in enormous changes in both political and scientific data throughout the process. Finally, extraneous events such as the Soviet invasion of Afghanistan can destroy the process. Very complicated international linkage exists on this crucial security issue. No possible verification procedures can convince a government or a public that is determined to mistrust its adversary because of extraneous international events.

In Chapter 8 we discussed the impact of the Catholic Church on arms control at the international, regional, national, and state levels. At the international level, direct papal action emphasizes the symbolic, calling attention to the need for disarmament and enunciating the parameters under which national Catholic hierarchies can adopt their own positions. More direct papal mediation would be an indicator that the world had exhausted normal channels and faced Armageddon again as in the case of the Cuban missile crisis. On December 4, 1983, shortly after the Soviet walkout at Geneva, Vatican Secretary of State Casaroli replied to reporters that the Vatican was attempting to mediate the crisis, but that he was not optimistic about attaining "very conciliatory results."[43] During the 1980s Soviet-American relations have never gotten quite horrible enough for direct Vatican mediation. At the level of "deliberate policy," neither John Paul II nor the Vatican has publicly condemned President Reagan's Strategic Defense Initiative (SDI), despite the personal lobbying of Gromyko and other Soviet diplomats. The absence of a Vatican condemnation should be considered a diplomatic victory for the United States. This victory has resulted less from

American lobbying than from the Vatican's general orientation toward Western European security policy.

The Western Europeans initially had difficulty taking SDI seriously ("a dream, not a real program" according to the FRG defense minister).[44] When it became clear that Reagan was indeed serious, the Europeans tried to raise their concerns without seeming to take the Soviet position. The most important of these statements have come from Great Britain, from Prime Minister Thatcher in private, and Foreign Secretary Howe in a March 15, 1985, address to the Royal United Services Institute. Another indirect response has been the formation of the European Eureka Seventeen to pursue advanced technological development independently of the United States.[45] Like the other European states, the Vatican does not wish to be perceived as taking the Soviet position. Nevertheless, the negative report on SDI by the Pontifical Academy allows the Vatican to be critical of the idea without commiting the entire institution to a Soviet position.

Regardless of the technical and political merit of the various SDI proposals,[46] the Reagan vision of a world no longer dependent upon deterrence has proved to be an excellent tactical position in the ethical debate. American spokespersons can now claim a superior moral position to the bishops themselves who had to "compromise" on deterrence.[47] The president himself maintained a general propaganda advantage from the Soviet walkout of November 1983 until the accession of Gorbachev gave him a more worthy competitor in the international media. Gorbachev, who gave the first open press conference by a Soviet leader in twenty-five years in Paris in November 1985, enunciated his own plan the following January to rid the world of nuclear weapons by the year 2000. Gorbachev has also constantly pressed his public call for a moratorium on nuclear testing.

In Soviet-American arms control negotiations, the Catholic Church plays different roles in Europe, the Soviet Union, and the United States. Catholic political initiatives almost always aim at stability in European politics. Vatican support of the Helsinki Accords and active fostering of relations between NATO and Warsaw Pact states remains especially significant for creating a climate for arms control. The more tense Soviet-American relations become, the more important are the "Catholic" links between other countries of NATO and the Warsaw Pact, and within these two great alliances themselves.

This book has illustrated the political importance of the rise of national hierarchies within the church. Western national Catholic hierarchies enter the arms control process by ethical statements, by their influence on Catholic peace movements, and through direct discussions with national leaders. The mix of these initiatives tends to differ according to the historical and societal background of the particular country, but in general Catholicism has distinguished itself among all religions in its preference for contacts between institutional leaders. In culturally Protestant nations like the Netherlands and the United States, Catholics have formed successful popular peace organizations. The American bishops, many of whom have joined Pax Christi, have combined all three modes of activity. The United States episcopate issued "The Challenge of Peace" after consulting with government officials and many members of the arms control establishment. In this way they mirrored John Paul's attempt to combine ethics, politics, and science in meetings of the Pontifical Academy of Sciences.

The decline of Western peace movements since 1982 has demonstrated the necessity for a broad-based "consensus" approach to arms control. The European peace protests of 1981-1983 focused attention on the defense issue, but they could not block the deployment of the Euromissiles. As the lack of a constituency for SALT II convinced many members of the American arms control establishment of the necessity of a peace movement, the election and policy reversals of 1983-1984 have convinced some members of the peace movement of the necessity of a more sophisticated political strategy. In West Germany, for example, the Protestant Action Reconciliation has battled to keep the emphasis on protesting nuclear weapons, resisting radical attempts to focus on disrupting NATO maneuvers, a highly unpopular cause with most Germans.[48]

Within the national context, the consistent policy orientation of Catholic hierarchies adds some stability to the waxing and waning of peace movements. Western episcopal conferences, with the possible exception of the Netherlands, have now taken arms control positions to the political left of the practicing Catholic laity, The episcopal letters have influenced that laity to change their views. Sociologist Andrew Greeley, relying on survey data from the National Opinion Research Center, has called the American letter "the most successful intervention to change attitudes ever measured by social science."[49] Because bishops are less dependent on the swings of public interest and opinion than politicians and newscasters, bishops can continue to act as a catalyst for ethical debate on defense issues. Such activity, of course, does not guarantee political victories. USCC opposition to the MX has not been able to defeat the Reagan strategy of tying the weapon to the Scowcroft Commission and the Geneva arms talks. On the other hand, the president has had to use up considerable political capital on each vote, and final victory is far from certain. At the November 1985 meeting of the NCCB, Bishop Gumbleton and five others introduced a resolution calling for a reexamination of the 1983 pastoral's provisional acceptance of deterrence. The resulting committee adds Archbishops Mahony and Roach to the four surviving members of the Bernardin committee.[50]

The major danger to successful arms control negotiations from the United States side stems from the fragmentation and volatility of the American culture and political system, which we described in Chapter 5. The prominence of the second draft of the American peace pastoral in November 1982 serves as a reminder of the serious weaknesses in the contemporary United States political system. A strong nongovernmental institution like the Catholic Church with its traditional style of including all groups from Pax Christi to the military is, therefore, functional for an arms control consensus. With most American political leaders spending considerable time just running for reelection, the continuity of other institutions with more permanent leadership such as the universities, professional organizations like PSR, and the churches can help foster national consensus. Such a function is not automatic, of course, as the chaotic Catholic episcopal participation in the 1984 presidential campaign amply demonstrated.

The American Catholic bishops' appreciation for collective deliberation and a unified response on arms contol is probably more important than their specific policy recommendations. Rapid technological change means that the American political system, founded on an eighteenth-century Constitution rarely amended, must constantly face new choices. Without a tempering of political individualism and its media manifestations, it will be difficult for the United States government and people to meet the serious challenges of arms reduction and peace. The principal Catholic dangers to arms control are the use of the traditional Catholic anticommunist crusade by the American and European laity, and the public uncertainty surrounding the origin of the attempt to assassinate John Paul II. The three Bulgarians and three Turks have been acquitted "for insufficient proof," but this "neither guilty nor innocent" verdict practically guarantees that the theory of a conspiracy by the deceased Andropov and his successors will continue to be used by the political right in all NATO countries. Linkage again damages arms control.

CONCLUSION: CATHOLIC POLITICS AND SOVIET-AMERICAN RELATIONS IN THE INTERNATIONAL SYSTEM

Gordon Craig and Alexander George have pointed out that "the Congress of Vienna in 1814-1815 created an international system that secured a fragile peace for two generations and then, as modified by Bismarck, for most of the rest of the century."[51] Chapter 1 has already described how the papacy had its lands restored by the Congress of Vienna. During the nineteenth century the popes generally supported the consort of powers, even to discouraging Catholic Irish and Polish rebellion against Protestant Britain and Orthodox Russia.

Twentieth-century attempts at collective security have failed, according to Craig and George, because there is no true international system. Contemporary international relations have lacked:

(1) an agreement among the principal states concerning aims and objectives that reflects the dominant values that they are seeking to preserve and enhance in creating and participating in the system; (2) a structure appropriate to the number of states interacting with each other, the geographical boundaries or scope of the system, the distribution of power among member states, and the stratification and status hierarchy among them; and (3) commonly accepted procedures—that is, norms, rules, practices, and institutions for the achievement of the aims and objectives of the system.[52]

Certainly, contemporary international politics offers a complexity of values, structures, and procedures unheard of in nineteenth-century Europe, let alone among the European elites at the Congress of Vienna, who had been terrified by the French Revolution and Napoleon. While Soviet and American values and lifestyles remain quite different, a major thrust of Soviet policy has been to secure "equal" treatment by the United States in international affairs. Soviet delegates, for example, insisted on the specification of equality in the Soviet-American "Basic Principles Agreement" of May 1972. That this term did not signify just "strategic parity" can be seen in Moscow's outrage at American attempts to exclude them from the formulation of a Middle East peace since 1973.

Neither the Soviet nor the American visions of "equality" extend to any third country, though the People's Republic of China remains hard to ignore in Soviet geopolitical calculations. Soviet intellectuals and leaders react as quickly as the more conservative elements of the Reagan Administration to denounce the policy bogey of "internationalism."[53] In this the Soviets reflect their fear that Reagan, "the most ideological of all recent American presidents," might take a chance in supporting ethnic subversion of the Soviet Union. Therefore, they argue, strong Soviet nationalism is a prerequisite for international stability. The Soviet leadership has always lived with the tension between the dual goals of furthering the common interests of the world proletariat (ideological internationalism) and of strengthening the strategic and economic interests of the Soviet Union (geopolitical nationalism). In almost every case since its World War I treaty with Germany, the Soviet leadership has favored national interest. The Soviet leadership suffers from the tension of these dual goals because it claims both instrumental and expressive power.

The Vatican differs from both superpowers in emphasizing the claims of the international system. This has been especially true since John XXIII's *Pacem in terris*, whose whole fourth section developed the Catholic argument for a worldwide public authority, and specifically advocated that "the United Nations—in its structure and in its means—may become ever more equal to the magnitude and nobility of its tasks."[54] The absence of such a global public authority, argued the pope, produces a structural defect in the international system. Thus, at every level from village politics to the international system, crises and structural defects activate institutionalized Catholic political initiatives.

The Vatican has thus placed its primary emphasis on supporting the structures and the prerogatives of the United Nations and the World Court, even while using specific opportunities to further bilateral relations. John Paul II used the occasion of World Peace Day (January 1, 1986) to reiterate to diplomats accredited to the Holy See his strong support for the United Nations. If the goals for which the UN was founded "remain yet today in large measure to be achieved, this must not be grounds for discouragement, but of renewed decisiveness and more convinced resolve."[55] In a speech to the World Court in May 1985, the pope urged a strengthening of the Court and "international administration of justice and arbitration" as an alternative to war. Despite the fact that the United States had recently refused the court's jurisdiction in its dispute with Nicaragua, the pope advocated "a wider acceptance of the so-called compulsory jurisdiction of the court."[56] In the single year of 1980, Vatican participants or observers attended 214 international meetings, an increase of 15 over the preceding year.[57] As the United Nations debate over the Law of the Sea Treaty reached its final stages in spring 1982, the Holy See's observer, Archbishop Giovanni Cheli made an impassioned plea for "a necessary compromise" between industrialized nations seeking to safeguard their mining rights and many developing countries seeking guarantees that seabed materials will be the common heritage of all nations. A compromise was necessary for the management of such resources "with a view to contributing to the survival and development of a great number of men, women and children."[58]

This chapter has emphasized the outside constraints on the possible solutions to Third World political crises. The question at issue was not which of the possible political coalitions to choose as in Western Europe, but whether a feasible core solution existed at all. The same parsimony of solutions is true of the current, even larger crisis in the international system. The first atomic explosion at Alamogordo introduced very real technological constraints on international politics. Any long-term international solution must now be reformist, based on an international consensus which supports elite state-to-state negotiations between national leaders who enjoy political legitimacy at home.[59] Any radical political or technological solution from either NATO or the Warsaw Pact brings with it an unacceptable risk of global destruction. Even more dangerous would be the breaking apart of the Nuclear Non-Proliferation Treaty or nuclear or biological terrorism. The Vatican has denounced Catholic sectarian terrorism, regardless of whether it has been directed against the West (Northern Ireland) or the East (Yugoslavia).

The Catholic political tradition is inalienably reformist. It always starts with the church as an institution fostering consensus between the leadership of states and national and transnational organizations. Vatican foreign policy most closely approximates that of Jordan in the Middle East, of Austria in its emphasis on fostering East-West relations, of the Netherlands in public support for a European rather than a nationalist orientation, and of the People's Republic of China in focusing on reformist solutions to North-South disparities.[60] There are real ironies in singling out the last two states, since the Vatican has damaged the popular legitimacy of the Dutch hierarchy, and China will not allow its native Catholic Church to have contact with Rome.

Soviet and American emphasis on national prerogatives have complicated the political role of the Catholic Church, even in the halcyon period of *détente*. It is no accident that historically the worst political years for the Catholic Church coincided with the heyday of the sovereign nation state in the West. As the nineteenth-century international system dissolved into the chaos of two World Wars, the Vatican again began to exercise influence in global affairs. Hiroshima added urgency to the search for a new world order. Finally, the Cuban missile crisis not only convinced the American and Soviet elites of the neccesity of "peaceful coexistence," but it also persuaded Pope John XXIII that *Peace on Earth* must be the church's first political priority. In this way, the Cuban missile crisis, carried live into hundreds of millions of homes by television, may have evoked the most significant political and religious responses to the technological challenges of the twentieth century.

Methodological Issues

THE INTRODUCTION to this book began by contrasting the instrumental power of Jaruzelski with the expressive power of John Paul II. Ivan Vallier first employed this theoretical distinction in an attempt to explain the role of the Catholic Church in Western political systems. His essay, "The Roman Catholic Church: A Transnational Actor,"[1] treats the church as a type of large, hierarchically organized and centrally directed bureaucracy performing specialized functions across international borders.[2]

Vallier's emphasis on the centralized bureaucratic nature of the church raised important questions. However, since the Second Vatican Council, national hierarchies have become increasingly significant. In his essay "Amending Vallier" (1978),[3] J. Bryan Hehir faulted Vallier for being too exclusively concerned with the flow of authority from Rome to the local churches and for ignoring changes in the church's ideological foundation which sustain and legitimize its actions in world affairs. In overemphasizing the organizational factor Vallier followed other eminent sociologists and political scientists who have been tempted to focus on the Roman church's wonderfully complex bureaucratic structure extending down from pope to bishop to parish priest.

This book attempts to compensate for Vallier's lack of emphasis on church ideology as an independent variable by using the ecclesiastical models of Avery Dulles (Chapter 3) to demonstrate the political impact of changed perceptions of the church. The same chapter demonstrates the transnational influence of various Catholic ideologies. Nevertheless, the primary analytical categories of this work derive from contemporary studies in comparative politics and international relations, not theology or political theory. Transnational, modernization, institutional, bureaucratic, and political party studies have all provided concepts as well as data.

Such an approach, of course, raises further theoretical questions, which themselves could be developed into a book-length manuscript. Here, however, we will treat some of these methodological issues under two headings: the Catholic Church as the Object of Social Science; and the Nature of Social Science and the Methodology of This Work. The first section points to dissonance between the paradigms traditionally employed by Catholic ecclesiastics and social scientists. As such it complements the discussion of conscious Catholic ideologies in Chapter 3.

THE CATHOLIC CHURCH AS THE OBJECT OF SOCIAL SCIENCE

Scholars like Vallier, Robert Bellah, and S. N. Eisenstadt[4] have all emphasized the capacity of religion to transform institutions and societies. In this way they differ from the predominant judgment about Catholicism held by nineteenth-century social scientists. Classical theorists like Durkheim, Marx, and Weber all stressed the conservative nature of the Catholic Church. This approach reflected both the predispositions of their own intellectual environment and the predominant political posture of the church during that century.

Despite recent changes in sociological theory and the *aggiornamento* of the Second Vatican Council, basic contradictions remain between the intellectual traditions of Catholicism and those of contemporary social science. Catholic scholarship, even among critical theologians like Karl Rahner, has remained anchored in the Thomistic tradition. Neo-Thomists like the French philosophers Jacques Maritain and Gilson rejected not only nineteenth-century Marxism and positivism, but much of Western philosophy since Machiavelli and Hobbes. The Canadian Jesuit Bernard Lonergan, the greatest Catholic methodologist of the twentieth century, has criticized the mechanistic basis of modern philosophy and social science as incompatible with both the truths understood by Aquinas and with the discoveries of contemporary natural science. Of the developments derived from Galileo, Lonergan says,

Thus Galilean methodology is penetrated with philosophic assumptions about reality and objectivity and, unfortunately, those assumptions are not too happy. Their influence is evident in Descartes. Their ambiguities appear in Hobbes and Locke, Berkeley and Hume. Their final inadequacy becomes clear in Kant, where the real and objective bodies of Galilean thought prove to constitute no more than a phenomenal world.[5]

This Catholic orientation toward the Thomist tradition has resulted not principally from the nineteenth-century Pope Leo XIII's adoption of Thomism as the official philosophy of the church, but from the creative scholarship of twentieth-century thinkers like Maritain, Rahner, and Lonergan.

Understanding the Catholic intellectual tradition remains particularly difficult for contemporary Americans. As Bellah et al. remark, the voluntary "sectarian"[6] type of religious organization has predominated in American Christianity, and a strong individualistic "mysticism" has arisen in the United States in contemporary times.[7] Therefore, recent cultural developments have led Americans even further away from traditional Catholic political culture, with its emphasis on "church" organization. The Catholic hierarchy, following this "church" model, has always stressed preaching the Gospel "to all living creatures," and including all people in church membership. This orientation has resulted in a truly "Catholic" religious organization which has tolerated large variations in the content and style of belief as long as its members professed ecclesiastical unity and loyalty to the institution.[8]

Catholic bishops perceive their loyalty to institutional unity as an integral part of their religious faith. As they take their faith seriously, they take their institution seriously. Celibacy strengthens this clerical and religious attachment to the institution, as does the formative socialization of seminary training. When faced with an attack on what are perceived to be essential features of the church, defense of the institution usually overrides all other goals. In missionary countries, especially, Roman education has served to inspire a life-long commitment to the center. Therefore, objective political scientists must take into account a strong episcopal devotion to the visible religious institution as a motivational force. Daniel Levine calls for a "phenomenological approach" by which he means starting from the hierarchy's own stated perceptions when analyzing these elites. Such an analysis, according to Levine, will enable the political scientist to avoid the twin subjectivisms of the "village atheist" and the "village preacher."[9]

Such a strong intellectual dissonance between the traditions of the disciplines involved (social sciences) and the object of study (the Catholic Church) should alert us to be very careful in analysis. An "objective" social science patterned on the natural sciences remains extremely problematic, especially in such volatile areas as religion and politics. In the Introduction to his study on "Comrades and Christians" in a small sector of Bologna, the American Jewish anthropologist David Kertzer remarks that "the Arborese (and Italians in general) see social scientists as a major part of the political landscape. . . . The Communist sociologist is expected to conduct re-

search that will benefit the Communist cause; the Catholic sociologist will benefit the interests of the Church."[10] Being Jewish allowed
him to attend mass without having that attendance perceived as an
anticommunist statement, but Kertzer's participation as an American in an anti-Vietnam War demonstration caused considerable political difficulties for his field research. Daniel Levine also describes
his own work on Venezuela and Colombia as "a study of Catholicism and politics in Latin America by a Jewish, North American professor of political science."[11]

Such an outside stance can contribute to objectivity, but it would
also be difficult to deny the richness of material and insight afforded
Jesuit priests John Coleman and Brian Smith by their roles within
the church. Kertzer, Levine, Coleman, and Smith all tap the academic resources of the modern sociology of religion while adding
insights from other disciplines. In addition to non-Catholic academics and Catholic scholars like Coleman and Smith who are sympathetic to the church, there is the reverse phenomenon of Catholics
who are angry at their church and who let that anger permeate the
manuscript and destroy its objectivity. This latter phenomenon has
become less prevalent in the United States as time has passed since
the virulent ecclesiastical controversies of the late 1960s.

A strong devotion to the church as institution would seem to constitute a natural basis for acquiescence to the political *status quo* in
both Capitalist and Communist countries. In the very least it would
encourage a covert conservatism masquerading as religious holiness and political neutrality. Vaillancourt, who describes his approach as "broadly speaking, a neo-Marxian one," emphasizes "attention to these important and often neglected structural and
infrastructural roots of ideological phenomena." He stresses the
close ties among the Vatican, Italian political and financial elites,
and American imperialism "cemented mostly during the last years
of World War II and in the late forties."[12] Such an analytical approach is associated with the Italian Antonio Gramsci, whose work
is often cited in Vaillancourt's second chapter, his historical survey
of "The Origins of the Lay Movement."

Many recent studies of Catholicism have employed theories of
political and social development to explain ecclesiastical change.
Sanders points out that three recent fine texts on Latin American
Catholicism (Levine, Bruneau, Smith) all contain "an implicit theory of development . . . namely, as a process that moves from conservatism through reformism and culminates in an outlook that fa-
vors radical structural change, cooperation with Marxists, and

political activism within a given historical process of liberation."[13] Coleman's work on Dutch Catholicism uses Vallier's two poles of missionary and cultural-pastoral strategies of influence as typologies. The Dutch church moves from the first strategy to the second through a seven-stage sequence of social change provided by the American sociologist Neil J. Smelser. As Coleman says, "The seven-sequence model is essentially an explanatory device for the study of structural differentiation." Thus, while the direction of the Latin American models points to radical structural change, Smelser's model describes "evolution from a multi-functional role structure to several more specialized structures."[14] Structural differentiation, of course, has been one of the crucial variables in Gabriel Almond's theories of political development.[15] The concept, while useful in Coleman's analysis of Dutch Catholicism, seems less applicable in non-Western political cultures, as many comparative theorists have pointed out in their critiques of Almond's work.

Bruneau, a student of Vallier, credits his mentor with producing "the most valuable analytical model of the Latin American church," but states that the evolutionary model failed to predict the repoliticization of the church. "He [Vallier] could not conceptualize politics as an autonomous sphere and thus failed to include it as a key variable in analysis of the church."[16] The development of Latin American politics during the last decade has also raised serious questions about the inevitability of ecclesiastical political radicalism. Catholic radicalism hit its apex at the Chilean Christians for Socialism Conference in 1972. In the interim Latin American politics has shifted to Counterrevoltuion and Reform. The official papal position at Puebla would be reduced to ingnominious compromise if viewed only from this univocal theory of Catholic evolution toward radicalism. The present manuscript relies on scholarship that employs these and other useful sociological and political theories, but it hopes to eschew any grand theory of national or international Catholic development, especially a "necessary" one.

THE NATURE OF SOCIAL SCIENCE AND THE METHODOLOGY OF THIS WORK

Moving from the political analysis employed in the text to the preceding discussion of the Catholic Church as an object of social science required asking a "meta" (in the sense of "meta" physics) question about the former inquiry. If one performs the same type of operation on the latter inquiry, one can ask about the nature of so-

cial science itself and the methodological ramifications of that nature. On this latter question, this appendix uses as a starting point
a similar appendix, "Social Science as Public Philosophy," in *Habits
of the Heart* (pp. 297-307). We agree with the position that although
all of us have benefited from the advances of contemporary professional scholarship, attempts to cast the social sciences in the mold
of the natural sciences have failed. The divorce of contemporary social science from the humanities has been particularly detrimental
to public philosophy and decision making in the public sphere.

This general stance has methodological and audience implica-
tion. The authors of *Habits* describe their own work as emphasizing
participant observation and the active interview over survey research (p. 305). This book would describe its own methodology as
ecclectic, reflecting the same general theoretical stance as *Habits*, the
nature of the Catholic Church, and the nature of this book's integra-
tive project, which reflects both the content and methodologies of
many other authors. The major methodological and analytical differences between this work and *Habits* stem from the fact that while
the latter work describes its "synopic view" as "at once philosophical, historical, and sociological" (p. 298), this work includes these
methods, but focuses on domestic and international politics.

This book, like *Habits*, employs concepts from classical sociologists like Troeltsch and Weber who stressed social theory. Quite a
bit of the background material would fall into the category of social
history since we agree with the Yugoslav scholar Bogdan Denitch's
declaration about his country, "Before a sociologist or political scientist can begin to assess the relationship of religion to social
change in Yugoslavia, he must turn to the social historian."[17] Recent
political scientists have tended to emphasize institutional analysis
(Vallier) or elite interviews (Levine). The former approach risks
slighting the religious aspect of the institution (Hehir's criticism),
while the latter raises questions about the actual political effect of
enunciated goals. Elite perceptions may be overemphasized, even
in the Catholic Church. It is also difficult to devise a politically significant interview coding system which does not do violence to religious language. Almost all of the above types of studies analyze
church documents, and many employ case studies. Smith adds the
methodologies of participant-observer and survey research. He
says the former gave him "the most sensitivity for the human dimensions involved in the formation of a new church."[18] The anthropologist Kertzer describes his book as "an attempt to demonstrate
the value of participant-observation research to modern, urban

study."[19] Survey research remains crucial in analyzing the practical mass effect of shifts in elite ideology. One of the major challenges in analyzing Catholic politics, especially in authoritarian and developing countries, is the lack of survey data.

To describe a methodology as eclectic gives no hint of the criteria for selection of a particular methodology for a particular issue. At times, since the book borrows from specific national and regional studies of the Catholic Church, the choice of methodology resides with the original author. Nevertheless, reliance on such area specialists is comfortable since the closest model to what we are attempting to achieve for the international Catholic Church would be the sections on Japanese politics in Edwin O. Reischauer's *The Japanese*. At the most fundamental level, then, we have sought to explain the political culture of the Catholic Church and its effect on world politics, especially the political systems of the United States and the Soviet Union. Methodologies have been chosen for their efficacy in attaining that particular goal.

In terms of audience, as Bellah et al. propose a national dialogue including both the "community of competence" and fellow citizens, this book is written for specialists in arms control, international relations, and religious studies, and for political and religious leaders and activists. On arms control, any substantial progress depends on a much greater mutual understanding between specialists from the "arms control priesthood" and activists from the "priesthood of the laity." As such, this book is envisioned as a small contribution to the political process which acts as "broker" between universal religious and ethical norms and the specific political and technological constraints of a particular decision at a particular moment.

INTRODUCTION

1. *New York Times* [hereafter NYT], July 18, 1983, p. 5.

2. Gabriel A. Almond and G. Bingham Powell, Jr., defined political culture as "the pattern of individual attitudes and orientations towards politics among the members of a political system." *Comparative Politics: A Developmental Approach*, p. 50. This text includes traditional organizational structure, and eschews the developmental assumptions of the modernization literature. It is in the context of political culture, however, that the valid insights of modernization theorists can be integrated. For a review of this perspective and its literature, see J. Samuel Valenzuela and Arturo Valenzuela, "Modernization and Dependency: Alternative Perspectives in the Study of Latin American Underdevelopment." This text defines political culture as "that unique amalgamation of historical memory, types of social organizations, and traditional modes of thought that provides the contemporary environment for political and economic institutions." Focusing on the political cultures of the Catholic Church and various nation states, a natural orientation for a book dealing with the interaction between ecclesiastical and political institutions, allows this work to benefit from recent "national character" analyses like Robert N. Bellah, Richard Madsen, William M. Sullivan, Ann Swidler, and Stephen Tipton, *Habits of the Heart: Individualism and Commitment in American Life*, which describes its own task as following "Tocqueville and other classical social theorists in focusing on the mores— the 'habits of the heart'—that include consciousness, culture, and the daily practices of life" (p. 275). Appendix One, below, relates its own methodology to that of Bellah et al.

3. Peter Nichols, *The Pope's Divisions*, p. 23.

4. Coit D. Blacker and Gloria Duffy, eds., *International Arms Control*, p. 3, n. 1 distinguishes "disarmament" and "arms control" in the following manner:

"Disarmament" involves the reduction or the elimination of armaments or armed forces. "Arms control" or "Arms limitation" involves limitations on the number or types of armaments or armed forces, on their deployment or disposition, or on the use of particular types of armaments; "arms control" also encompasses measures designed to reduce the danger of accidental war or to reduce concern about surprise attack. Although the terms are generally used in an international setting, they can also be applied to unilateral actions of states. Postwar negotiations have concerned both arms control and disarmament, but most of the agreements actually achieved have technically been measures of arms control.

5. For the contrast of instrumental and expressive power, see Ivan Vallier, "The Roman Catholic Church: A Transnational Actor" in Robert O.

Keohane and Joseph F. Nye, eds., *Transnational Relations and World Politics*, p. 145. Henryk Jabłoński was the president of the Polish State, but Jaruzelski wielded effective power as party secretary and state premier. Jaruzelski has since resigned as premier. Jabłoński and the pope had met the previous day at the airport.

6. The covers are *Newsweek*, June 20 and June 27, 1983, and *Time*, June 27, 1983. Photos of John Paul and Jaruzelski appeared in the July 27 issues above the story head (*Newsweek*) and opposite the headline (*Time*).

7. International Commission for the Study of Communications Problems, *Many Voices, One World*. Séan MacBride of Ireland was president of the commission.

8. NYT, February 13, 1984.

9. Marconi designed Vatican Radio and supervised it until his death. At present Father Robert Tucci, S.J., heads the staff of 350 of whom 40 are Jesuits. The station broadcasts 240 hours of programming per week in 35 languages. Although the purpose of Vatican Radio is "that the voice of the Supreme Pastor may be heard throughout the world by means of the ether waves, for the glory of Christ and the salvation of souls," neither Vatican Radio nor *L'Osservatore Romano* constitute official church organs since prior censorship is not exercised on all material. However, both follow current church policy very closely. Soviet specialists will recognize the above distinction. The Holy See's official publication is *Acta Apostolicae Sedis* (hereafter AAS), a monthly bulletin in Latin carrying papal decrees and other important curial decisions. The official ecclesiastical organ for press relations is the Commission for Social Communications. In April 1984 the pope raised Msgr. John P. Foley, editor of the Philadelphia *Catholic Standard and Times* to archbishop and president of the Commission for Social Communications. For an excellent description of the internal politics of the Vatican media and the frustrations of Vatican reporters, see Paul Hofmann, *O Vatican!* pp. 243-70.

10. Vasyl Markus, "Religion and Nationality: The Uniates of the Ukraine," in Bohdan R. Bociurkiw and John W. Strong, eds., *Religion and Atheism in the U.S.S.R. and Eastern Europe*, p. 110.

11. *Christian Science Monitor* (hereafter CSM), June 27, 1984.

12. Following the pope's second trip, the Warsaw government accused Western reporters of fabricating articles asserting that the papal trip had political aspects. NYT, June 26, 1983.

13. John A. Coleman, *The Evolution of Dutch Catholicism, 1958-74*, pp. 120, 101-102.

14. The articles have been collected in Francis X. Murphy [pseud. Xavier Rynne], *Vatican Council II*. Robert Blair Kaiser wrote *Pope, Council and World: The Story of Vatican II*. Henri Fesquet's work is available in English as *The Drama of Vatican II: The Ecumenical Council (June, 1962–December, 1965)*.

15. The pope's clout with the Western press is obvious from this book's frequent citations from the *New York Times*, its principal newspaper refer-

ence. The secondary news reference is another highly influential American paper, the *Christian Science Monitor*. Additional coverage comes from *Le Monde*, the *Washington Post*, the *Los Angeles Times*, and other international media. The *San Jose Mercury News* is used for the local politics of the high-tech Silicon Valley, home of electronic defense systems and a crucial "swing county" in California politics. The less influential but internally important Catholic media network is represented by the American National Catholic News Service (NC) as it was used half-way across the globe by the English-language Catholic *Hong Kong Sunday Examiner*. When this source is used, it usually indicates that the aspect of the event under discussion was not covered in the international secular media.

16. This increased emphasis on expressive power constitutes an acceleration rather than a change in direction. From the perspective of 1972 Vallier held that in the previous one hundred years the church had become a much more integrated, international organization. Although it had lost many traditional forms of established state political support, the church had reoriented itself to relying more for its prestige on its spiritual and moral leadership. This had meant a decreased emphasis on "confessional expansion" and a new sensitivity to the aspirations of the Catholic Laity. In other words, the Roman Catholic Church had become more purely expressive, having lost its major temporal power in 1870. Vallier, "Transnational Actor," pp. 129-52.

17. Juan J. Linz has defined authoritarian regimes as "political systems with limited, not responsible, political pluralism; without elaborate and guiding ideology (but with distinctive mentalities); without intensive or extensive political mobilization (except at some points in their development); and in which a leader (or occasionally a small group) exercises power within formally ill-defined limits but actually quite predictable ones." Linz, "An Authoritarian Regime: Spain," in Erik Allardt and Yrjo Littunen, eds., *Cleavages, Idologies, and Party Systems*. Linz was concerned to distinguish Franco's Spain from both democratic and totalitarian regimes.

18. This account is drawn from Roland Flamini, *Pope, Premier, President*, pp. 54-59; see especially Chs. Four, Five, and Seven. Hansjakob Stehle, *Eastern Politics of the Vatican 1917-1979*, pp. 305-307, bases his account on Zizola, although he says Zizola "overrates the importance of Norman Cousins and Felix Morlion in the papal mediation on Cuba" (note 42). Stehle starts the mediation with a call from Kennedy to Cousins on the evening of October 23. When Morlion called Rome, according to Stehle, the papacy was already active and delivered the papal message to the embassies on the morning of the 24th. When Cousins passed through Rome on the way to Moscow, he also met Archbishop Dell'Acqua, deputy secretary of state, and patron of Morlion. For Cousins's own account of the mediation, see *The Improbable Triumvirate*. The significance of the papal message also receives due emphasis in Peter Hebblethwaite, *Pope John XXIII*, pp. 445-48.

19. Morlion deserves a book to himself. He had served as an OSS agent

during World War II, and had many American contacts, including Clare Boothe Luce, who helped to finance his private Pro Deo Institute in Rome. The Vatican Secretary of State Tardini disliked his intelligence activities and forced him out of Rome, whereupon he went to the United States and became associated with Cousins.

20. Flamini, *Pope, Premier, President*, pp. 66-67. Conversely, the Russian Orthodox Church received much better treatment under Stalin, who needed nationalistic ecclesiastical support to withstand the German attack during World War II, than from Khrushchev, who conducted an antireligious campaign, 1959-1964. See Michael Bourdeaux and Kathleen Matchett, "The Russian Orthodox Church in Council 1945-1971," in Bociurkiw and Strong, *Religion and Atheism*, pp. 37-57.

21. In the 1950s the second and third generations of Catholic immigrants, many of them graduates of Midwestern and Eastern Catholic universities like Fordham, Georgetown, and Notre Dame, benefited from the unquestioned anticommunism of American Catholicism that partially reversed the traditional governmental favoritism for WASP graduates from Ivy League institutions. This was especially true in security organizations like the FBI and the CIA. During that period the CIA Rome station chief was the Catholic William E. Colby, who later developed good contacts to Vietnamese Catholics when he moved to Saigon in the 1960s. The Rome station chief in the early 1960s was Catholic convert and ex-New York rack-busting lawyer, Thomas Kalamasinas. Flamini cites CIA reports on the papacy in several places.

22. In addition, any association with the Vatican threatened Kennedy's further political career. Flamini remarks that while the president was "a practicing Catholic in the old-fashioned Irish sense that he still found occasional solace in mass," his intelligence remained "fundamentally secular." *Pope, Premier, President*, p. 61, and especially Ch. 5.

23. Associated Press (hereafter AP) from Moscow, December 29, 1982.

24. NYT, February 28, 1985.

25. For the text of these two documents see Joseph Gremillion, ed., *The Gospel of Peace and Justice*, pp. 143-241. Papal documents are known by the first few words of the official Latin text. Sometimes these words are easily translated without the rest of the sentence, as Peace on Earth for *Pacem in terris*. Sometimes they are not.

26. Reported in Jean-Guy Vaillancourt, *Papal Power*, pp. 206-207.

27. When the Catholic Church exercises the prime responsibility for ethical values within a society, this text will refer to that role as being the "primary ethical broker" within that society. See Chapters 7 and 9.

28. There is no such thing, of course, as an exclusively "national church" in Roman Catholicism. The term seems useful, however, to indicate that national level of analysis which has become increasing important since Vatican II. See Chapter 2.

29 In Brian Smith's book on Chile, which employs "international influ-

ences" as one of four major independent variables, this terms refers as often to the churches of West Germany and the United States as it does to the papacy. Both churches exercise considerable ecclesiastical influence through their bilateral financial aid, as Smith documents in the Chilean case. Smith, *The Church and Politics in Chile*.

30. My earlier work on Catholic politics in South Korea necessarily referred to the actions of the United States Catholic Conference because of its influence on American foreign policy toward the Republic of Korea, a nation already heavily dependent on American political and economic involvement in the Far East. Hanson, *Catholic Politics in China and Korea*, pp. 98-111.

31. Gary MacEoin and the Committee for the Responsible Election of the Pope, *The Inner Elite: Dossiers of Papal Candidates*, p. xviii.

32. For a narrative of the negotiations, see Strobe Talbot, *Endgame*. For the internal bureaucratic politics of the early Reagan years, see Talbot, *Deadly Gambits*.

33. Thomas G. Sanders, in his review of national Catholic studies by Bruneau (1982), Levine (1981), and Smith (1982), states "If there is any deficiency in these three excellent books, it lies in their failure to integrate the discussion of national churches into the current 'official' projection of the institutional church." Sanders, "The Politics of Catholicism in Latin America," p. 254.

CHAPTER 1

1. For excellent coverage and analysis of the pope's four-day visit, see *Le Monde*, beginning May 31, 1980. The NYT for the period has also been used for a few extra details.

2. NYT, May 31, 1980.

3. *Le Monde*, June 3, 1980. Following Le Bourget, John Paul spoke to the French bishops and condemned the two extremes of progressivism and integralism. The keynote phrase was, "Fille aînée de l'Eglise, es-tu fidèle?" For its use in the peace pastoral, see Joint Pastoral Letter of the French Bishops, "Winning the Peace," n. 58, translated with the German bishops letter (San Francisco: Ignatius Press, 1984), p. 119.

4. *Le Monde*, May 31, 1980.

5. For France during the late nineteenth and early twentieth centuries, see A. Latreille, E. Delaruelle, J. R. Palangue, and R. Rémond, *Histoire du Catholicisme en France*, pp. 455-530. In contrast, see Joseph Moody, "The Papacy: The Church and New Forces in Western Europe and Italy," in Moody, ed., *Church and Society*, p. 42, which stresses "the Italian genius for practical solutions."

6. Coleman, *Dutch Catholicism*, p. 10.

7. Garry Wills, *Bare Ruined Choirs*, pp. 38-60.

8. Walter Ullman, *A Short History of the Papacy in the Middle Ages*, p. 2.

This entire book stands as a superb synthesis of the development of the papacy as an institution and forms the basis for this section. The text also follows Ullman's earlier *The Growth of Papal Government in the Middle Ages*.

9. Hedrick Smith, *The Russians*, p. 679.

10. Ullman, *Short History*, pp. 4-5.

11. For a short treatment of Nicaea and its background, see Philip Hughes, *The Church in Crisis*, pp. 22-36.

12. For example, Bociurkiw discusses the effect of Khrushchev's religious policies on the legitimacy of the Moscow patriarch in his article on "Religious Dissent and the Soviet State." Bociurkiw and Strong, *Religion and Atheism*, pp. 58-90.

13. Ullman, *Growth*, pp. 44-86. Ullman discusses Charlemagne in pp. 87-118.

14. Ibid., p. 99. If Charlemagne had known about the pope's plan, of course, he would never have entered the church.

15. George Sabine, *A History of Political Theory*, p. 188.

16. Ibid., p. 193.

17. Ullman, *A Short History*, p. 157.

18. Ernst Troeltsch, *The Social Teaching of the Christian Churches*, p. 330.

19. The great classic on traditional Chinese sectarian rebellion is J.J.M. DeGroot, *Sectarianism and Religious Persecution in China*.

20. For this phenomenon, see Norman Cohn, *The Pursuit of the Millennium*. For the general period, see John A.F. Thomson, *Popes and Princes*.

21. Vaillancourt, *Papal Power*, p. 19. See pp. 1-59 for the history of the Catholic Church from this perspective.

22. "After the curing of the Schism the project of reforming the church by a General Council, though it could still be talked about even as late as the sixteenth and seventeenth centuries, was definitely not within the region of practical politics." Sabine, *History*, p. 317.

23. Ullman, *A Short History*, pp. 21-22.

24. For a brief account of the Council of Trent, see Hughes, *The Church in Crisis*, pp. 301-32. The definitive work on Trent is Hubert Jedin, *A History of the Council of Trent*.

25. Hughes, *Church in Crisis*, pp. 318-19.

26. William J. Callahan and David Higgs, eds., *Church and Society in Catholic Europe of the Eighteenth Century*, pp. 11-12.

27. Owen Chadwick, *The Popes and European Revolution*, p. 354, and 345-90, passim.

28. Ibid., p. 412.

29. *Risorgimento* contained three separate elements: desire for independence from foreign control, especially from Austria; unification of Italy under a papal, republican, or monarchist government; and liberal political and social change. The combinations of these elements varied for different actors and at different times. See Joseph Moody, "The Papacy," pp. 33-34.

30. See John Henry Whyte, *Catholics in Western Democracies*, pp. 33-34.

31. Cited in Avery Dulles, *Models of the Church*, p. 84.

32. Hughes, *Church in Crisis*, p. 338, offers this summary of the convoking bull *Aeterni Patris* (June 29, 1868). Hughes covers Vatican I on pp. 333-65.

33. The third was Cardinal De Champs (Mechlin), ibid., p. 356.

34. For the history of Cullen's struggle to remake the Irish church, see Emmet Larkin, *The Making of the Roman Catholic Church in Ireland, 1850-1860*.

35. Christopher Dawson, *The Making of Europe*, p. 198.

36. Benedict Fitzpatrick, *Ireland and the Foundations of Europe*, opposite p. 384.

37. Charles Duff, *Six Days to Shake an Empire*, pp. 3-7, covers the content, use, and authenticity of the document. I have relied on many histories of Ireland, including Terrence Brown, *Ireland*; Emmet Larkin, *The Historical Dimensions of Irish Catholicism*; T. W. Moody, ed., *A New History of Ireland*; John H. Whyte, *Church and State in Modern Ireland 1923-1970*. I am also indebted to excellent papers by Santa Clara University students John Haggerty and Gary Hopkins, and Richard Peoples and Robert Bigiogni.

38. Larkin, *Historical Dimensions*, p. 875.

39. Ibid., pp. 853-56.

40. Ibid., p. 1247. The marginal rural class experienced most of the drop in population. As a result of the Famine the numbers of farms under 30 acres dropped from 572,912 to 410, 651. The number of farms over 30 acres stayed constant at 157,000.

41. Brown, *Social and Cultural History*, p. 21.

42. See, for example, Larkin, *Historical Dimensions*, pp. 628, 862. For a complete treatment of the clergy and laity in pre-Famine Ireland, see S. J. Connolly, *Priests and People in Pre-Famine Ireland*.

43. Larkin, *Historical Dimensions*, p. 866.

44. Brown, *Social and Cultural History*, p. 32.

45. Larkin, *Historical Dimensions*, p. 649.

46. Ibid., p. 640.

47. Brown, *Social and Cultural History*, p. 29.

48. Hilaire Belloc, *Europe and the Faith*.

49. J. Derek Holmes, *More Roman than Rome*. See also Edward Norman, *The English Catholic Church in the Nineteenth Century*.

50. Peter Comen, *Catholics and the Welfare State*, p. 12.

51. Ibid., p. 13.

52. Francis X. Murphy, "Vatican Politics: Structure and Function," p. 549, n. 17.

53. Whyte, *Western Democracies*, p. 58, contrasts the social positions taken by Catholics in the 1880s.

54. Francis X. Murphy, *The Papacy Today*, p. 34.

55. Gerard Noel, *The Anatomy of the Catholic Church*, pp. 36-37.

56. For a discussion of Catholic participation in this event, see Latreille et al., *Histoire*, pp. 489-94.

57. The key to Pius XI's world vision is furnished by two encyclicals, *Ubi arcano Dei* (December 23, 1922) and *Quas primas* (December 23, 1925). Murphy, "Vatican Politics," p. 550.

58. Whyte, *Western Democracies*, pp. 83-85.

59. For an excellent treatment of papal diplomacy during this period, see Anthony Rhodes, *The Vatican in the Age of the Dictators 1922-1945.* Rhodes also has an excellent bibliography, pp. 359-68.

60. Murphy, *Papacy Today*, p. 70.

61. Guenther Lewy, *The Catholic Church and Nazi Germany*, p. 341. Lewy's case against the German episcopate is particularly strong.

62. Rhodes, *The Vatican in the Age of Dictators*, pp. 337-52.

63. See Chapter 7, below. One recent controversy has concerned the "Simon Wiesenthal Center Investigative Report on SS Colonel Walter Rauff: The Church Connection 1943-47," which allegedly links Rauff with high church officials, especially Cardinal Ildefonso Schuster of Milan. For a discussion of the charges, see NCR, May 18, 1984. *L'Ossevatore Romano* praised Elie Wiesel's play "The Trial of God," a strong attack on Christian attitudes toward Jews throughout the ages, when it was staged in San Miniato, Italy. The artistic director was Father Marco Bongioanni, who had been secretary to Montini before he became Pope Paul VI. NYT, September 11, 1983.

64. Murphy, *Papacy Today*, p. 13.

65. Ibid., pp. 80-81.

66. Coleman, *Dutch Catholicism*, p. 147.

67. Gremillion, *Gospel*, pp. 387-416 for *Populorum*, pp. 427-44 for *Humanae*. Numerous Latin American and African texts and commentaries are also available for *Populorum*. Even the Brazilian military government of that time, the archetype of a national security state, made a major show of welcoming the encyclical. See Thomas C. Bruneau, *The Political Transformation of the Brazilian Catholic Church*, p. 180. For the politics behind the document, see Robert Blair Kaiser, *The Politics of Sex and Religion*.

68. For a review of two books on the 1978 papal elections, see Raymond A. Schroth, S.J., "The Vicars of Christ on Earth," *New York Times Book Review*, June 24, 1979. Schroth prefers Peter Hebblethwaite, *The Year of Three Popes* to Andrew M. Greeley, *The Making of the Popes 1978.* I am also indebted to a term paper by Santa Clara University students Gary Gardner and Dan Martinelli analyzing the two elections.

69. Hebblethwaite, *Year*, p. 141-43.

70. For the circumstances surrounding the founding of the PPI, see Luigi Sturzo, "My Political Vocation," pp. 537-40. For the emergence of Italian Christian Democracy, see, among others, Giuseppe Mammarella, *Italy After Fascism*; John N. Molony, *The Emergence of Political Catholicism in Italy*; Gianfranco Poggi, *Catholic Action in Italy*; Luigi Sturzo, *Church and State.* I am also indebted to a report by Santa Clara University students Fabio Aversa and Chris Smart for some of the ideas in this chapter.

71. Vaillancourt, *Papal Power*, p. 185. Vaillancourt makes the case against Pius XI in pp. 183-89.

72. Michael Patrick Fogarty, *Christian Democracy in Western Europe, 1820-1953*, pp. 272-75, 105. In this classic, Fogarty stressed the basic importance of social and economic groups to the political development of Christian Democracy. For example, the Young Christian Workers (YCW) began with Father (later Cardinal) Cardijn's work in Brussels in 1912. Christian Democratic political parties have always relied heavily on the support of such Catholic social, cultural, and economic organizations. Fogarty also stresses Christian Democratic appreciation for the moral character of political problems, and the fact that "Christian Democratic movements have become the chief supporters of a United Europe" (p. 105). The unification of Europe became particularly important in the ideology of the postwar German Christian Democrats.

Fogarty's definition of Christian Democracy (p. 5) is as follows: "It might be crudely defined as the movement of those laymen, engaged on their own responsibility in the solution of political, economic, and social problems in the light of Christian principles, who conclude from these principles and from practical experience that in the modern world democracy is normally best: that government, in the State, the firm, the local community, or the family, should be not merely of and for the people but also by them. More precisely: Christian Democracy is the movement of these who, having regard to the Christian revelation, accept the personalist and pluralist principles to be outlined in later chapters, and conclude from these that conditions in the modern world call for the widespread use of such techniques as political democracy, joint responsibility in industry, or the withering away of the patriarchal family."

73. For a brief discussion of these two ways of intervention in Italian politics, see P. A. Allum, *Italy*, pp. 104-107. Allum follows La Palombara in his exposition.

74. Whyte, *Western Democracies*, pp. 83-90, 95.

75. Fogarty, *Christian Democracy*, p. 8.

76. Bruneau, *Political Transformation*, pp. 19, 23.

CHAPTER 2

1. *NYT*, January 28, 1979. The pope's homily at this mass is available in John Eagleson and Philip Scharper, ed., *Puebla and Beyond*, pp. 72-76.

2. For an excellent brief analysis of the Medellín documents see Philip Berryman, "Latin American Liberation Theology," in Sergio Torres and John Eagleson, eds. *Theology in the Americas*, pp. 21-26.

3. Virgilio Elizondo, "The Pope's Introductory Address: Introduction and Commentary," in Eagleson and Scharper, eds., *Puebla*, p. 47. For texts of the Opening Address, see pp. 57-71, and the speech to the Indians of Oaxaca and Chiapas, see pp. 81-83.

4. Jon Sobrino, S.J., "The Significance of Puebla for the Catholic Church in Latin America," ibid., p. 297.

5. The conflict between the Pontifical Commission on Latin America

(CAL) and the bishops of CELAM had a long history. The Vatican Latin American expert Samorè was a member of the preparatory commission for CELAM I (1955) but could not compete for influence with such progressive bishops as Dom Helder Câmara of Brazil. Samorè then worked to establish CAL at the Vatican to control regional trends. Samorè became vice president and then president of CAL.

6. Smith, *Chile*, p. 121.

7. See Daniel H. Levine, *Religion and Politics in Latin America*, pp. 56-96.

8. Murphy, *Papacy Today*, p. 191. López's letter was addressed to an old crony, Archbishop Cabral Duarte of Aracajú, Brazil. The letter was dictated but, by Trujillo's own admission, not sent.

9. Scholars like Bruneau, *The Church in Brazil*, p. 10, strongly support the significance of the diocesan level. In this book Bruneau focuses on Brazilian beliefs and practices and links them to the institutional patterns he treated in his first book (1974). A study of religious beliefs should emphasize the diocesan level, while the national security concerns of this book tend to be decided by national episcopal conferences. Both Rome and the national conferences have strongly discouraged individual bishops from deviating either to the left or the right on issues like arms control.

The levels of urbanization, mobility, and communications also influence the relative significance of levels of ecclesiastical analysis. In many advanced countries the heads of local dioceses have become less influential. First, the church has reduced the size of its dioceses in an attempt to bring local bishops closer to their people. Second, increased mobility has diluted the influence of individual bishops. In the San Francisco Bay Area, for example, a family might live in one diocese (San Jose) with the husband working in a second (San Francisco) and the wife in a third (Oakland). In addition other American and foreign bishops visit the Bay Area to give lectures and meet with local Catholics. Third, the national secular media may provide most of the information for the average individual.

10. For example, see the *Los Angeles Times*, February 2, 1979.

11. NYT, February 18, 1979.

12. The political reality of episcopal appointments is more complex than the official lines of command, of course. For an examination of the Vatican from the perspective of "the U.S. management press," see the special "Forum" section by Arthur Jones and Peter Hebblethwaite in NCR, May 24, 1985.

13. Nichols, *The Politics of the Vatican*, p. 134. Nichols's later work (*The Pope's Divisions*) contains fine treatments of the papacy, pp. 107-30, and the Curia and Synod, pp. 153-73.

14. For the most damning analysis of papal disregard of the conclusions of the Synod, see Jan Grootaers and Joseph A. Selling, *The 1980 Synod of Bishops "On the Role of the Family": An Exposition of the Event and an Analysis of the Text*. Peter Hebblethwaite reviews the book and narrates the contro-

versy surrounding its introduction at a press conference in Rome, NCR, October 28, 1983.

15. See coverage by Hebblethwaite in NCR, October 14, 1983. Also NYT, October 20, 1983.

16. First published as *Rapporto Sulla Fede* (Milan: Edizioni Paoline, 1985). Brought to the United States by Ratzinger's ex-student Joseph Fessio, S.J., for his Ignatian Press as *The Ratzinger Report* (San Francisco, 1985). The original manuscript authorized by Ratzinger was in German. For a critical review, see Peter Steinfels's attack on the "hermeneutics of suspicion" in *America* (November 30, 1985): 388-90.

17. See NYT, especially December 7, 9, 1985. NCR, December 20, 1985, has "Synod wrap-up" pullout section which included the National Catholic News Service (hereafter NCNS) translation of the final document.

18. For articles on Bernardin, his background, and the challenges in Chicago, see D.J.R. Bruckner, "Chicago's Activist Cardinal," *New York Times Magazine*, May 1, 1983 (just before the final vote on the peace pastoral); and Bruce Buursma, "Riding High," *Chicago Tribune Magazine*, August 21, 1983 (first anniversary of Bernardin's appointment to Chicago).

19. Murphy, *Papacy Today*, p. 13.

20. Nichols, *Politics of the Vatican*, p. 174.

21. The technical title for this second-in-command is "Substitute and Secretary of the Cypher."

22. Nichols, *Politics of the Vatican*, p. 169.

23. Cited in ibid., pp. 182-83.

24. Ibid., p. 188.

25. NYT, August 11, 1979.

26. Norman B. Cooper, *Catholicism and the Franco Regime*, p. 41.

27. Interview with former staff member of the Secretariat for Non-Believers under König. Santa Clara, California, Spring 1979.

28. Technically, Casaroli became pro-secretary of state and pro-prefect of the Council for the Public Affairs of the Church because he was not yet a cardinal.

29. In April 1984 the Congregation for Sacraments and Divine Worship was split into the Congregation for Sacraments and the Congregation for Divine Worship, but given to the same pro-prefect (Mayer).

30. Other major changes were: Ryan for Agnelo Rossi (Evangelization), Hamer for Pironio (Religious), Etchegaray for Gantin (Justice and Peace), and Pironio for Opilio Rossi (Laity). Monsignor John Foley, editor of the Philadelphia *Catholic Standard and Times*, became president of the Pontifical Commission for Social Communications. The full list of curial appointments with analysis by Peter Hebblethwaite can be found in NCR, April 20, 1984. The story in NYT, April 10, 1984, features Gantin, Foley, and the absence of a replacement for Marcinkus at the Vatican Bank. The banking practices of this native of Cicero, Illinois, had come under international scrutiny. Foley had written an article on Glemp's proposed agricultural fund for a recent

issue of *L'Osservatore Romano*. In September 1986 Glemp announced the failure of agricultural fund talks with the Polish government.

31. The bishop in charge of the diocese or archdiocese is called an "ordinary." Some large dioceses and archdioceses have assistant bishops known as "auxiliaries."

32. See Reese, "The Selection of Bishops," pp. 65-72. This fine analysis, based partially on an interview with Archbishop Jadot, even contains a copy of the questionnaire sent out at the national level.

33. Nichols, *Politics of the Vatican*, p. 132. His *The Pope's Divisions*, pp. 153-60, provides an excellent description of the important curial positions for the formulation of foreign policy.

34. Murphy, *Papacy Today*, p. 12.

35. The papal diplomatic corps consists of nuncios (ambassadorial rank in a country that automatically recognizes the Vatican's representative as head of the diplomatic corps), pro-nuncios (ambassadorial rank), internuncios (head of a legation), apostolic delegates (papal representatives not diplomatically accredited), and legates (special representative for a particular purpose). Lower officials are counselor, auditor, secretary, and attaché (in descending order). Papal diplomats generally receive training at the Pontifical Ecclesiastical Academy in Rome, where Casaroli taught diplomacy from 1958-1961. The future secretary of state studied simultaneously at the Pontifical Ecclesiastical Academy and the Lateran University (Canon Law) following his ordination in 1937.

36. In a summary review, Francis X. Murphy praises Nichols's *The Pope's Divisions* along with works by Bull and Hofmann, while excoriating the "fabrications" of *The Vatican Connection, La Popessa*, and *Pontiff*. F. X. Murphy, "Vaticanology: Separating Fact and Fiction," in NCR, February 24, 1984. Andrew Greeley's critical review of Luigi Di Fonzo's *St. Peter's Banker* and Paul I. Murphy's *La Popessa* in NCR, May 6, 1983, pp. 22-23. Antoni Gronowicz, *God's Broker: The Life of Pope John Paul II* (New York: Richardson and Snyder, 1984) proved so creative that its publisher withdrew the book.

37. Hofmann, *O Vatican!*, p. 264. In his classic *Ideology and Organization in Communist China*, pp. 63-67, Franz Schurmann lists six major types of articles that appear in Chinese newspapers: policy decisions, concrete experiences in policy implementation, discussions of general principles, criticisms, propaganda, and public information.

38. AP from Rome, June 24, 1983, in NYT, June 25, 1983.

39. NYT, June 26, 1983. The reliance of newsmen on "unnamed Vatican sources" parallels similar practices in most great Western bureaucracies. These activities of "Vaticanologists" approximates even more closely those of Kreminologists and China watchers who seek to piece together an understanding of the inner workings of secretive bureaucracies. Like their colleagues in Moscow and Beijing, Vatican analysts attempt to supplement the reticence of official sources by carefully cultivating contacts within the bu-

reaucracy. The quality of contacts and the level of professional standards among such writers vary enormously.

40. NYT, January 24, November 30, 1984.

41. Bruneau lists four characteristics: the total coverage of territory, the all-inclusiveness of groups and sectors to be focused on, the comprehensive relationship of church and society, and the ecclesiastical employment of societal structures and groups to exercise influence. *Political Transformation*, pp. 11-12.

42. Ibid., pp. 16, 23.

43. In 1889 the much smaller Catholic Church of the United States had eighty-four bishops and 8,000 priests. Bruneau gives the Brazilian figures as thirteen bishops and 700 priests in 1889. Ibid., p. 25.

44. Bruneau, *The Church in Brazil*, pp. 17-18. For a detailed treatment of this period, see Bruneau, *Political Transformation*, pp. 32-51.

45. Bruneau, *The Church in Brazil*, p. 48.

46. For the political and religious aspects of this victory, see Smith, *Chile*, pp. 106-25.

47. Bruneau, *The Church in Brazil*, p. 51. For Bruneau's detailed treatment of 1950-1964, see Bruneau, *Political Transformation*, pp. 53-104.

48. Moises Sandoval, "Report from the Conference," in Eagleson and Scharper, eds., *Puebla*, pp. 28-43.

49. Bruneau, *The Church in Brazil*, p. 129, emphasizes the connection between official support and the success of the CEBs. The April position paper is summarized in ibid., pp. 78-79. At the 1985 Synod, CELAM Executive Secretary Bishop Castrillón Hoyos (Pereira, Colombia) attacked Liberation Theology, while Brazilians Bishop Ivo Lorscheiter and Cardinal Aloísio Lorscheider defended it. NYT, December 4, 1985.

50. Text in Eagleson and Scharper, eds., *Puebla*, pp. 122-285. Analysis by Jon Sobrino, S.J., pp. 289-309.

51. Bruneau, *The Church in Brazil*, p. 159. The epilogue is titled "The Implications of the Pope's Visit in Summer 1980."

52. David Gross, Patrick Murray, and Paul Piccone, in "Introduction" to special issue on Religion and Politics, *Telos* 58 (Winter 1983-84): 4.

53. *Decree on the Pastoral Office of the Bishops*, 38:1, in *The Teachings of the Second Vatican Council* (Westminster, Md.: Newman Press, 1966), p. 302.

54. *Ecclesiae Sanctae* (August 6, 1966), No. 41 (one), translated in Flannery, ed., *Vatican Council II*, p. 609.

55. Hebblethwaite in NCR, April 29, 1983, on Ratzinger's position at the meeting of European and American bishops in Rome in January 1983. Ratzinger also attacked the national conferences in a 1984 article in the Italian magazine *Jesus* and his book *Report on Faith* the following year.

56. The Canon Law Society of Great Britain and Ireland in association with The Canon Law Society of Australia and New Zealand and The Canadian Canon Law Society, trans., *The Code of Canon Law in English Translation*, pp. 80-82. One of the major complaints against American curial offi-

cials is that they apply the "perfect norms" of Roman law with Anglo-Saxon rigidity.

57. Coleman, *Dutch Catholicism*, pp. 11-17, 109.

58. Ibid., pp. 88, 45-48.

59. See the Conclusion for Chs. 6 and 7 in ibid., pp. 259-61.

60. Ibid., pp. 35-36.

61. Ibid., p. 281.

62. Ibid., p. 289.

63. NYT, May 14, 1985.

64. Coleman, *Dutch Catholicism*, pp. 270-71. Simonis had been notified privately of his appointment on June 19. Gijsen had so alienated his fellow bishops that after the Dutch Synod the pope decided that Gijsen should no longer be involved in the work of the episcopal committee evaluating seminary training.

65. Patricia Scharber Lefevere from Antwerp, NCR, July 29, 1983.

66. Coleman, *Dutch Catholicism*, p. 235.

67. Interviews in the Netherlands, June 1984.

68. Belgian's Cardinal Suenens recommended Jadot, an ex-Belgian missionary to Africa, to Paul VI.

69. *San Jose Mercury News*, August 13, 1978. For the procedure preceding the sending of the three names to Rome by the papal representatives, see Reese, "Selection of Bishops." Reese lists seven general actors of whom the "pronuncio, as long as he maintains the confidence of the Vatican, is the key figure in the process" (pp. 71-72).

70. Ibid., p. 70.

71. NYT, March 27, 1984, has a biographical article.

72. Law, a graduate of Harvard, had a strong record of ecumenical activities in Missouri. A bibliographic article can be found in NYT, January 25, 1984. Kenneth Briggs's interpretation of the two appointments can be found in the February 14 issue. Of course, the wide distribution of the questionnaire ensures that candidates hold an acceptable position on ordination of women, optional celibacy, birth control, and social justice—all concerns of the present pope. According to Archbishop Jadot (Reese, "Selection of Bishops," p. 68): "If the priest's first reaction to *Humanae Vitae* was negative—he just blew up—and later came to accept it, this would not be a major objection."

73. NCR, February 10, 1984.

74. NYT, August 15, 1984, March 14, 1984. The *Village Voice* called O'Connor "Irish America's answer to (black Muslim leader Louis) Farrakhan." Quoted in NCR, July 20, 1984.

75. NYT, July 17, 1983. Reese, "Selection of Bishops," p. 72, characterizes the present process as "not a democratic process but an institutional process that attempts through wide consultation to find a candidate who will be a pastoral bishop sincerely concerned about the good of the people in his diocese." The laity contributes most in reports on the needs of the diocese and the kind of bishop they would like. For a delightful evaluation

of the various candidates for the archbishopric of Dublin, see O'Leary, "The Battle for the Diocese of Dublin," pp. 10-19.

76. For example, a commission of the Congregation met with Schillebeeckx in December 1979 over what the commission viewed as ambiguities in his views on Christ's divinity, the virgin birth, the resurrection, and related questions. In June 1981 the Congregation released its report which cleared Schillebeeckx, but also asked him to publish the clarifications he gave to the commission at the meeting. NCNS from Vatican City, in *Hong Kong Sunday Examiner* (hereafter HKSE), July 24, 1981.

77. See, for example, reports on the 1983 *ad limina* visits in NYT, September 5, October 30, 1983.

78. The study is headed by Archbishop John Quinn of San Francisco, who was named a pontifical delegate who would report directly to John Paul rather than through the Congregation of Religious. While the Congregation supported the naming of Quinn, such committees can act as as "buffer" for local religious against bureaucratic harrassments. *National Catholic Reporter*, July 29, 1983.

79. NYT, June 24, 1983.

80. Jesuit anti nuclear activist Father Jack Morris termed the investigation and appointment an "humiliation" to Hunthausen. "Rome is trying to do here what they did in Holland," said Morris. NCR, December 13, 1985. The conservative *Wanderer* had campaigned against Hunthausen, but the move resulted in a major outcry within the archdiocese.

81. NCR, April 27, 1984.

82. NCR, March 21, 1986. Fr. Bernard Häring, who taught Curran at the Gregorian, seconded Curran at the Rome meeting.

83. For excerpts from Ratzinger's letter justifying the action, see NYT, August 19, 1986.

84. Excerpts in NYT, March 21, 1985. Analysis by Hebblethwaite in NCR, May 17, 1985.

85. NYT, June 3, 1985. The conservative Cardinal Sales said, "Anyone who is not satisfied can leave the church."

86. NYT, March 17, April 1, 1986. NCR, March 28, 1986. The Brazilian bishops also gave input on political conditions in their country for the visit of Brazilian President José Sarney to John Paul II in July. For the pope's mediation between the CNBB and the government on agrarian land reform, see NYT, July 11, 1986.

87. NCR, November 4, 1983.

88. See Kelly, *Battle for the American Church*, and *The New Biblical Theorists*.

89. Coleman, *Dutch Catholicism*, p. 101.

90. Hofmann, *O Vatican!*, p. 209; see especially pp. 208-42.

91. The Dutch anthropologist Mart Bax has employed this friction as the primary variable in explaining sociocultural change in southern Dutch society. Whether or not his thesis will bear that much weight, it is true that these "competitors for the same clientele" have lined up on the opposite

sides of basic issues in this "politico-religious process." Bax connects the process to the long-lasting power struggle between the developing nation states and Rome." Mart Bax, "Religious Leadership and Social-Cultural Change in Southern-Dutch Society; The Dialects of a Politico-Religious Process," paper presented at Symposium on "Leadership and Social Change" of the XIth International Congress of Anthropological and Ethnological Sciences, Vancouver, August 20-25, 1983.

92. Cooper, *Franco*, p. 20.

93. For an analysis of this period see ibid., pp. 5-15, 20-23.

94. Cited in Hofmann, *O Vatican!*, p. 233.

95. Cooper remarks: "When one looks at the spectacular advance of Opus Dei from 1939 to 1964 one is once again struck by the way in which it took the organizations left behind by its defeated enemies in 1939, and distorted and inverted them." Cooper, *Franco*, pp. 27-28.

96. Antoniutti had been nuncio in Madrid. Hofmann, *O Vatican!*, pp. 229-30, relates an interview with Antoniutti's successor, Riberi (the ex-nuncio to China), in which Riberi cautioned Hofmann that the serving nun was an Opus member. Riberi replaced those assistants hired by Antoniutti.

97. The documents are summarized in ibid., pp 239-40. The election of John Paul, of course, influenced curial behavior. Baggio and others became more sympathetic to Opus concerns because they perceived the pope as friendly to the organization.

98. NCNS from Vatican City, in HKSE, September 10, 1982.

99. HKSE, Dec. 12, 1982.

100. Interview with Otto Maduro, New York City, January 1983, in *Telos* 58 (Winter 1983-84): 194-95.

101. Cooper, *Franco*, pp. 21-22.

102. Those philosophers on the "Not to be lent" shelves in the University's main library include Spinosa, Kant, Hegel, Kierkegaard, Nietzsche, Heidegger, Mill, and William James. Henry Kamm, "The Secret World of Opus Dei," *New York Times Magazine*, January 8, 1984. With the exception of Kamm's visit to Navarre, the article is a fine example of how little information a disciplined organization can give the media if it so chooses. Kamm had to wait nearly one year for his interview with del Portillo.

103. Interview by José Casanova, New York City, January 1983, in *Telos* 58 (Winter 1983-84): 195.

104. Cooper says the Jesuits in Spain "were now largely allied with the progressives," and mentions the cases of Fathers José Diez-Alegria and Bolado. Bolado was beaten up by rightists after a demonstration in the Barcelona cathedral. *Franco*, p. 38.

105. The Pontifical Gregorian University, founded by Gregory XIII in 1582, is the church's foremost university and key Jesuit institution in Rome. In addition, the Jesuits direct the highly respected Pontifical Biblical and Oriental Institutes, the Institute for Marxist Studies, Vatican Observatory, *Civiltà Cattolica*, and Vatican Radio.

106. Cited in Hofmann, *O Vatican!*, p. 218.

107. Cited in ibid., p. 220. Hofmann recounts the Diez-Alegria and Hebblethwaite cases on the preceding page.

108. NCNS from Rome, in HKSE, November 20, 1981. The complete text of the papal letter to Arrupe (October 5, 1981) is available in the same issue. The Jesuit Press Office released the letter on October 23.

109. The letter was dated October 27, 1981, and not released to the public. It was later leaked and appeared in the Italian Catholic monthly *Il Regno* in January 1982. NCNS from Bologna, in HKSE, December 3, 1982.

110. NCNS from Cincinatti, Ohio, in HKSE, February 19, 1982.

111. NYT, August 8, 1983, September 14, 1983.

112. The four general assistants did include an American, John O'Callaghan. The others were Larraín Juan Ochagavia (Chilean provincial when Pinochet took over), Michael Amaladoss (India) and Simon Dacloux (Belgium). The intervention of the papal delegate Archbishop Vincenzo Fagiolo did not prevent the Franciscans (Order of Friars Minor) from reelecting a progressive Californian, Father John Vaughan, as their minister general on May 25, 1985.

113. One delegate to the General Congregation described Kolvenbach as a man like Arrupe, who "knew where the Jesuits should go," but a better technical administrator.

114. Cited in NCR, December 21, 1984. The Central American Jesuit superior Peter Marchetti "happened" to be traveling in Ireland and unavailable for comment.

115. Paul VI opened Medellín (1968) and thus sanctioned its work, but his personal attendance did not change its outcome as John Paul II's did at Puebla.

116. Ballestrero, a member of the Congregation of Religious and Secular Institutes, is archbishop of Turin.

117. E. J. Dionne, Jr., in *New York Times Magazine*, May 12, 1985.

118. James Hitchcock states the conservative critique of what is perceived as the reinforcing nature of the ills of American society, Catholic progressivism, and the American Jesuits. *The Pope and the Jesuits.* This book, like his *Catholicism and Modernity*, attempts to convince by compiling many of what Hitchcock feels are outrageous examples. While recent papal concerns have centered on progressive and radical Jesuits, the order has also provided some eminent conservatives and reactionaries. In the 1970s some of the Spanish Jesuits petitioned Rome to form a traditionalist group.

119. MacEoin, *The Inner Elite*, p. 187, says "Benelli was given the primary credit for resolving one of the most serious crises the church has faced since Vatican II." One liberal Jesuit ex-Curia official listed Benelli's "good deeds" as his fight against Franco over Spanish episcopal appointments, his stand against older conservative Spanish Jesuits being allowed to form a seperate society, his resistance to expanded prerogatives for Opus Dei, and his attempts to increase curial efficiency by measures like banning two persons

from the same village from serving in the same secretariat or congregation. Interview, Santa Clara, California, February 1985.

120. Cooper, *Franco*, p. 41.

121. Levine, *Venezuela and Colombia*, p. 253.

CHAPTER 3

1. NYT, March 5, 1983.

2. This took place in late October 1982. NYT, December 3, 1982. The other priests were Foreign Minister D'Escoto, a Maryknoll priest; Jesuit Fernando Cardenal, then leader of the Sandinista youth movement; diocesan priest Edgar Parrales, ambassador to the OAS, and Alvaro Arquello Hurtado, representative of the clergy on the Council of State.

3. AP from Managua, March 4, 1983, in NYT, March 5, 1983.

4. NYT, March 5, 1983.

5. *Church and Politics in Chile*, Chs. 7 and 8.

6. Johnson, *Just War Tradition and the Restraint of War*, p. 257n. This and Johnson's earlier *Ideology, Reason, and the Limitation of War* provide superb treatments of the relationship of ideology to the development of the just war tradition.

7. Dulles, *Models*. Dulles's use of "paradigm" comes from T. S. Kuhn, *The Structure of Scientific Revolutions*, in which the shift of scientific paradigms begot scientific revolutions. Among those cited on the theological use of models, I. T. Ramsey receives prominence. In general, "paradigm" tends to denote a model receiving predominant acceptance.

8. In addition to *Models*, see Dulles, *The Catholicity of the Church*.

9. *De controversus*, tom. 2, liber 3, *De ecclesia militante*, cap. 2, "De definitione Ecclesiae" (Naples: Guiliano, 1857), vol. 2, p. 75, cited in Dulles, *Models*, p. 14.

10. Pope Pius XII, *The Mystical Body of Christ*.

11. Gremillion, *Gospel*, pp. 235-36.

12. Garaudy, *From Anathema to Dialogue*.

13. For a summary of the discussions, see Hebblethwaite, *The Christian-Marxist Dialogue and Beyond*, pp. 17-37. Hebblethwaite reported on the dialogues for *The Month*. See also Arthur F. McGovern, *Marxism*, pp. 113-15.

14. Wolfe is commenting on an article by the Italian Communist Marzani in which Marzani claimed John Paul II for the political left. Wolfe attributes the Vatican's traditionally stronger attack on leftist errors to four historical causes: the class background of ecclesiastical leaders; early radical Socialism's direct attack on the church; the amelioration of Capitalism; and the "softening" of the condemnation of absolute Liberalism at the local level. Wolfe, "The Vatican as Nobody's Ally," *This World*, No. 4 (Winter 1983): 80-81. *This World* is published by AEI and the Institute for Educational Affairs. Michael Novak is on the Editorial Board, and the Advisory Board includes Peter Berger, Paul Ramsey, and George Will.

15. Yves Congar, *Challenge to the Church*, pp. 15, 16.

16. Ibid., pp. 77-79.

17. The papal letters are in ibid., pp. 79-81. Bishop Adam is cited on p. 23. For the ordinations, see *La Croix*, August 20, 1976.

18. Traditionalists won a partial liturgical victory in October 1984 when John Paul II approved limited use of the Tridentine mass, though not in parish churches. For the ecclesiastical politics of the decision, see Hebblethwaite in the NCR, December 21, 1984.

19. NCNS from Rome, in HKSE, May 13, 1983.

20. See Congar, *Lefebvre*, p. 91.

21. NCNS from Montevideo, in HKSE, September 19, 1980.

22. Those interested in reading further about the exploits of the TFP should see Antonio Augusto Borelli Machado et al., *Tradition Family Property*.

23. Smith, *Chile*, p. 256, n. 58.

24. Jürgen Moltmann and Johannes B. Metz have been the major figures in the development of European political theology. For an excellent short discussion of their work and its relation to Liberation Theology, see John A. Coleman, *An American Strategic Theology*, pp. 59-70.

25. "Speaking Out After a Long Silence," complete text in NCR, October 11, 1985.

26. NCNS from London, in HKSE, March 25, 1983.

27. NYT, October 31, 1983.

28. NCR, August 12, 1983.

29. Report of an interview by Patricia Scharber Lefever, in NCR, August 12, 1983.

30. Philip Berryman, "Latin American Liberation Theology," in Torres and Engleson, *Theology in the Americas*, p. 21. Cardinal Ratzinger, however, emphasizes the European roots (Bultmann, Marxism) of Liberation Theology. See Ratzinger's address in 30 *Giorni* (March 1984), translated in *Catholicism in Crisis* (September 1984): 37-41.

31. Alberto Methol Ferre, *Iglesia y sociedad opulenta: Una crítica a Suenens desde América latina* [Church and Opulent Society: A Critique of Suenens from Latin America], special supplement to *Vespera* (September 1969).

32. Berryman, "Liberation Theology," p. 77, n. 2. Paulo Freire, *Pedagogy of the Oppressed*.

33. See the bibliographical article by Gonzalo Arroyo, "Pensiamento latino-americano sobre subdesarollo y dependencia," *Mesaje* (October 1968), pp. 516-17.

34. Gustavo Gutiérrez, *A Theology of Liberation*. The most widely read and most influential single essay is Gustavo Gutiérrez, "Notes for a Theology of Liberation." For a discussion of other authors like Bonino, Comblin, Segundo, Dussel, and Miranda, see Berryman, "Liberation Theology," pp. 54-75. For the experience of Christian guerrillas, see Philip Berryman, "Ca-

milo Torres, Revolutionay-Theologian." Camilo Torres, *Cristianismo y revolu-cion.* Nestor Paz, *My Life for My Friends: The Diary of Nestor Paz, Christian.*

35. "Trip to New York," in Ernesto Cardenal, *Zero Hour.* See also Ernesto Cardenal, *In Cuba,* and *The Gospel in Solentiname.*

36. Steven F. White, ed. *Poets of Nicaragua: A Bilingual Anthology, 1918-1979,* p. 155. White (p. 141) calls Cardenal "the main proponent of *la poesía exteriorista* which is, in his [Cardenal's] words, 'the only poetry that can express Latin American reality, reach the people, and be revolutionary.' "

37. Cited in Kim Chi Ha, *The Gold-Crowned Jesus and Other Writings,* p. xxvi.

38. Ibid., p. xxvii.

39. Ibid., pp. 26-27.

40. The Tonghak ("Eastern Learning") is compared to the Chinese Taiping in John K. Fairbank, Edwin O, Reischauer, and Albert M. Craig, *East Asia: The Modern Transformation,* pp. 463-64.

41. Peter Walshe, *Church Versus State in South Africa,* pp. 136-37.

42. Cited in Bernard Hassan, "Orbis Books," p. 55.

43. Charges by *The Mindszenty Report,* and both Buckley and Novak are cited in NCR, April 3, 1981. The governing councils of the Maryknoll missionaries strongly reaffirmed their dedication to social justice during fall 1984 in the two-month separate (priests and brothers, nuns) sessions which are convoked every six years. NCCB president Bishop Malone gave the order the firm backing of the American bishops in his opening address. NYT, December 10, 1984.

44. Torres and Eagleson, *Theology in the Americas,* ix-xxviii. Robert Mc-Alfee Brown, *Theology in a New Key,* and Gustavo Gutiérrez.

45. Eagleson and Scharper, *Puebla and Beyond,* pp. 330-46.

46. Marie Augusta Neal, *The Socio-Theology of Letting Go.*

47. Torres and Eagleson, *Theology in the Americas,* p. 84. Robert N. Bellah, *The Broken Covenant.*

48. The release was originally planned for January 5, but it was leaked at New Year's. The chairman of the eight-bishop commission was Bishop Remi De Roo of Victoria, British Columbia. Cardinal Carter of Toronto commented that "getting into the details of economic policy is, in my opinion, risky." NYT, January 5, 1983.

49. NCNS from Edmonton, Alberta, in HKSE, October 2, 1981.

50. *Washington Post,* January 30, 1983.

51. "It takes a Catholic to notice the ideas of association, community and cooperation which they expertly practiced but never mentioned." Interview in *New Perspectives* 2 (Summer 1985): 21.

52. Jacques Maritain, *The Peasant of the Garonne: An Old Layman Questions Himself About the Present Times* (New York: Holt, Rinehart and Winston, 1968).

53. Michael Novak, *Toward a Theology of the Corporation,* and *The Spirit of Democratic Capitalism.*

54. Novak, *Corporation*, pp. 23, 33.

55. Philip F. Lawler, "Michael Novak's Commercial Republic," *The American Spectator* 15 (October 1982): 13. This whole argument relates very closesly to Peter Berger's *Sacred Canopy* and Robert Bellah's *Civil Religion*.

56. Michael Novak, "Why Latin America is Poor," p. 67.

57. *Catholicism in Crisis* (September 1983): 41.

58. The letter constitutes the entire issue of *Origins* 14 (November 15, 1984). The NYT, November 12, 1984 devotes all of page 14 to excerpts. The entire letter was also an insert in NCR, November 23, 1984.

59. Short preliminary statement in *Origins*, November 15, 1984, p. 1. Summary in NYT, November 12, 1984. The persons who appeared before the committee are listed as Appendix I to the first draft.

60. Summary in NYT, November 12, 1984.

61. Eugene Kennedy, "America's Activist Bishops: Examining Capitalism," *New York Times Magazine*, August 12, 1984, p. 16. For the background of committee members, see NYT, November 12, 1984.

62. See NYT, November 15, 1984, for Kirkland and episcopal reaction. The strongest criticism came from Archbishop Hannan of New Orleans who argued that the draft "yields too much to government," while placing too little emphasis on private endeavors to fight poverty.

63. For excerpts and analysis, see NYT, November 7, 1984. The entire text is *Catholicism in Crisis* 2 (November 1984).

64. Simon, Luce, Grace, Haig, and CIA Director William E. Casey are all members of the Sovereign Military Order of Malta (SMOM), the Catholic charitable organization. For a report on the conservative contacts of SMOM members, the Contra aid issue, and the SMOM induction of Cardinal Bernard Law and 1982 New York candidate for governor, convert Lewis E. Lehrman, see Martin A. Lee and Kevin Coogan's report in NCR May 23, 1986. Cardinal John O'Connor is "Grand Protector and Spiritual Advisor" of the American chapter.

65. NYT, November 20, 1984.

66. Kennedy, "Examining Capitalism," p. 17.

67. One of the better offerings is J. Brian Benestad, *The Pursuit of a Just Social Order: Policy Statements of the U.S. Catholic Bishops 1966-80*, which takes the position that recent episcopal statements have tended to devalue evangelization and education as a means of pursuing justice.

68. For the comments of Weakland and Novak regarding the delay, see NYT, April 3, 1985. On the second draft and the bishops' reactions, see NYT, October 7, November 14, 1985.

69. NCR, June 6, 1986.

70. The nineteenth-century sociologist Max Weber placed the Catholic Church among those "distinctly developed and quantitatively large bureaucracies." H. H. Gerth and C. Wright Mills, eds., *From Max Weber*, p. 204.

71. Troeltsch, *Social Teaching*, esp. Vol. I, pp. 331-43. See also Ch. 1, above.

72. See, for example, Bruneau, *The Church in Brazil*, pp. 21-45.

73. See Maurice Meisner, "Leninism and Maoism: Some Populist Perspectives on Marxist-Leninism in China."

74. One liberal Jesuit ex-Curia official said that in the early 1970s he used to stress to Dutch ecclesiastics that Vatican conservatives wanted verbal compliance above all else. Interview, Santa Clara University, February 1985. Direct challenges in the *New York Times* like those of Küng and the American Catholics for Free Choice almost guarantees a curial response. Archbishops Bernardin and O'Connor, whose differing positions will be contrasted below in the analysis of the peace pastoral and the 1984 American presidential campaign, appeared together on WPIX-TV in New York on March 3, 1985. Their joint appearance featured praise of each other's virtues coupled with denunciation of each other's ecclesiastical critics. What is good Catholic episcopal style can be dreadfully boring television. Their joint appearance before Congress to present USCC criticism of the MX, of course, constituted effective political lobbying.

CHAPTER 4

1. NYT, November 10, 1982. More details are available in NCNS from Santiago de Compostela, in HKSE, November 26, 1982.

2. See, for example, Juan J. Linz, "Religion and Politics in Spain."

3. The Constitution of December 1978 recognized a right to divorce but provided no specific legislation. When the parliament debated a divorce bill in early 1981, the 21-member Permanent Commission of the Spanish Bishops' Conference denounced the legislation as "a grave threat to the stability of matrimonial bonds." The Christian Democratic factions associated with the 15-party coalition of the UCD attempted to strengthen the bill, but failed. After passage of the legislation, the bishops declared that Catholics could not in conscience avail themselves of the new law. NCNS from Madrid, in HKSE, March 13, 1981. NCNS from Madrid, in HKSE, July 24, 1981.

4. NCNS from Madrid, in HKSE, January 5, 1979.

5. NCNS from Madrid, in HKSE, February 2, 1979.

6. CSM, September 30, 1983.

7. These organizers had met with their French counterparts in Paris in September, and hoped to duplicate the French victory discussed in the following section. NYT, November 19, 1984. As in France, the Catholic educational system maintains a traditional constituency among many nonpracticing Catholics and even non-Catholics in a country where 36-37 percent of all pupils attend private schools with the figure rising to 50 percent for secondary pupils. Groups like the Spanish Federation of Clergy in Education (FERE) oppose the law principally because they fear loss of administrative

autonomy. Jesuit priest Santiago Martín Jiménez, secretary general of FERE, states that the proposed regulations would "take away the framework for truly Christian centers [schools]." Jiménez fears that "in the long run the Christian character will deteriorate because of the lack of a legal framework." Pond, "Spain settles into secular politics," CSM, September 12, 1984.

8. NCR, November 4, 1983.

9. Although 93 percent of private school students attend Catholic institutions, there are also 50 Jewish schools with 13,000 pupils. In addition, there are Protestant and secular private schools. Private schools enroll 17 percent of the primary and secondary students in France.

10. See NYT, December 21, 1983; March 5, 1984; June 25, 1984. The number of demonstrators follow police estimates. Organizers of the rallies claimed 800,000 for Versailles and 1.5 million for Paris.

11. NYT, April 19, 1984.

12. Jean-Pierre Chevènement, the new minister of education, saved Mitterand's face by "issuing statements so ambiguous that the proponents of public schools say the government remains faithful to its proclaimed ideals while the pro-private school people were happy because they had, in fact, won the day." CSM, October 4, 1984.

13. Reported in *America* 151 (August 25, 1984): 63.

14. "Social science research and surveys conducted at election time show that no variable accounts better for French political attitudes than religious integration." Annick Percheron, "Religious Acculturation and Political Socialization in France," in Suzanne Berger, ed., *Religion in Western European Politics*, p. 8. Renaud Dulong and Jean-Marie Donegani also cite this factor in their own analysis contained in the same volume. For a full discussion, see Guy Michelat and Michel Simon, *Classe, religion et comportement politique*.

15. CSM, March 9, 1984.

16. *"Le marxisme, l'homme et la foi chrétienne"* also warns Catholics of the dangers of accepting Marxism as a whole. The Spanish bishops have taken a similar line with the Italian bishops much more negative.

17. Antonio da Silva Rego, "Portugal," in Fitzsimmons, *Western Democracies*, pp. 162-66.

18. The Spanish case is best documented in Enrique Miret Magdalena, *La Revolución de lo Religión* (Madrid: Ediciónes Paulinas, 1976). Miret Magdalena is the former president of Acción Católica.

19. NYT, October 8, 1985, February 18, 1986.

20. NCNS from Lisbon, in HKSE, August 29, 1980.

21. For the bargaining to overcome the threat of a Greek veto, see NYT, March 30, 1985.

22. Other Western leaders have linked Spain's EEC membership with remaining in NATO. One Spanish magazine quoted Germany's Kohl as tell-

ing Spanish journalists that, "You can't hope to sell olives in the European market and not contribute to defense." NYT, June 13, 1984.

23. Spanish noun for "a general sense of letdown whose translation falls somewhere between the mistyness of 'disenchantment' and the hard edge of 'disillusionment.' " New York Times, June 26, 1984.

24. The remaining ballots were blank or invalid. See NYT, March 13, 1986, for Spanish and American reaction. The referendum did list three conditions under which Spain would remain in NATO: a continued ban on nuclear weapons, the maintenance of the Spanish military outside NATO's command structure, and a cutback in American troops stationed in Spain.

25. Other observers, however, deny that Italian politics lends itself to such an easy "rational" solution. Luigi Giorgio Barzini explains the progressive polarization of the political spectrum in terms of Italy's traditional political culture. While Italian cultural unity is strong, political unity is recent and weak. In addition to the ancient rivalry between North and South, Italians have traditionally identified with their families, regions, and special groups like the Catholic Church, the Freemasons, and the Mafia. Barzini proposes the thesis that the people have traditionally alternated between the church power (medieval Guelphs, contemporary Christian Democrats) and the antichurch power (medieval Ghibellines, contemporary Communists) to preserve their own local autonomy. Barzini, The Italians, pp. 333-36.

26. Berlinguer's letter, which also appeared in Renascita, is summarized the Washington Post, October 14, 1977.

27. Giovanni Guareschi, The Little World of Don Camillo, and numerous other collections of these short stories.

28. Vaillancourt, Papal Power, pp. 188-89. Paul's links to Christian Democracy are central to the thesis of this book.

29. NYT, May 14, 1978. The central photo on the front page shows Paul VI greeting Moro's sister after the funeral mass. Paul's decision to celebrate the mass surprised many since the Moro family had wanted to keep all ceremonies private.

30. NCNS from Rome, in HKSE, February 27, 1981.

31. NCNS from Rome, in HKSE, January 5, 1981.

32. John Paul warned that Italy was suffering from "the process of de-Christianization." For the talk and political reaction, NYT, April 13, 1985.

33. NYT, February 19, 1984. For conservative criticism of the concordat, see Roberto de Mattei, L'Italia cattolica e il Nuovo Concordato-Può un Cattolico preferire lo Stato ateo? (Rome, 1985). The concordat still did not go far enough for the Italian Radical Party. Deputy Massimo Theodori criticized remaining privileges in education, state subsidies, and financial dealings. The Protestant Waldensian weekly editorialized in February 1984: "The Constantinian principle of integration of church and state authority remains intact: Under the new Concordat the state still underwrites the cost of Catholic ministrations . . . and the state still authorizes one denomination—the

Catholic Church—to teach religion in public school." Both quoted in Pond, "Italy loosens some church-state ties," CSM, September 11, 1984.

34. NCNS from Bergamo, in HKSE, May 22, 1981. The preceding Christmas Cardinal Benelli of Florence had blasted the parliament for passing the 1978 law. Judge Piero Pirovano, acting as a private citizen, brought criminal charges of defamation against Benelli, but they were dismissed. When Cardinal Ursi of Naples preached against the abortion law at the annual liquification of St. Januarius' blood in 1980, the Radical Party protested sharply.

35. However, despite recent changes in the political role of the Italian Catholic Church, loss of support by the DC, and the continued secularization of Italian society, Douglas Wertman predicts that religion will continue "as the single most important base of DC electoral support." Douglas A. Wertman, "The Catholic Church and Italian Politics: The Impact of Secularization," in Berger, ed., *Religion*, p. 105.

36. NCNS from Bagheria, Sicily, in HKSE, November 12, 1982.

37. NYT, June 29, 1983. Still, the PSI had hoped for a much more substantial victory. The biggest winner in the 1983 election, therefore, was the small Republican Party, which increased its vote from 3 to 5.1 percent. The Republicans benefit from ex-prime minister Spadolini's leadership and the combination of liberal stands on civic and human rights with conservative economic policy.

38. NYT, August 5, 1983.

39. Italian Catholics did hold a peace march in Milan on New Year's Eve of 1982. In their announcement of the march, Bishop Betazzi, president of Pax Christi International, and Bishop Dante Bernini, president of the Commission for Justice and Peace of the Italian Bishops' Conference, referred to the deliberations of the NCCB: "We express our solidarity with the American bishops who have denounced the immorality of the unrestrained arms race, and we share the perplexity of those who fear the start of atomic rearmament in Europe with the installation of missiles in Comiso as well as the exploitation the South." AP from Rome, November 30, 1982, in NYT, December 1, 1982. The French episcopate also has a tradition of protest against arms sales and weapons testing. For example, in 1973 Cardinal Jean Guyot joined Bishop Guy-Marie Riobé and other prelates in condemning France's program of nuclear testing.

40. NYT, April 25, 1983.

41. The two parties formed a coalition that lasted until 1966. Government jobs are still distributed according to "Proporz," a system which allocates positions according to party. For example, the Creditanstalt-Bankverein is controlled by members of the People's Party, while Socialists direct Österreichische Länderbank. CSM, May 1, 1984.

42. The Schmidt government manifested its annoyance by making it very difficult to arrange a meeting between John Paul and the German leader on the pope's trip to the country in November 1980. Protestants complained about the overemphasis on the Catholic South in the papal itin-

erary. Even a special German-language edition of *L'Osservatore Romano* re-marked, "flatly stated, the atmosphere is typical of weather in November, cloudy and miserable."

43. Ratzinger, a student of Karl Rahner, was theological adviser to the liberal Cardinal Joseph Frings at Vatican II. Ratzinger taught theology until 1977. In trying to account for the disparity between the cardinal's past liberal reputation in Germany and his present activities as prefect of the CDF, Father Nobert Greinacher, Tübingen professor of practical theology and defender of his colleague Hans Küng, has commented: "I think in Ratzinger's life there was a turning point. It was, I think, in 1968 at the time of the Vietnam war and student protests. I think it was at the Congress of Catholic Students. One of his doctoral students attacked him very, very sharply, publicly, on the question of political activity by students, by the Catholic community and by the Catholic church." Interviewed in NCR, September 14, 1984. Another German church analyst pointed out that Ratzinger had already had conflicts with progressive clergy and laity in Munich. "But we German Catholics still think of him in connection with his more moderate past." Interview, Santa Clara University, February 1985.

44. Translated in *Christianity in Crisis* (April 1983): 20. Wolfgang Huber, "The Churches and the Debate on Nuclear Weapons and Disarmament in the Federal Republic of Germany," paper presented to the conference on The Churches' Influence on Disarmament Decisions in East and West, Evanston, Illinois, October 2-4, 1984, pp. 22-24, notes "a considerable progress in Catholic thought and judgment" between the November 1981 statement and the episcopal letter of June 1983 (see Ch. 8, below). Regardless of this progress, says Huber, "The statements issued by the Roman Catholic church in the FRG are less clear than some of the Protestant declarations—and far less so than the Pastoral Letter of the Catholic Bishops' Conference in the United States."

45. CSM, March 29, 1983.

46. NCR, September 14, 1984.

47. There is a fine three-column photo of Kerchschläger, König, and John Paul in the September 11, 1983 NYT. The bitterness of Austrian politics during the 1920s and 1930s was recalled by the Socialist youth in their criticism of John Paul's visit to Vienna in September 1983. Kreisky ordered a Socialist newspaper to withdraw its characterization of a previous prelate as an "old gagster." Kerchschläger then encouraged both sides to cool down.

48. Erwin Kleine, "Germany," in Fitzsimmons, *Western Europe*, p. 29.

49. Erika Weinzierl, "Austria," in ibid., p. 67.

50. Whyte, *Western Democracies*, p. 50-51.

51. Kleine, "Germany," in Fitzsimmons, *Western Europe*, pp. 43-44, 56.

52. Weinzierl, "Austria," in ibid., p. 76.

53. NYT, April 5, 1983. Lafontaine, the forty-one-year-old mayor of Saar-

brucken, led his party to an unexpected clear majority in Saarland state elections in March 1985. The Greens were excluded.

54. Quoted in James M. Markham, "Bonn Socialists Flirting With NATO," NYT, March 12, 1984.

55. NYT, October 21, 1983.

56. NYT, June 21, 1984.

57. Of the 18 to 20-year-olds, 41 percent voted SPD, and 38 percent for the CDU. NYT, August 14, 1983.

58. NYT, May 24, 1984.

59. NYT, August 14, 1983.

60. Jean Delfosse, "Belgium," in Fitzsimmons, *Western Europe*, p. 243.

61. Whyte, *Western Democracies*, p. 39.

62. Delfosse, "Belgium," in Fitzsimmons, *Western Europe*, p. 254.

63. Whyte, *Western Democracies*, p. 73.

64. Delfosse, "Belgium," in Fitzsimmons, *Western Europe*, p. 264. The Louvain controversy is narrated on pp. 261-66.

65. For an analysis of Belgian peace movements, see A. M. Vincke-Hendrick, "Les Mouvements de Paix en Belgique," *The Peace Movements* (Rome: Research Center of F.I.U.C., n.d.), pp. 224-43. This is a collection of papers presented at a conference of the same name sponsored by the International Federation of Catholic Universities (F.I.U.C.) and the Club of Rome, Salzburg, February 18-21, 1983.

66. CSM, March 18, 1985.

67. NYT, October 14, 1985.

68. Herman Bakvis, *Catholic Power in the Netherlands*, p. 59.

69. Cited in ibid., p. 135.

70. Bakvis presents tables for the elections of 1967, 1971, 1972, and 1977 in ibid., pp. 168-69.

71. NYT, September 9, 1982.

72. The formation of the coalition is reported in NYT, October 20, 1982.

73. NYT, June 3, 1984.

74. Bakvis, *Netherlands*, p. 129.

75. Hylke Tromp, "Pacifism in the Netherlands," *The Peace Movements*, p. 246.

76. The French Bishop Theas, who had been a German prisoner during World War II, started Pax Christi following that war to bring about peace and reconciliation between France and Germany. Pope Pius XII gave the movement his full approval as an international Catholic peace movement in 1952. Its presidents since then have been Cardinal Feltin (1952-1965), Cardinal Alfrink (1965-1978), Bishop Betazzi (1978-1985), and Cardinal Konig (1985-). Cardinal Konig retired as archbishop of Vienna in September 1986. Pax Christi became increasingly concerned with global justice and East-West relations during the 1960s.

77. Koos van der Bruggen, "Politics and Ethics of the Dutch Peace Movements," *The Peace Movements*, p. 261.

78. IKV is not a membership organization, with only about 25 members, the official representatives of the nine participating churches, as official members. The other member bodies are: Reformed Churches in the Netherlands (870,000); Evangelical-Lutheran Church (32,000); Mennonite Brotherhood (22,000); Remonstrant Brotherhood (12,000); Old Catholic Church (6,000); Moravian Church (3,000); and Quakers (150). Laurens Hogebrink, "The Churches in the Netherlands and Nuclear Disarmament," paper presented to consultation on The Churches' Influence on Disarmament in East and West, Evanston, Illinois, October 2-4, 1984.

79. Tromp, "Pacifism," *The Peace Movements*, pp. 248-50.

80. Hogebrink (n. 78, above, pp. 41-42) attributes Pax Christi's hesitancy about the IKV campaign to "the increasingly critical position of the bishops in the U.S.A., who in their pastoral letter, 'To Live in Christ Jesus' (late 1976), went much further than the Dutch bishops in condemning nuclear deterrence."

81. NYT, June 2, 1984.

82. NYT, June 14, 1984.

83. NYT, June 2, 1984.

84. NYT, September 11, 1983.

85. Ibid.

86. Results of poll by European newspapers, March 13–April 14, reported in NYT, May 28-29, 1984. The low opinion of Britain partially reflects anger at Mrs. Thatcher's recalcitrance in the 1983-1984 EEC negotiations.

87. Of the persons questioned, 87 percent could locate themselves on the scale. Of those, 65 percent picked one of the four central points, with 41 percent choosing the two points closest to the center. NYT, March 23, 1984.

88. CSM, December 12, 1983. The minister was Jean-Pierre Cot.

89. CSM, October 14, 1983.

90. The exact meaning of the passage is not clear. However, the current vicar of Madrid, Father José Martín Patino, characterizes the relationship as not "almost total separation of church and state on the French model," but "the system under the Spanish Constitution of collaboration and autonomy between church and state." Quoted in Pond, "Spain," CSM, September 12, 1984.

91. CSM, August 9, 1983. Strauss intervened with the Czech government for 20 Czechoslovakian Franciscans when he visited Prague in summer 1983.

92. Austrian interviews, July 1984. Other leftists who support the Communists do so as a counterweight to a neutral government "which really belongs to NATO."

93. CSM, May 1, 1984.

94. For the exchange between *Pravda* and *Neues Deutchland*, see NYT, August 26, 1984. For Honecker, see CSM, August 30, 1984. For the postponement, see NYT, September 5, 1984.

95. In one passage Glemp said: "If after 40 years of living in a country someone declares himself a foreigner without knowing the language of his

newly professed fatherland, then what we have is an artificial claim, motivated by greed, the thought of easy money, the desire for the easy life, and perhaps the desire to avoid toil and struggle." NYT, August 16, 1984.

96. NYT, August 18, 1984.

97. CSM, August 30, 1984.

98. Philip P. Everts, "The Influence of the Churches on Nuclear Disarmament in the Netherlands," paper presented to consultation on The Churches' Influence on Disarmament in East and West, pp. 32-36.

99. Everts, "Netherlands," pp. 14-20. See also Philip P. Everts and G. Walraven, De vredesbeweging [The Peace Movement].

100. See Hogebrink, "Netherlands," pp. 35-39 (n. 78, above), for the battle within The Reformed Churches in the Netherlands (Gereformeerde Kerken). The anti-IKV group in the larger Netherlands Reformed Church is the Reformed Council for Peace Questions (HBV).

101. Ibid., p. 43.

102. Monsignor Drs. R. P. Bär, "Christianity and Deterrence: Views of Church groups in the Netherlands on War and Peace," NATO Review 30 (February 1982): 23-27.

103. For a full report on the Antwerp meeting, see Bulletin, the quarterly of Pax Christi International (summer 1983).

CHAPTER 5

1. Quoted in Time, October 15, 1979, p. 15.

2. NYT, October 8, 1979.

3. NYT, October 8, 1979. For a recent analysis of American female religious, see Donna Singles, "Les Religieuses Americaines; Mais Qu'est-ce Qu'elles Veulent?"

4. The first quotation comes from the pope's speech and the second from the apologetic of Monsignor Neil Willard, chancellor of the archdiocese. NYT, September 12, 1984.

5. NYT, September 14, 1984.

6. Quoted in Time, October 15, 1979, p. 34.

7. For a standard work on the concept "civil religion," see Russell E. Richey and Donald G. Jones, eds., American Civil Religion. The collection includes Robert Bellah's two (1967, 1973) famous essays on the subject. See, also, A. James Reichley, Religion in American Public Life. For an excellent treatment of the place of Catholicism in the American context, see John A. Coleman, An American Strategic Theology, especially Chs. 7-14.

8. For example, the NCCB report for the 1985 Synod contained support for the activist stance of the American church and a special emphasis on the "rights and dignity" of women in the church to further "their advancement to positions of leadership and decision-making." The report did not advocate that women be made priests. NYT, September 16, 1985. For survey data on American Catholics in general, see Andrew Greeley, American Cath-

olics Since the Council, and NYT/CBS poll of November 18-19, 1985, published in NYT, November 25, 1985.

9. Canada as a whole presents a special case because of the strong concentration of French-speaking Québécois in the church. See Susan Mann Trofimenkoff, *The Dream of Nation: A Social and Intellectual History of Quebec*. Of all the elite groups, the French Catholic clergy survived the English Conquest the best (pp. 29-30). Both Irish Catholicism in Ireland and French Catholicism in Canada remained at the heart of national identity while dealing with British governments. In return for Catholic political support both London and Ottawa supported church control of education and morality.

10. Eric Brown, *The Catholic Church in South Africa*; John W. De Gruchy, *The Church Struggle in South Africa*; J. B. Brain, *Catholic Beginnings in Natal and Beyond*. I am also indebted to an excellent term paper by Santa Clara University student Matthew D. Feuer.

11. Whyte, *Western Democracies*, p. 18.

12. Ibid., p. 17. Whyte places French Canada in the 1940s and 1950s at the "closed" end of the spectrum, with Australia, Ireland, and the United States in the middle.

13. See Knox's obituary notice in NYT, June 27, 1983.

14. Dorothy Dohen, *Nationalism and American Catholicism*, p. 1. For an excellent summary of "The Anti-Communist Impulse in American Catholic Life, 1850-1950," see Donald J. Crosby, S.J., *God, Church, and Flag: Senator Joseph R. McCarthy and the Catholic Church, 1950-57*, pp. 3-25.

15. J. Brian Benestad and Francis J. Butler, eds., *Quest for Justice*, pp. 51-55.

16. Dohen, *Nationalism*, p. 5, defines nationalism as "the ideology which permits the nation to be the impersonal and final arbiter of human affairs."

17. See the *America* (November 30, 1985) special issue of "The Legacy of John Courtney Murray."

18. James Hennesey, *American Catholics*, p. 285. A great deal of controversy has surrounded the recent biography of Spellman by John Cooney. Charges of homosexuality that appeared in the galley proofs were softened to "an irresolvable debate" by the publisher when no direct evidence could be produced by the author.

19. Hennesey, *American Catholics*, p. 178.

20. John R.G. Hassard, *Life of the Most Rev. John Hughes*, p. 276, cited in Dohen, *Nationalism*, p. 67.

21. Hennesey, *American Catholics*, p. 124, n. 26. See also Jay Dolan, *The American Catholic Experience*, which stresses the role that various ethnic Catholicisms have played in the development of the American church.

22. Nathan Glazer and Daniel P. Moynihan, *Beyond the Melting Pot*, pp. lvii-lxx.

23. Hennesey, *American Catholics*, pp. 149-57.

24. Ibid., pp. 223-28.

25. With lines like "America, Our America! With dignity all sublime,

Thou art dedicated to Mary," this poem reflects Spellman's belief in the essential righteousness of America's destiny. The full poem can be found in Dohen, *Nationalism*, p. 123.

26. Hennesey, *American Catholics*, p. 188.

27. Cited in ibid., p. 259. The "Bishops' Program," written by Ryan, appeared on February 12, 1919. The program called for national government action on, among other policies: minimum wage legislation; unemployment, sickness, disability, and old-age insurance; minimum age limit for child labor; legal enforcement of the right of labor to organize; continuation of the War Labor Board; a national employment service; public housing for low-income workers; increased wages, even over wartime levels; regulation of public-utility rates and progressive taxes on inheritance, income, and excess profits; participation of labor in management and ownership; control of monopolies, even by government competition.

28. For Spellman's ancestry, see Gannon, *Cardinal Spellman*, pp. 2-3. Spellman's paternal grandparents came from Tipperary and Limerick. His maternal grandparents came from Cork and Carlow. His grocer father provided his family with "the life typical of a lucky American boy at the turn of the century."

29. Hennesey, *American Catholics*, p. 194.

30. Ibid., p. 240.

31. NYT, May 25, 1983.

32. Hennesey, *American Catholics*, p. 259.

33. John Tracy Ellis, "American Catholics and the Intellectual Life." For a contemporary critique of Catholic higher education, see Andrew Greeley, "Why Catholic Higher Learning Is Lower," NCR, September 23, 1983.

34. Kelly, *Battle*, p. 62. Kelly, of course, criticizes the declaration along with American Catholic educators like Theodore Hesburgh, president of Notre Dame.

35. Hennesey, *American Catholics*, p. 274.

36. Crosby, *God, Church, and Flag*, pp. 104-13, 197-98, 205-15, documents the personal and political response of the Kennedy family to McCarthy's rise and fall.

37. Theodore White, *The Making of the President 1960*.

38. However, the bishop of Cincinnati, 70-year-old John Baptist Purcell, did leave among the acts of the council an undelivered address that called American separation of church and state "the best form of human government." Hennesey, *American Catholics*, p. 215. Purcell's position seems advanced, even when compared with the great priest-social theoretician John A. Ryan in *The State and The Church* fifty years later. Ryan still relied on the church's European tradition, summarized in Leo XIII's *Immortale dei* (1885). It remained to the Jesuit John Courtney Murray to articulate the theological rationale for the American experience which became part of the heritage of the universal church in the Declaration of Religious Liberty at the Second Vatican Council.

39. Cited in Hennesey, *American Catholics*, p. 215.

40. Mel Piehl, *The Breaking of Bread*, p. 120.

41. For a history of the paper, see Nancy L. Roberts, *Dorothy Day and the Catholic Worker*.

42. Cited in Hennesey, *American Catholics*, p. 267. For Day's writings, see Robert Ellsberg, ed., *By Little and by Little*.

43. The entire address is Appendix C in Theodore H. White, *The Making of the President 1960*, pp. 391-93. The preceding weekend Kennedy adviser and Unitarian Ted Sorenson remarked, "We can win or lose the election right there in Houston on Monday night" (p. 260).

44. Michael Harrington's current reflections on the state of American society and on his life since leaving Catholicism and can be found in *The Politics at God's Funeral*. Richard John Neuhaus compares the book to George F. Will, *Soul and Statecraft*, in its neglect of "mediating structures." "In the Case of Michael Harrington."

45. Piehl, *The Breaking of Bread*, p. 197.

46. William D. Miller, *Dorothy Day*, pp. 478-92.

47. For the story of the founding of the Catholic Peace Fellowship, see Arthur Jones's interview of Jim Forest in the NCR, August 17, 1984. Forest, forty-three, directs the International Fellowship of Reconciliation (IFOR), which is headquartered in Alkmaar, Netherlands. Forest's father was an organizer for the American Communist Party, and his mother was a psychiatric social worker.

48. The organization is now called Clergy and Laity Concerned (still CALC), headed by United Methodist Minister John Collins and Maryknoll Sister Blaise Lupo. For a periodization of CALC (1965-1972, 1972-1979, 1979-), see NCR, September 7, 1984.

49. Miller, *Dorothy Day*, pp. 488-89.

50. Hennesey, *American Catholics*, pp. 226-31.

51. The NCCB is an ecclesiastical organization, a national episcopal conference as described in Chapter 2. The USCC is a civil entity of the American Catholic Bishops, incorporated in the District of Columbia, which assists in uniting American Catholics where voluntary collective action on a broad interdiocesan level is needed. This separation of the NCCB and the USCC allows the staff of the USCC greater latitude in political and social policies without committing the full prestige of the bishops. Malone's parents were Irish immigrants. Archbishop May of St. Louis is the present NCCB vice-president. The vice-president traditionally succeeds to the presidency.

52. Benestad and Butler, *Compendium*, p. 78.

53. Hanna, *American Politics*, pp. 148-99.

54. *San Francisco Chronicle*, June 1, 1981.

55. George F. Will criticizes Senator Moynihan, who "was after all, Irish before he acquired the convictions on behalf of which he employs his gift for disputation." *Los Angeles Times*, September 21, 1978.

56. For example, Robert G. Hoyt, "Learning a Lesson From the Catholic Schools," *New York* 10 (September 12, 1977): 48-55.

57. Minority students made up 20.4 percent of Catholic school students in 1982-1983 versus 10.8 percent in 1970-1971. Non-Catholics rose from 2.7 percent to 10.6 percent during the same period. *San Jose Mercury News*, July 8, 1983.

58. Article and excerpts from Bernardin's speech can be found in NYT, December 7, 1983. Citation of bishops on capital punishment can be found in a separate article. In November 1980 the Catholic bishops voted 145 to 31 with 14 abstentions to advocate eliminating capital punishment as "a manifestation of our belief in the unique worth and dignity of each person from the moment of conception, a creature made in the image and likeness of God."

59. NYT, May 12, 1983.

60. Nicholas Acocella, "Politics: The Vatican and Father Drinan."

61. Ms. Violet, a Republican, garnered 43 percent of the vote in 1982. The NYT, January 20, 1984, pointed to the anomaly of Democrat Sister Elizabeth Morancy, also a Sister of Mercy, planning to run for her fourth term as a state representative. Arlene Violet won 51 percent of the vote in 1984 and became the first woman elected attorney general of Rhode Island. On March 1, 1984, Canada's only priest in parliament announced that he would not seek reelection because of a letter from the papal nuncio that suggested such a reelection campaign would be contrary to the new code of canon law. NCR, March 16, 1984. See Madonna Kolbenschlag, ed., *Between God and Caesar: Priests, Sisters, and Political Office in the United States*.

62. Bellah et al., *Habits of the Heart*. The relation of politics and culture has become a major topic, even among politicians. See, for example, the interviews of Cuomo, Kemp, Bell, Bellah, and Novak in *New Perspectives* 2 (Summer 1985).

63. See Peter Steinfels's review of *Habits of the Heart* in NYT, April 14, 1985.

64. Committee on Political Parties of the American Political Science Association, "Toward a More Responsible Two-Party System," *American Political Science Review* (September 1950, supplement), p. 1. See also Everett Carl Ladd, *Where Have All the Voters Gone?*

65. NCR, February 8, 25, 1975. Thomas Flemming, "Divided Shepherds of a Restive Flock," *New York Times Magazine* (January 16, 1977): 9-44.

66. If Call to Action polarized ecclesiastical liberals and radicals, Cardinal Krol's Eucharistic Congress in the summer of 1976 successfully maintained Catholic conservative unity. 1.2 million Catholics participated in this event whose theme was the physical and spiritual hunger of the world. Parishes responded by donating $5 million for a program called Operation Rice Bowl. Catholic Pentecostals held fifteen events at which they cried out ecstatically, spoke in tongues and otherwise celebrated the presence of the Holy Spirit.

67. Kelly, *Battle*, p. 384.

68. Voting profiles from Rep. Vin Weber, "From the Hill."

69. Hanna, *American Politics*, pp. 203-208.

70. Ibid., pp. 101-47.

71. Ibid., p. 202.

72. *San Jose Mercury News*, October 21, 1983.

73. Catholics 55-44, public 59-51. The NYT-CBS News Poll, in NYT, November 8, 1984, for election percentages. American Protestantism has produced strong traditions of political service. The three major Democratic candidates of 1984 personified three of these traditions. Walter and Joan Mondale both came from Presbyterian ministerial families. Hart studied at Bethany Nazarene College (Oklahoma) and Yale Divinity School. Jackson, a Baptist minister, represents the strong communal tradition of black churches. Some Republican Conservatives are supporting evangelist Pat Robertson for 1988.

74. Casey, son of a Kerry creamery manager, became chairman of Trocaire in 1973, and "has since tilted at governments at home and abroad for more Third World aid. A fierce critic of U.S. policy in Central America, he has probably done more than any other single person to create Irish anger at U.S. interference in the region." O'Leary, "Diocese of Dublin," p. 19. The same article also mentions bishopric candidate Peter Lemass as "trenchantly against Reagan's policies in Central America," but criticized by others for uncompromising stands. The section on Lemass ends with the opinion that he will probably be allowed to go to Chile. "Ireland loves a far away radical" (p. 18).

75. NYT, June 5, 1984.

76. NYT, September 11, 1984. When considering Polish-American relations on August 1, Reagan brought the papal nuncio to Santa Barbara for consultations and newsphotos. Polish congressmen, however, belong to the Democratic Party and have generally liberal voting records. For a conservative protest against such congressmen, see Magnus J. Krynski, "What's Wrong with the Voting Record of Polish-Americans in the 98th Congress?"

77. NYT, July 27, 1984.

78. Quoted in Mary McGrory, "The Governor Battles the Archbishop to a Political Draw," *San Jose Mercury News*, August 8, 1984. McGrory also comments on the fact that Cuomo challenged Archbishop O'Connor, something even Catholic James Shannon and Jew Barney Frank failed to do against Cardinal Medeiros of Boston in the famous abortion case in the 1980 election. After Shannon was reelected, however, he did comment that his victory showed "single-issue candidacies won't work in Massachusetts."

79. NYT, August 3, 4, 1984. The first issue is based on an interview with Cuomo. The full text of O'Connor's statement and Cuomo's reaction to that statement can be found in the second issue.

80. NYT, August 12, 1984. Cuomo and Catholic Congressman Henry J.

Hyde (R-Ill.) both went to the University of Notre Dame to voice their vision of abortion, Catholic values and American society. For excerpts from the Cuomo speech, see NYT, September 14, 1984. NYT, September 15, 1984. For excerpts of Hyde's speech, see NYT September 25, 1984.

81. NYT, August 24, 1984. The lead photo shows the president at the prayer breakfast.

82. NYT, October 17, 1984.

83. NYT, September 13, 1984.

84. On December 18, the Congregation of Religious wrote to the nuns' superiors with the demand that the nuns recant the statement or face expulsion. NYT, December 19, 26, 1984. CFCC sponsored a follow-up ad on March 2, 1986, but the NCR in a September 27, 1985, editorial urged Catholics not to sign, charging that "The advertisement being proposed is a deceitful, dishonest and divisive effort by a small, single-issue group that may have started from a position of honest concern but seems to have degenerated into demagoguery." Richard Doerflinger, assistant director of the NCCB Office for Prolife Activities, criticized CFCC on three grounds: it was not only "prochoice," but "proabortion"; it had strong ties to secular population control groups; and it had avoided "dialogue" to present itself as "something akin to an alternative religious denomination." Doerflinger, "Who Are Catholics for a Free Choice?" Pro-Life Chairman Cardinal Bernardin spoke out strongly on the issue on October 2, 1985. NYT, October 3, 1985. CFCC Executive Director Frances Kissling said that incidents like the recent excommunication of the Catholic director of Planned Parenthood in Rhode Island had prompted the second ad. NYT, February 28, 1986.

85. NYT, September 6, 1984.

86. NYT, September 21, 1984. For Kennedy's defense of Cuomo and Ferraro, see NYT, September 11, 1984.

87. NYT, October 16, 1984.

88. NCR, November 2, 1984. NYT, September 28, 1984.

89. NCR, October 19, 1984.

90. NYT, October 24, 1984.

91. The Democrats gained two seats in the Senate, where the Republicans led 53-47. The Republicans won sixteen seats in the House, where the Democrats led 253-182. Democrats still control the great majority of governorships and state legislatures.

92. Sixty-seven percent of the general electorate was negative. WCED also disagreed 56-36 percent that "President Reagan was right in his Dallas speech when he suggested that instead of separating religion from politics, it is better to bring religion closer to politics, and government closer to religion." Results of Harris poll, *San Jose Mercury News*, October 4, 1984.

93. *San Jose Mercury News*, October 15, 1984.

94. NYT, November 13, 1984.

95. The NCCB issued its pastoral letter "The Hispanic Presence: Challenge and Commitment," on December 12, 1983. The drafting committee

consisted of Chairperson Archbishop Robert F. Sanchez and Bishops Roger Mahony, Ricardo Ramírez, and Rene Valero. Hispanic Catholic leadership has traditionally come from New Mexico and San Antonio. Father Virgil Elizondo, who as a young priest served as a *peritus* at Medellín, founded San Antonio's Mexican American Cultural Center (MACC) in 1972. San Antonio, whose Hispanic Mayor Henry Cisneros has been mentioned as a Democratic vice-presidential candidate in 1988, is also the location of Communities Organized for Public Service (COPS), the archdiocesan-supported community activist organization that has served as a model for similar efforts in other cities, e.g., Los Angeles' United Neighborhoods Organization (UNO). *Los Angeles Times*, December 26, 1977. The lack of Hispanic bishops has been an issue in California, but Mahony served as the first head of California's Agricultural Labor Relations Board, which was set up by then ex-Jesuit Governor Jerry Brown.

96. Trofimenkoff, *Dream of Nation*, pp. 288-96. The Catholic Church had responded to Canadian poverty in the first part of the century by establishing cooperatives, credit unions, and unions, on the universal church model of Catholic Action.

Demographic trends have long worried French-speaking Canadians. The French portion of the population fell from 31.1 percent in 1871 to 28.7 percent in 1971. The figures for Quebec were 78 percent in 1871, 82 percent in 1951, and 79 percent in 1971. In 1971 French Catholics made up 58.3 percent of the Canadian church, with 52.4 percent of Canadian Catholics living in Quebec. For the demographic trends of ethnics, religion, and language, see Richard Arès, *Les Positions—ethniques, linguistiques, et religieuses—des Canadiens français à la suite du recensement de 1971*. The 1983 Directory of the Canadian Conference of Catholic Bishops lists 10,433,849 of 24,347,400 Canadians as Catholics (42.9 percent).

97. Trofimenkoff, *Dream of Nation*, p. 299.

98. *America* 15 (August 25, 1984): 63.

99. Toronto, for example, has over 300,000 Italian-Canadians.

100. NYT, June 11, 1984.

101. NCR, September 21, 1984. NYT, September 17, 1984.

102. NYT, September 13, 1984.

103. Drogheda contains the relics of Bishop Oliver Plunkett, executed by the British in 1681. Excerpts from John Paul's speech can be found in NYT, September 30, 1979. The Irish bishops had prepared the pope's visit with a letter to the people which said, "May his visit challenge all Irishmen to put an end to our murdering hates and replace them by Christ's love and forgiveness."

104. NYT, September 29, 1979.

105. NCNS from Armagh, in HKSE, December 18, 1981.

106. NCNS from Aylesford, England, in HKSE, October 15, 1982.

107. NCNS from Belfast, in HKSE, February 4, 1983. When Cahal Daly was bishop of rural Ardagh and Clonmacnois, he called the IRA "a move-

ment alien to Irish values and tradition . . . a Frankenstein out of control."
Thomas Mahoney, "Ireland: Change and Challenge," p. 215.

108. Text in NYT, November 16, 1985. For analysis of the Unionist response, see Terence O'Keeffe, "Why Unionists Say No," *The Tablet* 240 (January 18, 1986): 52-54.

109. Will Herberg, *Protestant, Catholic, Jew*.

110. Robert N. Bellah, "Civil Religion in America," in Richey and Jones, *American Civil Religion*, pp. 21-44.

111. Piehl, *The Breaking of Bread*, p. 249.

CHAPTER 6

1. At the time of Wojtyła's election the Polish Communist Party was trying to promote an obscure army major, Poland's first astronaut, as "the world's most famous Pole." The election of John Paul II killed that campaign.

2. Kolbe offered his own life to save a fellow prisoner, Franciszek Gajowniczek, at the Birkenau concentration camp. Gajowniczek met John Paul II when the pope visited the former cell of Kolbe on his June 1979 visit.

3. The destruction of World War II, the increase in population, and the movement of peasants to industrial "new towns," all created a considerable need for new church buildings. Militant prelates like Bishop Ignacy Tokarczuk of Przemyśl forced the issue. Starting in the mid-1960s Tokarczuk urged his parishioners to assemble secretly small prefab churches overnight and present the authorities with a *fait accompli*. Tokarczuk put up more than one hundred illegal new churches. When a prosecutor tried to fine Tokarczuk, such a large number of Catholic housewives followed him and occupied the prosecutor's office that the harried official dismissed the case. Despite strong popular support for Tokarczuk as a successor for Wojtyła in Kraków or Wyszyński in Warsaw, state acquiescence was inconceivable.

4. "Everyone in Lithuania is a dissident. We don't have a few dissidents; we have a handful of collaborators." On November 22, 1978, Father Alfonsas Svarinskas, spokesman for five Lithuanian clergymen, addressed Western correspondents at a Moscow news conference. He announced the formation of a new Catholic Committee for the Defense of the Rights of Believers, established nine days earlier in Lithuania. Russian Orthodox priest Gleb Yakunin, a founding member of the Christian Committee for the Defense of Believers in the USSR (founded in December 1976), demonstrated his solidarity with the Lithuanian priests by attending the news conference.

5. John Paul's phrase during this visit. He also said, "It is impossible merely to visit [Auschwitz]. It is necessary to think with fear of how far hatred can go, how far man's destruction of man can go, how far cruelty

can go." As a member of the Polish underground Wojtyła had hid Jews from the Nazis.

6. On Pentecost John Paul spoke at Gniezno, Poland's first Christian capital. He stressed the link between Poland and Czechoslovakia by recalling the Polish patron St. Adalbert, born in Moravia and buried at Gniezno. The NYT provides extensive coverage of the entire trip.

7. Wałęsa continued, "my case itself would not exist and I would not be what I am. I'll say more: If I hadn't been a believing soul, I wouldn't have resisted because I had so many threats. So many." Wałęsa gave a personally revealing interview to the Italian journalist Oriana Fallaci in Warsaw on February 23-24, 1981.

8. NYT, July 3, 1983. This question remains particularly delicate for party and state youth policy.

9. Daniel Singer, *The Road to Gdansk*, p. 233.

10. HKSE, February 20, 1981.

11. NYT, September 3, 1980.

12. Father Joachim Kondziela, director of the Peace Research Center in Warsaw, says that "The Church had to play both the role of mediator between the State authorities and Solidarity and that of an agent calming radically anarchist take-over tendencies of extremist Jacobin moods." Kondziela, "What the Church in Poland Did for Peace in 1980 to 1983," p. 3, paper presented to consultation on The Churches' Influence on Disarmament Decisions in East and West. The Polish church's role as mediator received strong emphasis in the episcopal conference communiqué of December 12, 1980, and the special pastoral letter, "To the Polish Nation," read in all churches two days later. The former document stated, "Action must not be taken which could drive our fatherland into danger of losing its freedom or its existence as a sovereign state." Excerpts from both documents, Szajkowski, *Next to God*, pp. 112-13.

13. HKSE, February 20, 1981.

14. HKSE, September 26, 1980.

15. *San Jose Mercury News*, March 29, 1981.

16. Clifford R. Barnett, *Poland*, p. 48.

17. Ibid., p. 67. Singer, *Gdansk*, p. 190, emphasizes that John Paul's "triumph was the certificate of ideological and political bankruptcy for an allegedly communist regime." Although Poland has always been Catholic, earlier "there was also an anticlerical trend among socialists, communists, and a progressive intelligentsia which all opposed the church as an institution backing the landowners, blessing the capitalist, flirting with anti-Semitism and living in sin with Piłsudski and his colonels."

18. For this phenomenon, see Adam Bujak, *Journey to Glory*.

19. NYT, June 29, 1983.

20. For the battle over the Constitution of 1976, see Peter Osnos, *The Polish Road to Communism*, pp. 212-15. The clauses concerned: 1) inseparable and unbreakable ties to the Soviet Union; 2) the Communist Party as "the

leading political force in the country"; and 3) the fact that "citizens' rights are inseparately linked with honest fulfillment of their duties to the socialist motherland." Wyszyński's objections were to the implied uses of the phrases. Clause one was dropped and clauses two and three amended.

21. Interview on recent trip to Poland, Krassowski, June 1986. Censorship has always been unpredictable. The entire inauguration of John Paul II was televised live, but the pope's written Christmas message of *Tygodnik* was censored. The government objected to a reference to St. Stanislaus as "the defender of the most important rights of man and of the nation." Turowicz refused to publish the mutilated text. NCNS from Rome in HKSE, January 19, 1979. The strikers of Gdańsk and Szczecin won the concession of a mass broadcast nationally once a week starting in September 1980. NYT, September 21, 1980. Before the October papal inauguration and the two papal visits, minute censorship instructions were distributed to Polish journalists. As expected, Wojtyła's past battles with the party in Kraków was a forbidden subject.

22. *Polish Perspectives*, No. 6 (January 1979), p. 8. In August 1984 the church and Solidarity urged Poles to boycott vodka for one month as a patriotic act which would also deprive the government of its largest source of revenue. Bishop Mazur of Siedlce said: "No Christian and no Pole should drink alcohol this month, buy it or serve it. And let every drunk in this month be a reminder of the yoke of occupation and a symbol of those who oppressed, persecuted and exploited us at any given time." NYT, August 2, 1984.

23. Besides the Catholic University of Lublin, there are five Catholic secondary schools. Most of the university faculty are priests. The 3,500 students pay no tuition. The university is completely supported by parish and émigré donations. It is supervised by the Ministries of Education, Religious Affairs, and Interior. Since the secondary schools have strong reputations for academic excellence and firm discipline, many party officials send their children to the schools.

24. Bolesław Piasecki, founding chairman of PAX, died on January 1, 1979. Piasecki was first a rightist and then made a political about face. He built PAX into a profitable business empire of publications, factories, and shops. He had also been a member of the Polish Council of State and a deputy in parliament. NCNS from Warsaw, in HKSE, January 26, 1979.

25. PAX had six deputies, while ChSS and PZKS had four apiece. The new PAX chairman, Z. Komender, is a deputy premier. PZKS has been the official Catholic liaison with international Catholic organizations like "Pax Romana."

26. Barnett, *Poland*, pp. 78-79. Also, Alistair Kee, "Soft-Sell Ideology in Poland."

27. Workers and intellectuals are less literal in their faith than the peasants, but they retain the same strong nationalistic orientation. Barnett, *Poland*, p. 68. Workers are often critical of church statements and publications,

so they suffer much less from moral conflicts over religious questions. The intelligentsia remain skeptical of church authority and tend to define their own style of Catholicism. They are not as devoted to religious practices and often interpret religious dogma in their own way. However, educated Poles do not need to concern themselves with orthodoxy since the country has never had any popular heresies. Many analysts have stressed the important role Solidarity played in uniting intellectuals and workers. Krassowski, interview, May 1, 1981. NYT, May 23, 1983. During my interviews in Poland in July 1984, many people stressed that martial law had resulted in many of the most skeptical intellectuals returning to the protection of the church.

28. NYT, June 23, 1983.

29. NYT, March 8, 9, 11, 1984.

30. NYT, March 15, 1984.

31. NYT, March 21, 28, 31, 1984.

32. NYT, April 7, 1984.

33. Glemp transferred Rev. Mieczysław Nowak, who regularly gave antigovernment sermons while ministering to the workers at the big Ursus tractor plant, to the tiny new rural parish of Leki Kościelne. More than 2,000 people packed a protest mass on February 20 at St. Joseph the Worker parish in Ursus, an industrial suburb of Warsaw. The controversy, fueled by more protest masses and a hunger strike, lasted throughout Glemp's trip to South America. When the cardinal returned, he summoned Nowak and told him the transfer was "for the good of the church and the homeland," and eventually the protestors agreed to accept the cardinal's decision. NYT, February 21, 22, 23, 1984. The pastor Rev. Kazimierz Szklarczyk and some of the parishioners supported the cardinal against Nowak. In Glemp's absence Cardinal Macharski, archbishop of Kraków, met with the protestors. NYT, March 16, 1984. The widespread respect for Glemp, epitomized by the remark of one activist and intellectual that "He is a good Pole," was one of the major surprises of my July 1984 interviews. This intellectual and others, however, complained about the poor state of the cardinal's Polish grammar.

34. The Gromyko visit is covered in NYT, January 24, 1979. When John Paul visited Poland in June 1979, the Moscow television program "International Panorama" showed a 30-second clip of his arrival, but no crowd shots. The commentator Alexander Bovin remarked that there were good and bad features to the trip, but that "there are some circles in the Polish church which are trying to use it for antistate purposes." AP from Moscow, in NYT, June 4, 1979. For the papal letter to Brezhnev, see Szajkowski, Next to God, pp. 111-12.

35. NYT, July 9, 1983.

36. In addition, the June 1981 edition of URSS Oggi (USSR Today) charged U.S. involvement because of papal positions on disarmament, El Salvador, and the Middle East which were "diametrically opposed to the

political stand taken by the White House." Presidential envoy William W. Wilson protested the article to the Italian government which "raised this matter with the Soviet embassy." NCNS from Rome, in HKSE, September 25, 1981.

37. For the Bulgarian case, see Eric Bourne's interview of Boyan Traykov, journalist and member of the Bulgarian Central Committee, in CSM, September 26, 1984.

38. NYT, May 27, 1983. Italian-Bulgarian relations had deteriorated since the incident. The Bulgarian deputy foreign minister used the papal visit to appeal for better relations. The Vatican used the visit to arrange a Vatican delegation to Sofia in connection with the annual celebration of St. Cyril and St. Methodius.

39. NCNS from Moscow, in HKSE, September 17, 1982 covers the Czech reprint and other Tass anti-Vatican comments in June and July. The *Literaturnaya Gazeta* article is excerpted in NCNS from Moscow, in HKSE, November 12, 1982.

40. The September 18, 1982 issue of the party newspaper *Sovetskaya Byelourussia* (Soviet White Russia) denounced Catholic activists and priests near the Polish border for violating Soviet religious laws. "The violations included collecting building material for new churches, establishing religious schools for children, and the unauthorized soliciting of money." These activities, encouraged by Vatican Radio, are being ignored by local authorities, according to the article. The paper did not mention that these areas had belonged to Poland before 1939. NCNS from New York, in HKSE, October 15, 1982. For a good general summary of Soviet religious policy, see John Anderson, "Soviet Religious Policy under Brezhnev and After," *Religion in Communist Lands*, (hereafter RCL) 11 (Spring 1983): 25-30.

41. Quoted by Joan Landsbergis in Excursus III: "The Not So Silent Church in Lithuania," *Worldview* 22 (September 1979): 31.

42. NCNS from London, in HKSE, July 20, 1979. The text was provided by the Keston College Centre for the Study of Religion and Communism. Recent communications report small concessions by the government, such as an increased quota of seminary students, publication of a catechism, and open religious instruction in almost all parishes. Quotations from the 44th issue of the *Chronicle of the Catholic Church in Lithuania* are contained in NCNS from New York, HKSE, February 20, 1981. The main source of information on religious and national ferment in Lithuania is the *samizdat* journal, the *Chronicle of the Catholic Church in Lithuania*, which has been appearing since March 1972.

43. NCNS for Vatican City, in HKSE, April 29, 1983.

44. See, for example, Marite Saphets, "New Hard-Line Policy towards Catholic Clergy in Lithuania," RCL 11 (Winter 1983): 334-36.

45. See NCNS from Rome, in HKSE, February 25, 1983; "An Interview with the new Latvian Cardinal," RCL 11 (Summer 1983): 207-9.

46. Stehle, *Eastern Politics*, p. 308.

47. Ibid., pp. 367, 380.

48. NCNS from Vatican City, in HKSE, December 19, 1980.

49. NYT, September 17, 1984. The report of the cardinal's death can be found in NYT, September 8, 1984. The continued vitality of the Uniate church in the Ukraine is attested to by the eight issues of the *samizdat Chronicle of the the Catholic Church of the Ukraine* which have been smuggled out of the Soviet Union. This journal, which was first published in January 1984, notes that from early 1981 to early 1984 the secret ordination of 81 priests took place in the Transcarpathian region alone. Former political prisoner and editor Josyp Terelya, in a public letter to Lech Wałęsa, calls the Polish struggle "the hope which gives us strength for resistence." CSM, March 6, 1985.

50. Charles A. Frazee, "The Greek Catholic Islanders and the Revolution of 1821." The article demonstrates that for Greek Catholics, their religion, not their language or culture, gave them their identity as a community. Alan J. Reinerman, "Metternich, the Papacy, and the Greek Revolution." There were also other considerations. Papal support of the rebels would cause Turkish reprisals against the Greek Catholics. A Greek victory might encourage revolutions elsewhere. The papacy needed good relations with Austria. Although Metternich had some influence on papal policy, it is likely that Rome would have taken this position without his efforts.

51. The Romanian government has allowed Latin-Rite Catholics, mostly ethnic Hungarians, to exist, but suppressed the Romanian-Rite Catholics who are ethnically Romanian in 1948. For Bulgaria, see Janice Broun, "Catholics in Bulgaria," RCL 11 (Winter 1983): 310-20; and Broun, "Religious Survival in Bulgaria," *America* (November 16, 1985): 323-27.

52. Stehle remarks that "not once since Tito's break with Stalin had there been interference in the church's internal affairs." *Eastern Politics*, p. 326. Of course, some Croatian ecclesiastics would vigorously dispute that contention. The types of pressure used by the state will become clearer in the rest of this section.

53. The full text of the "protocol" is in ibid., pp. 445-47. For the question of nationalism, see Pedro Ramet, *Nationalism and Federalism in Yugoslavia*.

54. NYT, December 23, 1972.

55. Stehle, *Eastern Politics*, pp. 390-91. For a comprehensive survey, see also John M. Kramer, "The Vatican's Ostpolitik."

56. For a detailed analysis of Communist religious policies in the early postwar period, see Robert Tobias, *Communist-Christian Encounter in East Europe*.

57. Stehle, *Eastern Politics*, p. 353.

58. In March 1963 Hungarian Socialist Workers Party First Secretary János Kádár had indicated that he was open to some accommodation when he asserted "believers and nonbelievers are equal citizens. It is all the same whether one writes the word God with a capital letter and the other does

not, but it is important that everyone write the word 'person' with a capital letter." NYT, March 23, 1963.

59. Casaroli insisted on including the phrase "as is appropriate for a bishop or priest." Stehle, *Eastern Politics*, p. 315.

60. Ibid., p. 322. Although Mindszenty said he had Paul VI's personal assurances that he would keep his positions for life, the Vatican repeatedly sought the cardinal's voluntary retirement. Many Hungarian exiles were very disappointed in the Vatican's treatment of the cardinal. In 1979, on the anniversary of his trial, 400 Hungarian Catholic priests in the United States and Canada called on the Hungarian government to "publicly declare him to be innocent of all the trumped up charges leveled against him 30 years ago." NCNS from New Brunswick, N.J., in HKSE, March 2, 1979.

61. NYT, September 14, 1983. If the pope had wanted to make a statement on the suppression of ecclesiastical rights in Eastern Europe, he would undoubtedly have referred to the Czechoslovakian Catholic Church, whose Cardinal Tomášek had been kept from coming to Vienna to join fellow cardinals from East Germany, Hungary, Poland, and Yugoslavia.

62. Lékai was born in 1910, the son of an artisan. He went for studies at the German-Hungarian College in Rome. After returning to Hungary, he was a seminary professor and then secretary to Mindszenty. The Nazis arrested them both in 1944, but both prelates were released when the Soviets liberated the country the following February. Lékai then became apostolic administrator of Vezprém. From the beginning he pursued a policy of frank and loyal cooperation with the Socialist government to the extent that both church and state sought the betterment of society.

63. *Washington Post*, June 10, 1977.

64. The letter quotes from John Paul's remarks to the Hungarian bishops in October 1982. NCNS from Vatican City, in HKSE, June 17, 1983.

65. NYT, January 23, 1984.

66. HKSE, March 5, 1982, report on interview with five Italian journalists.

67. Stehle, *Eastern Politics*, p. 324.

68. The declaration was broadcast on Vatican Radio, NCNS from Vatican City, in HKSE, October 20, 1981.

69. See Christopher Cviic, "A Fatima in a Communist Land?" RCL 10 (Spring 1982): 4-10. Pedro Ramet, "Catholicism and Politics in Socialist Yugoslavia," RCL 10 (Winter 1982): 256-74.

70. For this interview, and conflicting interviews with church leaders, see NYT, November 18, 1985.

71. In 1945 Tito demanded that the Vatican replace the Croatian Archbishop Alojzije Stepinac of Zagreb with another prelate. When Pius XII refused, the government arrested Stepinac and sentenced him to sixteen years of forced labor in October 1946. At the end of 1951 Tito exiled the archbishop to his home village of Krašić. Yugoslavia broke relations with

the Vatican one year later when Pius XII announced that he was raising Stepinac to the cardinalate. When the cardinal died in 1960 as a simple village pastor, Tito allowed Stepinac to be buried in the Zagreb cathedral, where his grave has become a place of pilgrimage.

72. An offer Beran accepted. Stehle, *Eastern Politics*, pp. 331-33.

73. "We, the bishops of the Czech Socialist Republic, would like to make it unmistakably clear that we are not signatories to this charter. . . . As regards the sphere of religious life . . . we alone, together with the Holy Father, are competent to make a judgment. . . . Nobody else among the clergy or the laity is authorized to express the standpoint of the Church in our country." Quoted in Documentation for RCL 8 (Spring 1980): 48. This issue contains four important documents on the Czechoslovakian Catholic Church. Zvěřina's letter is on pp. 49-51. See also Milena Kalinovska, "The Religious Situation in Czechoslovakia," RCL 5 (Autumn 1977): 148-57.

74. A vicar capitular is the administrator of a vacant diocese, elected by a cathedral chapter. A vicar apostolic, on the other hand, is appointed by Rome, either to a diocese, e.g. some Spanish dioceses under Franco (Chapter 2), where politics makes the appointment of a bishop impossible, or to a missionary jurisdiction where the local church is insufficiently developed to become a diocese. Alexander Tomsky, " 'Pacem in Terris' Between Church and State in Czechoslovakia," RCL 10 (Winter 1982): 275-82. For a visit to the headquarters of Pacem in Terris, see Dan Fisher's article in the *Los Angeles Times*, July 18, 1983.

75. Interview in *La Republica* cited in NCNS from Rome, in HKSE, April 2, 1982. NCNS also quotes an unnamed Czech bishop who feared the political effect of the document: "If that declaration had been published the week before, we should not be here now." The Vatican's timing was deliberate.

76. "It is the quality of belief that is so important in Bohemia and Moravia." NYT, April 5, 1984. *Washington Post*, March 28, 1984.

77. CSM, August 26, 1983.

78. NCNS from New York, in HKSE, October 15, 1982.

79. HKSE, April 15, 1983. NYT, December 8, 1983.

80. Interview with Douglas Stranglin, *Newsweek*, June 20, 1983.

81. Despite the fact that ordinary Poles have not flocked to PRON, hard-line party members attack it as an unorthodox threat to party control because it is the first political body in the Eastern block which does not give the party a guaranteed majority. CSM, May 19, 1983.

Jaruzelski attended Jesuit boarding school before joining the party in 1947. While in Poland in July 1984 I asked all my interviewees what Jaruzelski was really like. The general consensus was that "he's a good Pole," but the party made it impossible for him to act correctly. All agreed that the army had suffered a loss of prestige from martial law, but that it was still much more highly regarded than the party. There was not the slightest optimism about the possibility of reforming the Polish Workers Party. One politician said that martial law might have worked if the party and Solidarity both had been dissolved immediately. However, the argument against such a move at the time was that the general did not have enough control to dissolve Solidarity, so that Solidarity's strength ended up saving the party. For an evaluation of Jaruzelski at the time he became prime minister (February 1981), see Garton Ash, *The Polish Revolution*, pp. 143-47.

82. Secretary of State Casaroli headed the Vatican delegation to Wyszyński's funeral. He immediately met with many of the Polish bishops. Glemp's experience in dealing with Party functionaries while a member of the primate's staff was his biggest political asset.

83. NYT, December 15, 18, 23, 1981; January 9, 1982.

84. "The visit of the pope, as head of the Vatican state, will make it much more difficult for them to continue their policy, which is unfriendly to us," said Łopatka. AP from Warsaw, in *San Jose Mercury News*, June 3, 1983.

85. NYT, May 10, 1983. CSM, May 19, 1983.

86. Church sources said that the government had requested the second meeting, and Polish television featured it. *Wall Street Journal*, June 27, 1983. Glemp stated that the nation "showed that if the foreigners don't stick their noses in the affairs of Poland, the church within the nation is able to stand up and walk on the road of its historic mission." AP from Rome, July 10, 1983, in NYT, July 11, 1983. The pope was very low key when he talked to Poles in Vienna in September 1983.

87. NYT, June 25, 1983.

88. Reuters from Warsaw, January 6, 1984, in NYT, January 7, 1984.

89. Reuters from Warsaw, January 27, 1984, in NYT, January 28, 1984. Prices rose by an average of 10 percent, but the government's prior consultation, increased supplies of meat, and the bishops' letter all contributed to a fairly quiet transition. Reuters from Warsaw, January 30, 1984, in NYT, January 31, 1984. On the attempt to use the consultation to bolster the new unions, see CSM, January 20, 1984. For John Kifner's report on popular response to the price increases, see NYT, February 14, 1984.

90. NYT, March 17, 1984.

91. The commission of the murder, as detailed in their trial, seemed both savage and inept. The unprecedented 25-day trial ended on February 7, 1985, with the conviction and sentencing of the four. Two received terms of 25 years, the longest under Polish law. However, the convictions went no higher than Colonel Adam Pietruszka, although the involvement of higher officials had been alleged during the proceedings. The entire trial received maximum domestic and international coverage. See, for example, NYT, December 28, 1984–February 8, 1985. Patrick Michel and G. Minx, *Mort d'un Prêtre* (Paris, 1985).

92. NYT, October 29, 1984.

93. NYT, November 1, 1984.

94. CSM, June 20, 1985.

95. NYT, November 12, 1985. However, in the July 1986 housecleaning

of the Central Committee, Rakowski was retained while Olszowski was dismissed. Diplomats mentioned this as an argument for Jaruzelski's liberal to centrist tendencies. NYT, July 4, 1986.

96. At the time, Cardinal Glemp said, "Even if the amnesty does not open the door to paradise, the contact with a man who has been freed fills us with joy."

97. The Polish-American Congress had been in the forefront against any concessions. Mazewski said the Polish authorities should extend the amnesty to several key dissidents, including Popiełuszko and Bogdan Lis, before the United States dropped all objections to Poland's readmittance to the IMF. He opposed giving Poland U.S. Commodity and Export-Import Bank Credits. CSM, August 2, 1984. The positions of the Congress also reflects the significant emotional ambiguity felt by many Poles about sanctions and the charcter of President Reagan. The president in his personality of tough bargainer with the Soviets is tremendously popular, even though many of the intellectuals I spoke with in July 1984 favored the lifting of sanctions. Other dissidents like Adam Michnik have said, "I have to thank the policy of sanctions, among other things, for the fact that we can talk here today, and I'm sitting here in my apartment and not in jailed on Rakowiecka Street." Quoted by Timothy Garton Ash, NYT, November 14, 1984.

98. NYT, July 25, August 1, 1984; CSM, September 24, 1984. How much Vatican wishes were taken into account is unclear, especially since the publicity surrounding the nuncio's trip to Santa Barbara was deemed useful for the presidential campaign (see Ch. 5). The other prominent American episcopal spokesperson on Polish affairs is the Polish-American Cardinal Krol. Krol has headed the "Tribute to the People of Poland" program of Catholic Relief Services which began in July 1981. In less than two years the program shipped more than $487 million worth of foodstuffs, 85 percent of which came from United States surpluses under Title II of Public Law 480. President Reagan invited Krol to the White House on May 11, 1983 to discuss the program. NCNS from Philadelphia, in HKSE, June 3, 1983. Krol, who accompanied John Paul to Poland in June 1983, later called on Reagan to present his own and the pope's views of the trip.

99. NYT, October 18, 1984.

100. NYT, December 14, 1985.

101. AP from Warsaw, April 24, 1986, in NYT, April 25, 1986.

102. CSM, January 26, 1984. Vice President Bush praised the human rights record of Budapest in a September 1983 visit. UPI from Budapest, September 19, 1983, in NYT, September 20, 1983.

103. CSM, November 30, 1983. Under János Kádár, Catholic Hungary has strengthened ties to neighboring Catholic Austria. On December 12, 1982, the first radio mass to be celebrated in Hungary since 1948 was broadcast from Budapest to Austria, West Germany, and Norway. Cardinal Lékai and Bishop Stefan László of Eisenstadt, Austria, concelebrated.

104. This was the first official direct contact since d'Herbigny's trip in 1926. Stehle, *Eastern Politics*, pp. 79-83, 86-102. With each country constituting such a special case it is no wonder that John Paul II on his way home from Austria denied that it was possible to generalize about the church in Communist countries. Then he added that nowhere have relations worsened, and in Hungary they have improved. NYT, September 14, 1983.

105. Stehle, *Eastern Politics*, pp. 365-66.

106. Ibid., pp. 361-64.

107. Jaruzelski was even permitted to visit Vilnius, the capital of Soviet Lithuania and an a cultural center of the old kingdom of Poland and Lithuania. NYT, March 10, 1986. For the Polish Congress, see NYT, July 2-4, 1986. Jaruzelski dominated the congress, introducing three more generals to the Politburo. Only 57 of the 214 old Central Committee members stayed on.

108. For comparative treatment of the role of the Catholic Church in dissent, see Jane Leftwich Curry, ed., *Dissent in Eastern Europe*. For the role of nationalism, see Pedro Ramet, ed., *Religion and Nationalism in Soviet and Eastern European Politics*.

109. NYT, September 29, 1984.

110. Interview, Warsaw, July 1984.

CHAPTER 7

1. NYT, September 16, 1982.

2. AP from Jerusalem, September 14, 1982, in NYT, September 13, 1982.

3. NYT, September 14, 1982.

4. NYT, September 16, 1982.

5. NCNS from Albany, N.Y., in HKSE, September 18, 1981. At the request of Cardinal Cooke, then president of the Catholic Near East Welfare Association, and the Holy See, Nolan visited the American hostages in Iran.

6. Reuters from Rome, April 19, 1984, in NYT, April 20, 1984. For an excellent history of the Catholic Church in the Middle East, see Charles A. Frazee, *Catholics and Sultans*.

7. Other arguments for recognition are: 1) Israel must be part of any comprehensive settlement; and 2) Such a move would ally the Vatican more closely with the United States, who will continue to protect the church's interests in Eastern Europe. The NYT, October 22, 1984, mentions Archbishop Andrzej Maria Deskur as a leading advocate of recognition. However, such groups reflect policy tendencies among certain nationalities, not frozen curial cliques.

8. NCNS from Vatican City, in HKSE, July 6, 1979, NCNS from Castelgandolfo, in HKSE, September 26, 1980.

9. NYT, February 20, 1985.

10. NYT, November 7, 1985. The cardinal's spokesman, Reverend Peter

Finn, said he did not think O'Connor had been apprised of Mr. Bronfman's remarks before the dinner and would have no comment. For another example, see Rabbi and World Jewish Congress Vice President Arthur Hertzberg's op-ed piece in the NYT, December 4, 1985.

11. NYT, March 20, 1986.

12. "Bethlehem University fights for survival," interview of Thomas Scanlan, F.S.C., by Morgan J. Vittengl, M.M., in *Maryknoll* 77 (May 1983): 35-37. The entire May 1983 issue was devoted to the Middle East, thus illustrating a new emphasis on this region by Maryknoll.

13. Middle Eastern Catholics belong primarily to the non-Latin rites associated with the five great patriarchs of Byzantium, Alexandria, Antioch, Chaldea, and Armenia. The principal Catholic groups in Lebanon, for example, belong to the Maronite and Melkite Rites, subgroups of the Antiochene and Byzantine Rites respectively. Catholics belonging to the non-Latin rites are very protective of their traditional liturgical and organizational prerogatives, for example, non-Latin rite Christians are grouped under the Vatican Congregation of Eastern Rite Christians.

14. While in Iran in 1980 Capucci delivered papal letters to the Ayatollah on the cases of Archbishop Barden and the Salesians. Iran had expelled the Irish Dominican Archbishop William Barden (seventy-two), head of the country's only Latin-rite diocese, in August 1980. During the preceding month the government had closed Catholic schools and accused ten Italian Salesian missionaries of spying. After negotiations with Capucci, who delivered several papal messages, Tehrān deported six of the Salesians and ordered the other four not to teach. NCNS from Rome, in HKSE, September 12, 1980. NCNS from Tehrān, in HKSE, September 19, 1980.

15. Carter lost the election (November 1980), Khomeini removed Bani-Sadr (June 1981), Ghotbzadeh was executed (September 1982). NYT, April 6, 7, 30, 1980. The April 6th issue has a photo of Ghotbzadeh embracing Capucci. After the failed attempt by the Americans to rescue the hostages in which eight Marines were killed, Ghotzbadeh invited Capucci to Tehrān to join with the Swiss embassy and the Red Cross in arranging the transfer of the American bodies.

16. *Il Tempo* on April 22, 1980, NCNS from Rome, in HKSE, May 16, 1980.

17. See, for example, the statements of Maronite Patriarch Antoine Pierre Khoraiche in NCNS from New York, in HKSE, October 9, 1981, and Melkite Patriarch Maximos V Hakim to British journalists that return of the West Bank and the Gaza Strip to the Arabs remains the key to peace in the Middle East.

18. Monsignor Nolan expressed the Vatican interest when he said, "In Lebanon Christianity is fighting for its life. As Lebanon goes, so goes Christianity in the Middle East." NCNS from Albany, N.Y., in HKSE, September 18, 1981.

19. Jonathan C. Randal, *Going All the Way*, p. 139, "Never before had the Maronites been represented by a single man or a single organization."

20. Ibid., p. 172.

21. The description fits Suleiman Franjieh. The seventy-three-year-old Maronite former president belonged to the National Salvation Front with Druze Jumblatt and Sunni Karami. NYT, November 2, 1983.

22. Reuters from Rome, November 28, 1983, in NYT, November 29, 1983.

23. Quoted by Cobban, CSM, January 6, 1978.

24. At the requiem Naaman said: "Sometimes a single person sums up an entire people and an entire nation with its aptitudes and its longings. The Lebanese Forces are the shield of Lebanon, its strength and its pride. He left us to become myth and example." Randal, *Going All the Way*, pp. 148-49.

25. Randal says the monk "always good-naturedly wagged his finger at me and called me 'naughty' for having described him as the 'architect of the Israeli alliance.' " Randal, *Going All the Way*, p. 140.

26. NCNS from Rome, HKSE September 12, 1980. Khoraiche, born in 1907, was elected and appointed patriarch in February 1975, just in time for the civil war.

27. The Druze are a tight-knit sectarian community, which coalesced in Lebanon in the mid-eleventh century from dissident Moslem sectarians and various ethnic groups. They have a long tradition of emnity with the Maronites.

28. Randal, *Going All the Way*, discussed Bashir's fateful decision to send his militia "to areas in the Lebanese provinces from which they had been expelled during the civil war, or in some cases, to places where the Phalangist Party had never maintained offices."

29. See NYT, February 9, 1984, for Italian, British, and French reaction to the American decision. The NYT page features a photo of a weary-looking John Paul II with the caption: "Appeal By Pope: Pope John Paul II after announcing yesterday at the Vatican that he had appealed to President Reagan to use his influence to bring about an immediate cease-fire in Lebanon." The pope also appealed to President Assad of Syria and others.

30. NYT, October 24, 1984.

31. The Shiite militia Amal is led by Nabih Berri, minister of hydroelectricity and justice in the Karami cabinet. See NYT, May 1, 1984, for the naming of this cabinet of five Christians and five Muslims.

32. CSM, April 9, 1984.

33. Commentators gave principal credit for Jenco's release to Syrian intervention. Monsignor John Nolan, national secretary of the Near East Welfare Association, accompanied O'Connor. NYT, June 14, 17, 19, July 27-30, 1986.

34. This section does not attempt a full comparative analysis of the political role of the Catholic Church in various Central American nations but fo-

cuses on the international links involved. A comparative analysis could be constructed starting with Tommie Sue Montgomery, *Revolution in El Salvador*, for two reasons: Montgomery's theory of the Salvadorean political cycle; and Montgomery's emphasis that "for the first time in Latin American history a popular mass organization came directly out of the evangelizing efforts of the Roman Catholic Church" (p. 117). See also Ch. 3, above.

35. *ENVIO* (April 1983), summarized in *Center Focus* 54 (May 1983): 3-4.

36. Reported in *Latin American Weekly Report* (March 18, 1983): 11.

37. See, for example, Lawrence E. Harrison, "How the Sandinistas Have Radicalized the Revolution," which begins, "The visit of Pope John Paul II to Nicaragua . . ." in CSM, March 21, 1983. Harrison was director of U.S. AID in Nicaragua, 1979-1981.

38. *Latin America Weekly Report* (March 18, 1983): 10-11.

39. NYT, March 4, 1983.

40. *Wall Street Journal*, March 9, 1983. See also Raymond Alcide Joseph, "The Church Challenges Baby Doc."

41. See, for example, CSM, February 11, 1986, which also provides background on the conservative and progressive wings of the Haitian church. Following the departure of Duvalier, Archbishop François W. Ligondé issued a pastoral letter which vividly described the ouster as a "victory of truth, justice, prayer and love" but urged Haitians not to seek revenge. One month later, Bishop François Gayot, president of the Haitian Bishops' Conference, launched a literacy campaign targeted at making three million (50 percent of the population) literate in five years. NYT, February 10, March 11, 1986.

42. At the same time the pope visited Latin America, NCCB President Malone led a high-ranking group (Archbishops Law, Flores) of American bishops to visit Cuba. The trip contributed to the moderation of Cuban religious policy. Within a month Castro fired two hardline Stalinists and closed their bureau of political education, opting for a new Office of Religious Affairs under the more flexible José Carneado. In August the president and secretary of the Cuban episcopal conference were invited to the Havana International Conference on rescheduling international debts. In December in their magazine *Vida Christiana* the Cuban bishops endorsed the position of Cardinal Arns of São Paulo, Brazil, which attacked the IMF. See Stanislas Maillard, "Le Pari de l'Église Cubaine," for an excellent firsthand report. Interview with Carneado, NYT, May 29, 1985. The Mexican bishops called for a moratorium on the nation's international debt on October 8, 1985.

43. NYT, May 25, 1984. A classified U.S. State Department report also concluded that there had been a Salvadoran government cover-up, and that it was "quite possible" that the current minister of defense, Carlos Eugenior Vides Casanova was aware of it. NYT, February 16, 1984.

44. In November 1978 government soldiers and party militiamen raided the Maryknoll radio station (Radio San Miguel) in El Prado, Bolivia. The

station broadcasts lessons in literacy, health, and agriculture to jungle Indians. NCNS from Riberalta, Bolivia, in HKSE, November 17, 24, 1978.

45. NCNS from Maryknoll, N.Y., in HKSE, July 8, 1982.

46. NYT, September 12, 1984, especially mentions Maryknoll missionary sister Peggy Healy of Managua and the Washington-based Nicaraguan Action Group, more than half of whose members are nuns. Religious with political and media skills are particularly effective spokespersons in Washington. Lisa Fitzgerald of the Religious of the Sacred Heart, and ex-assistant attorney-general of Massachusetts, returned from Jalapa, Nicaragua, to lobby the Congress against United States destabilization of the country. NYT, July 4, 1983.

47. CSM, November 23, 1984.

48. NCR, March 5, 1982.

49. NCR, November 11, 1983. The British Catholic Institute for International Relation (CIIR), an authorized agency of the British and Welsh bishops, published a strong defense of the Sandinista government in early 1983. The article in the CIIR periodical *Comment* criticized the "near-paranoia of the Reagan government" and lamented that "[t]he measures taken by the [Nicaraguan] bishops' conference to distance the Catholic Church from the Sandinistas have caused confusion and resentment among ordinary Catholics." NCNS from London, in HKSE, April 15, 1983. In early 1981, five Canadian religious leaders, including Monsignor Dennis J. Murphy, general secretary of the Canadian Conference of Catholic Bishops, sent a statement to Prime Minister Trudeau asking him to "protest in the clearest possible terms continued U.S. military intervention in El Salvador." NCNS from Toronto, in HKSE, March 13, 1981.

50. NCNS from Nicaragua, in HKSE, May 20, 1983.

51. NYT, December 23, 27, 1983. For analysis of the various attempts at political use of the exodus, including Bishop Vega's rejection of Bishop Obando's comparison of Schlaefer with Moses, see NCR, January 13, 1984. Report of an interview with Schlaefer is available in the NYT, January 3, 1984. Bishop Schlaefer's companion on the trek, Father Wendelin Shaker, appears in Lee Shapiro's 1986 PBS documentary on the Miskitos, "Nicaragua Was Our Home," which is very critical of the Sandinistas.

52. For Hickey's complete testimony, see Falcoff and Royal, *Crisis and Opportunity*, pp. 143-58. Cardinal Bernardin has also spoken out on Central America. On May 14, 1984, he told an Emory University audience that, "The fundamental basis of unrest in El Salvador exists prior to outside interference . . . the roots of the revolution are surely local. They reside in the soil of long-standing injustice and inequity in the perception of the majority that the country has been run against them, not for them." However, the NCCB has not been able to arrive at a unified position on the Sanctuary Movement for illegal Central American refugees in the United States. In June 1984 Stacey Lynn Merkt of Casa Romero was sentenced for transporting three Salvadoran refugees who had entered the country illegally. The

local bishop John J. Fitzpatrick of Brownsville supports sanctuary, as do many other bishops. Nevertheless, there is also significant opinion against the Sanctuary Movement within the NCCB on the grounds that such proclamations focus government attention on the refugees. The movement has developed from a decentralized informal base. Over 80,000 Salvadorans, most of whom have arrived since 1980, live in the San Francisco Bay Area, which has over forty churches in the movement. On May 1, 1986, a Tucson court convicted another eight of eleven defendants after a controversial and well-publicized trial.

53. NYT, April 18, 1985.

54. For a summary of the testimony and cross-examination, see NCR, April 26, 1985.

55. NYT, February 6, March 5, 1986. Religious opposition to the aid was led by Bishop Gumbleton and Episcopal Bishop Paul Moore, Jr., of New York. Altogether, the anti-aid statement was signed by 21 Roman Catholic, Methodist, Episcopal and Lutheran bishops, officials of the United Church of Christ, the Christian Church, the Mennonite Church, the Unitarian Universalist Association, the National Council of Churches, and about a dozen rabbis.

56. NYT, July 5, 6, 1986; CSM, July 7, 1986; NCR, July 18, 1986. For a fine report on church-state relations within Nicaragua including the current divisions within the Nicaraguan church, see Edward R.F. Sheehan, "The Battle for Nicaragua."

57. NCR, August 31, 1984. Misereor and Adveniat, directed by the West German bishops, receive funding from the taxes of Catholics in the FRG. This aid has supported many religious and social programs in the Third World. See Smith, *Chile*, pp. 53, 60, 123.

58. *San Jose Mercury News*, February 24, 1984.

59. See Deborah Huntington, "The Prophet Motive," and "God's Saving Plan," *NACLA Report* (January-February 1984): 2-36.

60. NCR, March 30, 1984. Geraldine O'Leary de Macías, wife of a former vice minister of labor in the Nicaraguan Revolutionary Government, has taken a leading role in opposing American missionary critics of United States policy. See, for example, "Foreign Christians are a Problem," Falcoff and Royal, *Crisis and Opportunity*, pp. 425-32.

61. NCR, October 26, 1984.

62. NYT, May 20, 1985.

63. NYT, March 27, 1982, has a nice three-column photo of Hesburgh and Senator Nancy Kassebaum arriving in El Salvador as part of the monitoring group. After the elections, Rivera y Damas appealed to guerrillas and their political arm, the Democratic Revolutionary Front, "to take the people's vote as a mandate for peace, democracy and justice . . . and leave the ways of armed struggle and destruction." The same speech reflected concern about the victory of D'Aubuisson when the bishop said the Constituent Assembly should tackle "the basic roots of the ongoing conflict:

mockery and frustration of past elections, the unfair distribution of wealth, the unpunished string of murders, the missing persons and the political prisoners, and the thousands displaced by war." NCNS from San Salvador, in HKSE, May 21, 1982. The bishop's preelection statement is reported in NCNS from San Salvador, in HKSE, March 19, 1982.

64. NCNS from San Salvador, in HKSE, March 13, 1981. On April 6, 1981, Rivera met with Vice President Bush and Under Secretary of State William Clark at the White House. Following the meeting Rivera wrote to Bush urging the United States to pressure the Salvadoran military into a negotiated settlement. NCR, February 17, 1984.

65. Rivera y Damas said: "Doing pastoral work among the armed forces does not mean that a priest becomes a soldier; doing the same work among non-believers does not mean he becomes one. And by engaging in pastoral work in conflict zones it does not mean that the priest becomes a guerrilla." NCNS from San Salvador, in HKSE, November 12, 1982. See CSM, January 5, 1984, on Belgian missionary Rogel Poncel, who serves with the People's Revolutionary Army (ERP). Poncel left for northern Morazan after a bomb exploded in his rectory.

66. NYT, September 12, 1983.

67. AP from San Salvador, December 25, 1983, in NYT, December 26, 1983.

68. A public radio broadcast by the Maximiliano Hernández Martínez Anticommunist Brigade demanded that the Sunday homilies be suspended, or "drastic sanctions" would be undertaken. During 1977-1983 nine priests were assassinated, and twenty-five fled the country. The 1977 death-squad campaign was keynoted by pamphlets which read: "Be a Patriot! Kill a priest." CSM, November 14, 1983.

69. NYT, June 12, 1984, also mentions the reestablishment of connections between the government and the church because of the archbishop's "evenhandedness" in denouncing the crimes of both the right and the left.

70. Shultz met with Duarte in San Salvador on October 10. Both stressed that the talks would "not involve power-sharing." NYT, October 11, 1984.

71. The archbishop had just concluded a one-week trip into these areas. On the first day, said the archbishop, a bomb had dropped within four miles of him, despite a statement by the Minister of Defense Casanova that no bombs were dropped in the area. NYT, January 13, 1986.

72. American Vice-President Bush attended Alfonsín's inauguration in December 1983, as did Uruguayan opposition leader Wilson Ferreyra Aldunate. The Reagan Administration lifted its arms embargo against Argentina, while maintaining the one against Chile. Bush said, "We would like to see more adherence to democratic principles in Chile." NYT, November 13, 1983. Chilean opposition leader Anselmo Sule also attended the ceremony.

73. Students of the Latin American National Security regimes of the 1970s produced a considerable literature on the "bureaucratic-authoritar-

ian" model. See, for example, David Collier, ed., *The New Authoritarianism in Latin America*.

74. Brian H. Smith, "Churches and Human Rights in Latin America: Recent Trends in the Subcontinent," p. 36.

75. Bruneau, *The Church in Brazil*, pp. 56-57.

76. Youngblood, "Church Opposition to Martial Law in the Philippines," p. 505.

77. Smith, *Chile*, p. 292. For the case of the church and the Christian Democrats under Pinochet, see Smith and Michael Fleet, *The Rise and Fall of Chilean Christian Democracy*.

78. NCNS from Asunción, in HKSE, July 13, 1979. The bishops' statement was released in June.

79. Bruneau, *The Church in Brazil*, p. 70.

80. Scott Mainwaring, *The Catholic Church and Politics in Brazil, 1916-1985*, p. 155.

81. Bruneau, *The Church in Brazil*, pp. 64-65.

82. Ibid., p. 71.

83. Mainwaring, *The Church and Brazil*, p. 173.

84. Ibid., pp. 170-74.

85. For comparative material on popular Catholicism, see Michael Dodson, "Comparing the Popular Church in Nicaragua and Brazil," pp. 131-36, and Daniel H. Levine, "Popular Organizations and the Church: Thoughts from Colombia," pp. 137-44.

86. Mainwaring, *The Church and Brazil*, p. 164.

87. Ibid., p. 166.

88. Ibid., p. 173. For a discussion of the movement to civilian rule, see Thomas C. Bruneau, "Consolidating Civilian Brazil."

89. Smith, "Churches and Human Rights." The others were Chile, Brazil, Paraguay, and Bolivia.

90. On August 15, 1982, the Argentinian bishops called on the military government to account for missing persons, return to the Constitution, and let civilians rule. For episcopal criticism of the "Whitewash paper," see NCNS from Buenos Aires, in HKSE, May 27, 1983. Vatican criticism is reported in NYT, May 4, 1983. In January 1983 the Brazilian Cardinal Arns released a list of 7,291 Argentinians missing for political reasons. AP from São Paolo, in *Los Angeles Times*, January 15, 1983.

91. "Broker" is used rather than "actor" since the positions of a national episcopal conference usually result from a complex informal dialogue among the bishops, their clergy, and lay representatives from significant and relevant segments of society.

92. NYT, May 3, 1980.

93. *Le Monde*, May 3, 1980.

94. *Los Angeles Times*, September 23, 1977.

95. Tanzania makes an excellent contrast. According to Nichols, *The Pope's Divisions*, p. 365: "The Church in Tanzania is very gentle with

Nyerere: 'We do very well from him,' was the phrase of a European missionary. There is still, nevertheless, this strange abyss between an institution that is old-fashioned in its structure, conservative in purely Catholic matters, and recognizeably European even if all but two bishops are black, and, on the other side of the abyss, authoritarian black socialism that has failed so far to give an effective basis to the economy or an acceptable level of living to the farmers involved in their collectivized villages." For Catholic politics in Zaire and Zimbabwe, see also Willy DeCraemer, *The Jamaa and the Church*; Ian Linden, *The Catholic Church and the Struggle for Zimbabwe*; Enda McDonagh, *Church and Politics*; and Marvin D. Markowitz, *Cross and Sword*.

96. James F. Conway, "John Paul II: Touching the Heart of Black Africa," p. 22. Conway says this decision constituted "the most serious break with history and protocol and belies deeper conflicts." Ibid., p. 23.

97. The Afrikaner Brotherhood serves as the organizational link between Dutch Reformed ideology and the ruling Nationalist Party. Membership in the Brotherhood includes most of the country's political elite, whose task it is to maintain Afrikaner tribal nationalism.

98. Walshe, *South Africa*, narrates the rise and fall of the Institute. The government lifted its ban on the sixty-nine-year-old Naudé in September 1984. Minister of Law and Order Le Grange said that even after seven years the decision to lift the ban "was not easy" but denied that it was an attempt to placate opponents during unrest. NYT, September 27, 1984. Naudé then became general secretary of the SACC.

99. For examples of Hurley's support, see Walshe, *South Africa*, pp. 122, 130, 143. On October 19, 1984, Archbishop Hurley pleaded innocent to government charges that he "falsely accused a police unit of committing atrocities against civilians in Namibia." The government later dropped the charges. The charges carried a maximum fine of $8,000 or eight years in prison or both. For a two-part interview of the archbishop by Richard A. Cuoto, see NCR, November 2, 9, 1984.

100. Walshe, *South Africa*, p. 41.

101. Ibid., p. 82.

102. Ibid., pp. 210-11.

103. NYT, February 12, 1977.

104. See Ch. 4, above, for a brief history of the Belgium Catholic university.

105. NYT, August 29, 1986.

106. Cited in Catholic Institute for International Relations and Pax Christi, *War and Conscience in South Africa*, pp. 47-48. For the 1982 statement of a Catholic universal pacifist conscientious objector, see Neil Mitchell, pp. 89-93. Under section 3, "The Teaching of the Catholic Church," Mitchell cites Vatican II and Popes Pius XII, John XXIII, Paul VI, and John Paul II.

107. CSM, October 31, 1983. Even more moderate blacks like Zulu Chief Gatsha Buthelezi have condemned the constitution, as has the SACBC. NYT, September 26, 1983. Philadelphia black minister Reverend Leon Sul-

livan joined the General Motors Board of Directors in 1970 after a distinguished career in the Civil Rights Movement. Almost immediately he separated himself from the rest of the directors on South Africa, and gradually
evolved a set of principles under which American corporations would be
justified in doing business in South Africa. In March 1977 many American
corporations formally adopted these principles, which emphasized the expansion of black employment opportunities and the integration of company facilities. In the early 1980s when Botha began to tighten influx control
and pass laws, Bishop Tutu called on American multinational corporations
to notify the South African government that they would remain only if they
were allowed to: ensure that all their black workers were permitted to live
with their families near their place of work, recognize black labor unions
whether or not they were registered with the government, freely hire black
labor without regard to the influx or homelands policies, implement fair labor practices, and invest "massively in black education and training."
American companies initially balked when the Reverend Sullivan wanted
to add these "enhancements" to his principles, but in November 1984 the
corporations tacitedly gave their approval. The Interfaith Center on Corporate Responsibility (ICCR) has coordinated the lobbying of most American churches on this issue within the United States.

108. NYT, June 20, 1984.

109. See, for example, USCC Committee on Social Development,
"Southern Africa: Peace or War?" in *Quest for Justice*, pp. 129-32. Catholic
Institute for International Relations and Pax Christi, *War and Conscience*, pp.
103-109, cites the USCC on conscientious objection.

110. Robert F. Drinan, S.J., *America* (August 11, 1984): 44.

111. NYT, September 15, 1984.

112. NYT, September 7, 1984, which reports the assertion of Le Grange
that the rent increase was not the real problem, but then cites "Roman
Catholic priests working in Sharpeville" to the contrary.

113. NYT, August 30, September 30, 1985. Earlier South African businessmen had gone to Zambia to meet with exiled leaders of the African National Congress.

114. For Reverend Sullivan, see n. 107, above. According to ICCR, "All
support the South African government either through products and services used by the police and military, by the size of their assets in the country, by their sales and number of employees, and by the strategic nature of
their involvement or financial services rendered." Cited in Timothy H.
Smith, "Church Activists in the 1980s: The Conscience of Corporate America," in "Church Activism and Corporate America," Special Report by the
Center for the Study of Business and Government, Baruch College, p. 16.
The twelve corporations are Burroughs, Chevron, Citicorp, Control Data,
Fluor, Ford, General Electric, General Motors, IBM, Mobil, Newmont Min-
ing, and Texaco.

115. NYT, December 7, 1985.

116. Hanson, *Catholic Politics*, p. 113, with additions from other parts of the book. This book contains an extensive bibliography of works on Catholic Church-Chinese state relations up to 1980.

117. "Orthodox" and "patriotic" are two terms used in English to distinguish those Chinese who have placed more emphasis on remaining united to Rome from those who have stressed a national course. Use of the terms does not indicate any judgment about the orthodoxy or patriotism of either group.

118. The *dazibao* (large character poster) movement began in Beijing in November 1978. For a detailed chronology and analysis of the Democracy Movement, see Kjeld Erik Brodsgaard, "The Democracy Movement in China, 1978-1979: Opposition Movements, Wall Poster Campaigns, and Underground Journals."

119. For analysis of Chinese religious policy toward the Catholic Church 1979-1982: *China News Analysis* 1156 (June 8, 1979); *China News Analysis* 1186 (August 1, 1980); Angelo Lazzarotto, *The Catholic Church in Post-Mao China*; Lazarrotto, "The Chinese Communist Party and Religion." For documentation, see *Religion in the People's Republic of China* (hereafter RPRC), published by the China Study Project, England, the Lutheran World Federation, Geneva, and Pro Mundi Vita, Brussels, in cooperation with members of the Ecumenical China Liaison Group.

120. *China News Analysis* 1156, p. 5.

121. The Religious Affairs Bureau started in 1951 as the Religious Affairs Office, belonging to the Committee on Cultural and Educational Affairs of the Government Administration Council, a state organization. See Hanson, *Catholic Politics*, pp. 60-71.

122. The New China News Agency (hereafter NCNA) releases can be found in RPRC 2-3 (July 1980): 43-46.

123. RPRC 2-3 (July 1980): 29-39.

124. RPRC 5 (May 1981): 10-15. On February 20, Casaroli said that John Paul hoped to visit China.

125. RPRC 5(May 1981): 14.

126. Chinese reaction to Tang's appointment can be found in RPRC 6 (October 1981): 7-12.

127. Lazzarotto, *Catholic Church*, pp. 143-45.

128. For the brief story of his family, see Hanson, *Catholic Politics*, pp. 50-51. An Amnesty International circular of December 4, 1981, stated that, "Amnesty International believes that the three priests are probably prisoners of conscience." A NCNA release indicated that Roman Catholics had been arrested for "following the wishes of the Roman Curia" and "trying to undermine the independence of Chinese churches." UCAN from Hong Kong, in HKSE, January 8, 1982.

129. NYT, May 2, 1983.

130. For a summary of Catholic events in China during 1985, see *Asian Focus* 2 (January 10, 1986): 5.

131. NYT, July 4, 5, 1985.

132. Hanson, *Catholic Politics*, p. 115.

133. NYT, May 11, 1984.

134. NYT, May 23, 1977. NCNS from Notre Dame, Ind., in HKSE, June 10, 1977.

135. Quoted in *Time*, October 30, 1979, p. 87.

136. *Far East Economic Review* (July 10, 1981): 12-13.

137. Michael Dodson, "Comparing the 'Popular Church' in Nicaragua and Brazil." See also Michael Dodson, and T. S. Montgomery, "The Churches and the Nicaraguan Revolution," in T. Walker, ed., *Nicaragua in Revolution*.

138. Smith, *Chile*, pp. 323-33.

139. Robert F. Drinan, "American Guns, Guatemalan Justice."

140. Smith, *Chile*, 189-90.

CHAPTER 8

1. Catholic Bishops' Conference of Japan, trans., *Appeal for Peace by Pope John Paul II at Hiroshima on February 25, 1981*. NYT, February 25, 1981. *Toronto Globe and Mail*, February 25, 1981.

2. Pius XII, Address to the International Office of Documentation for Military Medicine, 19 October 1953, in *Peace and Disarmament: Documents of the World Council of Churches and the Roman Catholic Church* (Vatican City: Tipographica Poliglotta Vaticana, 1982), p. 128. Cited in David Hollenbach, "The Challenge of Peace in the Context of Recent Church Teachings," in Philip J. Murnion, ed. *Catholics and Nuclear War*, p. 9. Hollenbach's essay has been very helpful in this section. See also David Hollenbach, *Nuclear Ethics*. Some other important recent ethical works and collections in the Christian tradition are James T. Johnson, *Just War Tradition*; Philip Lawler, ed. *Justice and War in the Nuclear Age*; Joseph F. Nye, Jr., *Nuclear Ethics*; William V. O'Brien, *The Conduct of Just and Limited War*; Thomas A. Shannon, ed., *War or Peace? The Search for New Answers*; Koos van der Bruggen, *Verzekerde vrede of verzekerde vernietiging*. See also Kenneth R. Melchin, "Military and Deterrence Strategy and the 'Dialectic of Community,' " paper presented to the International Symposium on Bernard Lonergan, University of Santa Clara, March 15-18, 1984. See also the special issue of the *New Catholic World* 226 (November-December 1983).

3. Pius XII, Address to Eighth Congress of World Medical Association, September 30, 1954. Cited in *The Challenge of Peace*, n. 147.

4. Pius XII, Christmas Message 1948, cited in NCCB, *The Challenge of Peace: God's Promise and Our Response* (May 3, 1983), no. 76.

5. Pius XII, Christmas Message 1956, in Vincent A. Yzermans, ed., *The Major Addresses of Pope Pius XII*, p. 225. John Paul II also remains skeptical about pacifism. When he visited Flanders field in May 1985, the pope warned against "unilateral slogans" and "simple sentimentalism" in the

pursuit of peace. "Involvement in the cause of peace must be accompanied by a clear understanding of the principles and values at stake. As the threat that hangs over humanity becomes greater, the moral maturity of mankind must grow stronger." NYT, May 18, 1985.

6. John XXIII, *Pacem in terris*, no. 127, in David J. O'Brien and Thomas A. Shannon, eds., *Renewing the Earth*, p. 154.

7. Flannery, *Vatican Council II*, pp. 988-89.

8. The full text is in NYT, October 3, 1979.

9. For a discussion of what the pope meant, see Bruce M. Russett, "Ethical Dilemmas of Nuclear Deterrence," pp. 40-42. Russett stresses that the operative words in the French original are " '*Une dissuasion*'—a deterrent, some deterrent, not any and all deterrents." It is not really clear that the pope *meant* to be quite so vague. The point is that he *was*. This allowed episcopal conferences to oppose many forms of deterrence while staying within the papal guidelines.

10. Flannery, *Vatican Council II*, pp. 986-87. *Gaudium et spes*, no. 78.

11. The question is even more complex when the nuances of different languages are added. For an op-ed piece on the connotations of the word in different languages, see Joseph A. Murphy, "Peace around the world," CSM, November 18, 1985.

12. L. Bruce van Voorst, "The Churches and Nuclear Deterrence," p. 829.

13. Jonathan Schell, *The Fate of the Earth*. Physicians for Social Responsibility leader Helen Caldicott called it the "Bible for Our Time" at Santa Clara University, October 5, 1982. The book first appeared in installments in the *New Yorker*. Schell quickly moved to a more nuanced political position. See the last section of this chapter.

14. In addition to California, Massachusetts, Rhode Island, New Jersey, North Dakota, Oregon, Montana, and Michigan voted on the Freeze Initiative. Only conservative Arizona rejected it. During the primary election of September 14, 1982, Wisconsin had approved a freeze proposal by a three to one margin.

Top Reagan Administration officials from California have included George Shultz, Casper Weinberger, Richard Allen, William French Smith, William Clark, and Ed Meese.

15. For the Progressives and the Initiative process, see John McFarland, "Protestant Reformers Who Thought Politics Was Sin." These early twentieth-century evangelical reformers, concentrated in Southern California, opposed unions which were often dominated by "priest-ridden" Catholics and the foreign-born.

16. Ian Thiermann, retired Los Angeles businessman and long-time Quaker activist, was so moved by the conference that he and his film-maker son produced the documentary by superimposing actual photographs from Hiroshima and Nagasaki over the taped track of the conference. The International Physicians for the Prevention of Nuclear War won the Nobel

Peace Prize in 1985. The IPPNW was founded on the American side by mainly Jewish and Catholic doctors. Dr. Bernard Lown is the son and grandson of rabbis and Dr. James Muller studied medicine and Russian at Notre Dame University.

17. The full text of Quinn's pastoral letter can be found in the *San Jose Mercury News*, December 10, 1981. The testimony to the Senate can be found in *San Jose Mercury News*, January 24, 1982. The text of the speech to the Commonwealth Club, "Church, State and the Arms Race," *The Commonwealth* 185 (July 12, 1982), is less remarkable than the fact that Quinn was asked to address this very proper establishment group on such a topic. The *San Jose Mercury News* published its series October 4-18, 1981. One journalistic coup was the official Soviet reply (by Zhurkin) to Reagan's message.

18. For a strong apologetic for the pacifist position as a critique of the pastoral letter, see Gordon Zahn, "Pacifism and the Just War," in Murnion, *Nuclear War*, pp. 119-31. Jim Wallis, ed., *Peacemakers*. The interventions of the various bishops appear throughout Jim Castelli, *The Bishops and the Bomb*.

19. Civil disobedience in support of disarmament has united Plowshares, a loose group of fifty-one people (thirty-eight of whom are Catholic) who, as of March 1985, had conducted twelve major actions. For a description of the group and the present activities of the Berrigan brothers, see NCR, March 1, 1985. When U.S. District Court Judge Brook Bartlett gave the four "Silo Pruning Hooks Plowshares" sentences ranging from eight to eighteen years, West German Judge Ulf Panzer, representing 800 judges and prosecutors in the FRG, wrote to Bartlett protesting the severity of the sentences. One of the four, Oblate Father Carl Kabat, had been involved in the destruction of a Pershing II missile launcher in Schwabish-Gmund in December 1983, but the German judge merely fined the protestors. NCR, May 10, 1985.

20. Jim Castelli, *The Bishops and the Bomb*, p. 166. Castelli's book remains the most complete narrative of the process of writing the letter, since he was given access to committee materials from the beginning. Castelli (p. 160) categorizes the bishops in ascending order of influence as: a) vocal, e.g., pacifist Kenny and conservative O'Rourke; b) respected, e.g., Weakland, McManus, Gumbleton; and c) heavyweights, e.g., Krol, Quinn, Hickey, Bernardin, Roach, Malone.

21. *The Challenge of Peace*, no. 170.

22. NYT, June 9, 1982.

23. The Vatican's designation of a particular bishop to care for the United States military forces dates to November 24, 1917 when Patrick Hayes was named "bishop ordinary of the United States Army and Navy chaplains." Hayes became archbishop of New York in 1919. Archbishop O'Connor was given the job of separating the archdiocese and the vicariate shortly after

being appointed to New York. Archbishop Ryan, formerly auxiliary bishop in New York, became the military vicar.

24. The then vicar general of the vicariate, Auxiliary Bishop (and now Archbishop) John O'Connor of New York, has written extensively on the just war theory. See Castelli, *The Bishops and the Bomb*, pp. 134-35:

O'Connor, assigned to revise the section on just war and pacifism, had ignored the second draft's framework and completely redone the section on deterrence. He sent Bernardin a forty-seven-page redraft with a cover letter saying: "It essentially reflects the position that in conscience I believe we must take. As always, I hope I am completely open to discussion and improvement. In integrity, however, I am not sure that I can deviate far from the basic position I attempt to express herein. And in honesty I must observe that I believe the format, structure and style of the enclosure better suit the issues treated than does the section in the Second Draft as currently presented."

The others interpreted O'Connor's letter as an implied threat to at least dissent, possibly resign, if he didn't get his way. (In an interview in November, O'Connor said that if he ever came to a point where he couldn't reconcile his concerns within the committee, he would ask Bernardin and Roach whether they wanted to replace him or have a minority report.) Russett told Hehir that if the committee accepted O'Connor's draft, he would resign, and not quietly.

25. Quotations from Cooke's letter to the chaplains and the reply can be found in NCNS from New York, in HKSE, January 15, 1982. For the transmittal letter, see NCNS from New York, in HKSE, July 8, 1983.

26. For House testimony, see NYT, June 27, 1984. For an interview of O'Connor along with analysis of the future of the Social Development and World Peace Committee, see NCR, January 27, 1984. In the interview O'Connor said he was "happy with the prudential judgment which strongly questions the . . . MX missile . . . I do not know enough about it technically to know if it would fall in the category of being condemned . . . but it would be very unwise for this or any other administration to proceed with production." On the B-1 bomber and Pershing II missile, O'Connor said: "I don't feel that I know enough to make a moral judgment (but) there seem to be . . . so many conflicting positions articulated by responsible people, pro and con, that I would have to question the prudence of the enormous expenditures required." O'Connor was appointed Archbishop of New York at the end of January.

27. Castelli, *The Bishops and the Bomb*, p. 175.

28. NCNS from New Orleans, in HKSE, May 27, 1983.

29. Van Voorst, "The Churches," pp. 833-34.

30. For this history of the pastoral, see Castelli, *The Bishops and the Bomb*. The *varia* of the three bishops are discussed in Ch. 1, pp. 13-25.

31. Russett, "Ethical Dilemmas," p. 38.

32. A complete list of those testifying can be found in the Appendix to the second draft (among other places, insert to NCR, November 5, 1982).

33. Castelli, *The Bishops and the Bomb*, p. 81.

34. Ibid., p. 43. Castelli summarizes points made in various speeches at the November 1981 meeting (pp. 40-50).

35. The draft said, "the MX missile might fit into this category."

36. NYT, November 17, 1982.

37. For the full text of the letter, see NYT, November 17, 1982. The letter was oddly addressed not to the bishops, but to Clare Boothe Luce. Clark is the subject of an article in *New York Times Magazine*, August 14, 1983.

38. The full text of Secretary Lehman's remarks can be found in the *Wall Street Journal*, November 15, 1982.

39. NYT, November 13, 1982. Excerpts of the Congressman's letter are in NYT, December 23, 1982. *Catholicism in Crisis* (February 1983) carries the whole text.

40. The full text is in *Catholicism in Crisis* (March 1983) and was issued by the Nashville publisher Thomas Nelson (1983). For earlier criticism by Novak, see "Nuclear Morality."

41. NCR, April 22, 1983. The *Reporter* letter, "What is Evil is Evil," can be found in the April 15, 1983, issue.

42. In his letter Hyde cited the *Baltimore Sun* headline, "Bishops Back Off Freeze Idea." Several pro-Freeze members of Congress, mostly Catholics, answered with a "Dear Colleague" letter that quoted Bernardin-Roach clarification (see p. 298) and included Pax Christi's list of 142 bishops who had supported the Freeze. Castelli, *The Bishops and the Bomb*, pp. 149-52.

43. Castelli comments, "Bernardin is unmatched as a church politician, but he has never been able to master the world of secular politics, the Washington land of 'blue-smoke and mirrors' in which perception is all and careers and movements live or die by the headlines." Castelli also includes the lament of one USCC aide that Roach did not hold the press conference. Ibid., pp. 148-49.

44. NYT, April 10, 1983. The original April 6 NYT (front page, two column) headline read, "Bishop's Letter on Nuclear Arms is Revised to 'More Flexible' View." The later press conference only received a one-column subhead.

45. Castelli, *The Bishops and the Bomb*, p. 165.

46. Ibid., pp. 169-70. Catholic votes on the House Freeze resolution can be found on p. 178.

47. The essays in Murnion, ed., *Nuclear War*, are an excellent introduction to the various religious issues involved. See especially J. Bryan Hehir, "From the Pastoral Constitution of Vatican II to *The Challenge of Peace*," which analyzes the pastoral as a theological document.

48. From "Summary," *The Challenge of Peace*.

49. The release of the USCC letter against the MX made the front page top of the NYT (March 16, 1985), with the text of the letter on p. 4.

50. NYT, May 5, 1983.

51. NYT, May 6, 1983. CSM, May 10, 1983. Russett, "Ethical Dilemmas," p. 50, n. 17, commented that neither the NYT editorial nor Albert Wohl-

stetter, "Bishops, Statesmen, and Other Strategists on the Bombing of Innocents," took into account the differences between the second and third or final drafts. "A charitable interpretation of their criticism is that they simply had not read the later versions carefully."

52. McGeorge Bundy, "The Bishops and the Bomb," p. 4. When the bipartisan commission on social security proved so successful politically, Reagan attempted to solve difficult foreign policy issues by appointing bipartisan groups on Latin America, the Kissinger Commission, and arms control, the Scowcroft Commission led by ex-Kissinger national security aide Brent Scowcroft. *Report of the President's Commission on Strategic Forces* (The Scowcroft Commission) (Washington, D.C.: Government Printing Office, 1983). See also NYT, April 12, 1983, for release and commentary.

53. Russett, "Ethical Dilemmas," p. 53, n. 19, lists some of the recent literature concerning the feasibility of a nonnuclear defense of Europe, besides referring to other articles listed in the pastoral.

54. Bundy, "The Bishops," p. 6.

55. Excerpted in Castelli, *The Bishops and the Bomb*, pp. 138-39. The committee received the memo in Washington on a March afternoon, casting a pall over the deliberations. The possibility of intervention from Rome was always on the mind of the committee and staff. On another occasion the committee was meeting at the cathedral in Chicago when a call came "from Rome." Everyone in the room held his breadth. It turned out to be a telegram for Bernardin: "Best wishes on your Saint's Day."

56. NCR, May 13, 1983.

57. Hume's letter, along with English translations of the German and French letter, can be found in James V. Schall, S.J., ed., *Bishops' Pastoral Letters*, which includes translations of *Out of Justice, Peace* (German letter) and *Winning the Peace* (French letter).

58. See Philipp Schmitz, S.J., "Friedenswort diesseits und jenseits des Atlantiks," and Bernhard Sutor, "Das Politische in den Friedenserklarungen katholischer Bischofskonferenzen."

59. *Le Monde*, November 10, 1983, contains extensive excerpts from the pastoral. See also the special section of *L'Actualité Religieuse dans le Monde* 7 (December 1983): 39-53.

60. *Der Spiegel*, May 9, 1983. Translation in NCNS from Hamburg, in HKSE, June 10, 1983.

61. Letter is available in Schall, *Peace*, pp. 121-24. The German letter also differed from the American one in the process used to write it. Rather than hold extensive hearings and publicize successive drafts, a committee of four plus one redactor constituted the majority input. See Schmitz, "Friedenswort."

62. Schall, ed., *Pastoral Letters*, p. 121.

63. See, for example, Walter Stein, ed., *Nuclear Weapons and Christian Conscience*.

64. Editorial, "The Mission of Bruce Kent," *The Month* 16 (May 1983):

147-48. On the American pastoral, this British Catholic journal comments, "The US bishops, whether one wholly agrees with them or not, have given a spectacular example of how the discussion should go" (p. 148).

65. NCNS from London in HKSE, May 20, 1983. The Scottish bishops had issued their own peace pastoral in 1982.

66. NCNS from Logumkloster, in HKSE, December 25, 1981.

67. This leaves the British Catholic Church and Conservative politicians at odds over the role of Bruce Kent, the possibility of restoring capital punishment (which is inextricably bound up with the question of Irish terrorism), and Conservative cuts in social welfare programs. In addition, in April 1983 London's eight Catholic auxiliary bishops criticized a Conservative police and criminal evidence bill, which, the bishops felt, "appears to erode deeply felt and important freedoms." NCNS from London, in HKSE, July 8, 1983. The British bishops have also issued a statement on the multi-racial character of British society.

68. The zone would encompass 400 million people between the U.S.S.R. in the East and France and the United Kingdom in the West. Summary in "Pax Christi Quest for Disarmament in 1983," *Bulletin* (Summer 1984): 6-7.

69. Those speaking were: Mark Neidergang, editor of the *Freeze Newsletter*, Albert De Smaele of the Security Zone proposal, and Willem Bartels.

70. See the report of the statements of De Jonghe and Laurens Hogenbrink, board member of IKV and IPCC in *Bulletin* (Summer 1984): 8.

71. Murnion, *Nuclear War*, pp. 339-44. Hesburgh was also one of the eight American members of the ad hoc Aspen committee which produced "Managing East-West Conflict," which advocated less NATO reliance on nuclear weapons. The committee included, among others, Kreisky, James Callaghan, Edward Heath, Trudeau, Edgar Faure, Saburo Okita, Soares, Kennan, McNamara, Cyrus Vance, and Schmidt. See NYT, November 27, 1984 for excerpts and news story.

72. NCNS from Vatican City, in HKSE, May 27, 1983.

73. NYT, January 24, July 8, 1985.

74. Preus later pronounced himself satisfied with the balance of the documents. For the internal politics that produced these documents, and severe criticism of the United States government and the American media, see articles by H. Lamar Gibble, James E. Will, and J. Martin Bailey in a special edition of *Occasional Papers on Religion in Eastern Europe* (hereafter OPREE) 2 (July 1982). Billy Graham's presence did guarantee media coverage, but distracted somewhat from the central focus of the meeting. Most of the Soviet propaganda was included in the "Greetings" (an old Orthodox tradition) by various Soviet church speakers. The most damaging decision for the credibility of the conference was the decision to deny the IKV representative Willem Bartels the opportunity to address the conference. Bartels withdrew.

All Eastern bloc countries have official peace committees as they have departments of religious affairs. One of the values of having a conference sponsored by the Russian Orthodox Church rather than the Soviet Peace Committee is the added legitimacy in the West. In general, the Soviet government and the Russian Orthodox Church have worked closely in promoting peace initiatives.

75. NCNS from Rome, in HKSE, June 11, 1982.

76. The Czechoslovakian government has supported the international Christian Peace Conference, whose Sixth All-Christian Peace Assembly took place in Prague, July 2-9, 1985. Bishop Dr. Károly Tóth (Hungarian Reformed Church) was reelected as president, and Metropolitan Mikhail A. D. Filaret of Kiev and Galicia as chairman of the Continuation Committee. The new secretary general is Rev. Dr. Lubomír Miřejovský (Evangelical Church of Czech Bretheran). Czech President Husák received a CPC delegation on July 4. The retired Mexican bishop Sergio Méndez Arceo was the only Catholic in the delegation and the only Catholic to present a plenary report, "Peaceful Coexistence and Liberation."

77. "Many European countries with a longstanding Christian culture are bristling with lethal missiles. It is immoral to frighten mankind in this way." NYT, January 7, 1984.

78. "Circumspect blessing" is the term of Kondziela, "What the Church in Poland Did for Peace in 1980-1983," consultation on The Churches' Influence on Disarmament Decisions in East and West, p. 4. Follow-up meetings were held in 1980 and 1981, but none have been held since. In his paper Kondziela designates Polish church actions for internal stability and European stability as its greatest contribution to peace.

79. For an "official" view lumping PZKS, ChSS, and PAX activities, see Janusz Symonides, "Structural and Functional Possibilities for the Churches to Influence Disarmament Issues in Poland," consultation on The Churches' Influence on Disarmament Decisions in East and West, pp. 13-17. Symonides is director of the Polish Institute of International Affairs.

80. NCNS from Washington, D.C., in HKSE, July 27, 1979. Baltic émigrés submitted documents to the Stockholm Conference on Disarmament and Confidence-Building Measures in Europe showing an estimated 174 land-based nuclear delivery systems stationed in the three countries. In 1981 thirty-eight Baltic citizens sent an open letter to the West asking to be included in any Nordic nuclear free zone. Several signatories of the letter in Latvia and Estonia were arrested and sentenced in late 1983. CSM, January 26, 1984.

81. J. A. Hebly, "Churches in Eastern Europe: Three Models of Church-State Relations and Their Relevance for the Ecumenical Movement."

82. Earl A. Pope, "The Romanian Orthodox Church."

83. NYT, November 26, 1983. The Romanians had originally advocated a "radical zero option," but then moved back closer to Soviet policy, calling for the withdrawal and destruction of Soviet SS-20s, but only down to the numbers of British and French missiles. In October 1984 Ceauşescu, on the

first visit to a NATO capital by a Warsaw Pact leader since deployment, called for the gradual dissolution of both alliances.

84. Hebly, "Churches in Eastern Europe," p. 24. He quotes the Reformed Bishop Lajos Bakos as addressing the Patriotic Front: "Socialism means the world of freedom, of justice, of equality, and of humanity."

85. The Peace Group for Dialogue demonstration attracted 150 supporters, while the official Peace Council march had 20,000 the same day. CSM, November 1, 1983.

86. NYT, January 22, 1984.

87. For an excellent comparison of the use of the anniversary made by both Germanies, see Elizabeth Pond's article in CSM, April 20, 1983.

88. Timothy Garton Ash, "Swords into Plowshares: The Unofficial 'Peace Movement' and the Churches in East Germany," RCL 11 (Winter 1983): 244.

89. A. James McAdams, "Preaching Peace in East Germany."

90. CSM, October 16, 1984.

91. Leonard Swindler, editor of the *Journal of Ecumenical Studies*, reported attending a small East German Catholic peace group in NCR, September 14, 1984. He writes, "they [the Catholic activists] also could point to a recent strong peace statement by the Catholic hierarchy of East Germany (said to have been forthcoming only at the command of the Vatican, lest the acknowledgedly very conservative Catholic church of East Germany totally lose credibility). Likewise, they were acting in concert with the Pax Christi movement headquartered in West Germany (as can be imagined, East-West relations are *sub rosa*), which buoyed them."

92. Senior Editor Vladimir Gorloch explained that such letters were a natural phenomenon. "It would have been astonishing if there had been no reaction. The letters were from people who showed they had no idea of modern war." NYT, March 30, 1984.

93. Kathpress (Austrian Catholic news agency) from Vienna, reported in CSM, February 9, 1984.

94. CSM, November 21, 1983.

95. In his summary paper for the consultation on The Churches' Influence on Disarmament Decisions in East and West, James W. Will employs the distinction (taken from WCC Faith and Order Paper No. 85) between the traditional Catholic collaborative and Lutheran complementary relationships between church and state. The Polish church must be strong because it is a partner in fashioning the *societas perfecta*.

96. "Prospects for Militarization and for Peace in Asia and the Pacific: An American Catholic View," p. 1, by Sister Ann Gormly. S.N.D. in a talk to Southern Asia Committee, Division of Ministries (D.O.M.), Committee for East Asia and Pacific, D.O.M., February 24, 1983.

97. Statement of Japanese Bishops' Conference presented to His Excellence the Secretary General of the U.N. by the Catholic Peace Pilgrimage Delegation from Japan, p. 1.

98. At the same time various Buddhist groups collected nearly 100 million signatures, which were also presented at the Second Session.

99. NCNS from Washington, in HKSE, June 18, 1982.

100. Cited in Gormly, "Prospects," p. 2.

101. UCAN (Union of Catholic Asian News) from Tokyo, in HKSE, October 10, 1980.

102. James M. Phillips, *From the Rising of the Sun*, pp. 45-46.

103. CW (Catholic Weekly)-TOSEI, in HKSE, November 28, 1980.

104. Archbishop Jadot, president of the Secretariat for Non-Christians, was leading the Vatican delegation. UCAN from Tokyo, in HKSE, July 10, 1981.

105. NYT, February 24, 1981.

106. Catholic Bishops' Conference of Japan, "The Desire for Peace: The Gospel Mission of the Japanese Catholic Church," pp. 1-2. The English translation from Reverend John Vinsko, M.M., international secretary of the Japanese Catholic Council for Justice and Peace, is not an official text, since only the Japanese text is so regarded.

107. "The Desire for Peace," p. 6. Jesuit priest Noel Yamada of the Japanese Catholic Council for Justice and Peace remarked, "In the Asian milieu, if you say 'peace,' the contents are human rights and the promotion of justice." Cited in Gormly, "Prospects," p. 2.

108. "The Desire for Peace," p. 4.

109. Interview in *Info for Human Development* (October 1982): 2-4. When the Jesuit Social and Pastoral Committee Secretariat held a discussion on the American pastoral letter, the second of their main points was: "Nevertheless, when they [the American bishops] touch on the evaluation of concrete policies such as the conditional recognition of nuclear deterrence theirs is a compromising weak stance." *Social and Pastoral Bulletin* 1 (May 15, 1984).

110. Phillips, *The Rising of the Sun*, p. 21.

111. Phillips gives four characteristics of Christian political activity since 1945: the direct involvement of Christians in politics was minimal; Christians participated in politics mostly as individuals and not as members of a group; Christians have tended to focus their attention on a few political issues that seemed to them of special significance; and the polarization that developed among some Christian groups was symptomatic of an underlying political polarization in Japanese society as a whole. Ibid., pp. 44-47.

112. Edwin O. Reischauer, *The Japanese*, p. 213. In a national survey of Asahi Shinbun 62 percent of the respondents said they professed no religion. Twenty-seven percent named Buddhism, 4 percent both Shinto and Buddhism, and 2 percent Christianity. HKSE, July 10, 1981.

113. Phillips, *The Rising of the Sun*, p. 38. I remember discussing the student take-over of some buildings at the Jesuit Sophia University with a faculty member in spring 1971. He described the debate between Japanese and foreign Jesuits over whether or not to turn off the heat in the occupied

buildings. The Japanese prevailed and the heat was not turned off. The UCCJ had been formed with government support during World War II.

114. Jonathan Schell, "The Abolition," is divided into two parts, "Defining the Great Predicament" (January 2, 1984): 36-75; and "A Deliberate Policy" (January 9, 1984): 43-94. Schell also comments extensively on the American pastoral throughout his article. He admires the bishops but concludes that, "the bishops' U-turn, in which they criticize but then embrace deterrence, although only provisionally and with barely contained revulsion, reflects the whole peace movement's rejection of the premises of deterrence and its simultaneous reliance on deterrence to justify the moderate and politically popular proposals that it has put forward" (January 2, p. 69).

115. As such it combines the strategic evaluation of the bomb first enunciated by Bernard Brodie in 1946 with some of Einstein's passion for escaping this horrible dilemma. For a comparison of Brodie and Einstein, see Schell, "The Abolition," pp. 50-54.

CHAPTER 9

1. Vocations to the priesthood and the religious life are increasing in the Third World, with the percentages of global vocations continuing to decline in the North Atlantic countries, especially continental Western Europe. Even in the United States, the increase in Spanish and Vietnamese-speaking candidates has brought about English as a Second Language training in some seminaries. At current rates Indians will soon replace Americans as the largest national group in the Jesuits.

2. Gary Wills, "Is the Pope Too Catholic?"

3. NYT, April 6, 1985. The selection of Navarro, a member of Opus Dei, caused controversy.

4. For the first time since 1945, the Chinese Communist Party reassessed its history at the Sixth Plenum of the Eleventh Central Committee, June 27-29, 1981. The Central Committee resolution condemned Mao's attack on Peng Dehuai, but praised Mao's effort to "energetically rectify the 'left' errors" during 1959-1962. For a full page of excerpts, see NYT, July 1, 1981.

5. See Kenneth Lieberthal, "Domestic Politics and Foreign Policy," in Harry Harding, ed., *China's Foreign Relations in the 1980s*, pp. 43-70.

6. The new video-cassette technology has produced difficulties for Second and Third World leaders. For example, Soviet leaders complain about the insidious invasion of Western "pop" culture on cassettes, and many Filipinos viewed a contraband video of Japanese news reports on the death of Aquino. Western politicians lack some control over the rate at which political issues are raised in public opinion. For example, antinuclear war groups used the video "The Last Epidemic" and the television movie "The Day After" to rally support for their cause. The former more primitive videotape, reinforced by small-group viewing, proved much more effective than ABC's slick presentation, even though "The Day After" brought on

attacks on the network by the conservative Accuracy in the Media. ABC's attempt at finessing the charge of bias has been to undertake production of "Amerika," a mini-series based on a hypothetical Soviet takeover of the United States.

7. *Washington Post*, February 25, 1986.

8. NYT, February 6, 1986. The headline on page 6 read, "Philippine Campaign Ends; Prelate Commends Aquino."

9. The accompanying story was the lead story on page 1, with a photo of Cardinal Ricardo Vidal, president of the CBCP. The CBCP also issued a pastoral following their meeting January 20-25 warning against election fraud. Cardinal Sin issued his second pastoral letter on the election January 19. See *Asian Focus* 2 (January 24): 1-5, and *Asian Focus* 2 (January 31): 1-5.

10. NYT, February 20, 1986.

11. For the cabinet, see NYT, February 27, 1986. The most important appointments from each group respectively would be Pimentel, Laurel, Concepción and Ongpin, and Enrile. For the view of the Jesuit and Harvard-trained Finance Minister James Ongpin, see *Wall Street Journal*, March 5, 1986. During the crisis Filipino Jesuits (retired bishop) Francisco Claver, Provincial Ben Nebres, and Ateneo de Manila President Joaquin Bernas wrote important letters and speeches for the episcopate, Sin, and Aquino.

12. The interview took place on February 21. After the ouster of Marcos, Sin went to Rome for an audience with the pope on March 6. See NYT, March 7, 1986. John Paul most fears close ties between the institutional church and *any* government in power, be it in the Philippines or Nicaragua. The church's role changes drastically, according to this perspective, as soon as the old regime is overthrown.

13. The cardinal said, "Before they argue that Korea is different from the Philippines, political leaders must first show to the Korean people that Korea is free of corruption, torture, political oppression, rule by a handful of families and violation of human rights, which were dominant in the Philippines." NYT, March 10, 1986.

14. Reagan Administration interest in Catholic politics was again demonstrated when Secretary of State Shultz flew to meet the pope in San Juan, Puerto Rico, at the beginning of John Paul's Latin American tour of October 1984. Shultz's wife is a Catholic.

15. The phrase belongs to Cardinal Sin of Manila during the period before the Aquino assassination. That Sin (ecclesiastical center) became so involved in the campaign to oust Marcos was an indication that the dictator had lost any claim to national expressive legitimacy. Bishop Claver (ecclesiastical left) maintained his anti-Marcos position throughout the 1970s and 1980s. That Claver and Enrile stood together under siege indicates the disparate nature of the final coalition.

16. On Chile, see Smith, *Chile*, and Michael Fleet, *The Rise and Fall of the Chilean Christian Democratic Party*.

17. The SACBC endorsed economic pressure in their May 1986 pastoral,

despite a petition drive against the move by the South African TFP. The bishops responded to union leaders who called for sanctions in their addresses to the plenary sessions of the SACBC. See NCR, May 9, 1986.

18. Aquino was drafted as an expressive symbol. Both Frei and Duarte belonged to the right wings of their parties. Duarte suffers from his lack of control of the military and the difficulties of the Salvadoran economy, both areas of concern for Aquino.

19. Area specialists might argue that most Third World societies are no more amenable to political coalitions than postwar China was to Marshall's suggestion of cooperation between Mao and Chiang Kai-shek. Under United States sponsorship both men toasted each other and prepared for the outbreak of full-scale Civil War. The major differences between that situation and those cited here are the existence of a strong primary ethical broker, the impact of the international media, and the extensive influence of Washington and the American business community. Fleet, *Chilean Christian Democracy*, pp. 236-46, foresees a prominent role for the PDC in the transition period immediately following Pinochet, but the loss of its centrist course as soon as moderate left- and right-wing blocks appear within the party. In this sense, says Fleet, Chilean Christian Democracy will follow the French, not the German experience. There is no question that a viable solution will be difficult for post-Pinochet Chile, but Fleet argues that the only chance lies in a center-oriented coalition whose legitimacy is based on a leadership which holds "such influence (that) assures effective realization of at least some of its (another group's) goals" (p. 231). Of course, such a center-oriented coalition would also be possible, if less probable, if the PDC did split into two parties.

20. Wilson denied that he had been forced to resign. Vatican spokesman Navarro said the Holy See was especially appreciative of Wilson's role in "the delicate duties" of establishing Vatican-American relations. NYT, May 22, 1986.

21. Interview with Senator Richard Lugar, Santa Clara University, January 1984.

22. NYT, January 11, 1984.

23. NYT, January 11, 1984.

24. For example, *Business Week*, January 23, 1984; CSM, January 13, 1984.

25. Laghi served as nuncio in Jerusalem, Cyprus, and Buenos Aires, the last assignment from 1974 to 1980.

26. Vallier, "The Roman Catholic Church: A Transnational Actor," in Robert O. Keohane and Joseph F. Nye, eds. *Transnational Relations and World Politics*, p. 145.

27. NYT, September 21, 1983.

28. See, for example, Ezra F. Vogel, *Japan as Number One*.

29. See, for example, the article and op-ed pieces in the CSM, March 11, 1986. The two headlines read, " 'Sensible and fair' Lugar makes his mark on foreign policy," and "Don't overlook Lugar." Catholic and alumnus of

the Jesuit Santa Clara University Laxalt said, "Since the Marcos phone call there's been a lot of speculation and editorials encouraging me to run [for president in 1988]." NYT, May 28, 1986.

30. Appointing Mahony meant major changes for the large multi-racial archdiocese. One of the archbishop's first acts was to relieve the vicar general, Monsignor Benjamin Hawkes, the powerful financial power broker. Hawkes, who had served as the model for Robert DeNiro in "True Confessions," was an ex-Lockheed accountant who oversaw the expansion of the archdiocese under Cardinals McIntyre and Manning. For Mahony's conservative stands on the "big three" theology cases (Curran, Buckley, and Provost), *Los Angeles Times*, August 25, 1986.

31. NYT, July 3, 1985.

32. These contacts occur at both diplomatic and academic levels. At the academic level, for example, the Institute for Peace Research of the Catholic Theological Faculty of the University of Vienna has cooperated with the Soviet-oriented Institute for Peace in sponsoring a series of international symposia since 1971.

33. Stehle, *Eastern Politics*, pp. 372-73. For theoretical considerations on human rights in the East-West dialogue, see the special issue of *Soundings* 67 (Summer 1984), edited by George R. Lucas, Jr., and James E. Will. The Lithuanian Catholic Church cited these accords, along with the Gospel of Christ, the decrees of the Second Vatican Council, the Soviet Constitution, and the Universal Declaration of Human Rights to protest against Soviet religious regulations. Four hundred sixty-eight of the country's 701 priests plus the apostolic administrator of Vilnius, Julijonas Steponavičius, had signed the document which was forwarded to the late President Brezhnev in November 1982. *Chronicle* (February 1983), cited in NCNS from Brooklyn, in HKSE, March 18, 1983.

34. Parts of the Helsinki Accords are called "Baskets." Basket Three concerns human rights. For commentary on the Madrid follow-up conference, see Jonathan Luxmoore, "Church and State after Madrid," *The Month* 17 (February 1984): 50-54.

35. CSM, February 28, 1985. The Association of Expellees unites former German residents of the Polish territory who live in West Germany. The Association lobbies, especially through the Christian Democratic Party, for a return to prewar boundaries.

36. NCR, July 15, 1983.

37. John Paul's first encyclical, *Redemptor hominis*, attacked both Western consumerism and Marxist economic determinism because they undermine the essential unity of the individual redeemed by Christ. The document also criticizes the industrial countries for offering the Third World modern weapons instead of bread and cultural aid. John Paul's second encyclical, *Dives in misericordia*, highlighted the importance of "merciful love" in bringing about just relationships between people and between societies. After *Laborem exercens* and *Slavorum apostoli* (treated at the beginning of this sec-

tion), John Paul issued *Dominum et vivificantem* on May 30, 1986. This fifth encyclical focused on the Holy Spirit, but also included attacks on materialism and Marxism as resistence to the Holy Spirit. English titles given to the five encyclicals make an excellent introduction to the concerns of John Paul: 1) *Redeemer of Man*; 2) *Rich in Mercy*; 3) *On Human Work*; 4) *The Apostles of the Slavs*; and 5) *The Lord and Giver of Life*.

38. For example, in May 1984 John Paul "with all my heart" called for prayers for the Soviet dissident Andrey Sakharov. NYT, May 28, 1984.

39. NCR, December 28, 1979.

40. On this point, see Paul Johnson, "The Strategy of John Paul II," p. 15. This does not mean, of course, that John Paul has not encouraged ecumenical endeavors with Protestants, especially Lutherans and Anglicans. See, for example, NYT, September 28, 1985.

41. Stehle, *Eastern Politics*, pp. 369-70.

42. Hungarian Primate Lékai is mentioned as the contact. CSM, March 12, 1986. Lékai died of a heart attack June 30, 1986.

43. The reporters' questions stemmed from Casaroli's recent trip to the United States, and papal meetings with Czech Foreign Minister Chňoupek and Italian Prime Minister Craxi. Casaroli did specify that he was not speaking of the Vatican's general willingness to be of diplomatic assistance. NYT, December 5, 1983.

44. On the European reaction to SDI, I am indebted to a seminar by Danish security professor Hans-Henrik Holm at Stanford, August 1985.

45. For the relation of this French-sponsored initiative to SDI, see Pierre-Henri Laurent, "The Thinking Behind Europe's Eureka," CSM, August 29, 1985.

46. The literature is enormous and varied. An introduction is Sidney D. Drell, Philip J. Farley, and David Holloway, *The Reagan Strategic Defense Initiative*.

47. SDI came too late for a full consideration by the Bernardin committee. At its last meeting before Chicago, the committee unanimously agreed to include a brief statement expressing support for the ABM Treaty, but the statement never made it into the final text.

48. CSM, December 24, 1984.

49. Andrew M. Greeley, "Why the Peace Pastoral Did Not Bomb," NCR, April 12, 1985. Greeley also highlights the fact that the national secular print and electronic media were the most significant conduits of influence, in other words, "the nuclear pastoral apparently succeeded because it was an effective media event at the right time."

50. Bishop Fulcher died in January 1984. Pressure has been added by the release of the pastoral letter of the Council of Bishops of the United Methodist Church which states "clear and unconditioned" opposition to any use of nuclear weapons. NYT, April 30, 1986.

51. Gordon A. Craig and Alexander L. George, *Force and Statecraft: Dip-*

lomatic Problems of Our Time (New York: Oxford University Press, 1983), p. x.

52. Ibid.

53. The Soviet Union and the United States do exercise veto power over international politics. When UN Secretary General Javier Pérez de Cuéllar was interviewed in August 1983, he expressed hope for an improvement in Soviet-American relations that would make possible his own mediation in the Middle Eastern, Afghanistan, Southeast Asian, South African, and Central American conflicts. A senior aide referred to the old African proverb, "When the elephants stop fighting, you can hear the other animals." CSM, August 16, 1983.

54. John XXIII, *Pacem in terris*, William J. Gibbons, S.J., ed. (New York: Paulist, 1963), p. 49.

55. NYT, January 2, 1986.

56. NYT, May 14, 1985.

57. NCNS from Vatican City, in HKSE, March 13, 1981.

58. NCNS from United Nations, in HKSE, May 21, 1982.

59. This formulation abstracts from how the leadership established that legitimacy. Democratic elections are not required. In the Eastern bloc, for example, Kádár enjoys a legitimacy that Gierek never had. It is at this point that national consensus must support international consensus.

60. For China's current reformist foreign policy, see Harry Harding, "China's Changing Roles in the Contemporary World," in Harding, ed., *China's Foreign Relations*, pp. 177-224.

APPENDIX

1. Vallier, "A Transnational Actor," pp. 129-52.

2. This is the use of the term in Samuel H. Huntington, "Transnational Organizations in World Politics." For Huntington's discussion on the difference between his use and that of Keohane and Nye, pp. 333-37.

3. J. Bryan Hehir, "The Roman Catholic Church as Transnational Actor: Amending Vallier," paper presented at the Annual Convention of the International Studies Association, Washington, D.C., February 22-26, 1978.

4. See, for example, S. N. Eisenstadt, ed., *The Protestant Ethic and Modernization*; Robert N. Bellah, *The Broken Covenant*.

5. Bernard J.F. Lonergan, *Insight*, p. 130. Of course, this epistemological question is separate from the church's long battle over Galileo's "heresies" about the place of the earth in the cosmos. For the latest on the latter question, see Reuters from Rome, May 9, 1983, in the NYT, May 10, 1983.

6. Ernst Troeltsch, *Social Teaching*. See, for example, "Sect-type and Church-type Contrasted," Vol. I, pp. 331-43.

7. Bellah et al., *Habits of the Heart*, pp. 244-45. The researchers of *Habits* even discovered an individual who consciously termed her own one-person religion "Sheilaism."

8. See, for example, Bruneau, "Religious Beliefs and Practices," *The Church in Brazil*, pp. 21-45.

9. Levine, *Venezuela and Colombia*, p. 9. Levine is quoting Geertz. For a discussion of the "phenomenological approach," see pp. 12-14.

10. David I. Kertzer, *Comrades and Christians*, p. 21.

11. Levine, *Venezuela and Colombia*, p. 6.

12. However, Vaillancourt does not hold that these structural and infrastructural roots can completely explain religion, so that his approach, he says, remains "compatible with that of Weber, Durkheim, and the functionalists." Vaillancourt, *Papal Power*, pp. 282-83.

13. Sanders, "The Politics of Catholicism in Latin America," pp. 254-55.

14. Coleman, *Dutch Catholicism*, p. 7.

15. The famous Little Brown series on comparative politics followed the general framework of Almond and Powell, *Comparative Politics*.

16. Bruneau, *The Church in Brazil*, pp. 6-7.

17. Bogdan Denitch, "Religion and Social Change in Yugoslavia," in Bociurkiw and Strong, *Religion and Atheism*, p. 369.

18. Smith, *Chile*, p. 13.

19. Kertzer, *Comrades and Christians*, p. xvi.

BOOKS

Abbott, Walter M., ed. *The Documents of Vatican II*. New York: America Press, 1966.

Adams, Richard. *Crucifixion by Power: Essays on Guatemalan National Social Structure, 1944-1966*. Austin: University of Texas Press, 1970.

Alix, Christine. *Le Saint-Siege et les nationalismes en Europe 1870-1960*. Paris: Sirey, 1962.

Allardt, Erik, and Littunen, Yrjo, eds. *Cleavages, Ideologies, and Party Systems*. Helsinki: Academic Bookstore, 1964.

Allum, P. A. *Italy: Republic Without Government*. New York: W. W. Norton, 1973.

Almond, Gabriel A., and Powell, G. Bingham, Jr. *Comparative Politics: A Developmental Approach*. Boston: Little, Brown, and Co., 1966.

Amery, Carl [pseud.], Mayer, Christian. *Capitulation: The Lesson of German Catholicism*. New York: Herder and Herder, 1967.

Anderson, Gerald H., ed. *Asian Voices in Christian Theology*. Maryknoll, N.Y.: Orbis Books, 1976.

Annuario Pontificio. Vatican City. Published annually since 1943.

Appiah-Kubi, Kofi, and Torres, Sergio. *African Theology En Route*. Maryknoll, N.Y.: Orbis Books, 1979.

Arès, Richard. *Les Positions—ethniques, linguistiques, et religieuses—des Canadiens français à la suite du recensement de 1971*. Montreal: Bellarmine, 1975.

Assman, Hugo. *Theology for a Nomad Church*. Maryknoll, N.Y.: Orbis Books, 1976.

Bakvis, Herman. *Catholic Power in the Netherlands*. Montreal: McGill-Queen University Press, 1981.

Bammel, E., and Moule, C.F.D., ed. *Jesus and the Politics of His Day*. New York: Cambridge University Press, 1983.

Barnett, Clifford R. *Poland: Its People, Its Society, Its Culture*. New York: Grove Press Books, 1958.

Barraclough, Geoffrey. *The Medieval Papacy*. London: Thames and Hudson, 1974.

Barzini, Luigi Giorgio. *The Italians*. New York: Atheneum, 1977.

Baum, Gregory. *Religion and Alienation*. New York: Paulist Press, 1976.

Bellah, Robert N. *Beyond Belief: Essays on Religion in a Post-Traditional World*. New York: Harper and Row, 1970.

———. *The Broken Covenant: American Civil Religion in Time of Trial*. New York: Seabury Press, 1975.

Bellah, Robert N.; Madsen, Richard; Sullivan, William M.; Swidler, Ann;

and Tipton, Stephen. *Habits of the Heart: Individualism and Commitment in American Life*. Berkeley: University of California Press, 1985.

Belloc, Hilaire. *Europe and the Faith*. London: Burns and Oates, 1962.

Benestad, J. Brian. *The Pursuit of a Just Social Order: Policy Statements of the U.S. Catholic Bishops, 1966-80*. Washington, D.C.: Ethics and Public Policy Center, 1982.

Benestad, J. Brian, and Butler, Francis J., eds. *Quest for Justice: A Compendium of Statements of the United States Catholic Bishops on the Political and Social Order 1966-80*. Washington, D.C.: United States Catholic Conference, 1981.

Berger, Peter. *The Sacred Canopy: Elements of a Sociological Theory of Religion*. Garden City: Doubleday & Co., 1967.

Berger, Suzanne, ed. *Religion in Western European Politics*. London: Frank Cass, 1982.

Berrigan, Daniel. *The Dark Night of Resistance*. Garden City, N.Y.: Doubleday, 1971.

Berrigan, Philip. *Prison Journals*. New York: Holt, Rinehart & Winston, 1970.

Berryman, Philip. *The Religious Roots of Rebellion: Christians in Central American Revolutions*. Maryknoll, N.Y.: Orbis Books, 1984.

Bialek, Robert W. *Catholic Politics: A History Based on Ecuador*. New York: Vantage Press, 1963.

Bickers, Bernard W., and Holmes, J. Derek. *A Short History of the Catholic Church*. New York: Paulist Press, 1984.

Biernatzki, William E., S.J.; Im, Luke Jin-Chang; and Min, Anselm K. *Korean Catholicism in the 70s*. Maryknoll, N.Y.: Orbis Books, 1975.

Bigo, Pierre. *The Church and Third World Revolution*. Maryknoll, N.Y.: Orbis Books, 1978.

Binchy, D. A. *Church and State in Fascist Italy*. London: Oxford University Press, 1970.

Blacker, Coit D., and Duffy, Gloria, eds. *International Arms Control: Issues and Agreements*. 2nd ed. Stanford: Stanford University Press, 1984.

Blanshard, Paul. *American Freedom and Catholic Power*. Boston: Beacon Press, 1958.

Bociurkiw, Bohdan R., and Strong, John W., eds. *Religion and Atheism in the U.S.S.R. and Eastern Europe*. Toronto: University of Toronto Press, 1975.

Bossy, John. *The English Catholic Community, 1570-1850*. New York: Oxford University Press, 1976.

Bosworth, William. *Catholicism and Crisis in Modern France: French Catholic Groups at the Threshold of the Fifth Republic*. Princeton: Princeton University Press, 1962.

Boxer, Charles Ralph. *The Church Militant and the Iberian Expansion, 1440-1770*. Baltimore: Johns Hopkins University Press, 1978.

Brain, J. B. *Catholic Beginnings in Natal and Beyond*. Durban, South Africa: T.W. Griggs and Co., 1975.

Brennan, Niall. *The Politics of Catholics*. Melbourne: Hill Publishing, 1972.

Broderick, John F. *The Holy See and the Irish Movement for the Repeal of the Union with England, 1829-1847*. Rome: Aedes Universitatis Gregorianae, 1951.

Brodrick, James. *St. Peter Canisius, S.J., 1521-1597*. Chicago: Loyola University Press, 1962.

Brown, Eric. *The Catholic Church in South Africa*. New York: P. J. Kennedy and Sons, 1960.

Brown, Robert McAfee. *Gustavo Gutiérrez*. Atlanta: John Knox Press, 1980.

―――. *Theology in a New Key: Responding to Liberation Themes*. Philadelphia: Westminster Press, 1978.

Brown, Terrence. *Ireland: A Social and Cultural History*. Glasgow: Collins, 1981.

Bruneau, Thomas C. *The Church in Brazil: The Politics of Religion*. Austin: University of Texas Press, 1982.

―――. *The Political Transformation of the Brazilian Catholic Church*. New York: Cambridge University Press, 1974.

Bujak, Adam. *Journey to Glory*. San Francisco: Harper and Row, 1976.

Bull, George. *Vatican Politics at the Second Vatican Council, 1962-1965*. Oxford: Oxford University Press, 1966.

Callahan, William J., and Higgs, David., ed. *Church and Society in Catholic Europe of the Eighteenth Century*. New York: Cambridge University Press, 1979.

Câmara, Helder. *The Church and Colonialism: The Betrayal of the Third World*. Denville, N.J.: Dimension, 1969.

―――. *Revolution Through Peace*. New York: Harper and Row, 1971.

Canon Law Society of Great Britain and Ireland, The, in association with The Canon Law Society of Australia and New Zealand and The Canadian Canon Law Society, trans. *The Code of Canon Law in English Translation*. London: Collins Liturgical Publications, 1983.

Cardenal, Ernesto. *The Gospel in Solentiname*. Trans. D. D. Walsh. 4 vols. Maryknoll: Orbis Books, 1976-80.

―――. *In Cuba*. Trans. D. D. Walsh. New York: New Directions, 1974.

―――. *Zero Hour*. Trans. P. W. Borgeson, Jr. New York: New Directions, 1980.

Carlyle, Robert Warrand. *A History of Medieval Political Theory in the West*. 6 vols. London: W. Blackwood, 1903-1936.

Carthy, Mary Peter. *Catholicism in English-speaking Lands*. New York: Hawthorne Books, 1964.

Castelli, Jim. *The Bishops and the Bomb*. Garden City, N.Y.: Image Books, 1983.

Catholic Institute for International Relations and Pax Christi. *War and Conscience in South Africa*. London: CIIR, 1982.

Chadwick, Owen. *The Popes and European Revolution*. New York: Oxford University Press, 1980.

Cleary, J. M. *Catholic Social Action in Britain, 1909-1959*. Oxford: Catholic Social Guild, 1961.

Cogley, John. *A Canterbury Tale: Experience and Reflections, 1916-1976*. New York: Seabury Press, 1976.

———. *Catholic America*. New York: Dial Press, 1973.

Cohen, Paul A. *China and Christianity: The Missionary Movement and the Growth of Chinese Antiforeignism, 1860-1870*. Cambridge: Harvard University Press, 1963.

Cohn, Norman. *The Pursuit of the Millennium*. New York: Harper and Row, 1961.

Coleman, John A. *An American Strategic Theology*. New York: Paulist, 1982.

———. *The Evolution of Dutch Catholicism, 1958-1974*. Berkeley: University of California Press, 1978.

Collier, David, ed. *The New Authoritarianism in Latin America*. Princeton: Princeton University Press, 1979.

Comblin, Jose. *The Church and the National Security State*. Maryknoll, N.Y.: Orbis Books, 1979.

Comen, Peter. *Catholics and the Welfare State*. London: Longman, 1977.

Congar, Yves Marie Joseph. *Challenge to the Church: The Case of Archbishop Lefebvre*. Huntington, Ind.: Our Sunday Visitor, 1976.

———. *The Mystery of the Church*. Baltimore: Helicon, 1960.

Connolly, S. J. *Priests and People in Pre-Famine Ireland*. Dublin: Gill and Macmillan, 1982.

Cooney, John. *The American Pope: The Life and Times of Francis Cardinal Spellman*. New York: Times Books, 1984.

Cooper, Norman B. *Catholicism and the Franco Regime*. Beverly Hills: Sage Publications, 1975.

Corbett, Edward M. *Quebec Confronts Canada*. Baltimore: John Hopkins Press, 1967.

Cousins, Norman. *The Improbable Triumvirate: John F. Kennedy, Pope John and Nikita Khrushchev*. New York: W. W. Norton, 1972.

Cox, Harvey. *The Secular City: Secularization and Urbanization in Theological Perspective*. Rev. ed. New York: Macmillan, 1965.

Craig, Gordon A., and George, Alexander L. *Force and Statecraft: Diplomatic Problems of Our Time*. New York: Oxford University Press, 1983.

Crosby, Donald F., S.J. *God, Church, and Flag: Senator Joseph R. McCarthy and the Catholic Church, 1950-57*. Chapel Hill, N.C.: University of North Carolina Press, 1978.

Curry, Jane Leftwich, ed. *Dissent in Eastern Europe*. New York: Praeger, 1983.

Dahlin, Therrin C.; Gillum, Gary P.; and Grover, Mark L. *The Catholic Left in Latin America: A Comprehensive Bibliography*. Boston: G. K. Hall, 1981.

Dawson, Christopher. *The Making of Europe: An Introduction to the History of European Unity*. New York: Sheed and Ward, 1952.

DeCraemer, Willy. *The Jamaa and the Church: A Bantu Catholic Movement in Zaire*. Oxford: Clarendon Press, 1977.

DeGroot, J.J.M. *The Religious System of China*. 6 vols. Leiden: E. J. Brill, 1892.

———. *Sectarianism and Religious Persecution in China*. Taipei: Ch'eng Wen Publishing Co., 1970.

De Gruchy, John W. *The Church Struggle in South Africa*. Grand Rapids, Mich.: William B. Ferdmans Pub. Co., 1979.

Diamant, Alfred. *Austrian Catholics and the First Republic*. Princeton: Princeton University Press, 1960.

———. *Austrian Catholics and the Social Question, 1918-1933*. Gainesville, Fla.: University of Florida Press, 1959.

Di Fonzo, Luigi. *St. Peter's Banker*. New York: Franklin Watts, 1983.

Dohen, Dorothy. *Nationalism and American Catholicism*. New York: Sheed and Ward, 1974.

Dolan, Jay. *The American Catholic Experience*. New York: Doubleday, 1986.

Domenach, Jean-Marie, and Montvalon, Robert de. *The Catholic Avant-Garde: French Catholicism since World War II*. New York: Holt, Rinehart, and Winston, 1967.

Drell, Sidney D.; Farley, Philip J.; and Holloway, David. *The Reagan Strategic Defense Initiative: A Technical, Political, and Arms Control Assessment*. New York: Ballinger, 1985.

Duff, Charles. *Six Days to Shake an Empire*. London: Dent, 1966.

Dulles, Avery Robert. *The Catholicity of the Church*. New York: Oxford University Press, 1985.

———. *Models of the Church*. Garden City, N.Y.: Doubleday, 1974.

Dulong, Renaud. *Une Église cassée: Essai sociologique sur la crise de l'Église catholique*. Paris: Editions Ouvrières, 1971.

Durkheim, Émile. *Les Formes élémentaires de la vie religieuse*. Paris: Alcan, 1912.

Dussel, Enrique. *Ethics and the Theology of Liberation*. Maryknoll, N.Y.: Orbis Books, 1978.

Eagleson, John, ed. *Christians and Socialism: Documentation of the Christians for Socialism Movement in Latin America*. Maryknoll, N.Y.: Orbis Books, 1975.

Eagleson, John, and Scharper, Philip, eds. *Puebla and Beyond*. Maryknoll, N.Y.: Orbis Books, 1979.

Eberstein, W. G. *Church and State in Franco Spain*. Princeton: Princeton University Press, 1960.

Eisenstadt, S. N. *The Protestant Ethic and Modernization*. New York: Basic Books, 1968.

Ellis, John Tracy. *American Catholicism*. 2nd. ed., rev. Chicago: University of Chicago Press, 1969.

———. *Perspectives in American Catholicism*. Baltimore: Helicon, 1963.

Ellsberg, Robert, ed. *By Little and by Little: The Selected Writings of Dorothy Day*. New York: Knopf, 1984.

Evans, Ellen Lovell. *The German Center Party, 1870-1933: A Study in Political Catholicism*. Carbondale: Southern Illinois University Press, 1974.

Everts, Philip P., and Walraven, G. *De vredesbeweging* [The Peace Movement]. Utrecht: Spectrum, 1984.

Fairbank, John K.; Reischauer, Edwin O.; Craig, Albert M. *East Asia: The Modern Transformation*. Boston: Houghton Mifflin, 1965.

Falcoff, Mark, and Royal, Robert, eds. *Crisis and Oportunity: U.S. Policy in Central America and the Caribbean*. Washington, D.C.: Ethics and Public Policy Center, 1984.

Falconi, Carlo. *The Popes in the Twentieth Century*. Boston: Little, Brown, 1967.

Fesquet, Henri. *The Drama of Vatican II: The Ecumenical Council, June 1962-December 1965*. New York: Random House, 1967.

Fitzpatrick, Benedict. *Ireland and the Foundations of Europe*. New York: Funk and Wagnalls, 1927.

Fitzpatrick, Brian. *Catholic Royalism in the Department of the Gard, 1814-1852*. New York: Cambridge University Press, 1983.

Fitzsimmons, M. A., ed. *The Catholic Church Today: Western Europe*. Notre Dame: University of Notre Dame, 1969.

Flamini, Roland. *Pope, Premier, President: The Cold War Summit That Never Was*. New York: Macmillan, 1980.

Flannery, Austin, O.P., ed. *Vatican Council II: The Conciliar and Post Conciliar Documents*. Collegeville, Minn.: The Liturgical Press, 1975.

Fleet, Michael. *The Rise and Fall of Chilean Christian Democracy*. Princeton: Princeton University Press, 1985.

Fogarty, Michael Patrick. *Christian Democracy in Western Europe, 1820-1953*. Notre Dame: University of Notre Dame Press, 1957.

Forman, Charles W. *The Island Churches of the South Pacific: Emergence in the Twentieth Century*. Maryknoll, N.Y.: Orbis Books, 1982.

Frazee, Charles A. *Catholics and Sultans: The Church and the Ottoman Empire, 1453-1923*. New York: Cambridge University Press, 1983.

Frei, Eduardo. *Latin America: The Hopeful Option*. New York: Orbis Books, 1978.

Freire, Paulo. *Pedagogy of the Oppressed*. New York: Herder and Herder, 1972.

Gannon, Robert I. *The Cardinal Spellman Story*. Garden City, N.Y.: Doubleday, 1962.

Garaudy, Roger. *From Anathema to Dialogue*. New York: Herder and Herder, 1966.

Garton Ash, Timothy. *The Polish Revolution: Solidarity 1980-82*. London: Jonathan Cape Ltd., 1983.

Geertz, Clifford. *The Interpretation of Cultures*. New York: Basic Books, 1973.

Gerth, H. H., and Mills, C. Wright, eds. *From Max Weber: Essays in Sociology*. New York: Oxford University Press, 1958.

Gheddo, Piero. *The Cross and the Bo Tree*. New York: Sheed and Ward, 1970.

Gilkey, Langdon. *Catholicism Confronts Modernity: A Protestant View*. New York: Seabury Press, 1975.

Gilson, Etienne, ed. *The Church Speaks to the Modern World: The Social Teachings of Leo XII*. Garden City, N.J.: Doubleday Image Books, 1954.

Glazer, Nathan, and Moynihan, Daniel P. *Beyond the Melting Pot*, 2nd ed. Cambridge: M.I.T. Press, 1970.

Glock, Charles Y.; Ringer, Benjamin R.; and Babbie, Earl R. *To Comfort and to Challenge: The Dilemma of the Contemporary Church*. Berkeley and Los Angeles: University of California Press, 1967.

Graham, Robert A., S.J. *Vatican Diplomacy: A Study of Church and State on the International Plane*. Princeton: Princeton University Press, 1959.

Gramsci, Antonio. *The Modern Prince and Other Writings*. New York: International Publishers, 1957.

Granfield, Patrick. *The Papacy in Transition*. Garden City, N.Y.: Doubleday, 1980.

Greeley, Andrew M. *The American Catholic: A Social Portrait*. New York: Basic Books, 1977.

———. *American Catholics Since the Council*. New York: Thomas More Press, 1985.

———. *The Making of the Popes 1978: The Politics of Intrigue in the Vatican*. Kansas City, Mo.: Andrews and McMeel, 1979.

Gremillion, Joseph, ed. *The Gospel of Peace and Justice: Catholic Social Teaching since Pope John*. Maryknoll, N.Y.: Orbis Books, 1976.

Gronowicz, Antoni. *God's Broker: The Life of Pope John Paul II*. New York: Richardson and Synder, 1984.

Grootaers, Jan, and Selling, Joseph A. *The 1980 Synod of Bishops "On the Role of the Family": An Exposition of the Event and an Analysis of the Text*. Louvain: Louvain University Press, 1983.

Guareschi, Giovanni. *The Little World of Don Camillo*. New York: Pellegrini and Cudahy, 1950.

Guitton, Jean. *The Pope Speaks: Dialogues of Paul VI with Jean Guitton*. New York: Meredith Press, 1968.

Gutiérrez, Gustavo. *A Theology of Liberation: History, Politics, and Salvation*. Trans. C. Inda and J. Eagleson. Maryknoll, N.Y.: Orbis Books, 1973.

Hales, E.E.Y. *Pio Nono*. Garden City, N.Y.: Image Books, 1962.

———. *Revolution and Papacy, 1769-1846*. Garden City, N.Y.: Hanover House, 1960.

Handy, Robert T. *A History of the Churches in the United States and Canada*. Oxford: Clarendon Press, 1976.

Hanna, Mary T. *Catholics and American Politics*. Cambridge: Harvard University Press, 1979.

Hanson, Eric O. *Catholic Politics in China and Korea*. Maryknoll, N.Y.: Orbis Books, 1980.

Harding, Harry, ed. *China's Foreign Relations in the 1980s*. New Haven: Yale University Press, 1984.

Harrington, Michael. *The Politics at God's Funeral*. New York: Holt, Rinehart, and Winston, 1983.

Hassard, John R.G. *Life of the Most Rev. John Hughes*. New York: Appleton, 1866.

Hay, Denys. *The Church in Italy in the Fifteenth Century*. New York: Cambridge University Press, 1977.

Hebblethwaite, Peter. *The Christian-Marxist Dialogue and Beyond*. London: Longman and Todd, 1977.

————. *"Inside" the Synod: Rome, 1967*. New York: Paulist Press, 1968.

————. *Pope John XXIII: Shepherd of the Modern World*. New York: Doubleday, 1985.

————. *The Year of Three Popes*. Cleveland: William Collins, 1979.

Hennesey, James. *American Catholics: A History of the Roman Catholic Community in the United States*. New York: Oxford University Press, 1981.

Henze, Paul. *The Plot to Kill the Pope*. New York: Charles Scribner's Sons, 1984.

Herberg, Will. *Protestant-Catholic-Jew*. 2nd ed. Garden City, N.Y.: Doubleday, 1960.

Hitchcock, James. *Catholicism and Modernity: Confrontation or Capitulation*. New York: Seabury Press, 1979.

————. *The Pope and the Jesuits: John Paul II and the New Order of the Society of Jesus*. New York: National Committee of Catholic Laymen, 1984.

Hofmann, Paul. *O Vatican! A Slightly Wicked View of the Holy See*. New York: Congdon and Weed, 1983.

Hollenbach, David. *Claims in Conflict: Retrieving and Renewing the Catholic Human Rights Tradition*. New York: Paulist Press, 1979.

————, ed. *Human Rights in the Americas: The Struggle for Consensus*. Washington, D.C.: Woodstock Theological Center, 1981.

————. *Nuclear Ethics*. New York: Paulist Press, 1983.

Hollis, Christopher A. *A History of the Jesuits*. Liverpool: Tinling and Co. Ltd., 1968.

Holmes, J. Derek. *More Roman than Rome: English Catholicism in the Nineteenth Century*. London: Burns and Oates, 1978.

Holmes, Peter. *Resistance and Compromise: The Political Thought of Elizabethan Catholics*. New York: Cambridge University Press, 1982.

Hope, Marjorie, and Young, James. *South African Churches in a Revolutionary Situation*. Maryknoll, N.Y.: Orbis Books, 1981.

Hughes, Philip. *The Catholic Question, 1688-1829: A Study in Political History*. London: Sheed and Ward, 1929.

————. *The Church in Crisis: A History of the General Councils 325-1870*. Garden City, N.Y.: Hanover House, 1960.

Huntington, Samuel P., and Moore, Clement H., eds. *Authoritarian Politics in Modern Society: The Dynamics of Established One-Party Systems*. New York: Basic Books, Inc. 1970.

International Commission for the Study of Communications Problems.

Many Voices, One World: Toward a New More Just and More Efficient World Information and Communication Order. London: Kogan Page, 1980.

International Federation of Catholic Universities. *The Peace Movements.* Rome: Research Center of F.I.U.C., n.d.

Jedin, Hubert. *History of the Church.* 10 vols. New York: Seabury Press, 1980-1981.

―――. *A History of the Council of Trent.* Trans. Dom Ernest Graf. St. Louis: Herder, 1957.

John XXIII, Pope. *Journal of a Soul.* New York: McGraw-Hill, 1965.

Johnson, James T. *Ideology, Reason, and the Limitation of War: Religious and Secular Concepts 1200-1740.* Princeton: Princeton University Press, 1975.

―――. *Just War Tradition and the Restraint of War.* Princeton: Princeton University Press, 1981.

Johnson, Paul. *Pope John Paul II and the Catholic Restoration.* London: Weidenfeld and Nicolson, 1982.

Kaiser, Robert Blair. *The Politics of Sex and Religion.* Kansas City, Mo.: Leaven Press, 1985.

―――. *Pope, Council and World: The Story of Vatican II.* New York: Macmillan, 1963.

Kelly, George A. *The Battle for the American Church.* Garden City, N.Y.: Doubleday, 1979.

―――. *The New Biblical Theorists: Raymond Brown and Beyond.* Ann Arbor, Mich.: Servant, 1983.

Kent, Peter C. *The Pope and the Duce: The International Impact of the Lateran Agreements.* London: Macmillan, 1981.

Kertzer, David I. *Comrades and Christians: Religion and Political Struggle in Communist Italy.* Cambridge: Cambridge University Press, 1980.

Keohane, Robert O., and Nye, Joseph F., Jr., eds. *Transnational Relations and World Politics.* Cambridge: Harvard University Press, 1972.

Kim Chi Ha. *The Gold Crowned Jesus and Other Writings.* Ed. Chong Sun Kim and S. Killen. Maryknoll, N.Y.: Orbis Books, 1978.

Klaiber, Jeffrey L. *Religion and Revolution in Peru, 1924-1976.* Notre Dame: University of Notre Dame Press, 1977.

Kolbenschlag, Madonna, ed. *Between God and Caesar: Priests, Sisters, and Political Office in the United States.* New York: Paulist Press, 1985.

König, Franz. *Worte zur Zeit.* Wien: Herder, 1968.

Konrad, Herman W. *A Jesuit Hacienda in Colonial Mexico: Santa Lucia, 1576-1767.* Stanford: Stanford University Press, 1980.

Koury, Enver. *The Crisis in the Lebanese System: Confessionalism and Chaos.* Washington, D.C.: American Enterprise Institute, 1976.

Kuhn, T. S. *The Structure of Scientific Revolutions.* 2nd. ed., enlarged. Chicago: University of Chicago Press, 1975.

Küng, Hans. *The Church.* Garden City, N.Y.: Doubleday, 1976.

Labanka, Miroslav, and Rudnytzky, Leonid. *The Ukrainian Catholic Church,*

1945-1975. Philadelphia: St. Sophia Religious Association of Ukrainian Catholics, 1976.

Ladd, Everett C. *Where Have All the Voters Gone?*. 2nd ed. New York: W. W. Norton and Co., 1981.

La Palombara, Joseph, and Winer, Myron. *Political Parties and Political Development*. Princeton: Princeton University Press, 1966.

Larkin, Emmet. *The Historical Dimensions of Irish Catholicism*. New York: Arno Press, 1976.

———. *The Making of the Roman Catholic Church in Ireland, 1850-1860*. Chapel Hill: University of North Carolina Press, 1980.

Latourette, Kenneth Scott. *Christianity in a Revolutionary Age: A History of Christianity in the Nineteenth and Twentieth Centuries*. 5 vols. New York: Harper & Brothers, 1958-62.

Latreille, A.; Palanque, J. R.; Delaruelle, E.; and Remond, R. *Histoire du Catholicisme en France, III: La periode contemporaine*. Paris: Editions Spes, 1962.

Lawler, Philip, ed. *Justice and War in the Nuclear Age*. Lanham, Md.: University Press of America, 1983.

Lazzarotto, Angelo S. *The Catholic Church in Post-Mao China*. Hong Kong: Holy Spirit Study Center, 1982.

Levine, Daniel H. *Religion and Politics in Latin America: The Catholic Church in Venezuela and Colombia*. Princeton: Princeton University Press, 1981.

———, ed. *Churches and Politics in Latin America*. Beverly Hills: Sage Publications, 1980.

Lewy, Guenther. *The Catholic Church and Nazi Germany*. New York: McGraw-Hill, 1964.

Lijphart, Arend. *Class Voting and Religious Voting in the European Democracies*. Occasional Paper No. 8. Glasgow: Survey Research Center, University of Strathclyde, 1971.

Linden, Ian. *The Catholic Church and the Struggle for Zimbabwe*. London: Longman, 1980.

———. *Church and Revolution in Rwanda*. Manchester: Manchester University Press, 1977.

Linehan, Peter, and Tierney, Brian, eds. *Authority and Power: Studies on Medieval Law and Government*. Cambridge: Cambridge University Press, 1980.

Linz, Juan J., and Stepan, Alfred, eds. *The Breakdown of Democratic Regimes*. 4 vols. Baltimore: John Hopkins University Press, 1978.

Lipset, Seymour M., and Rokkan, Stein, eds. *Party Systems and Voter Alignments*. New York: Free Press, 1968.

Lo Bello, Nino. *The Vatican Empire*. New York: Trident Press, 1968.

Lonergan, Bernard J.F. *Insight: A Study of Human Understanding*. New York: Longmans, 1957.

Lubac, Henri de. *The Splendour of the Church*. New York: Sheed and Ward, 1956.

McDonagh, Enda. *Church and Politics: From Theology to a Case Study of Zimbabwe*. Notre Dame: University of Notre Dame Press, 1980.

McDougall, Walter A. *The Heavens and the Earth: A Political History of the Space Age*. New York: Basic Books, 1985.

MacEoin, Gary. *The Inner Elite: Dossiers of Papal Candidates*. Kansas City: Sneed Andrews and McMeel, 1978.

Machado, Antonio Augusto Borelli, et al. *Tradition Family Property: Half a Century of Epic Anticommunism*. Trans. J. R. Spann and J.A.A. Schelini. Mount Kisco, N.Y.: The Foundation for a Christian Civilization, Inc., 1981.

McGovern, Arthur F. *Marxism: An American Christian Perspective*. Maryknoll, N.Y.: Orbis Books, 1980.

McIlwain, Charles Howard. *The Growth of Political Thought in the West, from the Greeks to the End of the Middle Ages*. New York: Macmillan, 1932.

MacInnis, Donald E., ed. *Religious Policy and Practice in Communist China*. New York: Macmillan, 1972.

McKenzie, John. *Authority in the Church*. New York: Sheed and Ward, 1966.

McManners, John. *Church and State in France, 1870-1914*. London: S.P.C.K. for the Church Historical Society, 1972.

————. *The French Revolution and the Church*. New York: Harper and Row, 1970.

Maier, Hans. *Revolution and Church: The Early History of Christian Democracy, 1789-1901*. Notre Dame: University of Notre Dame Press, 1969.

Mainwaring, Scott. *The Catholic Church and Politics in Brazil, 1916-1985*. Stanford: Stanford University Press, 1986.

Mammarella, Giuseppe. *Italy After Fascism: A Political History 1943-1963*. Montreal: Mario Casalini Ltd., 1964.

Maritain, Jacques. *The Peasant of the Garonne: An Old Layman Questions Himself About the Present Times*. New York: Holt, Rinehart, and Winston, 1968.

————. *True Humanism*. New York: Charles Scribner's Sons, 1938.

Markowitz, Marvin D. *Cross and Sword: The Political Role of Christian Missions in the Belgian Congo, 1908-1960*. Stanford: Hoover Institution Press, 1973.

Martin, Malachi. *The Delcine and Fall of the Roman Church*. New York: Putnam, 1981.

Meritt, Richard, and Rokkan, Stein, eds. *Comparing Nations: The Use of Quantitative Date in Cross-National Research*. New Haven: Yale University Press, 1966.

Michelat, Guy, and Simon, Michel. *Classe, religion et comportement politique*. Paris: La Presse de la Fondation Nationale des Sciences Politiques Editiones Sociales, 1977.

Miguez Bonino, José. *Christians and Marxists: The Mutual Challenge to Revolution*. Grand Rapids: William B. Eerdmans Publishing Co., 1976.

Miller, William D. *Dorothy Day: A Biography*. San Francisco: Harper and Row, 1982.

Mills, C. Wright. *The Sociological Imagination*. New York: Oxford University Press, 1959.

Miret Magdalena, Enrique. *La Revolución de lo Religión*. Madrid: Ediciónes Paulinas, 1976.

Mojtabai, A. G. *Blessed Assurance*. Boston: Houghton Mifflin, 1986.

Mol, J. J. *The Fixed and the Fickle: Religion and Identity in New Zealand*. Waterloo, Ont.: Wilfrid Laurier University Press, 1982.

Molony, John N. *The Emergence of Political Catholicism in Italy: Partito Populare, 1919-1926*. Totowa, N.J.: Rowman and Littlefield, 1977.

Moltmann, J. et al. *Religion and Political Society*. New York: Harper and Row, 1974.

Montgomery, Tommie Sue. *Revolution in El Salvador: Origins and Evolution*. Boulder: Westview Press, 1982.

Moody, Joseph N., ed. *Church and Society: Catholic Social and Political Thought and Movements, 1789-1950*. New York: Arts Inc., 1953.

Moody, T. W. *A New History of Ireland*. Oxford: Clarendon Press, 1982.

Mott, Michael. *The Seven Mountains of Thomas Merton*. Boston: Houghton Mifflin, 1984.

Murnion, Philip J., ed. *Catholics and Nuclear War*. New York: Crossroads, 1983.

Murphy, Francis X. *The Papacy Today*. New York: Macmillan, 1981.

Murphy, Francis X. [pseud. Xavier Rynne]. *Vatican Council II*. New York: Farrar, Straus and Giroux, 1968.

Murphy, Paul I. with Arlington, R. Rene. *La Popessa*. New York: Warner Books, 1983.

Murray, John Courtney. *We Hold These Truths: Catholic Reflections on the American Proposition*. New York: Sheed and Ward, 1960.

National Conference of Catholic Bishops [United States]. *The Challenge of Peace: God's Promise and Our Response*. Washington, D.C.: United States Catholic Conference, 1983.

Neal, Marie Augusta. *The Socio-Theology of Letting Go: A First World Church Facing Third World People*. New York: Paulist Press, 1977.

Nichols, Peter. *The Politics of the Vatican*. London: Pall Mall Press, 1968.

———. *The Pope's Divisions: The Roman Catholic Church Today*. New York: Holt, Rinehart and Winston, 1981.

Noel, Gerard. *The Anatomy of the Catholic Church*. New York: Doubleday, 1980.

Norman, Edward R. *The English Catholic Church in the Nineteenth Century*. Oxford: Clarendon Press, 1984.

———. *Church and Society in England 1770-1970: A Historical Study*. Oxford: Clarendon Press, 1976.

Novak, Michael. *Moral Clarity in the Nuclear Age*. Nashville: Thomas Nelson, 1983.

———. *The Spirit of Democratic Capitalism*. New York: Simon and Schuster, 1982.

————. *Toward a Theology of the Corporation*. Washington, D.C.: American Enterprise Institute, 1981.

Nye, Joseph F., Jr. *Nuclear Ethics*. New York: Free Press, 1986.

O'Brien, David J., and Shannon, Thomas A., eds. *Renewing the Earth: Catholic Documentation on Peace, Justice, and Liberation*. Garden City, N.Y.: Doubleday, 1977.

O'Brien, William V. *The Conduct of Just and Limited War*. New York: Praeger, 1981.

O'Dea, Thomas F. *The Catholic Crisis*. Boston: Beacon Press, 1968.

————. *The Sociology of Religion*. Englewood Cliffs: Prentice-Hall, 1966.

Osnos, Peter. *The Polish Road to Communism*. New York: Alfred Knopf, 1977.

Paz, Nestor. *My Life for My Friends: The Guerrilla Journal of Nestor Paz, Christian*. Maryknoll, N.Y.: Orbis Books, 1975.

Phillips, James M. *From the Rising of the Sun: Christians and Society in Contemporary Japan*. Maryknoll, N.Y.: Orbis Books, 1981.

Piehl, Mel. *The Breaking of Bread: The Catholic Worker and the Origin of Catholic Radicalism in America*. Philadelphia: Temple University Press, 1982.

Pius XII, Pope. *The Mystical Body of Christ*. New York: America Press, 1943. Introduction and notes by Joseph Bluett.

Poggi, Gianfranco. *Catholic Action in Italy*. Stanford: Stanford University Press, 1967.

Poulat, Émile. *Catholicisme, démocratie et socialisme: Le Mouvement catholique et Mgr Benigni de la naissance du socialisme à la victoire du fascisme*. Paris: Casterman, 1977.

Quigley, Thomas, ed. *American Catholics and Vietnam*. Grand Rapids, Mich.: William B. Eerdmans, 1968.

Quirk, Robert E. *The Mexican Revolution and the Church*. Bloomington: Indiana University Press, 1973.

Rahner, Karl. *The Christian of the Future*. New York: Herder and Herder, 1967.

Ramet, Pedro. *Nationalism and Federalism in Yugoslavia*. Bloomington: Indiana University Press, 1985.

————, ed. *Religion and Nationalism in Soviet and Eastern European Politics*. Durham, N.C.: Duke University Press, 1985.

Randal, Jonathan C. *Going All the Way: Christian Warlords, Israeli Adventurers, and War in Lebanon*. New York: Viking, 1983.

Ratzinger, Cardinal Joseph. *Rapporto Sulla Fede*. Milan: Edizioni Paoline, 1985.

Reardon, Bernard M.G., ed. *Roman Catholic Modernism*. Stanford: Stanford University Press, 1970.

Reichley, A. James. *Religion in American Public Life*. Washington: Brookings Institution, 1985.

Reischauer, Edwin O. *The Japanese*. Cambridge: Harvard University Press, 1977.

Reuther, Rosemary. *The Radical Kingdom: The Western Experience of Messianic Hope*. New York: Paulist Press, 1970.

Rhodes, Anthony. *The Vatican in the Age of the Dictators 1922-1945*. London: Hodder and Stroughton, 1973.

Richey, Russell E., and Jones, Donald G., eds. *American Civil Religion*. New York: Harper and Row, 1974.

Roberts, Nancy L. *Dorothy Day and the Catholic Worker*. Albany, N.Y.: SUNY Press, 1984.

Rose, Richard. *Northern Ireland: Time of Choice*. Washington, D.C.: American Enterprise Institute, 1976.

Ross, Ronald J. *Beleaguered Tower: The Dilemma of Political Catholicism in Wilhelmine Germany*. Notre Dame: University of Notre Dame Press, 1976.

Sabine, George. *A History of Political Theory*. 3d ed. New York: Holt, Rinehart and Winston, 1963.

Sanneh, Lamin. *West African Christianity: The Religious Impact*. Maryknoll, N.Y.: Orbis Books, 1983.

Sartori, Giovanni. *Parties and Party Systems: A Framework for Analysis*. Cambridge: Cambridge University Press, 1976.

Schall, James V., ed. *Bishop's Pastoral Letters*. San Francisco: Ignatius Press, 1984.

Schell, Jonathan. *The Fate of the Earth*. New York: Knopf, 1982.

Schurmann, Franz. *Ideology and Organization in Communist China*. Berkeley: University of California Press, 1966.

Segundo, J. L. *The Liberation of Theology*. Maryknoll, N.Y.: Orbis Books, 1976.

Shannon, Thomas A., ed. *War or Peace? The Search for New Answers*. Maryknoll, N.Y.: Orbis Books, 1980.

Sheen, Fulton J. *The Church, Communism and Democracy*. New York: Dell Publishing, 1964.

Shields, Currin V. *Democracy and Catholicism in America*. New York: McGraw-Hill, 1958.

Shields, W. Eugene. *King and Church: The Rise and Fall of the Patronato Real*. Chicago: Loyola University Press, 1961.

Singer, Daniel. *The Road to Gdansk: Poland and the U.S.S.R.* New York: Monthly Review Press, 1981.

Silvert, Kalman H., ed. *Churches and States: The Religious Institution and Modernization*. New York: American Universities Field Staff, 1967.

Simon, Gerald. *Catholic Church and Communist State*. New York: Harper and Row, 1974.

Smith, Brian. *The Church and Politics in Chile: Challenges to Modern Catholicism*. Princeton: Princeton University Press, 1982.

Smith, Donald E. *Religion and Political Development*. Boston: Little, Brown, 1970.

———, ed. *Religion and Political Modernization*. New Haven: Yale University Press, 1974.

Stehle, Hansjakob. *Eastern Politics of the Vatican, 1917-1979*. Trans. Sandra Smith. Athens: Ohio University Press, 1981.

Stein, Walter, ed. *Nuclear Weapons and Christian Conscience*. London: Merlin Press, 1965.

Sterling, Claire. *The Time of the Assassins*. New York: Holt, Rinehart, and Winston, 1983.

Sterns, Peter N. *Priest and Revolutionary: Lamennais and the Dilemma of French Catholicism*. New York: Harper and Row, 1967.

Sturzo, Luigi. *Church and State*. Notre Dame: University of Notre Dame Press, 1962.

————. *Il Partito Popolare Italiano*. 3 vols. Bologna: Zanicheli, 1956-57.

Suffert, Georges. *Les Catholiques et la gauche*. Paris: Maspero, 1960.

Sutton, Michael. *Nationalism, Positivism and Catholicism: The Politics of Charles Maurras and French Catholics 1890-1914*. New York: Cambridge University Press, 1983.

Szajkowski, Bogdan. *Next to God . . . Poland: Politics and Religion in Contemporary Poland*. New York: St. Martin's Press, 1983.

Talbot, Strobe. *Deadly Gambits: The Reagan Administration and the Stalemate in Nuclear Arms Control*. New York: Knopf, 1985.

————. *Endgame: The Inside Story of SALT II*. New York: Harper, 1979.

Tardini, Domenico. *Memories of Pius XII*. Westminster, Md.: Newman Press, 1961.

Thomas, Gordon and Morgan-Witts, Max. *Pontiff*. New York: Doubleday, 1983.

Thomson, John A.F. *Popes and Princes: Politics and Polity in the Late Medieval Church*. London: Allen and Unwin, 1980.

Tierney, Brian. *The Crisis of Church and State, 1050-1300*. Englewood Cliffs, N.J.: Prentice Hall, 1964.

Tobias, Robert. *Communist-Christian Encounter in East Europe*. Indianapolis: School of Religion Press, 1956.

Torres, Camilo. *Cristianismo y revolucion*. Ed. Oscar Maldonado Guitemie Oliveiri, German Zabala. Mexico, D.F.: Era, 1970.

Torres, Sergio, and Eagleson, John, eds. *Theology in the Americas*. Maryknoll, N.Y.: Orbis Books, 1976.

Troeltsch, Ernst. *The Social Teaching of the Christian Churches*. Trans. Olive Wyon. New York: Macmillan, 1931.

Trofimenkoff, Susan Mann. *The Dream of Nation: A Social and Intellectual History of Quebec*. Toronto: Macmillan of Canada, 1982.

Ullmann, Walter. *The Growth of Papal Government in the Middle Ages: A Study in the Ideological Relation of Clerical to Lay Power*. 2nd ed. London: Methuen, 1962.

————. *Medieval Papalism*. London: Methuen, 1949.

————. *Medieval Political Thought*. London: Penguin, 1970.

————. *A Short History of the Papacy in the Middle Ages*. 2nd ed. London: Methuen, 1962.

Vaillancourt, Jean-Guy. *Papal Power: A Study of Vatican Control over Lay Elites*. Berkeley: University of California Press, 1980.

van der Bruggen, Koos. *Verzekerde vrede of verzekerde vernietiging*. Kampen: Kok, 1986.

Van Kley, Dale K. *The Damiens Affair and The Unraveling of the Ancien Regime*. Princeton: Princeton University Press, 1984.

———. *The Jansenists and the Expulsion of the Jesuits From France, 1757-1765*. New Haven: Yale University Press, 1975.

Vekemans, Roger. *Marginalidad: promoción popular e integración latinoamericana*. Santiago: DESAL, 1970.

Vogel, Ezra F. *Japan as Number One*. Cambridge: Harvard University Press, 1979.

Walker, T., ed. *Nicaragua in Revolution*. New York: Praeger, 1982.

Wallis, Jim, ed. *Peacemakers: Christian Voices from the New Abolitionist Movement*. New York: Harper and Row, 1983.

Walshe, Peter. *Church Versus State in South Africa: The Case of the Christian Institute*. Maryknoll, N.Y.: Orbis Books, 1983.

Weber, Max. *The Protestant Ethic and the Spirit of Capitalism*. London: Allen and Unwin, 1930.

———. *The Sociology of Religion*. Boston: Beacon Press, 1964.

Weber, Stephen. *José Napoleón Duarte and the Christian Democratic Party in San Salvadorian Politics*. Baton Rouge: Louisiana University Press, 1979.

White, Steven F., ed. *Poets of Nicaragua: A Bilingual Anthology, 1918-1979*. Greensboro, N.C.: Unicorn Press, 1982.

White, Theodore. *The Making of the President, 1960*. New York: Atheneum, 1961.

Whyte, John Henry. *Catholics in Western Democracies: A Study in Political Behavior*. New York: St. Martin's Press, 1981.

———. *Church and State in Modern Ireland*, 2nd ed. Dublin: Gill and MacMillan, 1980.

Wilkes, Paul, ed. *Merton. By Those Who Knew Him Best*. San Francisco: Harper and Row, 1984.

Will, George F. *Soul and Statecraft*. New York: Simon and Schuster, 1983.

Wills, Gary. *Bare, Ruined Choirs: Doubt, Prophecy, and Radical Religion*. New York: Dell Publishing Co., 1974.

Wilson, Bryan R. *Magic and the Millennium: A Sociological Study of Religious Movements of Protest Among Tribal and Third World Peoples*. London: Heinemann Educational Books, 1973.

Wolf, Arthur P., ed. *Religion and Ritual in Chinese Society*. Stanford: Stanford University Press, 1974.

Wolf, Donald J., ed. *Toward Consensus: Catholic-Protestant Interpretations of Church and State*. Garden City, N.Y.: Doubleday and Co., Anchor Books, 1968.

Yang, C. K. *Religion in Chinese Society*. Berkeley: University of California Press, 1961.

Yzermans, Vincent A., ed. *The Major Addresses of Pope Pius XII*, Vol. II. St. Paul: North Central Publishing Co., 1961.

Zahn, Gordon Charles. *German Catholics and Hitler's War: A Study in Social Control*. New York: Sheed and Ward, 1962.

ARTICLES

Acocella, Nicholas. "Politics: The Vatican and Father Drinan," *Attenzione* 3 (May 1981): 16-20.

Anderson, John. "Soviet Religious Policy under Brezhnev and After," *Religion in Communist Lands* 11 (Spring 1983): 25-30.

Bär, R. P. "Christianity and Deterrence: Views of Church Groups in the Netherlands on War and Peace," *NATO Review* 30 (February 1982): 23-27.

Bax, Mart. "Religious Leadership and Social-Cultural Change in Southern Dutch Society; The Dialectics of a Politico-Religious Process," paper presented at Symposium on "Leadership and Social Change" of XIth International Congress of Anthropological and Ethnological Sciences, Vancouver, August 20-25, 1983.

Berryman, Philip. "Camilo Torres, Revolutionary-Theologian," *Commonweal* 96 (April 21, 1972): 164-67.

Brodsgaard, Kjeld Erik. "The Democracy Movement in China, 1978-1979: Opposition Movements, Wall Poster Campaigns, and Underground Journals," *Asian Survey* 21 (July 1981): 747-74.

Broun, Janice. 'Catholics in Bulgaria,' RCL 11 (Winter 1983): 310-20.

———. "Religious Survival in Bulgaria," *America* 153 (November 16, 1985): 323-27.

Bruckner, D.J.R. "Chicago's Activist Cardinal," *New York Times Magazine* (May 1, 1983): 43-92.

Bruneau, Thomas C. "Consolidating Civilian Brazil," *Third World Quarterly* 7 (October 1985): 973-87.

Bundy, McGeorge. "The Bishops and the Bomb," *New York Review of Books* (June 16, 1983): 3-8.

Buursma, Bruce. "Riding High," *Chicago Tribune Magazine* (August 21, 1983): 14-21.

Casanova, José. "Interview with Otto Maduro," *Telos* 58 (Winter 1983-84): 185-95.

Conway, James F. "John Paul II: Touching the Heart of Black Africa," *Worldview* 23 (July 1980): 21-23.

Cviic, Christopher. "A Fatima in a Communist Land?" RCL 10 (Spring 1982): 4-10.

Dodson, Michael. "Comparing the Popular Church in Nicaragua and Brazil," *Journal of Interamerican Studies and World Affairs* 26 (February 1984): 131-36.

Doerflinger, Richard. "Who Are Catholics for a Free Choice?" *America* 153 (November 16, 1985): 312-17.

Drinan, Robert F. "American Guns, Guatemalan Justice," *America* 144 (June 13, 1981): 478-80.

Ellis, John Tracy. "American Catholics and the Intellectual Life," *Thought* 30 (Autumn 1955): 351-88.

Flemming, Thomas. "Divided Shepherds of a Restive Flock," *New York Times Magazine* (January 16, 1977): 9-44.

Frazee, Charles A. "The Greek Catholic Islanders and the Revolution of 1821," *East European Quarterly* 13 (Fall 1979): 315-326.

Garton Ash, Timothy. "Swords into Plowshares: The Unofficial 'Peace Movement' and the Churches in East Germany," RCL 11 (Winter 1983): 244-50.

Gormley, Ann. "Prospects for Militarization and for Peace in Asia and the Pacific," talk to Southern Asia Committee, D.O.M., Committee for East Asia and Pacific, D.O.M., February 24, 1983.

Gross, David; Murray, Patrick; Piccone, Paul. "Introduction," *Telos* 58 (Winter 1983-84): 2-6.

Gutiérrez, Gustavo. "Notes for a Theology of Liberation," *Theological Studies* 31 (June 1970): 243-61.

Hassan, Bernard. "Orbis Books: A Line Where Politics and Theology Meet," *Publishers Weekly* 220 (October 2, 1981): 54-56.

Hebly, J. A. "Churches in Eastern Europe: Three Models of Church-State Relations and Their Relevance for the Ecumenical Movement," OPREE 4 (May 1984): 14-35.

Hehir, J. Bryan. "The Roman Catholic Church as Transnational Actor: Amending Vallier," paper presented at the Annual Convention of the International Studies Association, Washington, D.C., February 22-26, 1978.

Huntington, Deborah. "The Prophet Motive," and "God's Saving Plan," *NACLA Report* (January-February 1984): 2-36.

Huntington, Samuel H. "Transnational Organizations in World Politics," *World Politics* 25 (April 1973): 333-68.

Hvat, Ivan. "The Ukranian Catholic Church, the Vatican and the Soviet Union during the Pontificate of Pope John Paul II," *Religion in Communist Lands* 11 (Winter 1983): 264-80.

Johnson, Paul. "The Strategy of John Paul II," *Catholicism in Crisis* 2 (September 1984): 9-15.

Joseph, Raymond Alcide. "The Church Challenges Baby Doc," *The Nation* 236 (April 16, 1983): 463-82.

Kalinovaska, Milena. "The Religious Situation in Czechoslovakia," RCL 5 (Autumn 1977): 148-57.

Kamm, Henry. "The Secret World of Opus Dei," *New York Times Magazine* (January 8, 1984): 38-41, 75-85.

Kee, Alistair. "Soft-Sell Ideology in Poland," *The Christian Century* 97 (March 12, 1980): 289-91.

Kennedy, Eugene. "America's Activist Bishops: Examining Capitalism," *New York Times Magazine* (November 12, 1984): 14-30.

Kramer, John M. "The Vatican's Ostpolitik," *Review of Politics* 42 (July 1980): 283-308.

Krynski, Magnus J. "What's Wrong with the Voting Record of Polish-Americans in the 98th Congress?" *Catholicism in Crisis* 2 (September 1984): 31-34.

Lawler, Philip F. "Michael Novak's Commercial Republic," *The American Spectator* 15 (October 1982): 10-13.

Lazzarotto, Angelo S. "The Chinese Communist Party," *Missiology* 11 (July 1983): 267-90.

Levine, Daniel H. "Popular Organizations and the Church: Thoughts from Colombia," *Journal of Interamerican Studies and World Affairs* 26 (February 1984): 137-44.

Linz, Juan J. "Religion and Politics in Spain: From Conflict to Consensus Above Cleavage," *Social Compass* 27 (1980): 255-77.

McAdams, James A. "Preaching Peace in East Germany," *Worldview* (September 1982): 15-16.

McFarland, John. "Protestant Reformers Who Thought Politics Was Sin," *California Journal* 15 (October 1984): 388-89.

Mahoney, Thomas. "Ireland: Change and Challenge," *America* 142 (March 15, 1980): 215-16.

Maillard, Stanislas. "Le Pari de l'Eglise Cubaine," *L'Actualite Religieuse dans le monde* 32 (Mars 1986): 6-13.

Meisner, Maurice. "Leninism and Maoism: Some Populist Perspectives on Marxist-Leninism in China," *China Quarterly* 45 (January-March 1971): 2-36.

Melchin, Kenneth R. "Military and Deterrence Strategy and the 'Dialectic of Community,' " paper presented to the International Symposium on Bernard Lonergan, Santa Clara University, March 15-18, 1984.

Mojzes, Paul, ed. "Varieties of Christian-Marxist Dialogue," *Journal of Ecumenical Studies* 15 (Winter 1987).

Murphy, Francis X. "Vatican Politics: Structure and Function," *World Politics* 26 (July 1974): 542-59.

Neuhaus, Richard. "In the Case of Michael Harrington," *Catholicism in Crisis* 2 (May 1984): 39-44.

Novak, Michael. "Nuclear Morality," *America* 149 (July 3, 1982): 5-8.

———. "Why Latin America Is Poor," *The Atlantic Monthly* 249 (March 1982): 66-75.

O'Leary, Olivia. "The Battle for the Diocese of Dublin," *Magill* (June 1984): 10-19.

Pope, Earl A. "The Romanian Orthodox Church," OPREE 1 No. 3, pp. 7-12.

Quinn, John. "Church, State and the Arms Race," *The Commonwealth* 76 (July 12, 1982): 185-89.

Ramet, Pedro. "Catholicism and Politics in Socialist Yugoslavia," RCL 10 (Winter 1982): 256-74.

Reese, Thomas J., "The Selection of Bishops," America 151 (August 25, 1984): 65-72.

Reinerman, Alan J. "Metternich, the Papacy, and the Greek Revolution," East European Quarterly 12 (Summer 1978): 177-188.

Russett, Bruce M. "Ethical Dilemmas of Nuclear Deterrence," International Security 8 (Spring 1984): 36-54.

Sanders, Thomas G. "The Politics of Catholicism in Latin America," Journal of Interamerican Studies and World Affairs 24 (May 1982): 241-58.

Schell, Jonathan. "The Abolition," New Yorker 59 (January 2, 1984): 36-75; (January 9, 1984): 43-94.

Schmitz, Philipp. "Friedenswort diesseits und jenseits des Atlantiks," Stimmen der Zeit 201 (July 1983): 455-67.

Schroth, Raymond A. "The Vicars of Christ on Earth," New York Times Book Review (June 24, 1979): 11, 44.

Sheehan, Edward R.F. "The Battle for Nicaragua," Commonweal 113 (May 9, 1986): 264-68.

Singles, Donna. "Les Religieuses Americaines; Mais Qu'est-ce Qu'elles Veulent?" L'Actualite Religieuses dans le Monde 31 (February 1986): 52-54.

Smith, Brian. "Churches and Human Rights in Latin America: Recent Trends in the Subcontinent" (May 1978), paper, earlier version of which was presented at the Annual Convention of the International Studies Association, Washington, D.C., February 22-26, 1978.

Smith, Timothy H. "Church Activists in the 1980s: The Conscience of Corporate America," in "Church Activism and Corporate America," special report by the Center for the Study of Business and Government, Baruch College, No. 54 (Summer 1985): 15-20.

Sturzo, Luigi. "My Political Vocation," Commonweal 34 (September 26, 1941): 537-40.

Sutor, Bernhard. "Das Politische in den Friendenserklarungen katholischer Bischofskonferenzen," Stimmen der Zeit 202 (July 1984): 455-74.

Tomsky, Alexander. " 'Pacem in Terris' Between Church and State in Czechoslovakia," Religion in Communist Lands 10 (Winter 1982): 275-82.

Valenzuela, J. Samuel, and Valenzuela, Arturo. "Modernization and Dependency: Alternative Perspectives in the Study of Latin American Underdevelopment," Comparative Politics 10 (July 1978): 535-57.

van Voorst, L. Bruce. "The Churches and Nuclear Deterrence," Foreign Affairs 61 (Spring 1983): 825-52.

Vittengle, Morgan J. "Bethlehem University Fights for Survival," Maryknoll 77 (May 1983): 35-37.

Weber, Vin. "From the Hill," Catholicism in Crisis 1 (August 1983): 26-28.

Weisman, Steven R. "The Influence of William Clark: Setting a Hard Line in Foreign Policy," New York Times Magazine (August 14, 1983): 16-20, 41-47.

Wills, Gary. "Is the Pope Too Catholic?" *New York* 12 (October 1, 1979): 49-52.

Wohlstetter, Albert. "Bishops, Statesmen, and Other Strategists on the Bombing of Innocents," *Commentary* 75 (June 1983): 15-35.

Wolfe, Christopher. "The Vatican as Nobody's Ally," *This World*, No. 4 (Winter 1983): 63-85.

Youngblood, Robert L. "Church Opposition to Martial Law in the Philippines," *Asian Survey* 18 (May 1978): 505-20.

ACRONYMS

AAS	*Acta Apostolicae Sedis* (Acts of the Apostolic See)
ABC	atomic, biological, and chemical (warfare)
ACDA	Arms Control and Disarmament Agency
ACC	1) American Catholic Committee; 2) American Catholic Conference
ACCU	Association of Catholic Colleges and Universities
ACI	*Azione Cattolica Italiana* (Italian Catholic Action)
ACNP	*Asociación Católica Nacional de Propagandistas*
ACPO	*Acción Cultural Popular*
AEI	American Enterprise Institute
AFL-CIO	American Federation of Labor-Congress of Industrial Organizations
AID	Agency for International Development
AP	Associated Press
APDH	*Asamblea Permanente de Derechos Humanos* (Permanent Assembly for Human Rights)
APSA	American Political Science Association
ARENA	Alianza Republicana Nacionalista (Republican-Nationalist Alliance)
AZAPO	Azanian People's Organization
CAL	*Pontifica Commissione per l'America Latina* (Pontifical Commission on Latin America)
CALC	Clergy and Laity Concerned
CBCP	Catholic Bishops' Conference of the Philippines
CCP	Chinese Communist Party
CDA	*Christen-Democratisch Appel* (Christian Democratic Appeal)
CDF	*Congregazione per la Dottrina delle Fede* (Congregation for the Doctrine of the Faith)
CDU	*Christlich-Demokratische Union* (Christian Democratic Union)
CEB	*Comunidades eclesiais de base* (ecclesial base communities)
CELAM	*Consejo Episcopal Latinoamericano* (Latin Amerian Bishops' Conference)
CFCC	Catholics for a Free Choice
ChSS	*Chrześciuańskie Stowarzyszenie Społeczne* (Christian Social Association)
CIIR	Catholic Institute for International Relations
CIA	Central Intelligence Agency
CLAR	*Confederazione Latino-Americana dei Religiosi* (Latin American Confederation of Religious)
CNBB	*Conferencia Nacional dos Bispos do Brasil* (National Conference of Brazilian Bishops)
CND	Campaign for Nuclear Disarmament
CO	conscientious objector
COPROSA	*Comisión de Promoción Social* (Commission for Social Promotion)
COPS	Communities Organized for Public Service
CPF	Catholic Peace Fellowship
CPSU	Communist Party of the Soviet Union
CSM	*Christian Science Monitor*

CSN	*Confédération des syndicats nationaux* (National Confederation of Trade Unions)
CSU	*Christlich-Soziale Union* (Christian Social Union)
CTCC	*Confédération des travailleurs catholiques du Canada* (Confederation of Catholic Workers of Canada)
CUA	Catholic University of America
DC	*(Partito) Democrazia Cristiana* (Christian Democratic Party)
DOC	Documentation Center
EATWOT	Ecumenical Association of Third World Theologians
EEC	European Economic Community
END	European Nuclear Disarmament
ERP	*Ejército Revolucionario Popular* (People's Revolutionary Army)
ETA	*Euzkadi ta Azkatasuna* (Basque Land and Freedom)
FBI	1) Federal Bureau of Investigation; 2) Foreign Born Irish (humorous)
FDP	*Freie Demokratische Partei* (Free Democratic Party)
FDR	Franklin Delano Roosevelt
FLQ	*Front de libération du Québec* (Quebec Liberation Front)
FPÖ	*Freiheitliche Partei Österreichs* (Freedom Party of Austria)
FRG	Federal Republic of Germany
FSLN	*Frente Sandinista de Liberación Nacional* (Sandinista National Liberation Front)
FUCI	*Federazione Universitaria Cattolica Italiana* (Federation of Italian Catholic Universities)
FUIC	*Fédération Internationale des Universités Catholiques* (International Federation of Catholic Universities)
GDR	German Democratic Republic
GI bill	(General Issue), Veterans Benefits Act (1944)
GNP	gross national product
HBV	*Hervormd Beraad Vredesvraagstukken* (Reformed Council for Peace Questions)
HKSE	*Hong Kong Sunday Examiner*
ICCR	Interfaith Center on Corporate Responsibility
ICMICA	International Catholic Movement for Intellectual and Cultural Affairs
ICTO	*Interkerkelijk Comité Tweezijdige Ontwapening* (Interchurch Committee for Bilateral Disarmament)
IFOR	International Fellowship of Reconciliation
IKV	*Interkerkelijk Vredesberaad* (Interreligious Peace Fellowship)
IMF	International Monetary Fund
IPCC	International Peace Communication and Coordination Centre
IPPNW	International Physicians for the Prevention of Nuclear War
IRA	Irish Republican Army
IRD	Institute for Religion and Democracy
KBL	*Kilusan Bagong Lipunan* (New Society Movement)
KCIA	Korean Central Intelligence Agency
KGB	*Komitet Gosundarstvennoi Bezopasnosti* (Committee for State Security)
KMT	*Kuomintang* (Nationalist Party)
KOR	*Komitet Obrony Robotnikow* (Committee for the Defense of Workers)
KRO	*Katholieke Radio Omroep* (Catholic Radio Broadcasting Organization)
KVP	*Katholieke Volkspartij* (Catholic People's Party)
LCWR	Leadership Conference of Women Religious

LDP	Liberal Democratic Party
MACC	Mexican American Cultural Center
MEB	*Movimento de Educação de Base* (Basic Education Movement)
MEDH	*Movimiento Ecuménico de Derechos Humanos* (Ecumenical Movement for Human Rights)
MNC	multinational corporation
MRP	Mouvement républicain populaire
NAMFREL	National Movement for Free Elections
NATO	North Atlantic Treaty Organization
NCCB	National Conference of Catholic Bishops
NCNA	New China News Agency
NCNS	National Catholic News Service (officially, NC)
NCR	*National Catholic Reporter*
NCWC	National Catholic War (later Welfare) Conference
NG	*Nederduitse Gereformeerde* (Dutch Reformed)
NSDD	National Security Division Directive
NYT	*New York Times*
OAS	Organization of American States
OPREE	*Occasional Papers on Religion in Eastern Europe*
PAX	[peace]: 1) pro-party Catholic organizations in the Soviet bloc; 2) an international peace movement
PCF	*Parti Communiste Français* (Communist Party of France)
PCI	*Partito Communista Italiano* (Communist Party of Italy)
PD	Presidential Directive
PDC	*Partido Demócrata Cristiano* (Christian Democratic Party)
PDP	*Partido Demócrata Popular* (Popular Democratic Party)
PLO	Palestine Liberation Organization
PPI	*Partito Popolare Italiano* (Popular Party of Italy)
PPR	*Politieke Partij Radikalen* (Party of Political Radicals)
PQ	*Parti québécois* (Quebec Party)
PRC	People's Republic of China
PRI	*Partido Revolucionario Institucional* (Institutional Revolutionary Party)
PRON	*Patriotyczny Ruch Odrondzenia Narodowego* (Patriotic Order of National Rebirth)
PS	*Parti Socialiste* (Socialist Party)
PSI	*Partito Socialista Italiano* (Socialist Party of Italy)
PSR	Physicians for Social Responsibility
PVdA	*Partij van de Arbeid* (Labor Party)
PZKS	*Polski Związek Katolików Społecznych* (Polish Catholic Social Union)
RCL	*Religion in Communist Lands*
RKPN	*Rooms-Katholieke Partij Nederland* (Roman Catholic Party of the Netherlands)
ROC	Republic of China
ROK	Republic of Korea
RPRC	*Religion in the People's Republic of China*
SACBC	South African Catholic Bishops' Conference
SACC	South African Council of Churches
SADF	South African Defense Forces
SALT	Strategic Arms Limitation Talks
SASO	South African Students Association

SDI	Strategic Defense Initiative
SMOM	Soveriegn Military Order of Malta
SPD	*Sozialdemokratische Partei Deutschlands* (Social Democratic Party of Germany)
SPROCAS	Study Project of Christianity in Apartheid Society
START	Strategic Arms Reduction Talks
SUDENE	*Superintendência do Desenvolvimento do Nordeste* (Superintendency for the Development of the Northeast)
SWAPO	Southwest Africa People's Organization
Tass	*Telegraphnoye Agentstvo Sovyetskovo Soyuza* (Telegraph Agency of the Soviet Union)
UCA	University of Central America
UCAN	Union of Catholic Asian News
UCCJ	United Church of Christ in Japan
UCD	*Unión Centro Democrático* (Democratic Center Union)
UCM	University Christian Movement
UDF	United Democratic Front
UFW	United Farm Workers
UN	United Nations
UNESCO	United Nations Educational Social and Cultural Organization
UNO	United Neighborhoods Organization
UP	1) United Press; 2) Union Popular (Popular Union)
USCC	United States Catholic Conference
UTC	*Unión de Trabajadores Colombianos* (Union of Colombian Workers)
VCR	video cassette recorder
VVD	*Volkspartij voor Vrijheid en Democratie* (Liberal Party)
WASP	White Anglo-Saxon Protestant
WCC	World Council of Churches
WCED	White Catholics of European Descent
WOREC	World Religionists' Ethics Conference
YCW	Young Christian Workers

INDEX

Note: Because this entire book concerns the politics of the Catholic Church, it is necessary to specify the meaning of the subentries "Catholic Church" and "politics." "Catholic Church" refers to politics within the religious institution itself. "Politics" refers to national domestic politics, even when the Catholic Church is the major actor. The third subentry in this increasingly broader focus is "international relations," which designates the relations between nations, and the politics of various levels of the Catholic Church in these relations. The subentry "history" covers all three categories up to the mid-1960s. The notation "Page XXX(2)" refers to two separate endnotes on the same page. This index has been prepared for the general reader and for specialists in arms control, communication media, international business, political science, and religious studies.

LIBRARY OF CONGRESS CATALOGING-IN-PUBLICATION DATA

Hanson, Eric O.
The Catholic Church in world politics.

Bibliography: p.
Includes index.
1. Catholic Church and world politics—History—
20th century.   2. World politics—1945-   I. Title.

BX1793.H27 1987   322′.1   86-25430
ISBN 0-691-07729-0 (alk. paper)